ARMED FORCES RECIPE SERVICE:

A Cookbook for Large Groups

Volume I of II

by

The United States Department of Defense

KENNEBEC
PUBLISHING

www.KennebecPublishing.com

ISBN 978-0615862682

Printed in the United States of America

CONTENTS

S E C T I O N   B: Appetizers

S E C T I O N   C: Beverages

S E C T I O N   D: Breads and Sweet Doughs

S E C T I O N   E: Cereals and Pasta Products

S E C T I O N   H: Cookies

S E C T I O N   I: Pastry and Pies

S E C T I O N   J: Puddings and Other Desserts

S E C T I O N   K: Desserts (Sauces and Toppings)

INFORMATION FOR STANDARDIZED RECIPES

Standardized recipes are a necessity for a well-run food service operation. All of the recipes have been developed, tested and standardized for product quality, consistency and yield. Recipes are the most effective management tool for guiding the requisitioning of supplies and controlling breakouts and inventory. The U. S. Dietary Guidelines were among the many considerations in both the selection and development of the recipes included in the file. Many of the recipes have been modified to reduce fat, salt and calories. For new and experienced cooks, consistent use of standardized recipes is essential for quality and economy. The **Armed Forces Recipe Service** contains over 1600 tested recipes yielding 100 portions printed on cards.

Yield - The quantity of cooked product a recipe produces. The yield for each recipe in the Armed Forces Recipe is generally given as 100 portions and in some recipes in count or volume, e.g., 2 pans, 8 loaves, 6-1/2 gallons. Portion size is key to determining the quantity of food to be prepared. Many recipes also specify the weight per portion. For example, 3/4 cup (6-1/2 ounces) Beef Stroganoff.

Ingredients Column – Ingredients are listed in the order used. The specific form or variety of each ingredient is indicated. For example:

Flour, wheat, general purpose	Eggs, whole	Sugar, granulated
Flour, wheat, bread	Egg whites	Sugar, brown

Measure, Weights, and Issue Columns – Measures and Weights indicate the Edible Portion (E.P.) quantity of the ingredient required to prepare the recipe for 100 portions. The issue column represents the As Purchased (A.P.) quantity required if this amount is different from the E.P. quantity.

Method Column - Describes how the ingredients are to be combined and cooked. For example, the method will describe the order in which to sift dry ingredients, to thicken a sauce, or to fold in beaten egg whites. The method contains directions for the most efficient order of work, eliminating unnecessary tools and equipment and unnecessary steps in preparation.

INFORMATION FOR STANDARDIZED RECIPES
RECIPE CONVERSION

Since few dining facilities serve exactly 100 persons, and, in some instances, the acceptable size portion may be smaller or larger, it is often necessary to reduce or increase a recipe. You may adjust the recipe to yield the number of portions needed, or to use the amount of ingredients available, or to produce a specific number of smaller portions. When increasing or decreasing a recipe, the division or multiplication of pounds and ounces is simplified when decimals are used.

1. To convert the quantities to decimals, use this table:

Weight in Ounces	Decimal of Pound	Weight in Ounces	Decimal of Pound
1	.06	9	.56
2	.13	10	.63
3	.19	11	.69
4 (1/4 lb)	.25	12 (3/4 lb)	.75
5	.31	13	.81
6	.38	14	.88
7	.44	15	.94
8 (1/2 lb)	.50	16 (1 lb)	1.00

For example: 1 lb 4 oz is converted to 1.25 lb; 2 lb 10 oz is converted to 2.63 lb.

2. To adjust the recipe to yield a specific number of portions:
   First -- Obtain a working factor by dividing the number of portions needed by 100. For example:
         348 (portions needed) ÷ 100 = 3.48 (Working Factor)
   Then -- Multiply the quantity of each ingredient by the working factor. For example:
         1.25 lb (recipe) X 3.48 (Working Factor) = 4.35 lb (quantity needed).

   The part of the pound is converted to ounces by multiplying the decimal by 16. For example:
         .35 lb X 16 ounces = 5.60 ounces

   After the part of the pound has been converted to ounces, use the following scale to "round off":

.00 to .12 = 0	.63 to .87 = 3/4 ounce
.13 to .37 = 1/4 ounce	.88 to .99 = 1 ounce
.38 to .62 = 1/2 ounce	

   Thus 5.60 ounces will be "rounded off" to 5 1/2 ounces, and 4 lb 5 1/2 ounces will be the quantity needed (equal to 4.35 lb).

3. To adjust the recipe for volume:
   First -- Obtain a working factor by dividing the number of portions needed by 100 as shown in Step 2 of A.l, Recipe Conversion.
         333/100 = 3.33
   Then -- Multiply the quantity of each ingredient by the working factor. You will round off to the nearest 1/4 teaspoon. For example, the recipe calls for 6 gallons of water per 100 portions. Portions to prepare are 333.
         333 /100 = 3.33 Working Factor (W/F)

1.	W/F x No. of gallons = gallon	3.33 W/F x 6 = 19.98 GL
2.	Decimal (of gal) x 4 = quart (QT)	.98 GL x 4 = 3.92 QT
3.	Decimal (of quart) x 2 = pint (PT)	.92 QT x 2 = 1.84 PT
4.	Decimal (of pint) x 2 = cup (C)	.84 PT x 2 = 1.68 C
5.	Decimal (of tbsp) x 16 = tablespoon (TBSP)	.68 C x 16 = 10.88 TBSP
6.	Decimal (of tbsp) x 3 = teaspoon (TSP)	.88 TBSP x 3 = 2.64 TSP
7.	Round off decimal portion	.64 TSP = 3/4 TSP

(see paragraph 2)
The amount of water needed for 333 portions is: 19 GL, 3 QT, 1 PT, 1 C, 10 TBSP and 2 3/4 TSP.

NOTE:	4 QT = 1 GL	2 C = 1PT	3 TSP = 1 TBSP
	2 PT = 1 QT	16 TBSP = 1C	

4. To adjust the recipe on the basis of a quantity of an ingredient to be used:
   First -- Obtain a Working Factor by dividing the pounds you have to use by the pounds required to yield 100 portions.
         For example:
         102 lb ÷ 30 (lb per 100 servings) = 3.40 (Working Factor)
   Then -- Multiply the quantity of each ingredient in the recipe by the Working Factor.

5. To adjust the recipe to yield a specific number of portions of a specific size:
   First -- Divide the desired portion size by the standard portion of the recipe.
         3 oz (desired size) ÷ 4 oz (standard portion) = .75
         348 (servings needed) x .75   = 261
         261 ÷ 100   = 2.61 (Working Factor)

   Then -- Multiply the quantity of each ingredient in the recipe by the Working Factor

DEFINITION OF TERMS USED IN FOOD PREPARATION

Bake	To cook by dry heat in an oven, either covered or uncovered.
Barbecue	To roast or cook slowly, basting with a highly seasoned sauce.
Baste	To moisten food with liquid or melted fat during cooking to prevent drying of the surface and to add flavor.
Batch Preparation	A predetermined quantity or number of servings of food that is to be prepared at selected time intervals in progressive cookery for a given meal period to ensure fresh, high quality cooked food to customers.
Beat	To make a mixture smooth by using a fast regular circular and lifting motion which incorporates air into a product.
Blanch	To partially cook in deep fat, boiling water or steam.
Blend	To mix two or more ingredients thoroughly.
Boil	To cook in liquid at boiling point (212° F.) in which bubbles rise and break at the surface.
Braise	To brown in small amount of fat, then to cook slowly in small amount of liquid below the boiling point in a covered utensil.
Bread	To cover with crumbs or other suitable dry coating ingredient; or to dredge in a mixture of flour seasonings, and/or condiments, dip in a mixture of milk and slightly beaten eggs and then dredge in crumbs.
Broil	To cook by direct exposure to heat.
Brown	To produce a brown color on the surface of food by subjecting it to heat.
Chop	To cut food into irregular small pieces.
Cream	To mix until smooth, so that the resulting mixture is softened and thoroughly blended.
Crimp	To pinch together in order to seal.
Cube	To cut any food into square-shaped pieces.
Dice	To cut into small cubes or pieces.
Dock	To punch a number of vertical impressions in a dough with a smooth round stick about the size of a pencil to allow for expansion and permit gases to escape during baking.
Dredge	To coat with crumbs, flour, sugar or corn meal.
Fermentation	The process by which yeast acts on the sugar and starches in the dough to produce carbon dioxide gas and alcohol, resulting in expansion of the dough. During this period, the dough doubles in bulk.
Flake	To break lightly into small pieces.
Fold	To blend two or more ingredients together with a cutting and folding motion.
Fry	To cook in hot fat.
Garnish	To decorate with small pieces of colorful food.
Glaze	A glossy coat given to foods, as by covering with a sauce or by adding a sugary syrup, icing, etc.
Gluten	A tough elastic protein that gives dough its strength and ability to retain gas.
Grate	To rub food on a grater and thus break it into tiny pieces.
Grill	To cook, uncovered, on a griddle, removing grease as it accumulates. No liquid is added.
Knead	To work dough by folding and pressing firmly with palms of hands, turning between foldings.

Marinade	A preparation containing spices, condiments, vegetables, and aromatic herbs, and a liquid (acid or oil or combination of these) in which a food is placed for a period of time to enhance its flavor or to increase its tenderness.
Marinate	To allow to stand in a marinade to add flavor or tenderness.
Mince	To cut or chop into very small pieces.
Panbroil	To cook uncovered in a hot frying pan, pouring off fat as it accumulates.
Pare	To cut away outer covering.
Peel	To remove the outer layer of skin of a vegetable or fruit, etc.
Progressive Cookery	The continuous preparation of food in successive steps during the entire serving period (i.e., continuous preparation of vegetables, cook-to-order hamburgers, steaks, fried eggs, pancakes). This procedure ensures fresh, high quality cooked food to customers on a continuous basis. See Batch Preparation.
Proof	To allow shaped and panned yeast products like bread and rolls to double in size under controlled atmospheric conditions.
Reconstitute	To restore to liquid state by adding water. Also to reheat frozen prepared foods.
Rehydrate	To soak, cook, or use other procedures with dehydrated foods to restore water lost during drying.
Roast	To cook by dry heat; usually uncovered, in an oven.
Roux	Roux is a French word for a mixture of flour and fat, cooked to eliminate the raw, uncooked taste of flour.
Sauté	To brown or cook in small amount of fat.
Scald	To heat a liquid over hot water or direct heat to a temperature just below the boiling point.
Scale	To measure a portion of food by weighing.
Scant	Not quite up to stated measure.
Score	To make shallow cuts across top of a food item.
Seasoned Flour or Crumbs	A mixture of flour or crumbs with seasonings.
Shred	To cut or tear into thin strips or pieces using a knife or a shredder attachment.
Sift	To put dry ingredients through a sieve.
Simmer	To cook gently in a liquid just below the boiling point (190° F. - 210° F.); bubbles will form slowly and break at the surface.
Slurry	A lump-free mixture made by whipping cornstarch or flour into cold water or other liquids
Steam	To cook over or surrounded by steam.
Stew	To simmer in enough liquid to cover solid foods.
Stir	To mix two or more ingredients with a circular motion.
Temper	To remove from freezer and place under refrigeration for a period of time sufficient to facilitate separation and handling of frozen product. Internal temperature of the food should be approximately 26° F. to 28° F.
Thaw	To remove from freezer and place under refrigeration approximately 18-48 hours. Internal temperature should be above 30° F.
Toss	To mix ingredients lightly.
Wash	The liquid brushed on the surface of unbaked pies or turnovers to give a golden brown color to the crust or on the surface of proofed breads and rolls before baking and on baked bread and rolls to give a shine to the crust.
Whip	To beat rapidly with wire whip to increase volume by incorporating air.

MEASURING PROCEDURE

Weights are more accurate than measures and recipe ingredients should be weighed whenever possible. If scales for weighing are not available, follow the rules for measuring to ensure accurate measures.

Flour, general purpose or bread. . . . . . When specified, sift before measuring. Place flour lightly in measuring utensil. Level with straight edge of knife. DO NOT shake utensil; DO NOT pack flour.

Sugar, granulated . . . . Fill measuring utensil. Level with straight edge of knife. If sugar is lumpy, sift before measuring.

Sugar, brown. . . . . Pack lightly into measuring utensil. If sugar is lumpy, roll with a rolling pin to break up any lumps before measuring.

Sugar, brown, packed. . . . . Press sugar firmly into measuring utensil.

Milk, nonfat, dry. . . . . Stir lightly with a fork or spoon. Place lightly in measuring utensil. DO NOT shake utensil. Level with straight edge of knife.

Baking powder, herbs and spices . . . . Stir lightly with fork or spoon. Dip dry measuring spoon into container, bringing it up heaping full. Level with straight edge of knife.

Solid fats. . . . . Press fat firmly into measuring utensil. Level with straight edge of knife.

TABLE OF MEASURING EQUIVALENTS

TSP	TBSP	FLUID OUNCES	CUPS	SCOOPS	LADLES	FLUID MEASURE
3	1	1/2		1 – No. 40		
	1 – 1/2	3/4		1 – No. 30	Size 0	
	2	1		1 – No. 24		
	2 – 2/3	1 – 1/3		1 – No. 20		
	3	1 – 1/2		1 – No. 16	Size 1	
	4	2	¼	1 – No. 12		
	5 – 1/3	2 – 2/3	1/3	1 – No. 10		
	6	3	3/8	1 – No. 8	Size 2	
	8	4	½	1 – No. 6		
	10 – 2/3	5 – 1/3	2/3			
	12	6	¾			
	14	7	7/8			
	16	8	1		Size 3	1/2 pt
	18	9	1 – 1/8			
		12	1 – 1/2		Size 4	3/4 pt
		16	2			1 pt
		24	3			1 – 1/2 pt
		32	4			1 qt
		64	8			2 qt
		128	16			1 gal

NOTE: 1. Use ladles to serve individual portions of liquid or semi-liquid foods.
2. Scoop number indicates the number of portions per quart.

TABLE OF WEIGHTS AND MEASURES FOR CAN SIZES

CAN SIZE	AVERAGE NET WEIGHT OR FLUID MEASURE PER CAN (SEE NOTE)	AVERAGE CUPS PER CAN	APPROX. CANS PER CASE	NO. CANS EQUIV. NO. 10 CN
No. 10	6 lb 8 oz	12-1/2	6	1
No. 3 cyl	3 lb 2 oz (46 fl oz)	5-3/4	12	2
No. 3 (vacuum)	1 lb 7 oz	2-3/4	24	4-1/2
No. 2-1/2	1 lb 12 oz	3-1/2	24	4
No. 2	1 lb 4 oz	2-1/3	24	5
No. 303	1 lb	2	24	7
No. 300	14 oz	1-3/4	24	7
No. 2 (vacuum)	12 oz	1-1/2	24	8
No. 1 picnic	11 oz	1-1/4	48	10

NOTE: The net weight on can or jar labels differs among foods due to different densities of foods. For example: A No. 10 cn contains 6 lb 3 oz sauerkraut or 7 lb 5 oz cranberry sauce.

TABLE OF CONVERSION FACTORS FOR CONVERTING "EDIBLE PORTION" WEIGHTS OF FOODS TO "AS PURCHASED" WEIGHTS OF FOODS VEGETABLES

The E.P. (Edible Portion) weight of all vegetables, unless otherwise specified, is used in the recipes. This table lists raw items and easy, one-step conversion factors to determine how much A.P. (As Purchased) weight of vegetables to process.

To use these factors, multiply the E.P. quantity of ingredients listed in the recipe by the appropriate conversion factor given below to arrive at the quantity of the item (A. P.) to process.

EXAMPLE: 3 lb sliced cucumbers (pared) E.P. (ingredient weight) x 1.19 (conversion factor) = 3.57 lb (3 lb 9 OZ) fresh cucumbers A.P. The E.P. quantity maybe determined from an A.P. quantity by dividing the A.P. by the conversion factor as follows:

3.57 lb (3 lb 9 OZ) fresh cucumbers A.P. + 1.19 (conversion factor) = 3 lb cucumbers (pared) E.P.

	Conversion Factor E.P. to A.P.		Conversion Factor E.P. to A.P.
VEGETABLES, FRESH:		Cabbage (trimmed)	1.16
Alfalfa sprouts	1.00	Cabbage (trimmed and cored)	1.25
Asparagus (trimmed)	1.89	Carrots (peeled)	1.22
Beans, green, whole (trimmed)	1.14	Cauliflower (trimmed and cored)	1.20
Beansprouts	1.00	Celery (trimmed)	1.37
Broccoli (trimmed)	1.64	Celery leaves	34.48
Broccoli, flowerets (trimmed)	2.20	Corn-on-Cob (husked and silked)	1.43
Brussels sprouts (trimmed)	1.11	Cucumbers (peeled and seeded)	1.67
Cucumbers (pared)	1.19	Pea pods, Chinese, snow (trimmed)	1.06
Cucumbers (unpared)	1.05	Peppers, sweet (stemmed, seeded, cored)	1.22
Eggplant (pared)	1.23	Peppers, sweet (stemmed, seeded, ends removed)	2.08
Eggplant (unpared)	1.03	Potatoes, white (pared)	1.23
Endive (trimmed)	1.11	Potatoes, sweet (pared)	1.25
Escarole (trimmed)	1.11	Radishes (trimmed)	1.09
Garlic, dry (peeled)	1.15	Romaine (trimmed)	1.06
Greens, collard (trimmed)	1.35	Rutabagas (pared)	1.18
Greens, kale (trimmed)	1.41	Spinach (trimmed)	1.09
Lettuce (trimmed and cored)	1.08	Squash, summer (trimmed & unpared)	1.05
Mushrooms, sliced (trimmed)	1.10	Squash, fall and winter:	
Mushrooms, whole (trimmed)	1.10	Acorn (seeded)	1.15
Onions, dry(peeled)	1.11	Butternut (pared and seeded)	1.19
Onions, green with tops (trimmed)	1.20	Hubbard (seeded)	1.12
Parsley (trimmed)	1.05	Tomatoes (stemmed)	1.02
Parsnips (pared)	1.18	Turnips (pared)	1.23

TABLE OF CONVERSION FACTORS FOR CONVERTING "EDIBLE PORTION' WEIGHTS OF FOODS TO "AS PURCHASED" WEIGHTS OF FOODS FRUITS

The E.P. (Edible Portion) weight of all fruits, unless otherwise specified, is used in the recipes. This table lists raw items and easy, one-step conversion factors to determine how much A.P. (As Purchased) weight of fruits to process.

To use these factors, multiply the E.P. quantity of ingredients listed in the recipe by the appropriate conversion factor given below to arrive at the quantity of the item (A. P.) to process.

EXAMPLE: 3 lb sliced cherries (pared) E.P. (ingredient weight) x 1.19 (conversion factor) = 3.57 lb (3 lb 9 OZ) fresh cherries A.P. The E.P. quantity maybe determined from an A.P. quantity by dividing the A.P. by the conversion factor as follows:

3.57 lb (3 lb 9 OZ) fresh cherries A.P. + 1.19 (conversion factor) = 3 lb cherries (stemmed and pitted) E.P.

FRUITS, FRESH:	Conversion Factor E.P. to A.P.		Conversion Factor E.P. to A.P.
		Cantaloupe (pared and seeded)	1.96
Apples (pared and cored)	1.28	Cantaloupe (unpared and seeded)	1.11
Apples (unpared and cored)	1.18	Casaba melon (pared and seeded)	1.67
Apricots (unpared and pitted)	1.08	Casaba melon (unpared and seeded)	1.12
Avocados (pared and seeded)	1.45	Cherries, sweet (stemmed and pitted)	1.19
Bananas (peeled)	1.54	Cranberries (culled)	1.05
Grapefruit (segments only)	1.92	Oranges (peeled, seeded sections with membrane)	1.41
Grapefruit (peeled, seeded with membrane)	1.34	Papaya (pared and seeded)	1.49
Grapes (stemmed and seeded)	1.12	Peaches (pared and pitted)	1.32
Honeyball melon or Honeydew melon (pared and seeded)	2.17	Peaches (unpared and pitted)	1.10
Honeyball melon or Honeydew melon (unpared and seeded)	1.05	Pears (pared and cored)	1.28
Kiwi fruit, pared	1.16	Pears (unpared and cored)	1.09
Lemons (juice only)	2.33	Persian melon (pared and seeded)	2.38
Limes (juice only)	2.13	Persian melon (unpared and seeded)	1.05
Mangoes (pared and seeded)	1.45	Pineapple (pared and cored)	1.92
Nectarines (unpared and pitted)	1.10	Plums (pitted)	1.06
Oranges (juice only or sections without membrane)	2.00	Strawberries (capped and stemmed)	1.06
		Tangelos (sections)	1.35
		Tangerines (sections)	1.39
		Watermelons (pared and seeded)	1.92

TABLE OF EGG EQUIVALENTS

FRESH WHOLE EGGS (SHELLED)			DEHYDRATED EGG MIX		
Medium Size	Weight	Volume	Weight	Volume (Approx.)	Water to be Added
1 egg	1.6 oz	3 tbsp	1/2 oz	2 tbsp	2-1/2 tbsp
2 eggs	3.2 oz	6 tbsp	1 oz	1/4 cup	5 tbsp
10 eggs*	1 lb	1-7/8 cups	5 oz	1-1/4 cups	1-1/2 cups
12 eggs	1 lb 3.2 oz	2-1/4 cups	6 oz	1-1/2 cups	scant - 2 cups
20 eggs	2 lb	3-3/4 cups	10 oz	2-1/2 cups	3 cups
40 eggs	4 lb	7-1/2 cups	20 oz	1-1/4 qt (1-No. 3 cyl can)	1-1/2 qt

* 10 large eggs = 1 lb 2 oz

NOTES:
1. Frozen Whole Eggs and Frozen Egg Whites may be used in equivalent weights to shelled fresh whole eggs.
2. Dehydrated Egg Mix may be used in most recipes requiring whole eggs as shown in the table above. DO NOT USE RECONSTITUTED EGGS IN UNCOOKED SALAD DRESSINGS OR OTHER RECIPES WHICH DO NOT REQUIRE COOKING. RECONSTITUTED DEHYDRATED EGG MIX SHOULD BE USED WITHIN ONE HOUR UNLESS REFRIGERATED. DO NOT HOLD OVERNIGHT. For greater accuracy, weigh dehydrated egg mix.

3. *Reconstitution Methods for Dehydrated Egg Mix*
   a. Method 1. Place dehydrated egg mix in bowl; stir with a wire whip; add 1/2 of the water; whip until a smooth paste is formed; add remaining water; whip until mixture is blended.

   b. Method 2. Add dehydrated egg mix to water; stir to moisten; let stand 5 minutes; whip until smooth.

For Baked Products

   a. Method 1. Reconstitute dehydrated egg mix; substitute for eggs in recipe.
   b. Method 2. Sift dehydrated egg mix with dry ingredients; add water in step in Method column where whole eggs are incorporated.

For Batter Dips. Dehydrated egg mix may be reconstituted and used.

GUIDELINES FOR CONTAINER YIELDS FOR CANNED FRUITS

TYPE OF FRUIT	PORTION SIZE (Approximate)	CAN SIZE	# OF CANS FOR 100 PORTIONS
Applesauce	1/2 cup	No. 303 cn	25
		No. 10 cn	4
Applesauce, Instant	1/2 cup	No. 2-1/2 cn	4
Apricots, halved	3 to 5 halves	No. 2-1/2 cn	16
		No. 10 cn	4
Blueberries	1/2 cup	No. 10 cn	4
Cherries, sweet, dark or light, pitted or unpitted	1/2 cup	No. 303 cn	25
		No. 10 cn	4
Cranberry Sauce, strained	1/4 cup	No. 303 cn or 300 cn	13
Cranberry Sauce, whole	1/4 cup	No. 10 cn	2
Figs, Kadota	3 to 4 figs	No. 303 cn	25
Fruit Cocktail	1/2 cup	No. 2-1/2 cn	16
		No. 10 cn	4
Fruit Mix, chunks	1/2 cup	No. 303 cn	25
		No. 10 cn	4
Grapefruit	1/2 cup	No. 303 cn	25
		No. 3 cyl cn	8

TYPE OF FRUIT	PORTION SIZE (Approximate)	CAN SIZE	# OF CANS FOR 100 PORTIONS
Peaches, halves	2 halves	No. 2-1/2 cn	16
		No. 10 cn	4
Peaches, quarters or slices	1/2 cup	No. 2-1/2 cn	16
		No. 10 cn	4
Pears, halves	2 halves	No. 2-1/2 cn	16
		No. 10 cn	4
Pears, quarters or slices	1/2 cup	No. 2-1/2 cn	16
		No. 10 cn	4
Pineapple, chunks or tidbits	1/2 cup	No. 2 cn	20
		No. 10 cn	4
Pineapple slices	1 large or 2 small slices	No. 2 cn	20
		No. 10 cn	4
Plums, whole	2 to 3 plums	No. 2-1/2 cn	16
		No. 10 cn	4
Prunes, whole, unpitted	3 prunes	No. 10 cn	1-1/2

NONFAT DRY MILK
RECONSTITUTION CHART FOR COOKING

Nonfat Dry Milk + (Conventional)	Water =	Fluid Skim Milk
1-2/3 tbsp	1/2 cup	1/2 cup
3 tbsp	1 cup	1 cup
1-2/3 oz (6 tbsp)	1-7/8 cups	2 cups
3-1/4 oz (3/4 cup)	3-3/4 cups	1 qt
5 oz (1-1/8 cups)	5-3/4 cups	1-1/2 qt
6-1/2 oz (1-1/2 cups)	7-1/2 cups	2 qt
8 oz (1-7/8 cups)	9-1/2 cups	2-1/2 qt
10 oz (2-1/4 cups)	11-1/2 cups	3 qt
11-1/4 oz (2-2/3 cups)	3-1/3 qt	3-1/2 qt
13 oz (3 cups)	3-3/4 qt	1 gal
1 lb 10 oz (1-1/2 qt)	1-7/8 gal	2 gal
2 lb 7 oz (2-1/4 qt)	2-7/8 gal	3 gal
4 lb 2 oz (3-3/4 qt)	4-3/4 gal	5 gal
5 lb 2 oz (4-3/4 qt)	6 gal	6-1/4 gal

NOTE:

1. Recipes in this file use conventional nonfat dry milk.

2. Instant nonfat dry milk may be substituted on a pound for pound basis for the nonfat dry milk specified in any recipe. It should be weighed because the measures for instant nonfat dry milk are different from measures for nonfat dry milk (conventional). Nonfat dry milk, instant settles. If instant milk must be measured, follow directions on the container.

3. For best results, nonfat dry milk should be weighed instead of measured. Measures vary from one manufacturer to another. However, as a general rule, 1 ounce of nonfat dry milk will measure 3-2/3 tablespoons, and 4-1/2 ounces of nonfat dry milk will measure 1 cup.

4. Dry milk must be reconstituted in clean containers using clean utensils and must be treated like fresh milk after it is reconstituted. It must be refrigerated and protected from contamination.

5. Dry milk reconstitutes more easily in warm water. It should be stirred into the water with a circular motion using a whip or slotted spoon. It may also be reconstituted in a mixer if a large quantity is being prepared. However, it should be mixed at low speed to prevent excessive foaming.

6. If nonfat dry milk is to be used for a beverage, it should be weighed using 1 lb dry milk and 3-3/4 qt water per gallon. Chill thoroughly before serving. For 100 portions (8 oz), use 6 lb 4 oz nonfat dry milk and 23-1/2 qt water.

GUIDELINES FOR USE OF DEHYDRATED ONIONS, GREEN PEPPERS, AND PARSLEY

ONIONS

Dehydrated, chopped and dehydrated compressed, chopped onions may be used in any recipe which specifies "onions, fresh, chopped or sliced."

REHYDRATION GUIDE:	Dehydrated Onions +	Water = (70-90° F.)	Rehydrated Onions OR	Fresh Onion Equivalent*
Dehydrated chopped onions	2 oz (9-2/3 tbsp) 3-1/3 oz (1 cup) 1 lb (4-7/8 cups) 2 lb 8 oz (3 qt-1 No. 10 cn)	1-1/2 cups 2-1/2 cups 3 qt 7-1/2 qt	8 oz (1-1/4 cups) 13 oz (2 cups) 4 lb (2-1/2 qt) 10 lb (6-1/4 qt)	1 lb (3 cups) (1 lb 1-3/4 oz A.P.) 1 lb 10 oz (4-3/4 cups) (1 lb 13 oz A.P.) 8 lb (1-1/2 gal) (8 lb 14 oz A.P.) 20 lb (3-3/4 gal) (22 lb 3 oz A.P.)
Dehydrated, compressed chopped onions	1-3/4 oz 2-1/3 oz 1 lb 1 lb 3 oz (1 No. 2-1/2 cn)	1-1/2 cups 2 cups 3 qt 3-1/2 qt	8 oz (1-1/8 cups) 10-1/2 oz (1-3/8 cups) 4 lb 8 oz (2-1/2 qt) 5 lb 5-1/2 oz (3 qt)	1 lb (3 cups) (1 lb 1-3/4 oz A.P.) 1 lb 5 oz (1 qt) (1 lb 7 oz A.P.) 9 lb (6-3/4 qt) (10 lb A.P.) 10 lb 11 oz (2 gal) (11 lb 14 oz A.P.)

* Volume is for chopped onions.

FOR RECIPES WITH SMALL AMOUNTS OF LIQUID: Cover dehydrated onions with 70° F. to 90 F. water. Stir dehydrated compressed onions occasionally to break apart. Let dehydrated onions stand 30 minutes; compressed dehydrated onions 1 hour or more. Drain. Note: Weight of rehydrated onions will be less than weight of dry onions but appearance and flavor will be similar.

FOR SOUPS, STEWS, SAUCES OR RECIPES WITH A LOT OF LIQUID: Add dehydrated chopped or dehydrated compressed onions directly.

GREEN PEPPERS

Dehydrated green peppers may be used in any recipe which specifies "peppers, sweet, diced or chopped."

REHYDRATION GUIDE:	Dehydrated Peppers +	Cold Water = (35-55° F.)	Rehydrated Peppers OR	Sweet Peppers Equivalent*
	1 oz (2/3cup)	2 cups	6-1/2 oz (1-1/3 cups)	6-1/2 oz (1-1/4 cups) (8 oz A.P.)
	1 lb (2-1/2qt)	2 gal	6 lb 8 oz (5-1/2 qt)	6 lb 8 oz (1-1/4 gal)(7 lb 15 oz A.P.)

* Volume is for chopped peppers

FOR SALADS OR UNCOOKED DISHES:
Cover with cold water. Refrigerate 1 hour or overnight. Drain.

FOR RECIPES WITH SMALL AMOUNTS OF LIQUID:
Cover with cold water. Let stand 30 minutes. Drain.

FOR SOUPS, STEWS, SAUCES OR RECIPES WITH A LOT OF LIQUID:
Add dehydrated peppers directly.

PARSLEY

Dehydrated parsley may be used in any recipe which specifies "chopped, fresh parsley."

REHYDRATION GUIDE:	Dehydrated Parsley +	Cold Water = (35-55° F.)	Rehydrated Parsley OR	Fresh Parsley Equivalent*
	1 oz (1-2/3 cup)	3-1/3 cups	8 oz (1-3/4 cups)	9 oz (4-1/4 cups) (9-1/2 oz A.P.)

* Volume is for chopped parsley

FOR SALADS OR UNCOOKED DISHES:
Cover with ice cold water. Let stand 3 to 5 minutes. Drain.

FOR SOUPS, STEWS, SAUCES OR RECIPES WITH A LOT OF LIQUID:
Add dehydrated parsley directly.

RECONSTITUTING SOUP AND GRAVY BASES

Beef Soup and Gravy Base, Chicken Soup and Gravy Base, and Ham Soup and Gravy Base may be reconstituted and used as bouillon to extend natural meat juices, or as stock in recipes for soups, gravies, and sauces.
The powdered bases are seasoned and when reconstituted in boiling water will have the characteristic flavor and appearance of a beef broth or chicken broth or ham stock. When used in preparing a recipe, always check the seasoning before adding salt.

	BASE	+ BOILING WATER
	WEIGHT	MEASURE
	2 tsp (1-7 gm env)	1 cup
1 oz	3 tbsp	1 qt
4 oz	12 tbsp	1 gal
8 oz	1 – 8 oz jar	2 gal
24 oz	1 – No. 21/2 can	6 gal

GUIDELINES FOR FRUIT BARS

Fruit bars provide important sources of nutrients such as Vitamins A and C, and fiber. All fruits are low in fat and calories and none contain cholesterol. They may be set up for service at breakfast, lunch, dinner and brunch meals. A variety of fresh, canned and frozen fruits may be used.

Preparation: Wash all fresh fruits except bananas. Drain well. Refrigerate until ready to serve. Keep bananas in a cool, dry place until ready to serve.

ITEM	PORTION SIZE	100 PORTIONS	
		A.P. WEIGHT OR CONTAINER	E.P.
Apples, canned, drained	1/4 cup (1-1/2 oz)	13 lb 8 oz (2-No. 10 cn)	12 lb
Apples, fresh, eating	1 apple (6 oz)	37 lb 8 oz	
Applesauce, canned	1/4 cup (2 oz)	14 lb 10 oz (2-1/6-No. 10 cn)	
Apricots, canned, halves, drained	3 halves (1-1/2 oz)	20 lb 4 oz (3-No. 10 cn)	11 lb 10 oz
Apricots, fresh	2 apricots (2-1/2 oz)	16 lb 11 oz	
Bananas, fresh, peeled, sliced	1/2 cup (2-1/2 oz)	28 lb	18 lb 3 oz
Bananas, fresh	1 banana (6 oz)	40 lb	
Blueberries, canned drained	1/2 cup (4-1/2 oz)	52 lb 10 oz (8-1/4-No. 10 cn)	28 lb 6 oz
Cantaloupe, fresh, quartered, unpared	1/4 small cantaloupe (3 oz)	21 lb 14 oz	
Cantaloupe, fresh, pared, 1 inch pieces	1/2 cup (2-1/2 oz)	35 lb	17 lb 14 oz
Casaba melons, fresh, unpared, sliced	1/10 melon (4 oz)	31 lb 4 oz	
Casaba melons, fresh, pared 1 inch pieces	1/2 cup (2-1/2 oz)	29 lb 11 oz	17 lb 12 oz
Cherries, canned, sweet, drained	1/2 cup (3-1/2 oz)	38 lb 13 oz (5-3/4 No.-10 cn)	23 lb 14 oz
Cherries, fresh, sweet	1/2 cup (2-1/2 oz)	17 lb 10 oz	
Coconut, prepared, sweetened, flakes	1 tbsp	1 lb 5 oz	
Coconut, prepared, sweetened, flakes	1 tbsp	1 lb 5 oz	
Fruit cocktail, canned, drained	1/2 cup (4 oz)	42 lb 3 oz (6-1/4-No. 10 cn)	27 lb 12 oz
Fruits, chunks, mixed, canned, drained	1/2 cup (3 oz)	39 lb 2 oz (5-3/4-No. 10 cn)	26 lb 3 oz
Grapefruit, canned, drained	1/2 cup (4 oz)	46 lb 14 oz (15-No. 3 cyl cn or 47-No. 303 cn)	25 lb 10 oz

ITEM	PORTION SIZE	100 PORTIONS	
		A.P. WEIGHT OR CONTAINER	E.P.
Grapefruit, fresh, segments	1/2 cup (4 oz)	48 lb	25 lb
Grapes, fresh	1/2 cup (2-1/2 oz)	16 lb 11 oz	
Honeyball melons, fresh, unpared, sliced	1/10 melon (3 oz)	40 lb 15 oz	
Honeyball melons, fresh, pared, 1 inch pieces	1/2 cup (2-1/2 oz)	37 lb 14 oz	17 lb 7 oz
Honeydew melons, fresh, pared, 1 inch pieces	1/2 cup (2-1/2 oz)	37 lb 14 oz	17 lb 7 oz
Kiwifruit, fresh, pared, sliced	2 slices (1/2 oz)	5 lb 14 oz	5 lb 1 oz
Mangoes, fresh, pared, diced	1/2 cup (3 oz)	27 lb 12 oz	19 lb 3 oz
Mangoes, fresh, pared, sliced	4 slices (2 oz)	18 lb 9 oz	12 lb 12 oz
Nectarines, fresh	1 nectarine (4-1/2 oz)	28 lb 2 oz	
Oranges, fresh, peeled, sliced	3 slices (2 oz)	20 lb 9 oz	14 lb 9 oz
Oranges, fresh	1 orange (6 oz)	37 lb 8 oz	
Oranges, Mandarin, canned, drained	1/4 cup (1-1/2 oz)	20 lb 4 oz (3 No. 10 cn)	10 lb 15 oz
Papaya, fresh, pared, seeded, cubed	1/2 cup (2-1/2 oz)	24 lb	15 lb 11 oz
Papaya, fresh, pared, sliced	3 slices (2 oz)	22 lb 8 oz	14 lb 11 oz
Peaches, canned, halves, drained	2 halves (4 oz)	45 lb 9 oz (6-3/4-No 10 cn)	27 lb 7 oz
Peaches, canned, quarters/slices, drained	1/2 cup (4 oz)	43 lb 14 oz (6-1/2-No. 10 cn)	27 lb
Peaches, fresh	1 peach (4 oz)	25 lb	
Peaches, frozen	1/2 cup (4 oz)	27 lb 13 oz (4-1/4-No. 10 cn)	
Pears, canned, halves, drained	2 halves (3-1/2 oz)	41 lb 7 oz (6-1/4-No. 10 cn)	25 lb
Pears, canned, quarters/slices, drained	1/2 cup (3-1/2 oz)	36 lb 7 oz (5-1/2-No. 10 cn)	22 lb 8 oz
Pears, fresh	1 pear (5-1/2 oz)	36 lb	
Persian melons, fresh, unpared, sliced	1/10 melon (3 oz)	45 lb 13 oz	
Persian melons, fresh, pared, diced	1/2 cup (2-1/2 oz)	41 lb 4 oz	17 lb 5 oz
Pineapple, canned, chunks/tidbits, drained	1/2 cup (3-1/2 oz)	37 lb 2 oz (5-1/2-No. 10 cn)	22 lb 10 oz

ITEM	PORTION SIZE	100 PORTIONS	
		A.P. WEIGHT OR CONTAINER	E.P.
Pineapple, fresh, pared, cored, 1 inch pieces	1/2 cup (2-1/2 oz)	33 lb 4 oz	17 lb 5 oz
Plums, canned, drained	3 plums (2-1/2 oz)	32 lb 1 oz (4-3/4 No. 10 cn)	17 lb 13 oz
Plums, fresh	1 plum (2-1/2 oz)	15 lb 10 oz	
Raisins	1 tbsp	2 lb 4 oz (1/2-No. 10 cn)	
Raspberries, frozen	1/2 cup (4 oz)	27lb 13oz (4-1/4 No.10 cn)	
Strawberries, fresh, sliced	1/2 cup (2-1/2 oz)	18 lb 4 oz	17 lb 3 oz
Strawberries, fresh, whole	1/2 cup (2-1/2 oz)	16 lb 9 oz	15 lb 10 oz
Strawberries, frozen, sliced	1/2 cup (4 oz)	27 lb 13 oz (4-1/4-No. 10 cn)	
Tangelos, fresh	1 tangelo (6 oz)	37 lb 8 oz	
Tangerines, fresh	1 tangerine (3-1/2 oz)	22 lb 15 oz	
Watermelons, fresh, unpared, wedge (1 inch by 4 inches)	1 wedge (4 oz)	51 lb	
Watermelons, fresh, pared, 1 inch pieces	1/2 cup (2-1/2 oz)	34 lb	17 lb 11 oz

GUIDELINES FOR USE OF MICROWAVE OVENS

A microwave oven heats, cooks, or thaws food by means of short energy waves called microwaves. Oven-proof glass, paper, oven-proof dinnerware and plastic are transparent to microwaves and will permit microwaves to pass through them with little or no absorption. It is recommended that food be placed inside the microwave oven on a plate or container made of one of these materials. AVOID heating or cooking foods in metal or metallic containers and the use of metallic covers such as aluminum foil. Do not use melamine plastic tableware as a cooking/heating container in the microwave oven. Melamine tableware absorbs microwave energy. It becomes dangerously hot and could explode.

Cooking, heating or thawing time in a microwave oven depends on the amount of food, its density, shape, initial temperature (i. e. , frozen, thawed), desired final temperature and the power level of the oven. Time and portion control are important. Because of microwave cooking speed, greater care must be taken to prevent over-cooking/heating. A general rule is to underestimate cooking/heating time, then add time if necessary. As with conventional methods, there is often some temperature rise (additional cooking) after food is removed from the oven, and this should be taken into consideration. The manufacturer's operating manual for cooking guidelines should be followed for approximate cooking times.

SAFETY PRECAUTIONS: Microwave ovens will not emit dangerous levels of microwave energy if properly used and maintained. The manufacturer's operating manual should be thoroughly read and guidelines followed for safe and efficient use of the microwave oven. If not available, follow these general guidelines:

   a. DO NOT operate oven with the door open. Open-door operation can result in harmful exposure to microwave energy. Do not break or tamper with the safety interlocks.
   b. Never close the oven door on utensils, cloths and other objects, or allow soil or cleaner residue to accumulate on the sealing surfaces.
   c. DO NOT operate oven with an empty cavity. Keep all metal utensils out of the oven cavity at all times.
   d. DO NOT obstruct cooling vents in the oven housing.
   e. DO NOT operate the oven if it is damaged. It is particularly important that the oven door close properly and that there is no damage to the (1) door (bent) (2) hinges and latches (broken or loosened) (3) door seals and sealing surfaces.

The oven should not be adjusted or repaired by anyone except properly qualified personnel. The oven shall be inspected at least quarterly for radiation leakage or as required by each service. Any repairs involving the oven door or exterior housing should be followed by recertification for microwave leakage.

GENERAL OPERATION: Operating instructions may differ depending on the manufacturer and model of the microwave oven. The manufacturer's operating manual should be consulted for instructions on the particular make/model of microwave oven. If not available, follow these general instructions:

   a. Place food on a suitable container (oven-proof glass or dinnerware or paper). DO NOT use metal or metallic containers or aluminum foil.
   b. Most food item(s) should be covered with a suitable cover (glass, china, or paper) for faster heating/cooking and to prevent spattering the oven. DO NOT cover bakery items, sandwiches or breaded products. These products become soggy when covered.
   c. Place item in center of microwave oven. Close oven door securely; select proper time setting.

CLEANING: A buildup of food and grease on the interior oven surfaces can result in damage to the materials and surfaces as well as a loss in cooking power. To keep the microwave oven safe and operational, follow the manufacturer's operating manual.

GUIDELINES FOR USE OF MICROWAVE OVENS

SANITARY PRECAUTIONS:

FRESH PORK: Fresh pork (pork chops, pork sausage, diced pork, pork loin, pork spareribs, pork tenderloin, pork steaks) should not be cooked in a microwave oven.

Fresh pork should be cooked to a consistent internal temperature of 170°F. With rapid cooking methods such as microwaving, heat may not be evenly distributed resulting in "cold spots." "Cold spots" can harbor infectious trichinae organisms that might be present in fresh pork.

MICROWAVE OVEN THAWING: Frozen foods may be thawed in microwave ovens provided they are immediately cooked thereafter as a part of a continuous cooking process. Some microwave ovens may include a thawing or defrost setting. Consult the manufacturer's directions for use.

CONVERSION OF QUANTITIES IN RECIPES

Weight Conversion Chart

The following chart for weights permit easy adjustment of recipes to yield the number of portions actually needed. Since recipes are based on 100 portions, find the amount as specified in the recipe under the column headed 100 portions, and then use the amount shown in the column with the heading for the number of portions to be prepared, i.e., if a recipe for 100 uses 1 pound of flour, find 1 pound under the column headed 100 portions and then look in the column under 125 portion and you will see that your should use 1 pound 4 ounces to prepare 125 portions of the item.

Oz = ounce lb = pound

10 Portions	25 Portions	50 Portions	75 Portions	100 Portions	125 Portions	150 Portions	175 Portions	250 Portions	275 Portions	300 Portions
1/10 oz	1/4 oz	1/2 oz	3/4 oz	1 oz	1-1/4 oz	1-1/2 oz	1-3/4 oz	2-1/2 oz	2-3/4 oz	3 oz
1/5 oz	1/2 oz	1 oz	1-1/2 oz	2 oz	2-1/2 oz	3 oz	3-1/2 oz	5 oz	5-1/2 oz	6 oz
3/10 oz	3/4 oz	1-1/2 oz	2-1/4 oz	3 oz	3-3/4 oz	4-1/2 oz	5-1/4 oz	7-1/2 oz	8-1/4 oz	9 oz
2/5 oz	1 oz	2 oz	3 oz	4 oz	5 oz	6 oz	7 oz	10 oz	11 oz	12 oz
1/2 oz	1-1/4 oz	2-1/2 oz	3-3/4 oz	5 oz	6-1/4 oz	7-1/2 oz	8-3/4 oz	12-1/2 oz	13-3/4 oz	15 oz
3/5 oz	1-1/2 oz	3 oz	4-1/2 oz	6 oz	7-1/2 oz	9 oz	10-1/2 oz	15 oz	1 lb	1 lb 2 oz
7/10 oz	1-3/4 oz	3-1/2 oz	5-1/4 oz	7 oz	8-3/4 oz	10-1/2 oz	12-1/4 oz	1 lb 2 oz	1 lb 4 oz	1 lb 5 oz

CONVERSION OF QUANTITIES IN RECIPES

Weight Conversion Chart

10 Portions	25 Portions	50 Portions	75 Portions	100 Portions	125 Portions	150 Portions	175 Portions	250 Portions	275 Portions	300 Portions
4/5 oz	2 oz	4 oz	6 oz	8 oz	10 oz	12 oz	14 oz	1 lb 4 oz	1 lb 6 oz	1 lb 8 oz
7/8 oz	2-1/4 oz	4-1/2 oz	6-3/4 oz	9 oz	11-1/4 oz	13-1/2 oz	15-3/4 oz	1 lb 6 oz	1 lb 8 oz	1 lb 11 oz
1 oz	2-1/2 oz	5 oz	7-1/2 oz	10 oz	12-1/2 oz	15 oz	1 lb 2 oz	1 lb 10 oz	1 lb 12 oz	1 lb 14 oz
1-1/8 oz	2-3/4 oz	5-1/2 oz	8-1/4 oz	11 oz	13-3/4 oz	1 lb	1 lb 4 oz	1 lb 12 oz	1 lb 14 oz	2 lb 2 oz
1-1/4 oz	3 oz	6 oz	9 oz	12 oz	15 oz	1 lb 2 oz	1 lb 5 oz	1 lb 14 oz	2 lb 2 oz	2 lb 4 oz
1-1/3 oz	3-1/4 oz	6-1/2 oz	9-3/4 oz	13 oz	1 lb	1 lb 4 oz	1 lb 6 oz	2 lb	2 lb 4 oz	2 lb 8 oz
1-3/8 oz	3-1/2 oz	7 oz	10-1/2 oz	14 oz	1 lb 2 oz	1 lb 5 oz	1 lb 8 oz	2 lb 4 oz	2 lb 6 oz	2 lb 10 oz
1-1/2 oz	3-3/4 oz	7-1/2 oz	11 oz	15 oz	1 lb 2 oz	1 lb 6 oz	1 lb 10 oz	2 lb 5 oz	2 lb 10 oz	2 lb 14 oz
1-5/8 oz	4 oz	8 oz	12 oz	1 lb	1 lb 4 oz	1 lb 8 oz	1 lb 12 oz	2 lb 8 oz	2 lb 12 oz	3 lb
2 oz	5 oz	10 oz	15 oz	1 lb 4 oz	1 lb 10 oz	1 lb 14 oz	2 lb 4 oz	3 lb 2 oz	3 lb 8 oz	3 lb 12 oz
2-2/5 oz	6 oz	12 oz	1 lb 2 oz	1 lb 8 oz	1 lb 14 oz	2 lb 4 oz	2 lb 10 oz	3 lb 12 oz	4 lb 2 oz	4 lb 8 oz
2-4/5 oz	7 oz	14 oz	1 lb 5 oz	1 lb 12 oz	2 lb 4 oz	2 lb 10 oz	3 lb 2 oz	4 lb 6 oz	4 lb 14 oz	5 lb 4 oz
3-1/5 oz	8 oz	1 lb	1 lb 8 oz	2 lb	2 lb 8 oz	3 lb	3 lb 8 oz	5 lb	5 lb 8 oz	6 lb
3-3/5 oz	9 oz	1 lb 2 oz	1 lb 11 oz	2 lb 4 oz	2 lb1 4 oz	3 lb 6 oz	4 lb	5 lb 10 oz	6 lb 4 oz	6 lb 12 oz
4 oz	10 oz	1 lb 4 oz	1 lb 14 oz	2 lb 8 oz	3 lb 2 oz	3 lb 12 oz	4 lb 6 oz	6 lb 4 oz	6 lb 14 oz	7 lb 8 oz

CONVERSION OF QUANTITIES IN RECIPES

Weight Conversion Chart

10 Portions	25 Portions	50 Portions	75 Portions	100 Portions	125 Portions	150 Portions	175 Portions	250 Portions	275 Portions	300 Portions
4-2/5 oz	11 oz	1 lb 6 oz	2 lb 2 oz	2 lb 12 oz	3 lb 8 oz	4 lb 2 oz	4 lb 14 oz	6 lb 14 oz	7 lb 10 oz	8 lb 4 oz
4-4/5 oz	12 oz	1 lb 8 oz	2 lb 4 oz	3 lb	3 lb 12 oz	4 lb 8 oz	5 lb 4 oz	7 lb 8 oz	8 lb 4 oz	9 lb
5-1/5 oz	13 oz	1 lb 10 oz	2 lb 8 oz	3 lb 4 oz	4 lb 2 oz	4 lb 14 oz	5 lb 11 oz	8 lb 2 oz	9 lb	9 lb 12 oz
5-3/5 oz	14 oz	1 lb 12 oz	2 lb 10 oz	3 lb 8 oz	4 lb 6 oz	5 lb 4 oz	6 lb 2 oz	8 lb 12 oz	9 lb 10 oz	10 lb 8 oz
6 oz	15 oz	1 lb 14 oz	2 lb 14 oz	3 lb 12 oz	4 lb 11 oz	5 lb 10 oz	6 lb 10 oz	9 lb 6 oz	10 lb 5 oz	11 lb 4 oz
6-2/5 z	1 lb	2 lb	3 lb	4 lb	5 lb	6 lb	7 lb	10 lb	11 lb	12 lb
8 oz	1 lb 4 oz	2 lb 8 oz	3 lb 12 oz	5 lb	6 lb 4 oz	7 lb 8 oz	8 lb 12 oz	12 lb 8 oz	13 lb 12 oz	15 lb
9-3/5 oz	1 lb 8 oz	3 lb	4 lb 8 oz	6 oz	7 lb 8 oz	9 lb	10 lb 8 oz	15 lb	16 lb 8 oz	18 lb
11-1/5 oz	1 lb 12 oz	3 lb 8 oz	5 lb 4 oz	7 lb	8 lb 12 oz	10 lb 8 oz	12 lb 4 oz	17 lb 8 oz	19 lb 4 oz	21 lb
12-4/5 oz	2 lb	4 lb	6 lb	8 lb	10 lb	12 lb	14 lb	20 lb	22 lb	24 lb
1 lb	2 lb 8 oz	5 lb	7 lb 8 oz	10 oz	12 lb 8 oz	15 lb	17 lb 8 oz	25 lb	27 lb 8 oz	36 lb
1 lb 4 oz	3 lb	6 lb	9 lb	12 lb	15 lb	18 lb	21 lb	30 lb	33 lb	36 lb
1 lb 8 oz	3 lb 12 oz	7 lb 8 oz	11 lb 4 oz	15 lb	18 lb 12 oz	22 lb 8 oz	26 lb 4 oz	37 lb 8 oz	41 lb 4 oz	45 lb
2 lb	5 lb	10 lb	15 lb	20 lb	25 lb	30 lb	35 lb	50 lb	55 lb	60 lb
3 lb	7 lb 8 oz	15 lb	22 lb 8 oz	30 lb	37 lb 8 oz	45 lb	52 lb 8 oz	75 lb	82 lb 8 oz	90 lb

CONVERSION OF QUANTITIES IN RECIPES

Measure Conversion Chart

The following chart for measures permits easy adjustments of recipes to yield the number of portions actually needed. Since recipes are based on 100 portions, find the amount as specified in the recipe under column headed 100 portions and then use the amount shown in the column with the heading for the number of portions to be prepared, i.e., if a recipe for 100 uses 3 cups of flour, find 3 cups under the column headed 100 portions and then look in the column under 125 portions and you will see that you should use 3 ¾ cups to prepare 125 portions of the item.

tsp – teaspoon   tbsp – tablespoon   qt – quart   gal - gallon

10 Portions	25 Portions	50 Portions	75 Portions	100 Portions	125 Portions	150 Portions	175 Portions	250 Portions	275 Portions	300 Portions
....	¼ tsp	½ tsp	¾ tsp	1 tsp	1 ¼ tsp	1 ½ tsp	1 ¾ tsp	2 ½ tsp	2 ¾ tsp	1 tbsp
....	½ tsp	1 tsp	1 ½ tsp	2 tsp	2 ½ tsp	1 tbsp	3 ½ tsp	1-2/3 tbsp	1-7/8 tbsp	2 tbsp
¼ tsp	¾ tsp	1 ½ tsp	2 tsp	1 tbsp	3 ¾ tsp	1-1/3 tbsp	1-2/3 tbsp	2-1/3 tbsp	2-2/3 tbsp	3 tbsp
½ tsp	1 ½ tsp	1 tbsp	1-2/3 tbsp	2 tbsp	2-2/3 tbsp	3 tbsp	3-2/3 tbsp	5 tbsp	5-2/3 tbsp	6 tbsp
¾ tsp	2 ¼ tsp	1-2/3 tbsp	2-1/3 tbsp	3 tbsp	¼ cup	4-2/3 tbsp	5 tbsp	7-2/3 tbsp	½ cup	9 tbsp
1 tsp	1 tbsp	2 tbsp	3 tbsp	¼ cup	5 tbsp	6 tbsp	7 tbsp	10 tbsp	11 tbsp	¾ cup
1 ½ tsp	3 ¾ tsp	2-2/3 tbsp	4 tbsp	5 tbsp	6 tbsp	7-2/3 tbsp	9 tbsp	12-2/3 tbsp	14 tbsp	1 cup
1 ¾ tsp	4 ½ tsp	3 tbsp	4-2/3 tbsp	6 tbsp	7-2/3 tbsp	½ cup	10-2/3 tbsp	15 tbsp	1 cup	1 cup + 2 tbsp
2 tsp	5 ¼ tsp	3-2/3 tbsp	5 tbsp	7 tbsp	9 tbsp	10-2/3 tbsp	¾ cup	1 cup + 1-2/3 tbsp	1 cup + 3 tbsp	1-1/3 cups
2 ¼ tsp	2 tbsp	4 tbsp	6 tbsp	½ cup	10 tbsp	¾ cup	14 tbsp	1 ¼ cups	1 cup + 6 tbsp	1 ½ cups
2 ½ tsp	2 tbsp	4-2/3 tbsp	7 tbsp	9 tbsp	11 tbsp	13-2/3 tbsp	1 cup	1 cup + 6 tbsp	1 ½ cups	1 ¾ cup
1 tbsp	2-2/3 tbsp	5 tbsp	7-2/3 tbsp	10 tbsp	¾ cup	1 cup	1 cup + 2 tbsp	1 ½ cups	1 ¾ cups	2 cups
3 ¼ tsp	3 tbsp	5-2/3 tbsp	8 tbsp	11 tbsp	14 tbsp	1 cup	1 cup + 3 tbsp	1 ¾ cups	2 cups	2-1/8 cups
3 ½ tsp	3 tbsp	6 tbsp	9 tbsp	¾ cup	1 cup	1 cup + 2 tbsp	1 ¼ cups	2 cups	2 cups + 2 tbsp	2 ½ cups
3 ¾ tsp	3 tbsp	6-2/3 tbsp	10 tbsp	13 tbsp	1 cup	1 ¼ cups	1 ½ cups	2 cups	2 ¼ cups	2 ½ cups
1-1/3 tbsp	3-2/3 tbsp	7 tbsp	10-2/3 tbsp	14 tbsp	1 cup + 2 tbsp	1-1/3 cups	1 ½ cups	2 cups + 3 tbsp	2-1/3 cups	2 ½ cups
4 ½ tsp	3 ¾ tbsp	7-2/3 tbsp	11 tbsp	15 tbsp	1 ¼ cups	1 ½ cups	1 ¾ cups	2-1/3 cups	2 ¾ cups	2-7/8 cups
4 ¾ tsp	¼ cup	½ cup	¾ cup	1 cup	1 ¼ cups	1 ½ cups	1 ¾ cups	2 ½ cups	2 ¾ cups	3 cups
2 tbsp	5 tbsp	10 tbsp	1 cup	1 ¼ cups	1 ½ cups	2 cups	2 ¼ cups	3 cups	3 ½ cups	3 ¾ cups
7 tbsp	6 tbsp	¾ cup	1 cup + 2 tbsp	1 ½ cups	2 cups	2 ¼ cups	2 ¾ cups	3 ¾ cups	1 qt	4 ½ cups

CONVERSION OF QUANTITIES IN RECIPES

Measure Conversion Chart

10 Portions	25 Portions	50 Portions	75 Portions	100 Portions	125 Portions	150 Portions	175 Portions	250 Portions	275 Portions	300 Portions
8 ¼ tsp	7 tbsp	14 tbsp	1-1/3 cups	1 ¾ cups	2 ¼ cups	2 ¾ cups	3 cups	4 ½ cups	4 ¾ cups	5 ¼ cups
9 ½ tsp	½ cup	1 cup	1 ½ cups	2 cups	2 ½ cups	3 cups	3 ½ cups	5 cups	5 ½ cups	1 ½ qt
10 ¾ tsp	½ cup + 1 tbsp	1 cup + 2 tbsp	1 ¾ cups	2 ¼ cups	2 ¾ cups	3 ½ cups	1 qt	5 ¾ cups	1 ½ qt	6 ¾ cups
¼ cup	10 tbsp	1 ¼ cups	2 cups	2 ½ cups	3 cups + 2 tbsp	3 ¾ cups	4 ½ cups	6 ¼ cups	1 ¾ qt	7 ½ cups
4 ¾ tbsp	¾ cup	1 ½ cups	2 ¼ cups	3 cups	3 ¾ cups	4 ½ cups	5 ¼ cups	7 ½ cups	8 ¼ cups	2 ¼ qt
5-2/3 tbsp	14 tbsp	1 ¾ cups	2 ½ cups	3 ½ cups	4 ½ cups	1 ¼ qt	1 ½ qt	2 ¼ qt	9 ¾ cups	10 ½ cups
6 ¼ tbsp	1 cup	2 cups	3 cups	1 qt	1 ¼ qt	1 ½ qt	1 ¾ qt	2 ½ qt	2 ¾ qt	3 qt
½ cup	1 ¼ cups	2 ½ cups	3 ¾ cups	1 ¼ qt	6 ¼ cups	7 ½ cups	8 ¾ cups	12 ½ cups	3 ½ qt	3 ¾ qt
9 ¾ tbsp	1 ½ cups	3 cups	4 ½ cups	1 ½ qt	7 ½ cups	2 ¼ qt	10 ½ cups	3 ¾ qt	1 gal	4 ½ qt
11 tbsp	1 ¾ cups	3 ½ cups	5 ¼ cups	7 cups	8 ¾ cups	10 ½ cups	3 qt	1 gal + 1 ½ cups	1 gal + 3 ¼ cups	5 ¼ qt
12 ¾ tbsp.	2 cups	1 qt	1 ½ qt	2 qt	2 ¼ qt	3 qt	3 ½ qt	1 ¼ gal	5 ½ qt	1 ½ gal
1 ¼ cups	3 cups	1 ½ qt	2 ¼ qt	3 qt	3 ¾ qt	4 ½ qt	5 ¼ qt	7 ½ qt	2 gal	2 ¼ gal
1 ½ cups	1 qt	2 qt	3 qt	1 gal	1 ¼ gal	1 ½ gal	1 ¾ gal	2 ½ gal	2 ¾ gal	3 gal
3 cups	2 qt	1 gal	1 ½ gal	2 gal	2 ¼ gal	3 gal	3 ½ gal	5 gal	5 ½ gal	6 gal
4 ½ cups	3 qt	1 ½ gal	2 ¼ gal	3 gal	3 ¾ gal	4 ½ gal	5 ¼ gal	7 ¼ gal	8 gal	9 gal
1 ½ qt	1 gal	2 gal	3 gal	4 gal	5 gal	6 gal	7 gal	10 gal	11 gal	12 gal
7 ½ cups	1 ¼ gal	2 ½ gal	3 ¾ gal	5 gal	6 ¼ gal	7 ½ gal	8 ¾ gal	12 ½ gal	13 ¾ gal	15 gal

USE OF DEHYDRATED GARLIC AND HORSERADISH

DEHYDRATED GARLIC

Dehydrated garlic may be added directly to recipes as a substitute for dry (fresh) garlic. For more garlic flavor, dissolve garlic in an equal volume of water.

SUBSTITUTION GUIDE:

Dehydrated		Dry (Fresh) Garlic
1/4 tsp	=	1 tsp minced (1 average clove)
3/4 tsp	=	1 tbsp minced (3 average cloves)
2-2/3 tbsp (1 oz)	=	10 tbsp (3-1/2 oz) minced (30 average cloves)

DRY (FRESH) GARLIC

Follow specific recipe for substitution of dry (fresh) garlic for dehydrated garlic. DO NOT SUBSTITUTE DRY (FRESH) GARLIC FOR DEHYDRATED GARLIC IN SALAD DRESSING RECIPES.

DEHYDRATED HORSERADISH

Dehydrated horseradish should be rehydrated before use in a recipe as follows:
To one part by volume dehydrated horseradish add two parts by volume of warm water.
The rehydrated horseradish is about twice as potent in strength as prepared horseradish; use the following substitution: One part by volume rehydrated horseradish for two parts by volume prepared horseradish.

SUBSTITUTION GUIDE:

Dehydrated Horseradish	+	Warm Water	=	Rehydrated Volume	=	Prepared Horseradish Equivalent
1/2 oz (2-1/3 tbsp)		4-2/3 tbsp		6 tbsp		3/4 cup
1-2/3 oz (62/3 tbsp)		13 tbsp		1 cup		2 cups
2-1/2 oz bottle (10 tbsp)		1-1/4 cups		1-1/2 cups		3 cups

Recipes using prepared horseradish will have a decreased volume when dehydrated horseradish is used. Additional water should NOT be used to yield a product equal in volume to the prepared horseradish.

GUIDELINES FOR USE OF FLOURS

All quantities in the Measures column of the recipes should be sifted before measuring. If flour weights rather than measures are used, the flour should be sifted after weighing to aerate the flour and to remove any foreign particles.

BREAD FLOUR is milled from blends of hard spring wheat and hard winter wheat or from either of these types alone. It is fairly high in protein and slightly granular to the touch. Bread flour is milled chiefly for making bread. Bread flour also is used in fruit cakes, cream puffs, and similar products which require strength in dough structure. One pound sifted bread flour measures 1 quart.

GENERAL PURPOSE FLOUR is milled from blends of hard and soft wheat. This flour is used for cookies, pie crust, biscuits, muffins, cakes, sauces, and gravies. One pound sifted general purpose flour measures 1 quart.

GUIDELINES FOR HANDLING FROZEN FOODS

Proper storage and thawing procedures for frozen foods are essential for keeping foods safe and palatable. Some foods, such as vegetables, do not need to be thawed before cooking. Many recipes require meat to be only partially thawed or tempered, to facilitate separation before cooking; this prevents excessive moisture loss. Unless otherwise indicated, preparation methods and cooking times are for thawed meat, fish and poultry.

Frozen foods should be stored at or below 0° F. and thawed at 36° F. DO NOT refreeze foods that have been thawed; cook and serve as soon as possible to promote maximum quality and safety.

FROZEN FRUITS: Thaw unopened under refrigeration (36° F. to 38° F.) or covered with cold water.

FROZEN FRUIT JUICES AND CONCENTRATES: These do not require thawing.

FROZEN VEGETABLES: These do not require thawing before cooking. For faster cooking, Brussels sprouts, broccoli, asparagus, cauliflower, and leafy greens may be partially thawed under refrigeration.

FROZEN MEATS: Improper thawing of meat encourages bacterial growth and also results in unnecessary loss of meat juices, poor quality and loss of yield and nutrients. To thaw meat, remove from shipping container, but leave inside wrappings (usually polyethylene bags) on meat. Thaw under refrigeration (36° F. to 38° F.) until almost completely thawed. Spread out large cuts, such as roasts, to allow air to circulate. The length of the thawing period will vary accordingly to the size of meat cut, the temperature and degree of air circulation in the chill space, and the quantity of meat being thawed in a given space. Boneless meats generally require 26 to 48 hours to thaw at 36° F. to 38° F.

Meat may be cooked frozen or tempered except for a few cuts which require complete thawing (i.e., bulk ground beef, bulk beef patty mix, braising Swiss steak, bulk pork sausage and diced beef for stewing.)

Roasts, when cooked from the frozen state, will require one-third to one-half more cooking time than thawed roasts. The addition of seasonings, if required, must be delayed until the outside is somewhat thawed and the surface is sufficiently moist to retain the seasonings. The insertion of meat thermometers must also be delayed until roasts are partially thawed. Grill steaks, pork chops and liver should be tempered before cooking to ensure a moist, palatable product. (Temper - To remove from freezer and place under refrigeration for a period of time sufficient to facilitate separation and handling of frozen product. Internal temperature of the food should be approximately 26° F. to 28° F.). Pork sausage patties and pork and beef sausage links should be cooked frozen.

FROZEN SEAFOOD: Fish fillets and steaks may be cooked frozen or thawed. Any fish that is to be breaded or batter dipped should be thawed. Clams, crabmeat, oysters, scallops and shrimp should be kept wrapped while thawing. Fish and shellfish should be thawed under refrigeration (36° F. to 38° F.) and require 12 hours to thaw.

Frozen, whole lobster, king crab legs, spiny lobster tail, breaded fish portions or nuggets, batter-dipped fish portions, or breaded oysters and shrimp SHOULD NOT be thawed before cooking.

FROZEN POULTRY: Poultry must be thawed under refrigeration (36° F. to 38° F.). Proper thawing of poultry reduces bacterial growth, maintains quality and retains nutrients through less drip loss.

GUIDELINES FOR HANDLING FROZEN FOODS

RAW CHICKEN: Remove whole chickens from shipping containers and thaw in individual wrappers (plastic bags). To thaw parts or quarters, remove intermediate containers from shipping containers; remove overwrapping from intermediate containers and open intermediate containers to expose inner wrapping. Length of thawing period under refrigeration (36° F. to 38° F.) will vary according to size of chicken and refrigeration conditions.

Approximate Thawing Times: Chicken, whole - 37 hours; Chicken, quarters - 52 hours; Chicken, cut-up - 52 hours

PRECOOKED BREADED CHICKEN, NUGGETS OR FILLETS: DO NOT THAW before cooking.

PRECOOKED UNBREADED CHICKEN FILLETS: Temper. DO NOT THAW before cooking.

PREPARED FROZEN CHILIES RELLENOS, BURRITOS, PIZZAS, ENCHILADAS, LASAGNA, TAMALES, MANICOTTI, CANNELLONI: DO NOT THAW before cooking.

TURKEY: Remove turkeys from shipping containers. Thaw in individual wrappers under refrigeration (36° F. to 38° F.)

Approximate Thawing Times: Turkey, whole (16 lbs or less - 2 days; Turkey, whole (over 16 lbs) - 3 to 4 days; Turkey, boneless - 12 to 16 hours; Turkey, ground – thaw; Turkey sausage patties and links - cook frozen

FROZEN EGGS: Thaw under refrigeration (36 F. to 38 F.) or covered with cold water. Thirty pound cans require at least 2 days to thaw, 10 lb cans or cartons require at least 1 day.

FROZEN PIZZA BLEND CHEESE: If pizza blend cheese is received and stored as a frozen product, it should be thawed under refrigeration (36° F. to 38° F.) to ensure retention of its characteristic flavor, texture, and appearance. Thawing at room temperature will encourage bacterial growth (inherent in the product) resulting in an undesirable flavor and swelling of the container.

GUIDELINES FOR USE OF ANTIBROWNING AGENT
(NON-SULFATING AGENTS)

The purpose of an antibrowning agent is to prevent browning and maintain color and crispness in fresh potatoes and fruits.

DIRECTIONS FOR USE
1. Dissolve 1-3/4 oz (3 tbsp) antibrowning agent per gallon of cold water in a clean stainless steel, glass or plastic container. DO NOT use galvanized metal containers.
2. Dip fresh white potatoes (peeled, whole, quarters, French fry cut, slices) or fruits (apples, avocados, bananas, peaches, pears) peeled, sliced and free from bruises in the antibrowning solution. Soak for 3 minutes.
3. Drain and refrigerate product until ready to use.

NOTE:
1. Keep antibrowning agent stored in its original container. Make the solution fresh daily. A plastic measuring spoon should be kept with the antibrowning agent for easy measuring.
2. Antibrowning agent is not required for lettuce, cauliflower, green peppers, cabbage, celery or pineapple.

GUIDELINES FOR USE OF STEAM COOKERS

Use of steamers in quantity food preparation can save cooking time, labor, help maintain appearance of food, and preserve nutrients normally lost by other cooking methods. Steamers are ideal for batch preparation. Foods may be steamed and served in the same pan, if steam table pans are used for preparation.

Steamers are either 5 lb pressure or 15 lb pressure (high speed) type. When food is steamed at 5 lb pressure, the internal temperature of the steamer is 225° F. to 228° F. At 15 lb pressure, the temperature is 245° F. to 250° F.

Most canned, fresh or frozen vegetables, in addition to other foods such as rice, pasta, poultry, meats, fish, and shellfish, can be cooked in steamers.
Foods may be steamed in perforated or solid pans. Perforated pans are usually used, particularly for vegetables, unless the cooking liquid is retained or manufacturer's directions specify solid type pans. Pans are normally filled no more than 2/3 full to allow steam to circulate for even cooking.

Cooking times will vary depending on the type steamer, food, and temperature and quantity of the product. For best results follow the manufacturer's cooking times and directions. Cooking time should be scheduled to include bringing food up to cooking temperature, as well as steaming time. Timing begins when the pressure gauge registers 3 lb on the 5 lb steamer and 9 lb on the 15 lb steamer. Be sure to use timer, if available, to prevent overcooking.

After cooking is completed, the steam should be exhausted slowly for safety and to preserve skins of vegetables such as peas. Leave steamer doors ajar for cooling and to preserve door gaskets.

GUIDELINES FOR GARNISHES

A garnish is a food item or part of a food item featured in such a way as to enhance the food served. Garnishing is an art. It can be done well with little time or effort by following a few simple guidelines. Generally, garnishes should be edible and should be an integral part of the food so that they will not be left on the plate. Not all food requires garnishing. Many recipes have built-in garnishes; examples are: beef stew with vegetables, creole shrimp, tossed vegetable salads, and desserts such as pies and cakes. They should be handled carefully to prevent spoilage and food-borne illness. (Note: always wash a vegetable before preparing it as a garnish).
Garnishes should be:

1. Simple, natural, and fresh in appearance.
2. Suitable in texture and size to the food.
3. Flavorful. Bland foods require a more highly seasoned garnish.
4. Arranged in a manner to enhance the food with which they are used.
5. Used sparingly. Sprinkle or place in small groupings.
6. Harmonious. Colors should never clash. Care should be used to produce combinations that will be pleasing to the eye.

The following list indicates some of the wide variety possible in edible garnishes:

Apples-unpared, slices, wedges
Croutons
Cheese-cubes, grated, wedges
Bacon, cooked-crumbled

Celery-sticks, curls, fans
Asparagus-spears
Cucumbers-rings, slices, sticks
Cherry tomatoes-whole, halves

Dates–halves, pieces, whole
Coconut–flaked
Cabbage, red–shredded
Grapes–whole, slices
Cranberry sauce–slices, wedges
Onions–rings, mums
Lemon–wedges, slices, grated rind, twists
Maraschino cherries–halves, minced, whole
Marshmallows–miniature
Melon balls
Pineapple–chunks, tidbits, slices, rings
Peppers, pickled–cherry or jalapeno
Radishes–slices, roses, tulips
Tomatoes–slices, wedges, roses

Beets–slices, julienne, grated
Dessert topping–whipped
Crabapples, spiced
Carrots–sticks, curls, ribbons
Kiwi fruit–slices
Peppers, sweet, green–rings, slices, sticks
Oranges–slices, grated rind, wedges, twists
Pickles–sticks, slices
Paprika Pimientos–strips, minced
Parsley–sprig, chopped, minced
Nuts–chopped, whole
Olives–green, ripe, whole, slices, chopped
Raisins

<u>Garnishes need not require special equipment</u>: only simple tools are needed; for example, a sharp pointed knife for paring, a serrated knife for bread and tomatoes, and a vegetable peeler for paring fruits and vegetables. Special garnishing tools, such as a V-cutter for zigzag finish or a garnishing knife for making "crinkle or waffle" cuts, may be purchased, if desired. The following are ideas and instructions for creating more garnishes from fruits and vegetables.

GUIDELINES FOR GARNISHES

Onion Mum

1. Select a medium-sized, well-rounded white onion.
2. Peel the outer skin of the onion. Leave the root end intact but cut off any roots.
3. Using a sharp knife, start at the top of the onion and make a cut downward toward the root end. Be careful not to go all the way to the root end but stop the cut about 1/2 inch from it. Make this cut deep into the center of the vegetable. Make additional cuts until you have gone completely around the onion.
4. When cutting is completed, place onion in a bowl of hot water. This will start the petals spreading and remove the onion smell.
5. Let soak for 5 minutes, then replace the hot water with ice water to allow the flower to bloom further.
6. Color the onion mum by placing food coloring in the ice water. Let soak until the desired tint is obtained.
7. Remove from ice water. Drain.

Radish Tulip

1. Cut a thin slice off the bottom and top of the radish.
2. Make 3 cuts from the top of the radish almost to the base, making 6 equal segments.
3. Place in ice water until open (overnight if possible). Remove from ice water. Drain.

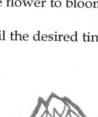

Lemon or Orange Twists

1. Cut fruit into 1/4 inch horizontal slices.
2. Slit each slice and twist.

Tomato Rose

1. Use a sharp paring knife. With the stem end of the tomato down, begin peeling on the smooth end. Cut around the tomato in a spiral, making a continuous strip about 3/4 inch wide. Do not be concerned if the peel breaks.
2. To form the rose, roll one end of the peel tightly to make the center. Loosely roll the remaining peel around the center.
3. Use a pick to secure rose base. Cut off excess pick. CAUTION: Be sure pick is firmly secured in the rose, so pick will not fall into the food during service.

NOTE: Storing tomato garnishes is not recommended.

GUIDELINES FOR GARNISHES

Carrot Ribbons or Curls

1. Slice carrot in half length-wise.
2. With a peeler. peel one strip at a time from the cut surface.
3. Drop in ice water and the strip will curl by itself.
4. Remove from ice water. Drain.

Celery Fans

1. Cut celery stalk into 2 or 3 equal lengths.
2. Make t1/4 inch slashes into one end or both ends of stalk.
3. Fan one end or both ends of stalk.
4. Drop in ice water. .
5. Remove from ice water. Drain

Radish Rose

1. Cut a thin slice of the bottom and top of the radish.
2. Make 4 cuts across the radish horizontally almost to the bottom and then make 4 cuts across the radish vertically.
3. Place in ice water until open (overnight if possible). Remove from ice water. Drain.

GUIDELINES FOR CONVECTION OVENS

A convection oven has a blower fan which circulates hot air throughout the oven, eliminating cold spots and promoting rapid cooking. Overall, cooking temperatures and times are shorter than in conventional ovens. The size, thickness, type of food, and amount loaded into the oven at one time will influence the cooking time.

TEMPERATURE SETTINGS: Follow the recommended temperature guide provided in the manufacturer's operating manual. If not available, follow the guidelines furnished on this card or check specific recipe for convection oven information. Note: At this time, not all AFRS oven recipes contain convection information. If food is cooked around the edges, but the center is still raw or not thoroughly cooked, or if there is much color variation, reduce the heat by 15° F. to 25° F. and return food to the oven. If necessary, continue to reduce the heat on successive loads until the desired results are achieved. Record most successful temperature on the recipe card for future reference.

TIME SETTING: Follow the recommended times provided in the manufacturer's operating manual. Should the manual not be available, follow the guidelines furnished on this card or check the specific recipe for convection oven information. Check progress halfway through the cooking cycle since time will vary with the quantity of food loaded, the temperature, and the type of pan used. NOTE: meat thermometers for roasting and visual examination of baked products are the most accurate methods of determining cooking times, both in convection ovens and in conventional ovens. Record most successful cooking time on the recipe card for future reference.

VENT DAMPER CONTROL SETTING: The vent damper control is located on or near the control panel. The damper should be kept closed for most foods of low moisture content such as roasts. If open during roasting, meats will be dry with excessive shrinkage.
The damper should be kept open when baking high moisture content foods (cakes, muffins, yeast bread, etc.). Leaving the damper closed throughout a baking cycle will produce cakes which are too moist and will not rise. A "cloud" or water droplets on the window indicate excessive moisture which should be vented out of the oven through the open damper.

FAN SPEED SETTINGS: SEE GENERAL NOTES BELOW.

INTERIOR OVEN LIGHTS: Turn on lights only when loading, unloading, or checking product. Continual burning of lights will result in short bulb life.

TIMER: The oven timer will ring only as a reminder; it has no control over the functioning of the oven. To ensure proper operation, wind the timer to the maximum setting, then turn back to the desired setting for the product.

GENERAL OPERATION:

1. Select and make the proper rack arrangement for the product to be cooked.
2. Turn or push the main power switch "ON" (gas oven - turn burner valve "ON"). Set thermostat to the recommended temperature. The thermostat signal light will light. Adjust fan speed on two-speed blower, if available (see General Notes below).
3. PREHEAT oven until thermostat signal light goes out indicating that the oven has reached the desired temperature. The oven should preheat to 350° F. within 10 to 15 minutes. (Note: To conserve energy, DO NOT turn on the oven until absolutely necessary - about 15 minutes before actual cooking is to start.)
4. OPEN oven doors and load the oven quickly to prevent excessive loss of heat. Load the oven from the top, centering the pans on the rack toward the front of the oven. Place partial loads in the center of the oven. Allow 1 to 2 inches between pans and along oven sides to permit good air circulation. Remember - overloading is the major cause of non-uniform baking and roasting.
5. Close oven doors and set the timer for the desired cooking time. Check the baking/roasting progress periodically until product is ready.

CLEANING AND MAINTENANCE: Refer to the manufacturer's operating manual for cleaning and maintenance instructions.

GENERAL NOTES: Most convection ovens are equipped with an electric interlock which energizes/de-energizes both the heating elements and the fan motor when the doors are closed/open. Therefore, the heating elements and fan will not operate independently and will only operate with the doors closed. (Only one known company manufactures an oven in which the fan can be controlled independently.) Some convection ovens are equipped with single-speed fan motors while others are equipped with two-speed fan motors. This information is particularly important to note when baking cakes, muffins or meringue pies, or similar products, and when oven-frying bacon. High speed air circulation may cause damage to the food (e.g., cakes slope to one side of the pan) or blow melted fat throughout the oven. Read the manufacturer's manuals and determine exactly what features you have and then, for the above products, proceed as follows.

<u>Two-Speed Interlocked Fan Motor:</u> Set fan speed to "low."

<u>Single-Speed Interlocked Fan Motor:</u> Preheat oven 50° F. higher than the recommended cooking temperature. Load oven quickly, close doors, and reduce thermostat to recommended cooking temperature. (This action will allow the product to "set up" before the fan/heating elements come on again.)

<u>Single-Speed Independent Fan Motor:</u>

1. Preheat oven 25° F. above temperature specified in recipe.
2. Turn fan "OFF."
3. Reduce heat 25° F.
4. Load oven quickly and close doors.
5. Turn fan "ON" after 7 to 10 minutes and keep "ON" for remaining cooking time.

EXCEPTION: Leave fan "OFF" for bacon to prevent fat from blowing throughout the oven. READ AND

UNDERSTAND THE MANUFACTURER'S MANUALS. THEY WILL MAKE YOUR JOB EASIER.

Note: Equipment is becoming more and more complex as the "state-of-the-art" progresses. It is absolutely essential that proper operating manuals be read and understood by everyone who either uses or maintains food service equipment. If you do not have the proper manuals available, proceed with extreme caution so as not to damage or misuse this equipment. Local food service equipment dealers, and/or your service's food service office should be contacted for assistance.

GUIDELINES FOR CONVECTION OVENS

FOOD	PAN SIZE (INCHES)	RECOMMENDED NO. OF SHELVES FOR ONE LOAD	RECOMMENDED TEMPERATURE (° F.)	TIME
BREADS				
Breads, yeast	10-1/2 by 5 by 3-1/2	3	375	30 min
Coffee cakes	18 by 26	4	325	15 min
Muffins	12-cup muffin pan	4	350	30 min
Rolls, yeast	18 by 26	4	350	10 to 15 min
Sweet rolls	18 by 26	4	325	15 min
CAKES				
Angel food	16 by 4-1/2 by 4-1/8	3	300	25 to 30 min
Layer	8 or 9	4	300	25 to 35 min
Loaf	16 by 4-1/2 by 4-1/8	3	325	65 min
Sheet	18 by 26	4	300 to 325	25 to 35 min
DESSERTS				
Brownies	18 by 26	4	325	25 to 35 min
Cookies, bar	18 by 26	5	325	15 min
Cookies, drop	18 by 26	5	325	12 min
Cookies, sliced	18 by 26	5	350	8 to 10 min
Pies, fruit	9	4	375	25 min
MEATS				
Bacon, oven fried	18 by 26	5	325	15 to 20 min
Chicken, quarters or pieces	18 by 26	5	350	30 min
Fish, baked or oven fried	18 by 26	4	325	15 to 20 min
Meatloaf	18 by 26	3	300	1 hr 15 min
Roasts, boneless,				
Beef	18 by 26	3	325	1 hr 45 min
Pork	18 by 26	3	325	1-1/2 hr to 2 hrs
Steak, grill (strip loin, ribeye roll, top sirloin butt)	18 by 26	7	400	See Recipe No. L00700
Turkey, boneless	18 by 26	3	325	3-1/2 to 4 hrs
MISCELLANEOUS				
Pizza	18 by 26	4	450	15 min
Potatoes, baked	18 by 26	5	400	35 to 40 min

GUIDELINES FOR USE OF TILTING FRY PANS

The tilting fry pan is a versatile piece of equipment. Although usually described as an oversized skillet because of its large flat cooking surface, this piece of equipment can perform almost any type of cooking except deep fat frying. The tilting fry pan can be used for braising, grilling, sautéing, pan frying, simmering, steaming, boiling, warming, and holding.

The ability to tilt the pan allows for easy removal of food to the serving pans without heavy lifting. It can be used for successive cooking functions without having to move the food from one piece of equipment to another. The temperature dial is adjustable over a range of 200 F. to 400 F.

GENERAL OPERATION:
1. Turn or push main power switch to "on" position. The red light will signal that power is on.

2. Set thermostat to desired temperature. Yellow light will signal when heating unit has reached temperature. It will cycle on and off to maintain the temperature.
3. Preheat approximately 12 minutes before using as a griddle or fry pan.
4. To use as a steamer use 1 to 2 inches water with a rack for holding food above the water. Leave cover closed while steaming.
5. To use as a griddle, follow directions and temperature as shown on the recipe card.
6. For sautéing or pan frying, temperature should be between 300 F. and 365 F.
7. For simmering, temperature should be 200 F.

CLEANING AND MAINTENANCE: Refer to the manufacturer's operating manual for instructions.

GUIDELINES FOR CAPACITIES OF STEAM TABLE AND BAKING AND ROASTING PANS

PANS	DEPTH (Inches)	USABLE CAPACITY (Quarts)	USABLE CAPACITY (1/2 Cup Portions)
STEAM TABLE: 12 by 20 inch (full size)	2 ½	7	56
	4	13	104
	6	18 ½	148
	8	27	216
12 by 10 inch (1/2 size)	2 ½	3 ½	28
	4	6 ½	52
	6	9	72
	8	12	96
6 by 12 inch (1/3 size)	2 ½	2 ½	20
	4	4	16
	6	6	24
6 by 10 inch (1/4 size)	2 ½	1-2/3	13
	4	2-2/3	21
	6	4	32
BAKING AND ROASTING: 18 by 24 inch	4 ½	24	192
16 by 16 inch	4	8	64

NOTE: Usable capacity: Pans are filled to about 1/2 inch from the brim. If pans are to be used for carrying liquids (i.e., soups, gravies), the capacity should be reduced to half full.

GUIDELINES FOR CALORIES

Guidelines for calories employs two principles: (1) average calories based on food groups or categories rather than calorie counting of individual recipes; and (2) controlling calories by simple modifications. These modifications include serving method, smaller portion sizes, and eliminating or minimizing high calorie accompaniments such as gravy and sauces and the fat added in food preparation.
Food Categories and portion sizes follow: [1]

BREAKFAST APPETIZERS (Small fruit serving)
The sample meal pattern on the last card of this guideline information suggests one of the following fruit servings with the breakfast meal. (Items in bold face are good sources of Vitamin C). Average calories per serving = 60:

Canned fruit	1/2 cup, drained of syrup
Fruit juice, unsweetened	1/2 cup
(orange, grapefruit, grapefruit and orange, pineapple, apple, **tomato,** vegetable, grape)	

[1]Army users can refer to a listing of weight control portion sizes of AFRS recipes by recipe number in "Nutrition Education and Calorie Awareness."

Apple	1 small
Banana	1/2 small
Berries, except strawberry	1/2 cup
Berries, strawberry (unsweetened)	3/4 cup
Cranberry juice cocktail	1/2 cup
Fruit cup	1/2 cup
Grapefruit	1/2
Grapefruit sections	1/2 cup
Grapefruit and pineapple juice cocktail	1/2 cup
Grapes	12
Melon	
Cantaloupe	1/4
Honeydew	1/8
Orange	1 small
Orange and pineapple juice cocktail	1/2 cup
Pear	1 small
Plums	2 medium
Prunes	2 medium
Raisins	2 tablespoons
Tangerine	1 medium

GUIDELINES FOR CALORIES

BREAKFAST ENTREES (Equivalent to one-ounce meat serving)
Average calories per serving = 75-100

*Bacon, crisp	2 strips
Cheese	1 ounce slice or 1 inch cube
Egg (poached, soft cooked, hard cooked)	1
*Egg (fried, scrambled)	1
Ham or other lean meat	1 ounce slice
Peanut butter	2 tablespoons
Sausage	1 link or pattie
Corned beef hash or	1/3 cup (No. 12 scoop)
*Creamed ground beef	
*Creamed chipped beef	

*Higher in fat and higher in calories. As little fat as possible should be used in egg preparation. (Shortening compound used for pan coating can be used to reduce fat in foods requiring grill preparation.) Poached, soft cooked and hard cooked eggs are lowest in calories, because no fat is involved in their preparation. Hot sandwiches may be served at breakfast for variety. Two slices of bread or 1 English muffin, 1 ounce of meat or cheese and 1 strip bacon (250 to 300 calories), form a complete breakfast except for milk and Breakfast Appetizer servings.

STARCH SERVINGS (Bread/Cereal foods, principally)
This menu category includes breads, cereal and cereal products, legumes and starchy vegetables.
Average calories per serving = 80.

A.   **Breads**

Bagel (whole wheat or plain)	1/2
Biscuit (2" diameter)	1
Bread (white, French, Italian, whole wheat, rye, pumpernickel, raisin)	1 slice
English muffin	1/2
Roll, dinner	1 medium (1 ounce)
Roll, hamburger, hot dog, Kaiser (2 oz roll)	1/2
Tortilla/taco shell (6" diameter)	1
Cornbread	2 inch square
Dumplings	1 average
Pancakes	1/4 inch (without butter or syrup)
French toast	1 slice without butter is equivalent to one breakfast entree plus one starch serving
Coffee cake	2 inch square

B.   **Cereal Products**

Baked macaroni and cheese	1/3 cup (counts as one starch serving and one fat)
Cereal, cooked	1/2 cup
Cereal, ready-to-eat, unsweetened	1 individual box or 1 ounce
Crackers, saltine, 2 inch square	6
Crackers, soda, 2-1/2 inch square	4
Grits	1/2 cup
Mexican rice	1/2 cup
Pasta, cooked (spaghetti, noodles, macaroni)	1/2 cup
Rice, steamed	1/2 cup
Rice pilaf	1/2 cup
Spanish rice	1/2 cup (counts as one starch serving and one fat)

C.   **Starchy Vegetables**

Beans (lima, pinto, kidney, white)	1/3 cup
Corn	1/2 cup
Corn on the cob	1 medium ear
Potato, baked or boiled	1 small
*Potatoes, hashed brown, lyonnaise, cottage fried	1/2 cup
*Potato griddle cake (German)	1 cake
Sweet potato, baked	1/2 potato
Sweet potato, mashed	1/2 cup
Succotash	1/2 cup
Peas	1/2 cup
Winter squash	1/2 cup

*Fat serving should be eliminated from the meal

GUIDELINES FOR CALORIES

FAT SERVINGS

Fats are concentrated sources of calories. Average calories per serving = 45.

Avocado (4″ diameter)	1/8
Bacon, crisp	1 strip
Bacon fat	1 teaspoon
Blue Cheese Dressing	1 tablespoon
Butter or margarine	1 pat or 1 teaspoon
Cream for coffee	2 tablespoons
Cream, sour	2 tablespoons
Cream, whipping	1 tablespoon
Cream cheese	1 tablespoon
Creamy Italian dressing	1 tablespoon
French dressing	1 tablespoon
Green Goddess dressing	1 tablespoon
Italian dressing	1 tablespoon
Low-calorie dressing	2 tablespoons
Salad dressing	1 teaspoon
Thousand Island dressing	1 tablespoon
Olives	5 small

BEVERAGES

A. Milk Servings

Two 8-ounce glasses of milk or other dairy product equivalent are recommended daily for adults to meet calcium requirements. One Milk Serving equals one 8-ounce glass milk or equivalent. Approximate calories per serving = 90.

Milk, skim	1 cup (1/2 pint or 8 fluid ounces)
Milk, low fat	3/4 cup (6 fluid ounces)
Milk, whole	1/2 cup (4 fluid ounces)
Buttermilk	1 cup
Yogurt, low fat (without fruit)	1 cup

B. Other Beverages

Unsweetened black coffee, unsweetened tea, sugar-free soft drinks, and bouillons range from 0 to 25 calories.

Sweetened soft drinks, milk shakes, and hot cocoa are high in sugar and calories. Milk shakes range in calories from approximately 290-450 calories depending on the ingredients used. Milk shakes contribute calcium. Dehydrated ice milk-milk shake mix (approximately 290 calories per serving) is a source of both calcium and Vitamin A–a consideration for Navy afloat patrons when milk is not available to supply these nutrients.

GUIDELINES FOR CALORIES

APPETIZERS (lunch/dinner)
A fruit or fruit juice or vegetable juice serving, large or small, is a good appetizer. Other possible appetizers containing about 120 calories include:

Soup
Broth-based soups (e.g., chicken noodle)	1 cup
Creamy soups	1/2 cup
Stuffed celery (filled with cheese spread or peanut butter)	2-4 sticks
Fruit cup	1/2 cup

LARGE FRUIT SERVINGS (for lunch/dinner appetizer or dessert)
Serve fresh fruits whenever possible to avoid the sugar added to most canned and frozen fruits. When only canned fruits are available, serve 1/2 cup and drain off the syrup. The following fruit servings are twice the size of the breakfast fruit servings and provide about 120 calories per serving.

Apple	1 medium
Banana	1 small or 1/2 large
Berries (except strawberry)	1 cup
Grapes	10
Melon	
Cantaloupe	1/2
Honeydew	1/4
Watermelon	2 cups (chunks)
Nectarine	1 large
Orange	1 medium
Peach	1 large
Pear	1 medium
Pineapple	1 cup (chunks)
Plums	2 large or 4 medium
Prunes	2 large or 4 medium
Raisins	1/4 cup
Tangerine	1 large
Fruit juice, unsweetened	1 cup
Tomato or vegetable juice	1 cup

MEAT SERVINGS (3 ounce lunch/dinner entree)
An ounce of cooked meat provides approximately 75 calories. Lean meats such as bottom round, roast veal, chicken without skin and fish contain approximately 55 calories per ounce. High-fat meats such as cold cuts, spareribs, sausage, corned beef and frankfurters have about 100 calories per ounce.
Serve lean meats whenever possible to reduce saturated fats, cholesterol and calories. Trim off visible fat. Remember that sauces and gravies, except tomato, seafood cocktail, and mustard, should be avoided by weight-conscious personnel. The following meats have about 225 calories per serving.
For the most part, plain meat portions are 3 ounces cooked (4 ounces raw meat makes a 3-ounce portion when cooked); mixed dishes (casseroles) are 1 cup. Use slotted spoon to serve casserole dishes such as beef stew to minimize calories from the gravy.

GUIDELINES FOR CALORIES

A. **Beef Portion Size**

Beef, ground, meatballs	3-1 1/3 ounce meatballs
Beef, ground, meat loaf	3 ounces (1 inch thick slice)
Beef, ground, pattie	1 pattie
Beef, oven roast	3 ounces
Beef, pot roast	3 ounces
Beef stew	1 cup (use slotted spoon)
Chili con carne	1 cup
Liver	4 ounces
Meat sauce (for spaghetti)	1 cup
Steak, grilled	3 ounces
Steak, Swiss	3 ounces

B. **Fish/Seafood**

Baked fish	4-4 1/2 ounces
Salmon cakes	1 cake
Salmon loaf	1 inch slice
Scallop creole	1 cup
Seafood newburg	1 cup
Shrimp creole	1 cup
Shrimp curry	3/4 cup
Tuna salad	3/4 cup
Baked tuna and noodles (counts as entree plus starch serving)	1 cup

C. **Pork**

Ham, sliced	3 ounces
Ham, chunks	1 cup
Ham, loaf	3 ounces
Pork chop	1 small
Pork chop suey	1 cup (use slotted spoon)
Pork roast	3 ounces

D. **Poultry**

Chicken, baked	1/4 chicken (thigh and drumstick or 1 breast piece and wing)
Chicken, BBQ, without extra sauce	1/4 chicken
Chicken (or turkey) salad	3/4 cup
Duck, roast (high in fat)	1/4 duck
Rock Cornish hen	1/2 hen
Turkey, cutlet	1 cutlet
Turkey, roast, sliced	3 ounces

E. **Veal**

Veal steak, breaded	1 small steak
Veal parmesan	3 ounces
Veal roast, sliced	3 ounces

Cottage cheese, 3/4 cup, is nutritionally similar to 3 ounces of meat.

GUIDELINES FOR CALORIES

VEGETABLE SERVINGS (cooked)

Vegetables prepared without added fats or sugar are very low in calories, about 25 per half-cup serving. The somewhat starchy vegetables, such as green peas and winter squash, contain about 70 calories per half-cup serving. Dark green and deep yellow vegetables are good sources of Vitamin A. Most dark green vegetables, if not overcooked, are also reliable sources of Vitamin C.

Asparagus	6 to 7 spears
Beans, green or wax	1/2 cup
Beets, sliced	1/2 cup
Broccoli	1 large stalk or 1/2 cup
Brussels sprouts	5 to 6 sprouts
Cabbage	1/2 cup
Carrots, sliced	1/2 cup
Cauliflower	1/2 cup
Eggplant	1/2 cup
Greens	1/2 cup
Mushrooms	1/2 cup
Okra	1/2 cup
Onions	1/2 cup
Peas, green	1/2 cup
Spinach	1/2 cup
Squash, yellow or zucchini, sliced	1/2 cup
Tomatoes, stewed	1/2 cup
SALADS (including raw vegetables)	

Most salads fall into the Vegetable/Fruit Group of the Basic Four Food Groups. Salads can be low in calories, if consumption of dressings and starchy salad bar items is limited. Fruits and vegetables add fiber to the diet; raw vegetables have negligible calories. For a tossed salad of very few calories, lemon juice, vinegar and seasonings, or Zero Dressing can be substituted for regular salad dressings.

The following Armed Forces Recipe Service salads provide 45 to 80 calories per 1/2 cup serving.

Carrot salad (shredded carrots with dressing, raisins or pineapple)	1/2 cup
Cole slaw	1/2 cup
Cottage cheese	1/4 cup plus 3 slices fruit as desired
Cucumber and onion salad	1/2 cup
Fruit salad	1/2 cup
Pickled beet and onion salad	1/2 cup
Pickled green bean salad	1/2 cup
Three bean salad	1/3 cup drained
Tossed salads	Greens as desired plus 1 tablespoon dressing or 2 tablespoons low-calorie dressing
Waldorf salad	1/2 cup

Relishes: celery sticks, carrot sticks, green peppers, radishes, cherry tomatoes and tomato wedges, cucumber and dill pickles have negligible calories.

GUIDELINES FOR CALORIES

DESSERTS

Fruit is a low fat, low calorie dessert with a greater ratio of essential vitamins and minerals to calories than many other common desserts, and is preferable for weight-conscious personnel as a dessert choice. Generally, the portions for cake, brownies, cookies and pie are one-half the Armed Forces Recipe Service portion. Approximate calories per serving is 150.

Cake, angel food, plain	4 inch square, 1 1/2 inches thick
Cake, unfrosted	2 inch square
Cobbler, any flavor	2 inch square
Cookie, 3 inch diameter	1
Cookie, bar type	2 inch square
Doughnut (not filled)	1 small or 1/2 large (1 ounce)
Gelatin dessert, plain	1/2 cup or a 3 inch square
Ice cream, sherbet, or frozen yogurt, plain	1/2 cup
Pie	1/12 of 9 inch pie (1/2 regular serving)
Pudding or custard without topping	1/2 cup

Sandwiches–Portions Recommended for Weight Control

Sandwiches provide entree variety for dieters. They replace the usual entree, starch, and fat serving of a meal. One sandwich or 1/2 submarine is a portion. (The exception is Beef Tacos. Two tacos equal the entree, starch, and fat serving.) Butter and salad dressing should be omitted from the recipe. Breads–rye, French, whole wheat, sandwich and pumpernickel that weigh about 1 ounce per slice are permitted. One-half of a 6-inch submarine roll equals 2 slices of bread. One Kaiser roll, hamburger bun, hot dog roll, or English muffin is equivalent to 2 slices of bread.

SAMPLE 1500-1700 CALORIE MEAL PLAN

Breakfast Pattern

1–Breakfast Appetizer (Fruit or Juice)
1–Breakfast Entree
2–Starch Servings
1–Fat Serving[1]
1 Cup Skim or 2% Lowfat Milk, or 1/2 cup whole
Coffee or Tea–as desired (without cream or sugar)

Lunch Pattern

1–Lunch Appetizer
1–Lunch Entree
1–Starch Serving
Vegetables–(plain–as desired or 1/2 cup buttered or starchy vegetable)
1–Salad (lettuce–as desired plus 2 tbsp low calorie salad dressing or 1/2 cup fruit or other vegetable salad)
1–Fat serving[1]
1 Cup Skim or 2% Lowfat Milk or 1/2 cup whole
Coffee or Tea–as desired (without cream or sugar)

GUIDELINES FOR CALORIES

Dinner Pattern

1-Dinner Entree
1-Starch Serving
Vegetables (plain–as desired or 1/2 cup buttered or starchy vegetable)
1-Salad (lettuce–as desired plus 2 tbsp low calorie salad dressing or 1/2 cup fruit or
       other vegetable salad)
1-Fat Serving[1]
1-Dessert Serving
Coffee or Tea–as desired (without cream or sugar)

[1]Fat servings are optional. By selecting those items at the lower end of the average calorie range, i.e., fresh fruit rather than a small portion of dessert, the meal plan more nearly approximates 1500 calories. (Lettuce salads and fresh fruit are not always available in Navy general messes afloat.)

NOTE: Navy and Marine Corps food service personnel can use this meal pattern as the basis of the Healthy Choices Plan. Army and Air Force users should refer to the Fitness and Short Order Menu Pattern in Department of the Army Supply Bulletin SB 10-260, and the Sensible Limited Intake Menu (SLIM) in United States Air Force Worldwide Menu AFP 146-17, respectively.

METRIC CONVERSION

The metric system is an international language of measurement. Its symbols are based on the International System of Units (SI). Of these, food service preparation will be primarily involved with the following metric base units:

Weight (mass)	gram (g)
	kilogram (kg)
Volume	milliliter (mL)
	liter (L)
Length	centimeter (cm)
	meter (m)
Temperature	degree Celsius (°C.)

While the U. S. metric system is voluntary and the food service industry in the United States has not converted to metric system, except for a few soft conversions (e. g., labeling), military food service dining facilities/general messes outside CONUS may experience the metric system in food and equipment support provided by the host country. The information furnished in this guideline card is primarily for these food service personnel.

CONVERSION OF U. S. CUSTOMARY TO METRIC UNITS

	U. S. Customary	Metric
Weight (or Mass)	1 ounce (oz) =	28.35 grams (g)
	1 pound (lb) =	453.6 grams (g) or .4536 kilograms
	2.2 pound (lb) =	1 kilogram (kg) or 1000 grams (g)
Volume	1 tsp =	4.93 milliliters (mL)
	1 tbsp =	14.79 milliliters (mL)
	1 cup =	236.59 milliliters (mL) or .237 liters (L)
	1 pint =	.473 liters (L)
	1 quart =	.946 liters (L)
	1 gallon =	3.785 liters (L)
	1.06 quarts =	1 liter (L) or 1000 milliliters (mL)
Length	1 inch =	2.54 centimeters (cm)
	1 foot =	.3048 meters (m)
	1 yard =	30.48 centimeters (cm) or .9144 meters (m)
	1.1 yards =	1 meter (m) or 100 centimeters (cm)

GUIDELINES FOR METRIC CONVERSION

Temperature Conversions

°F.	°C.	°F.	°C.
0	-18	212	100
26	-3	225	107
28	-2	228	109
30	-1	245	118
32	0	250	121
36	2	275	135
38	3	300	149
40	4	325	163
70	21	350	177
90	32	360	182
140	60	365	185
160	71	375	191
170	77	400	204
175	79	425	218
180	82	450	232
185	85	500	260
		550	288

GUIDELINES FOR CHEESES

USE OF DEHYDRATED CHEESES

Two types of dehydrated cheeses are used - dehydrated American cheese and dehydrated cottage cheese.

a. Cheese, Cottage, Dehydrated

1) USE - Dehydrated cottage cheese may be substituted in any recipe using fresh cottage cheese.
2) PREPARATION - Measure 8-1/2 cups water (70° F.) into a shallow serving pan. Pour 1-No. 10 cn (1 lb 1 oz) canned dehydrated cottage cheese evenly over the water. Stir gently to wet all particles of cheese. Let stand 5 minutes, then stir gently. If more water is needed, sprinkle 1/2 to 1 cup water over cheese. Chill rehydrated cheese thoroughly before serving (3 to 4 hours).
3) SUBSTITUTION - Rehydration ratio - 1 pound dehydrated cottage cheese to 4 pounds (2 qt) water.

Dehydrated Cheese	Water Added	= Rehydrated Cheese	OR Fresh Cheese Equivalent
1-No. 10cn (1 lb 1oz (2-3/4qt))	8-1/2 cups	5 1b oz (3 qt)	6 lb (3qt)
2-No. 10cn (2 lb 2oz (5-1/2qt))	4-1/4 qt	10 lb 2 oz (6-1/4 qt)	12 lb (1-1/2 gal)

b. Cheese, American, Processed, Dehydrated

1) USE - Dehydrated American processed cheese may be substituted in any recipe using processed American cheese. Rehydrate cheese before adding to any recipe to eliminate any un-rehydrated cheese in the end product. To store dehydrated cheese after being opened, place unused portion in a tightly covered container to prevent absorption of moisture. Refrigerate if possible.
2) PREPARATION - Add water to cheese and mix until blended. For a moist semi-solid cheese, such as for an appetizer or omelet, use 1 lb (1 qt) dehydrated cheese and 1 cup water. For a semi-fluid cheese for sauces (better volume substitute), use 1 pound (1 qt) dehydrated cheese and 2 cups water.
3) SUBSTITUTION:

Dehydrated Cheese	+ WARM Water Added	= Rehydrated Cheese	OR Fresh Cheese Equivalent
Semi-solid 6oz (1-1/2cups)	3/8 cup	1-1/8 cups	1 lb
3 1b (3qt) 1-No. 10cn	3 cups	2-1/4 qt	8 lb
Fluid 6oz (1-1/2 cups)	3/4 cup	1-1/2 cups	1 lb
3 1b (3qt) 1-No. 10cn	1-1/2 qt	3 qt	8 lb

GUIDELINES FOR USING EGGS

SANITARY PRECAUTIONS:

1. Fresh clean eggs only should be accepted from supply points. DO NOT ACCEPT DIRTY or DIRTY, CRACKED EGGS. Fresh eggs should be refrigerated until ready to use. Under no circumstances should fresh eggs be stored unrefrigerated. Frozen whole eggs and whites, once thawed, SHOULD NOT BE REFROZEN.
2. Cracked whole fresh eggs should be used only in recipes requiring cooking. To avoid possible contamination, never use in salad dressings and other uncooked dishes.
3. Dehydrated egg mix and frozen bakery-type eggs should be used only in recipes requiring cooking.
4. Remember, fresh eggs are a potentially hazardous food item and must be handled carefully during storage, preparation and serving.

PREPARATION:

1. Remove from refrigeration about 30 minutes before use. This will ensure uniform cooking when eggs are fried or baked, prevent cracked shells when soft or hard cooked in their shells, and will increase the volume of beaten egg whites.
2. When eggs are to be an ingredient in a recipe, or when two or more eggs are to be mixed or beaten together, the eggs should be broken separately into a small bowl. If one egg has a bad odor, appearance or color, it can be discarded without spoiling the remaining eggs or other ingredients.

PREPARATION AND COOKING:

1. Follow the times and temperatures prescribed in specific recipes for egg cookery.
2. Fried, poached, scrambled, and soft cooked eggs, using fresh whole eggs, may be prepared to order. For individual orders, no more than 6 eggs will be cracked at once. Use a clean bowl for each 6 eggs. Cook until desired consistency. For batch preparation of scrambled eggs, using fresh whole eggs, ensure eggs are cooked until firm (dry). No more than 3 qt (about 60 eggs) should be used per batch when scrambling eggs. DO NOT add a batch of just-cooked scrambled eggs to leftover eggs in steam table. Hold at 140°F. or higher. Frozen whole table eggs or a mixture of frozen whole table eggs and egg whites may be used. Cook according to directions on Recipe No. F-10.
3. Add other recipe ingredients gradually when folding into stiffly beaten egg whites.
4. To keep yolks of hard cooked eggs from discoloring, plunge eggs into cold running water immediately after cooking. Add ice, if necessary, to cool eggs.
5. When slicing hard cooked eggs, dip knife blade into cold water and the yolks will not crumble.

STORAGE AND LEFTOVERS:

1. Leftover shelled, uncooked eggs must be refrigerated and used within 24 hours. The total time at room temperature must not exceed 3 hours. Use leftover, shelled, uncooked eggs only in recipes requiring cooking. To keep leftover uncooked yolks from drying out, beat slightly with a fork; add 1 tablespoon cold water for each 2 yolks; cover and store in refrigerator and use within 24 hours. Use only in recipes requiring cooking.
2. Store hard cooked eggs in their shells in the refrigerator until they are served. Shelled, hard cooked eggs will darken if stored for any length of time. Use within 36 hours.

GUIDELINES FOR USING HERBS

The following information is provided as a guide in developing familiarity and creativity with using herbs. Start with a small amount, taste, then add more if necessary.

Herb	Appetizers Salad	Breads/Eggs Sauces/Cheese	Vegetables Pasta	Meat Poultry	Fish Shellfish
Basil	Green, Potato & Tomato Salads, Salad Dressing, Stewed Fruit	Breads, Fondue & Egg Dishes, Dips, Marinades, Sauces	Mushrooms, Tomatoes, Squash, Pasta, Bland Vegetables	Broiled, Roast Meat & Poultry Pies, Stews, Stuffing	Baked, Broiled & Poached Fish, Shellfish
Bay Leaf	Seafood Cocktail, Seafood Salad, Tomato Aspic, Stewed Fruit	Egg Dishes, Gravies, Marinades, Sauces	Dried Bean Dishes, Beets, Carrots, Onions, Potatoes, Rice, Squash	Corned Beef, Tongue Meat & Poultry Stews	Poached Fish, Shellfish Fish Stews
Chives	Mixed Vegetables, Green, Potato & Tomato Salads, Salad Dressings	Egg & Cheese Dishes, Cream Cheese, Cottage Cheese, Gravies, Sauces	Hot Vegetables, Potatoes	Broiled Poultry, Rissoles, Poultry & Meat Pies, Stews, Casseroles	Baked Fish, Fish Casseroles, Fish Stews, Shellfish
Dill	Seafood Cocktail, Green, Potato & Tomato Salads, Salad Dressings	Breads, Egg & Cheese Dishes, Cream Cheese, Fish and Meat Sauces	Beans, Beets, Cabbage, Carrots, Cauliflower, Peas, Squash, Tomatoes	Beef, Veal Roasts, Lamb, Steaks, Chips, Stews, Roast & Creamed Poultry	Baked, Broiled, Poached & Stuffed Fish, Shellfish
Garlic	All Salads, Salad Dressings	Fondue Poultry Sauces, Fish and Meat Marinades	Beans, Eggplant, Potatoes, Rice, Tomatoes	Roast Meats, Meat & Poultry Pies, Hamburgers, Stews & Casseroles	Broiled Fish, Shellfish, Fish Stews, Casseroles
Marjoram	Seafood Cocktail, Green, Poultry & Seafood Salads	Breads, Cheese Spreads, Egg & Cheese Dishes, Gravies, Sauces	Carrots, Eggplant, Peas, Onions, Potatoes, Dried Bean Dishes, Spinach	Roast Meats & Poultry Meat & Poultry Pies, Stews & Casseroles	Baked, Broiled & Stuffed Fish, Shellfish
Mustard	Fresh Green Salads, Prepared Meat, Macaroni & Potato Salads, Salad Dressing	Biscuits, Egg & Cheese Dishes, Sauces	Baked Beans, Cabbage, Eggplant, Squash, Dried Beans, Mushrooms, Pasta	Chops, Steaks, Ham, Pork, Poultry Cold Meats	Shellfish
Oregano	Green, Poultry & Seafood Salads	Breads, Egg & Cheese Dishes, Meat, Poultry & Vegetable Sauces	Artichokes, Cabbage, Eggplant, Squash, Dried Beans, Mushrooms, Pasta	Broiled, Roast Meats, Meat & Poultry Pies, Stews, Casseroles	Baked, Broiled & Poached Fish, Shellfish
Parsley	Green, Potato Seafood & Vegetable Salads	Biscuits, Breads, Egg & Cheese Dishes, Gravies, Sauces	Asparagus, Beets, Eggplant, Squash, Dried Beans, Mushrooms, Pasta	Meat Loaf, Meat & Poultry Pies, Stews and Casseroles, Stuffing	Fish Stews, Stuffed Fish
Rosemary	Fruit Cocktail, Fruit & Green Salads	Biscuits, Egg Dishes, Herb Butter, Cream Cheese, Marinades, Sauces	Beans, Broccoli, Peas, Cauliflower, Mushrooms, Baked Potatoes, Parsnips	Roast Meat, Poultry & Meat Loaf, Meat & Poultry Pies, Stews & Casseroles, Stuffing	Stuffed Fish, Shellfish
Sage		Breads, Fondue, Egg & Cheese Dishes, Spreads, Gravies, Sauces	Beans, Beets, Onions, Peas, Spinach, Squash, Tomatoes	Roast Meat, Poultry, Meat Loaf, Stews, Stuffing	Baked, Poached, & Stuffed Fish
Tarragon	Seafood Cocktail, Avocado Salads (all), Salad Dressings	Cheese Spreads, Marinades, Sauces, Egg Dishes	Asparagus, Beans, Beets, Carrots, Mushrooms, Peas, Squash, Spinach	Steaks, Poultry, Roast Meats, Casseroles & Stews	Baked, Broiled & Poached Fish, Shellfish
Thyme	Seafood Cocktail, Green, Poultry, Seafood & Vegetable Salads	Biscuits, Breads Egg & Cheese Dishes, Sauces, Spreads	Beets, Carrots, Mushrooms, Onions, Peas, Eggplant, Spinach, Potatoes	Roast Meat, Poultry & Meat Loaf, Meat & Poultry Pies, Stews & Casseroles	Baked, Broiled & Stuffed Fish, Shellfish, Fish Stews

GUIDELINES FOR PREPARING FRESH VEGETABLES AND FRUITS

General Guidelines

Keep fresh fruits and vegetables cold at all times except bananas. DO NOT remove from shipping containers unless needed within 24 hours. When vegetables, except onions, and fruits are removed from shipping containers, sort, trim, wash, drain well and refrigerate in covered containers. Wash all fruits and vegetables except alfalfa sprouts, bean sprouts, mushrooms, and bananas. Soak vegetables, such as cauliflower, broccoli, cabbage and Brussels sprouts, 30 minutes in cold water containing a tablespoon of salt per gallon to loosen soil and remove insects. DO NOT leave greens in water for more than 6 to 7 minutes. DO NOT soak cherries, grapes or strawberries.

To cut vegetables and fruits, use a stainless steel knife to prevent discoloration. Pare or peel and cut as recipe directs. Refrigerate well-drained vegetables in covered containers at least 1 hour to crisp before individual salad make-up or placing on salad bars. If greens are to be held, drain excess water from pans.

Specific Guidelines:

LEAFY VEGETABLES:

1. When sorting and discarding damaged salad greens, keep as many outer salad green leaves as possible to make the salad attractive and provide nutrients/vitamins.
2. Core, stem and separate salad greens before washing. Wash greens by lifting up and down in an excessive amount of water. Soak wilted greens in ice water 10 minutes or only until crisp. Drain thoroughly to prevent watery salad.
3. Place heads of lettuce (core side down) to drain.
   a. Iceberg lettuce - Remove core except when shredded or used for wedges. Hit each head (core side directly down) on counter; lift or twist out core; or cut out.
   b. Big Boston, green leaf and red leaf lettuce - Remove base core and separate leaves.
   c. Cabbage and Chinese cabbage - Trim wilted outer leaves; cut in quarters and remove hard core (leave enough of the core to hold the head together).
   d. Romaine, endive and escarole - Remove base core and separate leaves.
   e. Collards, kale, parsley and spinach - Remove tough stems.
4. Tear or cut salad greens into bite-size pieces or as otherwise directed in recipe. Remove outer iceberg lettuce leaves for use as lettuce cups with individual salads.

NON-LEAFY VEGETABLES:

1. Wash and scrub thoroughly to remove dirt.
2. Use a vegetable brush for cleaning celery, carrots and potatoes when they are not peeled.
3. Trim bruised and blemished parts.
4. Cut tomatoes in slices or wedges shortly before using.
5. Radishes, carrots, celery and cucumbers may be crisped in ice water. Drain before using.
   Alfalfa sprouts - DO NOT wash.
   Asparagus - Trim woody ends.
   Beans, green - Trim ends and remove strings.
   Bean sprouts - DO NOT wash.
   Broccoli - Cut off tough ends and remove tough outer leaves, separate into flowerets.
   Brussels sprouts - Trim ends and yellowed or coarse outer leaves.
   Carrots - Trim tops, pare.
   Cauliflower - Trim end and separate into flowerets.
   Celery - Separate branches from stalk, trim heavy strings or midribs; for celery hearts, DO NOT trim leaves.
   Corn - Remove corn husks and silk; keep cold; DO NOT soak.

Cucumbers - Pare.

Eggplant - Pare if recipe indicates.

Garlic – Separate cloves from bud; trim clove end, peel off outer skin of clove.

Mushrooms - Trim stem end. DO NOT wash. Brush with soft brush to remove dirt.

Onions, dry - Trim ends, peel off outer skin.

Onions, green - Separate bunches. Remove wilted tops, outer layer of bulb, and root end.

Parsnips - Trim tops, pare.

Peas, snow - Trim stem end.

Peppers, sweet, green - Remove stems and seeds.

Potatoes, red - Best used well scrubbed and unpared.

Potatoes, sweet - Remove sprouts, best cooked in skins and then pared.

Potatoes, white - Remove sprouts, for baking scrub well, for others pare.

Radishes - Trim tops, pare.

Rutabagas - Trim tops, pare.

Squash, fall or winter type - Cut as recipe indicates, remove seeds.

Squash, summer type - Trim ends.

Tomatoes – Cut out stem end.

Tomatoes, cherry - Remove stems.

Turnips - Trim tops, pare.

FRUITS:

1. Wash thoroughly to remove dirt.
2. Trim bruised and blemished parts.

Apples - Cut or pare if recipe indicates; core.

Apricots - Remove pit.

Avocados - Pare and remove seed.

Bananas - Peel. DO NOT wash.

Cherries, sweet - Remove stems and pits. DO NOT soak.

Cranberries - Sort to remove damaged berries and stems.

Grapefruit - Pare and section or cut as recipe indicates.

Grapes - DO NOT soak. Remove stems.

Kiwifruit - Pare. Cut as recipe indicates.

Lemons - Grate rind. Cut in half to squeeze juice or cut as recipe indicates.

Limes - Grate rind. Cut in half to squeeze juice or cut as recipe indicates.

Mangos - Pare and remove seed. Cut as recipe indicates.

Melons - Cut in half to remove seeds. Pare if recipe indicates. Cut as recipe indicates.

Nectarines - Remove pit.

Oranges - Peel and section or cut as recipe indicates.

Papaya - Pare and remove seeds. Cut as recipe indicates.

Peaches - Pare if recipe indicates. Remove pit.

Pears - Pare if recipe indicates; core.

Pineapple - Pare, remove eyes and top tuft, remove core if tough.

Plums - Remove pit.

Strawberries - Remove caps and stems. DO NOT soak.

Tangelos - Peel and section or cut as recipe indicates.

Tangerines - Peel and section or cut as recipe indicates.

Watermelons - Pare and seed if recipe indicates. Cut as recipe indicates

HAZARD ANALYSIS CRITICAL CONTROL POINT

(HACCP)

HACCP System: A food safety system that identifies hazards and develops control points throughout the receiving, storage, preparation, service and holding of food. This system is designed to prevent foodborne illness.

- **Critical Control Point (CCP):** A point in a specific food service process where loss of control may result in an unacceptable health risk. Implementing a control measure at this point may eliminate or prevent the food safety hazard.
- **Critical Limits:** Elements such as time and temperature that must be adhered to in order to keep food safe. The Temperature Danger Zone is defined by the Food and Drug Administration's Food Code as 41° F. to 140° F.
- **Foodborne Illness:** An illness transmitted to humans through food. Any food may cause a foodborne illness, however potentially hazardous foods are responsible for most foodborne illnesses. Symptoms may include abdominal pain/cramps, nausea and vomiting.
- **Potentially Hazardous Food:** A food that is used as an ingredient in recipes or served alone that is capable of supporting the growth of organisms responsible for foodborne illness. Typical foods include high protein foods such as meat, fish, poultry, eggs and dairy products.

COOKING TEMPERATURES	
These temperatures represent the minimum required temperature. The time represents the minimum amount of time the temperature must be maintained.	
Eggs, Raw shell eggs	155° F. for 15 seconds
Eggs, Egg products, pasteurized	145° F. for 15 seconds
Poultry	165° F. for 15 seconds
Pork	145° F. for 15 seconds
Whole Beef Roasts and Corned Beef Roasts	145° F. for 3 minutes
Fish	145° F. for 15 seconds
Stuffed meat, fish, poultry or pasta, OR stuffings containing meat, fish or poultry	165° F. for 15 seconds
Meat or fish that has been reduced in size by methods such as chopping (i.e., beef cubes), grinding (i.e., ground beef, sausage), restructuring (i.e., formed roast beef, gyro meat), or a mixture of two or more meats (i.e., sausage made from two or more meats)	155° F. for 15 seconds
CCP: SERVING AND HOLDING (hot foods)	140° F.
COOLING	
FDA recommends a cooled product temperature of 41° F. In order to achieve a cooled internal product temperature of 34-38° F., the temperature of the refrigerator must be lower than 41° F.	Cooling from 140° F. to 70° F. should take no longer than 2 hours. Cooling from 70° F. to 41° F. should take no longer than 4 hours.

GUIDELINES FOR COMBI-OVENS

A combi-oven is a versatile piece of equipment that combines three modes of cooking in one oven: steam, circulated hot air or a combination of both. The combi mode is used to re-heat foods and to roast, bake and "oven fry." The steam mode is ideal for rapid cooking of vegetables and shellfish. The hot air mode operates as a normal convection oven for baking cookies, cakes and pastries. The combi mode decreases overall cooking times, reduces product shrinkage and eliminates flavor transfer when multiple items are cooked simultaneously.

OVEN MODES

COMBI MODE: Use to roast and braise meats, bake poultry and fish and reheat prepared foods. The combination of steam and hot air will improve yield and reduce overall cooking times. To **OVEN FRY,** use food items that are labeled "ovenable" by the manufacturer. Refer to cooking guidelines for oven frying individual items. Place items on perforated sheet pan in a single layer. DO NOT place excess amount of product on pan. A solid sheet pan may be placed under perforated pan to catch excess oils and eliminate smoke.

HOT AIR MODE: Use to bake cakes, cookies and breads and to roast and bake meats and poultry. The hot air mode circulates air in the same manner as a convection oven.

STEAMING MODE: Use to steam fresh, frozen or canned vegetables and shellfish. Use of the Combi-oven to steam foods can save time, labor, and help maintain appearance, and preserve nutrients normally lost by other cooking methods. The oven is ideal for steaming more than one type of vegetable at the same time without flavor transfer. Foods may be steamed in perforated or solid pans. Perforated pans are generally used, particularly for vegetables, unless the cooking liquid is retained or manufacturer's directions specify solid pans. Pans are normally filled no more than 2/3 full to allow steam to circulate for even cooking.
Steam temperature is preset at 212° F. The cooking time will vary depending on the type of food and the number of pans in the oven. The cooking time should include the time it requires to heat food up to cooking temperature, as well as steaming.

TEMPERATURE SETTING: At this time the AFRS recipes do not contain combi-oven information. Refer to the attached cooking guidelines for individual items or begin by using the recommended convection oven temperature noted on individual recipes. If food is cooked around the edges, but the center is still raw or not thoroughly cooked, or if there is too much color variation (some is normal), turn pan or reduce the heat by 10° F. to 15° F. and return food to the oven and continue cooking until done.

TIME SETTING: Follow the recommended convection cooking times on recipe cards. Check progress halfway through the cooking cycle since times will vary in the Combi mode with the quantity of food being cooked, the temperature, and the type of pan used.

MEAT PROBE: The meat probe measures a product core temperature during the cooking process.

FAN SPEED SETTING: See general operations notes below.

GENERAL OPERATION NOTES:

1. **OVEN RACKS:** Position oven racks for the number of pans and product to be cooked.
2. **WATER SUPPLY:** Verify water supply is on.
3. **SELECT COOKING MODE AND TEMPERATURE:** Turn oven on; SELECT the cooking mode. To cook in the combi or hot air mode, set thermostat to desired temperature. To cook in the steam

mode, set thermostat to 200° F. The thermostat light will come on indicating oven temperature is below set point.

4. **PREHEAT:** Heat oven until thermostat light goes out indicating that the oven has reached the set temperature. The oven should preheat to 350° F. within 10 to 15 minutes.

5. **FAN SPEED:** If two-speed fan is available, adjust the fan to recommended speed noted on individual recipe card. NOTE: The Combi-oven is equipped with electric interlock, which energizes/de-energizes both the heating element and fan motor when the doors are closed and open. Therefore, the heating elements and fan will not operate with the doors open, only when closed.

6. **MEAT PROBE:** Insert the meat probe in the thickest section of the product. NOTE: The tip of the probe should not be placed near bone or fat. This will result in inaccurate temperature readings. Turn the meat probe switch on and set the desired core temperature by using the up or down arrows. Press the set button to store the set point temperature. Set the timer to the STAY ON position. When the selected core temperature is reached the buzzer will sound and the oven automatically turns off.

7. **CLEANING AND MAINTENANCE:** Refer to the manufacturer's operating manual for cleaning and maintenance instructions. NOTE: Wipe out all spills as soon as they occur for ease of cleaning.

COMBI-OVEN COOKING GUIDELINES

Food	Cook Mode	Recommended Temperature	Time
MEATS			
Steak	Hot Air	400	See Recipe No. L 007 00
Bacon, oven fried	Hot Air	325	25-30 minutes
Roasts, boneless			
Beef	Combi	325	1 hr 45 minutes
Pork	Combi	325	2 to 2-1/2 hours
Spareribs	Combi	350	1 to 1-1/2 hours
Meatloaf	Combi	300	1 hour
POULTRY			
Turkey, boneless	Combi	325	2 to 2-1/2 hours
Chicken, pieces (with bone)	Combi	350	20-30 minutes
FISH			
Fish, baked	Combi	325	10-20 minutes
Shrimp, raw, frozen	Steam	Preset	3-5 minutes
MISCELLANEOUS			
Casserole type dishes			
Macaroni & cheese	Combi	325	15-20 minutes
Lasagna	Combi	300	40-50 minutes
BREADS			
Breads, yeast	Hot Air	375	30 minutes
Coffee cakes	Hot Air	325	15 minutes
Muffins	Hot Air	350	30 minutes
Rolls Yeast	Hot Air	350	10-15 minutes
Sweet rolls	Hot Air	325	15 minutes

EGGS			
Hard Cooked Eggs	Steam	Preset	12 minutes
CAKES			
Angel Food	Hot Air	300	30-35 minutes
Layer	Hot Air	300	25-35 minutes
Loaf	Hot Air	325	65-75 minutes
Sheet	Hot Air	300-325	25-35 minutes
DESSERTS			
Brownies	Hot Air	325	25-30 minutes
Cookies	Hot air	325	12-15 minutes
Pies, Fruit	Hot air	375	25 minutes
VEGETABLES			
Frozen	Steam	Preset	12-15 minutes
Canned	Steam	Preset	10-12 minutes
Fresh*	Steam	Preset	*See individual recipe cards
OVEN FRYING			
French Fries	Combi	400	7-9 minutes
Fish Portions	Combi	400	10-12 minutes
Shrimp, Battered	Combi	400	7-8 minutes
Chicken Pieces	Combi	400	20 minutes
Chicken Nuggets	Combi	400	8-14 minutes
Onion Rings	Combi	400	6-8 minutes
Jalapeno Popper	Combi	400	9-12 minutes
Egg rolls	Combi	400	12-18 minutes

GUIDELINES FOR SKITTLE

A skittle is a multipurpose piece of equipment that can be used as a pressureless steamer, braising pan or griddle. The griddle mode is ideal for cooking steaks, sandwiches, eggs, pancakes, breakfast meats and potatoes. The steam mode may be used to cook vegetables, seafood, rice and pasta. The braising mode is used for slow moist-heat cooking of meats, poultry and vegetables.

TO OPERATE AS A STEAMER:
1. Add 5 gallons (2"- 3") of water to the skittle using the spray hose.
2. Position steaming racks for the number of pans and product to be cooked.
3. Close the lid and the steam vent.
4. Set the thermostat at 350° Fahrenheit and allow 6-8 minutes to preheat. The skittle is ready when the heater power light goes out.
5. When the skittle is preheated, raise the lid to the top of the steamer racks and place food pans in the racks and close the lid. (NOTE: To retain maximum steam, do not raise the lid beyond steamer racks. The lid should be kept in a horizontal position)
6. If steam escapes from the closed lid, open the rear vent until excess is released.

The skittle is ideal for steaming more than one type of vegetable at the same time without flavor transfer. Foods may be steamed in perforated or solid pans. Perforated pans are normally used, particularly for vegetables, unless the cooking liquid is retained or manufacturer's directions specify solid pans. Pans should not be filled more than 2/3 to the top to allow steam to circulate for even cooking.

Cooking times will vary depending on the type of food and the number of pans used. The cooking time should include the time it requires to heat food up to cook temperature, as well as steaming. Be sure to record the most successful steaming times on individual recipe cards for future reference.

TO OPERATE AS A BRAISING PAN:

1. Set the thermostat at 375° Fahrenheit and allow 6-8 minutes to preheat. The skittle is ready when the heater power light goes out. Brown food according to individual AFRS recipe card instructions.
2. Lower temperature to 325° Fahrenheit and add cooking liquid. Lower hood and cook according to individual recipe card instructions.
3. To remove liquid, tilt the pan 10° using the tilt handle and drain the liquid through the drain valve into a food pan.

The Skittle may be used for braising pot roast, Swiss steaks, spareribs, stews and for preparing gravy, soups and sauces. Cooking times will vary according to individual foods and amount prepared.

TO OPERATE AS A GRIDDLE:

1. Set the thermostat to 350° Fahrenheit and allow 6-8 minutes to preheat. The griddle is ready when the heater power light goes out.
2. Raise the lid and cook foods according to individual AFRS guideline cards.
3. To drain any accumulated grease, place a #10 can into the can holder attached to the drain valve. Tilt the pan 10° using the tilt handle and allow grease to drain into the can. The griddle can be used to cook hamburgers, steak, sandwiches, eggs, pancakes, breakfast meats and potatoes. Heat is distributed evenly over the entire pan surface ensuring food products cook uniformly.

GENERAL OPERATION NOTES:

1. STEAMING MODE: The recommended thermostat temperature for steaming is 350° Fahrenheit. Higher temperatures may be used but water will evaporate quickly and cooking time will not be decreased.
2. WATER SUPPLY: The easiest way to fill the skittle with water is with the attached flexible spray hose.
3. SELECT COOKING TEMPERATURE: SELECT desired cooking temperature according to cook mode or individual recipe cards. The thermostat light will come on indicating oven temperature is below set point.
4. PREHEAT: Heat Skittle until thermostat light goes out indicating that the unit has reached the set temperature. The Skittle should preheat to 350° F. within 6 to 8 minutes. (Note: Lower the lid for faster preheating.)
5. CLEANING AND MAINTENANCE: Remove food waste. Fill the pan with warm water using the spray hose. Add mild detergent and scrub with a nylon scrub pad if necessary. Tilt the pan 10° using the tilt handle and allow water to drain into container placed directly under the drain valve. Rinse with clean water and drain again. Refer to the manufacturer's operating manual for cleaning and maintenance instructions.

GUIDELINES FOR USE OF CONVENIENCE PREPARED FOODS

Convenience prepared foods reduce labor since they only require heating. Specific cooking instructions should be located on each advanced foods package. Items to be considered when using convenience prepared foods are cooking times, nutrient content and serving size. Cooking times, nutrient content and serving size will vary among manufacturers for identical food items, therefore, in order to maintain the quality of these convenience prepared foods, instructions must be read and followed every time a convenience prepared food is utilized.

CRANBERRY AND ORANGE JUICE COCKTAIL

Yield 100   **Portion** 1/2 Cup

Calories	Carbohydrates	Protein	Fat	Cholesterol	Sodium	Calcium
69 cal	17 g	0 g	0 g	0 mg	3 mg	9 mg

Ingredient	Weight	Measure	Issue
CRANBERRY JUICE COCKTAIL	14-7/8 lbs	1 gal 2-2/3 qts	
JUICE,ORANGE,FROZEN,CONCENTRATE,3/1,THAWED	4-1/8 lbs	1 qts 2-5/8 cup	
WATER,COLD	9-7/8 lbs	1 gal 3/4 qts	

Method
Combine juices and water; stir until blended. Cover and refrigerate at 41 F. or lower.

CRANBERRY AND APPLE JUICE COCKTAIL

Yield 100   **Portion** 1/2 Cup

Calories	Carbohydrates	Protein	Fat	Cholesterol	Sodium	Calcium
70 cal	17 g	0 g	0 g	0 mg	7 mg	7 mg

Ingredient	Weight	Measure	Issue
CRANBERRY JUICE COCKTAIL	14-7/8 lbs	1 gal 2-2/3 qts	
JUICE,APPLE,FROZEN,CONCENTRATE,3/1,THAWED	4-1/8 lbs	1 qts 2-5/8 cup	
WATER,COLD	9-7/8 lbs	1 gal 3/4 qts	

Method
Combine juices and water; stir until blended. Cover and refrigerate at 41 F. or lower.

CHINESE EGG ROLLS (BAKED)

Yield 100   **Portion** 1 Egg Roll

Calories	Carbohydrates	Protein	Fat	Cholesterol	Sodium	Calcium
140 cal	13 g	10 g	5 g	50 mg	247 mg	22 mg

Ingredient	Weight	Measure	Issue
EGG ROLLS,CHINESE,FROZEN	18-3/4 lbs		

Method
1. Place 50 egg rolls on each sheet pan.
2. Using a convection oven, bake at 350 F. for 20 to 25 minutes or until brown on high fan, closed vent. CCP: Internal temperature must reach 145 F. or higher for 15 seconds. Hold for service at 140 F. or higher.

CHINESE EGG ROLLS (FRIED)

Yield 100   **Portion** 1 Egg Roll

Calories	Carbohydrates	Protein	Fat	Cholesterol	Sodium	Calcium
180 cal	13 g	10 g	10 g	50 mg	247 mg	22 mg

Ingredient	Weight	Measure	Issue
EGG ROLLS,CHINESE,FROZEN	18-3/4 lbs		

Method

1. Fry egg rolls in deep fat at 350 F. for 7 minutes or until golden brown and heated through. DO NOT OVERCOOK. Egg rolls will rise to the surface when cooked. CCP: Internal temperature must reach 145 F. or higher for 15 seconds.
2. Drain well in basket or on absorbent paper. CCP: Hold for service at 140 F. or higher.

PHILIPPINE STYLE EGG ROLLS (BAKED)

Yield 100   Portion 1 Egg Roll

Calories	Carbohydrates	Protein	Fat	Cholesterol	Sodium	Calcium
93 cal	8 g	7 g	4 g	33 mg	165 mg	15 mg

Ingredient	Weight	Measure	Issue
EGG ROLLS,PHILIPPINE,FROZEN	12-1/2 lbs		

Method

1. Place 50 egg rolls per sheet pan.
2. Using a convection oven, bake at 350 F. for 10 to 15 minutes or until heated through on high fan, closed vent. CCP: Internal temperature must reach 145 F. or higher for 15 seconds. Hold for service at 140 F. or higher.

PHILIPPINE STYLE EGG ROLLS (FRIED)

Yield 100   Portion 1 Egg Roll

Calories	Carbohydrates	Protein	Fat	Cholesterol	Sodium	Calcium
133 cal	8 g	7 g	8 g	33 mg	165 mg	15 mg

Ingredient	Weight	Measure	Issue
EGG ROLLS,PHILIPPINE STYLE,FROZEN	12-1/2 lbs		

Method

1. Fry Philippine egg rolls in deep fat at 350 F. for 4 to 5 minutes, or until golden brown and heated through. DO NOT OVERCOOK.
2. Drain well in basket or on absorbent paper. CCP: Hold for service at 140 F. or higher.

TOMATO JUICE COCKTAIL

Yield 100   Portion 1/2 Cup

Calories	Carbohydrates	Protein	Fat	Cholesterol	Sodium	Calcium
22 cal	6 g	1 g	0 g	0 mg	457 mg	12 mg

Ingredient	Weight	Measure	Issue
JUICE,TOMATO,CANNED	27-7/8 lbs	3 gal 1 qts	
JUICE,LEMON	6-1/2 oz	3/4 cup	

Method
Combine tomato juice and lemon juice; cover; refrigerate at 41 F. or lower for several hours or overnight.

VEGETABLE JUICE COCKTAIL

Yield 100   Portion 1/2 Cup

Calories	Carbohydrates	Protein	Fat	Cholesterol	Sodium	Calcium
24 cal	6 g	1 g	0 g	0 mg	340 mg	14 mg

Ingredient	Weight	Measure	Issue
JUICE,VEGETABLE,CANNED	27-3/4 lbs	3 gal 1 qts	
JUICE,LEMON	6-1/2 oz	3/4 cup	

Method
1. Combine canned vegetable juice and lemon juice; cover; refrigerate at 41 F. or lower for several hours or overnight.
2. Stir well before serving.

SPICY TOMATO JUICE COCKTAIL

Yield 100   Portion 1/2 Cup

Calories	Carbohydrates	Protein	Fat	Cholesterol	Sodium	Calcium
21 cal	6 g	1 g	0 g	0 mg	467 mg	12 mg

Ingredient	Weight	Measure	Issue
JUICE,TOMATO,CANNED	27-7/8 lbs	3 gal 1 qts	
SAUCE,TABASCO	6 oz	3/4 cup	
JUICE,LEMON	6-1/2 oz	3/4 cup	

Method
1. Combine tomato juice, hot sauce and lemon juice; cover; refrigerate at 41 F. or lower for several hours or overnight.
2. Stir well before serving.

SHRIMP COCKTAIL

Yield 100   Portion 4 Shrimp

Calories	Carbohydrates	Protein	Fat	Cholesterol	Sodium	Calcium
83 cal	12 g	10 g	1 g	84 mg	480 mg	43 mg

Ingredient	Weight	Measure	Issue
SHRIMP,FROZEN,RAW,PEELED,DEVEINED	12 lbs		
WATER,BOILING	6-1/4 lbs	3 qts	
SEAFOOD COCKTAIL SAUCE		3 qts 1-3/8 cup	
LETTUCE,ICEBERG,FRESH	4 lbs	4-1/3 lbs	
LEMONS,FRESH	5-1/8 lbs	13 each	

Method

1. Place shrimp in boiling water and cover. Return to a boil; uncover; reduce heat; simmer 2 to 3 minutes. CCP: Internal temperature must reach 145 F. or higher for 15 seconds. DO NOT OVERCOOK. Drain immediately.
2. Place shrimp in single layer on pans. CCP: Refrigerate at 41 F. or lower for use in Step 5.
3. Prepare 1 recipe Seafood Cocktail Sauce, Recipe No. O 011 00. Cover; refrigerate for use in Step 6.
4. Line individual serving dishes with lettuce.
5. Arrange 4 shrimp on lettuce in each dish.
6. Place 2 tablespoons of sauce in each souffle cup. Serve shrimp with 1 lemon wedge. Cut 8 wedges per lemon. CCP: Hold for service at 41 F. or lower.

Notes

1. In Step 3, prepared seafood cocktail sauce may be used.

SPICED SHRIMP

Yield 100   Portion 4 Shrimp

Calories	Carbohydrates	Protein	Fat	Cholesterol	Sodium	Calcium
60 cal	5 g	10 g	1 g	84 mg	100 mg	56 mg

Ingredient	Weight	Measure	Issue
SHRIMP,FROZEN,RAW,PEELED,DEVEINED	12 lbs		
WATER,BOILING	2-1/8 lbs	1 qts	
VINEGAR,DISTILLED	4-1/8 lbs	2 qts	
PEPPER,RED,GROUND	1-1/8 oz	1/4 cup 2-1/3 tbsp	
MUSTARD,DRY	2-3/8 oz	1/4 cup 2-1/3 tbsp	
CELERY SEED	7/8 oz	1/4 cup 1/3 tbsp	
PAPRIKA,GROUND	1/2 oz	2 tbsp	
GINGER,GROUND	1/4 oz	1 tbsp	
MACE,GROUND	1/4 oz	1 tbsp	
CINNAMON,GROUND	1/4 oz	1 tbsp	
CLOVES,GROUND	1/8 oz	1/3 tsp	
BAY LEAF,WHOLE,DRIED	3/8 oz	12 lf	
LETTUCE,FRESH,LEAF,RED	4 lbs	2 gal 1/8 qts	6-1/4lbs
LEMONS,FRESH	5-1/8 lbs	13 each	

Method

1. Place shrimp in boiling water, add vinegar and spices, cover; return to a boil. Uncover; reduce heat; simmer 2 to 3 minutes. CCP: Internal temperature must reach 145 F. or higher for 15 seconds. DO NOT OVERCOOK. Drain immediately.
2. Place shrimp in single layer on pans. CCP: Refrigerate at 41 F. or lower for use in Step 5.
3. Line individual serving dishes with lettuce.
4. Arrange 4 shrimp on lettuce in each dish. CCP: Hold for service at 41 F. or lower.
5. Serve shrimp with 1 lemon wedge. Cut 8 wedges per lemon.

Notes

1. In Step 3, prepared seafood cocktail sauce may be used.

PIZZA TREATS

Yield 100   **Portion** 1 Slice

Calories	Carbohydrates	Protein	Fat	Cholesterol	Sodium	Calcium
147 cal	17 g	8 g	5 g	10 mg	322 mg	158 mg

Ingredient	Weight	Measure	Issue
CHEESE,PIZZA BLEND,SHREDDED	4 lbs	1 gal	
TOMATO PASTE,CANNED	1 lbs	1-3/4 cup	
OIL,SALAD	3-7/8 oz	1/2 cup	
OLIVES,RIPE,PITTED,SLICED,DRAINED	7-1/8 oz	1-1/2 cup	
ONIONS,FRESH,CHOPPED	1 lbs	2-5/8 cup	1 lbs
PEPPERS,GREEN,FRESH,CHOPPED	11-7/8 oz	2-1/4 cup	14-3/8oz
BREAD,FRENCH,SLICED 1/2 INCH	6-1/4 lbs	100 sl	

Method

1. Combine cheese, tomato paste, salad oil, olives, onions and peppers. Blend well.
2. Spread 3 tablespoons of mixture on each slice of bread.
3. Place on ungreased pans. Using a convection oven, bake at 350 F. 5 minutes or until cheese is melted on low fan, open vent.

GUIDELINES FOR BREWING COFFEE

1. Measure or weigh quantities of water and coffee carefully. Prepare only in amounts necessary to maintain continuous service. Urn coffee held 1 hour or longer and automatic coffee maker coffee held 30 minutes or longer deteriorates in flavor and loses its aroma.
2. Use the proportion of 3/4 pound of coffee to 23/4 gallons of water for a standard strength brew. 1 lb 14 oz of coffee and 63/4 gallons of freshly drawn boiling water will yield approximately 100 (8 ounce) servings.
3. Ingredients for a good coffee brew are fresh coffee and freshly boiling water. Water that has been boiled a long time will have a flat taste which will affect the brew.
4. For an ideal brew, boiling water should pass through coffee within 4 to 6 minutes.
5. Keep equipment clean. Clean immediately after each use to prevent rancidity.
6. Urns and urn baskets should be washed with hot water and special urn cleaner or baking soda. (DO NOT use soap or detergent powder.) Rinse with clear water. When not in use, leave 1 or 2 gallons of clear water in urn. Drain before making coffee.
7. When using new urn bags: A new urn bag should be thoroughly rinsed in hot water before using. After using, urn bags should be thoroughly rinsed in clear, hot water; keep submerged in cold water until next use.
8. Faucets and glass gauges should be cleaned often with gauge brushes, hot water, and urn cleaner or baking soda. Rinse with clear water. Caps on faucets and gauges are removable to permit cleaning.

NOTE: For a stronger brewed cup of coffee, use the proportion of 2 lb 8 oz coffee to 63/4 gal water.

GUIDELINES FOR FRUIT AND VEGETABLE JUICES

(Single Strength, Concentrated and Instant)

TYPE	CAN SIZE	AMOUNTS FOR 1 GALLON (128 oz)	AMOUNTS FOR 31/8 GALLONS (100-4 oz portions)
1. Juice, Canned, Single Strength Apple, cranberry juice cocktail, grape, grapefruit, grapefruit and orange, orange, pineapple, tomato and vegetable	46 fl oz (No. 3 cyl)	2-3/4 cans	8-3/4 cans
2. Juice, Canned, Concentrated (3 plus 1) Tomato. . . . . Water	36 oz	1 can 3 qt	3 cans 9 qt
3. Juice, Canned, Frozen, Concentrated(3 plus 1) Apple, grape, grapefruit, orange Water	32 oz	1 can 3 qt	3-1/8 cans 9-3/8 qt
4. Juice, Canned, Instant Grape. . . . . Water. . . . . Grapefruit, orange. . . . . Water.	No. 2-1/2 15 1/2 oz	2 cans 3-3/4 qt 1 can 3-3/4 qt	6-1/4 cans 11-3/4 qt 3-1/8 cans 11-3/4 qt

NOTE: 1. For 6 oz portion, prepare 11/2 recipes; for 8 oz portion, prepare 2 recipes.
2. Prepare and refrigerate instant fruit juices overnight to ensure thorough chilling.
DO NOT ADD ICE as it produces a diluted unacceptable product.

GUIDELINES FOR USE OF POWDERED BEVERAGE BASES (FRUIT FLAVORED)

YIELD: 100 Portions (61/4 Gallons) Ounces)				EACH PORTION: 1 Cup (8
INGREDIENTS	WEIGHTS	MEASURES		METHOD
Beverage base, powdered, fruit punch flavor	2 oz	1/4 cup (1-1/4-5 gal yield pkg)	. . . .	1. Combine beverage base and sugar.
Sugar, granulated	5 lb	2-3/4 qt	. . . .	
Water, cold	. . . .	6 gal	. . . .	2. Add water. Stir until dissolved.

NOTE: 1.   In Step 1, other flavors (orange, lemonade, grape, cherry, lemon-lime, strawberry) may be used.
2.   In Step 2, 3 gal (12 lb) ice, crushed or cubed and 51/4 gal water may be used.

HOT COCOA

Yield 100   **Portion** 1 Cup

Calories	Carbohydrates	Protein	Fat	Cholesterol	Sodium	Calcium
112 cal	24 g	4 g	0 g	2 mg	112 mg	137 mg

Ingredient	Weight	Measure	Issue
COCOA	12-1/8 oz	1 qts	
SALT	1/3 oz	1/4 tsp	
SUGAR,GRANULATED	3-1/2 lbs	2 qts	
WATER,COLD	3-1/8 lbs	1 qts 2 cup	
MILK,NONFAT,DRY	2-1/4 lbs	3 qts 3 cup	
WATER,WARM	43-7/8 lbs	5 gal 1 qts	
EXTRACT,VANILLA	7/8 oz	2 tbsp	

Method
1.   Combine cocoa, salt, and sugar.
2.   Add water; mix. Heat to boiling point; reduce heat and simmer 5 minutes.
3.   Reconstitute milk; add to cocoa syrup, stirring constantly. Add vanilla (optional); mix until well blended.
4.   Heat to just below boiling. DO NOT BOIL.
5.   Serve hot.

Notes
1.   Cocoa may be served with miniature marshmallows.

HOT WHIPPED COCOA

Yield 100   **Portion** 3/4 Cup

Calories	Carbohydrates	Protein	Fat	Cholesterol	Sodium	Calcium
62 cal	15 g	5 g	4 g	0 mg	6 mg	35 mg

Ingredient	Weight	Measure	Issue
COCOA	6 lbs	1 gal 3-7/8 qts	

Method
1. Place Cocoa Beverage Powder in dispenser container. Follow manufacturer's directions for preparation and dispensing of cocoa.
2. Serve hot.

Notes
1. Cocoa may be served with miniature marshmallows. 8 ounce marshmallows will yield 4 to 5 marshmallows per serving of cocoa.

COFFEE (INSTANT)

Yield 100   **Portion** 1 Cup

Calories	Carbohydrates	Protein	Fat	Cholesterol	Sodium	Calcium
5 cal	1 g	0 g	0 g	0 mg	8 mg	8 mg

Ingredient	Weight	Measure	Issue
COFFEE,INSTANT,FREEZE DRIED	8 oz	2-5/8 cup	
WATER,BOILING	52-1/4 lbs	6 gal 1 qts	

Method
1. Add coffee to water. Stir until dissolved.
2. Keep hot. DO NOT BOIL.

Notes
1. Omit Steps 1 and 2 if using an instant coffee dispenser. Place 8 ounces of freeze-dried instant coffee in dispenser jar. Follow dispenser manufacturer's directions for preparation and dispensing of coffee.

COFFEE (AUTOMATIC COFFEE MAKER)

Yield 100   **Portion** 8 Ounces

Calories	Carbohydrates	Protein	Fat	Cholesterol	Sodium	Calcium
11 cal	2 g	1 g	0 g	0 mg	2 mg	6 mg

Ingredient	Weight	Measure	Issue
COFFEE,ROASTED,GROUND	1 lbs	2 qts 2-1/2 cup	

Method
1. Place filter paper in brewing funnel.
2. Spread coffee evenly in filter.
3. Slide funnel into brewer; place empty pot on heating element.
4. Press switch to start automatic brewing cycle.
5. Let water drip through completely; discard grounds.

Notes
1. Serve coffee within 30 minutes.
2. Check water temperature. The water filtered through the grounds must be 200 F. to ensure that the coffee from the brewing chamber will be at least 190 F.
3. For 1 pot: Use 2-1/2 ounces or 3/4 cup roasted, ground coffee. One pot makes 11 5-ounce portions or 7 8-ounce portions.
4. Coffee Maker Production Rates: 2 to 3 minutes to reach water temperature. 4 minutes average brewing time. 1 pot in average of 7 minutes. 8 pots per hour.

5. For 5-ounce portions: In Step 1, use 1-1/2 pound or 1-7/8 quarts roasted, ground coffee to make 10 pots.
6. For stronger brew, use 2-13/16 pounds or 3-1/2 quarts roasted, ground coffee for 8-ounce portion; for 5-ounce portion, use 2 pounds or 2-1/2 quarts roasted, ground coffee.

HOT TEA

Yield 100   **Portion** 1 Cup

Calories	Carbohydrates	Protein	Fat	Cholesterol	Sodium	Calcium
0 cal	0 g	0 g	0 g	0 mg	7 mg	5 mg

Ingredient	Weight	Measure	Issue
TEA,BLACK,LOOSE	8 oz	1-1/4 cup	
WATER,BOILING	54-1/3 lbs	6 gal 2 qts	

Method
1. Place tea in a cloth bag large enough to hold three times the amount.
2. Tie top of bag with cord long enough to facilitate removal; tie cord to handle of urn or kettle.
3. Place tea bag in urn or kettle.
4. Boil water. Pour water over tea bag. Cover. Allow to steep 3 to 5 minutes. Do not agitate or stir.
5. Remove tea bag.
6. Cover; keep hot, but do not boil.

Notes
1. If loose tea, not enclosed in a cloth bag, is placed in the urn or kettle, strain tea after it has steeped 5 minutes.
2. Tea must never be boiled as this produces a bitter flavor.
3. Schedule preparation so not more than 15 minutes will elapse between preparation and service; hold tea at temperatures 175 F. to 185 F.
4. For 5-ounce portions, use 1-3/4 cups tea, loose and 4 gallons of water.
5. 100 8-ounce individual tea bags may be used. Place on serving line for self-service.

COFFEE (AUTOMATIC URN)

Yield 100   **Portion** 1 Cup

Calories	Carbohydrates	Protein	Fat	Cholesterol	Sodium	Calcium
9 cal	2 g	0 g	0 g	0 mg	1 mg	5 mg

Ingredient	Weight	Measure	Issue
COFFEE,ROASTED,GROUND	13-3/4 oz	2 qts 1 cup	

Method
1. Make sure water level in urn liner does not exceed 2 inches from top or is lower than the center of glass water gauge.
2. Push HEAT SELECTOR switch to BREW position.
3. Rinse urn liner by placing spray arm over top of urn. Push START button. Push STOP button after 30 seconds and drain liner.
4. Set timer for desired amount of water, 3 quarts of water for every minute; weigh coffee and spread evenly in filter paper. See Guidelines for Coffee Urn Capacities.

5. Place wire basket containing filter paper and coffee in top of urn. Cover and position spray arm through hole in cover.
6. When BREW TEMPERATURE light is on, press START button.
7. Five minutes after brewing is completed, turn heat selector to HOLD position. Discard grounds and filter paper; rinse wire basket.
8. When empty, rinse out urn.

Notes
1. Always thoroughly drain leftover coffee from urn; do not make fresh coffee on top of old.
2. Never operate the urn without water. Damage to the heating elements and/or the thermostat control may result.
3. For a 5-ounce portion, use 5-1/2 cups roasted, ground coffee per 100 portions in Step 4.
4. Cleaning after each batch of coffee should be a regular routine. Coffee urns should have a special cleaning twice a week. See the operating manual for cleaning instructions.

COFFEE (MANUAL URN)

Yield 100   **Portion** 1 Cup

Calories	Carbohydrates	Protein	Fat	Cholesterol	Sodium	Calcium
9 cal	2 g	0 g	0 g	0 mg	1 mg	5 mg

Ingredient	**Weight**	**Measure**	**Issue**
COFFEE,ROASTED,GROUND	13-3/4 oz	2 qts 1 cup	

Method
1. Fill boiler with water to desired level. See Guidelines for Coffee Urn Capacities. Turn on heat.
2. Spread ground coffee evenly in urn bag or filter paper in wire basket; set in top of urn. Close urn cover.
3. When boiler water reaches a vigorous boil, open blow-over valve and spray water over coffee for 3 to 4 minutes. Close blow-over valve. Remove and discard grounds.
4. If urn has no agitation system, re-pour about 1/3 of the coffee directly back into boiler. Rinse urn bag and store in cold water.
5. Gradually replenish water no more than 1 gallon at a time whenever gauge shows less than half full.

Notes
1. 1-7/8 pound or 2-1/4 quarts roasted and ground coffee and 6-3/4 gallon water will yield 100 8-ounce portions or 6-1/4 gallon coffee.

FRUIT PUNCH

Yield 100   **Portion** 1-1/4 Cup

Calories	Carbohydrates	Protein	Fat	Cholesterol	Sodium	Calcium
117 cal	30 g	0 g	0 g	0 mg	10 mg	15 mg

Ingredient	**Weight**	**Measure**	**Issue**
SUGAR,GRANULATED	4-1/4 lbs	2 qts 1-5/8 cup	
WATER	12-1/2 lbs	1 gal 2 qts	
JUICE,GRAPEFRUIT,CONCENTRATE,FROZEN	3-2/3 lbs	1 qts 2 cup	
JUICE,LEMON	1-1/8 lbs	2 cup	
JUICE,PINEAPPLE,CANNED,UNSWEETENED	6-5/8 lbs	3 qts	
WATER,COLD	33-1/2 lbs	4 gal	
ICE CUBES	9-5/8 lbs	3 gal	

Method

1. Dissolve sugar in water. Cool.
2. Add juices and water to sugar solution. Mix thoroughly. Cover and refrigerate.
3. Add ice just before serving.

Notes

1. In Step 2, 1-1/2 gallons of canned grapefruit juice may be used. Reduce water to 2-3/4 gallons per 100 servings.
2. In Step 2, 2 quarts of fresh lemon juice may be used. Reduce water to 3-1/2 gallon per 100 servings.

LIME LEMON PUNCH

Yield 100   **Portion** 1 Cup

Calories	Carbohydrates	Protein	Fat	Cholesterol	Sodium	Calcium
130 cal	34 g	0 g	0 g	0 mg	14 mg	10 mg

Ingredient	Weight	Measure	Issue
SUGAR,GRANULATED	7 lbs	1 gal	
WATER	12-1/2 lbs	1 gal 2 qts	
JUICE,LEMON	1-1/8 lbs	2 cup	
JUICE,LIME	5-7/8 lbs	2 qts 3-3/4 cup	
WATER	39-3/4 lbs	4 gal 3 qts	
FOOD COLOR,GREEN	1/2 oz	1 tbsp	
ICE CUBES	9-5/8 lbs	3 gal	

Method

1. Dissolve sugar in water. Cool.
2. Add juices, food coloring, and water to sugar solution. Mix thoroughly. Cover and refrigerate.
3. Add ice just before serving.

Notes

1. In Step 2, 2 quarts of fresh lemon juice may be used. Reduce water to 3-1/2 gallon per 100 servings.

ORANGE AND PINEAPPLE JUICE COCKTAIL

Yield 100   **Portion** 1/2 Cup

Calories	Carbohydrates	Protein	Fat	Cholesterol	Sodium	Calcium
66 cal	16 g	1 g	0 g	0 mg	3 mg	17 mg

Ingredient	Weight	Measure	Issue
JUICE,ORANGE	15-3/8 lbs	1 gal 3 qts	
JUICE,PINEAPPLE,CANNED,UNSWEETENED	14-1/3 lbs	1 gal 2-1/2 qts	
ICE CUBES	4 lbs	1 gal 1 qts	

Method

1. Combine orange and pineapple juices; stir.
2. Add ice just before serving.

GRAPEFRUIT AND PINEAPPLE JUICE COCKTAIL

Yield 100   Portion 1 Cup

Calories	Carbohydrates	Protein	Fat	Cholesterol	Sodium	Calcium
63 cal	15 g	1 g	0 g	0 mg	3 mg	18 mg

Ingredient	Weight	Measure	Issue
JUICE,GRAPEFRUIT,CONCENTRATE,FROZEN	4-1/8 lbs	1 qts 2-5/8 cup	
JUICE,PINEAPPLE,CANNED,UNSWEETENED	14-1/3 lbs	1 gal 2-1/2 qts	
WATER	12-1/2 lbs	1 gal 2 qts	
ICE CUBES	4 lbs	1 gal 1 qts	

Method
1. Combine grapefruit and pineapple juices with water; stir.
2. Cover and refrigerate.
3. Add ice just before serving.

LEMONADE

Yield 100   Portion 1-1/4 Cups

Calories	Carbohydrates	Protein	Fat	Cholesterol	Sodium	Calcium
126 cal	33 g	0 g	0 g	0 mg	11 mg	7 mg

Ingredient	Weight	Measure	Issue
SUGAR,GRANULATED	7 lbs	1 gal	
WATER	12-1/2 lbs	1 gal 2 qts	
JUICE,LEMON	2-1/8 lbs	1 qts	
WATER,COLD	37-5/8 lbs	4 gal 2 qts	
ICE CUBES	9-5/8 lbs	3 gal	

Method
1. Dissolve sugar in water. Cool.
2. Add juice and water to sugar solution. Mix thoroughly. Cover and refrigerate.
3. Add ice just before serving.

LIMEADE

Yield 100   Portion 1-1/4 Cups

Calories	Carbohydrates	Protein	Fat	Cholesterol	Sodium	Calcium
131 cal	34 g	0 g	0 g	0 mg	14 mg	10 mg

Ingredient	Weight	Measure	Issue
SUGAR,GRANULATED	7 lbs	1 gal	
WATER	12-1/2 lbs	1 gal 2 qts	
JUICE,LIME	7-1/2 lbs	3 qts 3 cup	
WATER,COLD	37-5/8 lbs	4 gal 2 qts	
ICE CUBES	9-5/8 lbs	3 gal	

Method

1. Dissolve sugar in water. Cool.
2. Add juice and water to sugar solution. Mix thoroughly. Cover and refrigerate.
3. Add ice just before serving.

ICED TEA (INSTANT)

Yield 100   **Portion** 1-1/4 Cups

Calories	Carbohydrates	Protein	Fat	Cholesterol	Sodium	Calcium
6 cal	1 g	0 g	0 g	0 mg	14 mg	8 mg

Ingredient	Weight	Measure	Issue
TEA MIX,INSTANT,UNSWEETENED	8-3/4 oz		1 qts 3-3/8 cup
WATER,COLD	66-7/8 lbs	8 gal	
ICE CUBES	9-5/8 lbs	3 gal	

Method

1. Add tea to water; stir until dissolved.
2. Serve over crushed or cubed ice.

Notes

1. For each 8-ounce glass, use about 5 ounces of strong tea. Fill glass with crushed ice. Serve 2 8-ounce glasses per portion.

ICED TEA (INSTANT FOR DISPENSER)

Yield 100   **Portion** 1-1/4 Cups

Calories	Carbohydrates	Protein	Fat	Cholesterol	Sodium	Calcium
5 cal	1 g	0 g	0 g	0 mg	4 mg	2 mg

Ingredient	Weight	Measure	Issue
TEA MIX,INSTANT,UNSWEETENED	6-3/4 oz	1 qts 1-5/8 cup	
ICE CUBES	9-5/8 lbs	3 gal	

Method

1. Place instant tea, on dispenser. Follow manufacturer's directions for preparation, dispensing of tea, and cleaning of dispenser.
2. Serve over crushed or cubed ice.

Notes

1. For each 8-ounce glass, use about 5 ounces of strong tea. Fill glass with crushed ice. Serve 2 8-ounce glasses per portion.

ICED TEA (INSTANT W/LEMON AND SUGAR FOR DISPENSER)

Yield 100   **Portion** 1-1/4 Cups

Calories	Carbohydrates	Protein	Fat	Cholesterol	Sodium	Calcium
175 cal	44 g	0 g	0 g	0 mg	4 mg	2 mg

Ingredient	Weight	Measure	Issue
TEA MIX,INSTANT,W/LEMON AND SUGAR	10 lbs		
ICE CUBES	9-5/8 lbs	3 gal	

Method
1. Place instant tea mix with lemon and sugar on dispenser. Follow directions for preparation and dispensing of tea.
2. Serve over crushed or cubed ice.

Notes
1. For each 8-ounce glass, use about 5 ounces of strong tea. Fill glass with crushed ice. Serve 2 8-ounce glasses per portion.

ORANGEADE

Yield 100   **Portion** 1-1/4 Cups

Calories	Carbohydrates	Protein	Fat	Cholesterol	Sodium	Calcium
131 cal	34 g	0 g	0 g	0 mg	14 mg	10 mg

Ingredient	Weight	Measure	Issue
SUGAR,GRANULATED	4 lbs	2 qts 1 cup	
WATER	12-1/2 lbs	1 gal 2 qts	
JUICE,ORANGE	35-1/8 lbs	4 gal	
ICE CUBES	9-5/8 lbs	3 gal	

Method
1. Dissolve sugar in water. Cool.
2. Add juice to sugar solution. Mix thoroughly. Cover and refrigerate.
3. Add ice just before serving.

Notes
1. In Step 1, use 5 pounds or 2-3/4 quarts of granulated sugar and 2 gallons of hot water for 100 servings.

RECIPE CONVERSION

Most bread and sweet dough recipes have an additional column on the left side of each recipe card for TRUE PERCENTAGES. These are based on the total weight of all the ingredients, the sum of which is 100 percent. True percentages are used in adjusting a recipe to yield a specific number of servings to produce a specific number of smaller or larger servings, or to use the amount of ingredients available. To adjust a recipe to yield a specific number of servings, use this method:

For example using Sweet Dough (Recipe D–36)––

A. TRUE PERCENTAGE METHOD
Step 1–obtain a working factor by dividing the number of servings needed by 100.
For example: 438 servings needed ÷ 100 = 4.38 working factor. See Recipe Conversion No. A-1.
Step 2–multiply the working factor by the total weight of the recipe to obtain the pounds desired. (Note: the total weight of the recipe is listed at the bottom of the weight column on each recipe card.)
For example: 4.38 (working factor) x 12.958 (weight of recipe) = 56.76 (lbs desired).
Step 3–Multiply 56.76 (lbs desired) by the percent of each ingredient in the recipe.

Ingredient	Percent		Weight
Yeast............	2.37% × 56.76	=	1.34 lb = 1 lb 5 1/2 oz
Water............	18.92% × 56.76	=	10.74 lb = 10 lb 12 oz
Sugar...........	8.99% × 56.76	=	5.10 lb = 5 lb 1 1/2 oz
Salt.............	95% × 56.76	=	.54 lb = 8 3/4 oz
Shortening.......	7.57% × 56.76	=	4.30 lb = 4 lb 5 oz
Eggs............	9.46% × 56.76	=	5.37 lb = 5 lb 6 oz
Flour...........	50.16% × 56.76	=	28.47 lb = 28 lb 7 1/2 oz
Milk...........	1.58% × 56.76	=	.90 lb = 14 1/2 oz
TOTAL	100.00%		56.76 lb

GUIDELINES FOR PREPARATION OF YEAST DOUGHS

1. The water temperature in which the yeast is dissolved is important. If temperatures above 110°F. are used, the yeast will be killed. If under 105°F. the yeast's growth or development will be retarded.
2. The amount of water required may vary from that specified in the recipe due to variable amounts of moisture in the flour.
3. Full mixing or dough development produces better volume and lighter yeast products.
4. Lightly grease the bowl in which the dough is allowed to rise. Heavy greasing may cause streaks in the bread.
5. Yeast dough is ready to be punched when it is light and about double in bulk. To test, press the dough lightly with a finger tip. If the impression remains and the dough recedes slightly, it is ready to be punched.
6. Punching should be just enough to expel gases.
7. The dough for rolls is usually softer than that for bread.

RETARDED SWEET DOUGH METHODS

Retarded sweet dough is yeast dough that is refrigerated for a period of time prior to baking. Refrigeration temperatures retard fermentation of the dough. The quality of the end product is not changed. Retarded sweet dough may be held in refrigeration below 40°F. as long as 24 hours.

Retarded sweet dough may be prepared using Sweet Dough (Recipe No. D-36). Two methods of preparation are:

Method 1
1. Follow Steps 1 through 4, Recipe No. D-36. Omit Steps 5 through 7.
2. FERMENT: Set in warm place (80°F.) about 50 to 55 minutes.
3. PUNCH: Divide dough into desired working-size pieces (See Recipe No. D-G-7; shape each piece into a smooth rectangular piece. Let rest 15 minutes.
4. MAKE UP: As desired. See Recipe No. D-G-7 for specific shapes.
5. Cover; refrigerate immediately.
6. When ready to use, remove from refrigeration; PROOF until pieces are double in bulk.
7. BAKE: See Recipe No. D-G-7 for specific shapes, baking times and temperatures.
8. FINISH: As desired.

NOTE: Made up pieces prepared by this method can be stored safely for about 60 hours at 32°F.

Method 2
1. Follow Steps 1 through 3, Recipe No. D-36. Omit Steps 4 through 9.
2. FERMENT: Set in warm place (80°F.) about 50 to 55 minutes.
3. PUNCH: Divide dough into 3 pieces, about 4 lb 5 oz each (See Recipe No. D-G-7); shape each piece into a smooth rectangular piece. Let rest 15 minutes.
4. Flatten each piece; brush lightly with melted shortening or salad oil. Place on greased sheet pans; cover and refrigerate.
5. When ready to use, remove dough from refrigeration; make up as desired (See Recipe No. D-G-7). IT IS NOT NECESSARY TO BRING DOUGH TO ROOM TEMPERATURE BEFORE MAKE UP.
6. PROOF: Until pieces are double in bulk.
7. BAKE: See Recipe No. D-G-7 for specific shapes, baking times, and temperatures.
8. FINISH: As desired.

CHARACTERISTICS OF GOOD QUALITY BREAD PRODUCTS AND ROLLS

CHARACTERISTIC	BISCUITS	MUFFINS	YEAST BREADS AND ROLLS
Color.........	Uniform golden brown top and bottom. Inside creamy white. Free from yellow or brown spots.	Uniform golden brown out-side. Inside creamy white or slightly yellow but free from streaks.	Even rich brown color, creamy white inside and free from streaks.
Shape and size..	Uniform in shape and size, with straight sides and a smooth level top. The volume is at least twice the size of the unbaked product.	Uniform shape and size. Well-rounded pebbled top, free from peaks or cracks.	Well proportioned, symmetrical with a well-rounded top.
Crust.........	Tender and moderately smooth. Free from excess flour.	Tender, with a thin, slightly rough or pebbled shiny appearance.	Crisp-tender with an even thickness over entire surface. Free from cracks and bulges.
Texture.......	Slightly moist, tender and flaky crumb, with a medium fine grain.	Moist, tender and light crumb, with medium fine, evenly distributed air spaces.	Soft, springy texture, tender and slightly moist with fine grain, thin walled cells.
Flavor........	Pleasing, well-blended flavor with no bitterness.	Pleasing, well-blended flavor with no bitterness or off-flavors.	Wheaty, sweet nut-like other flavor. No off-flavors.

CHARACTERISTICS OF POOR QUALITY BREAD PRODUCTS AND ROLLS

CHARACTERISTIC	BISCUITS	MUFFINS	YEAST BREADS AND ROLLS
Outside Appearance Shape irregular	Too much liquid. Dough not rolled to uniform thickness. Improper cutting of dough. Uneven oven heat.	Too much flour. Not enough liquid. Overmixing. Too much batter in pan. Oven too hot.	Improper shaping. Too much dough for bread pan. Insufficient proofing time.
Color Too dark	Oven too hot. Overbaking.	Too much sugar. Oven too hot. Overbaking.	Too much sugar or milk. Insufficient fermentation time. Oven too hot.
Too pale	Dough too stiff. Oven not hot enough, insufficient sugar.	Overmixing. Oven not hot enough. Underbaking.	Not enough sugar or milk. Dough too warm during mixing and excessive fermentation. Oven not hot enough.
Crusts Tough or hard	Too much flour. Overmixing. Oven too hot. Overbaking.	Too much flour or not enough sugar or shortening. Overmixing.	Not enough shortening. Overbaking. Insufficient fermentation. Too much rolling in flour.
Irregular	Rough or blisters due to too much liquid, incorrect kneading or rolling.	Peaks due to mixture being too stiff, overmixing or oven hot.	Blisters due to improper make-up. Too much too rolling in flour.
Too smooth	. . . .	Too much liquid or overmixing.	. . . .
Inside Appearance Color streaks or spots	Too much leavening. Ingredients not well mixed.	Eggs and milk not well blended.	"Crusting" during fermentation of dough. Undermixing. Too much dusting flour during make-up.
Coarse or uneven grain	Too much leavening, not enough liquid, or improper mixing. "Not flaky" due to not enough shortening or improper mixing of shortening and flour.	Insufficient beating of eggs. Too much or not enough leavening. Overmixing. Tunnels due to not enough liquid or shortening or overmixing.	Improper make-up, excessive water or under-or overmixing.
Texture Too dry	Dough too stiff. Overbaking. Oven not hot enough. Not enough sugar or shortening.	Batter too stiff. Overbaking. Too much leavening. Not enough sugar and/or shortening.	Overproofing. Not enough water or improper mixing time.
Crumbly	Too much leavening, sugar or shortening. Not enough liquid.	Not enough liquid. Too much baking powder. Oven not hot enough.	Not enough water, improper mixing time.
Tough	Not enough shortening or leavening. Too much liquid. Dough too cold or oven not hot enough. Overmixing.	Not enough shortening or sugar. Overmixing.	Not enough shortening. Insufficient proofing time. Overbaking.
Heavy	Wrong proportion of ingredients. Improper mixing. Oven not hot enough or dough too stiff.	Not enough baking powder or shortening. Overmixing.	Underproofing or overmixing.
Poor Flavor	Wrong proportion of ingredients or improper mixing.	Wrong proportion of ingredients or improper mixing.	Wrong proportion of ingredients or improper mixing. Fermentation time too long.

GUIDE FOR HOT ROLL MAKE-UP

1. Cloverleaf or Twin Rolls

1. Follow Steps 1 through 7 of Recipe No.D-33 or D-34.
2. Divide each dough piece into thirds for cloverleaf rolls or in halves for twin rolls.
3. Shape into balls by rolling with a circular motion on work table.
4. Place in greased muffin pans, (Figure 1). Each cup: 3 balls for cloverleaf or 2 for twin; brush with 4 oz (1/2 cup) melted butter or 1/3 recipe Milk Wash (Recipe No. I-4-2).
5. Proof at 90°F. until double in bulk.
6. Bake at 400°F. 15 to 20 minutes or in 350°F. convection oven 10 to 15 minutes or until golden brown on high fan, open vent.
7. Brush with 4 oz (1/2 cup) melted butter (optional) immediately after baking. (EACH PORTION: 2 Rolls)

Figure 1

2. Frankfurter Rolls

1. Prepare 2/3 Recipe No. D-33 or D-34.Follow Steps 1 through 6.
2. Roll 21/2 oz pieces of dough into oblong rolls, 5 to 6 inches long.
3. Place on greased sheet pans in rows 4 by 9 (Figure 2). Brush with 1/3 recipe Milk Wash (Recipe No. I-4-2) or 1/4 recipe Egg Wash (Recipe No. D-17).
4. Proof at 90°F. until double in bulk.
5. Bake at 400°F. 15 to 20 minutes or in 350°F. convection oven 10 to 15 minutes or until golden brown on high fan, open vent. Cool. EACH PORTION: 1 Roll.

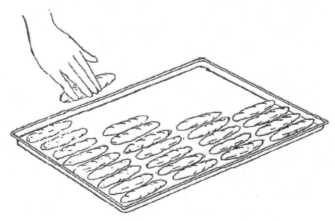

Figure 2

Frankfurter Rolls (Semi-Automatic Equipment)

1. Prepare 2/3 Recipe No. D-33. Follow Steps 1 through 3; add 2/3 oz (11/2 tbsp) bakery emulsifier to flour and milk. Follow Steps 4 and 5. Omit Steps 6 through 10.
2. Divide dough into 5 lb 1 oz pieces. Round; let rest 5 to 10 minutes.
3. Place each piece of dough into roll divider and rounding machine. Divide into 36 balls. Let rest 5 to 10 minutes.
4. Feed balls, one at a time, into a bread molder-sheeter machine with a 55/8 inch pressure dough plate.
5. Place on greased sheet pans in rows 4 by 7; brush with 1/3 recipe Milk Wash (Recipe No. I-4-2) or ¼ recipe Egg Wash (Recipe No. D-17).
6. Proof at 90°F. about 30 minutes or until double in bulk.
7. Bake at 400°F. 15 to 20 minutes or in 350°F. convection oven 10 to 15 minutes or until golden brown on high fan, open vent. Cool.
8. Slice rolls partially through using bun slicer.

EACH PORTION: 1 Roll.

3. Hamburger or Sandwich Rolls

1. Prepare 2/3 Recipe No. D-33 or D-34. Follow Steps 1 through 6.
2. Shape 21/2 oz pieces of dough into balls by rolling with a circular motion on work table.
3. Place on greased sheet pans in rows 4 by 6.
4. When half-proofed, flatten with hand or small can to about 1/2 inch thickness and 31/2 inch diameter (Figure 3); brush with 1/3 recipe Milk Wash (Recipe No. I-4-2) or 1/4 recipe Egg Wash (Recipe No. D-17).
5. Proof at 90°F. until double in bulk.
6. Bake at 400°F. 15 to 20 minutes in 350°F. convection oven 10 to 15 minutes or until golden brown on high fan, open vent. Cool.

EACH PORTION: 1 Roll.

Figure 3

GUIDE FOR HOT ROLL MAKE-UP

Hamburger Rolls (Semi-Automatic Equipment)

1. Prepare 2/3 Recipe No. D-33. Follow Steps 1 through 3; add 2/3 oz (11/2 tbsp) bakery emulsifier to flour and milk. Follow Steps 4 and 5. Omit Steps 6 through 10.
2. Divide dough into 5 lb 1 oz pieces. Round; let rest 5 to 10 minutes.
3. Place each piece of dough into roll divider and rounding machine. Divide into 36 balls. Let rest 5 to 10 minutes.
4. Place on greased sheet pans in rows 4 by 6.
5. Flatten with hand or small can to about 1/2 inch thickness and 31/2 inch diameter; brush with 1/3 recipe Milk Wash (Recipe No. I-4-2) or 1/4 recipe Egg Wash (Recipe No. D-17).
6. Proof at 90°F. about 30 minutes or until double in bulk.
7. Bake at 400°F. 15 to 20 minutes or in 350°F. convection oven 10 to 15 minutes or until golden brown on high fan, open vent. Cool.
8. Slice rolls using bun slicer.

EACH PORTION: 1 Roll

4. Pan, Cluster or Pull Apart Rolls

1. Follow Steps 1 through 7 of Recipe No. D-33 or D-34.
2. Shape 11/2 to 2 oz dough pieces into balls by rolling with a circular motion on work table.
3. Place on greased sheet pans in rows 6 by 9. Brush with 4 oz (1/2 cup) melted butter or 1/4 recipe Egg Wash (Recipe No. D-17), (Figure 4).
4. Proof at 90°F. until double in bulk.
5. Bake at 400°F. 15 to 20 minutes or in 350°F. convection oven 10 to 15 minutes or until golden brown on high fan, open vent.
6. Brush with 4 oz (1/2 cup) melted butter (optional) immediately after baking.

EACH PORTION: 2 Rolls.

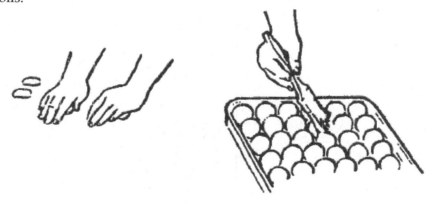

Figure 4

5. Parker House Rolls

1. Follow Steps 1 through 7 of Recipe No. D-33 or D-34.
2. Shape 11/2 to 2 oz dough pieces into balls by rolling with a circular motion on work table (Figure 4).
3. Cover with clean damp cloth; let rest 5 to 10 minutes.

4. Press center of each ball with a small rolling pin (Figure 5).
5. Brush with 4 oz (1/2 cup) melted butter; fold in half. Press edges together with thumb or palm of hand.
6. Place on greased sheet pans in rows 5 by 10; brush with 4 oz (1/2 cup) melted butter.
7. Proof at 90°F. until double in bulk.
8. Bake at 400°F. 15 to 20 minutes or in 350°F. convection oven 10 to 15 minutes or until golden brown on high fan, open vent.

EACH PORTION: 2 Rolls.

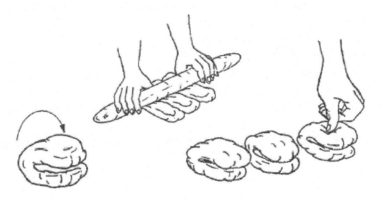

Figure 5

6. Poppy Seed or Sesame Seed Rolls

1. Follow Steps 1 through 7 of Recipe No. D-33 or D-34.
2. Shape rolls as desired.
3. Place on greased sheet pans. Brush top of rolls lightly with water or 1/6 recipe Egg White Wash (Recipe No. D-17-1). Use 3 oz (3/4 cup) poppy or sesame seeds; sprinkle top of roll with seeds (Figure 6).
4. Proof at 90°F. until double in bulk.
5. Bake at 400°F. 15 to 20 minutes or in 350°F. convection oven 10 to 15 minutes or until golden brown on high fan, open vent.

EACH PORTION: 2 Rolls.

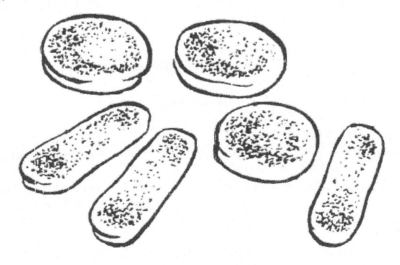

Figure 6

GUIDE FOR SWEET DOUGH MAKE-UP

Sweet Roll (Round) Varieties

1. Glazed Rolls (2 Pans)

1. Follow Steps 1 through 6 of Recipe No. D-36.
2. Roll each 4 lb 5 oz piece of dough into a long rope of uniform diameter. (For D-36-1, use 4 lb 2 oz pieces.)
3. Slice into 34 pieces, weighing 13/4 to 2 oz each.
4. Shape into balls by rolling with a circular motion.
5. Place on lightly greased sheet pans in rows 6 by 9.
6. Melt 8 oz (1 cup) butter or margarine. Brush 1/2 cup on rolls in each pan.
7. Proof at 90°F. to 100°F. until double in bulk.
8. Bake at 375°F. 20 to 25 minutes or until golden brown or in 325°F. convection oven 15 minutes on high fan, open vent. Cool.
9. Prepare 1 recipe Vanilla Glaze (Recipe No. D-46); brush about 11/3 cups on baked rolls in each pan.

EACH PORTION: 1 Roll.

2. Pecan Rolls (2 Pans)

1. Follow Steps 1 through 6 of Recipe No. D-36.
2. Roll each 4 lb 5 oz piece of dough into a long rope of uniform diameter. (For D-36-1, use 4 lb 2 oz pieces.)
3. Slice into 34 pieces, weighing 13/4 to 2 oz each.
4. Shape into balls by rolling with a circular motion.
5. Prepare 1 recipe Pecan Topping (Recipe No. D-49-1). Spread 11/4 qt in each pan.
6. Flatten balls. Place on topping mixture in rows 6 by 9.
7. Melt 8 oz (1 cup) butter or margarine. Brush 1/2 cup on rolls in each pan.
8. Proof at 90°F. to 100°F. until double in bulk.
9. Bake at 375°F. 20 to 25 minutes or until golden brown or in 325°F. convection oven 15 minutes on high fan, open vent.
10. Invert pans as soon as removed from oven; bottom of roll becomes top. EACH PORTION: 1 Roll.

Cinnamon Roll Varieties

3. Cinnamon Rolls (3 Pans)

1. Follow Steps 1 through 6 of Recipe No. D-36.
2. Roll each 4 lb 5 oz piece of dough into a rectangular sheet, about 18 inches wide, 36 inches long, and 1/4 inch thick. (For D-36-1, use 4 lb 2 oz pieces).
3. Melt 1 lb (2 cups) butter or margarine. Brush 1/2 cup on each sheet of dough. Set aside remainder for use in Step 4.

(a) **Cinnamon Rolls**
Prepare 1 recipe Cinnamon Sugar Filling (Recipe No.D-42). Sprinkle 11/2 cups cinnamon sugar mixture over each sheet of dough.

(b) **Cinnamon Nut Rolls**
Prepare 1 recipe Cinnamon Sugar Nut Filling (Recipe No. D-42-1). Sprinkle 11/2 cups cinnamon sugar mixture and 2 cups chopped unsalted nuts over each sheet of dough.

(c)   **Cinnamon Raisin Rolls**
   Prepare 1 recipe Cinnamon Sugar Raisin Filling
   (Recipe No. D-42-2). Sprinkle 1 1/2 cups cinnamon
   sugar and 2 cups raisins over each sheet of dough.

4. Roll each piece tightly to make a long slender roll. Seal
    edges by pressing firmly. Elongate roll to 35 inches by
    rolling back and forth on work table. (See Figure 7). Brush
    2 tbsp butter or margarine on each roll.
5. Slice each roll into 34 pieces about 1 inch wide, using
    dough cutter (See Figure 7).
6. Place cut side down on lightly greased sheet pans in rows
    5 by 8. (See Figure 7).
7. Proof at 90°F. to 100°F. until double in bulk.
8. Bake at 375°F. 20 to 25 minutes or until golden brown or in
    325°F. convection oven 15 minutes on high fan, open vent.
    Cool.
9. Glaze, if desired, with 1 recipe Vanilla Glaze (Recipe No.
    D-46). Brush about 1 cup on rolls in each pan.

Figure 7

EACH PORTION: 1 Roll.

4. Butterfly Rolls (3 Pans)

1. Follow Steps 1 through 6 of Recipe No. D-36 except divide into 6-2 lb 2 oz pieces. (For D-36-1, divide
    into 2 lb 1 oz pieces.)
2. Roll each piece of dough into a rectangular sheet, about 10 inches wide, 30 inches long, and 1/4 inch
    thick.
3. Melt 12 oz (1 1/2 cups) butter or margarine.
    Brush ¼ cup on each sheet of dough.

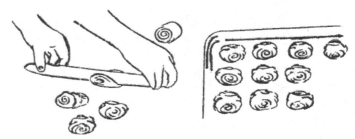

4. Roll each piece tightly to make a long slender
    roll. Seal edges by pressing firmly. Elongate
    roll to 30 inches by rolling back and forth on
    work table.
5. Slice each roll into 17 pieces about 1 3/4
    inches wide.
6. Press each piece firmly in center parallel to
    cut side of roll with back of knife or small
    rolling pin. (See Figure 8).
7. Place on lightly greased sheet pans in rows 4
    by 8. Prepare 1/4 recipe Egg Wash (Recipe
    No. D-17). Brush 1/4 cup on rolls in each pan.

Figure 8

8. Proof at 90°F. to 100°F. until double in bulk.
9. Bake at 375°F. 20 to 25 minutes or until golden brown or in 325°F. convection oven 15 minutes on high
    fan, open vent. Cool.
10. Glaze, if desired, with 1 recipe Vanilla Glaze (Recipe No. D-46). Brush about 1 cup on rolls in each pan.

EACH PORTION: 1 Roll.

5. Sugar Rolls (3 Pans)

1. Follow Steps 1 through 6 of Recipe No. D-36.
2. Roll out each 4 lb 5 oz piece of dough into a rectangular sheet, about 18 inches wide, 36 inches long, and 1/4 inch thick. (For D-36-1, use 4 lb 2 oz pieces.)
3. Melt 1 lb (2 cups) butter or margarine. Brush 1/2 cup on each sheet of dough.
4. Roll each piece tightly to make a long slender roll. Seal edges by pressing firmly. Elongate roll to 35 inches by rolling back and forth on work table. Brush 2 tbsp butter or margarine on each roll.
5. Slice each roll into 34 pieces, about 1 inch wide, using dough cutter (See Figure 9).
6. Press cut side of each slice in 14 oz (2 cups) granulated sugar so that surface is well coated. (See Figure 9).
7. Place sugar side up on lightly greased sheet pans in rows 5 by 8 (See Figure 9).
8. Proof at 90°F. to 100°F. until double in bulk.
9. Bake at 375°F. 20 to 25 minutes or until golden brown or in 325°F. convection oven 15 minutes on high fan, open vent. Cool.
10. Glaze, if desired, with 1 recipe Vanilla Glaze (Recipe No. D-46). Brush about 1 cup on rolls in each pan.

Figure 9

EACH PORTION: 1 Roll.

6. Streusel Coffee Cake (2 Pans)

1. Follow Steps 1 through 6 of Recipe No. D-36 except divide into 2-6 lb 8 oz pieces. (For D-36-1, divide into 6 lb 4 oz pieces.)
2. Roll each piece of dough into a rectangular sheet, about 18 inches wide, 25 inches long and 1/2 inch thick; fit into greased sheet pans, pressing against sides (edges should not be thicker than center).
3. Dock dough with fork or docker, if available.
4. Prepare 1/4 recipe Egg Wash (Recipe No. D-17). Brush about 1/3 cup on dough in each pan. Prepare 1 recipe Streusel Topping (Recipe No. D-49); sprinkle 11/2 qt topping over dough in each pan.
5. Proof dough 20 to 35 minutes.
6. Bake at 375°F. 30 to 35 minutes or until golden brown or in 325°F. convection oven 15 minutes on high fan, open vent.
7. Prepare 2/3 recipe Vanilla Glaze (Recipe No. D-46); drizzle about 1 cup over each cake while hot.
8. Cut 6 by 9.

EACH PORTION: 1 Piece.

7. Small Coffee Cake (18 Cakes) (5 Pans)

1. Follow Steps 1 through 6 of Recipe No. D-36 except divide dough into 6-2 lb 2 oz pieces. (For D-36-1, divide into 2 lb 1 oz pieces.)
2. Roll each piece of dough into a rectangular sheet about 9 inches wide, 36 inches long, and 1/4 inch thick.

3. Melt 12 oz (11/2 cups) butter or margarine; brush ¼ cup on each sheet of dough. Prepare 1 recipe Cinnamon Sugar Filling (Recipe No. D-42-2); use 2 lb (61/4 cups) raisins; sprinkle 3/4 cup filling and 1 cup raisins over each sheet of dough.
4. Roll each piece tightly to make a long slender roll. Seal edges by pressing firmly. Elongate roll to 36 inches by rolling back and forth on work table. (See Figure 7).
5. Cut rolls into 3-12 inch pieces (See Figure 10), weighing about 10 oz each.
6. Place 4 coffee cakes on each lightly greased sheet pan.
7. Make a deep 9-inch slit down center of each piece, about 1/2 through folds of dough. (See Figure 10). DO NOT CUT COMPLETELY THROUGH ALL LAYERS.

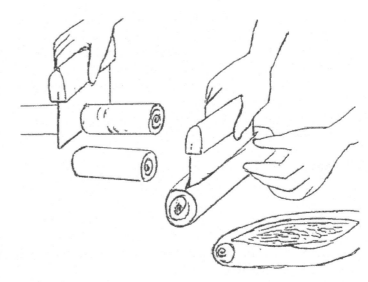

Figure 10

8. Prepare 1/4 recipe Egg Wash (Recipe No. D-17). Brush about 2 tsp on each cake.
9. Proof at 90°F. to 100°F. until double in bulk.
10. Bake at 375°F. 25 to 30 minutes or until golden brown or in 325°F. convection oven 15 minutes on high fan, open vent. Cool.
11. Glaze, if desired, with 1 recipe Vanilla Glaze (Recipe No. D-46)). Drizzle about 2 tbsp on cakes in each pan.
12. Cut each cake into 6-2 inch pieces.

EACH PORTION: 1 Piece.

8. Twist Coffee Cakes (18 Cakes) (5 Pans)

1. Follow Steps 1 through 6 of Recipe No. D-36.
2. Roll each 4 lb 5 oz piece of dough into a rectangular sheet, about 13 inches wide, 45 inches long and ¼ inch thick. (For D-36-1, use 4 lb 2 oz pieces.)
3. Melt 12 oz (11/2 cups) melted butter or margarine. Brush 1/2 cup over dough in each pan. Prepare 1 recipe Cinnamon Sugar Raisin Filling (Recipe No. D-42-2). Sprinkle 11/2 cups over each sheet of dough. Sprinkle about 1 cup raisins over center third of dough.
4. Fold 1/3 dough over center. Sprinkle 1 cup raisins on top of folded dough. Fold remaining 1/3 dough over raisins to form a strip 13 by 15 inches.
5. Cut each strip into 6-15 inch long, 2 inch wide pieces weighing about 1 lb each. (See Figure 11.)
6. Slit roll down center to within 1 inch of each end (See Figure 11).
7. Twist pieces in one direction and then in opposite direction (see Figure 11) stretching to about 19 inches.

Figure 11

8. Place each piece in a circle on lightly greased sheet pans; seal ends securely by fitting one end into other (See Figure 11). Rings should not touch each other.
9. Prepare 1/4 recipe Egg Wash (Recipe No. D-17). Brush about 2 tsp on each cake.
10. Proof at 90°F. to 100°F. until double in bulk.
11. Bake at 375°F. 25 to 30 minutes or until golden brown or in 325°F. convection oven 15 minutes on high fan, open vent. Cool.
12. Glaze, if desired, with 1 recipe Vanilla Glaze (Recipe No. D-46). Drizzle about 2/3 cup on each cake. Cut each cake into 6 pieces.

EACH PORTION: 1 Piece.

9. Bear Claws (4 Pans)

1. Follow Steps 1 through 6 of Recipe No. D-36, except divide into 6-2 lb 2 oz pieces. (For D-36-1, divide into 2 lb 1 oz pieces.)
2. Roll each piece of dough into a rectangular sheet, about 5 inches wide, 44 inches long and 1/3 inch thick.
3. Prepare 1 recipe Cherry Filling (Recipe No. D-41), Pineapple Filling (Recipe No. D-47), or Nut Filling (Recipe No. D-43). Spread 11/2 cups Cherry or Pineapple or 11/4 cups Nut Filling over center of each sheet of dough.
4. Fold dough over once, lengthwise; seal along edge by pressing firmly.
5. Cut dough into 17-21/2 inch pieces. Make 3 cuts, 3/4 inch in depth, on sealed side of each piece to form a claw (See Figure 12).
6. Place on lightly greased sheet pans in rows 3 by 8. Spread claws slightly. Claws should not touch each other.
7. Prepare 1/4 recipe Egg Wash (Recipe No. D-17). Brush 3 tbsp on claws in each pan.
8. Proof at 90°F. to 100°F. until double in bulk.
9. Bake at 375°F. 20 to 25 minutes or until golden brown or in 325°F. convection oven 15 minutes on high fan, open vent. Cool.
10. Glaze, if desired, with 1 recipe Vanilla Glaze (Recipe No. D-46). Brush about 2/3 cup over rolls in each pan.

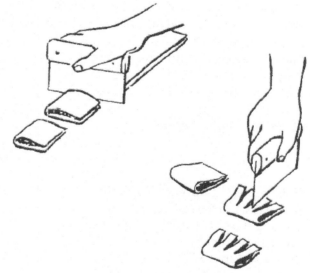

Figure 12

EACH PORTION: 1 Roll.

10. Snails (3 Pans)

1. Follow Steps 1 through 6 of Recipe No. D-36.
2. Roll each 4 lb 5 oz piece of dough into a rectangular sheet about 18 inches wide, 36 inches long, and 1/4 inch thick. (For D-36-1, use 4 lb 2 oz pieces.)
3. Melt 12 oz (11/2 cups) butter or margarine. Brush ½ cup on each sheet of dough. Prepare 1 recipe Cinnamon Sugar Filling (Recipe No. D-42); sprinkle 11/2 cups over each sheet of dough.
4. Fold each sheet of dough in thirds lengthwise to make a strip, about 6 inches wide, 35 inches long, and 3/4 inch thick.
5. Cut strips crosswise into 34 pieces about 1 inch wide (See Figure 13).

6. Twist pieces in one direction and then in opposite direction. Form snails by holding one end on greased pan and winding other end around and around loosely keeping roll flat (See Figure 13).
7. Place on lightly greased sheet pans in rows 4 by 8.
8. Prepare 1/4 recipe Egg Wash (Recipe No. D-17); brush about 1/4 cup on snails in each pan; let rise slightly.
9. Make slight depression with back of spoon in center of each snail. Use 2 cups jelly or jam; place about 1 tsp in each depression.
10. Proof at 90°F. to 100°F. until double in bulk.
11. Bake at 375°F. 20 to 25 minutes or until golden brown or in 325°F. convection oven 15 minutes on high fan, open vent. Cool.
12. Glaze, if desired, with 1 recipe Vanilla Glaze (Recipe No. D-46). Brush about 3/4 cup on rolls in each pan.

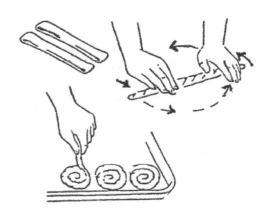

Figure 13

EACH PORTION: 1 Roll.

11. Bowknots, Chain Twists, Figure Eights, and "S" Shapes (3 Pans)

1. Follow Steps 1 through 6 of Recipe No. D-36.
2. Roll each 4 lb 5 oz piece of dough into a rectangular sheet about 18 inches wide, 36 inches long, and 1/4 inch thick. (For D-36-1, use 4 lb 2 oz pieces.)
3. Fold each sheet of dough in thirds lengthwise to make a strip about 6 inches wide, 35 inches long, and 3/4 inch thick.
4. Cut strips crosswise into 34 pieces about 1 inch wide (See Figure 13).
5. Twist pieces in one direction and then in opposite direction stretching to about 11 inches (See Figure 13).
6. Form into various shapes (See Figure 14). Place on lightly greased sheet pans in rows 4 by 8.
7. Prepare 1/4 recipe Egg Wash (Recipe No. D-17); brush about 1/4 cup on rolls in each pan.
8. Proof at 90°F. to 100°F. until double in bulk.
9. Bake at 375°F. oven 20 to 25 minutes or until golden brown or in 325°F. convection oven 15 minutes on high fan, open vent. Cool.
10. Glaze, if desired, with 1 recipe Vanilla Glaze (Recipe No. D-46). Brush about 3/4 cup on rolls in each pan.

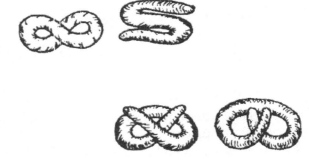

Figure 14

EACH PORTION: 1 Roll.

12. Cinnamon Twists

1. Follow Steps 1 through 6 of Recipe No. D-36.
2. Roll each 4 lb 5 oz piece of dough into a rectangular sheet about 18 inches wide, 36 inches long, and 1/4 inch thick. (For D-36-1, use 4 lb 2 oz pieces.)
3. Melt 12 oz (11/2 cups) butter or margarine. Brush ½ cup on each sheet of dough. Prepare 1 recipe
1. Cinnamon Sugar Filling (Recipe No. D-42); sprinkle 11/2 cups over each sheet of dough.
4. Fold each sheet of dough in thirds lengthwise to make a strip about 6 inches wide, 35 inches long, and 3/4 inch thick.
5. Cut strips crosswise into 34 pieces about 1 inch wide (See Figure 15).
6. Twist pieces in one direction and then in opposite direction (See Figure 15).
7. Place on lightly greased sheet pans in rows 4 by 8.
8. Prepare 1/4 recipe Egg Wash (Recipe No. D-17); brush 1/4 cup on rolls in each pan.
9. Proof at 90°F. to 100°F. until double in bulk.
10. Bake at 375°F. oven 20 to 25 minutes or until golden brown or in 325°F. convection oven 15 minutes on high fan, open vent. Cool.
11. Glaze, if desired, with 1 recipe Vanilla Glaze (Recipe No. D-46). Brush about 3/4 cup on rolls in each pan.

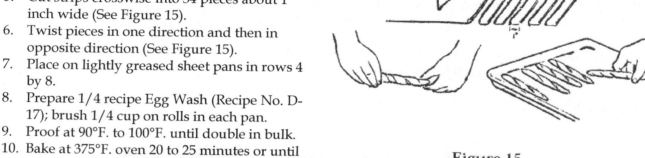

Figure 15

EACH PORTION: 1 Roll.

Wedge Roll-Up Varieties

13. Butterhorns (3 Pans)

1. Follow Steps 1 through 6 of Recipe No. D-36 except divide into 9-1 lb 7 oz pieces. (For D-36-1, divide into 9-1 lb 6 oz pieces.)
2. Roll each piece of dough into a rectangular sheet about 9 inches wide, 24 inches long, and about ¼ inch thick (See Figure 16).
3. Melt 12 oz (11/2 cups) butter or margarine. Brush about 3 tbsp on each sheet of dough.
4. Cut each strip into 12 wedges about 4 inches wide at widest end (See Figure 16).
5. Roll up each wedge from wide edge to point (See Figure 16).
6. Place on lightly greased sheet pans in rows 4 by 8 with point end under roll; press firmly in place.
7. Proof at 90°F. to 100°F. until double in bulk.
8. Bake at 375°F. 20 to 25 minutes or in 325°F. convection oven 15 minutes on high fan, open vent. Cool.
9. Glaze, if desired, with 1 recipe Vanilla Glaze (Recipe No. D-46). Brush about 3/4 cup on rolls in each pan.

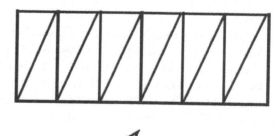

Figure 16

EACH PORTION: 1 Roll.

14. Crescents (3 Pans)

1. Follow Steps 1 through 6 of Recipe No. D-36 except divide in 9-1 lb 7 oz pieces. (For D-36-1, divide into 9-1 lb 6 oz pieces.)
2. Roll each piece of dough into a rectangular sheet about 9 inches wide, 24 inches long, and 1/4 inch thick (See Figure 16).
3. Melt 12 oz (11/2 cups) butter or margarine. Brush about 3 tbsp on each sheet of dough.
4. Cut each strip into 12 wedges about 4 inches wide at widest end (See Figure 16).
5. Roll up each wedge from wide edge to point. Shape each roll into a curve.
6. Place on lightly greased sheet pans in rows 4 by 8 with point end under roll; press firmly in place.
7. Proof at 90°F. to 100°F. until double in bulk.
8. Bake at 375°F. 20 to 25 minutes or until golden brown or in 325°F. convection oven 15 minutes on high fan, open vent. Cool.
9. Glaze, if desired, with 1 recipe Vanilla Glaze (Recipe No. D-46). Brush 3/4 cup on rolls in each pan.

EACH PORTION: 1 Roll.

BAKING POWDER BISCUITS

Yield 100   Portion 1 Biscuit

Calories	Carbohydrates	Protein	Fat	Cholesterol	Sodium	Calcium
148 cal	24 g	4 g	4 g	0 mg	345 mg	115 mg

Ingredient	Weight	Measure	Issue
FLOUR,WHEAT,GENERAL PURPOSE	6-5/8 lbs	1 gal 2 qts	
MILK,NONFAT,DRY	3-5/8 oz	1-1/2 cup	
BAKING POWDER	5-7/8 oz	3/4 cup	
SALT	1-1/2 oz	2-1/3 tbsp	
SHORTENING	12 oz	1-5/8 cup	
WATER	3-7/8 lbs	1 qts 3-1/2 cup	
COOKING SPRAY,NONSTICK	2 oz	1/4 cup 1/3 tbsp	

Method
1. Sift together flour, milk, baking powder, and salt into mixer bowl.
2. Blend shortening at low speed into dry ingredients until mixture resembles coarse cornmeal.
3. Add water; mix at low speed only enough to form soft dough.
4. Place dough on lightly floured board. Knead lightly 1minute or until dough is smooth.
5. Roll or pat out to a uniform thickness of 1/2-inch.
6. Lightly spray each pan with non-stick cooking spray. Cut with 2-1/2 inch floured biscuit cutter. Place 50 biscuits on each pan.
7. Using a convection oven, bake at 350 F. for 15 minutes or until lightly browned on low fan, open vent.

Notes
1. For browner tops: In Step 1, add 1/2 cup granulated sugar per 100 portions to dry ingredients.

BAKING POWDER BISCUITS (BISCUIT MIX)

Yield 100   **Portion** 1 Biscuit

Calories	Carbohydrates	Protein	Fat	Cholesterol	Sodium	Calcium
153 cal	23 g	3 g	6 g	1 mg	456 mg	64 mg

Ingredient	Weight	Measure	Issue
BISCUIT MIX	7-7/8 lbs	1 gal 3-1/2 qts	

Method

1. Prepare biscuit mix according to instructions on container. Using a convection oven, bake at 350 F. 15 minutes or until lightly browned on low fan, open vent.

CHEESE BISCUITS

Yield 100   **Portion** 1 Biscuit

Calories	Carbohydrates	Protein	Fat	Cholesterol	Sodium	Calcium
166 cal	24 g	5 g	6 g	5 mg	373 mg	147 mg

Ingredient	Weight	Measure	Issue
FLOUR,WHEAT,GENERAL PURPOSE	6-5/8 lbs	1 gal 2 qts	
MILK,NONFAT,DRY	3-5/8 oz	1-1/2 cup	
BAKING POWDER	5-7/8 oz	3/4 cup	
SALT	1-1/2 oz	2-1/3 tbsp	
CHEESE,CHEDDAR,GRATED	1 lbs	1 qts	
SHORTENING	12 oz	1-5/8 cup	
WATER	3-7/8 lbs	1 qts 3-1/2 cup	
COOKING SPRAY,NONSTICK	2 oz	1/4 cup 1/3 tbsp	

Method

1. Sift together flour, milk, baking powder, and salt into mixer bowl. Add grated cheddar cheese to sifted dry ingredients.
2. Blend shortening at low speed into dry ingredients until mixture resembles coarse cornmeal.
3. Add water; mix at low speed only enough to form soft dough.
4. Place dough on lightly floured board. Knead lightly, 1 minute or until dough is smooth.
5. Roll or pat out to a uniform thickness of 1/2 inch.
6. Lightly spray each pan with non-stick cooking spray. Cut with 2-1/2 inch floured biscuit cutter. Place 50 biscuits on each pan.
7. Using a convection oven, bake at 350 F. for 15 minutes or until lightly browned on low fan, open vent.

Notes

1. For browner tops: In Step 1, add 1/2 cup of granulated sugar per 100 portions to dry ingredients.

DROP BISCUITS

Yield 100   **Portion** 1 Biscuit

Calories	Carbohydrates	Protein	Fat	Cholesterol	Sodium	Calcium
148 cal	24 g	4 g	4 g	0 mg	345 mg	115 mg

Ingredient	Weight	Measure	Issue
FLOUR,WHEAT,GENERAL PURPOSE	6-5/8 lbs	1 gal 2 qts	
MILK,NONFAT,DRY	3-5/8 oz	1-1/2 cup	
BAKING POWDER	5-7/8 oz	3/4 cup	
SALT	1-1/2 oz	2-1/3 tbsp	
SHORTENING	12 oz	1-5/8 cup	
WATER	3-7/8 lbs	1 qts 3-1/2 cup	
COOKING SPRAY,NONSTICK	2 oz	1/4 cup 1/3 tbsp	

Method
1. Sift together flour, milk, baking powder, and salt into mixer bowl.
2. Blend shortening at low speed into dry ingredients until mixture resembles coarse cornmeal.
3. Add water; mix at low speed only enough to form a soft dough.
4. Lightly spray each pan with non-stick cooking spray. Drop biscuit dough by heaping tablespoon, 1 inch apart, on sprayed sheet pans in rows 6 by 9.
5. Using a convection oven, bake at 350 F. for 15 minutes or until lightly browned on low fan, open vent.

Notes
1. For browner tops: In Step 1, add 1/2 cup granulated sugar per 100 portions to dry ingredients.

IRISH SODA BREAD

Yield 100   Portion 1 Slices

Calories	Carbohydrates	Protein	Fat	Cholesterol	Sodium	Calcium
335 cal	59 g	6 g	9 g	44 mg	456 mg	70 mg

Ingredient	Weight	Measure	Issue
MILK,NONFAT,DRY	4-1/4 oz	1-3/4 cup	
WATER	4-2/3 lbs	2 qts 1 cup	
VINEGAR,DISTILLED	5-5/8 oz	1/2 cup 2-2/3 tbsp	
FLOUR,WHEAT,GENERAL PURPOSE	8-7/8 lbs	2 gal	
SUGAR,GRANULATED	3 lbs	1 qts 2-3/4 cup	
BAKING SODA	1-1/3 oz	2-2/3 tbsp	
BAKING POWDER	1-3/4 oz	1/4 cup	
SALT	1-7/8 oz	3 tbsp	
RAISINS	3-7/8 lbs	3 qts	
CARAWAY SEED	2-1/2 oz	1/2 cup 2-2/3 tbsp	
BUTTER	2 lbs	1 qts	
EGGS,WHOLE,FROZEN,BEATEN,ROOM TEMPERATURE	1-1/4 lbs	2-1/4 cup	
COOKING SPRAY,NONSTICK	2 oz	1/4 cup 1/3 tbsp	

Method
1. Reconstitute milk; add vinegar. Let stand 15 minutes. Set aside for use in Step 4.
2. Place flour, sugar, baking soda, baking powder, salt, raisins, and caraway seeds in mixer bowl. Mix at low speed just enough to blend.
3. Using pastry knife attachment, cut butter or margarine into dry ingredients until it resembles coarse meal.
4. Stir eggs into milk. Add egg-milk mixture to dry ingredients; blend until just mixed, about 45 seconds. DO NOT OVERMIX.

5. Lightly spray each pan with non-stick cooking spray. Place 3 pounds or 1-1/2 quarts batter in each sprayed loaf pan.
6. Bake 55 to 60 minutes at 375 F. or until done.
7. Cool thoroughly before slicing.
8. Cut 25, 1/2 inch thick slices per loaf.

SUBMARINE ROLLS (HOAGIE, TORPEDO)

Yield 100   **Portion** 1 Roll

Calories	Carbohydrates	Protein	Fat	Cholesterol	Sodium	Calcium
389 cal	73 g	12 g	5 g	0 mg	423 mg	17 mg

Ingredient	Weight	Measure	Issue
YEAST,ACTIVE,DRY	6-3/4 oz	1 cup	
WATER,WARM	2-1/8 lbs	1 qts	
WATER,COLD	8-7/8 lbs	1 gal 1/4 qts	
SUGAR,GRANULATED	8-7/8 oz	1-1/4 cup	
SALT	3-3/4 oz	1/4 cup 2-1/3 tbsp	
FLOUR,WHEAT,BREAD	21-1/8 lbs	4 gal 1-1/2 qts	
SHORTENING,SOFTENED	9 oz	1-1/4 cup	
COOKING SPRAY,NONSTICK	2 oz	1/4 cup 1/3 tbsp	

Method
1. Sprinkle yeast over water. DO NOT USE TEMPERATURES ABOVE 110 F. Mix well. Let stand 5 minutes; stir. Set aside for use in Step 3.
2. Place water, sugar, salt, and flour in mixer bowl.
3. Mix at low speed 1 minute or until all flour is incorporated into liquid, using dough hook. Add yeast solution; mix at low speed 1 minute.
4. Add shortening; mix at medium speed 10 minutes or until dough is smooth and elastic. Dough temperature should be between 78 F. and 82 F.
5. FERMENT: Cover. Set in warm place, 80 F. for 1-1/2 hours or until double in bulk.
6. PUNCH: Fold sides into center. Turn dough over. Divide dough into approximately 3-pound pieces. Let rest about 10 minutes.
7. MAKEUP: Divide each ball into 10 4-1/2-ounce pieces; flatten. Roll up like jelly roll into 1-1/4x8-inch rolls. Lightly spray pans with non-stick cooking spray. Place 15 rolls about 2 inches apart on each sprayed pan.
8. Prepare 1/2 Recipe Cornstarch Wash, Recipe No. D 040 00. Brush on top and sides of each roll.
9. PROOF: At 90 F. until double in size, about 40 minutes.
Using a convection oven, bake at 350 F. for 12 to 15 minutes or until lightly browned on high fan, open vent. Immediately brush with Cornstarch Wash. Cool on wire racks.
Notes
1. Rolls may be prepared using semi-automatic bakery equipment (roll divider and rounding machine, bread molder-dough sheeter machine and bun slicer). Follow Step 1. In Step 2, combine1 1/3 oz (3 tbsp) bakery emulsifier with flour and milk. Follow Steps 3 through 6. In Step 7, divide dough into 5 lb 6 oz pieces. Place in roll divider and rounding machine. Divide into 36 balls. Press 2 balls together to form 4-1/2 oz balls. Let rest 5 to 10 minutes. Feed balls, one at a time into bread molder-dough sheeter machine, with a 9-inch pressure plate. Follow Steps 8 through 10. Slice rolls partially through using bun slicer.

SUBMARINE ROLLS (ROLL MIX)

Yield 100   **Portion** 1 Roll

Calories	Carbohydrates	Protein	Fat	Cholesterol	Sodium	Calcium
340 cal	61 g	10 g	7 g	0 mg	532 mg	56 mg

Ingredient	Weight	Measure	Issue
YEAST,ACTIVE,DRY	8-1/2 oz	1-1/4 cup	
WATER,WARM	2-1/3 lbs	1 qts 1/2 cup	
ROLL,MIX	19-1/8 lbs		
WATER,COLD	8-1/3 lbs	1 gal	
COOKING SPRAY,NONSTICK	2 oz	1/4 cup 1/3 tbsp	

Method

1. Sprinkle yeast over water. Do not use temperatures above 110 F. Mix well. Let stand 5 minutes; stir. Prepare roll mix according to directions on package.
2. PUNCH: Fold sides into center. Turn dough over. Divide dough into approximately 3 pound pieces. Let rest about 10 minutes.
3. Lightly spray each pan with non-stick cooking spray. MAKEUP: Divide each ball into 10 4-1/2 ounce pieces; flatten. Roll up like jelly roll into 1-1/4x8 inch rolls. Place 15 rolls about 2 inches apart on each sprayed pan.
4. Prepare 1/2 recipe Cornstarch Wash, Recipe No. D 040 00. Brush on top and sides of each roll.
5. PROOF: At 90 F. until double in bulk, about 40 minutes.
6. Using a convection oven, bake 12 to 15 minutes at 350 F. or until lightly browned on high fan, open vent. Immediately brush with Cornstarch Wash. Cool on wire racks.

Notes

1. Rolls may be prepared using semi-automatic bakery equipment. Follow Step 1. In Step 1, add bakery emulsifier to roll mix. Follow Step 2. In Step 3 divide dough into 5lb 6 oz pieces. Place in roll divider and rounding machine. Divide into 36 balls. Press 2 balls together to form 4-1/2 oz balls. Let rest 5 to 10 minutes. Feed balls one at a time into bread molder-dough sheeter machine, with a 9-inch pressure plate. Follow Steps 4 through 5. Slice rolls partially through using bun slicer

FRENCH BREAD

Yield 100   **Portion** 2 Slices

Calories	Carbohydrates	Protein	Fat	Cholesterol	Sodium	Calcium
189 cal	37 g	6 g	2 g	0 mg	328 mg	8 mg

Ingredient	Weight	Measure	Issue
YEAST,ACTIVE,DRY	2 oz	1/4 cup 1 tbsp	
WATER,WARM	12-1/2 oz	1-1/2 cup	
WATER,COLD	4-5/8 lbs	2 qts 3/4 cup	
SUGAR,GRANULATED	2-2/3 oz	1/4 cup 2-1/3 tbsp	
SALT	3 oz	1/4 cup 1 tbsp	
FLOUR,WHEAT,BREAD	10-7/8 lbs	2 gal 1 qts	
SHORTENING	2-3/4 oz	1/4 cup 2-1/3 tbsp	

Method

1. Sprinkle yeast over water. DO NOT USE TEMPERATURES ABOVE 110 F. Mix well. Let stand 5 minutes; stir. Set aside for use in Step 3.

2. Place water, sugar, salt, and flour in mixer bowl.
3. Using dough hook, mix at low speed 1 minute or until all flour mixture is incorporated into liquid; add yeast solution; mix at medium speed 5 minutes.
4. Add shortening; continue mixing at medium speed 3 minutes. Dough temperature should be between 78 F. and 82 F.
5. FERMENT: Cover and set in warm place, 80 F. for 2-1/4 hours or until double in bulk.
6. PUNCH: Fold sides into center and turn completely over. Let rest 15 minutes.
7. MAKE-UP: Scale into 12-19 ounce pieces; shape each piece into a smooth ball; let rest 10 minutes. Form each piece into a rope, 1-1/4 inches in diameter and 18 inches long. Place 3 loaves on each cornmeal dusted pan. Use 1/8 cup cornmeal per pan.
8. PROOF: At 90 F. to 100 F. for 50 to 60 minutes or until double in bulk.
9. Brush top of each loaf with Cornstarch Wash, Recipe No. D 040 00 or Egg White Wash, Recipe No. D 017 01. Cut 6 diagonal slashes, 1/4-inch deep, on top of each loaf.

BAKE: 30 minutes at 425 F. or until done.

When cool, cut 17 one-inch thick slices per loaf.

RAISIN BREAD

Yield 100   **Portion** 2 Slices

Calories	Carbohydrates	Protein	Fat	Cholesterol	Sodium	Calcium
201 cal	40 g	6 g	2 g	0 mg	264 mg	26 mg

Ingredient	Weight	Measure	Issue
YEAST,ACTIVE,DRY	2-7/8 oz	1/4 cup 3 tbsp	
WATER,WARM	1-1/8 lbs	2-1/4 cup	
WATER,COLD	3-1/8 lbs	1 qts 2 cup	
SUGAR,GRANULATED	5-1/4 oz	3/4 cup	
SALT	2-1/3 oz	1/4 cup	
MILK,NONFAT,DRY	3-1/4 oz	1-3/8 cup	
CINNAMON,GROUND	1/2 oz	2 tbsp	
FLAVORING,LEMON	1/2 oz	1 tbsp	
FLOUR,WHEAT,BREAD	8-1/8 lbs	1 gal 2-3/4 qts	
SHORTENING	6-1/3 oz	3/4 cup 2 tbsp	
RAISINS	2-7/8 lbs	2 qts 1 cup	

Method

1. Sprinkle yeast over water. DO NOT USE TEMPERATURES ABOVE 110 F. Mix well. Let stand five minutes; stir. Set aside for use in Step 4.
2. Place water, sugar, salt, milk, cinnamon, and lemon flavoring in mixer bowl. Using dough hook, mix at low speed just enough to blend.
3. Add flour. Mix at low speed 1 minute or until all flour is incorporated into liquid.
4. Add yeast solution; mix at low speed 1 minute.
5. Add shortening; mix at low speed 1 minute. Continue mixing at medium speed 10 to 15 minutes or until dough is smooth and elastic. Dough temperature should be between 78 F. and 82 F.
6. Soak raisins in 3 quarts lukewarm water 15 minutes. Drain. Mix at low speed 1 minute.
7. FERMENT: Cover and set in a warm place, 80 F. for 2 hours or until double in bulk.
8. PUNCH: Fold sides into center and turn dough completely over. Let rest 20 minutes.
9. MAKE UP: Scale into approximately 8-2 pound pieces; shape each piece into a smooth ball; let rest 10 minutes. Mold each piece into a loaf; place each loaf into lightly greased bread pan.

PROOF: At 90 F. to 100 F. for 50 to 60 minutes or until double in bulk.

BAKE: If convection oven is used, bake at 325 F. for 30 minutes or until done on high fan, closed vent. Prepare 1/4 recipe Syrup Glaze, Recipe No. D 045 00 (optional). Brush top of each loaf with hot Syrup Glaze.

When cool, slice 25 slices (about 1/2 inch thick) per loaf.

Notes
1. In Step 9, when using 9x4-1/2x2-3/4 bread pans, scale into 10-25-ounce pieces.

TOASTED GARLIC BREAD

Yield 100   **Portion** 2 Slices

Calories	Carbohydrates	Protein	Fat	Cholesterol	Sodium	Calcium
259 cal	31 g	5 g	13 g	0 mg	487 mg	48 mg

Ingredient	Weight	Measure	Issue
MARGARINE,SOFTENED	3 lbs	1 qts 2 cup	
GARLIC POWDER	1/2 oz	1 tbsp	
BREAD,FRENCH	13 lbs		

Method
1. Place butter or margarine in mixer bowl. Whip at medium speed until creamy. Add garlic powder; blend thoroughly.
2. Slice each loaf in half lengthwise. Spread each half loaf with about 2 ounces or 1/4 cup of garlic-butter mixture. Cut each half loaf into 8 slices. Place 5 half loaves on each sheet pan.
3. Using a convection oven, bake at 350 F. for 10 to 12 minutes or until lightly browned on high fan, open vent.
4. Serve hot.

Notes
1. In Step 2, 100 hard rolls may be split and used for 100 portions.

TOASTED PARMESAN BREAD

Yield 100   **Portion** 2 Slices

Calories	Carbohydrates	Protein	Fat	Cholesterol	Sodium	Calcium
277 cal	31 g	7 g	14 g	3 mg	561 mg	103 mg

Ingredient	Weight	Measure	Issue
MARGARINE,SOFTENED	3 lbs	1 qts 2 cup	
CHEESE,PARMESAN,GRATED	14-1/8 oz	1 qts	
BREAD,FRENCH	13 lbs		

Method
1. Place butter or margarine in mixer bowl. Whip at medium speed until creamy. Add grated Parmesan cheese; mix thoroughly.
2. Slice each loaf in half lengthwise. Spread each half loaf with about 2 ounces or 1/4 cup cheese-butter mixture. Cut each half loaf into 8 slices. Place 5 half loaves on each sheet pan.
3. Using a convection oven, bake at 350 F. for 10 to 12 minutes or until lightly browned on high fan, open vent.
4. Serve hot.

TEXAS TOAST

Yield 100   Portion 2 Slices

Calories	Carbohydrates	Protein	Fat	Cholesterol	Sodium	Calcium
202 cal	31 g	5 g	6 g	0 mg	359 mg	44 mg

Ingredient	Weight	Measure	Issue
BREAD,FRENCH	13 lbs		

Method
1. Use unsliced French Bread. Diagonally cut each loaf into 8 even slices.
2. Using a convection oven, bake at 350 F. for 10 to 12 minutes or until lightly browned on high fan, open vent.
3. Serve hot.

Notes
1. Toast may be grilled. Place on lightly greased 400 F. griddle Grill 2 to 3 minutes until lightly browned.

WHITE BREAD

Yield 100   Portion 2 Slices

Calories	Carbohydrates	Protein	Fat	Cholesterol	Sodium	Calcium
181 cal	33 g	6 g	2 g	0 mg	334 mg	22 mg

Ingredient	Weight	Measure	Issue
YEAST,ACTIVE,DRY	1-2/3 oz	1/4 cup 1/3 tbsp	
WATER,WARM	12-1/2 oz	1-1/2 cup	
WATER,COLD	4-1/8 lbs	2 qts	
SUGAR,GRANULATED	5-1/4 oz	3/4 cup	
SALT	3 oz	1/4 cup 1 tbsp	
MILK,NONFAT,DRY	4-1/4 oz	1-3/4 cup	
FLOUR,WHEAT,BREAD	9-1/3 lbs	1 gal 3-3/4 qts	
SHORTENING	6-1/3 oz	3/4 cup 2 tbsp	

Method
1. Sprinkle yeast over water. DO NOT USE TEMPERATURES ABOVE 110 F. Mix well. Let stand 5 minutes; stir. Set aside for use in Step 4.
2. Place water, sugar, salt, and milk in mixer bowl. Mix at low speed just enough to blend.
3. Add flour. Using dough hook, mix at low speed 1 minute or until all flour is incorporated into liquid.
4. Add yeast solution; mix at low speed 1 minute.
5. Add shortening; mix at low speed 1 minute. Continue mixing at medium speed 10 to 15 minutes or until dough is smooth and elastic. Dough temperature should be between 78 F. to 82 F.
6. FERMENT: Cover and set in warm place, 80 F. for 2 hours or until double in bulk.
7. PUNCH: Fold sides into center and turn dough completely over. Let rest 30 minutes.

8. MAKE UP: Scale into approximately 8 1-3/4 pound pieces; shape each piece into a smooth ball; let rest 12 to 15 minutes. Mold each piece into an oblong loaf; place each loaf seam-side down into lightly greased pan.
9. PROOF: At 90 F. to 100 F. about 1 hour or until double in bulk.

BAKE: Using a convection oven, bake at 375 F. until done, on low fan with open vent.

When cool, slice 25 slices, about 1/2 inch thick, per loaf.

Notes
1. In Step 8, when using 9 x 4-1/4 x 2-3/4 bread pans, scale into 12-18 ounce pieces.
2. For Semi-Automated Equipment: Follow Steps 1 through 7. In Step 8, scale into 8-27-ounce pieces; shape each piece into a smooth ball; let rest 12 to 15 minutes. Using a 10-inch pressure plate, feed balls one at a time into bread molding machine. Pan seam-side down into lightly greased bread pans. Follow Steps 9 through 11.

WHITE BREAD (SHORT-TIME FORMULA)

Yield 100   **Portion** 2 Slices

Calories	Carbohydrates	Protein	Fat	Cholesterol	Sodium	Calcium
184 cal	34 g	6 g	2 g	0 mg	217 mg	20 mg

Ingredient	Weight	Measure	Issue
YEAST,ACTIVE,DRY	3 oz	1/4 cup 3-1/3 tbsp	
WATER,WARM	1 lbs	2 cup	
SUGAR,GRANULATED	3/4 oz	1 tbsp	
WATER	4-1/8 lbs	2 qts	
MILK,NONFAT,DRY	3-5/8 oz	1-1/2 cup	
SUGAR,GRANULATED	3-1/2 oz	1/2 cup	
FLOUR,WHEAT,BREAD	7-1/4 lbs	1 gal 2 qts	
SHORTENING,SOFTENED	5-7/8 oz	3/4 cup 1 tbsp	
FLOUR,WHEAT,BREAD	2-3/8 lbs	2 qts	
SALT	1-7/8 oz	3 tbsp	

Method
1. Sprinkle yeast over water. DO NOT USE TEMPERATURES ABOVE 110 F. Mix well. Let stand 5 minutes. Add sugar; stir until dissolved. Let stand 10 minutes; stir. Set aside for use in Step 3.
2. Place water in mixer bowl. Add milk and sugar. Using a dough hook, mix at low speed about 1 minute until blended.
3. Add flour; mix at low speed about 2 minutes or until flour is incorporated; add shortening and yeast solution. Mix at low speed about 2 minutes until smooth.
4. Mix at medium speed 10 minutes.
5. Let rise in mixer bowl 20 minutes.
6. Sift together flour and salt; add to mixture in mixer bowl. Mix at low speed 2 minutes or until flour in incorporated. Mix at medium speed 10 minutes or until smooth and elastic.
7. FERMENT: Cover. Set in warm place (80 F.) 25 to 30 minutes or until double in bulk.
8. MAKE UP: Scale into 8-28 ounce pieces. Roll scaled dough to pan size; place 1 loaf into each lightly greased bread pan.
9. PROOF: At 90 F. for 25 to 30 minutes or until double in bulk.

BAKE: Using a convection oven, bake at 400 F. for 3 to 5 minutes on high fan, open vent. Reduce oven temperature to 325 F. and bake 15 to 18 minutes or until done.

When cool, slice 25 slices, about 1/2-inch thick, per loaf.

Notes
1. In Step 8, when using 9 x 4-1/2 x 2-3/4 bread pans, scale into 10-22 ounce pieces

PUMPKIN BREAD

Yield 100   **Portion** 1 Slice

Calories	Carbohydrates	Protein	Fat	Cholesterol	Sodium	Calcium
272 cal	40 g	4 g	12 g	30 mg	302 mg	23 mg

Ingredient	Weight	Measure	Issue
EGGS,WHOLE,FROZEN	1-1/2 lbs	2-7/8 cup	
FLOUR,WHEAT,GENERAL PURPOSE	3-1/3 lbs	3 qts	
SALT	1-1/4 oz	2 tbsp	
BAKING POWDER	1/3 oz	1/3 tsp	
BAKING SODA	1-1/3 oz	2-2/3 tbsp	
CINNAMON,GROUND	1/3 oz	1 tbsp	
ALLSPICE,GROUND	1/4 oz	1 tbsp	
NUTMEG,GROUND	1/3 oz	1 tbsp	
CLOVES,GROUND	1/4 oz	1 tbsp	
SUGAR,GRANULATED	5-1/4 lbs	3 qts	
OIL,SALAD	1-7/8 lbs	1 qts	
PUMPKIN,CANNED,SOLID PACK	3-3/4 lbs	1 qts 3 cup	
WATER	1 lbs	2 cup	
NUTS,UNSALTED,CHOPPED,COARSELY	10-1/3 oz	2 cup	
RAISINS	10-1/4 oz	2 cup	
COOKING SPRAY,NONSTICK	2 oz	1/4 cup 1/3 tbsp	

Method
1. Beat eggs in mixer bowl at medium speed 3 minutes or until lemon colored.
2. Blend flour, salt, baking powder, baking soda, cinnamon, allspice, nutmeg, and cloves together in separate bowl.
3. Add flour mixture, sugar, salad oil, pumpkin, water, nuts, and raisins to beaten eggs.
4. Beat at low speed about 1/2 minute. Beat 1 minute or until well blended. DO NOT OVER BEAT.
5. Lightly spray each pan with non-stick cooking spray. Pour about 7-1/2 cups of batter into each sprayed pan.
6. Using a convection oven, bake at 325 F. about 70 minutes or until done on low fan, open vent. Let cool in pans 5 to 10 minutes before removing from pans.
7. Cool thoroughly; wrap in waxed paper; store overnight before slicing.
8. Cut 25 slices per loaf.

CRUMB CAKE SNICKERDOODLE

Yield 100   **Portion** 1 Piece

Calories	Carbohydrates	Protein	Fat	Cholesterol	Sodium	Calcium
303 cal	46 g	5 g	12 g	36 mg	212 mg	81 mg

Ingredient	Weight	Measure	Issue
SHORTENING	1-1/8 lbs	2-1/2 cup	
SUGAR,GRANULATED	3 lbs	1 qts 2-3/4 cup	
EGGS,WHOLE,FROZEN	1-3/4 lbs	3-1/4 cup	
FLOUR,WHEAT,GENERAL PURPOSE	5 lbs	1 gal 1/2 qts	
BAKING POWDER	2-3/4 oz	1/4 cup 2 tbsp	
MILK,NONFAT,DRY	1-3/4 oz	3/4 cup	

NUTMEG,GROUND	1/4 oz	1 tbsp
SALT	3/4 oz	1 tbsp
WATER	2 lbs	3-3/4 cup
EXTRACT,VANILLA	3/4 oz	1 tbsp
RAISINS	1-3/4 lbs	1 qts 1-1/2 cup
NUTS,UNSALTED,CHOPPED,COARSELY	1-1/4 lbs	1 qts
COOKING SPRAY,NONSTICK	2 oz	1/4 cup 1/3 tbsp
SUGAR,BROWN,PACKED	1-1/3 lbs	1 qts 1/4 cup
MARGARINE	8 oz	1 cup
CINNAMON,GROUND	1 oz	1/4 cup 1/3 tbsp
YELLOW CAKE (CRUMBS)		3 cup

Method
1. Place shortening and sugar in mixer bowl; cream at medium speed until light and fluffy.
2. Add eggs; beat at medium speed 2 minutes or until light and fluffy.
3. Sift together flour, baking powder, milk, nutmeg, and salt.
4. Add vanilla to water; add alternately with dry ingredients to mixture. Mix 1-1/2 minutes at low speed.
5. Fold raisins and nuts into batter.
6. Lightly spray each pan with non-stick cooking spray. Pour about 3-1/2 quarts of batter into each lightly sprayed pan.
7. Mix brown sugar, butter or margarine, cinnamon, and cake crumbs until mixture resembles cornmeal. Sprinkle about 1 quart of mixture over batter in each pan.
8. Using a convection oven, bake at 300 F. for 20 to 25 minutes or until done on low fan, open vent.
9. Cool; cut 6 by 9. If desired, top with Vanilla Glaze, Recipe No. D 046 00.

CRUMB CAKE SNICKERDOODLE (CK MIX, YELLOW)

Yield 100   Portion 1 Piece

Calories	Carbohydrates	Protein	Fat	Cholesterol	Sodium	Calcium
257 cal	36 g	3 g	12 g	11 mg	290 mg	25 mg

Ingredient	Weight	Measure	Issue
CAKE MIX,YELLOW	10 lbs		
NUTMEG,GROUND	1/4 oz	1 tbsp	

Method
1. Prepare mix according to instructions on container.
2. Add nutmeg.
3. Using a convection oven, bake at 300 F. for 25 minutes or until done on low fan, open vent.

BAGELS

Yield 100   Portion 1 Bagel

Calories	Carbohydrates	Protein	Fat	Cholesterol	Sodium	Calcium
242 cal	48 g	8 g	2 g	0 mg	375 mg	11 mg

Ingredient	Weight	Measure	Issue
YEAST,ACTIVE,DRY	3-3/8 oz	1/2 cup	
WATER,WARM	5-3/4 lbs	2 qts 3 cup	
SUGAR,GRANULATED	7 oz	1 cup	
SALT	3-3/8 oz	1/4 cup 1-2/3 tbsp	
FLOUR,WHEAT,BREAD	13-7/8 lbs	2 gal 3-1/2 qts	
COOKING SPRAY,NONSTICK	2 oz	1/4 cup 1/3 tbsp	

Method

1. Sprinkle yeast over water in mixer bowl. DO NOT USE TEMPERATURES ABOVE 110 F. Mix well. Let stand 5 minutes; stir.
2. Using a wire whip, add sugar and salt to yeast solution; stir until ingredients are dissolved.
3. Using a dough hook, add flour; mix at low speed 1 minute or until all flour is incorporated into liquid. Continue mixing at medium speed 13 to 15 minutes until dough is smooth and elastic. (Dough will be very stiff). Dough temperature should be 78 F. to 82 F.
4. Cover; let rest 15 minutes.
5. Place dough on unfloured work surface; divide dough into 3 ounce pieces; knead briefly; shape into balls by rolling in circular motion on work surface.
6. Place balls, in rows 4 by 6, on 4 ungreased sheet pans.
7. FERMENT: Cover. Set in warm place (80 F.) about 15 to 20 minutes or until dough increases slightly in bulk.
8. MAKE UP: Shape bagels like a doughnut; flatten to 2-1/2-inch circles, 3/4-inch thick. Pinch center of each bagel with thumb and forefinger and pull gently to make a 1-inch diameter hole and a total 3-1/2-inch diameter, keeping uniform shape. Place on 4 ungreased sheet pans in rows 4 by 6 per pan.
9. PROOF: At 90 F. until bagels begin to rise, about 20 to 30 minutes.
10. Lightly spray 5 sheet pans with non-stick cooking spray. Sprinkle each pan with 1/2 cup cornmeal.
11. Add water to steam-jacketed kettle or stock pot; bring to a boil; reduce heat to a simmer. Add 1/2 cup granulated sugar to water. Stir until dissolved. Gently drop bagels, one at a time, into water. Cook 30 seconds; turn; cook 30 seconds. Remove bagels with slotted spoon; drain. Place on sheet pans in rows 4 by 5.
12. BAKE: 30 to 35 minutes or until golden brown and crisp in 400 F. oven. Remove from pans; cool on wire racks.

Notes

1. In Step 1, a 60-quart mixer should be used for 100 portions as dough is very stiff. If using 20 to 30 quart mixers, prepare no more than 50 portions at a time.
2. In Steps 7 and 9, bagels should not double in bulk.
3. In Step 12, if convection oven is used, bake at 350 F. for 15 to 20 minutes on high fan, open vent.

CORN BREAD

Yield 100   **Portion** 1 Piece

Calories	Carbohydrates	Protein	Fat	Cholesterol	Sodium	Calcium
212 cal	30 g	5 g	8 g	30 mg	359 mg	127 mg

Ingredient	Weight	Measure	Issue
FLOUR,WHEAT,GENERAL PURPOSE	3-7/8 lbs	3 qts 2 cup	
CORN MEAL	3-2/3 lbs	3 qts	
MILK,NONFAT,DRY	6 oz	2-1/2 cup	
SUGAR,GRANULATED	7 oz	1 cup	
BAKING POWDER	5-7/8 oz	3/4 cup	

SALT	1-1/2 oz	2-1/3 tbsp
EGGS,WHOLE,FROZEN	1-1/2 lbs	2-7/8 cup
WATER	7-7/8 lbs	3 qts 3 cup
OIL,SALAD	1-1/2 lbs	3 cup
COOKING SPRAY,NONSTICK	2 oz	1/4 cup 1/3 tbsp

Method
1. Blend flour, cornmeal, milk, sugar, baking powder, and salt in mixer bowl.
2. Combine eggs and water; add to ingredients in mixer bowl. Blend at low speed about 1 minute. Scrape down bowl.
3. Add oil; mix at medium speed until blended.
4. Lightly spray each pan with non-stick cooking spray. Pour 1 gallon of batter into each pan.
5. Using a convection oven, bake at 375 F. for 20 minutes or until done on low fan, open vent.
6. Cool; cut into 6 by 9.

Notes
1. In step 1, omit sugar if southern-style cornbread is desired.

CORN MUFFINS

Yield 100   **Portion** 1 Muffin

Calories	Carbohydrates	Protein	Fat	Cholesterol	Sodium	Calcium
160 cal	22 g	4 g	6 g	24 mg	252 mg	95 mg

Ingredient	Weight	Measure	Issue
FLOUR,WHEAT,GENERAL PURPOSE	2-7/8 lbs	2 qts 2-1/2 cup	
CORN MEAL	2-3/4 lbs	2 qts 1 cup	
MILK,NONFAT,DRY	4-1/2 oz	1-7/8 cup	
SUGAR,GRANULATED	5-1/4 oz	3/4 cup	
BAKING POWDER	4-3/8 oz	1/2 cup 1 tbsp	
SALT	1 oz	1 tbsp	
EGGS,WHOLE,FROZEN	1-1/4 lbs	2-1/4 cup	
WATER	6 lbs	2 qts 3-1/2 cup	
OIL,SALAD	1-1/8 lbs	2-1/4 cup	
COOKING SPRAY,NONSTICK	2 oz	1/4 cup 1/3 tbsp	

Method
1. Blend flour, cornmeal, milk, sugar, baking powder, and salt in mixer bowl.
2. Combine eggs and water; add to ingredients in mixer bowl. Blend at low speed about 1 minute. Scrape down bowl.
3. Add oil; mix at medium speed until blended.
4. Lightly spray 9-12 cup muffin pans with non-stick cooking spray. Fill each cup 2/3 full.
5. Bake for 15 to 20 minutes at 425 F. or at 375 F. in a convection oven for 15 minutes or until done on low fan, open vent.

HUSH PUPPIES

Yield 100   **Portion** 3 each

Calories	Carbohydrates	Protein	Fat	Cholesterol	Sodium	Calcium
200 cal	28 g	5 g	7 g	30 mg	359 mg	129 mg

Ingredient	Weight	Measure	Issue
FLOUR,WHEAT,GENERAL PURPOSE	3-7/8 lbs	3 qts 2 cup	
CORN MEAL	3-2/3 lbs	3 qts	
MILK,NONFAT,DRY	6 oz	2-1/2 cup	
BAKING POWDER	5-7/8 oz	3/4 cup	
SALT	1-1/2 oz	2-1/3 tbsp	
EGGS,WHOLE,FROZEN	1-1/2 lbs	2-7/8 cup	
WATER	5-3/4 lbs	2 qts 3 cup	
ONIONS,FRESH,CHOPPED	2-1/8 lbs	1 qts 2 cup	2-1/3 lbs
PEPPER,BLACK,GROUND	1/3 oz	1 tbsp	
SHORTENING,VEGETABLE,MELTED	1-1/3 lbs	3 cup	

Method

1. Blend flour, cornmeal, milk, baking powder, and salt in mixer bowl.
2. Combine eggs, water, onions, and pepper; add to ingredients in mixer bowl. Blend at low speed for minute. Scrape down bowl.
3. Add shortening; mix at medium speed until blended.
4. Drop batter by rounded tablespoon into deep fat at around 360 F.; fry about 3 minutes. Drain on absorbent paper.

JALAPENO CORN BREAD

Yield 100   **Portion** 1 Piece

Calories	Carbohydrates	Protein	Fat	Cholesterol	Sodium	Calcium
224 cal	30 g	5 g	9 g	33 mg	391 mg	143 mg

Ingredient	Weight	Measure	Issue
FLOUR,WHEAT,GENERAL PURPOSE	3-7/8 lbs	3 qts 2 cup	
CORN MEAL	3-2/3 lbs	3 qts	
MILK,NONFAT,DRY	6 oz	2-1/2 cup	
SUGAR,GRANULATED	7 oz	1 cup	
BAKING POWDER	5-7/8 oz	3/4 cup	
SALT	1-1/2 oz	2-1/3 tbsp	
EGGS,WHOLE,FROZEN	1-1/2 lbs	2-7/8 cup	
WATER	7-7/8 lbs	3 qts 3 cup	
OIL,SALAD	1-1/2 lbs	3 cup	
CORN,CANNED,WHOLE KERNEL,DRAINED	11-5/8 oz	2 cup	
CHEESE,CHEDDAR,GRATED	8 oz	2 cup	
PEPPERS,JALAPENOS,CANNED,DRAINED,CHOPPED	2-3/8 oz	1/2 cup	
ONIONS,FRESH,GRATED	1-3/8 oz	1/4 cup 1/3 tbsp	1-5/8 oz
COOKING SPRAY,NONSTICK	2 oz	1/4 cup 1/3 tbsp	

Method

1. Blend flour, cornmeal, milk, sugar, baking powder, and salt in mixer bowl.
2. Combine eggs and water; add to ingredients in mixer bowl. Blend at low speed about 1 minute. Scrape down bowl.
3. Add shortening, drained corn, cheese, drained jalapeno peppers, and onions to mixture. Blend only until ingredients are distributed throughout mixture.
4. Lightly spray each pan with non-stick cooking spray. Pour 4-3/4 quarts batter into each pan.

5. Bake for 30 minutes at 425 F. or at 375 F. in a convection oven 20 minutes or until done on low fan, open vent.
6. Cool, cut 6 by 9.

CORN BREAD (CORN BREAD MIX)

Yield 100   **Portion** 1 Piece

Calories	Carbohydrates	Protein	Fat	Cholesterol	Sodium	Calcium
218 cal	36 g	4 g	7 g	1 mg	567 mg	29 mg

Ingredient	Weight	Measure	Issue
CORN BREAD MIX	11-1/4 lbs	2 gal 1/3 qts	
COOKING SPRAY,NONSTICK	2 oz	1/4 cup 1/3 tbsp	

Method
1. Prepare mix according to instructions on container.
2. Lightly spray each pan with non-stick cooking spray. Pour 1 gallon of batter into each pan.
3. Bake 20 to 25 minutes at 425 F. or if a convection oven is used, bake at 375 F. for 20 minutes or until done on low fan, open vent or until done.
4. Cool; cut 6 by 9.

Notes
1. Cornbread Mix is a slightly sweetened product. In Step 1, 2-1/8 cup of granulated sugar may be added to mix if a sweeter product is desired.

CORN MUFFINS (CORN BREAD MIX)

Yield 100   **Portion** 1 Muffin

Calories	Carbohydrates	Protein	Fat	Cholesterol	Sodium	Calcium
189 cal	32 g	3 g	5 g	1 mg	454 mg	23 mg

Ingredient	Weight	Measure	Issue
CORN BREAD MIX	9 lbs	1 gal 2-2/3 qts	
SUGAR,GRANULATED	12-1/3 oz	1-3/4 cup	
COOKING SPRAY,NONSTICK	2 oz	1/4 cup 1/3 tbsp	

Method
1. Prepare Cornbread Mix and combine with granulated sugar.
2. Lightly spray 9-12 cup muffin pans with non-stick cooking spray. Fill each cup 2/3 full.
3. Bake 15 to 20 minutes at 425 F. or in a 375 F. convection oven for 15 minutes or until done on low fan, open vent.

HUSH PUPPIES (CORN BREAD MIX)

Yield 100   **Portion** 3 Pieces

Calories	Carbohydrates	Protein	Fat	Cholesterol	Sodium	Calcium
257 cal	36 g	4 g	11 g	1 mg	567 mg	31 mg

Ingredient	Weight	Measure	Issue
CORN BREAD MIX	11-1/4 lbs	2 gal 1/3 qts	
ONIONS,FRESH,CHOPPED	2-1/8 lbs	1 qts 2 cup	2-1/3 lbs
PEPPER,BLACK,GROUND	1/3 oz	1 tbsp	

Method

1. Prepare mix according to instructions on container. Add finely chopped onions and black or white pepper.
2. Drop batter by rounded tablespoon into deep fat, at around 360 F.; fry about 3 minutes. Drain on absorbent paper.

JALAPENO CORN BREAD (CORN BREAD MIX)

Yield 100   **Portion** 1 Piece

Calories	Carbohydrates	Protein	Fat	Cholesterol	Sodium	Calcium
230 cal	36 g	4 g	8 g	3 mg	599 mg	46 mg

Ingredient	Weight	Measure	Issue
CORN BREAD MIX	11-1/4 lbs	2 gal 1/3 qts	
CORN,CANNED,WHOLE KERNEL,DRAINED	11-5/8 oz	2 cup	
CHEESE,CHEDDAR,GRATED	8 oz	2 cup	
PEPPERS,JALAPENOS,CANNED,DRAINED,CHOPPED	2-3/8 oz	1/2 cup	
ONIONS,FRESH,GRATED	2-7/8 oz	1/2 cup	3-1/8 oz
COOKING SPRAY,NONSTICK	2 oz	1/4 cup 1/3 tbsp	

Method

1. Prepare mix according to instructions on container. Add drained whole kernel corn, grated Cheddar or American cheese, jalapeno peppers, and onions. Blend only until ingredients are distributed.
2. Lightly spray each pan with non-stick cooking spray. Pour 4-3/4 quarts of batter into each pan.
3. Bake 30 minutes at 425 F. or in a 375 F. convection oven for 20 minutes or until done on low fan, open vent.
4. Cool; cut 6 by 9.

CROUTONS

Yield 100   **Portion** 8 Croutons

Calories	Carbohydrates	Protein	Fat	Cholesterol	Sodium	Calcium
24 cal	4 g	1 g	0 g	0 mg	49 mg	10 mg

Ingredient	Weight	Measure	Issue
BREAD,WHITE,STALE,SLICED	2 lbs	1 gal 2-1/2 qts	

Method

1. Trim crusts from bread; cut bread into 1/2-inch cubes.
2. Place bread cubes on sheet pans. Brown lightly in 325 F. oven, about 20 to 25 minutes or in 375 F. convection oven, about 6 minutes on high fan, open vent.

Notes

1. In Step 1, 2 lbs bread will yield about 1 gallons lightly browned croutons.

GARLIC CROUTONS

Yield 100   **Portion** 1/4 Cup

Calories	Carbohydrates	Protein	Fat	Cholesterol	Sodium	Calcium
49 cal	4 g	1 g	3 g	8 mg	77 mg	11 mg

Ingredient	Weight	Measure	Issue
BREAD,WHITE,STALE,SLICED	2 lbs	1 gal 2-1/2 qts	
BUTTER,MELTED	12 oz	1-1/2 cup	
GARLIC CLOVES,FRESH,MINCED	1/8 oz	1/4 tsp	

Method
1. Trim crusts from bread; cut bread into 1/2-inch cubes.
2. Place bread cubes on sheet pans. Brown lightly in 325 F. oven, about 20 to 25 minutes or in 375 F. convection oven for about 6 minutes on high fan, open vent.
3. Melt butter or margarine; blend in minced garlic. Pour mixture evenly over lightly browned croutons in steam table pans; toss lightly.

Notes
1. In Step 1, 2 lbs bread will yield about 1 gallon lightly browned croutons.

PARMESAN CROUTONS

Yield 100   **Portion** 8 Croutons

Calories	Carbohydrates	Protein	Fat	Cholesterol	Sodium	Calcium
55 cal	4 g	1 g	4 g	9 mg	105 mg	31 mg

Ingredient	Weight	Measure	Issue
BREAD,WHITE,STALE,SLICED	2 lbs	1 gal 2-1/2 qts	
BUTTER,MELTED	12 oz	1-1/2 cup	
CHEESE,PARMESAN,GRATED	5-1/4 oz	1-1/2 cup	

Method
1. Trim crusts from bread; cut bread into 1/2-inch cubes.
2. Place bread cubes on sheet pans. Brown lightly in 325 F. oven, 20 to 25 minutes or in 375 F. convection oven, 6 minutes on high fan, open vent.
3. Melt butter or margarine; blend in grated Parmesan cheese. Pour mixture over lightly browned croutons in steam table pans; toss lightly.

Notes
1. In Step 1, 2 lbs bread will yield about 1 gallon lightly browned croutons.

EGG WASH

Yield 100   **Portion** 3 Cups

Calories	Carbohydrates	Protein	Fat	Cholesterol	Sodium	Calcium
428 cal	16 g	36 g	23 g	989 mg	457 mg	458 mg

Ingredient	Weight	Measure	Issue
EGGS,WHOLE,FROZEN	8 oz	3/4 cup 3 tbsp	

| MILK,NONFAT,DRY | 7/8 oz | 1/4 cup 2-1/3 tbsp |
| WATER | 1 lbs | 2 cup |

Method
1. Combine eggs, milk, and water; mix well. CCP: Refrigerate at 41 F. or lower until ready to use.
2. Brush over shaped dough before or after proofing.

Notes
1. In Step 1, 2-1/2 ounces canned dehydrated egg mix combined with 3/4 cup warm water may be used for whole eggs.

EGG WHITE WASH

Yield 100   **Portion** 1 Piece

Calories	Carbohydrates	Protein	Fat	Cholesterol	Sodium	Calcium
81 cal	2 g	17 g	0 g	0 mg	280 mg	20 mg

Ingredient	Weight	Measure	Issue
EGG WHITES	5-2/3 oz	1/2 cup 2-2/3 tbsp	
WATER	1-1/8 lbs	2-1/4 cup	

Method
1. Beat egg whites and water together. CCP: Refrigerate at 41 F. or lower until ready for use.
2. Brush over shaped dough before or after proofing.

CAKE DOUGHNUTS (HOMEMADE)

Yield 100   **Portion** 1 Doughnut

Calories	Carbohydrates	Protein	Fat	Cholesterol	Sodium	Calcium
186 cal	26 g	3 g	7 g	24 mg	197 mg	78 mg

Ingredient	Weight	Measure	Issue
FLOUR,WHEAT,GENERAL PURPOSE	5-1/2 lbs	1 gal 1 qts	
BAKING POWDER	3-7/8 oz	1/2 cup	
MILK,NONFAT,DRY	1-5/8 oz	1/2 cup 2-2/3 tbsp	
SALT	5/8 oz	1 tbsp	
NUTMEG,GROUND	1/4 oz	1 tbsp	
SHORTENING	7-1/4 oz	1 cup	
SUGAR,GRANULATED	1-1/2 lbs	3-3/8 cup	
EGGS,WHOLE,FROZEN	1-1/4 lbs	2-1/4 cup	
WATER	2 lbs	3-3/4 cup	
EXTRACT,VANILLA	1/2 oz	1 tbsp	

Method
1. Sift together flour, baking powder, milk, salt, and nutmeg. Set aside for use in Step 5.
2. Place shortening and sugar in mixer bowl; cream at medium speed until light and fluffy.
3. Add eggs; beat at medium speed until light and fluffy.
4. Combine water and vanilla. Add to creamed mixture.
5. Add dry ingredients to creamed mixture alternately with liquids; add about 1/3 flour mixture each time. Blend at low speed after each addition. DO NOT OVERMIX. Let dough rest 10 minutes.

6. Roll dough 3/8-inch thick on well-floured board; cut with doughnut cutter.
7. Fry 1 minute on each side or until golden brown. Drain on absorbent paper.

Notes
1. In Step 5, dough may be chilled 1 hour for ease in handling.
2. Omit Steps 6 and 7 if dough machine is used.

SUGAR COATED DOUGHNUTS

Yield 100   Portion 1 Doughnut

Calories	Carbohydrates	Protein	Fat	Cholesterol	Sodium	Calcium
203 cal	31 g	3 g	7 g	24 mg	197 mg	78 mg

Ingredient	Weight	Measure	Issue
FLOUR,WHEAT,GENERAL PURPOSE	5-1/2 lbs	1 gal 1 qts	
BAKING POWDER	3-7/8 oz	1/2 cup	
MILK,NONFAT,DRY	1-5/8 oz	1/2 cup 2-2/3 tbsp	
SALT	5/8 oz	1 tbsp	
NUTMEG,GROUND	1/4 oz	1 tbsp	
SHORTENING	7-1/4 oz	1 cup	
SUGAR,GRANULATED	1-1/2 lbs	3-3/8 cup	
EGGS,WHOLE,FROZEN	1-1/4 lbs	2-1/4 cup	
WATER	2 lbs	3-3/4 cup	
EXTRACT,VANILLA	1/2 oz	1 tbsp	
SUGAR,GRANULATED	1 lbs	2-1/4 cup	

Method
1. Sift together flour, baking powder, milk, salt, and nutmeg. Set aside for use in Step 5.
2. Place shortening and sugar in mixer bowl; cream at medium speed until light and fluffy.
3. Add eggs; beat at medium speed until light and fluffy.
4. Combine water and vanilla. Add to creamed mixture.
5. Add dry ingredients to creamed mixture alternately with liquids; add about 1/3 flour mixture each time. Blend at low speed after each addition. DO NOT OVERMIX. Let dough rest 10 minutes.
6. Roll dough 3/8 inch thick on well-floured board; cut with doughnut cutter.
7. Fry 1 minute on each side or until golden brown. Drain on absorbent paper. While doughnuts are warm, roll in granulated sugar or in sifted powdered sugar.

Notes
1. In Step 5, dough may be chilled 1 hour for ease in handling.
2. Omit Steps 6 and 7 if dough machine is used.

CAKE DOUGHNUTS (DOUGHNUT MIX)

Yield 100   Portion 1 Doughnut

Calories	Carbohydrates	Protein	Fat	Cholesterol	Sodium	Calcium
199 cal	31 g	4 g	7 g	0 mg	323 mg	36 mg

Ingredient	Weight	Measure	Issue
DOUGHNUT MIX,CANNED	9 lbs	1 gal 4 qts	

Method
1. Use canned Doughnut Mix. Prepare according to instructions on container.

CHOCOLATE DOUGHNUTS

Yield 100   **Portion** 1 Doughnut

Calories	Carbohydrates	Protein	Fat	Cholesterol	Sodium	Calcium
190 cal	27 g	4 g	8 g	24 mg	198 mg	80 mg

Ingredient	Weight	Measure	Issue
FLOUR,WHEAT,GENERAL PURPOSE	5-1/2 lbs	1 gal 1 qts	
COCOA	6-1/8 oz	2 cup	
BAKING POWDER	3-7/8 oz	1/2 cup	
MILK,NONFAT,DRY	1-5/8 oz	1/2 cup 2-2/3 tbsp	
SALT	5/8 oz	1 tbsp	
NUTMEG,GROUND	1/4 oz	1 tbsp	
SHORTENING	7-1/4 oz	1 cup	
SUGAR,GRANULATED	1-1/2 lbs	3-3/8 cup	
EGGS,WHOLE,FROZEN	1-1/4 lbs	2-1/4 cup	
WATER	2 lbs	3-3/4 cup	
EXTRACT,VANILLA	1/2 oz	1 tbsp	

Method
1. Sift together flour, cocoa, baking powder, milk, salt, and nutmeg. Set aside for use in Step 5.
2. Place shortening and sugar in mixer bowl; cream at medium speed until light and fluffy.
3. Add eggs; beat at medium speed until light and fluffy.
4. Combine water and vanilla. Add to creamed mixture.
5. Add dry ingredients to creamed mixture alternately with liquids; add about 1/3 flour mixture each time. Blend at low speed after each addition. DO NOT OVERMIX. Let dough rest 10 minutes.
6. Roll dough 3/8-inch thick on well-floured board; cut with doughnut cutter.
7. Fry 1 minute on each side or until golden brown. Drain on absorbent paper towels. Glaze or coat if desired.

Notes
1. In Step 5, dough may be chilled 1 hour for ease in handling.
2. Omit Steps 6 and 7 if dough machine is used.

CINNAMON SUGAR DOUGHNUTS

Yield 100   **Portion** 1 Doughnut

Calories	Carbohydrates	Protein	Fat	Cholesterol	Sodium	Calcium
154 cal	28 g	3 g	3 g	24 mg	198 mg	81 mg

Ingredient	Weight	Measure	Issue
FLOUR,WHEAT,GENERAL PURPOSE	5-1/2 lbs	1 gal 1 qts	
BAKING POWDER	3-7/8 oz	1/2 cup	
MILK,NONFAT,DRY	1-5/8 oz	1/2 cup 2-2/3 tbsp	
SALT	5/8 oz	1 tbsp	
NUTMEG,GROUND	1/4 oz	1 tbsp	
SHORTENING	7-1/4 oz	1 cup	
SUGAR,GRANULATED	1-1/2 lbs	3-3/8 cup	
EGGS,WHOLE,FROZEN	1-1/4 lbs	2-1/4 cup	
WATER	2 lbs	3-3/4 cup	
EXTRACT,VANILLA	1/2 oz	1 tbsp	
CINNAMON SUGAR FILLING		2 cup	

Method

1. Sift together flour, baking powder, milk, salt, and nutmeg. Set aside for use in Step 5.
2. Place shortening and sugar in mixer bowl; cream at medium speed until light and fluffy.
3. Add eggs; beat at medium speed until light and fluffy.
4. Combine water and vanilla. Add to creamed mixture.
5. Add dry ingredients to creamed mixture alternately with liquids; add about 1/3 flour mixture each time. Blend at low speed after each addition. DO NOT OVERMIX. Let dough rest 10 minutes.
6. Roll dough 3/8 inch thick on well-floured board; cut with doughnut cutter.
7. Fry 1 minute on each side or until golden brown. Drain on absorbent paper towels. While doughnuts are still warm, roll in Cinnamon Sugar Filling, Recipe No. D 042 00.

Notes

1. In Step 5, dough may be chilled 1 hour for ease in handling.
2. Omit Steps 6 and 7 if dough machine is used.

GLAZED NUT DOUGHNUTS

Yield 100   Portion 1 Doughnut

Calories	Carbohydrates	Protein	Fat	Cholesterol	Sodium	Calcium
298 cal	47 g	5 g	11 g	26 mg	208 mg	82 mg

Ingredient	Weight	Measure	Issue
FLOUR,WHEAT,GENERAL PURPOSE	5-1/2 lbs	1 gal 1 qts	
BAKING POWDER	3-7/8 oz	1/2 cup	
MILK,NONFAT,DRY	1-5/8 oz	1/2 cup 2-2/3 tbsp	
SALT	5/8 oz	1 tbsp	
NUTMEG,GROUND	1/4 oz	1 tbsp	
SHORTENING	7-1/4 oz	1 cup	
SUGAR,GRANULATED	1-1/2 lbs	3-3/8 cup	
EGGS,WHOLE,FROZEN	1-1/4 lbs	2-1/4 cup	
WATER	2 lbs	3-3/4 cup	
EXTRACT,VANILLA	1/2 oz	1 tbsp	
VANILLA GLAZE		2-3/4 cup	
NUTS,UNSALTED,CHOPPED,COARSELY	1 lbs	3-1/8 cup	

Method

1. Sift together flour, baking powder, milk, salt, and nutmeg. Set aside for use in Step 5.
2. Place shortening and sugar in mixer bowl; cream at medium speed until light and fluffy.
3. Add eggs; beat at medium speed until light and fluffy.
4. Combine water and vanilla. Add to creamed mixture.
5. Add dry ingredients to creamed mixture alternately with liquids; add about 1/3 flour mixture each time. Blend at low speed after each addition. DO NOT OVERMIX. Let dough rest 10 minutes.
6. Roll dough 3/8-inch thick on well-floured board; cut with doughnut cutter.
7. Fry 1 minute on each side or until golden brown. Drain on absorbent paper.
8. Prepare Vanilla Glaze, Recipe No. D 046 00. Keep glaze warm; dip 1 side of doughnut into glaze, then into chopped, unsalted nuts. Place on racks to drain.

Notes

1. In Step 5, dough may be chilled 1 hour for ease in handling.
2. Omit Steps 6 and 7 if dough machine is used.

GLAZED COCONUT DOUGHNUTS

Yield 100   **Portion** 1 Doughnut

Calories	Carbohydrates	Protein	Fat	Cholesterol	Sodium	Calcium
300 cal	49 g	4 g	10 g	26 mg	222 mg	79 mg

Ingredient	Weight	Measure	Issue
FLOUR,WHEAT,GENERAL PURPOSE	5-1/2 lbs	1 gal 1 qts	
BAKING POWDER	3-7/8 oz	1/2 cup	
MILK,NONFAT,DRY	1-5/8 oz	1/2 cup 2-2/3 tbsp	
SALT	5/8 oz	1 tbsp	
NUTMEG,GROUND	1/4 oz	1 tbsp	
SHORTENING	7-1/4 oz	1 cup	
SUGAR,GRANULATED	1-1/2 lbs	3-3/8 cup	
EGGS,WHOLE,FROZEN	1-1/4 lbs	2-1/4 cup	
WATER	2 lbs	3-3/4 cup	
EXTRACT,VANILLA	1/2 oz	1 tbsp	
VANILLA GLAZE		2-3/4 cup	
COCONUT,PREPARED,SWEETENED FLAKES	1-1/4 lbs	1 qts 2 cups	

Method
1. Sift together flour, baking powder, milk, salt, and nutmeg. Set aside for use in Step 5.
2. Place shortening and sugar in mixer bowl; cream at medium speed until light and fluffy.
3. Add eggs; beat at medium speed until light and fluffy.
4. Combine water and vanilla. Add to creamed mixture.
5. Add dry ingredients to creamed mixture alternately with liquids; add about 1/3 flour mixture each time. Blend at low speed after each addition. DO NOT OVERMIX. Let dough rest 10 minutes.
6. Roll dough 3/8-inch thick on well-floured board; cut with doughnut cutter.
7. Fry 1 minute on each side or until golden brown. Drain on absorbent paper.
8. Prepare Vanilla Glaze, Recipe No. D 046 00. Keep glaze warm; dip 1 side of doughnut into glaze, then into prepared, sweetened flaked coconut. Place on racks to drain.

Notes
1. In Step 5, dough may be chilled 1 hour for ease in handling.
2. Omit Steps 6 and 7 if dough machine is used.

GLAZED DOUGHNUTS

Yield 100   **Portion** 1 Doughnut

Calories	Carbohydrates	Protein	Fat	Cholesterol	Sodium	Calcium
217 cal	34 g	3 g	8 g	25 mg	201 mg	78 mg

Ingredient	Weight	Measure	Issue
FLOUR,WHEAT,GENERAL PURPOSE	5-1/2 lbs	1 gal 1 qts	
BAKING POWDER	3-7/8 oz	1/2 cup	
MILK,NONFAT,DRY	1-5/8 oz	1/2 cup 2-2/3 tbsp	
SALT	5/8 oz	1 tbsp	
NUTMEG,GROUND	1/4 oz	1 tbsp	
SHORTENING	7-1/4 oz	1 cup	
SUGAR,GRANULATED	1-1/2 lbs	3-3/8 cup	
EGGS,WHOLE,FROZEN	1-1/4 lbs	2-1/4 cup	

WATER	2 lbs	3-3/4 cup
EXTRACT,VANILLA	1/2 oz	1 tbsp
VANILLA GLAZE		2-3/4 cup

Method
1. Sift together flour, baking powder, milk, salt, and nutmeg. Set aside for use in Step 5.
2. Place shortening and sugar in mixer bowl; cream at medium speed until light and fluffy.
3. Add eggs; beat at medium speed until light and fluffy.
4. Combine water and vanilla. Add to creamed mixture.
5. Add dry ingredients to creamed mixture alternately with liquids; add about 1/3 flour mixture each time. Blend at low speed after each addition. DO NOT OVERMIX. Let dough rest 10 minutes.
6. Roll dough 3/8-inch thick on well-floured board; cut with doughnut cutter.
7. Fry 1 minute on each side or until golden brown. Drain on absorbent paper.
8. Prepare Vanilla Glaze, Recipe No. D 046 00. Keep glaze warm; dip doughnuts to cover. Place on racks to drain.

Notes
1. In Step 5, dough may be chilled 1 hour for ease in handling.
2. Omit Steps 6 and 7 if dough machine is used.

RAISED DOUGHNUTS

Yield 100   **Portion** 1 Doughnut

Calories	Carbohydrates	Protein	Fat	Cholesterol	Sodium	Calcium
191 cal	26 g	4 g	8 g	11 mg	170 mg	13 mg

Ingredient	Weight	Measure	Issue
YEAST,ACTIVE,DRY	3-3/4 oz	1/2 cup 1 tbsp	
WATER,WARM	1-5/8 lbs	3 cup	
SUGAR,GRANULATED	1 lbs	2-1/4 cup	
SALT	1-1/2 oz	2-1/3 tbsp	
SHORTENING	9 oz	1-1/4 cup	
EGGS,WHOLE,FROZEN	8-5/8 oz	1 cup	
WATER,COLD	1-1/4 lbs	2-3/8 cup	
EXTRACT,VANILLA	1-3/8 oz	3 tbsp	
FLOUR,WHEAT,BREAD	3-7/8 lbs	3 qts 1 cup	
FLOUR,WHEAT,GENERAL PURPOSE	2-1/4 lbs	2 qts	
MILK,NONFAT,DRY	1-3/4 oz	3/4 cup	
NUTMEG,GROUND	1/4 oz	1 tbsp	

Method
1. Sprinkle yeast over water. DO NOT USE TEMPERATURES ABOVE 110 F. Mix well. Let stand for 5 minutes; stir. Set aside for use in Step 3.
2. Cream sugar, salt, and shortening in mixer bowl at medium speed.
3. Add eggs, yeast solution, water, and vanilla; mix at low speed until blended.
4. Sift together flours, milk, and nutmeg; add to mixture. Using dough hook, mix at low speed 1 minute or until all flour mixture is incorporated into liquid. Continue mixing at medium speed 10 minutes or until dough is smooth and elastic. Dough temperature should be between 78 F. to 82 F.
5. FERMENT: Cover. Set in warm place (80 F.) for 1-1/2 hours or until double in bulk.
6. PUNCH: Divide into 3 pieces (3 lb 8 oz); shape each piece into a smooth ball; let rest 10 to 20 minutes.

7. MAKE-UP: Roll each piece to 1/2-inch thickness. Cut with floured 3 inch doughnut cutter.
8. PROOF: Place on floured sheet pan; let rise 30 minutes or until light.
9. FRY: Until golden brown on underside. Turn; fry on other side. Drain on absorbent paper.
10. When cool, roll in granulated sugar or sifted powdered sugar or in Cinnamon Sugar Filling, Recipe No. D 042 00, or dip in Vanilla Glaze, Almond Glaze, or Rum Glaze, Recipe Nos. D 046 00, D 046 01, D 046 02. Place glazed doughnuts on racks to drain.

BEIGNETS (NEW ORLEANS DOUGHNUTS)

Yield 100   Portion 2 Each

Calories	Carbohydrates	Protein	Fat	Cholesterol	Sodium	Calcium
289 cal	38 g	5 g	13 g	13 mg	219 mg	17 mg

Ingredient	Weight	Measure	Issue
YEAST,ACTIVE,DRY	5-1/8 oz	3/4 cup	
WATER,WARM	2 lbs	3-3/4 cup	
SUGAR,GRANULATED	1-1/4 lbs	2-3/4 cup	
SALT	1-7/8 oz	3 tbsp	
SHORTENING	10-7/8 oz	1-1/2 cup	
EGGS,WHOLE,FROZEN	10-3/4 oz	1-1/4 cup	
WATER,COLD	1-1/2 lbs	2-3/4 cup	
EXTRACT,VANILLA	1-7/8 oz	1/4 cup 1/3 tbsp	
FLOUR,WHEAT,BREAD	4-7/8 lbs	1 gal	
FLOUR,WHEAT,GENERAL PURPOSE	2-3/4 lbs	2 qts 2 cup	
MILK,NONFAT,DRY	2-3/8 oz	1 cup	
SUGAR,POWDERED,SIFTED	1-1/3 lbs	1 qts 1 cup	

Method
1. Sprinkle yeast over water. DO NOT USE TEMPERATURES ABOVE 110 F. Mix well. Let stand for 5 minutes; stir. Set aside for use in Step 3.
2. Cream sugar, salt, and shortening in mixer bowl at medium speed.
3. Add eggs, yeast solution, water, and vanilla; mix at low speed until blended.
4. Sift together flours and milk; add to mixture. Using dough hook, mix at low speed 1 minute or until all flour mixture is incorporated into liquid. Continue mixing at medium speed 10 minutes or until dough is smooth and elastic. Dough temperature should be 78 F. to 82 F.
5. FERMENT: Cover and set in warm place, about 80 F., 1-1/2 hours or until double in bulk.
6. PUNCH: Divide into even pieces; shape each piece into a smooth ball; let rest 10 to 20 minutes.
7. MAKE-UP: Roll each piece onto a rectangular sheet, about 18 inches wide, 29 inches long, and 1/8-inch thick. Cut 6 by 9.
8. FRY: Until golden brown on underside. Turn and fry on other side. Drain on absorbent paper.
9. Sprinkle with sifted powdered sugar.

RAISED DOUGHNUTS (SWEET DOUGH MIX)

Yield 100   Portion 1 Doughnut

Calories	Carbohydrates	Protein	Fat	Cholesterol	Sodium	Calcium
194 cal	29 g	6 g	8 g	0 mg	323 mg	13 mg

Ingredient	Weight	Measure	Issue
SWEET DOUGH MIX	9 lbs	2 gal 1/8 qts	
YEAST,ACTIVE,DRY	3-3/4 oz	1/2 cup 1 tbsp	
EXTRACT,VANILLA	1/3 oz	1/3 tsp	
NUTMEG,GROUND	1/8 oz	1/3 tsp	
WATER	3-1/8 lbs	1 qts 2 cup	
SUGAR,POWDERED,SIFTED	1 lbs	1 qts	

Method

1. Prepare doughnuts according to directions on the container of Sweet Dough Mix.
2. When cool, roll in granulated sugar or sifted powdered sugar or in Cinnamon Sugar Filling, Recipe No. D 042 00, or dip in Vanilla Glaze, Almond Glaze, or Rum Glaze, Recipe Nos. D 046 00, D 046 01, D 046 02. Place glazed doughnuts on racks to drain.

LONGJOHNS

Yield 100   **Portion** 1 Each

Calories	Carbohydrates	Protein	Fat	Cholesterol	Sodium	Calcium
191 cal	26 g	4 g	8 g	11 mg	170 mg	13 mg

Ingredient	Weight	Measure	Issue
YEAST,ACTIVE,DRY	3-3/4 oz	1/2 cup 1 tbsp	
WATER,WARM	1-5/8 lbs	3 cup	
SUGAR,GRANULATED	1 lbs	2-1/4 cup	
SALT	1-1/2oz	2-1/3 tbsp	
SHORTENING	9 oz	1-1/4 cup	
EGGS,WHOLE,FROZEN	8-5/8 oz	1 cup	
WATER,COLD	1-1/4 lbs	2-3/8 cup	
EXTRACT,VANILLA	1-3/8 oz	3 tbsp	
FLOUR,WHEAT,BREAD	3-7/8 lbs	3 qts 1 cup	
FLOUR,WHEAT,GENERAL PURPOSE	2-1/4 lbs	2 qts	
MILK,NONFAT,DRY	1-3/4 oz	3/4 cup	
NUTMEG,GROUND	1/4 oz	1 tbsp	

Method

1. Sprinkle yeast over water. DO NOT USE TEMPERATURES ABOVE 110 F. Mix well. Let stand for 5 minutes; stir. Set aside for use in Step 3.
2. Cream sugar, salt, and shortening in mixer bowl at medium speed.
3. Add eggs, yeast solution, water, and vanilla; mix at low speed until blended.
4. Sift together flours, milk, and nutmeg; add to mixture. Using dough hook, mix at low speed 1 minute or until all flour mixture is incorporated into liquid. Continue mixing at medium speed 10 minutes or until dough is smooth and elastic. Dough temperature should be between 78 F. to 82 F.
5. FERMENT: Cover and set in warm place (80 F.), 1-1/2 hours or until double in bulk.
6. PUNCH: Divide into 3 (3 lb 8 oz) pieces; shape each piece into a smooth ball; let rest 10 to 20 minutes.
7. MAKE-UP: Roll each piece into rectangular strips, 5 inches wide, 50 inches long, and 1/2-inch thick; cut into strips 1 inch wide.
8. PROOF: Place on floured sheet pan; let rise 30 minutes or until light.
9. FRY: Until golden brown on underside. Turn and fry on other side. Drain on absorbent paper.

10. When cool, roll in granulated sugar or sifted powdered sugar or in Cinnamon Sugar Filling, Recipe No. D 042 00 or dip in Vanilla Glaze, Rum Glaze, Almond Glaze, Recipe Nos. D 046 00, D 046 01, D 046 02. Place glazed doughnuts on racks to drain.

CRULLERS

Yield 100   **Portion** 1 Doughnut

Calories	Carbohydrates	Protein	Fat	Cholesterol	Sodium	Calcium
191 cal	26 g	4 g	8 g	11 mg	170 mg	13 mg

Ingredient	Weight	Measure	Issue
YEAST,ACTIVE,DRY	3-3/4 oz	1/2 cup 1 tbsp	
WATER,WARM	1-5/8 lbs	3 cup	
SUGAR,GRANULATED	1 lbs	2-1/4 cup	
SALT	1-1/2oz	2-1/3 tbsp	
SHORTENING	9 oz	1-1/4 cup	
EGGS,WHOLE,FROZEN	8-5/8 oz	1 cup	
WATER,COLD	1-1/4 lbs	2-3/8 cup	
EXTRACT,VANILLA	1-3/8 oz	3 tbsp	
FLOUR,WHEAT,BREAD	3-7/8 lbs	3 qts 1 cup	
FLOUR,WHEAT,GENERAL PURPOSE	2-1/4 lbs	2 qts	
MILK,NONFAT,DRY	1-3/4 oz	3/4 cup	
NUTMEG,GROUND	1/4 oz	1 tbsp	

Method

1. Sprinkle yeast over water. DO NOT USE TEMPERATURES ABOVE 110 F. Mix well. Let stand for 5 minutes; stir. Set aside for use in Step 3.
2. Cream sugar, salt, and shortening in mixer bowl at medium speed.
3. Add eggs, yeast solution, water, and vanilla; mix at low speed until blended.
4. Sift together flours, milk, and nutmeg; add to mixture. Using dough hook, mix at low speed 1 minute or until all flour mixture is incorporated into liquid. Continue mixing at medium speed 10 minutes or until dough is smooth and elastic. Dough temperature should be between 78 F. to 82 F.
5. FERMENT: Cover and set in warm place (80 F.), 1-1/2 hours or until double in bulk.
6. PUNCH: Divide into 3 (3 lb 8 oz) pieces; shape each piece into a smooth ball; let rest 10 to 20 minutes.
7. MAKE-UP: Roll each piece into rectangular strips, 5 inches wide, 50 inches long, and 1/2-inch thick; cut into strips 1 inch wide.
8. PROOF: Place on floured sheet pan; let rise 30 minutes or until light.
9. FRY: Until golden brown on underside. Turn and fry on other side. Drain on absorbent paper.
10. When cool, roll in granulated sugar or sifted powdered sugar or in Cinnamon Sugar Filling, Recipe No. D 042 00 or dip in Vanilla Glaze, Rum Glaze, Almond Glaze, Recipe Nos. D 046 00, D 046 01, D 046 02. Place glazed doughnuts on racks to drain.

DUMPLINGS

Yield 100   **Portion** 2 Each

Calories	Carbohydrates	Protein	Fat	Cholesterol	Sodium	Calcium
175 cal	26 g	3 g	6 g	1 mg	521 mg	73 mg

Ingredient				Weight	Measure	Issue
BISCUIT MIX				9 lbs	2 gal 1/2 qts	

Method
1. Mix according to instructions on container.
2. Drop a scant 1/8-cup batter on top of simmering stew or into shallow simmering stock. Cover; cook 15 minutes. DO NOT remove cover during cooking time.

Notes
1. Shallow simmering stock should not be more than 1 inch in depth.

ENGLISH MUFFINS

Yield 100   **Portion** 1 Muffin

Calories	Carbohydrates	Protein	Fat	Cholesterol	Sodium	Calcium
281 cal	43 g	8 g	8 g	20 mg	130 mg	25 mg

Ingredient	Weight	Measure	Issue
YEAST,ACTIVE,DRY	2-7/8 oz	1/4 cup 3 tbsp	
WATER,WARM	1-1/8 lbs	2-1/4 cup	
SUGAR,GRANULATED	3/4 oz	1 tbsp	
SUGAR,GRANULATED	4 oz	1/2 cup 1 tbsp	
SALT	1 oz	1 tbsp	
SHORTENING,SOFTENED	1-1/2 lbs	3-3/8 cup	
WATER,WARM	4-1/3 lbs	2 qts 1/4 cup	
FLOUR,WHEAT,BREAD	1-3/4 lbs	1 qts 2 cup	
MILK,NONFAT,DRY	3-5/8 oz	1-1/2 cup	
FLOUR,WHEAT,BREAD	10-5/8 lbs	2 gal 3/4 qts	
EGGS,WHOLE,FROZEN	1 lbs	1-7/8 cup	

Method
1. Sprinkle yeast over water. DO NOT USE TEMPERATURES ABOVE 110 F. Mix well. Let stand 5 minutes. Add sugar; stir until dissolved. Let stand 10 minutes, then stir again. Set aside for use in Step 3.
2. Place sugar, salt, and shortening in mixer bowl. Add water; stir until shortening is melted.
3. Sift together flour and milk; add to sugar and shortening mixture. Beat at medium speed until smooth. Add yeast solution.
4. Add 1/2 of the flour mixture; mix well. Add eggs, two at a time, beating well after each addition. Add 2 remaining flour; beat to form a smooth dough.
5. FERMENT: Cover; set in a warm place (80 F.), 1-1/2 to 2 hours or until double in bulk.
6. PUNCH: Let stand 1 hour.
7. MAKE UP: Divide dough into 5 balls. Let rest 10 minutes. Roll dough to 1/2-inch thickness. Cut each dough piece into 20-4 inch circles.
8. Place cut circles in rows 4 by 6 about 1 inch apart on pans, which have been sprinkled lightly with cornmeal, about 1/2 cup per pan.
9. PROOF: At 80 F. for 45 minutes or until double in size.
10. BAKE: Brown muffins on lightly greased griddle 5 minutes per side. Place browned muffins on sheet pans; bake 15 to 20

CINNAMON RAISIN ENGLISH MUFFINS

Yield 100   **Portion** 1 Muffin

Calories	Carbohydrates	Protein	Fat	Cholesterol	Sodium	Calcium
321 cal	53 g	8 g	8 g	20 mg	132 mg	34 mg

Ingredient	Weight	Measure	Issue
YEAST,ACTIVE,DRY	2-7/8 oz	1/4 cup 3 tbsp	
WATER,WARM	1-1/8 lbs	2-1/4 cup	
SUGAR,GRANULATED	3/4 oz	1 tbsp	
SUGAR,GRANULATED	4 oz	1/2 cup 1 tbsp	
SALT	1 oz	1 tbsp	
SHORTENING,SOFTENED	1-1/2 lbs	3-3/8 cup	
WATER,WARM	4-1/3 lbs	2 qts 1/4 cup	
CINNAMON,GROUND	3/4 lbs	3 tbsp	
RAISINS	2-7/8 oz	2 qts 1 cup	
FLOUR,WHEAT,BREAD	1-3/4 lbs	1 qts 2 cup	
MILK,NONFAT,DRY	3-5/8 lbs	1-1/2 cup	
FLOUR,WHEAT,BREAD	10-5/8 lbs	2 gal 3/4 qts	
EGGS,WHOLE,FROZEN	1 lbs	1-7/8 cup	

Method

1. Sprinkle yeast over water. DO NOT USE TEMPERATURES ABOVE 110 F. Mix well. Let stand 5 minutes. Add sugar; stir until dissolved. Let stand 10 minutes, then stir again. Set aside for use in Step 3.
2. Place sugar, salt, and shortening in mixer bowl. Add water; stir until shortening is melted.
3. Sift together flour, cinnamon, raisins, and milk; add to sugar and shortening mixture. Beat at medium speed until smooth. Add yeast solution.
4. Add 1/2 of the flour mixture; mix well. Add eggs, two at a time, beating well after each addition. Add remaining flour; beat to form a smooth dough.
5. FERMENT: Cover and set in a warm place, about 80 F., 1-1/2 to 2 hours or until double in bulk.
6. PUNCH: Let stand 1 hour.
7. MAKE UP: Divide dough into 5 balls. Let rest 10 minutes. Roll dough to 1/2-inch thickness. Cut each dough piece into 20-4 inch circles.
8. Place cut circles in rows 4 by 6 about 1 inch apart on pans, which have been sprinkled lightly with cornmeal, using about 1/2 cup per pan.
9. PROOF: At 80 F. for 45 minutes or until double in size.

BAKE: Brown muffins on lightly greased griddle 5 minutes per side. Place browned muffins on sheet pans; bake 15 to 20 minutes.

FRENCH TOAST

Yield 100   **Portion** 2 Slices

Calories	Carbohydrates	Protein	Fat	Cholesterol	Sodium	Calcium
206 cal	29 g	9 g	6 g	148 mg	324 mg	94 mg

Ingredient	Weight	Measure	Issue
WATER	5-3/4 lbs	2 qts 3 cup	
SUGAR,GRANULATED	10-5/8 oz	1-1/2 cup	
MILK,NONFAT,DRY	5-5/8 oz	2-3/8 cup	

EGGS,WHOLE,FROZEN	7-1/2 lbs	3 qts 2 cup
BREAD,WHITE,SLICED	11 lbs	200 sl
COOKING SPRAY,NONSTICK	2 oz	1/4 cup 1/3 tbsp

Method
1. Place water in a mixer bowl.
2. Combine water, milk and sugar; blend well. Whip on low speed until dissolved, about 1 minute.
3. Add eggs to ingredients in mixer bowl; whip on medium speed until well blended, about 2 minutes.
4. Dip bread in egg mixture to coat both sides. DO NOT SOAK.
5. Lightly spray grill with non-stick spray. Place bread on griddle; cook on each side about 1-1/2 minutes or until golden brown. CCP: Internal temperature must reach 145 F. or higher for 15 seconds.

FRENCH TOAST (THICK SLICE)

Yield 100   Portion 2 Slices

Calories	Carbohydrates	Protein	Fat	Cholesterol	Sodium	Calcium
305 cal	48 g	12 g	6 g	147 mg	573 mg	104 mg

Ingredient	Weight	Measure	Issue
WATER	5-3/4 lbs	2 qts 3 cup	
SUGAR,GRANULATED	10-5/8 oz	1-1/2 cup	
MILK,NONFAT,DRY	5-5/8 oz	2-3/8 cup	
EGGS,WHOLE,FROZEN	7-1/2 lbs	3 qts 2 cup	
BREAD,FRENCH,THICK SLICE	18-3/4 lbs	200 sl	
COOKING SPRAY,NONSTICK	2 oz	1/4 cup 1/3 tbsp	

Method
1. Place water in a mixer bowl.
2. Combine water, milk and sugar; blend well. Whip on low speed until dissolved, about 1 minute.
3. Add eggs to ingredients in mixer bowl; whip on medium speed until well blended, about 2 minutes.
4. Cut each loaf diagonally into 16 slices, ¾ inch thick (ends removed). Dip bread in egg mixture to coat both sides. DO NOT SOAK.
5. Lightly spray grill with non-stick spray. Place bread on griddle; cook on each side about 1-1/2 minutes or until golden brown. CCP: Internal temperature must reach 145 F. or higher for 15 seconds.

ENGLISH MUFFIN FRENCH TOAST

Yield 100   Portion 1 Muffin

Calories	Carbohydrates	Protein	Fat	Cholesterol	Sodium	Calcium
206 cal	30 g	9 g	5 g	147 mg	319 mg	139 mg

Ingredient	Weight	Measure	Issue
WATER	5-3/4 lbs	2 qts 3 cup	
SUGAR,GRANULATED	10-5/8 oz	1-1/2 cup	
MILK,NONFAT,DRY	5-5/8 oz	2-3/8 cup	
EGGS,WHOLE,FROZEN	7-1/2 lbs	3 qts 2 cup	
ENGLISH MUFFIND, SPLIT OR CUT	12-5/8 lbs	100 each	
COOKING SPRAY,NONSTICK	2 oz	1/4 cup 1/3 tbsp	

Method

1. Place water in a mixer bowl.
2. Combine water, milk and sugar; blend well. Whip on low speed until dissolved, about 1 minute.
3. Add eggs to ingredients in mixer bowl; whip on medium speed until well blended, about 2 minutes.
4. Cut muffins in half; dip split muffins in batter 30 seconds. DO NOT SOAK.
5. Lightly spray grill with non-stick spray. Place muffins on griddle; cut side down. Grill about 3; turn, grill on crust side about 1-1/2 minutes. CCP: Internal temperature must reach 145 F. or higher for 15 seconds.

FRENCH TOAST (FROZEN EGGS AND EGG WHITES)

Yield 100   **Portion** 2 Slices

Calories	Carbohydrates	Protein	Fat	Cholesterol	Sodium	Calcium
186 cal	29 g	8 g	4 g	69 mg	324 mg	85 mg

Ingredient	Weight	Measure	Issue
WATER	5-3/4 lbs	2 qts 3 cup	
SUGAR,GRANULATED	10-5/8 oz	1-1/2 cup	
MILK,NONFAT,DRY	5-5/8 oz	2-3/8 cup	
EGG WHITES,FROZEN,THAWED	3-1/2 lbs	1 qts 2-1/2 cup	
EGGS,WHOLE,FROZEN	3-1/2 lbs	1 qts 2-1/2 cup	
BREAD,WHITE,SLICED	11 lbs	200 sl	
COOKING SPRAY,NONSTICK	2 oz	1/4 cup 1/3 tbsp	

Method

1. Place water in a mixer bowl.
2. Combine water, milk and sugar; blend well. Whip on low speed until dissolved, about 1 minute.
3. Add whole eggs and egg whites to ingredients in mixer bowl; whip on medium speed until well blended, about 2 minutes.
4. Dip bread in egg mixture to coat both sides. DO NOT SOAK.
5. Lightly spray grill with non-stick spray. Place bread on griddle; cook on each side about 1-1/2 minutes or until golden brown. CCP: Internal temperature must reach 145 F. or higher for 15 seconds.

FRENCH TOAST PUFF

Yield 100   **Portion** 2 Halves

Calories	Carbohydrates	Protein	Fat	Cholesterol	Sodium	Calcium
284 cal	48 g	7 g	6 g	30 mg	570 mg	175 mg

Ingredient	Weight	Measure	Issue
EGGS,WHOLE,FROZEN	1-1/2 lbs	2-3/4 cup	
SUGAR,GRANULATED	1-1/4 lbs	2-3/4 cup	
SALT	1-7/8 oz	3 tbsp	
EXTRACT,VANILLA	1-1/4 oz	2-2/3 tbsp	
MILK,NONFAT,DRY	6-7/8 oz	2-7/8 cup	
WATER,WARM	7-7/8 lbs	3 qts 3 cup	
FLOUR,WHEAT,GENERAL PURPOSE	8-1/4 lbs	1 gal 3-1/2 qts	
BAKING POWDER	6-3/4 oz	3/4 cup 2 tbsp	
BREAD,WHITE,SLICE	5-1/2 lbs	100 sl	

Method

1. Combine eggs, sugar, salt, vanilla, milk, and water in mixer bowl. Beat at medium speed until well blended.
2. Add slowly flour and baking powder; mix at medium speed until smooth.
3. Cut bread in half diagonally. Dip half slices of bread in batter. Drain.
4. Fry until golden brown. Drain on absorbent paper.

Notes

1. In Step 5, serve with maple, blueberry or strawberry syrup, marmalade, jam, or jelly.
2. In Step 5, serve with well-drained canned sliced peaches, fruit cocktail or thawed, well-drained strawberries.
3. Puffs, while warm, may be rolled in Cinnamon Sugar Filling, Recipe No. D 042 00 or dusted with powdered sugar

APPLE FRITTERS

Yield 100   Portion 2 Fritters

Calories	Carbohydrates	Protein	Fat	Cholesterol	Sodium	Calcium
248 cal	34 g	3 g	12 g	20 mg	273 mg	73 mg

Ingredient	Weight	Measure	Issue
FLOUR,WHEAT,GENERAL PURPOSE	4 lbs	3 qts 2-1/2 cup	
BAKING POWDER	3-1/4 oz	1/4 cup 3 tbsp	
MILK,NONFAT,DRY	3-1/4 oz	1-3/8 cup	
SALT	1-1/2 oz	2-1/3 tbsp	
SUGAR,GRANULATED	1-1/4 lbs	2-3/4 cup	
NUTMEG,GROUND	1/4 oz	1 tbsp	
CINNAMON,GROUND	1/4 oz	1 tbsp	
EGGS,WHOLE,FROZEN	1 lbs	1-7/8 cup	
WATER	3-3/4 lbs	1 qts 3-1/4 cup	
OIL,SALAD	5-3/4 oz	3/4 cup	
APPLES,CANNED,SLICED,DRAINED	6 lbs	3 qts	
SUGAR,POWDERED,SIFTED	2-1/8 lbs	2 qts	

Method

1. Sift together flour, baking powder, milk, salt, sugar, nutmeg, and cinnamon into mixer bowl.
2. Combine eggs, water, shortening or salad oil, and add to dry ingredients. Mix at low speed until well blended.
3. Drain apples and chop apples coarsely; add to batter; mix lightly.
4. Using a well rounded tablespoon, drop batter into deep fat. Fry 4 to 6 minutes. Drain on absorbent paper. Sprinkle with sifted powdered sugar.

Notes

1. In Step 3, 6 lb (7 lb 11 oz A.P.) pared, cored and diced fresh apples may be used per 100 portions.

PANCAKES

Yield 100   Portion 2 Cakes

Calories	Carbohydrates	Protein	Fat	Cholesterol	Sodium	Calcium
253 cal	41 g	7 g	6 g	53 mg	512 mg	207 mg

Ingredient	Weight	Measure	Issue
FLOUR,WHEAT,GENERAL PURPOSE	9-7/8 lbs	2 gal 1 qts	

BAKING POWDER	8-3/4 oz	1-1/8 cup
MILK,NONFAT,DRY	13-1/4 oz	1 qts 1-1/2 cup
SALT	1-7/8 oz	3 tbsp
SUGAR,GRANULATED	12-1/3 oz	1-3/4 cup
EGGS,WHOLE,FROZEN	2-2/3 lbs	1 qts 1 cup
WATER	13 lbs	1 gal 2-1/4 qts
OIL,SALAD	1 lbs	2 cup
COOKING SPRAY,NONSTICK	2 oz	1/4 cup 1/3 tbsp

Method

1. Sift together flour, baking powder, milk, salt, and sugar into mixer bowl.
2. Add eggs and water; mix at low speed about 1 minute or until blended.
3. Blend in salad oil or melted shortening about 1 minute.
4. Lightly spray griddle with non-stick spray. Pour 1/4 cup batter onto hot griddle. Cook on one side 1-1/2 to 2 minutes or until top is covered with bubbles and underside is browned. Turn; cook on other side 1-1/2 to 2 minutes.

BUTTERMILK PANCAKES (DRY BUTTERMILK)

Yield 100   **Portion** 2 Cakes

Calories	Carbohydrates	Protein	Fat	Cholesterol	Sodium	Calcium
281 cal	44 g	10 g	7 g	60 mg	478 mg	211 mg

Ingredient	Weight	Measure	Issue
FLOUR,WHEAT,GENERAL PURPOSE	9-7/8 lbs	2 gal 1 qts	
BAKING POWDER	3-7/8 oz	1/2 cup	
MILK,BUTTERMILK,DRY	2-3/8 lbs	1 qts 1/2 cup	
BAKING SODA	1 oz	2 tbsp	
SALT	1-7/8 oz	3 tbsp	
SUGAR,GRANULATED	12-1/3 oz	1-3/4 cup	
EGGS,WHOLE,FROZEN	2-2/3 lbs	1 qts 1 cup	
WATER	13 lbs	1 gal 2-1/4 qts	
OIL,SALAD	1 lbs	2 cup	
COOKING SPRAY,NONSTICK	2 oz	1/4 cup 1/3 tbsp	

Method

1. Sift together flour, baking powder, dry buttermilk, salt, sugar, and baking soda.
2. Add eggs and water; mix at low speed about 1 minute or until blended.
3. Blend in salad oil or melted shortening about 1 minute.
4. Lightly spray griddle with non-stick cooking spray. Pour 1/4 cup batter onto hot griddle. Cook on one side 1-1/2 to 2 minutes or until top is covered with bubbles and underside is browned. Turn; cook on other side 1-1/2 to 2 minutes.

BLUEBERRY PANCAKES

Yield 100   **Portion** 2 Cakes

Calories	Carbohydrates	Protein	Fat	Cholesterol	Sodium	Calcium
265 cal	43 g	8 g	7 g	53 mg	512 mg	209 mg

Ingredient	Weight	Measure	Issue
FLOUR,WHEAT,GENERAL PURPOSE	9-7/8 lbs	2 gal 1 qts	
BAKING POWDER	8-3/4 oz	1-1/8 cup	
MILK,NONFAT,DRY	13-1/4 oz	1 qts 1-1/2 cup	
SALT	1-7/8 oz	3 tbsp	
SUGAR,GRANULATED	12-1/3 oz	1-3/4 cup	
EGGS,WHOLE,FROZEN	2-2/3 lbs	1 qts 1 cup	
WATER	13 lbs	1 gal 2-1/4 qts	
OIL,SALAD	1 lbs	2 cup	
BLUEBERRIES,FROZEN,UNSWEETENED	5-1/8 lbs	3 qts 3 cup	
COOKING SPRAY,NONSTICK	2 oz	1/4 cup 1/3 tbsp	

Method
1. Sift together flour, baking powder, milk, salt, and sugar into mixer bowl.
2. Add eggs and water; mix at low speed about 1 minute or until blended.
3. Blend in salad oil or melted shortening about 1 minute. Use partially thawed frozen blueberries, or drain and rinse canned blueberries in cold water. Drain thoroughly and fold into batter.
4. Lightly spray non-stick cooking spray on griddle. Pour 1/4 cup batter onto hot griddle. Cook on one side 1-1/2 to 2 minutes or until top is covered with bubbles and underside is browned. Turn; cook on other side 1-1/2 to 2 minutes. Stir between batches to redistribute berries.

BUTTERMILK PANCAKES (PANCAKE MIX)

Yield 100   **Portion** 2 Cakes

Calories	Carbohydrates	Protein	Fat	Cholesterol	Sodium	Calcium
296 cal	48 g	7 g	8 g	14 mg	827 mg	164 mg

Ingredient	Weight	Measure	Issue
PANCAKE MIX,BUTTERMILK	12-1/2 lbs	3 gal 1-1/8 qts	

Method
1. Prepare pancakes according to instructions on container.

PANCAKES (PANCAKE MIX)

Yield 100   **Portion** 2 Cakes

Calories	Carbohydrates	Protein	Fat	Cholesterol	Sodium	Calcium
226 cal	42 g	6 g	3 g	12 mg	716 mg	142 mg

Ingredient	Weight	Measure	Issue
PANCAKE MIX	13 lbs	2 gal 3-1/3 qts	

Method
1. Prepare pancakes according to instructions on container.

WAFFLES, FROZEN (BROWN AND SERVE)

Yield 100   **Portion** 2 Each

Calories	Carbohydrates	Protein	Fat	Cholesterol	Sodium	Calcium
176 cal	27 g	4 g	6 g	22 mg	524 mg	155 mg

Ingredient		Weight	Measure	Issue
WAFFLES,BROWN & SERVE,FROZEN		15-3/8 lbs	200 each	

Method

1. Prepare according to instructions on container.

WAFFLES (PANCAKE MIX)

Yield 100   Portion 2 Cakes

Calories	Carbohydrates	Protein	Fat	Cholesterol	Sodium	Calcium
226 cal	42 g	6 g	3 g	12 mg	716 mg	142 mg

Ingredient	Weight	Measure	Issue
PANCAKE MIX	13 lbs	2 gal 3-1/3 qts	

Method

1. Prepare waffles according to instructions on container.

WAFFLES

Yield 100   Portion 1 Each

Calories	Carbohydrates	Protein	Fat	Cholesterol	Sodium	Calcium
253 cal	41 g	7 g	6 g	53 mg	512 mg	207 mg

Ingredient	Weight	Measure	Issue
FLOUR,WHEAT,GENERAL PURPOSE	9-7/8 lbs	2 gal 1 qts	
BAKING POWDER	8-3/4 oz	1-1/8 cup	
MILK,NONFAT,DRY	13-1/4 oz	1 qts 1-1/2 cup	
SALT	1-7/8 oz	3 tbsp	
SUGAR,GRANULATED	12-1/3 oz	1-3/4 cup	
EGGS,WHOLE,FROZEN	2-2/3 lbs	1 qts 1 cup	
WATER	13 lbs	1 gal 2-1/4 qts	
OIL,SALAD	1 lbs	2 cup	

Method

1. Sift together both flours, baking powder, milk, salt, and sugar into mixer bowl.
2. Add eggs and water; mix at low speed about 1 minute or until blended.
3. Blend in salad oil or melted shortening about 1 minute.
4. Pour 1/2 cup batter on preheated waffle iron. Bake until steaming stops, about 3 to 4 minutes.

WHOLE WHEAT PANCAKES

Yield 100   Portion 2 Cakes

Calories	Carbohydrates	Protein	Fat	Cholesterol	Sodium	Calcium
236 cal	37 g	8 g	7 g	53 mg	513 mg	210 mg

Ingredient	Weight	Measure	Issue
FLOUR,WHOLE WHEAT	4-1/4 lbs	1 gal	

Ingredient	Weight	Measure	Issue
FLOUR,WHEAT,GENERAL PURPOSE	5 lbs	1 gal 1/2 qts	
BAKING POWDER	8-3/4 oz	1-1/8 cup	
MILK,NONFAT,DRY	13-1/4 oz	1 qts 1-1/2 cup	
SALT	1-7/8 oz	3 tbsp	
SUGAR,GRANULATED	12-1/3 oz	1-3/4 cup	
EGGS,WHOLE,FROZEN	2-2/3 lbs	1 qts 1 cup	
WATER	13 lbs	1 gal 2-1/4 qts	
OIL,SALAD	1 lbs	2 cup	

Method
1. Sift together both flours, baking powder, milk, salt, and sugar into mixer bowl.
2. Add eggs and water; mix at low speed about 1 minute or until blended.
3. Blend in salad oil or melted shortening about 1 minute.
4. Pour 1/4 cup batter onto lightly greased hot griddle. Cook on one side 1-1/2 to 2 minutes or until top is covered with bubbles and underside is browned. Turn; cook on other side 1-1/2 to 2 minutes.

PANCAKES (FROZEN EGGS AND EGG WHITES)

Yield 100   **Portion** 2 Cakes

Calories	Carbohydrates	Protein	Fat	Cholesterol	Sodium	Calcium
247 cal	41 g	7 g	6 g	27 mg	513 mg	204 mg

Ingredient	Weight	Measure	Issue
FLOUR,WHEAT,GENERAL PURPOSE	9-7/8 lbs	2 gal 1 qts	
BAKING POWDER	8-3/4 oz	1-1/8 cup	
MILK,NONFAT,DRY	13-1/4 oz	1 qts 1-1/2 cup	
SALT	1-7/8 oz	3 tbsp	
SUGAR,GRANULATED	12-1/3 oz	1-3/4 cup	
EGGS,WHOLE,FROZEN	1-1/3 lbs	2-1/2 cup	
EGG WHITES,FROZEN,THAWED	1-1/3 lbs	2-1/2 cup	
WATER	13 lbs	1 gal 2-1/4 qts	
OIL,SALAD	1 lbs	2 cup	

Method
1. Sift together flour, baking powder, milk, salt, and sugar into mixer bowl.
2. Add eggs and water; mix at low speed about 1 minute or until blended.
3. Blend in salad oil or melted shortening about 1 minute.
4. Pour 1/4 cup batter onto lightly greased hot griddle. Cook on one side 1-1/2 to 2 minutes or until top is covered with bubbles and underside is browned. Turn; cook on other side 1-1/2 to 2 minutes.

PANCAKES (EGG SUBSTITUTE)

Yield 100   **Portion** 2 Cakes

Calories	Carbohydrates	Protein	Fat	Cholesterol	Sodium	Calcium
246 cal	41 g	8 g	6 g	1 mg	518 mg	207 mg

Ingredient	Weight	Measure	Issue
FLOUR,WHEAT,GENERAL PURPOSE	9-7/8 lbs	2 gal 1 qts	
BAKING POWDER	8-3/4 oz	1-1/8 cup	
MILK,NONFAT,DRY	13-1/4 oz	1 qts 1-1/2 cup	

SALT	1-7/8 oz	3 tbsp
SUGAR,GRANULATED	12-1/3 oz	1-3/4 cup
EGG SUBSTITUTE,PASTEURIZED	2-3/4 lbs	1 qts 1 cup
WATER	13 lbs	1 gal 2-1/4 qts
OIL,SALAD	1 lbs	2 cup

Method

1. Sift together flour, baking powder, milk, salt, and sugar into mixer bowl.
2. Add egg substitute and water; mix at low speed about 1 minute or until blended.
3. Blend in salad oil or melted shortening about 1 minute.
4. Pour 1/4 cup batter onto lightly greased hot griddle. Cook on one side 1-1/2 to 2 minutes or until top is covered with bubbles and underside is browned. Turn; cook on other side 1-1/2 to 2 minutes.

HOT CROSS BUNS

Yield 100   **Portion** 1 Each

Calories	Carbohydrates	Protein	Fat	Cholesterol	Sodium	Calcium
147 cal	28 g	5 g	3 g	0 mg	270 mg	17 mg

Ingredient	Weight	Measure Issue
YEAST,ACTIVE,DRY	2-1/4 oz	1/4 cup 1-2/3 tbsp
WATER,WARM	3-1/8 lbs	1 qts 2 cup
SWEET DOUGH MIX	7-1/2 lbs	1 gal 2-7/8 qts
RAISINS	2-1/4 lbs	1 qts 3 cup
CINNAMON,GROUND	1/2 oz	2 tbsp
CLOVES,GROUND	<1/16th oz	<1/16th tsp
NUTMEG,GROUND	<1/16th oz	<1/16th tsp
COOKING SPRAY,NONSTICK	2 oz	1/4 cup 1/3 tbsp

Method

1. Sprinkle yeast over water. DO NOT USE TEMPERATURES ABOVE 110 F. Mix well. Let stand 5 minutes; stir.
2. Add Sweet Dough Mix, raisins, cinnamon, cloves, and nutmeg.
3. Using dough hook, mix at low speed until water is absorbed. Mix at medium speed until dough is developed and cleans the bowl. Dough temperature should be 78 F. to 82 F.
4. FERMENT: Cover. Set in warm place (80 F.) 1-1/2 to 2 hours or until double in bulk.
5. PUNCH: Divide dough into 8-2 pound pieces on lightly floured work surface; shape each piece into a smooth ball. Let rest 10 to 20 minutes.
6. MAKE-UP: Roll each piece into a long rope of uniform diameter. Cut rope into pieces about 1 inch thick, weighing 1-1/2 ounces each. Shape into balls by rolling with circular motion on work surface.
7. Lightly spray pans with non-stick cooking spray. Place on pans in rows 6 by 9. Prepare 1/8 recipe Egg Wash, Recipe No. D 017 00. Brush buns in each pan with wash.
8. PROOF: At 90 F. to 100 F. about 45 minutes or until almost double in bulk.
9. BAKE: 30 minutes at 400 F. or until lightly browned. If convection oven is used, bake at 350 F. for 10 minutes on high fan, closed vent.
10. Prepare 1/8 recipe Syrup Glaze, Recipe No. D 045 00 per 100 servings. Brush buns in each pan with 1/4 cup hot glaze immediately after removal from oven.
11. When cool, prepare 1/8 recipe Decorator's Frosting, Recipe No. G 007 00 per 100 servings. Frost each bun with frosting in a cross design using a pastry bag with a small plain tip.

Notes

1. In Step 2, 1 tbsp lemon flavoring may be added per 100 servings.

116

KOLACHES

Yield 100   **Portion** 1 Roll

Calories	Carbohydrates	Protein	Fat	Cholesterol	Sodium	Calcium
240 cal	39 g	5 g	7 g	20 mg	177 mg	21 mg

Ingredient	Weight	Measure	Issue
YEAST,ACTIVE,DRY	5-1/8 oz	3/4 cup	
WATER,WARM	1-7/8 lbs	3-1/2 cup	
SUGAR,GRANULATED	7/8 oz	2 tbsp	
SUGAR,GRANULATED	1-1/4 lbs	2-3/4 cup	
SALT	1-1/2 oz	2-1/3 tbsp	
SHORTENING	1-1/3 lbs	3 cup	
EGGS,WHOLE,FROZEN	1 lbs	1-7/8 cup	
WATER	2-1/8 lbs	1 qts	
FLOUR,WHEAT,BREAD	7-1/4 lbs	1 gal 2 qts	
MILK,NONFAT,DRY	2-2/3 oz	1-1/8 cup	
CHERRY FILLING (PIE FILLING, PREPARED)	2-3/4 kg	3 unit	

Method

1. Sprinkle yeast over water. DO NOT USE TEMPERATURES ABOVE 110 F. Mix well. Let stand 5 minutes. Add sugar; stir until dissolved. Let stand 10 minutes; stir again. Set aside for use in Step 3.
2. Mix sugar, salt, and shortening in mixer bowl at medium speed 1 minute.
3. Blend in eggs, water, and yeast solution at low speed.
4. Sift flour and milk together, add to egg mixture. Mix at low speed 7 to 10 minutes or until dough is formed.
5. FERMENT: Set in warm place (80 F.) for about 1 hour.
6. PUNCH: Let rest 10 minutes. Divide dough into 2 pieces. Shape each piece into a smooth ball; let rest 10 minutes.
7. MAKE UP: Form into a rope 1-1/2 inches in diameter. Cut into 1-1/2 inch pieces. Shape into 2-ounce balls. Place 2 inches apart on greased pans. Flatten out slightly with palm of hand.
8. PROOF: About 30 minutes or until pieces are double in bulk.
9. Press down center of each piece with back of spoon. Leave a rim about 1/4-inch wide.
10. Fill center of each Kolache with about 1 ounce (2 tbsp) of Cherry Filling, Recipe No. D 041 01.
11. Brush rim with Egg Wash, Recipe No. D 017 00.
12. PROOF: 20 minutes at 350 F. or until double in bulk.
13. BAKE: At 350 F. for 25 minutes or until done. For convection oven, bake 15 minutes at 300 F.
14. If desired, cool; sprinkle with 1 lb (3 1/2 cups) sifted powder sugar or brush out edges with 1 recipe Vanilla Glaze (Recipe No. D 046 00) per 100 servings.

Notes

1. In Step 10, 7 lb (1-No. 10 cn) prepared pie filling, apple, blueberry, cherry or peach, or bakery filling, raspberry, may be used, per 100 servings.

KOLACHES (SWEET DOUGH MIX)

Yield 100   **Portion** 1 Roll

Calories	Carbohydrates	Protein	Fat	Cholesterol	Sodium	Calcium
166 cal	32 g	6 g	3 g	0 mg	325 mg	15 mg

Ingredient	Weight	Measure	Issue
SWEET DOUGH MIX	9 lbs	2 gal 1/8 qts	

| YEAST,ACTIVE,DRY | 3-3/4 oz | 1/2 cup 1 tbsp |
| CHERRY FILLING (PIE FILLING, PREPARED) | 2-3/4 kg | 3 unit |

Method

1. Use sweet dough mix and active dry yeast. Prepare dough according to instructions on container.
2. PUNCH: Let rest 10 minutes. Divide dough into 2 pieces. Shape each piece into a smooth ball; let rest 10 minutes.
3. MAKE UP: Form into a rope 1-1/2 inches in diameter. Cut into 1-1/2 inch pieces. Shape into 2-ounce balls. Place 2 inches apart on greased pans. Flatten out slightly with palm of hand.
4. PROOF: About 30 minutes or until pieces are double in size.
5. Press down center of each piece with back of spoon. Leave a rim about 1/4-inch wide.
6. Fill center of each Kolache with about 1 ounce (2 tbsp) filling. Use 1 recipe Cherry Filling (Recipe No. D 041 01).
7. Brush rim with Egg Wash, Recipe No. D 017 00.
8. PROOF: 20 minutes or until double in size.
9. BAKE: 25 minutes at 350 F. or until done. For convection oven, bake 15 minutes at 300 F.

If desired, cool; sprinkle with 1 lb (3 1/2 cups) sifted powder sugar or brush out edges with 1 recipe Vanilla Glaze (Recipe No. D 046 00) per 100 servings.

Notes

1. In Step 10, 7 lb (1-No. 10 cn) prepared pie filling, apple, blueberry, cherry or peach, or 7 lb 4 oz (7/8-No. 10 cn) bakery filling, raspberry, may be used, per 100 servings.

BRAN MUFFINS

Yield 100   **Portion** 1 Muffin

Calories	Carbohydrates	Protein	Fat	Cholesterol	Sodium	Calcium
173 cal	34 g	3 g	4 g	12 mg	240 mg	110 mg

Ingredient	Weight	Measure Issue
APPLESAUCE,CANNED,SWEETENED	5-1/4 lbs	2 qts 1-3/8 cup
WATER	2-1/8 lbs	1 qts
CEREAL,ALL BRAN,BULK	1-7/8 lbs	2 qts 2 cup
FLOUR,WHEAT,GENERAL PURPOSE	3-5/8 lbs	3 qts 1 cup
SUGAR,GRANULATED	2-1/4 lbs	1 qts 1 cup
BAKING POWDER	4-3/8 oz	1/2 cup 1 tbsp
SALT	3/4 oz	1 tbsp
CINNAMON,GROUND	1/2 oz	2 tbsp
NUTMEG,GROUND	1/8 oz	1/3 tsp
EGGS,WHOLE,FROZEN	9-1/2 oz	1-1/8 cup
EGG WHITES,FROZEN,THAWED	9-1/2 oz	1-1/8 cup
OIL,SALAD	9-5/8 oz	1-1/4 cup
COOKING SPRAY,NONSTICK	2 oz	1/4 cup 1/3 tbsp

Method

1. Mix applesauce with water; add to bran. Let stand for 5 minutes.
2. Sift together flour, sugar, baking powder, salt, cinnamon, and nutmeg into mixer bowl. Batter will be lumpy.
3. Add bran applesauce mixture, eggs, and salad oil or shortening; mix at low speed about 15 seconds; scrape down sides and bottom of mixer bowl. Mix until dry ingredients are moistened, about 15 seconds. DO NOT OVER MIX.

118

4. Lightly spray muffin cup with non-stick cooking spray. Fill each muffin cup 2/3 full.
5. Bake 25 to 30 minutes at 400 F. or until lightly brown.

RAISIN BRAN MUFFINS

Yield 100   **Portion** 1 Muffin

Calories	Carbohydrates	Protein	Fat	Cholesterol	Sodium	Calcium
199 cal	41 g	4 g	4 g	10 mg	240 mg	114 mg

Ingredient	Weight	Measure	Issue
APPLESAUCE,CANNED,SWEETENED	5-1/4 lbs	2 qts 1-3/8 cup	
WATER	2-1/8 lbs	1 qts	
CEREAL,ALL BRAN,BULK	1-7/8 lbs	2 qts 2 cup	
FLOUR,WHEAT,GENERAL PURPOSE	3-5/8 lbs	3 qts 1 cup	
SUGAR,GRANULATED	2-1/4 lbs	1 qts 1 cup	
BAKING POWDER	4-3/8 oz	1/2 cup 1 tbsp	
SALT	3/4 oz	1 tbsp	
CINNAMON,GROUND	1/2 oz	2 tbsp	
NUTMEG,GROUND	1/8 oz	1/3 tsp	
EGGS,WHOLE,FROZEN	8-5/8 oz	1 cup	
EGG WHITES,FROZEN,THAWED	8-1/2 oz	1 cup	
OIL,SALAD	9-5/8 oz	1-1/4 cup	
RAISINS	1-7/8 lbs	1 qts 2 cup	
COOKING SPRAY,NONSTICK	2 oz	1/4 cup 1/3 tbsp	

Method
1. Mix applesauce with water; add to bran. Let stand for 5 minutes.
2. Sift together flour, sugar, baking powder, salt, cinnamon, and nutmeg into mixer bowl. Batter will be lumpy.
3. Add bran applesauce mixture, eggs, and salad oil or shortening; mix at low speed for 15 seconds; scrape down sides and bottom of mixer bowl. Mix until dry ingredients are moistened, about 15 seconds. DO NOT OVER MIX. Fold in raisins.
4. Lightly spray each muffin cup with non-stick cooking spray. Fill each muffin cup 2/3 full.
5. Bake 25 to 30 minutes at 400 F. or until lightly brown.

BLUEBERRY BRAN MUFFINS

Yield 100   **Portion** 1 Muffin

Calories	Carbohydrates	Protein	Fat	Cholesterol	Sodium	Calcium
174 cal	34 g	3 g	4 g	10 mg	239 mg	110 mg

Ingredient	Weight	Measure	Issue
APPLESAUCE,CANNED,SWEETENED	5-1/4 lbs	2 qts 1-3/8 cup	
WATER	2-1/8 lbs	1 qts	
CEREAL,ALL BRAN,BULK	1-7/8 lbs	2 qts 2 cup	
FLOUR,WHEAT,GENERAL PURPOSE	3-5/8 lbs	3 qts 1 cup	
SUGAR,GRANULATED	2-1/4 lbs	1 qts 1 cup	
BAKING POWDER	4-3/8 oz	1/2 cup 1 tbsp	

SALT	3/4 oz	1 tbsp
CINNAMON,GROUND	1/2 oz	2 tbsp
NUTMEG,GROUND	1/8 oz	1/3 tsp
EGGS,WHOLE,FROZEN	8-5/8 oz	1 cup
EGG WHITES,FROZEN,THAWED	8-1/2 oz	1 cup
OIL,SALAD	9-5/8 oz	1-1/4 cup
BLUEBERRIES,FROZEN,UNSWEETENED	10-7/8 lbs	2 cup
COOKING SPRAY,NONSTICK	2 oz	1/4 cup 1/3 tbsp

Method

1. Mix applesauce with water; add to bran. Let stand for 5 minutes.
2. Sift together flour, sugar, baking powder, salt, cinnamon, and nutmeg into mixer bowl. Batter will be lumpy.
3. Add bran applesauce mixture, eggs, and salad oil or shortening; mix at low speed for 15 seconds. DO NOT OVER MIX. Fold in blueberries.
4. Lightly spray each muffin cup with non-stick cooking spray. Fill each muffin cup 2/3 full.
5. Bake 25 to 30 minutes at 400 F. or until lightly brown.

BANANA BRAN MUFFINS

Yield 100   Portion 1 Muffin

Calories	Carbohydrates	Protein	Fat	Cholesterol	Sodium	Calcium
181 cal	36 g	3 g	4 g	10 mg	239 mg	111 mg

Ingredient	Weight	Measure	Issue
APPLESAUCE,CANNED,SWEETENED	5-1/4 lbs	2 qts 1-3/8 cup	
WATER	2-1/8 lbs	1 qts	
CEREAL,ALL BRAN,BULK	1-7/8 lbs	2 qts 2 cup	
FLOUR,WHEAT,GENERAL PURPOSE	3-5/8 lbs	3 qts 1 cup	
SUGAR,GRANULATED	2-1/4 lbs	1 qts 1 cup	
BAKING POWDER	4-3/8 oz	1/2 cup 1 tbsp	
SALT	3/4 oz	1 tbsp	
CINNAMON,GROUND	1/2 oz	2 tbsp	
NUTMEG,GROUND	1/8 oz	1/3 tsp	
EGGS,WHOLE,FROZEN	8-5/8 oz	1 cup	
EGG WHITES,FROZEN,THAWED	8-1/2 oz	1 cup	
OIL,SALAD	9-5/8 oz	1-1/4 cup	
BANANA,FRESH	2 lbs		3-1/8 lbs
COOKING SPRAY,NONSTICK	2 oz	1/4 cup 1/3 tbsp	

Method

1. Mix applesauce with water; add to bran. Let stand for 5 minutes.
2. Sift together flour, sugar, baking powder, salt, cinnamon, and nutmeg into mixer bowl. Batter will be lumpy.
3. Add bran applesauce mixture, eggs, and salad oil or shortening; mix at low speed for 15 seconds; scrape down sides and bottom of mixer bowl. Mix until dry ingredients are moistened, about 15 seconds. DO NOT OVER MIX. Fold bananas into batter.
4. Lightly spray each muffin cup with non-stick cooking spray. Fill each muffin cup 2/3 full.
5. Bake 25 to 30 minutes at 400 F. or until lightly brown.

APRICOT BRAN MUFFINS

Yield 100   **Portion** 1 Muffin

Calories	Carbohydrates	Protein	Fat	Cholesterol	Sodium	Calcium
199 cal	41 g	4 g	4 g	10 mg	240 mg	114 mg

Ingredient	Weight	Measure	Issue
APPLESAUCE,CANNED,SWEETENED	5-1/4 lbs	2 qts 1-3/8 cup	
WATER	2-1/8 lbs	1 qts	
CEREAL,ALL BRAN,BULK	1-7/8 lbs	2 qts 2 cup	
FLOUR,WHEAT,GENERAL PURPOSE	3-5/8 lbs	3 qts 1 cup	
SUGAR,GRANULATED	2-1/4 lbs	1 qts 1 cup	
BAKING POWDER	4-3/8 oz	1/2 cup 1 tbsp	
SALT	3/4 oz	1 tbsp	
CINNAMON,GROUND	1/2 oz	2 tbsp	
NUTMEG,GROUND	1/8 oz	1/3 tsp	
EGGS,WHOLE,FROZEN	8-5/8 oz	1 cup	
EGG WHITES,FROZEN,THAWED	8-1/2 oz	1 cup	
OIL,SALAD	9-5/8 oz	1-1/4 cup	
APRICOT,DRIED,HALVES,PITTED	1-5/8 lbs	1 qts 2 cup	
COOKING SPRAY,NONSTICK	2 oz	1/4 cup 1/3 tbsp	

Method

1. Mix applesauce with water; add to bran. Let stand for 5 minutes.
2. Sift together flour, sugar, baking powder, salt, cinnamon, and nutmeg into mixer bowl. Batter will be lumpy.
3. Add bran applesauce mixture, eggs, and salad oil or shortening; mix at low speed for 15 seconds; scrape down sides and bottom of mixer bowl. Mix until dry ingredients are moistened, about 15 seconds. DO NOT OVER MIX. Fold in dried, chopped apricots.
4. Lightly spray each muffin cup with non-stick cooking spray. Fill each muffin cup 2/3 full.
5. Bake 25 to 30 minutes at 400 F. or until lightly brown.

CRANBERRY BRAN MUFFINS

Yield 100   **Portion** 1 Muffin

Calories	Carbohydrates	Protein	Fat	Cholesterol	Sodium	Calcium
177 cal	35 g	3 g	4 g	10 mg	239 mg	111 mg

Ingredient	Weight	Measure	Issue
APPLESAUCE,CANNED,SWEETENED	5-1/4 lbs	2 qts 1-3/8 cup	
WATER	2-1/8 lbs	1 qts	
CEREAL,ALL BRAN,BULK	1-7/8 lbs	2 qts 2 cup	
FLOUR,WHEAT,GENERAL PURPOSE	3-5/8 lbs	3 qts 1 cup	
SUGAR,GRANULATED	2-1/4 lbs	1 qts 1 cup	
BAKING POWDER	4-3/8 oz	1/2 cup 1 tbsp	
SALT	3/4 oz	1 tbsp	
CINNAMON,GROUND	1/2 oz	2 tbsp	
NUTMEG,GROUND	1/8 oz	1/3 tsp	
EGGS,WHOLE,FROZEN	8-5/8 oz	1 cup	
EGG WHITES,FROZEN,THAWED	8-1/2 oz	1 cup	
OIL,SALAD	9-5/8 oz	1-1/4 cup	

CRANBERRIES,FRESH	1-3/4 lbs	2 qts 3/8 cup	1-7/8lbs
COOKING SPRAY,NONSTICK	2 oz	1/4 cup	
		1/3 tbsp	

Method

1. Mix applesauce with water; add to bran. Let stand for 5 minutes.
2. Sift together flour, sugar, baking powder, salt, cinnamon, and nutmeg into mixer bowl. Batter will be lumpy.
3. Add bran applesauce mixture, eggs and salad oil or shortening; mix at low speed about 15 seconds. DO NOT OVER MIX. Fold cranberries into batter.
4. Lightly spray each muffin cup with non-stick cooking spray. Fill each muffin cup 2/3 full.
5. Bake 25 to 30 minutes at 400 F. or until lightly brown.

MUFFINS

Yield 100   **Portion** 1 Muffin

Calories	Carbohydrates	Protein	Fat	Cholesterol	Sodium	Calcium
178 cal	30 g	4 g	5 g	34 mg	204 mg	86 mg

Ingredient	Weight	Measure	Issue
FLOUR,WHEAT,GENERAL PURPOSE	5 lbs	1 gal 1/2 qts	
SUGAR,GRANULATED	2-1/2 lbs	1 qts 1-5/8 cup	
MILK,NONFAT,DRY	3-5/8 oz	1-1/2 cup	
BAKING POWDER	3-7/8 oz	1/2 cup	
SALT	5/8 oz	1 tbsp	
WATER,WARM	3-2/3 lbs	1 qts 3 cup	
EGGS,WHOLE,FROZEN	1-3/4 lbs	3-1/4 cup	
APPLESAUCE,CANNED,UNSWEETENED	1-5/8 lbs	3 cup	
OIL,SALAD	11-1/2 oz	1-1/2 cup	
COOKING SPRAY,NONSTICK	1-1/2 oz	3 tbsp	

Method

1. In mixer bowl, sift together flour, sugar, milk, baking powder and salt.
2. Add warm water, eggs, applesauce, and salad oil; mix at low speed until dry ingredients are moistened about 15 seconds; scrape down sides and bottom of mixer bowl; continue to mix at low speed another 15 seconds. DO NOT OVER MIX. Batter will be lumpy.
3. Lightly spray muffin cups with non-stick cooking spray. Fill each muffin cup 2/3 full.
4. Using a convection oven, bake at 350 F. 23 to 26 minutes with open vent, fan turned off the first 10 minutes, and then low fan. Remove muffins from oven and let cool.

BLUEBERRY MUFFINS

Yield 100   **Portion** 1 Muffin

Calories	Carbohydrates	Protein	Fat	Cholesterol	Sodium	Calcium
187 cal	33 g	4 g	5 g	34 mg	204 mg	87 mg

Ingredient	Weight	Measure	Issue
FLOUR,WHEAT,GENERAL PURPOSE	5 lbs	1 gal 1/2 qts	
SUGAR,GRANULATED	2-1/2 lbs	1 qts 1-5/8 cup	
MILK,NONFAT,DRY	3-5/8 oz	1-1/2 cup	

BAKING POWDER	3-7/8 oz	1/2 cup
SALT	5/8 oz	1 tbsp
WATER,WARM	3-2/3 lbs	1 qts 3 cup
EGGS,WHOLE,FROZEN	1-3/4 lbs	3-1/4 cup
APPLESAUCE,CANNED,UNSWEETENED	1-5/8 lbs	3 cup
OIL,SALAD	11-1/2 oz	1-1/2 cup
BLUEBERRIES,CANNED,DRAINED	2-1/4 lbs	1 qts
COOKING SPRAY,NONSTICK	1-1/2 oz	3 tbsp

Method
1. In mixer bowl, sift together flour, sugar, milk, baking powder and salt.
2. Add warm water, eggs, applesauce and salad oil; mix at low speed until dry ingredients are moistened about 15 seconds; scrape down sides and bottom of mixer bowl; continue to mix at low speed another 15 seconds. DO NOT OVER MIX. Batter will be lumpy.
3. Rinse blueberries, drain well. Fold into batter.
4. Lightly spray muffin cups with non-stick cooking spray. Fill each muffin cup 2/3 full.
5. Using a convection oven, bake at 350 F. 23 to 26 minutes with open vent, fan turned off the first 10 minutes, and then low fan. Remove muffins from oven and let cool. NOTES: 1. In Step 3, 2 lb A.P. (1-1/2 quarts) blueberries, frozen, IQF, thawed, may be subsitituted.

RAISIN MUFFINS

Yield 100   **Portion** 1 Muffin

Calories	Carbohydrates	Protein	Fat	Cholesterol	Sodium	Calcium
204 cal	37 g	4 g	5 g	34 mg	205 mg	90 mg

Ingredient	Weight	Measure	Issue
FLOUR,WHEAT,GENERAL PURPOSE	5 lbs	1 gal 1/2 qts	
SUGAR,GRANULATED	2-1/2 lbs	1 qts 1-5/8 cup	
MILK,NONFAT,DRY	3-5/8 oz	1-1/2 cup	
BAKING POWDER	3-7/8 oz	1/2 cup	
SALT	5/8 oz	1 tbsp	
WATER,WARM	3-2/3 lbs	1 qts 3 cup	
EGGS,WHOLE,FROZEN	1-3/4 lbs	3-1/4 cup	
APPLESAUCE,CANNED,UNSWEETENED	1-5/8 lbs	3 cup	
RAISINS	1-7/8 lbs	1 qts 2 cup	
OIL,SALAD	11-1/2 oz	1-1/2 cup	
COOKING SPRAY,NONSTICK	1-1/2 oz	3 tbsp	

Method
1. In mixer bowl, sift together flour, sugar, milk, baking powder and salt.
2. Add warm water, eggs, applesauce, salad oil and raisins; mix at low speed until dry ingredients are moistened about 15 seconds; scrape down sides and bottom of mixer bowl; continue to mix at low speed another 15 seconds. DO NOT OVER MIX. Batter will be lumpy.
3. Lightly spray each muffin cup with non-stick cooking spray. Fill each muffin cup 2/3 full.
4. Using a convection oven, bake at 350 F. 23 to 26 minutes with open vent, fan turned off the first 10 minutes, and then low fan. Remove muffins from oven and let cool.

BANANA MUFFINS

Yield 100   **Portion** 1 Muffin

Calories	Carbohydrates	Protein	Fat	Cholesterol	Sodium	Calcium
186 cal	32 g	4 g	5 g	34 mg	204 mg	87 mg

Ingredient	Weight	Measure	Issue
FLOUR,WHEAT,GENERAL PURPOSE	5 lbs	1 gal 1/2 qts	
SUGAR,GRANULATED	2-1/2 lbs	1 qts 1-5/8 cup	
MILK,NONFAT,DRY	3-5/8 oz	1-1/2 cup	
BAKING POWDER	3-7/8 oz	1/2 cup	
SALT	5/8 oz	1 tbsp	
WATER,WARM	3-2/3 lbs	1 qts 3 cup	
EGGS,WHOLE,FROZEN	1-3/4 lbs	3-1/4 cup	
APPLESAUCE,CANNED,UNSWEETENED	1-5/8 lbs	3 cup	
OIL,SALAD	11-1/2 oz	1-1/2 cup	
BANANA,FRESH,MASHED	2 lbs	1 qts	3-1/8lbs
COOKING SPRAY,NONSTICK	1-1/2 oz	3 tbsp	

Method

1. In mixer bowl, sift together flour, sugar, milk, baking powder and salt.
2. Add warm water, eggs, applesauce, and salad oil; mix at low speed until dry ingredients are moistened about 15 seconds; scrape down sides and bottom of mixer bowl; continue to mix at low speed another 15 seconds. DO NOT OVER MIX. Batter will be lumpy.
3. Add mashed bananas to batter; mix at low speed another 15 seconds until blended.
4. Lightly spray muffin cups with non-stick cooking spray. Fill each muffin cup 2/3 full.
5. Using a convection oven, bake at 350 F. 23 to 26 minutes with open vent, fan turned off the first 10 minutes, and then low fan. Remove muffins from oven and let cool.

APPLE MUFFINS

Yield 100   **Portion** 1 Muffin

Calories	Carbohydrates	Protein	Fat	Cholesterol	Sodium	Calcium
191 cal	34 g	4 g	5 g	34 mg	204 mg	87 mg

Ingredient	Weight	Measure	Issue
FLOUR,WHEAT,GENERAL PURPOSE	5 lbs	1 gal 1/2 qts	
SUGAR,GRANULATED	2-1/2 lbs	1 qts 1-5/8 cup	
MILK,NONFAT,DRY	3-5/8 oz	1-1/2 cup	
BAKING POWDER	3-7/8 oz	1/2 cup	
SALT	5/8 oz	1 tbsp	
WATER,WARM	3-2/3 lbs	1 qts 3 cup	
EGGS,WHOLE,FROZEN	1-3/4 lbs	3-1/4 cup	
APPLESAUCE,CANNED,UNSWEETENED	1-5/8 lbs	3 cup	
OIL,SALAD	11-1/2 oz	1-1/2 cup	
APPLES,FRESH,MEDIUM,PEELED,CORED,CHOPPED	2 lbs	1qts 3-1/4cup	2-1/2lbs
SUGAR,GRANULATED	7 oz	1 cup	
CINNAMON,GROUND	1/8 oz	1/3 tsp	
COOKING SPRAY,NONSTICK	1-1/2 oz	3 tbsp	

Method

1. In mixer bowl sift together flour, sugar, milk, baking powder and salt.
2. Add warm water, eggs, applesauce and salad oil; mix at low speed until dry ingredients are moistened about 15 seconds; scrape down sides and bottom of mixer bowl; continue to mix at low speed another 15 seconds. DO NOT OVERMIX. Batter will be lumpy.
3. Fold apples into batter.
4. Mix sugar and cinnamon; sprinkle 1/2 teaspoon of cinnamon sugar mixture over each muffin.
5. Lightly spray muffin cups with non-stick cooking spray. Fill each muffin cup 2/3 full.
6. Using a convection oven, bake 23 to 26 minutes with open vent, fan turned off the first 10 minutes, and then low fan. Remove muffins from oven and let cool.

Notes

1. In Step 3, 2 lb 4 oz A.P. (1 qt-1/3 No. 10 cn) drained, chopped apple slices may be substituted.

CINNAMON CRUMB TOP MUFFINS

Yield 100   **Portion** 1 Muffin

Calories	Carbohydrates	Protein	Fat	Cholesterol	Sodium	Calcium
195 cal	33 g	4 g	5 g	36 mg	212 mg	90 mg

Ingredient	Weight	Measure	Issue
FLOUR,WHEAT,GENERAL PURPOSE	5 lbs	1 gal 1/2 qts	
SUGAR,GRANULATED	2-1/2 lbs	1 qts 1-5/8 cup	
MILK,NONFAT,DRY	3-5/8 oz	1-1/2 cup	
BAKING POWDER	3-7/8 oz	1/2 cup	
SALT	5/8 oz	1 tbsp	
WATER,WARM	3-2/3 lbs	1 qts 3 cup	
EGGS,WHOLE,FROZEN	1-3/4 lbs	3-1/4 cup	
APPLESAUCE,CANNED,UNSWEETENED	1-5/8 lbs	3 cup	
OIL,SALAD	11-1/2 oz	1-1/2 cup	
COOKING SPRAY,NONSTICK	1-1/2 oz	3 tbsp	
SUGAR,BROWN,PACKED	9 oz	1-3/4 cup	
BUTTER	3 oz	1/4 cup 2-1/3 tbsp	
FLOUR,WHEAT,GENERAL PURPOSE	1-2/3 oz	1/4 cup 2-1/3 tbsp	
CINNAMON,GROUND	1/2 oz	2 tbsp	

Method

1. In mixer bowl sift together flour, sugar, milk, baking powder and salt.
2. Add warm water, eggs, applesauce and salad oil; mix at low speed until dry ingredients are moistened about 15 seconds; scrape down sides and bottom of mixer bowl; continue to mix at low speed another 15 seconds. DO NOT OVERMIX. Batter will be lumpy.
3. Lightly spray muffin cups with non-stick cooking spray. Fill each muffin cup 2/3 full.
4. Mix brown sugar, butter or margarine, flour and cinnamon until mixture is crumbly. Sprinkle 1 teaspoon mixture on top of each muffin.
5. Using a convection oven, bake at 350 F. 23 to 26 minutes with open vent, fan turned on for the first 10 minutes, and then on low fan. Remove muffins from oven and cool.

CRANBERRY MUFFINS

Yield 100   **Portion** 1 Muffin

Calories	Carbohydrates	Protein	Fat	Cholesterol	Sodium	Calcium
182 cal	32 g	4 g	5 g	34 mg	204 mg	87 mg

Ingredient	Weight	Measure	Issue
FLOUR,WHEAT,GENERAL PURPOSE	5 lbs	1 gal 1/2 qts	
SUGAR,GRANULATED	2-1/2 lbs	1 qts 1-5/8 cup	
MILK,NONFAT,DRY	3-5/8 oz	1-1/2 cup	
BAKING POWDER	3-7/8 oz	1/2 cup	
SALT	5/8 oz	1 tbsp	
WATER,WARM	3-2/3 lbs	1 qts 3 cup	
EGGS,WHOLE,FROZEN	1-3/4 lbs	3-1/4 cup	
APPLESAUCE,CANNED,UNSWEETENED	1-5/8 lbs	3 cup	
OIL,SALAD	11-1/2 oz	1-1/2 cup	
CRANBERRIES,FRESH	2 lbs	2qts 1-1/2cup	3-1/8lbs
COOKING SPRAY,NONSTICK	1-1/2 oz	3 tbsp	

Method

1. In mixer bowl, sift together flour, sugar, milk, baking powder and salt.
2. Add warm water, eggs, applesauce, and salad oil; mix at low speed until dry ingredients are moistened about 15 seconds; scrape down sides and bottom of mixer bowl; continue to mix at low speed another 15 seconds. DO NOT OVER MIX. Batter will be lumpy.
3. Fold cranberries into batter.
4. Lightly spray muffin cups with non-stick cooking spray. Fill each muffin cup 2/3 full.
5. Using a convection oven, bake at 350 F. 23 to 26 minutes with open vent, fan turned off the first 10 minutes, and then low fan. Remove muffins from oven and let cool.

Notes

1. In Step 3, 2 lb 1 oz A.P. (8-1/3 cup) cranberries, brozen, IQF, thawed, may be substituted.

DATE MUFFINS

Yield 100   **Portion** 1 Muffin

Calories	Carbohydrates	Protein	Fat	Cholesterol	Sodium	Calcium
196 cal	35 g	4 g	5 g	34 mg	204 mg	88 mg

Ingredient	Weight	Measure	Issue
FLOUR,WHEAT,GENERAL PURPOSE	5 lbs	1 gal 1/2 qts	
SUGAR,GRANULATED	2-1/2 lbs	1 qts 1-5/8 cup	
MILK,NONFAT,DRY	3-5/8 oz	1-1/2 cup	
BAKING POWDER	3-7/8 oz	1/2 cup	
SALT	5/8 oz	1 tbsp	
WATER,WARM	3-2/3 lbs	1 qts 3 cup	
EGGS,WHOLE,FROZEN	1-3/4 lbs	3-1/4 cup	
APPLESAUCE,CANNED,UNSWEETENED	1-5/8 lbs	3 cup	
OIL,SALAD	11-1/2 oz	1-1/2 cup	
DATES,DRIED,PITTED,CHOPPED	1-1/2 lbs		
COOKING SPRAY,NONSTICK	1-1/2 oz	3 tbsp	

Method

1. In mixer bowl, sift together flour, sugar, milk, baking powder and salt.
2. Add warm water, eggs, applesauce, salad oil and dates; mix at low speed until dry ingredients are moistened about 15 seconds; scrape down sides and bottom of mixer bowl; continue to mix at low speed another 15 seconds. DO NOT OVER MIX. Batter will be lumpy.
3. Add mashed bananas to batter; mix at low speed another 15 seconds until blended.

4. Lightly spray muffin cups with non-stick cooking spray. Fill each muffin cup 2/3 full.
5. Using a convection oven, bake at 350 F. 23 to 26 minutes with open vent, fan turned off the first 10 minutes, and then low fan. Remove muffins from oven and let cool.

NUT MUFFINS

Yield 100   **Portion** 1 Muffin

Calories	Carbohydrates	Protein	Fat	Cholesterol	Sodium	Calcium
272 cal	34 g	5 g	14 g	39 mg	169 mg	67 mg

Ingredient	Weight	Measure	Issue
FLOUR,WHEAT,GENERAL PURPOSE	5-1/2 lbs	1 gal 1 qts	
SUGAR,GRANULATED	2-1/4 lbs	1 qts 1 cup	
MILK,NONFAT,DRY	1-3/4 oz	3/4 cup	
BAKING POWDER	2-3/4 oz	1/4 cup 2 tbsp	
SALT	5/8 oz	1 tbsp	
EGGS,WHOLE,FROZEN	2 lbs	3-3/4 cup	
APPLESAUCE,CANNED,UNSWEETENED	1-5/8 lbs	3 cup	
WATER,WARM	2-1/8 lbs	1 qts	
OIL,SALAD	11-1/2 oz	1-1/2 cup	
PECANS,CHOPPED	3 lbs		
COOKING SPRAY,NONSTICK	2 oz	1/4 cup 1/3 tbsp	

Method
1. In mixer bowl, sift together flour, sugar, milk, baking powder and salt.
2. Add warm water, eggs, applesauce, salad oil and pecans; mix at low speed until dry ingredients are moistened about 15 seconds; scrape down sides and bottom of mixer bowl; continue to mix at low speed another 15 seconds. DO NOT OVER MIX. Batter will be lumpy.
3. Lightly spray each muffin cup with non-stick cooking spray. Fill each muffin cup 2/3 full.
4. Using a convection oven, bake at 350 F. 23 to 26 minutes with open vent, fan turned off the first 10 minutes, and then low fan. Remove muffins from oven and let cool.

OATMEAL RAISIN MUFFINS

Yield 100   **Portion** 1 Muffin

Calories	Carbohydrates	Protein	Fat	Cholesterol	Sodium	Calcium
216 cal	38 g	5 g	5 g	34 mg	205 mg	95 mg

Ingredient	Weight	Measure	Issue
FLOUR,WHEAT,GENERAL PURPOSE	3-1/2 lbs	3 qts 3/4 cup	
SUGAR,GRANULATED	2-1/2 lbs	1 qts 1-5/8 cup	
MILK,NONFAT,DRY	3-5/8 oz	1-1/2 cup	
BAKING POWDER	3-7/8 oz	1/2 cup	
SALT	5/8 oz	1 tbsp	
CINNAMON,GROUND	1/4 oz	1 tbsp	
CEREAL,OATMEAL,ROLLED	2 lbs	1 qts 1-3/4 cup	
RAISINS	1-7/8 lbs	1 qts 2 cup	
WATER,WARM	3-2/3 lbs	1 qts 3 cup	
EGGS,WHOLE,FROZEN	1-3/4 lbs	3-1/4 cup	
APPLESAUCE,CANNED,UNSWEETENED	1-5/8 lbs	3 cup	

OIL,SALAD	11-1/2 oz	1-1/2 cup
EXTRACT,VANILLA	1-7/8 oz	1/4 cup 1/3 tbsp
COOKING SPRAY,NONSTICK	1-1/2 oz	3 tbsp

Method

1. In mixer bowl, sift together flour, sugar, milk, baking powder and salt.
2. Add warm water, eggs, applesauce, salad oil and vanilla; mix at low speed until dry ingredients are moistened about 15 seconds; scrape down sides and bottom of mixer bowl; continue to mix at low speed another 15 seconds. DO NOT OVER MIX. Batter will be lumpy.
3. Lightly spray muffin cups with non-stick cooking spray. Fill each muffin cup 2/3 full.
4. Using a convection oven, bake at 350 F. 23 to 26 minutes with open vent, fan turned off the first 10 minutes, and then low fan. Remove muffins from oven and let cool.

BANANA BREAD

Yield 100   **Portion** 1 Slice

Calories	Carbohydrates	Protein	Fat	Cholesterol	Sodium	Calcium
258 cal	33 g	6 g	12 g	37 mg	140 mg	64 mg

Ingredient	Weight	Measure	Issue
SHORTENING	1 lbs	1-1/8 cup	
SUGAR,GRANULATED	2-2/3 lbs	1 qts 2 cup	
EGGS,WHOLE,FROZEN	1-7/8 lbs	3-1/2 cup	
APPLESAUCE,CANNED,SWEETENED	5-1/4 lbs	1 cup	
BANANA,FRESH,MASHED	2-5/8 lbs	2 qts 2-5/8 cup	
NUTS,UNSALTED,CHOPPED,COARSELY	3-7/8 lbs	2 qts	
FLOUR,WHEAT,GENERAL PURPOSE	2-2/3 oz	3 qts 2 cup	
BAKING POWDER	3/8 oz	1/4 cup 2 tbsp	
SALT	2 oz	1/3 tsp	
COOKING SPRAY,NONSTICK	8-1/8 lbs	1/4 cup 1/3 tbsp	

Method

1. Cream shortening and sugar in mixer bowl at medium speed 2 minutes until light and fluffy.
2. Add eggs and applesauce to mixture. Mix at medium speed 1 minute.
3. Add bananas and nuts to egg mixture. Mix at medium speed until blended.
4. Sift together flour, baking powder and salt.
5. Add dry ingredients to banana mixture; beat at low speed about 1/2 minute. Continue beating 1/2 minute longer or until blended. DO NOT OVER MIX.
6. Lightly spray each pan with non-stick cooking spray. Pour about 2 quarts of batter into each sprayed and floured loaf pan. Spread batter evenly.
7. Using a convection oven, bake at 325 F. for 70 to 75 minutes or until done on low fan, open vent.
8. Let bread cool in pans 5 minutes; then remove from pan and place on wire rack to cool completely. To enhance flavor and moistness, product may be prepared in advance. CCP: Refrigerate at 41 F. or lower overnight.

HARD ROLLS

Yield 100   **Portion** 2 Rolls

Calories	Carbohydrates	Protein	Fat	Cholesterol	Sodium	Calcium
259 cal	49 g	8 g	3 g	0 mg	425 mg	11 mg

Ingredient	Weight	Measure	Issue
YEAST,ACTIVE,DRY	2-1/2 oz	1/4 cup 2-1/3 tbsp	
WATER,WARM	1-2/3 lbs	3-1/4 cup	
WATER,COLD	6-1/4 lbs	3 qts	
EGG WHITES	8-1/2 oz	1 cup	
SUGAR,GRANULATED	3-1/2 oz	1/2 cup	
SALT	3-3/4 oz	1/4 cup 2-1/3 tbsp	
SHORTENING,SOFTENED	4-1/8 oz	1/2 cup 1 tbsp	
FLOUR,WHEAT,BREAD	14-1/2 lbs	3 gal	
COOKING SPRAY,NONSTICK	2 oz	1/4 cup 1/3 tbsp	

Method

1. Sprinkle yeast over water. DO NOT USE TEMPERATURES ABOVE 110 F. Mix well. Let stand 5 minutes; stir.
2. Place water, egg whites, sugar, salt, shortening, and flour in mixer bowl. Add yeast solution.
3. Using dough hook, mix at low speed 1 minute or until all flour mixture is incorporated into liquid. Continue mixing at medium speed 10 minutes or until dough is smooth and elastic. Dough temperature should be between 78 F. to 82 F.
4. FERMENT: Cover. Set in warm place (80 F.) about 1-1/2 hours or until double in bulk.
5. PUNCH: Divide dough into 8 2-1/2 pound pieces. Shape each piece into a smooth ball; let rest 10 to 20 minutes.
6. Roll each piece into a long rope, about 25 inches, of uniform diameter. Cut rope into pieces about 1-inch thick, weighing 1-1/2 ounces each.
7. MAKE-UP: Lightly spray sheet pans with non-stick cooking spray. Place rolls on sheet pans in rows 5 by 7 so rolls do not touch each other during proofing or baking.
8. PROOF: At 90 F. to 100 F. until double in bulk. Brush with 1 recipe hot Cornstarch Wash, Recipe No. D 040 00.
9. BAKE: 25 to 30 minutes at 400 F. or in 350 F. convection oven 15 minutes or until golden brown, on high fan, open vent. Brush with hot Cornstarch Wash, Recipe No. D 040 00 immediately after removal from oven.

HOT ROLLS

Yield 100   Portion 2 Rolls

Calories	Carbohydrates	Protein	Fat	Cholesterol	Sodium	Calcium
325 cal	56 g	9 g	7 g	0 mg	358 mg	26 mg

Ingredient	Weight	Measure	Issue
YEAST,ACTIVE,DRY	4-1/2 oz	1/2 cup 2-2/3 tbsp	
WATER,WARM	1-7/8 lbs	3-1/2 cup	
WATER,COLD	5-3/4 lbs	2 qts 3 cup	
SUGAR,GRANULATED	1-1/2 lbs	3-1/2 cup	
SALT	3-1/8 oz	1/4 cup 1-1/3 tbsp	
FLOUR,WHEAT,BREAD	14-1/2 lbs	3 gal	
MILK,NONFAT,DRY	4-1/4 oz	1-3/4 cup	
SHORTENING,SOFTENED	1-1/4 lbs	2-3/4 cup	
COOKING SPRAY,NONSTICK	1 oz	2 tbsp	

Method

1. Sprinkle yeast over water. DO NOT USE TEMPERATURES ABOVE 110 F. Mix well. Let stand 5 minutes; stir.
2. Place cold water in mixer bowl; add sugar and salt; stir until dissolved. Add yeast solution.
3. Combine flour and milk; add to liquid solution. Using dough hook, mix at low speed 1 minute or until flour mixture is incorporated into liquid.
4. Add shortening; mix at medium speed 10 minutes or until dough is smooth and elastic. Dough temperature should be between 78 F. to 82 F.
5. FERMENT: Cover. Set in warm place, about 80 F., 1-1/2 hours or until double in size.
6. PUNCH: Divide dough into 8 2 lb 14 oz pieces. MAKEUP: Shape each piece into a smooth ball; let rest 10 to 20 minutes.
7. Roll each piece into a long rope, about 32 inches, of uniform diameter. Cut rope into 25 1-3/4 oz pieces about 1-1/4 inch long. Place rolls on a lightly sprayed sheet pan.
8. PROOF: At 90 F. about 1 hour or until double in bulk.
9. BAKE: Using a 350 F. convection oven, bake for 10 to 15 minutes or until golden brown, on high fan, open vent.

HOT ROLLS (BROWN AND SERVE)

Yield 100   **Portion** 2 Rolls

Calories	Carbohydrates	Protein	Fat	Cholesterol	Sodium	Calcium
325 cal	56 g	9 g	7 g	0 mg	358 mg	26 mg

Ingredient	Weight	Measure	Issue
YEAST,ACTIVE,DRY	4-1/2 oz	1/2 cup 2-2/3 tbsp	
WATER,WARM	1-7/8 lbs	3-1/2 cup	
WATER,COLD	5-3/4 lbs	2 qts 3 cup	
SUGAR,GRANULATED	1-1/2 lbs	3-1/2 cup	
SALT	3-1/8 oz	1/4 cup 1-1/3 tbsp	
FLOUR,WHEAT,BREAD	14-1/2 lbs	3 gal	
MILK,NONFAT,DRY	4-1/4 oz	1-3/4 cup	
SHORTENING,SOFTENED	1-1/4 lbs	2-3/4 cup	
COOKING SPRAY,NONSTICK	1 oz	2 tbsp	

Method

1. Sprinkle yeast over water. DO NOT USE TEMPERATURES ABOVE 110 F. Mix well. Let stand 5 minutes; stir.
2. Place cold water in mixer bowl; add sugar and salt; stir until dissolved. Add yeast solution.
3. Combine flour and milk; add to liquid solution. Using dough hook, mix at low speed 1 minute or until flour mixture is incorporated into liquid.
4. Add shortening; mix at medium speed 10 minutes or until dough is smooth and elastic. Dough temperature should be between 78 F. to 82 F.
5. FERMENT: Cover. Set in warm place, about 80 F., 1-1/2 hours or until double in size.
6. PUNCH: Divide dough into 8 2 lb 14 oz pieces. Shape each piece into a smooth ball; let rest 10 to 20 minutes.
7. Roll each piece into a long rope, about 32 inches, of uniform diameter about 2 inches thick. Cut rope into 25 1-3/4 oz pieces about 1-1/4 inch long.
8. MAKEUP: Shape dough pieces into balls by rolling with a circular motion. Lightly spray sheet pans with non-stick cooking spray.
9. PROOF: At 90 F. about 30 minutes or until double in size.

10. PREBAKE: 25 minutes at 325 F. or in 300 F. convection oven for 12 to 15 minutes or until rolls begin to brown on low fan, open vent.
11. Cool on pans; wrap in aluminum foil. Refrigerate at 40 F. for up to 2 days.
12. BAKE: Bring covered rolls to room temperature about 1 hour before baking. Finish baking in 350 F. convection oven about 10 to 12 minutes or until golden brown on high fan, open vent.

HOT ROLLS (ROLL MIX)

Yield 100   Portion 1 Slice

Calories	Carbohydrates	Protein	Fat	Cholesterol	Sodium	Calcium
264 cal	48 g	8 g	5 g	0 mg	416 mg	44 mg

Ingredient	Weight	Measure	Issue
ROLL,MIX	15 lbs		
YEAST,ACTIVE,DRY	6-3/4 oz	1 cup	
WATER	1-3/4 lbs	3-3/8 cup	

Method
1. Prepare dough according to instructions on container.
2. PUNCH: Divide dough into 8-2 lb 14 oz pieces. Shape each piece into a smooth ball; let rest 10 to 20 minutes.
3. Roll each piece into a long rope, about 32 inches, of uniform diameter about 2 inches thick. Cut rope into 25 1-3/4 oz pieces about 1-1/4 inch long.
4. MAKE-UP: Shape each piece into a smooth ball; let rest 10 to 20 minutes.
5. PROOF: At 90 F. about 1 hour or until double in bulk.
6. BAKE: 15 to 20 minutes at 400 F. or in 350 F. convection oven for 10 to 15 minutes or until golden brown, on high fan, open vent.

OATMEAL ROLLS

Yield 100   Portion 2 Rolls

Calories	Carbohydrates	Protein	Fat	Cholesterol	Sodium	Calcium
300 cal	46 g	8 g	9 g	0 mg	358 mg	28 mg

Ingredient	Weight	Measure	Issue
YEAST,ACTIVE,DRY	4-1/2 oz	1/2 cup 2-2/3 tbsp	
WATER,WARM	1-7/8 lbs	3-1/2 cup	
WATER,COLD	5-3/4 lbs	2 qts 3 cup	
SUGAR,GRANULATED	1-1/2 lbs	3-1/2 cup	
SALT	3-1/8 oz	1/4 cup 1-1/3 tbsp	
FLOUR,WHEAT,BREAD	9-2/3 lbs	2 gal	
CEREAL,OATMEAL,ROLLED	2 lbs	1 qts 2 cup	
MILK,NONFAT,DRY	4-1/4 oz	1-3/4 cup	
SHORTENING,SOFTENED	1-2/3 lbs	3-3/4 cup	
COOKING SPRAY,NONSTICK	1 oz	2 tbsp	

Method
1. Sprinkle yeast over water. DO NOT USE TEMPERATURES ABOVE 110 F. Mix well. Let stand 5 minutes; stir.
2. Place cold water in mixer bowl; add sugar and salt; stir until dissolved. Add yeast solution.

3. Combine flour, rolled oats and milk; add to liquid solution. Using dough hook, mix at low speed 1 minute or until flour mixture is incorporated into liquid.
4. Add shortening; mix at medium speed 10 minutes or until dough is smooth and elastic. Dough temperature should be between 78 F. to 82 F.
5. FERMENT: Cover. Set in warm place (80 F.) 1-1/2 hours or until double in size.
6. PUNCH: Divide dough into 8 2 lb 14 oz pieces. Shape each piece into a smooth ball; let rest 10 to 20 minutes.
7. Roll each piece into a long rope, about 32 inches, of uniform diameter about 2 inches thick. Cut rope into 25 1-3/4 oz pieces about 1-1/4 inches long.
8. MAKE-UP: Shape dough pieces into balls rolling with a circular motion on a worktable. Place rolls on lightly sprayed sheet pans.
9. PROOF: At 90 F. about 1 hour or until double in bulk.

BAKE: Using a 350 F. convection oven, bake 10 to 12 minutes on high fan, open vent.

CLOVERLEAF OR TWIN ROLLS

Yield 100   **Portion** 2 Rolls

Calories	Carbohydrates	Protein	Fat	Cholesterol	Sodium	Calcium
357 cal	56 g	9 g	11 g	5 mg	377 mg	27 mg

Ingredient	Weight	Measure Issue
YEAST,ACTIVE,DRY	4-1/2 oz	1/2 cup 2-2/3 tbsp
WATER,WARM	1-7/8 lbs	3-1/2 cup
WATER,COLD	5-3/4 lbs	2 qts 3 cup
SUGAR,GRANULATED	1-1/2 lbs	3-1/2 cup
SALT	3-1/8 oz	1/4 cup 1-1/3 tbsp
FLOUR,WHEAT,BREAD	14-1/2 lbs	3 gal
MILK,NONFAT,DRY	4-1/4 oz	1-3/4 cup
SHORTENING,SOFTENED	1-2/3 lbs	3-3/4 cup
BUTTER,MELTED	4 oz	1/2 cup
BUTTER,MELTED	4 oz	1/2 cup

Method
1. Sprinkle yeast over water. DO NOT USE TEMPERATURES ABOVE 110 F. Mix well. Let stand 5 minutes; stir.
2. Place water in mixer bowl; add sugar and salt; stir until dissolved. Add yeast solution.
3. Combine flour and milk; add to liquid solution. Using dough hook, mix at low speed 1 minute until flour mixture is incorporated into liquid.
4. Add shortening; mix at medium speed 10 minutes or until dough is smooth and elastic. Dough temperature should be between 78 F. to 82 F.
5. FERMENT: Cover. Set in warm place (80 F.) for 1-1/2 hours or until double in bulk.
6. PUNCH: Divide dough into 8 2 lb 14 oz pieces. Shape each piece into a smooth ball; let rest 10 to 20 minutes.
7. Roll each piece into a long rope, about 32 inches, of uniform diameter about 2 inches thick. Cut rope into 25 1-3/4 oz pieces about 1-1/4 inch long.
8. Divide each dough piece into thirds for cloverleaf rolls or in halves for twin rolls.
9. Shape into balls by rolling with a circular motion on work table.
10. Place in greased muffin pans. In each cup: 3 balls for cloverleaf or 2 for twin; brush with 4 ounces or 1/2 cup of melted butter or 1/3 recipe Milk Wash, Recipe No. I 004 02.
11. PROOF: At 90 F. until double in bulk.

12. BAKE: At 400 F. for 15 to 20 minutes or in a 350 F. convection oven for 10 to 15 minutes or until golden brown on high fan, open vent.
13. If desired, brush with 4 ounces or 1/2 cup of melted butter immediately after baking.

FRANKFURTER ROLLS

Yield 100   **Portion** 1 Roll

Calories	Carbohydrates	Protein	Fat	Cholesterol	Sodium	Calcium
227 cal	37 g	6 g	6 g	0 mg	239 mg	18 mg

Ingredient	Weight	Measure	Issue
YEAST,ACTIVE,DRY	3-3/8 oz	1/2 cup	
WATER,WARM	1-1/4 lbs	2-3/8 cup	
WATER,COLD	1 lbs	1-7/8 cup	
SUGAR,GRANULATED	1 lbs	2-3/8 cup	
SALT	2-1/8 oz	3-1/3 tbsp	
FLOUR,WHEAT,BREAD	9-2/3 lbs	2 gal	
MILK,NONFAT,DRY	2-2/3 oz	1-1/8 cup	
SHORTENING,SOFTENED	1-1/8 lbs	2-1/2 cup	
MILK AND WATER WASH		1/2 cup	

Method
1. Sprinkle yeast over water. DO NOT USE TEMPERATURES ABOVE 110 F. Mix well. Let stand 5 minutes; stir.
2. Place water in mixer bowl; add sugar and salt; stir until dissolved. Add yeast solution.
3. Combine flour and milk; add to liquid solution. Using dough hook, mix at low speed 1 minute or until flour mixture is incorporated into liquid.
4. Add shortening; mix at medium speed 10 minutes or until dough is smooth and elastic. Dough temperature should be between 78 F. to 82 F.
5. FERMENT: Cover. Set in warm place, about 180 F., 1-1/2 hours or until double in bulk.
6. PUNCH: Divide dough into 8 2 lb 14 oz pieces. Shape each piece into a smooth ball; let rest 10 to 20 minutes.
7. Roll 2-1/2-ounce pieces of dough into oblong rolls, 5 to 6 inches long.
8. Place on greased sheet pans in rows 4 by 9. Brush with 1/3 recipe Milk Wash, Recipe No. I 004 02 per 100 servings.
9. Proof at 90 F. until double in bulk.
10. Bake at 400 F. for 15 to 20 minutes or in a 350 F. convection oven for 10 to 15 minutes or until golden brown on high fan, open vent. Cool.

HAMBURGER ROLLS

Yield 100   **Portion** 1 Roll

Calories	Carbohydrates	Protein	Fat	Cholesterol	Sodium	Calcium
227 cal	37 g	6 g	6 g	0 mg	239 mg	18 mg

Ingredient	Weight	Measure	Issue
YEAST,ACTIVE,DRY	3-3/8 oz	1/2 cup	

133

WATER,WARM	1-1/4 lbs	2-3/8 cup
WATER,COLD	1 lbs	1-7/8 cup
SUGAR,GRANULATED	1 lbs	2-3/8 cup
SALT	2-1/8 oz	3-1/3 tbsp
FLOUR,WHEAT,BREAD	9-2/3 lbs	2 gal
MILK,NONFAT,DRY	2-2/3 oz	1-1/8 cup
SHORTENING,SOFTENED	1-1/8 lbs	2-1/2 cup
MILK AND WATER WASH		1/2 cup

Method

1. Sprinkle yeast over water. DO NOT USE TEMPERATURES ABOVE 110 F. Mix well. Let stand 5 minutes; stir.
2. Place water in mixer bowl; add sugar and salt; stir until dissolved. Add yeast solution.
3. Combine flour and milk; add to liquid solution. Using dough hook, mix at low speed 1 minute or until flour mixture is incorporated into liquid.
4. Add shortening; mix at medium speed 10 minutes or until dough is smooth and elastic. Dough temperature should be between 78 F. to 82 F.
5. FERMENT: Cover. Set in warm place, about 180 F., 1-1/2 hours or until double in bulk.
6. PUNCH: Divide dough into 8 2 lb 14 oz pieces. Shape each piece into a smooth ball; let rest 10 to 20 minutes.
7. Roll 2-1/2-ounce pieces of dough into oblong rolls, 5 to 6 inches long.
8. Place on greased sheet pans in rows 4 by 9. Brush with 1/3 recipe Milk Wash, Recipe No. I 004 02 per 100 servings.
9. Proof at 90 F. until double in bulk.
10. Bake at 400 F. for 15 to 20 minutes or in a 350 F. convection oven for 10 to 15 minutes or until golden brown on high fan, open vent. Cool.

PAN, CLUSTER, OR PULL APART ROLLS

Yield 100   **Portion** 2 Rolls

Calories	Carbohydrates	Protein	Fat	Cholesterol	Sodium	Calcium
357 cal	56 g	9 g	11 g	0 mg	380 mg	27 mg

Ingredient	Weight	Measure	Issue
YEAST,ACTIVE,DRY	4-1/2 oz	1/2 cup 2-2/3 tbsp	
WATER,WARM	1-7/8 lbs	3-1/2 cup	
WATER,COLD	5-3/4 lbs	2 qts 3 cup	
SUGAR,GRANULATED	1-1/2 lbs	3-1/2 cup	
SALT	3-1/8 oz	1/4 cup 1-1/3 tbsp	
FLOUR,WHEAT,BREAD	14-1/2 lbs	3 gal	
MILK,NONFAT,DRY	4-1/4 oz	1-3/4 cup	
SHORTENING,SOFTENED	1-2/3 lbs	3-3/4 cup	
MARGARINE,MELTED	4 oz	1/2 cup	
MARGARINE,MELTED	4 oz	1/2 cup	

Method

1. Sprinkle yeast over water. DO NOT USE TEMPERATURES ABOVE 110 F. Mix well. Let stand 5 minutes; stir.
2. Place water in mixer bowl; add sugar and salt; stir until dissolved. Add yeast solution.

3. Combine flour and milk; add to liquid solution. Using dough hook, mix at low speed 1 minute until flour mixture is incorporated into liquid.
4. Add shortening; mix at medium speed 10 minutes or until dough is smooth and elastic. Dough temperature should be between 78 F. to 82 F.
5. FERMENT: Cover. Set in warm place (80 F.) for 1-1/2 hours or until double in bulk.
6. PUNCH: Divide dough into about 3 pound pieces. Shape each piece into a smooth ball; let rest 10 to 20 minutes.
7. Roll each piece into a long rope, about 32 inches, of uniform diameter about 2 inches thick. Cut rope into 25 1-3/4 oz pieces about 1-1/4 inch long.
8. Shape 1-1/2 to 2-ounce dough pieces into balls by rolling with a circular motion on work table.
9. Place on greased sheet pans in rows 6 by 9. Brush with 4 ounces of melted butter or 1/4 recipe Egg Wash, Recipe No. D 017 00.
10. Proof at 90 F. until double in bulk.
11. Bake at 400 F., 15 to 20 minutes or in 350 F. convection oven 10 to 15 minutes or until golden brown on high fan, open vent.
12. Brush with 4 oz melted butter, optional, immediately after baking.

PARKER HOUSE ROLLS

Yield 100   **Portion** 2 Rolls

Calories	Carbohydrates	Protein	Fat	Cholesterol	Sodium	Calcium
357 cal	56 g	9 g	11 g	5 mg	377 mg	27 mg

Ingredient	Weight	Measure	Issue
YEAST,ACTIVE,DRY	4-1/2 oz	1/2 cup 2-2/3 tbsp	
WATER,WARM	1-7/8 lbs	3-1/2 cup	
WATER,COLD	5-3/4 lbs	2 qts 3 cup	
SUGAR,GRANULATED	1-1/2 lbs	3-1/2 cup	
SALT	3-1/8 oz	1/4 cup 1-1/3 tbsp	
FLOUR,WHEAT,BREAD	14-1/2 lbs	3 gal	
MILK,NONFAT,DRY	4-1/4 oz	1-3/4 cup	
SHORTENING,SOFTENED	1-2/3 lbs	3-3/4 cup	
BUTTER,MELTED	4 oz	1/2 cup	
BUTTER,MELTED	4 oz	1/2 cup	

Method
1. Sprinkle yeast over water. Do not use temperatures above 110 F. Mix well. Let stand 5 minutes; stir.
2. Place water in mixer bowl; add sugar and salt; stir until dissolved. Add yeast solution.
3. Combine flour and milk; add to liquid solution. Using dough hook, mix at low speed 1 minute until flour mixture is incorporated into liquid.
4. Add shortening; mix at medium speed 10 minutes or until dough is smooth and elastic. Dough temperature should be between 78 F. to 82 F.
5. FERMENT: Cover. Set in warm place, about 80 F., for 1-1/2 hours or until double in bulk.
6. PUNCH: Divide dough into about 3 pound pieces. Shape each piece into a smooth ball; let rest 10 to 20 minutes.
7. Roll each piece into a long rope, about 32 inches, of uniform diameter. Cut rope into pieces about 1-1/4 inch thick.
8. Shape 1-1/2 to 2-ounce dough pieces into balls by rolling with a circular motion on work table.
9. Cover with clean damp cloth; let rest 5 to 10 minutes.
10. Press center of each ball with a small rolling pin.

11. Brush with 4 ounces of melted butter; fold in half. Press edges together with thumb or palm of hand.
12. Place on greased sheet pans in rows 5 by 10; brush with 4 ounces of melted butter.
13. Proof at 90 F. until double in bulk.
14. Bake at 400 F., 15 to 20 minutes or in 350 F. convection oven 10 to 15 minutes or until golden brown on high fan, open vent.

POPPY SEED ROLLS

Yield 100   **Portion** 2 Rolls

Calories	Carbohydrates	Protein	Fat	Cholesterol	Sodium	Calcium
346 cal	56 g	9 g	9 g	0 mg	359 mg	42 mg

Ingredient	Weight	Measure Issue
YEAST,ACTIVE,DRY	4-1/2 oz	1/2 cup 2-2/3 tbsp
WATER,WARM	1-7/8 lbs	3-1/2 cup
WATER,COLD	5-3/4 lbs	2 qts 3 cup
SUGAR,GRANULATED	1-1/2 lbs	3-1/2 cup
SALT	3-1/8 oz	1/4 cup 1-1/3 tbsp
FLOUR,WHEAT,BREAD	14-1/2 lbs	3 gal
MILK,NONFAT,DRY	4-1/4 oz	1-3/4 cup
SHORTENING,SOFTENED	1-2/3 lbs	3-3/4 cup
EGG WHITE WASH		1/2 cup
POPPY SEEDS	3-3/4 oz	3/4 cup

Method
1. Sprinkle yeast over water. Do not use temperatures above 110 F. Mix well. Let stand 5 minutes; stir.
2. Place water in mixer bowl; add sugar and salt; stir until dissolved. Add yeast solution.
3. Combine flour and milk; add to liquid solution. Using dough hook, mix at low speed 1 minute until flour mixture is incorporated into liquid.
4. Add shortening; mix at medium speed 10 minutes or until dough is smooth and elastic. Dough temperature should be between 78 F. to 82 F.
5. FERMENT: Cover. Set in warm place, about 80 F., for 1-1/2 hours or until double in bulk.
6. PUNCH: Divide dough into about 8 2 lb 14 oz pieces. Shape each piece into a smooth ball; let rest 10 to 20 minutes.
7. Roll each piece into a long rope, about 32 inches, of uniform diameter about 2 inches thick. Cut rope into 25 1-3/4 oz pieces about 1-1/4 inch long.
8. Shape rolls as desired.
9. Place on greased sheet pans. Brush top of rolls lightly with water or 1/6 recipe Egg White Wash, Recipe No. D 017 01. Sprinkle top of rolls with poppy seeds.
10. Proof at 90 F. until double in bulk.
11. Bake at 400 F. for 15 to 20 minutes or in a 350 F. convection oven 10 to 15 minutes or until golden brown on high fan, open vent.

SESAME SEED ROLLS

Yield 100   **Portion** 2 Rolls

Calories	Carbohydrates	Protein	Fat	Cholesterol	Sodium	Calcium
347 cal	56 g	9 g	9 g	0 mg	359 mg	28 mg

Ingredient	Weight	Measure Issue
YEAST,ACTIVE,DRY	4-1/2 oz	1/2 cup 2-2/3 tbsp

Ingredient	Weight	Measure
WATER,WARM	1-7/8 lbs	3-1/2 cup
WATER,COLD	5-3/4 lbs	2 qts 3 cup
SUGAR,GRANULATED	1-1/2 lbs	3-1/2 cup
SALT	3-1/8 oz	1/4 cup 1-1/3 tbsp
FLOUR,WHEAT,BREAD	14-1/2 lbs	3 gal
MILK,NONFAT,DRY	4-1/4 oz	1-3/4 cup
SHORTENING,SOFTENED	1-2/3 lbs	3-3/4 cup
EGG WHITE WASH		1/2 cup
SESAME SEEDS	3-3/4 oz	3/4 cup

Method

1. Sprinkle yeast over water. Do not use temperatures above 110 F. Mix well. Let stand 5 minutes; stir.
2. Place water in mixer bowl; add sugar and salt; stir until dissolved. Add yeast solution.
3. Combine flour and milk; add to liquid solution. Using dough hook, mix at low speed 1 minute until flour mixture is incorporated into liquid.
4. Add shortening; mix at medium speed 10 minutes or until dough is smooth and elastic. Dough temperature should be between 78 F. to 82 F.
5. FERMENT: Cover. Set in warm place, about 80 F., for 1-1/2 hours or until double in bulk.
6. PUNCH: Divide dough into about 8 2 lb 14 oz pieces. Shape each piece into a smooth ball; let rest 10 to 20 minutes.
7. Roll each piece into a long rope, about 32 inches, of uniform diameter about 2 inches thick. Cut rope into 25 1-3/4 oz pieces about 1-1/4 inch long.
8. Shape rolls as desired.
9. Place on greased sheet pans. Brush top of rolls lightly with water or 1/6 recipe Egg White Wash, Recipe No. D 017 01. Sprinkle top of rolls with poppy seeds.
10. Proof at 90 F. until double in bulk.
11. Bake at 400 F. for 15 to 20 minutes or in a 350 F. convection oven 10 to 15 minutes or until golden brown on high fan, open vent.

HOT ROLLS (SHORT-TIME FORMULA)

Yield 100   **Portion** 2 Rolls

Calories	Carbohydrates	Protein	Fat	Cholesterol	Sodium	Calcium
276 cal	51 g	9 g	4 g	0 mg	325 mg	30 mg

Ingredient	Weight	Measure Issue
YEAST,ACTIVE,DRY	4-1/2 oz	1/2 cup 2-1/3 tbsp
WATER,WARM	1-5/8 lbs	3 cup
SUGAR,GRANULATED	1-1/8 oz	2-2/3 tbsp
WATER	6-1/4 lbs	3 qts
MILK,NONFAT,DRY	5-3/8 oz	2-1/4 cup
SUGAR,GRANULATED	5-1/4 oz	3/4 cup
FLOUR,WHEAT,BREAD	10-7/8 lbs	2 gal 1 qts
SHORTENING,SOFTENED	9 oz	1-1/4 cup
FLOUR,WHEAT,BREAD	3-5/8 lbs	3 qts
SALT	2-7/8 oz	1/4 cup 2/3 tbsp

Method

1. Sprinkle yeast over water. DO NOT USE TEMPERATURES ABOVE 110 F. Mix well. Let stand 5 minutes. Add sugar and stir until dissolved. Let stand for 10 minutes; stir. Set aside for use in Step 3.

2. Place water in mixer bowl. Add milk and sugar. Using dough hook, mix at low speed about 1 minute until blended.
3. Add flour; mix at low speed about 2 minutes or until flour is incorporated. Add shortening and yeast solution. Mix at low speed about 2 minutes until smooth.
4. Mix at medium speed 10 minutes.
5. Let rise in mixer bowl 20 minutes.
6. Sift flour and salt; add to mixture in mixer bowl. Mix at low speed 2 minutes or until flour is incorporated. Mix at medium speed 10 minutes or until smooth and elastic.
7. FERMENT: Cover. Set in warm place (80 F.) 1-1/2 hours or until double in bulk.
8. MAKE-UP: Line pans with parchment paper. Divide dough into 2 2 lb-10 oz pieces. Shape each piece into a smooth ball; let rest 15 minutes.
9. Roll each piece into a long rope, about 38 inches, of uniform diameter, about 1-1/2-inch thick. Cut rope into 25 1-2/3 inch pieces, about 1-1/3 inches long.
10. MAKE-UP: Shape each piece into a smooth ball; let rest 10 to 20 minutes.
11. PROOF: At 90 F. until double in bulk, about 45 minutes.
12. BAKE: 15 to 20 minutes at 400 F. or in 350 F. convection oven 10 to 12 minutes or until golden brown on high fan, open vent.

BROWN AND SERVE ROLLS (SHORT-TIME FORMULA)

Yield 100   **Portion** 2 Rolls

Calories	Carbohydrates	Protein	Fat	Cholesterol	Sodium	Calcium
284 cal	51 g	9 g	5 g	3 mg	335 mg	31 mg

Ingredient	Weight	Measure	Issue
YEAST,ACTIVE,DRY	4-1/2 oz	1/2 cup 2-1/3 tbsp	
WATER,WARM	1-5/8 lbs	3 cup	
SUGAR,GRANULATED	1-1/8 oz	2-2/3 tbsp	
WATER	6-1/4 lbs	3 qts	
MILK,NONFAT,DRY	5-3/8 oz	2-1/4 cup	
SUGAR,GRANULATED	5-1/4 oz	3/4 cup	
FLOUR,WHEAT,BREAD	10-7/8 lbs	2 gal 1 qts	
SHORTENING,SOFTENED	9 oz	1-1/4 cup	
FLOUR,WHEAT,BREAD	3-5/8 lbs	3 qts	
SALT	2-7/8 oz	1/4 cup 2/3 tbsp	
BUTTER,MELTED	4 oz	1/4 cup	

Method
1. Sprinkle yeast over water. DO NOT USE TEMPERATURES ABOVE 110 F. Mix well. Let stand 5 minutes. Add sugar; stir until dissolved. Let stand for 10 minutes; stir. Set aside for use in Step 3.
2. Place water in mixer bowl. Add milk and sugar. Using dough hook, mix at low speed about 1 minute until blended.
3. Add flour; mix at low speed about 2 minutes or until flour is incorporated. Add shortening and yeast solution. Mix at low speed about 2 minutes until smooth.
4. Mix at medium speed 10 minutes.
5. Let rise in mixer bowl 20 minutes.
6. Sift together flour and salt; add to mixture in mixer bowl. Mix at low speed 2 minutes or until flour is incorporated. Mix at medium speed 10 minutes or until smooth and elastic.
7. FERMENT: Cover. Set in warm place (80 F.) 1-1/2 hours or until double in bulk.

8. MAKE-UP: Line pans with parchment paper. Divide dough into 8 2 lb 10 oz pieces. Shape each piece into a smooth ball; let rest 15 minutes.
9. Roll each piece into a long rope, about 38 inches, of uniform diameter, about 1-1/2-inch thick. Cut rope into 25 1-2/3 oz pieces about 1-1/3 inches long.
10. Shape each piece into a smooth ball; let rest 10 to 20 minutes.
11. PROOF: At 90 F. until double in bulk, about 45 minutes.
12. Bake at 325 F. for 25 to 30 minutes or in 300 F. convection oven 12 to 15 minutes or until rolls begin to brown on low fan, open vent. Brush with melted margarine or butter. Cool on pans; wrap in aluminum foil. Bring covered rolls to room temperature about 1 hour before baking. Finish baking at 400 F. about 14 to 17 minutes or in 350 F. convection oven about 10 to 12 minutes or until golden brown on high fan, open vent.

WHOLE WHEAT ROLLS (SHORT-TIME FORMULA)

Yield 100   Portion 2 Rolls

Calories	Carbohydrates	Protein	Fat	Cholesterol	Sodium	Calcium
263 cal	48 g	8 g	4 g	0 mg	325 mg	30 mg

Ingredient	Weight	Measure	Issue
YEAST,ACTIVE,DRY	4-1/2 oz	1/2cup 2-1/3tbsp	
WATER,WARM	1-5/8 lbs	3 cup	
SUGAR,GRANULATED	1-1/8 oz	2-2/3 tbsp	
WATER	6-3/4 lbs	3 qts 1 cup	
MILK,NONFAT,DRY	5-3/8 oz	2-1/4 cup	
SUGAR,GRANULATED	7 oz	1 cup	
FLOUR,WHEAT,BREAD	3-5/8 lbs	3 qts	
FLOUR,WHEAT,BREAD	6-1/3 lbs	1 gal 1-1/4 qts	
SHORTENING,SOFTENED	9 oz	1-1/4 cup	
FLOUR,WHEAT,BREAD	3-5/8 lbs	3 qts	
SALT	2-7/8 oz	1/4cup 2/3tbsp	

Method
1. Sprinkle yeast over water. DO NOT USE TEMPERATURES ABOVE 110 F. Mix well. Let stand 5 minutes. Add sugar and stir until dissolved. Let stand for 10 minutes; stir. Set aside for use in Step 3.
2. Place water in mixer bowl. Add milk and sugar. Using dough hook, mix at low speed about 1 minute until blended.
3. Add flour; mix at low speed about 2 minutes or until flour is incorporated. Add shortening and yeast solution. Mix at low speed about 2 minutes until smooth.
4. Mix at medium speed 10 minutes.
5. Let rise in mixer bowl 20 minutes.
6. Sift flour and salt; add to mixture in mixer bowl. Mix at low speed 2 minutes or until flour is incorporated. Mix at medium speed 10 minutes or until smooth and elastic.
7. FERMENT: Cover. Set in warm place (80 F.) 1-1/2 hours or until double in bulk.
8. MAKE-UP: Line pans with parchment paper. Divide dough into 8 2 lb-10 oz pieces. Shape each piece into a smooth ball; let rest 15 minutes.
9. Roll each piece into a long rope, about 38 inches, of uniform diameter, about 1-1/2 inches thick. Cut rope into 25 1-2/3 oz pieces about 1-1/3 inches long.
10. Shape each piece into a smooth ball; let rest 10 to 20 minutes.
11. PROOF: At 90 F. until double in bulk, about 45 minutes.
12. BAKE: 20 to 25 minutes at 400 F. or in 350 F. convection oven 12 to 15 minutes or until golden brown on high fan, open vent.

ONION ROLLS

Yield 100   **Portion** 2 Rolls

Calories	Carbohydrates	Protein	Fat	Cholesterol	Sodium	Calcium
312 cal	58 g	8 g	5 g	0 mg	428 mg	41 mg

Ingredient	Weight	Measure	Issue
YEAST,ACTIVE,DRY	3-3/8 oz	1/2 cup	
WATER,WARM	1-1/3 lbs	2-1/2 cup	
WATER	4-2/3 lbs	2 qts 1 cup	
SUGAR,GRANULATED	1-1/4 lbs	2-3/4 cup	
MILK,NONFAT,DRY	3-1/4 oz	1-3/8 cup	
SALT	3-3/4 oz	1/4 cup 2-1/3 tbsp	
ONIONS,DEHYDRATED,CHOPPED	1-5/8 lbs	3 qts 1 cup	
WATER	4-1/8 lbs	2 qts	
FLOUR,WHEAT,GENERAL PURPOSE	13-1/4 lbs	3 gal	
SHORTENING,SOFTENED	1 lbs	2-1/4 cup	

Method

1. Sprinkle yeast over water. DO NOT USE TEMPERATURES ABOVE 110 F. Mix well; let stand 5 minutes; stir. Set aside for use in Step 3.
2. Place water in mixer bowl. Add sugar, milk, and salt. Mix at low speed until smooth.
3. Soak and drain the dehydrated onions.
4. Add flour; mix at low speed. Add shortening, yeast solution, and onions; mix until well blended.
5. Mix at medium speed 15 minutes or until dough is smooth and elastic.
6. FERMENT: Cover. Set in warm place (80 F.) 2 hours or until double in bulk.
7. PUNCH: Let rest 20 minutes.
8. MAKE-UP: Shape each piece into a smooth ball; let rest 10 to 20 minutes.
9. PROOF: Until rolls are double in bulk.
10. BAKE: At 425 F. 12 to 15 minutes or until done.

ONION ROLLS (ROLL MIX)

Yield 100   **Portion** 2 Rolls

Calories	Carbohydrates	Protein	Fat	Cholesterol	Sodium	Calcium
262 cal	49 g	7 g	4 g	0 mg	376 mg	58 mg

Ingredient	Weight	Measure	Issue
ONIONS,DEHYDRATED,CHOPPED	1-5/8 lbs	3 qts 1 cup	
WATER	4-1/8 lbs	2 qts	
ROLL,MIX	13-1/2 lbs		
YEAST,ACTIVE,DRY	5-1/8 oz	3/4 cup	

Method

1. Soak and drain dehydrated onions. Add onions to Roll Mix and active dry yeast.
2. Prepare mix according to instructions on container.
3. PUNCH: Let rest 20 minutes.
4. MAKE-UP: Shape each piece into a smooth ball; let rest 10 to 20 minutes.
5. PROOF: Until rolls are double in bulk.
6. BAKE: At 425 F. 12 to 15 minutes or until done.

SWEET DOUGH

Yield 100   **Portion** 1 Roll

Calories	Carbohydrates	Protein	Fat	Cholesterol	Sodium	Calcium
201 cal	32 g	6 g	5 g	24 mg	221 mg	16 mg

Ingredient	Weight	Measure	Issue
YEAST,ACTIVE,DRY	6-3/4 oz	1 cup	
WATER,WARM	1 lbs	2 cup	
WATER	1-5/8 lbs	3 cup	
EGGS,WHOLE,FROZEN	1-1/4 lbs	2-1/4 cup	
SUGAR,GRANULATED	1-1/8 lbs	2-5/8 cup	
MILK,NONFAT,DRY	1-3/4 oz	3/4 cup	
SALT	1-7/8 oz	3 tbsp	
FLOUR,WHEAT,BREAD	7-7/8 lbs	1 gal 2-1/2 qts	
SHORTENING,SOFTENED	14-1/2 oz	2 cup	

Method

1. Sprinkle yeast over water. DO NOT USE TEMPERATURES ABOVE 110 F. Mix well. Let stand 5 minutes; stir. Set aside for use in Step 3.
2. Place water, eggs, sugar, milk, and salt in mixer bowl. Using dough hook, mix at low speed just until blended.
3. Add flour and yeast solution. Mix at low speed 1 minute or until all flour mixture is incorporated into liquid.
4. Add shortening; mix at low speed 1 minute. Continue mixing at medium speed 10 minutes or until dough is smooth and elastic. Dough temperature should be between 78 F. to 82 F.
5. FERMENT: Cover. Set in warm place (80 F.) about 1-1/2 hours or until double in bulk.
6. PUNCH: Divide dough into 3 pieces, shape into a rectangular piece. Let rest 10 to 20 minutes.

SWEET DOUGH (SWEET DOUGH MIX)

Yield 100   **Portion** 1 Roll

Calories	Carbohydrates	Protein	Fat	Cholesterol	Sodium	Calcium
135 cal	24 g	6 g	3 g	0 mg	323 mg	13 mg

Ingredient	Weight	Measure	Issue
SWEET DOUGH MIX	9 lbs	2 gal 1/8 qts	
YEAST,ACTIVE,DRY	4-1/4 oz	1/2 cup 2 tbsp	
WATER	3-2/3 lbs	1 qts 3 cup	

Method

1. Use Sweet Dough Mix and active dry yeast. Prepare dough according to instructions on container.
2. FERMENT: Cover. Set in warm place (80 F.) about 1-1/2 hours or until double in bulk.
3. PUNCH: Divide dough into 3 pieces, let rest 10 to 20 minutes.

GLAZED ROLLS

Yield 100   **Portion** 1 Roll

Calories	Carbohydrates	Protein	Fat	Cholesterol	Sodium	Calcium
244 cal	38 g	6 g	8 g	29 mg	243 mg	17 mg

Ingredient	Weight	Measure	Issue
YEAST,ACTIVE,DRY	6-3/4 oz	1 cup	
WATER,WARM	1 lbs	2 cup	
WATER	1-5/8 lbs	3 cup	
EGGS,WHOLE,FROZEN	1-1/4 lbs	2-1/4 cup	
SUGAR,GRANULATED	1-1/8 lbs	2-5/8 cup	
MILK,NONFAT,DRY	1-3/4 oz	3/4 cup	
SALT	1-7/8 oz	3 tbsp	
FLOUR,WHEAT,BREAD	7-7/8 lbs	1 gal 2-1/2 qts	
SHORTENING,SOFTENED	14-1/2 oz	2 cup	
BUTTER	8 oz	1 cup	
VANILLA GLAZE		2-3/8 cup	

Method

1. Sprinkle yeast over water. DO NOT USE TEMPERATURES ABOVE 110 F. Mix well. Let stand 5 minutes; stir. Set aside for use in Step 3.
2. Place water, eggs, sugar, milk, and salt in mixer bowl. Using dough hook, mix at low speed just until blended.
3. Add flour and yeast solution. Mix at low speed 1 minute or until all flour mixture is incorporated into liquid.
4. Add shortening; mix at low speed 1 minute. Continue mixing at medium speed 10 minutes or until dough is smooth and elastic. Dough temperature should be between 78 F. to 82 F.
5. FERMENT: Cover. Set in a warm place (80 F.) about 1-1/2 hours or until double in bulk.
6. PUNCH: Divide dough into 3 pieces, 4 lb 5 oz each; shape into a rectangular piece. Let rest 10 to 20 minutes.
7. MAKE-UP: Roll each 4 lb 5 oz piece of dough into a long rope of uniform diameter. (If using D 036 01, Sweet Dough Mix, use 4 lb 2 oz pieces.)
8. Slice into 34 pieces, weighing 1-3/4 to 2 oz each.
9. Shape into balls by rolling with a circular motion.
10. Place on lightly greased sheet pans in rows 6 by 9.
11. Melt butter or margarine. Brush 1/2 cup on rolls in each pan.
12. PROOF: At 90 F. to 100 F. until double in bulk.
13. BAKE: At 375 F. for 20 to 25 minutes or until golden brown or in a 325 F. convection oven for 15 minutes on high fan, open vent. Cool.
14. Prepare 1 recipe Vanilla Glaze, Recipe No. D 046 00; brush about 1-1/3 cups on baked rolls in each pan for each 100 servings.

PECAN ROLLS

Yield 100   **Portion** 1 Roll

Calories	Carbohydrates	Protein	Fat	Cholesterol	Sodium	Calcium
302 cal	40 g	6 g	13 g	34 mg	261 mg	25 mg

Ingredient	Weight	Measure	Issue
YEAST,ACTIVE,DRY	6-3/4 oz	1 cup	
WATER,WARM	1 lbs	2 cup	
WATER	1-5/8 lbs	3 cup	
EGGS,WHOLE,FROZEN	1-1/4 lbs	2-1/4 cup	
SUGAR,GRANULATED	1-1/8 lbs	2-5/8 cup	
MILK,NONFAT,DRY	1-3/4 oz	3/4 cup	
SALT	1-7/8 oz	3 tbsp	
FLOUR,WHEAT,BREAD	7-7/8 lbs	1 gal 2-1/2 qts	
SHORTENING,SOFTENED	14-1/2 oz	2 cup	
PECAN TOPPING		2 qts 2 cup	
BUTTER	8 oz	1 cup	

Method

1. Sprinkle yeast over water. DO NOT USE TEMPERATURES ABOVE 110 F. Mix well. Let stand 5 minutes; stir. Set aside for use in Step 3.
2. Place water, eggs, sugar, milk, and salt in mixer bowl. Using dough hook, mix at low speed just until blended.
3. Add flour and yeast solution. Mix at low speed 1 minute or until all flour mixture is incorporated into liquid.
4. Add shortening; mix at low speed 1 minute. Continue mixing at medium speed 10 minutes or until dough is smooth and elastic. Dough temperature should be between 78 F. to 82 F.
5. FERMENT: Cover. Set in a warm place (80 F.) about 1-1/2 hours or until double in bulk.
6. PUNCH: Divide dough into 3 pieces, 4 lb 5 oz each; shape into a rectangular piece. Let rest 10 to 20 minutes.
7. Roll each 4 lb 5 oz piece of dough into a long rope of uniform diameter. (If using D 036 01, Sweet Dough Mix, use 4 lb 2 oz pieces.)
8. Slice into 34 pieces weighing 1-3/4 to 2 ounces each.
9. Shape into balls by rolling with a circular motion.
10. Prepare 1 recipe Pecan Topping, Recipe No. D 049 01 per 100 portions. Spread 1-1/4 quart in each pan.
11. Flatten balls. Place on topping mixture in rows 6 by 9.
12. Melt butter or margarine and brush 1/2 cup on rolls in each pan.
13. Proof at 90 F. to 100 F. until double in bulk.
14. Bake at 375 F. for 20 to 25 minutes or until golden brown or in 325 F. convection oven for 15 minutes on high fan, open vent.
15. Invert pans as soon as removed from oven; bottom of roll becomes top.

CINNAMON ROLLS

Yield 100   **Portion** 1 Roll

Calories	Carbohydrates	Protein	Fat	Cholesterol	Sodium	Calcium
289 cal	47 g	6 g	9 g	34 mg	265 mg	40 mg

Ingredient	Weight	Measure	Issue
YEAST,ACTIVE,DRY	6-3/4 oz	1 cup	
WATER,WARM	1 lbs	2 cup	
WATER	1-5/8 lbs	3 cup	
EGGS,WHOLE,FROZEN	1-1/4 lbs	2-1/4 cup	
SUGAR,GRANULATED	1-1/8 lbs	2-5/8 cup	

MILK,NONFAT,DRY	1-3/4 oz	3/4 cup
SALT	1-7/8 oz	3 tbsp
FLOUR,WHEAT,BREAD	7-7/8 lbs	1 gal 2-1/2 qts
SHORTENING,SOFTENED	14-1/2 oz	2 cup
BUTTER	1 lbs	2 cup
CINNAMON SUGAR FILLING		3 cup

Method

1. Sprinkle yeast over water. DO NOT USE TEMPERATURES ABOVE 110 F. Mix well. Let stand 5 minutes; stir. Set aside for use in Step 3.
2. Place water, eggs, sugar, milk, and salt in mixer bowl. Using dough hook, mix at low speed just until blended.
3. Add flour and yeast solution. Mix at low speed 1 minute or until all flour mixture is incorporated into liquid.
4. Add shortening; mix at low speed 1 minute. Continue mixing at medium speed 10 minutes or until dough is smooth and elastic. Dough temperature should be between 78 F. to 82 F.
5. FERMENT: Cover. Set in a warm place (80 F.) about 1-1/2 hours or until double in bulk.
6. PUNCH: Divide dough into 3 pieces, 4 lb 5 oz each; shape into a rectangular piece. Let rest 10 to 20 minutes.
7. MAKE-UP: Roll each 4 lb 5 oz piece of dough into a rectangular sheet, about 18 inches wide, 36 inches long, and 1/4 inch thick. (If using D 036 01, Sweet Dough Mix, use 4 lb 2 oz pieces.)
8. Melt butter or margarine. Brush 1/2 cup on each sheet of dough. Set aside remainder for use in Step 4.
9. Prepare 1 recipe Cinnamon Sugar Filling, Recipe No. D 042 00 for 100 servings. Sprinkle 1-1/2 cups cinnamon sugar mixture over each sheet of dough.
10. Roll each piece tightly to make a long slender roll. Seal edges by pressing firmly. Elongate roll to 35 inches by rolling back and forth on work table. Brush 2 tablespoons of butter or margarine on each roll.
11. Slice each roll into 34 pieces about 1 inch wide, using dough cutter.
12. Place cut side down on lightly greased sheet pans in rows 5 by 8.
13. Proof at 90 F. to 100 F. until double in bulk.
14. Bake at 375 F. for 20 to 25 minutes or until golden brown or in 325 F. convection oven 15 minutes on high fan, open vent. Cool.
15. Glaze, if desired, with 1 recipe Vanilla Glaze, Recipe No. D 046 00 per 100 portions. Brush about 1 cup on rolls in each pan.

CINNAMON NUT ROLLS

Yield 100   Portion 1 Roll

Calories	Carbohydrates	Protein	Fat	Cholesterol	Sodium	Calcium
306 cal	38 g	7 g	15 g	34 mg	260 mg	26 mg

Ingredient	Weight	Measure	Issue
YEAST,ACTIVE,DRY	6-3/4 oz	1 cup	
WATER,WARM	1 lbs	2 cup	
WATER	1-5/8 lbs	3 cup	
EGGS,WHOLE,FROZEN	1-1/4 lbs	2-1/4 cup	
SUGAR,GRANULATED	1-1/8 lbs	2-5/8 cup	
MILK,NONFAT,DRY	1-3/4 oz	3/4 cup	
SALT	1-7/8 oz	3 tbsp	

Ingredient	Weight	Measure
FLOUR,WHEAT,BREAD	7-7/8 lbs	1 gal 2-1/2 qts
SHORTENING,SOFTENED	14-1/2 oz	2 cup
BUTTER	1 lbs	2 cup
CINNAMON SUGAR FILLING		3 cup
PECANS,CHOPPED	2 lbs	

Method

1. Sprinkle yeast over water. DO NOT USE TEMPERATURES ABOVE 110 F. Mix well. Let stand 5 minutes; stir. Set aside for use in Step 3.
2. Place water, eggs, sugar, milk, and salt in mixer bowl. Using dough hook, mix at low speed just until blended.
3. Add flour and yeast solution. Mix at low speed 1 minute or until all flour mixture is incorporated into liquid.
4. Add shortening; mix at low speed 1 minute. Continue mixing at medium speed 10 minutes or until dough is smooth and elastic. Dough temperature should be between 78 F. to 82 F.
5. FERMENT: Cover. Set in a warm place (80 F.) about 1-1/2 hours or until double in bulk.
6. PUNCH: Divide dough into 3 pieces, 4 lb 5 oz each; shape into a rectangular piece. Let rest 10 to 20 minutes.
7. MAKE-UP: Roll each 4 lb 5 oz piece of dough into a rectangular sheet, about 18 inches wide, 36 inches long, and 1/4 inch thick. (If using D 036 01, Sweet Dough Mix, use 4 lb 2 oz pieces.)
8. Melt butter or margarine. Brush 1/2 cup on each sheet of dough. Set aside remainder for use in Step 4.
9. Prepare 1 recipe Cinnamon Sugar Filling, Recipe No. D 042 00 for 100 servings. Sprinkle 1-1/2 cups cinnamon sugar mixture and 2 cups of pecans over each sheet of dough.
10. Roll each piece tightly to make a long slender roll. Seal edges by pressing firmly. Elongate roll to 35 inches by rolling back and forth on work table. Brush 2 tablespoons of butter or margarine on each roll.
11. Slice each roll into 34 pieces about 1 inch wide, using dough cutter.
12. Place cut side down on lightly greased sheet pans in rows 5 by 8.
13. Proof at 90 F. to 100 F. until double in bulk.
14. Bake at 375 F. for 20 to 25 minutes or until golden brown or in 325 F. convection oven 15 minutes on high fan, open vent. Cool.
15. Glaze, if desired, with 1 recipe Vanilla Glaze, Recipe No. D 046 00 per 100 portions. Brush about 1 cup on rolls in each pan.

CINNAMON RAISIN ROLLS

Yield 100   **Portion** 1 Roll

Calories	Carbohydrates	Protein	Fat	Cholesterol	Sodium	Calcium
298 cal	49 g	6 g	9 g	34 mg	265 mg	41 mg

Ingredient	Weight	Measure	Issue
YEAST,ACTIVE,DRY	6-3/4 oz	1 cup	
WATER,WARM	1 lbs	2 cup	
WATER	1-5/8 lbs	3 cup	
EGGS,WHOLE,FROZEN	1-1/4 lbs	2-1/4 cup	
SUGAR,GRANULATED	1-1/8 lbs	2-5/8 cup	
MILK,NONFAT,DRY	1-3/4 oz	3/4 cup	
SALT	1-7/8 oz	3 tbsp	
FLOUR,WHEAT,BREAD	7-7/8 lbs	1 gal 2-1/2 qts	
SHORTENING,SOFTENED	14-1/2 oz	2 cup	

BUTTER	1 lbs	2 cup
CINNAMON SUGAR FILLING		3 cup
RAISINS	10-1/4 oz	2 cup

Method

1. Sprinkle yeast over water. DO NOT USE TEMPERATURES ABOVE 110 F. Mix well. Let stand 5 minutes; stir. Set aside for use in Step 3.
2. Place water, eggs, sugar, milk, and salt in mixer bowl. Using dough hook, mix at low speed just until blended.
3. Add flour and yeast solution. Mix at low speed 1 minute or until all flour mixture is incorporated into liquid.
4. Add shortening; mix at low speed 1 minute. Continue mixing at medium speed 10 minutes or until dough is smooth and elastic. Dough temperature should be between 78 F. to 82 F.
5. FERMENT: Cover. Set in a warm place (80 F.) about 1-1/2 hours or until double in bulk.
6. PUNCH: Divide dough into 3 pieces, 4 lb 5 oz each; shape into a rectangular piece. Let rest 10 to 20 minutes.
7. MAKE-UP: Roll each 4 lb 5 oz piece of dough into a rectangular sheet, about 18 inches wide, 36 inches long, and 1/4 inch thick. (If using D 036 01, Sweet Dough Mix, use 4 lb 2 oz pieces.)
8. Melt butter or margarine. Brush 1/2 cup on each sheet of dough. Set aside remainder for use in Step 4.
9. Prepare 1 recipe Cinnamon Sugar Filling, Recipe No. D 042 00 for 100 servings. Sprinkle 1-1/2 cups cinnamon sugar mixture and 2 cups of raisins over each sheet of dough.
10. Roll each piece tightly to make a long slender roll. Seal edges by pressing firmly. Elongate roll to 35 inches by rolling back and forth on work table. Brush 2 tablespoons of butter or margarine on each roll.
11. Slice each roll into 34 pieces about 1 inch wide, using dough cutter.
12. Place cut side down on lightly greased sheet pans in rows 5 by 8.
13. Proof at 90 F. to 100 F. until double in bulk.
14. Bake at 375 F. for 20 to 25 minutes or until golden brown or in 325 F. convection oven 15 minutes on high fan, open vent. Cool.
15. Glaze, if desired, with 1 recipe Vanilla Glaze, Recipe No. D 046 00 per 100 portions. Brush about 1 cup on rolls in each pan.

BUTTERFLY ROLLS

Yield 100   **Portion** 1 Roll

Calories	Carbohydrates	Protein	Fat	Cholesterol	Sodium	Calcium
312 cal	52 g	6 g	9 g	36 mg	261 mg	19 mg

Ingredient	Weight	Measure	Issue
YEAST,ACTIVE,DRY	6-3/4 oz	1 cup	
WATER,WARM	1 lbs	2 cup	
WATER	1-5/8 lbs	3 cup	
EGGS,WHOLE,FROZEN	1-1/4 lbs	2-1/4 cup	
SUGAR,GRANULATED	1-1/8 lbs	2-5/8 cup	
MILK,NONFAT,DRY	1-3/4 oz	3/4 cup	
SALT	1-7/8 oz	3 tbsp	
FLOUR,WHEAT,BREAD	7-7/8 lbs	1 gal 2-1/2 qts	
SHORTENING,SOFTENED	14-1/2 oz	2 cup	
BUTTER	12 oz	1-1/2 cup	

EGG WASH   3/4 cup
VANILLA GLAZE   2-3/4 cup

Method

1. Sprinkle yeast over water. DO NOT USE TEMPERATURES ABOVE 110 F. Mix well. Let stand 5 minutes; stir. Set aside for use in Step 3.
2. Place water, eggs, sugar, milk, and salt in mixer bowl. Using dough hook, mix at low speed just until blended.
3. Add flour and yeast solution. Mix at low speed 1 minute or until all flour mixture is incorporated into liquid.
4. Add shortening; mix at low speed 1 minute. Continue mixing at medium speed 10 minutes or until dough is smooth and elastic. Dough temperature should be between 78 F. to 82 F.
5. FERMENT: Cover. Set in a warm place (80 F.) about 1-1/2 hours or until double in bulk.
6. PUNCH: Divide dough into 6-2 lb 2 oz pieces; shape into a rectangular piece. Let rest 10 to 20 minutes.
7. Roll each piece of dough into a rectangular sheet, about 10 inches wide, 30 inches long and 1/4 inch thick.
8. Melt butter or margarine. Brush 1/4 cup on each sheet of dough.
9. MAKE-UP: Roll each piece tightly to make long slender roll. Seal edges by pressing firmly. Elongate roll to 30 inches by rolling back and forth on work table.
10. Slice each roll into 17 pieces about 1-3/4 inches wide.
11. Press each piece firmly in center parallel to cut side of roll with back of knife or small rolling pin.
12. Place on lightly greased sheet pans in rows 4 by 8. Prepare 1/4 recipe Egg Wash, Recipe No. D 017 00 per 100 portions and brush 1/4 cup on rolls in each pan.
13. Proof at 90 F. to 100 F. until double in bulk.
14. Bake at 375 F. for 20 to 25 minutes or until golden brown or in a 325 F. convection oven for 15 minutes on high fan, open vent. Cool.
15. Glaze, if desired, with 1 recipe Vanilla Glaze, Recipe No. D 046 00 per 100 portions. Brush about 1 cup on rolls in each pan.

SUGAR ROLLS

Yield 100   Portion 1 Roll

Calories	Carbohydrates	Protein	Fat	Cholesterol	Sodium	Calcium
335 cal	56 g	6 g	10 g	36 mg	269 mg	18 mg

Ingredient	Weight	Measure	Issue
YEAST,ACTIVE,DRY	6-3/4 oz	1 cup	
WATER,WARM	1 lbs	2 cup	
WATER	1-5/8 lbs	3 cup	
EGGS,WHOLE,FROZEN	1-1/4 lbs	2-1/4 cup	
SUGAR,GRANULATED	1-1/8 lbs	2-5/8 cup	
MILK,NONFAT,DRY	1-3/4 oz	3/4 cup	
SALT	1-7/8 oz	3 tbsp	
FLOUR,WHEAT,BREAD	7-7/8 lbs	1 gal 2-1/2 qts	
SHORTENING,SOFTENED	14-1/2 oz	2 cup	
BUTTER	1 lbs	2 cup	
SUGAR,GRANULATED	14-1/8 oz	2 cup	
VANILLA GLAZE		2-3/4 cup	

Method

1. Sprinkle yeast over water. DO NOT USE TEMPERATURES ABOVE 110 F. Mix well. Let stand 5 minutes; stir. Set aside for use in Step 3.
2. Place water, eggs, sugar, milk, and salt in mixer bowl. Using dough hook, mix at low speed just until blended.
3. Add flour and yeast solution. Mix at low speed 1 minute or until all flour mixture is incorporated into liquid.
4. Add shortening; mix at low speed 1 minute. Continue mixing at medium speed 10 minutes or until dough is smooth and elastic. Dough temperature should be between 78 F. to 82 F.
5. FERMENT: Cover. Set in a warm place (80 F.) about 1-1/2 hours or until double in bulk.
6. PUNCH: Divide dough into 3 pieces, 4 lb 5 oz each; shape into a rectangular piece. Let rest 10 to 20 minutes.
7. Roll out each 4 lb 5 oz piece of dough into a rectangular sheet, about 18 inches wide, 36 inches long, and 1/4 inch thick. (If using D 036 01, Sweet Dough Mix, use 4 lb 2 oz pieces).
8. Melt butter or margarine. Brush 1/2 cup on each sheet of dough.
9. Roll each piece tightly to make a long slender roll. Seal edges by pressing firmly. Elongate roll to 35 inches by rolling back and forth on the work table. Brush 2 tbsp butter or margarine on each roll.
10. Slice each roll into 34 pieces, about 1 inch wide, using dough cutter.
11. Press cut side of each slice in 14 ounces or 2 cups granulated sugar so that surface is well coated.
12. Place sugar side up on lightly greased sheet pans in rows 5 by 8.
13. Proof at 90 F. to 100 F. until double in bulk.
14. Bake at 375 F. for 20 to 25 minutes or until golden brown or in 325 F. convection oven 15 minutes on high fan, open vent. Cool.
15. Glaze, if desired, with 1 recipe Vanilla Glaze, Recipe No. D 046 00 per 100 portions. Brush about 1 cup on rolls in each pan.

STREUSEL COFFEE CAKE

Yield 100   **Portion** 1 Piece

Calories	Carbohydrates	Protein	Fat	Cholesterol	Sodium	Calcium
319 cal	50 g	7 g	10 g	39 mg	274 mg	26 mg

Ingredient	Weight	Measure	Issue
YEAST,ACTIVE,DRY	6-3/4 oz	1 cup	
WATER,WARM	1 lbs	2 cup	
WATER	1-5/8 lbs	3 cup	
EGGS,WHOLE,FROZEN	1-1/4 lbs	2-1/4 cup	
SUGAR,GRANULATED	1-1/8 lbs	2-5/8 cup	
MILK,NONFAT,DRY	1-3/4 oz	3/4 cup	
SALT	1-7/8 oz	3 tbsp	
FLOUR,WHEAT,BREAD	7-7/8 lbs	1 gal 2-1/2 qts	
SHORTENING,SOFTENED	14-1/2 oz	2 cup	
EGG WASH		3/4 cup	
STREUSEL TOPPING		3 qts	
VANILLA GLAZE		2 cup	

Method

1. Sprinkle yeast over water. DO NOT USE TEMPERATURES ABOVE 110 F. Mix well. Let stand 5 minutes; stir. Set aside for use in Step 3.

2. Place water, eggs, sugar, milk, and salt in mixer bowl. Using dough hook, mix at low speed just until blended.
3. Add flour and yeast solution. Mix at low speed 1 minute or until all flour mixture is incorporated into liquid.
4. Add shortening; mix at low speed 1 minute. Continue mixing at medium speed 10 minutes or until dough is smooth and elastic. Dough temperature should be between 78 F. to 82 F.
5. FERMENT: Cover. Set in warm place (80 F.) about 1-1/2 hours or until double in bulk.
6. PUNCH: Divide dough into 2-6 lb 8 oz pieces. (If using D 036 01, Sweet Dough Mix, divide into 6 lb 4 oz pieces). Shape into a rectangular piece. Let rest 10 to 20 minutes.
7. Roll each piece of dough into a rectangular sheet, about 18 inches wide, 25 inches long and 1/2-inch thick; fit into greased sheet pans, pressing against sides; edges should be thicker than center.
8. Dock dough with fork or docker, if available.
9. Prepare 1/4 recipe Egg Wash, Recipe No. D 017 00 per 100 portions. Brush about 1/3 cup on dough in each pan. Prepare 1 recipe Streusel Topping, Recipe No. D 049 00; sprinkle 1-1/2 quart topping over dough in each pan.
10. Proof dough 20 to 35 minutes.
11. Bake at 375 F., 30 to 35 minutes or until golden brown or in 325 F. convection oven 15 minutes on high fan, open vent.
12. Prepare 2/3 recipe Vanilla Glaze, Recipe No. D 046 00 per 100 portions; drizzle about 1 cup over each cake while hot.
13. Cut 6 by 9.

SMALL COFFEE CAKE

Yield 100   **Portion** 1 Piece

Calories	Carbohydrates	Protein	Fat	Cholesterol	Sodium	Calcium
423 cal	81 g	6 g	9 g	36 mg	270 mg	57 mg

Ingredient	Weight	Measure	Issue
YEAST,ACTIVE,DRY	6-3/4 oz	1 cup	
WATER,WARM	1 lbs	2 cup	
WATER	1-5/8 lbs	3 cup	
EGGS,WHOLE,FROZEN	1-1/4 lbs	2-1/4 cup	
SUGAR,GRANULATED	1-1/8 lbs	2-5/8 cup	
MILK,NONFAT,DRY	1-3/4 oz	3/4 cup	
SALT	1-7/8 oz	3 tbsp	
FLOUR,WHEAT,BREAD	7-7/8 lbs	1 gal 2-1/2 qts	
SHORTENING,SOFTENED	14-1/2 oz	2 cup	
BUTTER	12 oz	1-1/2 cup	
CINNAMON SUGAR FILLING		1 qts 1/2 cup	
RAISINS	2 lbs	1 qts 2-1/4 cup	
EGG WASH		3/4 cup	
VANILLA GLAZE		2-3/4 cup	

Method
1. Sprinkle yeast over water. DO NOT USE IN TEMPERATURES ABOVE 110 F. Mix well. Let stand 5 minutes; stir. Set aside for use in Step 3.
2. Place water, eggs, sugar, milk, and salt in mixer bowl. Using dough hook, mix at low speed just until blended.

3. Add flour and yeast solution. Mix at low speed 1 minute or until all flour mixture is incorporated into liquid.
4. Add shortening; mix at low speed 1 minute. Continue mixing at medium speed 10 minutes or until dough is smooth and elastic. Dough temperature should be between 78 F. to 82 F.
5. FERMENT: Cover. Set in a warm place (80 F.) about 1-1/2 hours or until double in bulk.
6. PUNCH: Divide dough into 6-2 lb 2 oz pieces; (if using D 036 01, Sweet Dough Mix, divide into 2 lb 1 oz pieces). Shape into a rectangular piece. Let rest 10 to 20 minutes.
7. Roll each piece of dough into a rectangular sheet about 9 inches wide, 36 inches long, and 1/4 inch thick.
8. Melt butter or margarine; brush 1/4 cup on each sheet of dough. Prepare Cinnamon Sugar Filling, Recipe No. D 042 02; use 2 pounds or 6-1/4 cups of raisins; sprinkle 3/4 cup filling and 1 cup raisins over each sheet of dough.
9. Roll each piece tightly to make a long slender roll. Seal edges by pressing firmly. Elongate roll to 36 inches by rolling back and forth on work table.
10. Cut rolls into 12-inch pieces weighting about 10 ounces each.
11. Place 4 coffee cakes on each lightly greased sheet pan.
12. Make a deep 9-inch slit down the center of each piece, about 1/2 through folds of dough. Do not cut completely through all layers.
13. Prepare 1/4 recipe Egg Wash, Recipe No. D 017 00 per 100 portions. Brush about 2 teaspoons on each cake.
14. Proof at 90 F. to 100 F. until double in bulk.
15. Bake at 375 F. for 25 to 30 minutes or until golden brown or in 325 F. convection oven for 15 minutes on high fan, open vent.
16. Glaze, if desired, with 1 recipe Vanilla Glaze, Recipe No. D 046 00. Drizzle about 2 tablespoons on cakes in each pan.
17. Cut each cake into 6, 2-inch pieces.

TWIST COFFEE CAKE

Yield 100   **Portion** 1 Roll

Calories	Carbohydrates	Protein	Fat	Cholesterol	Sodium	Calcium
303 cal	51 g	6 g	9 g	35 mg	257 mg	29 mg

Ingredient	Weight	Measure	Issue
YEAST,ACTIVE,DRY	6-3/4 oz	1 cup	
WATER,WARM	1 lbs	2 cup	
WATER	1-5/8 lbs	3 cup	
EGGS,WHOLE,FROZEN	1-1/4 lbs	2-1/4 cup	
SUGAR,GRANULATED	1-1/8 lbs	2-5/8 cup	
MILK,NONFAT,DRY	1-3/4 oz	3/4 cup	
SALT	1-7/8 oz	3 tbsp	
FLOUR,WHEAT,BREAD	7-7/8 lbs	1 gal 2-1/2 qts	
SHORTENING,SOFTENED	14-1/2 oz	2 cup	
BUTTER	12 oz	1-1/2 cup	
CINNAMON SUGAR RAISIN FILLING		2-3/4 cup	
RAISINS	10-1/4 oz	2 cup	
RAISINS	10-1/4 oz	2 cup	
EGG WASH		3/4 cup	
VANILLA GLAZE		2-3/4 cup	

Method

1. Sprinkle yeast over water. DO NOT USE TEMPERATURES ABOVE 110 F. Mix well. Let stand 5 minutes; stir. Set aside for use in Step 3.
2. Place water, eggs, sugar, milk, and salt in mixer bowl. Using dough hook, mix at low speed just until blended.
3. Add flour and yeast solution. Mix at low speed 1 minute or until all flour mixture is incorporated into liquid.
4. Add shortening; mix at low speed 1 minute. Continue mixing at medium speed 10 minutes or until dough is smooth and elastic. Dough temperature should be between 78 F. to 82 F.
5. FERMENT: Cover. Set in a warm place (80 F.) about 1-1/2 hours or until double in bulk.
6. PUNCH: Divide dough into 3 pieces, 4 lb 5 oz pieces; shape into a rectangular piece. Let rest 10 to 20 minutes.
7. Roll each 4 lb 5 oz piece of dough into a rectangular sheet, about 13 inches wide, 45 inches long, and 1/4-inch thick. (If using D 036 01, Sweet Dough Mix, use 4 lb 2 oz pieces).
8. Melt butter or margarine. Brush 1/2 cup over dough in each pan. Prepare Cinnamon Sugar Raisin Filling, Recipe No. D 042 02. Sprinkle 1-1/2 cups over each sheet of dough. Sprinkle about 1 cup of raisins over center third of dough.
9. Fold 1/3 dough over center. Sprinkle 1 cup raisins on top of folded dough. Fold remaining 1/3 dough over raisins to form a strip 13 by 15 inches.
10. Cut each strip into 6-15 inch long, 2 inch wide pieces weighing about 1 pound each.
11. Slit roll down center to within 1 inch of end.
12. Twist pieces in one direction and then in opposite direction, stretching to about 19 inches.
13. Place each piece in a circle on lightly greased sheet pans; seal ends securely by fitting one end into other. Rings should not touch each other.
14. Prepare 1/4 recipe Egg Wash, Recipe No. D 017 00 per 100 portions. Brush about 2 teaspoons on each cake.
15. Proof at 90 F. to 100 F. until double in bulk.
16. Bake at 375 F. for 25 to 30 minutes or until golden brown or in 325 F .convection oven 15 minutes on high fan, open vent. Cool.
17. Glaze, if desired, with 1 recipe Vanilla Glaze, Recipe No. D 046 00 per 100 portions. Drizzle about 2/3 cup on each cake. Cut each cake into 6 pieces.

BEAR CLAWS

Yield 100   Portion 1 Roll

Calories	Carbohydrates	Protein	Fat	Cholesterol	Sodium	Calcium
308 cal	53 g	8 g	7 g	87 mg	254 mg	48 mg

Ingredient	Weight	Measure	Issue
YEAST,ACTIVE,DRY	6-3/4 oz	1 cup	
WATER,WARM	1 lbs	2 cup	
WATER	1-5/8 lbs	3 cup	
EGGS,WHOLE,FROZEN	1-1/4 lbs	2-1/4 cup	
SUGAR,GRANULATED	1-1/8 lbs	2-5/8 cup	
MILK,NONFAT,DRY	1-3/4 oz	3/4 cup	
SALT	1-7/8 oz	3 tbsp	
FLOUR,WHEAT,BREAD	7-7/8 lbs	1 gal 2-1/2 qts	
SHORTENING,SOFTENED	14-1/2 oz	2 cup	
CHERRY FILLING (CORNSTARCH)		2 qts 1 cup	
EGG WASH		1 gal 3/4 qts	
VANILLA GLAZE		2-3/8 cup	

Method

1. Sprinkle yeast over water. DO NOT USE TEMPERATURES ABOVE 110 F. Mix well. Let stand 5 minutes; stir. Set aside for use in Step 3.
2. Place water, eggs, sugar, milk, and salt in mixer bowl. Using dough hook, mix at low speed just until blended.
3. Add flour and yeast solution. Mix at low speed 1 minute or until all flour mixture is incorporated into liquid.
4. Add shortening; mix at low speed 1 minute. Continue mixing at medium speed 10 minutes or until dough is smooth and elastic. Dough temperature should be 78 F. to 82 F.
5. FERMENT: Cover. Set in a warm place (80 F.) about 1-1/2 hours or until double in bulk.
6. PUNCH: Divide dough into 2 pound 2 ounce pieces; shape into a rectangular piece. Let rest 10 to 20 minutes. (If using D 036 01, Sweet Dough Mix, use 2 lb 1 oz pieces.)
7. Roll each piece of dough into a rectangular sheet about 5 inches wide, 44 inches long, and 1/3-inch thick.
8. Prepare Cherry Filling, Recipe No. D 041 00, Pineapple Filling, Recipe No. D 047 00, or Nut Filling, Recipe D 043 00. Spread 1-1/2 cups cherry or pineapple or 1-1/4 cups nut filling over center of each sheet of dough.
9. Fold dough over once, lengthwise; seal along edge by pressing firmly.
10. Cut dough into 17 2-1/2-inch pieces. Make 3 cuts, 3/4-inch in depth, on sealed side of each piece to form a claw.
11. Place on lightly greased sheet pans in rows 3 by 8. Spread claws slightly. Claws should not touch each other.
12. Prepare 1/4 Recipe Egg Wash, Recipe No. D 017 00. Brush 3 tablespoons on claws in each pan.
13. Proof at 90 F. to 100 F. until double in bulk.
14. Bake at 375 F. for 20 to 25 minutes or until golden brown or in a 325 F. convection oven for 15 minutes on high fan, open vent. Cool.
15. Glaze, if desired, with 1 Recipe Vanilla Glaze, Recipe No. D 046 00. Brush about 2/3 cup over rolls in each pan.

SNAILS

Yield 100   **Portion** 1 Roll

Calories	Carbohydrates	Protein	Fat	Cholesterol	Sodium	Calcium
321 cal	54 g	6 g	9 g	29 mg	266 mg	20 mg

Ingredient	Weight	Measure	Issue
YEAST,ACTIVE,DRY	6-3/4 oz	1 cup	
WATER,WARM	1 lbs	2 cup	
WATER	1-5/8 lbs	3 cup	
EGGS,WHOLE,FROZEN	1-1/4 lbs	2-1/4 cup	
SUGAR,GRANULATED	1-1/8 lbs	2-5/8 cup	
MILK,NONFAT,DRY	1-3/4 oz	3/4 cup	
SALT	1-7/8 oz	3 tbsp	
FLOUR,WHEAT,BREAD	7-7/8 lbs	1 gal 2-1/2 qts	
SHORTENING,SOFTENED	14-1/2 oz	2 cup	
MARGARINE	12 oz	1-1/2 cup	
EGG WASH		3/4 cup	
JELLY	1-1/3 lbs	2 cup	
VANILLA GLAZE		2-1/2 cup	

Method

1. Sprinkle yeast over water. DO NOT USE TEMPERATURES ABOVE 110 F. Mix well. Let stand 5 minutes; stir. Set aside for use in Step 3.
2. Place water, eggs, sugar, milk, and salt in mixer bowl. Using dough hook, mix at low speed just until blended.
3. Add flour and yeast solution. Mix at low speed 1 minute or until all flour mixture is incorporated into liquid.
4. Add shortening; mix at low speed 1 minute. Continue mixing at medium speed 10 minutes or until dough is smooth and elastic. Dough temperature should be 78 F. to 82 F.
5. FERMENT: Cover. Set in a warm place (80 F.) about 1-1/2 hours or until double in bulk.
6. PUNCH: Divide dough into 3 pieces, 4 lb 5 oz each; shape into a rectangular piece. Let rest 10 to 20 minutes.
7. Roll each 4 lb 5 oz piece of dough into a rectangular sheet about 18 inches wide, 36 inches long, and 1/4-inch thick. (If using D 036 01, Sweet Dough Mix, use 4 lb 2 oz pieces.)
8. Melt butter or margarine. Brush 1/2 cup on each sheet of dough. Prepare 1 recipe Cinnamon Sugar Filling, Recipe No. D 042 00; sprinkle 1-1/2 cups over each sheet of dough.
9. Fold each sheet of dough in thirds lengthwise to make a strip, about 6 inches wide, 35 inches long, and 3/4 inches thick.
10. Cut strips crosswise into 34 pieces about 1-inch wide.
11. Twist pieces in one direction and then in the opposite direction. Form snails by holding one end on greased pan and winding other end around and around loosely keeping roll flat.
12. Place on lightly greased sheet pans in rows 4 by 8.
13. Prepare 1/4 Recipe Egg Wash, Recipe D 017 00; brush about 1/4 cup on snails in each pan; let rise slightly.
14. Make slight depression with back of spoon in center of each snail. Use 2 cups of jelly or jam; place about 1 teaspoon in each depression.
15. Proof at 90 F. to 100 F. until double in bulk.
16. Bake at 375 F. for 20 to 25 minutes or until golden brown or in a 325 F. convection oven for 15 minutes on high fan, open vent. Cool.
17. Glaze, if desired, with 1 Recipe Vanilla Glaze, Recipe No. D 046 00. Brush about 3/4 cup on rolls in each pan.

BOWKNOTS, FIGURE 8's, AND S SHAPES

Yield 100   Portion 1 Roll

Calories	Carbohydrates	Protein	Fat	Cholesterol	Sodium	Calcium
288 cal	52 g	6 g	6 g	29 mg	233 mg	18 mg

Ingredient	Weight	Measure	Issue
YEAST,ACTIVE,DRY	6-3/4 oz	1 cup	
WATER,WARM	1 lbs	2 cup	
WATER	1-5/8 lbs	3 cup	
EGGS,WHOLE,FROZEN	1-1/4 lbs	2-1/4 cup	
SUGAR,GRANULATED	1-1/8 lbs	2-5/8 cup	
MILK,NONFAT,DRY	1-3/4 oz	3/4 cup	
SALT	1-7/8 oz	3 tbsp	
FLOUR,WHEAT,BREAD	7-7/8 lbs	1 gal 2-1/2 qts	
SHORTENING,SOFTENED	14-1/2 oz	2 cup	
EGG WASH		3/4 cup	
VANILLA GLAZE		2-3/4 cup	

Method

1. Sprinkle yeast over water. DO NOT USE TEMPERATURES ABOVE 110 F. Mix well. Let stand 5 minutes; stir. Set aside for use in Step 3.
2. Place water, eggs, sugar, milk, and salt in mixer bowl. Using dough hook, mix at low speed just until blended.
3. Add flour and yeast solution. Mix at low speed 1 minute or until all flour mixture is incorporated into liquid.
4. Add shortening; mix at low speed 1 minute. Continue mixing at medium speed 10 minutes or until dough is smooth and elastic. Dough temperature should be 78 F. to 82 F.
5. FERMENT: Cover. Set in a warm place (80 F.) about 1-1/2 hours or until double in bulk.
6. PUNCH: Divide dough into 3 pieces, 4 lb 5 oz pieces; shape into a rectangular piece. Let rest 10 to 20 minutes.
7. Roll each 4 lb 5 oz piece of dough into a rectangular sheet about 18 inches wide, 36 inches long, and 1/4-inch thick. (If using D 036 01, Sweet Dough Mix, use 4 lb 2 oz pieces.)
8. Fold each sheet of dough in thirds lengthwise to make a strip about 6 inches wide, 35 inches long, and 3/4-inch thick.
9. Cut strips crosswise into 34 pieces about 1 inch wide.
10. Twist pieces in one direction, then in the opposite direction, stretching to about 11 inches.
11. Form into various shapes. Place on lightly greased sheet pans in rows 4 by 8.
12. Prepare 1/4 Recipe Egg Wash, Recipe No. D 017 00; brush about 1/4 cup on rolls in each pan.
13. Proof at 90 F. to 100 F. until double in bulk.
14. Bake at 375 F. for 20 to 25 minutes or until golden brown or in a 325 F. convection oven for 15 minutes on high fan, open vent. Cool.
15. Glaze, if desired, with 1 recipe Vanilla Glaze, Recipe No. D 046 00. Brush about 3/4 cup on rolls in each pan.

CINNAMON TWISTS

Yield 100   **Portion** 1 Roll

Calories	Carbohydrates	Protein	Fat	Cholesterol	Sodium	Calcium
368 cal	66 g	6 g	9 g	36 mg	266 mg	41 mg

Ingredient	Weight	Measure	Issue
YEAST,ACTIVE,DRY	6-3/4 oz	1 cup	
WATER,WARM	1 lbs	2 cup	
WATER	1-5/8 lbs	3 cup	
EGGS,WHOLE,FROZEN	1-1/4 lbs	2-1/4 cup	
SUGAR,GRANULATED	1-1/8 lbs	2-5/8 cup	
MILK,NONFAT,DRY	1-3/4 oz	3/4 cup	
SALT	1-7/8 oz	3 tbsp	
FLOUR,WHEAT,BREAD	7-7/8 lbs	1 gal 2-1/2 qts	
SHORTENING,SOFTENED	14-1/2 oz	2 cup	
BUTTER	12 oz	1-1/2 cup	
CINNAMON SUGAR FILLING		3 cup	
EGG WASH		3/4 cup	
VANILLA GLAZE		2-3/4 cup	

Method

1. Sprinkle yeast over water. DO NOT USE TEMPERATURES ABOVE 110 F. Mix well. Let stand 5 minutes; stir. Set aside for use in Step 3.

2. Place water, eggs, sugar, milk, and salt in mixer bowl. Using dough hook, mix at low speed just until blended.
3. Add flour and yeast solution. Mix at low speed 1 minute or until all flour mixture is incorporated into liquid.
4. Add shortening; mix at low speed 1 minute. Continue mixing at medium speed 10 minutes or until dough is smooth and elastic. Dough temperature should be 78 F. to 82 F.
5. FERMENT: Cover. Set in a warm place (80 F.) about 1-1/2 hours or until double in bulk.
6. PUNCH: Divide dough into 3 pieces, 4 lb 5 oz each; shape into a rectangular piece. Let rest 10 to 20 minutes.
7. Roll each 4 pounds 5 ounce pieces of dough into a rectangular sheet about 18 inches wide, 36 inches long, and 1/4-inch thick. If using D 036 01, use 4 lb 2 oz pieces.
8. Melt butter or margarine. Brush 1/2 cup on each sheet of dough. Prepare Cinnamon Sugar Filling, Recipe No. D 042 00; sprinkle 1-1/2 cups on each sheet of dough.
9. Fold each sheet of dough in thirds lengthwise to make a strip about 6 inches wide, 35 inches long, and 3/4-inch thick.
10. Cut strips crosswise into 34 pieces about 1 inch wide.
11. Twist pieces in one direction and then in opposite direction.
12. Place on lightly greased sheet pans in rows 4 by 8.
13. Prepare 1/4 Recipe Egg Wash, Recipe No. D 017 00; brush 1/4 cup on rolls in each pan.
14. Proof at 90 F. to 100 F. until double in bulk.
15. Bake at 375 F. for 20 to 25 minutes or in 325 F. convection oven for 15 minutes on high fan, open vent. Cool.
16. Glaze, if desired, with 1 Recipe Vanilla Glaze, Recipe No. D 046 00. Brush about 3/4 cup on rolls in each pan.

BUTTERHORNS

Yield 100   **Portion** 1 Roll

Calories	Carbohydrates	Protein	Fat	Cholesterol	Sodium	Calcium
311 cal	52 g	6 g	9 g	34 mg	260 mg	18 mg

Ingredient	Weight	Measure	Issue
YEAST,ACTIVE,DRY	6-3/4 oz	1 cup	
WATER,WARM	1 lbs	2 cup	
WATER	1-5/8 lbs	3 cup	
EGGS,WHOLE,FROZEN	1-1/4 lbs	2-1/4 cup	
SUGAR,GRANULATED	1-1/8 lbs	2-5/8 cup	
MILK,NONFAT,DRY	1-3/4 oz	3/4 cup	
SALT	1-7/8 oz	3 tbsp	
FLOUR,WHEAT,BREAD	7-7/8 lbs	1 gal 2-1/2 qts	
SHORTENING,SOFTENED	14-1/2 oz	2 cup	
BUTTER	12 oz	1-1/2 cup	
VANILLA GLAZE		2-3/4 cup	

Method
1. Sprinkle yeast over water. DO NOT USE TEMPERATURES ABOVE 110 F. Mix well. Let stand 5 minutes; stir. Set aside for use in Step 3.
2. Place water, eggs, sugar, milk, and salt in mixer bowl. Using dough hook, mix at low speed just until blended.

3. Add flour and yeast solution. Mix at low speed 1 minute or until all flour mixture is incorporated into liquid.
4. Add shortening; mix at low speed 1 minute. Continue mixing at medium speed 10 minutes or until dough is smooth and elastic. Dough temperature should be 78 F. to 82 F.
5. FERMENT: Cover. Set in a warm place (80 F.) about 1-1/2 hours or until double in bulk.
6. PUNCH: Divide dough into 1 pound 7 ounce pieces; shape into a rectangular piece. Let rest 10 to 20 minutes.
7. Roll each piece of dough into a rectangular sheet about 9 inches wide, 24 inches long, and about 1/4-inch thick. (For D 036 01, divide into 9-1 lb 6 oz pieces.)
8. Melt butter or margarine. Brush about 3 tablespoons on each sheet of dough.
9. Cut each strip into 12 wedges about 4 inches wide at the widest end.
10. Roll up each wedge from wide edge to point.
11. Place on lightly greased sheet pans in rows 4 by 8 with point end under roll; press firmly in place.
12. Proof at 90 F. to 100 F. until double in bulk.
13. Bake at 375 F. for 20 to 25 minutes or in a 325 F. convection oven for 15 minutes on high fan, open vent. Cool.
14. Glaze, if desired, with 1 Recipe Vanilla Glaze, Recipe No. D 046 00. Brush about 3/4 cup on rolls in each pan.

CRESCENTS

Yield 100   **Portion** 1 Roll

Calories	Carbohydrates	Protein	Fat	Cholesterol	Sodium	Calcium
311 cal	52 g	6 g	9 g	34 mg	260 mg	18 mg

Ingredient	Weight	Measure	Issue
YEAST,ACTIVE,DRY	6-3/4 oz	1 cup	
WATER,WARM	1 lbs	2 cup	
WATER	1-5/8 lbs	3 cup	
EGGS,WHOLE,FROZEN	1-1/4 lbs	2-1/4 cup	
SUGAR,GRANULATED	1-1/8 lbs	2-5/8 cup	
MILK,NONFAT,DRY	1-3/4 oz	3/4 cup	
SALT	1-7/8 oz	3 tbsp	
FLOUR,WHEAT,BREAD	7-7/8 lbs	1 gal 2-1/2 qts	
SHORTENING,SOFTENED	14-1/2 oz	2 cup	
BUTTER	12 oz	1-1/2 cup	
VANILLA GLAZE		2-3/4 cup	

Method
1. Sprinkle yeast over water. DO NOT USE TEMPERATURES ABOVE 110 F. Mix well. Let stand 5 minutes; stir. Set aside for use in Step 3.
2. Place water, eggs, sugar, milk, and salt in mixer bowl. Using dough hook, mix at low speed just until blended.
3. Add flour and yeast solution. Mix at low speed 1 minute or until all flour mixture is incorporated into liquid.
4. Add shortening; mix at low speed 1 minute. Continue mixing at medium speed 10 minutes or until dough is smooth and elastic. Dough temperature should be 78 F. to 82 F.
5. FERMENT: Cover. Set in a warm place (80 F.) about 1-1/2 hours or until double in bulk.
6. PUNCH: Divide dough into 9 pieces, 1 lb 7 oz pieces; shape into a rectangular piece. Let rest 10 to 20 minutes. If using D 036 01, divide into 9 1 lb 6 oz pieces.

7. Roll each piece of dough into a rectangular sheet about 9 inches wide, 24 inches long, and about 1/4-inch thick.
8. Melt butter or margarine. Brush about 3 tablespoons on each sheet of dough.
9. Cut each strip into 12 wedges about 4 inches wide at the widest end.
10. Roll up each wedge from wide edge to point.
11. Place on lightly greased sheet pans in rows 4 by 8 with point end under roll; press firmly in place.
12. Proof at 90 F. to 100 F. until double in bulk.
13. Bake at 375 F. for 20 to 25 minutes or in a 325 F. convection oven for 15 minutes on high fan, open vent. Cool.
14. Glaze, if desired, with 1 Recipe Vanilla Glaze, Recipe No. D 046 00. Brush about 3/4 cup on rolls in each pan.

QUICK COFFEE CAKE (BISCUIT MIX)

Yield 100   **Portion** 1 Piece

Calories	Carbohydrates	Protein	Fat	Cholesterol	Sodium	Calcium
276 cal	44 g	4 g	9 g	24 mg	443 mg	76 mg

Ingredient	Weight	Measure	Issue
FLOUR,WHEAT,GENERAL PURPOSE	1-2/3 lbs	1 qts 2 cup	
MARGARINE,SOFTENED	12 oz	1-1/2 cup	
CINNAMON,GROUND	1/4 oz	1 tbsp	
SUGAR,BROWN,PACKED	7-2/3 oz	1-1/2 cup	
BISCUIT MIX	6-3/4 lbs	1 gal 2-3/8 qts	
SUGAR,GRANULATED	1-1/2 lbs	3-1/2 cup	
MILK,NONFAT,DRY	3-5/8 oz	1-1/2 cup	
WATER	3-1/8 lbs	1 qts 2 cup	
EGGS,WHOLE,FROZEN	1-1/4 lbs	2-1/4 cup	
EXTRACT,VANILLA	7/8 oz	2 tbsp	
COOKING SPRAY,NONSTICK	2 oz	1/4 cup 1/3 tbsp	
SUGAR,POWDERED	2-1/8 lbs	2 qts	
WATER,BOILING	8-1/3 oz	1 cup	
MARGARINE,SOFTENED	2 oz	1/4 cup 1/3 tbsp	
EXTRACT,VANILLA	1/8 oz	1/8 tsp	

Method
1. TOPPING: In mixer bowl, combine flour, butter or margarine, brown sugar, cinnamon; mix at low speed 3 minutes until mixture resembles coarse cornmeal. Remove topping from mixer bowl and set aside for use in Step 6.
2. CAKE: In mixer bowl, combine Biscuit Mix, sugar and nonfat dry milk; mix at low speed 1 minute or until well blended.
3. Combine water, eggs, vanilla; add egg mixture gradually to dry mixture while mixing at low speed for 2 minutes.
4. Scrape down sides and bottom of mixer bowl; continue to mix at low speed an additional 1 minute. DO NOT OVERMIX.
5. Lightly spray pan with non-stick cooking spray. Pour 3-1/2 quarts of batter into each floured pan. Spread batter evenly.
6. Sprinkle 1 quart topping over batter in each pan.
7. Using a convection oven, bake at 325 F. for about 30 minutes on low fan, open vent. Remove cakes from oven and let cool slightly.

8. GLAZE: Combine powdered sugar, hot water, butter or margarine and vanilla; mix until smooth.
9. Drizzle about 2 cups glaze over each baked cake while cakes are still warm. Cut 6 by 9.

QUICK APPLE COFFEE CAKE (BISCUIT MIX)

Yield 100   **Portion** 1 Piece

Calories	Carbohydrates	Protein	Fat	Cholesterol	Sodium	Calcium
214 cal	37 g	4 g	6 g	24 mg	405 mg	76 mg

Ingredient	Weight	Measure	Issue
SUGAR,GRANULATED	1 lbs	2-1/4 cup	
CINNAMON,GROUND	1 oz	1/4 cup 1/3 tbsp	
NUTMEG,GROUND	1/8 oz	1/3 tsp	
BISCUIT MIX	6-3/4 lbs	1 gal 2-3/8 qts	
SUGAR,GRANULATED	1-1/2 lbs	3-1/2 cup	
MILK,NONFAT,DRY	3-5/8 oz	1-1/2 cup	
WATER	3-1/8 lbs	1 qts 2 cup	
EXTRACT,VANILLA	7/8 oz	2 tbsp	
EGGS,WHOLE,FROZEN	1-1/4 lbs	2-1/4 cup	
COOKING SPRAY,NONSTICK	2 oz	1/4 cup 1/3 tbsp	
APPLES,CANNED,SLICED,DRAINED	6-3/4 lbs	3 qts 1-5/8 cup	

Method

1. TOPPING: Combine sugar, cinnamon and nutmeg. Set aside for use in Steps 6 and 8.
2. Cake: In mixer bowl, combine biscuit mix, sugar and nonfat dry milk; mix at low speed 1 minute or until well blended.
3. Combine water, eggs and vanilla. Add egg mixture gradually to dry mixture while mixing at low speed for 2 minutes.
4. Scrape down sides and bottom of mixer bowl; continue to mix at low speed an additional 1 minute. DO NOT OVERMIX.
5. Lightly spray each pan with non-stick cooking spray. Pour 3-1/2 quarts of batter into each floured pan. Spread batter evenly.
6. Sprinkle 1/2 cup of topping over batter in each pan.
7. Arrange 3 pounds of apple slices evenly over batter and topping in each pan.
8. Sprinkle 3/4 cup of sugar mixture over apple slices in each pan.
9. Using a convection oven, bake 30 minutes at 325 F. on low fan, open vent.
10. Remove cakes from oven and let cool. Cut 6 by 9.

QUICK FRENCH COFFEE CAKE (BISCUIT MIX)

Yield 100   **Portion** 1 Piece

Calories	Carbohydrates	Protein	Fat	Cholesterol	Sodium	Calcium
343 cal	53 g	6 g	12 g	24 mg	444 mg	87 mg

Ingredient	Weight	Measure	Issue
FLOUR,WHEAT,GENERAL PURPOSE	1-2/3 lbs	1 qts 2 cup	
MARGARINE,SOFTENED	12 oz	1-1/2 cup	
SUGAR,BROWN,PACKED	7-2/3 oz	1-1/2 cup	
CINNAMON,GROUND	1/4 oz	1 tbsp	
BISCUIT MIX	6-3/4 lbs	1 gal 2-3/8 qts	

RAISINS	1-7/8 lbs	1 qts 2 cup
SUGAR,GRANULATED	1-1/2 lbs	3-1/2 cup
NUTS,UNSALTED,CHOPPED,COARSELY	1-1/2 lbs	1 qts 5/8 cup
MILK,NONFAT,DRY	3-5/8 oz	1-1/2 cup
NUTMEG,GROUND	1/2 oz	2 tbsp
WATER	3-1/8 lbs	1 qts 2 cup
EXTRACT,VANILLA	7/8 oz	2 tbsp
EGGS,WHOLE,FROZEN	1-1/4 lbs	2-1/4 cup
COOKING SPRAY,NONSTICK	2 oz	1/4 cup 1/3 tbsp
SUGAR,POWDERED	2-1/8 lbs	2 qts
WATER,BOILING	8-1/3 oz	1 cup
MARGARINE,SOFTENED	2 oz	1/4 cup 1/3 tbsp
EXTRACT,VANILLA	1/8 oz	1/8 tsp

Method

1. TOPPING: In mixer bowl, combine flour, butter or margarine, brown sugar, cinnamon; mix at low speed 3 minutes until mixture resembles coarse cornmeal. Remove topping from mixer bowl and set aside for use in Step 6.
2. CAKE: In mixer bowl, combine Biscuit Mix, raisins, sugar, walnuts, nonfat dry milk and nutmeg; mix at low speed 1 minute or until well blended.
3. Combine water, eggs and vanilla. Add egg mixture gradually to dry mixture whiile mixing at low speed 2 minutes.
4. Scrape down sides and bottom of mixer bowl. Continue to mix at low speed an additional 1minute. DO NOT OVERMIX.
5. Pour 1 gallon batter into each lightly sprayed and floured pan. Spread batter evenly.
6. Sprinkle 1 quart of topping over batter in each pan.
7. Using a convection oven, bake 30 minutes on low fan, open vent. Remove cakes from oven and let cool slightly.
8. GLAZE: Combine powdered sugar, hot water, butter or margarine and vanilla; mix until smooth.
9. Drizzle 2 cups glaze over each baked cake while cakes are still warm. Cut 6 by 9.

QUICK CHERRY COFFEE CAKE (BISCUIT MIX)

Yield 100   **Portion** 1 Piece

Calories	Carbohydrates	Protein	Fat	Cholesterol	Sodium	Calcium
290 cal	48 g	4 g	9 g	24 mg	443 mg	79 mg

Ingredient	Weight	Measure	Issue
FLOUR,WHEAT,GENERAL PURPOSE	1-2/3 lbs	1 qts 2 cup	
MARGARINE,SOFTENED	12 oz	1-1/2 cup	
SUGAR,BROWN,PACKED	7-2/3 oz	1-1/2 cup	
CINNAMON,GROUND	1/4 oz	1 tbsp	
BISCUIT MIX	6-3/4 lbs	1 gal 2-3/8 qts	
SUGAR,GRANULATED	1-1/2 lbs	3-1/2 cup	
MILK,NONFAT,DRY	3-5/8 oz	1-1/2 cup	
WATER	3-1/8 lbs	1 qts 2 cup	
EGGS,WHOLE,FROZEN	1-1/4 lbs	2-1/4 cup	
EXTRACT,VANILLA	7/8 oz	2 tbsp	
COOKING SPRAY,NONSTICK	2 oz	1/4 cup 1/3 tbsp	
CHERRIES,CANNED,RED,TART,WATER PACK,INCL	6-1/2 lbs	2 qts 3-7/8 cup	

LIQUIDS

SUGAR,POWDERED	2-1/8 lbs	2 qts
WATER,BOILING	8-1/3 oz	1 cup
MARGARINE,SOFTENED	2 oz	1/4 cup 1/3 tbsp
EXTRACT,VANILLA	1/8 oz	1/8 tsp

Method

1. TOPPING: In mixer bowl, combine flour, butter or margarine, brown sugar, cinnamon; mix at low speed 3 minutes until mixture resembles coarse cornmeal. Remove topping from mixer bowl and set aside for use in Step 7.
2. CAKE: In mixer bowl, combine Biscuit Mix, sugar and nonfat dry milk; mix at low speed 1 minute or until well blended.
3. Combine water, eggs and vanilla. Add egg mixture gradually to dry mixture while mixing at low speed for 2 minutes.
4. Scrape down sides and bottom of mixer bowl; continue to mix low speed an additional 1 minute. DO NOT OVERMIX.
5. Pour 3-1/2 quart batter into each lightly sprayed and floured pan. Spread batter evenly.
6. Arrange 2-1/2 pounds cherries evenly over batter in each pan.
7. Sprinkle 1 quart of topping over batter and cherries in each pan.
8. Using a convection oven, bake about 30 minutes on low fan, open vent at 325 F. Remove cakes from oven and let cool slightly.
9. GLAZE: Combine powdered sugar, hot water, butter or margarine, vanilla; mix until smooth.
10. Drizzle 2 cups glaze over each baked cake while cakes are still warm. Cut 6 by 9.

QUICK ORANGE-COCONUT COFFEE CAKE (BISCUIT MIX)

Yield 100   **Portion** 1 Piece

Calories	Carbohydrates	Protein	Fat	Cholesterol	Sodium	Calcium
405 cal	53 g	4 g	20 g	37 mg	519 mg	66 mg

Ingredient	Weight	Measure	Issue
SUGAR,GRANULATED	1-1/2 lbs	3-1/2 cup	
MARGARINE,SOFTENED		1 cup	
BISCUIT MIX	6-3/4 lbs	1 gal 2-3/8 qts	
SUGAR,GRANULATED		2-1/4 cup	
MILK,NONFAT,DRY		1-1/2 cup	
WATER	3-1/8 lbs	1 qts 2 cup	
EGGS,WHOLE,FROZEN	1-1/4 lbs	2-1/4 cup	
EXTRACT,VANILLA	7/8 oz	2 tbsp	
ORANGE-COCONUT TOPPING		2 qts 2 cup	
COOKING SPRAY,NONSTICK	2 oz	1/4 cup 1/3 tbsp	

Method

1. TOPPING: In mixer bowl, cream sugar and butter or margarine at medium speed 2 minutes. Add coconut, orange juice, flour and orange rind; mix at low speed 2 minutes. Remove topping from mixer bowl and set aside for use in Step 6.
2. CAKE: In mixer bowl, combine bisquick mix, sugar and nonfat dry milk; mix at low speed 1 minute or until well blended.
3. Combine water, eggs and vanilla. Add egg mixture gradually to dry mixture while mixing at low speed 2 minutes.

160

4. Scrape down sides and bottom of mixer bowl; continue to mix low speed an additional 1 minute. DO NOT OVERMIX.
5. Lightly spray each pan with non-stick spray. Pour 3-1/2 quarts of batter into each sprayed and floured pan. Spread batter evenly.
6. Sprinkle 1 quart topping over batter in each pan.
7. Using a convection oven, bake about 30 minutes on low fan, open vent at 325 F. Remove cakes from oven and let cool slightly. Cut 6 by 9.

QUICK COFFEE CAKE

Yield 100   **Portion** 1 Piece

Calories	Carbohydrates	Protein	Fat	Cholesterol	Sodium	Calcium
288 cal	45 g	4 g	11 g	32 mg	246 mg	68 mg

Ingredient	Weight	Measure	Issue
FLOUR,WHEAT,GENERAL PURPOSE	1-2/3 lbs	1 qts 2 cup	
BUTTER,SOFTENED	12 oz	1-1/2 cup	
SUGAR,BROWN,PACKED	7-2/3 oz	1-1/2 cup	
CINNAMON,GROUND	1/4 oz	1 tbsp	
FLOUR,WHEAT,GENERAL PURPOSE	3-7/8 lbs	3 qts 2 cup	
SUGAR,GRANULATED	3 lbs	1 qts 2-3/4 cup	
MILK,NONFAT,DRY	3 oz	1-1/4 cup	
BAKING POWDER	2-3/4 oz	1/4 cup 2 tbsp	
SALT	1 oz	1 tbsp	
WATER	3-1/8 lbs	1 qts 2 cup	
OIL,SALAD	1-1/2 lbs	3 cup	
EGGS,WHOLE,FROZEN	1-1/4 lbs	2-1/4 cup	
EXTRACT,VANILLA	7/8 oz	2 tbsp	
SUGAR,POWDERED	2-1/8 lbs	2 qts	
WATER,BOILING	8-1/3 oz	1 cup	
BUTTER,SOFTENED	2 oz	1/4 cup 1/3 tbsp	
EXTRACT,VANILLA	1/8 oz	1/8 tsp	

Method
1. TOPPING: In mixer bowl, combine flour, butter or margarine, brown sugar, cinnamon; mix at low speed 3 minutes until mixture resembles coarse cornmeal. Remove topping from mixer bowl and set aside for use in Step 6.
2. CAKE: In mixer bowl, sift together flour, sugar and nonfat dry milk, baking powder and salt; mix at low speed 1 minute or until well blended.
3. Combine water, salad oil, eggs and vanilla. Add egg mixture gradually to dry mixture while mixing at low speed 2 minutes.
4. Scrape down sides and bottom of mixer bowl; continue to mix low speed an additional 1 minute. DO NOT OVERMIX.
5. Pour 3-1/2 quart into each lightly sprayed and floured pan. Spread batter evenly.
6. Sprinkle 1 quart of topping over batter in each pan.
7. Using a convection oven, bake on low fan, open vent at 325 F. for about 30 minutes. Remove cakes from oven and let cool slightly.
8. GLAZE: Combine powdered sugar, hot water, butter or margarine and vanilla; mix until smooth.
9. Drizzle 2 cups glaze over each baked cake while cakes are still warm. Cut 6 by 9.

TEMPURA BATTER

Yield 100   **Portion** 1 Gallon

Calories	Carbohydrates	Protein	Fat	Cholesterol	Sodium	Calcium
5796 cal	1069 g	204 g	66 g	2231 mg	27078 mg	3545 mg

Ingredient	Weight	Measure	Issue
FLOUR,WHEAT,GENERAL PURPOSE	3 lbs	2 qts 3 cup	
BAKING POWDER	1-3/4 oz	1/4 cup	
SALT	1-7/8 oz	3 tbsp	
EGGS,WHOLE,FROZEN	1-1/8 lbs	2-1/8 cup	
WATER,COLD	5-1/4 lbs	2 qts 2 cup	

Method

1. Sift together flour, baking powder, and salt into mixer bowl.
2. Add water to beaten eggs.
3. Add egg mixture to dry ingredients; whip at high speed until smooth.
4. Fry in small batches. Tempura-fried foods lose crispness if allowed to stand on steam-table. DO NOT SAVE.

Notes

1. Batter may be used for Tempura Fried Shrimp, Recipe No. L 137 01 and Tempura Fried Onion Rings, Recipe No. Q 035 02.

DANISH DIAMONDS (DANISH PASTRY DOUGH)

Yield 100   **Portion** 1 Danish

Calories	Carbohydrates	Protein	Fat	Cholesterol	Sodium	Calcium
228 cal	23 g	3 g	14 g	5 mg	168 mg	15 mg

Ingredient	Weight	Measure	Issue
DANISH DOUGH,FROZEN	11 lbs	100 each	
EGG WASH	181-7/8 gm	3/4 unit	
PIE FILLING,APPLE,PREPARED	6 lbs	3 qts	
EGG WASH	181-7/8 gm	3/4 unit	

Method

1. Prepare 50 Danish squares in a batch. Thaw at room temperature 5 minutes on a lightly floured working surface. Rolling out is not necessary.
2. Prepare 1/2 Recipe (1-1/2 cups) Egg Wash, Recipe No. D 017 00. Use 3/4 cup of egg wash. Lightly brush entire surface of each square. Set aside remaining 3/4 cup egg wash for use in Step 6.
3. Place pie filling in mixer bowl. Using whip, mix on medium speed 15 seconds to break up large pieces. Place about 2 tbsp filling in center of each square. Fold lower left corner to center; fold upper right corner over top of first corner. Press firmly to seal; repeat by folding lower right corner to center; press firmly to seal. Fold upper left corner to center; press tip to seal.
4. Place squares on lightly greased pans in rows 4 by 6.
5. Brush lightly with remaining egg wash.
6. Proof at 90 F. for 30 to 45 minutes or until double in bulk.
7. Using a convection oven, bake at 325 F. for 10 minutes or until golden brown on low fan, open vent.
8. Cool. Glaze if desired, with Vanilla Glaze or Variations, Recipe Nos. D 046 00, D 046 01, D 046 02.

Notes

1. In Step 3, any type of fruit pie filling may be used.
2. In Step 3, 7 lb 11 oz of cherry, pineapple or strawberry jam may be used, per 100 portions.
3. Prepare in batches as dough becomes difficult to work with in 15 minutes.

BEAR CLAWS (DANISH PASTRY DOUGH)

Yield 100   **Portion** 1 Danish

Calories	Carbohydrates	Protein	Fat	Cholesterol	Sodium	Calcium
219 cal	20 g	3 g	15 g	5 mg	162 mg	14 mg

Ingredient	Weight	Measure	Issue
DANISH DOUGH,FROZEN	11 lbs	100 each	
EGG WASH	181-7/8 gm	3/4 unit	
PIE FILLING,APPLE,PREPARED	3-1/8 lbs	1 qts 2-1/4 cup	
COOKING SPRAY,NONSTICK	2 oz	1/4 cup 1/3 tbsp	
EGG WASH	181-7/8 gm	3/4 unit	

Method

1. Prepare 50 Danish squares in a batch. Thaw at room temperature 5 minutes on a lightly floured working surface. Rolling out is not necessary.
2. Prepare 1/2 Recipe Egg Wash, Recipe No. D 017 00. Use 3/4 cup of egg wash. Lightly brush entire surface of each square. Set aside remaining 3/4 cup egg wash for use in Step 6.
3. Place about 1 tablespoon of filling over half of each square. Fold in half; seal edge by pressing firmly.
4. Make 3 cuts, 3/4-inch in depth, on 4-inch sealed side of each piece to form a claw.
5. Lightly spray pans with non-stick cooking spray. Place dough on pans. Bend into slight horseshoe shape and spread claws slightly.
6. Brush lightly with remaining egg wash.
7. Proof at 90 F. to 100 F. for 30 to 45 minutes or until double in size.
8. Using a convection oven, bake at 325 F. for 10 minutes or until golden brown on low fan, open vent.
9. Cool. Glaze if desired, with Vanilla Glaze or Variations, Recipe Nos. D 046 00, D 046 01, D 046 02.

Notes

1. Prepare in batches as dough becomes difficult to work with in 15 minutes.

FRUIT TURNOVERS (FROZEN PUFF PASTRY DOUGH)

Yield 100   **Portion** 1 Danish

Calories	Carbohydrates	Protein	Fat	Cholesterol	Sodium	Calcium
346 cal	33 g	4 g	22 g	5 mg	155 mg	9 mg

Ingredient	Weight	Measure	Issue
PUFF PASTRY DOUGH,SQUARES,FROZEN	12-1/2 lbs	100 each	
EGG WASH	181-7/8 gm	3/4 unit	
PIE FILLING,APPLE,PREPARED	6 lbs	3 qts	
COOKING SPRAY,NONSTICK	2 oz	1/4 cup 1/3 tbsp	
EGG WASH	181-7/8 gm	3/4 unit	

Method

1. Prepare 50 Danish squares in a batch. Thaw at room temperature 5 minutes on a lightly floured working surface. Rolling out is not necessary.
2. Prepare 1/2 recipe Egg Wash (Recipe No. D 017 00). Use 3/4 cup egg wash. Lightly brush entire surface of each square. Set aside remaining 3/4 cup egg wash for use in Step 5.
3. Place about 2 tbsp filling in center of each square. Fold upper right corner over lower left corner to form a triangle. Seal by crimping edges together.
4. Make two 1-inch slits in the center.
5. Lightly spray each pan with non-stick cooking spray. Place 24 turnovers on each pan.
6. Brush lightly with remaining egg wash.
7. Using a convection oven, bake 15 minutes in a 350 F. with low fan, open vent or until golden brown.
8. Cool. Glaze if desired, with Vanilla Glaze or Variations, Recipe Nos. D 046 00, D 046 01, D 046 02.

Notes

1. In Step 3, pie filling, prepared, fruit (apple, blueberry, cherry, or peach) may be used as filling. Place in mixer bowl. Using whip, mix on medium speed 15 seconds to break up large pieces.
2. In Step 3, 7 pounds 11 ounces of cherry, pineapple, or strawberry jam may be used, per 100 portions.
3. Prepare in batches as dough becomes difficult to work with in 15 minutes.

FRUIT PUFFS (FROZEN PUFF PASTRY DOUGH)

Yield 100   Portion 1 Danish

Calories	Carbohydrates	Protein	Fat	Cholesterol	Sodium	Calcium
357 cal	37 g	4 g	22 g	0 mg	153 mg	7 mg

Ingredient	Weight	Measure	Issue
PUFF PASTRY DOUGH,SQUARES,FROZEN	12-1/2 lbs	100 each	
WATER	12-1/2 oz	1-1/2 cup	
SUGAR,GRANULATED	1 lbs	2-1/4 cup	
PIE FILLING,APPLE,PREPARED	6 lbs	3 qts	

Method

1. Prepare 50 Danish squares in a batch. Thaw at room temperature 5 minutes on a lightly floured working surface. Rolling out is not necessary.
2. Place squares in rows 3 by 5 on pans. Brush water over each square. Sprinkle sugar over each square.
3. Place about 2 tbsp filling in center of each square. Fold lower left corner to center; fold upper right corner over top of first corner. Press firmly to seal; repeat by folding lower right corner to center; press firmly to seal. Fold upper left corner to center; press tip to seal.
4. Using a convection oven, bake in 350 F. for 15 minutes with low fan and open vent or until golden brown.
5. Cool.

Notes

1. In Step 3, pie filling, prepared, fruit (apple, blueberry, cherry, or peach) may be used as filling. Place in mixer bowl. Using whip, mix on medium speed 15 seconds to break up large pieces.
2. In Step 3, 7 lbs 11 oz cherry, pineapple or strawberry jam may be used, per 100 portions.
3. Prepare in batches as dough becomes difficult to work within 15 minutes.

CORNSTARCH WASH

Yield 100   **Portion** 1 Quart

Calories	Carbohydrates	Protein	Fat	Cholesterol	Sodium	Calcium
122 cal	29 g	0 g	0 g	0 mg	31 mg	20 mg

Ingredient	Weight	Measure	Issue
CORNSTARCH	1-1/8 oz	1/4 cup 1/3 tbsp	
WATER	2-1/8 lbs	1 qts	

Method
1. Combine cornstarch and water. Bring to a boil; cook until clear.
2. Brush on bread and rolls before and immediately after baking.

Notes
1. Keep wash warm. Reheat if necessary.

CHERRY FILLING (CORNSTARCH)

Yield 100   **Portion** 3 Quarts

Calories	Carbohydrates	Protein	Fat	Cholesterol	Sodium	Calcium
7081 cal	1816 g	23 g	4 g	0 mg	76 mg	358 mg

Ingredient	Weight	Measure	Issue
CHERRIES,CANNED,RED,TART,WATER	6-1/2 lbs	3 qts	
PACK,DRAINED	1-5/8 lbs	3 cup	
RESERVED LIQUID	4-1/2 oz	1 cup	
CORNSTARCH	3 lbs	1 qts 2-3/4 cup	
SUGAR,GRANULATED	1/8 oz	1/8 tsp	
FOOD COLOR,RED			

Method
1. Drain cherries. Dissolve cornstarch in juice. Set juice and cornstarch mixture aside for use in Step 4.
2. Mash cherries with wire whip 1 minute at medium speed; combine with sugar and food coloring.
3. Bring to a boil in steam-jacketed kettle or stock pot stirring constantly to prevent scorching. Reduce heat. Simmer about 10 minutes.
4. Add reserved juice and cornstarch mixture to cherries while stirring. Cook 2 to 3 minutes until clear and thickened, stirring constantly. Remove from heat; cool.

CHERRY FILLING (PIE FILLING, PREPARED)

Yield 100   **Portion** 3 Quarts

Calories	Carbohydrates	Protein	Fat	Cholesterol	Sodium	Calcium
3132 cal	798 g	14 g	5 g	0 mg	245 mg	300 mg

Ingredient	Weight	Measure	Issue
PIE FILLING,CHERRY,PREPARED	6 lbs	3 qts	

Method
1. Mash prepared filling with a wire whip for 1 minute at medium speed.

APPLE FILLING (PIE FILLING, PREPARED)

Yield 100   **Portion** 3 Quarts

Calories	Carbohydrates	Protein	Fat	Cholesterol	Sodium	Calcium
2749 cal	713 g	3 g	3 g	0 mg	1197 mg	109 mg

Ingredient	Weight	Measure	Issue
PIE FILLING,APPLE,PREPARED	6 lbs	3 qts	

Method
1. Break up large pieces of prepared apple pie filling with wire whip one minute at medium speed.

BLUEBERRY FILLING (PIE FILLING, PREPARED)

Yield 100   **Portion** 3 Quarts

Calories	Carbohydrates	Protein	Fat	Cholesterol	Sodium	Calcium
2871 cal	754 g	0 g	0 g	0 mg	1615 mg	718 mg

Ingredient	Weight	Measure	Issue
PIE FILLING,BLUEBERRY,PREPARED	7 lbs	3 qts	

Method
1. Use accordingly.

RASPBERRY FILLING (PREPARED BAKERY)

Yield 100   **Portion** 3 Quarts

Calories	Carbohydrates	Protein	Fat	Cholesterol	Sodium	Calcium
2947 cal	774 g	0 g	0 g	0 mg	1657 mg	737 mg

Ingredient	Weight	Measure	Issue
RASPBERRY BAKERY FILLING	7-1/4 lbs	3 qts 3/8 cup	

Method
1. Use accordingly.

CINNAMON SUGAR FILLING

Yield 100   **Portion** 4-1/2 Cups

Calories	Carbohydrates	Protein	Fat	Cholesterol	Sodium	Calcium
1843 cal	480 g	1 g	1 g	0 mg	191 mg	1843 mg

Ingredient	Weight	Measure	Issue
CINNAMON,GROUND	1 oz	1/4 cup 1/3 tbsp	
SUGAR,BROWN,PACKED	1 lbs	3-1/4 cup	

Method
1. Combine cinnamon and brown sugar.
Notes
1. Granulated sugar may be substituted for brown sugar.

CINNAMON SUGAR NUT FILLING

Yield 100   Portion 4-1/2 Cups

Calories	Carbohydrates	Protein	Fat	Cholesterol	Sodium	Calcium
6933 cal	646 g	232 g	433 g	0 mg	244 mg	1506 mg

Ingredient	Weight	Measure	Issue
CINNAMON,GROUND	1 oz	1/4 cup 1/3 tbsp	
SUGAR,BROWN,PACKED	1 lbs	3-1/4 cup	
NUTS,UNSALTED,CHOPPED,COARSELY	1-7/8 lbs	1 qts 2 cup	

Method
1. Combine cinnamon and brown sugar.
2. Sprinkle chopped nuts over cinnamon sugar mixture.

Notes
1. In Step 1, granulated sugar may be substituted for brown sugar.

CINNAMON SUGAR RAISIN FILLING

Yield 100   Portion 4-1/2 Cups

Calories	Carbohydrates	Protein	Fat	Cholesterol	Sodium	Calcium
4562 cal	1197 g	30 g	5 g	0 mg	300 mg	1179 mg

Ingredient	Weight	Measure	Issue
CINNAMON,GROUND	1 oz	1/4 cup 1/3 tbsp	
SUGAR,BROWN,PACKED	1 lbs	3-1/4 cup	
RAISINS	2 lbs	1 qts 2-1/4 cup	

Method
1. Combine cinnamon and brown sugar.
2. Sprinkle raisins over cinnamon sugar mixture.

Notes
1. In Step 1, granulated sugar may be substituted for brown sugar.

NUT FILLING

Yield 100   Portion 7-1/2 Cups

Calories	Carbohydrates	Protein	Fat	Cholesterol	Sodium	Calcium
10666 cal	1214 g	95 g	641 g	1118 mg	4412 mg	970 mg

Ingredient	Weight	Measure	Issue
FLOUR,WHEAT,GENERAL PURPOSE	13-1/4 oz	3 cup	
CINNAMON,GROUND	3/8 oz	1 tbsp	
SUGAR,GRANULATED	1-1/8 lbs	2-1/2 cup	
SUGAR,BROWN,PACKED	12-3/4 oz	2-1/2 cup	
BUTTER,MELTED	1-1/8 lbs	2-1/4 cup	
WALNUTS,SHELLED,CHOPPED	12-2/3 oz	3 cup	

Method
1. Sift together flour and cinnamon in mixer bowl; blend in sugars.
2. Add butter or margarine to dry ingredients; mix at low speed until well blended.
3. Add nuts, mixing at low speed. Use about 1 tbsp filling for each pastry.

OAT BRAN RAISIN MUFFINS

Yield 100   **Portion** 1 Muffin

Calories	Carbohydrates	Protein	Fat	Cholesterol	Sodium	Calcium
196 cal	29 g	5 g	7 g	40 mg	189 mg	88 mg

Ingredient	Weight	Measure	Issue
FLOUR,WHEAT,GENERAL PURPOSE	1-2/3 lbs	1 qts 2 cup	
MILK,NONFAT,DRY	5-1/8 oz	2-1/8 cup	
BAKING POWDER	2-3/4 oz	1/4 cup 2 tbsp	
SALT	5/8 oz	1 tbsp	
RAISINS	1-7/8 lbs	1 qts 2 cup	
CEREAL,OATMEAL,ROLLED	2-7/8 lbs	2 qts 1/2 cup	
CEREAL,OAT BRAN	12 oz	1 qts 2 cup	
SUGAR,BROWN,PACKED	1 lbs	3 cup	
WATER,WARM	4-2/3 lbs	2 qts 1 cup	
EGGS,WHOLE,FROZEN	2 lbs	3-3/4 cup	
OIL,SALAD	1 lbs	2 cup	
COOKING SPRAY,NONSTICK	2 oz	1/4 cup 1/3 tbsp	

Method
1. Sift together flour, milk, baking powder, and salt into mixer bowl.
2. Blend in raisins, rolled oats, oat bran, and brown sugar at low speed for 1/2 minute.
3. Add water, eggs, and oil or shortening to dry ingredients; mix at low speed until dry ingredients are moistened, about 15 seconds. DO NOT OVER MIX.
4. Lightly spray each muffin cup with non-stick cooking spray. Fill each muffin cup 2/3 full (1-No. 16 scoop).
5. Using a convection oven, bake at 350 F. for 20 minutes or until lightly browned with open vent and fan turned off first 5 minutes, then low fan.

SYRUP GLAZE

Yield 100   **Portion** 1 Quart

Calories	Carbohydrates	Protein	Fat	Cholesterol	Sodium	Calcium
2930 cal	790 g	1 g	1 g	0 mg	1106 mg	146 mg

Ingredient	Weight	Measure	Issue
SYRUP	2-1/3 lbs	3-3/8 cup	
WATER	1 lbs	2 cup	

Method
1. Combine syrup and water. Bring to a boil; boil about 5 minutes, stirring constantly.
2. Brush warm glaze over rolls or coffee cakes immediately after baking.

VANILLA GLAZE

Yield 100   Portion 2-3/4 Cups

Calories	Carbohydrates	Protein	Fat	Cholesterol	Sodium	Calcium
3125 cal	717 g	0 g	35 g	93 mg	365 mg	22 mg

Ingredient	Weight	Measure	Issue
SUGAR,POWDERED,SIFTED	1-5/8 lbs	1 qts 2 cup	
BUTTER,SOFTENED	1-1/2 oz	3 tbsp	
WATER,BOILING	6-1/4 oz	3/4 cup	
EXTRACT,VANILLA	1/4 oz	1/4 tsp	

Method
1. Combine powdered sugar, butter, boiling water, and vanilla; mix until smooth.
2. Spread glaze over baked sweet rolls or coffee cakes. Coat or dip fried doughnuts in glaze.

ALMOND GLAZE

Yield 100   Portion 2-3/4 Cups

Calories	Carbohydrates	Protein	Fat	Cholesterol	Sodium	Calcium
3115 cal	717 g	0 g	35 g	93 mg	364 mg	21 mg

Ingredient	Weight	Measure	Issue
SUGAR,POWDERED,SIFTED	1-5/8 lbs	1 qts 2 cup	
BUTTER,SOFTENED	1-1/2 oz	3 tbsp	
WATER,BOILING	6-1/4 oz	3/4 cup	
EXTRACT,ALMOND	1/8 oz	1/8 tsp	

Method
1. Combine powdered sugar, butter, boiling water, and vanilla; mix until smooth.
2. Spread glaze over baked sweet rolls or coffee cakes. Coat or dip fried doughnuts in glaze.

RUM GLAZE

Yield 100   Portion 2-3/4 Cups

Calories	Carbohydrates	Protein	Fat	Cholesterol	Sodium	Calcium
3125 cal	717 g	0 g	35 g	93 mg	365 mg	22 mg

Ingredient	Weight	Measure	Issue
SUGAR,POWDERED,SIFTED	1-5/8 lbs	1 qts 2 cup	
BUTTER,SOFTENED	1-1/2 oz	3 tbsp	
WATER,BOILING	6-1/4 oz	3/4 cup	
EXTRACT,RUM	1/4 oz	1/4 tsp	

Method
1. Combine powdered sugar, butter, boiling water, and vanilla; mix until smooth.
2. Spread glaze over baked sweet rolls or coffee cakes. Coat or dip fried doughnuts in glaze.

PINEAPPLE FILLING (CORNSTARCH)

Yield 100   **Portion** 2-1/2 Quarts

Calories	Carbohydrates	Protein	Fat	Cholesterol	Sodium	Calcium
2942 cal	680 g	10 g	36 g	93 mg	389 mg	331 mg

Ingredient	Weight	Measure	Issue
PINEAPPLE,CANNED,CRUSHED	5 lbs	2 qts 1 cup	
BUTTER,MELTED	1-1/2 oz	3 tbsp	
SUGAR,GRANULATED	8-7/8 oz	1-1/4 cup	
CORNSTARCH	3 oz	1/2 cup 2-2/3 tbsp	
WATER	5-5/8 oz	1/2 cup 2-2/3 tbsp	

Method
1. Combine pineapple, butter, and sugar and combine over heat.
2. Dissolve cornstarch in cool water; add to hot pineapple mixture while stirring; bring to a boil; cook until thick and clear, about 5 minutes.
3. Cool slightly before using.

Notes
1. If desired, filling may be used for cake. Use 3 quarts filling for each sheet cake or 2 cups for each 9-inch layer cake.

ORANGE-COCONUT TOPPING

Yield 100   **Portion** 2-1/4 Quarts

Calories	Carbohydrates	Protein	Fat	Cholesterol	Sodium	Calcium
9327 cal	1063 g	42 g	581 g	497 mg	4811 mg	314 mg

Ingredient	Weight	Measure	Issue
BUTTER,SOFTENED	8 oz	1 cup	
SUGAR,GRANULATED	1 lbs	2-1/4 cup	
FLOUR,WHEAT,GENERAL PURPOSE	2-1/4 oz	1/2 cup	
JUICE,ORANGE,CANNED,UNSWEETENED	8-3/4 oz	1 cup	
ORANGE,RIND,GRATED	1-1/4 oz	1/4 cup 2-1/3 tbsp	
COCONUT,PREPARED,SWEETENED FLAKES	2-1/2 lbs	3 qts	

Method
1. Cream butter or margarine and sugar together at medium speed in mixer bowl.
2. Add flour, orange juice, orange rind, and coconut; blend.
3. Spread over sweet rolls or coffee cakes after proofing.

STREUSEL TOPPING

Yield 100   **Portion** 3 Quarts

Calories	Carbohydrates	Protein	Fat	Cholesterol	Sodium	Calcium
1242 cal	83 g	468 g	1242 g	37 mg	4892 mg	818 mg

Ingredient	Weight	Measure	Issue
FLOUR,WHEAT,GENERAL PURPOSE	1-2/3 lbs	1 qts 2 cup	
SUGAR,BROWN,PACKED	1 lbs	3-1/4 cup	
SUGAR,GRANULATED	7 oz	1 cup	
CINNAMON,GROUND	1/2 oz	2 tbsp	
BUTTER	1-1/4 lbs	2-1/2 cup	

Method
1. Place flour, sugars, and cinnamon in mixer bowl; blend thoroughly at low speed 2 minutes.
2. Add butter or margarine to dry ingredients; blend at low speed 1-1/2 to 2 minutes or until mixture resembles coarse cornmeal. DO NOT OVERMIX.
3. Sprinkle over sweet rolls and coffee cakes before baking.

Notes
1. If butter or margarine is too soft, a mass will form and mixture will not be crumbly.

PECAN TOPPING

Yield 100   Portion 2-1/2 Quarts

Calories	Carbohydrates	Protein	Fat	Cholesterol	Sodium	Calcium
8428 cal	752 g	56 g	624 g	497 mg	2122 mg	816 mg

Ingredient	Weight	Measure	Issue
BUTTER	8 oz	1 cup	
SUGAR,BROWN,PACKED	1-1/3 lbs	1 qts 1/4 cup	
PECANS,CHOPPED	1-1/2 lbs		

Method
1. Combine softened butter or margarine, brown sugar, and chopped pecans.
2. Use as a topping for Pecan Rolls, Recipe No. D 036 03.

Notes
1. If butter or margarine is too soft, a mass will form and mixture will not be crumbly.

MAPLE SYRUP

Yield 100   Portion 1 Gallon

Calories	Carbohydrates	Protein	Fat	Cholesterol	Sodium	Calcium
7143 cal	1835 g	0 g	0 g	0 mg	1364 mg	1612 mg

Ingredient	Weight	Measure	Issue
SUGAR,BROWN,PACKED	4-1/8 lbs	3 qts 3/4 cup	
WATER	4-1/8 lbs	2 qts	
SALT	<1/16th oz	<1/16th tsp	
CORNSTARCH	1-1/3 oz	1/4 cup 1 tbsp	
FLAVORING,MAPLE	5/8 oz	1 tbsp	

Method
1. Combine brown sugar, water, salt, and cornstarch. Bring to a boil; reduce heat; simmer about 10 minutes or until thickened.

2. Remove from heat; add maple flavoring.

Notes
1. Hot syrup will be thin, but will thicken upon cooling.

FRYING BATTER

Yield 100   **Portion** 1 Gallon

Calories	Carbohydrates	Protein	Fat	Cholesterol	Sodium	Calcium
10896 cal	2068 g	350 g	114 g	2246 mg	67950 mg	3966 mg

Ingredient	Weight	Measure	Issue
FLOUR,WHEAT,GENERAL PURPOSE	5-1/2 lbs	1 gal 1 qts	
SUGAR,GRANULATED	3-1/2 oz	1/2 cup	
SALT	5-3/4 oz	1/2 cup 1 tbsp	
MILK,NONFAT,DRY	3 oz	1-1/4 cup	
BAKING POWDER	1-1/3 oz	2-2/3 tbsp	
EGGS,WHOLE,FROZEN	1-1/8 lbs	2-1/8 cup	
OIL,SALAD	1-1/4 oz	2-2/3 tbsp	
WATER	4-1/8 lbs	2 qts	

Method
1. Sift together flour, sugar, salt, milk, and baking powder into mixer bowl.
2. Combine eggs and salad oil or melted shortening; add to dry ingredients.
3. Slowly add water; beat at medium speed until smooth.

Notes
1. Batter may be used for fruits and vegetables such as apples, eggplant, and tomatoes. Moist foods should be dredged in flour before dipping into batter. When ready to fry, dip into batter; drain slightly. Fry in 350 F. to 375 F. deep fat until lightly browned.
2. Use batter the day prepared. DO NOT SAVE.

OATMEAL BREAD

Yield 100   **Portion** 2 Slices

Calories	Carbohydrates	Protein	Fat	Cholesterol	Sodium	Calcium
211 cal	37 g	7 g	4 g	0 mg	216 mg	21 mg

Ingredient	Weight	Measure	Issue
YEAST,ACTIVE,DRY	5-1/8 oz	3/4 cup	
WATER,WARM	1-1/3 lbs	2-1/2 cup	
WATER,COLD	3-7/8 lbs	1 qts 3-1/2 cup	
SUGAR,GRANULATED	8 oz	1-1/8 cup	
MILK,NONFAT,DRY	2-2/3 oz	1-1/8 cup	
SALT	1-7/8 oz	3 tbsp	
FLOUR,WHEAT,BREAD	8-1/2 lbs	1 gal 3 qts	
SHORTENING	7-1/4 oz	1 cup	
CEREAL,OATMEAL,ROLLED	2 lbs	1 qts 1-5/8 cup	
COOKING SPRAY,NONSTICK	2 oz	1/4 cup 1/3 tbsp	

Method

1. Sprinkle yeast over water. DO NOT USE TEMPERATURES ABOVE 110 F. Mix well. Let stand 5 minutes; stir. Set aside for use in Step 4.
2. Place water, sugar, milk, and salt in mixer bowl; blend thoroughly with a wire whip.
3. Add flour. Using dough hook, mix at low speed 1 minute or until all flour is incorporated into liquid.
4. Add yeast solution; mix at low speed 1 minute.
5. Add shortening; mix at low speed 1 minute. Continue mixing at medium speed 10 to 15 minutes or until dough is smooth and elastic. Dough temperature should be 78 F. to 82 F.
6. Add oats; mix at low speed 2 minutes. Mix at medium speed 1 minute.
7. FERMENT: Cover. Set in warm place (80 F.), 1 hour and 45 minutes or until double in bulk.
8. PUNCH: Fold sides into center and turn dough completely over. Let rest 15 minutes.
9. MAKE UP: Scale into 8 1-3/4 pound pieces; shape each piece into a smooth ball; let rest 10 minutes. Mold each piece into an oblong loaf; place each loaf seam-side down into a pan sprayed with non-stick cooking spray.
10. PROOF: At 90 F. to 100 F. about 45 minutes or until double in bulk.
11. Bake 45 to 50 minutes in 375 F. oven or in 325 F. convection oven for 30 minutes on high fan, open vent, or until done.
12. When cool, slice 25 slices, about 1/2-inch thick per loaf.

Notes

1. If using 9x4-1/2x2-3/4-inch bread pans, scale into 10 1-3/8 pound pieces; proof at 90 F. to 100 F. for 30 minutes or until double in bulk. Slice 20 slices, about 1/2-inch thick per loaf.

APPLESAUCE MUFFINS

Yield 100   **Portion** 1 Muffin

Calories	Carbohydrates	Protein	Fat	Cholesterol	Sodium	Calcium
181 cal	33 g	3 g	4 g	12 mg	213 mg	73 mg

Ingredient	Weight	Measure	Issue
FLOUR,WHEAT,GENERAL PURPOSE	5-3/4 lbs	1 gal 1-1/4 qts	
SUGAR,GRANULATED	2-1/4 lbs	1 qts 1 cup	
BAKING POWDER	3-7/8 oz	1/2 cup	
SALT	3/4 oz	1 tbsp	
CINNAMON,GROUND	1/2 oz	2 tbsp	
NUTMEG,GROUND	1/8 oz	1/3 tsp	
APPLESAUCE,CANNED,UNSWEETENED	5 lbs	2 qts 1-3/8 cup	
EGGS,WHOLE,FROZEN	9-5/8 oz	1-1/8 cup	
EGG WHITES,FROZEN,THAWED	9-5/8 oz	1-1/8 cup	
OIL,SALAD	10-1/4 oz	1-3/8 cup	
COOKING SPRAY,NONSTICK	2 oz	1/4 cup 1/3 tbsp	

Method

1. Sift together flour, sugar, baking powder, salt, cinnamon, and nutmeg into mixer bowl.
2. Add applesauce, eggs, egg whites, and salad oil or shortening; mix at low speed 15 seconds or until dry ingredients are moistened. DO NOT OVER MIX. Batter will be lumpy.
3. Lightly spray each muffin cup with non-stick cooking spray. Fill each muffin cup 2/3 full.
4. Bake 25 to 30 minutes in 400 F. oven or in 350 F. convection oven for 23 to 26 minutes until done, open vent, fan turned off first 10 minutes, then low fan.

APPLESAUCE RAISIN MUFFINS

Yield 100   **Portion** 1 Muffin

Calories	Carbohydrates	Protein	Fat	Cholesterol	Sodium	Calcium
207 cal	40 g	4 g	4 g	12 mg	214 mg	77 mg

Ingredient	Weight	Measure	Issue
FLOUR,WHEAT,GENERAL PURPOSE	5-3/4 lbs	1 gal 1-1/4 qts	
SUGAR,GRANULATED	2-1/4 lbs	1 qts 1 cup	
BAKING POWDER	3-7/8 oz	1/2 cup	
SALT	3/4 oz	1 tbsp	
CINNAMON,GROUND	1/2 oz	2 tbsp	
NUTMEG,GROUND	1/8 oz	1/3 tsp	
RAISINS	1-7/8 lbs	1 qts 2 cup	
APPLESAUCE,CANNED,UNSWEETENED	5 lbs	2 qts 1-3/8 cup	
EGGS,WHOLE,FROZEN	9-5/8 oz	1-1/8 cup	
EGG WHITES,FROZEN,THAWED	9-5/8 oz	1-1/8 cup	
OIL,SALAD	10-1/4 oz	1-3/8 cup	
COOKING SPRAY,NONSTICK	2 oz	1/4 cup 1/3 tbsp	

Method

1. Sift together flour, sugar, baking powder, salt, cinnamon, and nutmeg into mixer bowl.
2. Add applesauce, eggs, egg whites, and salad oil or shortening; mix at low speed 15 seconds until dry ingredients are moistened. Fold in raisins. DO NOT OVER MIX. Batter will be lumpy.
3. Lightly spray each muffin cup with non-stick cooking spray. Fill each muffin cup 2/3 full.
4. Bake 25 to 30 minutes in 400 F. oven or in 350 F. convection oven for 23 to 26 minutes until done, open vent, fan turned off first 10 minutes, then low fan.

APPLESAUCE ORANGE MUFFINS

Yield 100   **Portion** 1 Muffin

Calories	Carbohydrates	Protein	Fat	Cholesterol	Sodium	Calcium
191 cal	35 g	4 g	4 g	12 mg	213 mg	76 mg

Ingredient	Weight	Measure	Issue
FLOUR,WHEAT,GENERAL PURPOSE	5-3/4 lbs	1 gal 1-1/4 qts	
SUGAR,GRANULATED	2-1/4 lbs	1 qts 1 cup	
BAKING POWDER	3-7/8 oz	1/2 cup	
SALT	3/4 oz	1 tbsp	
CINNAMON,GROUND	1/2 oz	2 tbsp	
NUTMEG,GROUND	1/8 oz	1/3 tsp	
APPLESAUCE,CANNED,UNSWEETENED	3-1/4 lbs	1 qts 2 cup	
JUICE,ORANGE,FROZEN,CONCENTRATE,3/1,THAWED	1-7/8 lbs	3 cup	
EGGS,WHOLE,FROZEN	9-5/8 oz	1-1/8 cup	
EGG WHITES,FROZEN,THAWED	9-5/8 oz	1-1/8 cup	
OIL,SALAD	10-1/4 oz	1-3/8 cup	
COOKING SPRAY,NONSTICK	2 oz	1/4 cup 1/3 tbsp	

Method

1. Sift together flour, sugar, baking powder, salt, cinnamon, and nutmeg into mixer bowl.

2. Add applesauce, orange juice concentrate, eggs, egg whites, and salad oil or shortening; mix at low speed for 15 seconds or until dry ingredients are moistened. DO NOT OVERMIX. Batter will be lumpy.
3. Lightly spray each muffin cup with non-stick cooking spray. Fill each muffin cup 2/3 full.
4. Bake 25 to 30 minutes in 400 F. oven or in 350 F. convection oven for 23 to 26 minutes until done, open vent, fan turned off first 10 minutes, then low fan.

PINEAPPLE CARROT MUFFINS

Yield 100   Portion 1 Muffin

Calories	Carbohydrates	Protein	Fat	Cholesterol	Sodium	Calcium
145 cal	24 g	4 g	4 g	0 mg	205 mg	99 mg

Ingredient	Weight	Measure	Issue
FLOUR,WHEAT,GENERAL PURPOSE	3-1/8 lbs	2 qts 3-1/2 cup	
CEREAL,OAT BRAN	11-1/2 oz	1 qts 1-3/4 cup	
BAKING POWDER	3-1/8 oz	1/4cup 2-2/3tbsp	
BAKING SODA	1 oz	2 tbsp	
YOGURT,PLAIN,NONFAT	3-3/4 lbs	1 qts 3 cup	
SUGAR,BROWN,PACKED	1-1/4 lbs	1 qts	
OIL,SALAD	11-1/2 oz	1-1/2 cup	
EGG WHITES,FROZEN,THAWED	14-7/8 oz	1-3/4 cup	
PINEAPPLE,CANNED,CRUSHED,JUICE PACK,DRAINED	3-7/8 lbs	1 qts 3 cup	
CARROTS,FRESH,GRATED	1-1/2 lbs	1 qts 2-1/4cup	1-7/8lbs
COOKING SPRAY,NONSTICK	2 oz	1/4cup 1/3tbsp	

Method
1. Sift together flour, oat bran, baking powder, and baking soda. Set aside for use in Step 5.
2. Combine yogurt, brown sugar, and oil in mixer bowl. Beat at medium speed about 1 minute or until well blended.
3. Add egg whites; mix at low speed about 30 seconds.
4. Add pineapple and carrots; mix at low speed for 30 seconds.
5. Add flour mixture; mix at low speed about 15 seconds, scrape down sides and bottom of mixer bowl. Mix about 15 seconds or until ingredients are moistened. Do not overmix.
6. Lightly spray each muffin cup with non-stick cooking spray. Fill each muffin cup 2/3 full.
7. Bake 25 to 30 minutes at 400 F. or until lightly browned, or using a 350 F. convection oven, bake for 18 to 20 minutes or until lightly browned with open vent, low fan.

WHOLE WHEAT BREAD

Yield 100   Portion 2 Slices

Calories	Carbohydrates	Protein	Fat	Cholesterol	Sodium	Calcium
158 cal	29 g	5 g	3 g	0 mg	288 mg	25 mg

Ingredient	Weight	Measure	Issue
YEAST,ACTIVE,DRY	1-2/3 oz	1/4 cup 1/3 tbsp	
WATER,WARM	12-1/2 oz	1-1/2 cup	
WATER	4-1/8 lbs	2 qts	
MILK,NONFAT,DRY	4-1/2 oz	1-7/8 cup	

SUGAR,GRANULATED	10-5/8 oz	1-1/2 cup
SALT	2-1/2 oz	1/4 cup 1/3 tbsp
FLOUR,WHEAT,BREAD	4-1/4 lbs	3 qts 2 cup
FLOUR,WHOLE WHEAT	3-1/2 lbs	3 qts 1 cup
SHORTENING,SOFTENED	7-1/4 oz	1 cup

Method

1. Sprinkle yeast over water. DO NOT USE TEMPERATURES ABOVE 110 F. Mix well. Let stand 5 minutes. Stir. Set aside for use in Step 4.
2. Place water, milk, sugar, and salt in mixer bowl. Using dough hook, mix at low speed about 1 minute until blended.
3. Combine flours thoroughly; add to liquid in mixer bowl. Using dough hook, mix at low speed 1 minute or until the dry ingredients are incorporated into liquid.
4. Add yeast solution; mix at low speed for one minute.
5. Add shortening; mix at low speed 1 minute. Continue mixing at medium speed for 10 to 15 minutes or until dough is smooth and elastic. Dough temperature should be 78 F. to 82 F.
6. FERMENT: Cover. Set in warm place (80 F.) 2 hours or until double in bulk.
7. PUNCH: Fold sides into center and turn dough completely over. Let rest 15 minutes.
8. PROOF: At 90 F. to 100 F. for about 1 hour or until double in size.
9. BAKE: 35 to 40 minutes at 375 F. or 30 to 35 minutes in a 325 F. convection oven until bread is done on high fan, open vent.
10. When cool, slice 25 slices, about 1/2-inch thick, per loaf.

WHOLE WHEAT BREAD (WHOLE WHEAT FLOUR SHRT TM FORM)

Yield 100   **Portion** 2 Slices

Calories	Carbohydrates	Protein	Fat	Cholesterol	Sodium	Calcium
158 cal	29 g	6 g	3 g	0 mg	218 mg	24 mg

Ingredient	Weight	Measure Issue
YEAST,ACTIVE,DRY	3 oz	1/4 cup 3-1/3 tbsp
WATER,WARM	1 lbs	2 cup
SUGAR,GRANULATED	3/4 oz	1 tbsp
WATER	4-1/8 lbs	2 qts
MILK,NONFAT,DRY	3-5/8 oz	1-1/2 cup
SUGAR,GRANULATED	5 oz	1/2 cup 3-1/3 tbsp
FLOUR,WHEAT,BREAD	2-1/4 lbs	1 qts 3-1/2 cup
FLOUR,WHOLE WHEAT	3-2/3 lbs	3 qts 2 cup
SHORTENING,SOFTENED	6 oz	3/4 cup 1-1/3 tbsp
FLOUR,WHOLE WHEAT	2-1/8 lbs	2 qts
SALT	1-7/8 oz	3 tbsp
COOKING SPRAY,NONSTICK	2 oz	1/4 cup 1/3 tbsp

Method

1. Sprinkle yeast over water. DO NOT USE TEMPERATURES ABOVE 110 F. Mix well. Let stand 5 minutes. Add sugar. Stir until dissolved. Let stand 10 minutes; stir. Set aside for use in Step 3.
2. Place water in mixer bowl. Add milk, sugar, and yeast food. Using dough hook, mix at low speed until smooth.
3. Combine flours, add to bowl. Mix at low speed 2 minutes or until flour is incorporated; add shortening and yeast solution. Mix at low speed about 2 minutes until smooth.

4. Mix at medium speed 10 minutes.
5. Let rise in mixer bowl 20 minutes.
6. Sift together flour and salt; add to mixture in mixer bowl. Mix at low speed for 2 minutes or until flour is incorporated. Mix at medium speed 10 minutes or until dough is smooth and elastic.
7. FERMENT: Cover. Set in warm place (80 F.), for 25 to 30 minutes or until double in bulk.
8. MAKE UP: Scale into 8-28 ounce pieces. Roll scaled dough to pan size; place 1 loaf into each lightly greased pan.
9. PROOF: At 90 F. for 25 to 30 minutes or until double in bulk.
10. BAKE: 5 minutes at 450 F. Reduce temperature to 375 F. and bake 40 to 45 minutes or until done or in a convection oven 3 to 5 minutes on high fan, open vent. Reduce temperature to 325 F., bake 22 to 26 minutes or until done on high fan, open vent.
11. When cool, slice 25 slices, about 1/2-inch thick, per loaf.

APPLE COFFEE CAKE

Yield 100   **Portion** 1 Piece

Calories	Carbohydrates	Protein	Fat	Cholesterol	Sodium	Calcium
206 cal	39 g	4 g	5 g	0 mg	213 mg	65 mg

Ingredient	Weight	Measure	Issue
APPLES,CANNED,DRAINED,CHOPPED	8 lbs	1 gal	
JUICE,ORANGE	2-3/4 lbs	1 qts 1 cup	
CINNAMON,GROUND	3/4 oz	3 tbsp	
FLOUR,WHEAT,GENERAL PURPOSE	3-5/8 lbs	3 qts 1 cup	
SUGAR,GRANULATED	3 lbs	1 qts 2-3/4 cup	
FLOUR,WHOLE WHEAT	1-1/8 lbs	1 qts 1/4 cup	
MILK,NONFAT,DRY	1-3/4 oz	3/4 cup	
BAKING POWDER	2-3/4 oz	1/4 cup 2 tbsp	
SALT	5/8 oz	1 tbsp	
NUTMEG,GROUND	1/4 oz	1 tbsp	
MARGARINE,SOFTENED	1 lbs	2 cup	
WATER	2 lbs	3-3/4 cup	
EXTRACT,VANILLA	3/4 oz	1 tbsp	
EGG WHITES,FROZEN,THAWED	1-3/4 lbs	3-1/4 cup	
COOKING SPRAY,NONSTICK	2 oz	1/4 cup 1/3 tbsp	
SUGAR,BROWN,PACKED	3-7/8 oz	3/4 cup	

Method
1. Coarsely chop apples. Toss with orange juice and cinnamon. Cover.
2. Sift together flour, sugar, whole wheat flour, milk, baking powder, salt, and nutmeg into mixer bowl.
3. Add margarine, water, and vanilla to dry ingredients. Beat at low speed 1 minute until blended. Scrape down bowl; continue beating 2 minutes. Scrape down bowl.
4. Slowly add egg whites to mixture while beating at low speed 2 minutes. Scrape down bowl. Beat at medium speed 3 minutes.
5. Pour 2-1/2 quarts of batter into each lightly sprayed pan. Spread to evenly distribute batter.
6. Spread about 2-1/2 quarts apple mixture evenly over batter in each pan. Sprinkle 3 ounces or 1/3 cup of brown sugar over apples in pan.
7. Bake about 1 hour at 400 F. or until done or using a convection oven, bake at 325 F. for about 35 minutes or until done on low fan, open vent.

8. Prepare 1 recipe Vanilla Glaze, Recipe No. D 046 00. Drizzle 8 ounces or 1 cup of glaze over warm cake in each pan.
9. Cut 6 by 9.

OVEN BAKED FRENCH TOAST

Yield 100   **Portion** 2 Slices

Calories	Carbohydrates	Protein	Fat	Cholesterol	Sodium	Calcium
199 cal	31 g	9 g	4 g	1 mg	365 mg	99 mg

Ingredient	Weight	Measure	Issue
WATER	5-3/4 lbs	2 qts 3 cup	
EXTRACT,VANILLA	2-1/2 oz	1/4 cup 1-2/3 tbsp	
MILK,NONFAT,DRY	5-5/8 oz	2-3/8 cup	
SUGAR,GRANULATED	10-5/8 oz	1-1/2 cup	
CINNAMON,GROUND	3/8 oz	1 tbsp	
EGG SUBSTITUTE,PASTEURIZED	7-3/4 lbs	3 qts 2 cup	
BREAD,WHITE,SLICED	12 lbs	9 gal 2-7/8 qts	
COOKING SPRAY,NONSTICK	2 oz	1/4 cup 1/3 tbsp	

Method
1. Place water and vanilla in mixer bowl.
2. Combine milk, sugar, and cinnamon; blend well. Add to water; mix at low speed until dissolved or for about 1 minute.
3. Add egg substitute to ingredients in mixer bowl; mix at low speed until well blended, about 1 minute.
4. Stir egg mixture before using to redistribute cinnamon. Dip bread slices in egg mixture to coat both sides. Do not soak.
5. Lightly spray sheet pans with non-stick spray. Place dipped bread slices on pans 4 by 6.
6. Bake 20 to 25 minutes or until toast is golden brown in 450 F. oven or using a convection oven, bake at 425 F. for 12 to 14 minutes on high fan, open vent or until golden brown. Use batch method of preparation. Toast becomes tough when held more than 15 minutes.

WHOLE WHEAT ROLLS

Yield 100   **Portion** 2 Rolls

Calories	Carbohydrates	Protein	Fat	Cholesterol	Sodium	Calcium
261 cal	50 g	8 g	4 g	0 mg	383 mg	31 mg

Ingredient	Weight	Measure	Issue
YEAST,ACTIVE,DRY	4-1/2 oz	1/2 cup 2-2/3 tbsp	
WATER,WARM	1-7/8 lbs	3-1/2 cup	
WATER,COLD	6-3/4 lbs	3 qts 1 cup	
SUGAR,GRANULATED	1-1/2 lbs	3-3/8 cup	
SALT	3-3/8 oz	1/4 cup 1-2/3 tbsp	
FLOUR,WHOLE WHEAT	5-1/2 lbs	1 gal 1-1/4 qts	
FLOUR,WHEAT,BREAD	7-1/4 lbs	1 gal 2 qts	
MILK,NONFAT,DRY	4-1/2 oz	1-7/8 cup	
SHORTENING,SOFTENED	9 oz	1-1/4 cup	

Method

1. Sprinkle yeast over water. Do not use in temperatures above 110 F. Mix well. Let stand for 5 minutes. Stir.
2. Place water in mixer bowl; add sugar and salt; stir until dissolved. Add yeast solution.
3. Combine whole wheat flour, bread flour, and milk. Add to liquid solution. Using dough hook, mix at low speed 1 minute or until flour mixture is incorporated into liquid.
4. Add shortening; mix at medium speed 10 minutes or until dough is smooth and elastic. Dough temperature should be 78 F. to 82 F.
5. FERMENT: Cover. Set in warm place (80 F.) for 1-1/2 hours or until double in bulk.
6. PUNCH: Divide dough into 8 2-lb 14-oz pieces. Shape each piece into a smooth ball; let rest 10 to 20 minutes.
7. Roll each piece into a long rope, about 32 inches, of uniform diameter about 2 inches thick. Cut rope into 25 1-3/4 oz pieces about 1-1/4 inches long.
8. MAKE-UP: Shape into balls by rolling with a circular motion on work table.
9. PROOF: At 90 F. until double in bulk, about 1 hour.
10. BAKE: 15 to 20 minutes at 400 F., or in 350 F. convection oven for 10 to 15 minutes until golden brown, on high fan, open vent.

OATS AND FRUIT BREAKFAST SQUARES

Yield 100   **Portion** 1 Each

Calories	Carbohydrates	Protein	Fat	Cholesterol	Sodium	Calcium
254 cal	42 g	6 g	8 g	0 mg	116 mg	36 mg

Ingredient	Weight	Measure	Issue
FRUIT COCKTAIL,CANNED,JUICE PACK,INCL LIQUIDS	8-7/8 lbs	1 gal 1/4 qts	
FLOUR,WHEAT,GENERAL PURPOSE	2-1/4 lbs	2 qts	
CINNAMON,GROUND	1-7/8 oz	1/2 cup	
BAKING SODA	1/2 oz	1 tbsp	
MARGARINE,SOFTENED	1-1/2 lbs	3 cup	
SUGAR,BROWN,PACKED	1-5/8 lbs	1 qts 1 cup	
SUGAR,GRANULATED	1-1/8 lbs	2-5/8 cup	
RESERVED LIQUID	12-1/2 oz	1-1/2 cup	
EXTRACT,VANILLA	1-1/4 oz	2-2/3 tbsp	
EGG SUBSTITUTE,PASTEURIZED	1-1/8 lbs	2 cup	
CEREAL,OATMEAL,ROLLED	5-3/8 lbs	3 qts 3-5/8 cup	
COOKING SPRAY,NONSTICK	3/8 oz	3/8 tsp	

Method

1. Drain fruit; reserve liquid for use in Step 3 and fruit for use in Step 6.
2. Sift together flour, cinnamon, and baking soda; set aside for use in Step 5.
3. Place margarine, sugars, egg substitute, reserved liquid, and vanilla in a mixer bowl. Beat at high speed for 1 to 2 minutes or until well blended. Scrape down bowl.
4. Add oats; mix at low speed 1 minute until well blended. Scrape down bowl.
5. Add flour mixture; mix at low speed 1 to 2 minutes or until well blended. Scrape down bowl.
6. Add fruit; mix at low speed 30 seconds or until just mixed.
7. Lightly spray sheet pans. Place about 1-1/4 gallons in each sheet pan. Spread evenly.
8. Bake 35 minutes at 325 F. or until lightly browned and toothpick comes out clean on high fan, open vent.
9. Loosen from pans while still warm. Cut 6 by 9.

PUMPKIN PATCH MUFFINS

Yield 100   **Portion** 1 Muffin

Calories	Carbohydrates	Protein	Fat	Cholesterol	Sodium	Calcium
154 cal	25 g	3 g	5 g	0 mg	208 mg	64 mg

Ingredient	Weight	Measure	Issue
FLOUR,WHEAT,GENERAL PURPOSE	1-2/3 lbs	1 qts 2 cup	
FLOUR,WHOLE WHEAT	1-5/8 lbs	1 qts 2 cup	
SUGAR,GRANULATED	1-3/4 lbs	1 qts	
BAKING POWDER	2-5/8 oz	1/4 cup 1-2/3 tbsp	
SALT	7/8 oz	1 tbsp	
CINNAMON,GROUND	5/8 oz	2-2/3 tbsp	
NUTMEG,GROUND	1/2 oz	2 tbsp	
EGG SUBSTITUTE,PASTEURIZED	1-1/8 lbs	2 cup	
MILK,NONFAT,DRY	1-3/4 oz	3/4 cup	
WATER	2 lbs	3-3/4 cup	
PUMPKIN,CANNED,SOLID PACK	2-1/8 lbs	1 qts	
OIL, CANOLA	1 lbs	2 cup	
RAISINS	1-1/4 lbs	1 qts	
COOKING SPRAY,NONSTICK	2 oz	1/4 cup 1/3 tbsp	

Method
1. Combine all purpose flour, whole-wheat flour, sugar, baking powder, salt, cinnamon, and nutmeg, set aside.
2. Reconstitute milk. In a mixer bowl, combine milk, pumpkin, oil, and egg substitute, mix on low speed until blended.
3. Add flour mixture to mixer bowl; mix on low speed until dry ingredients are moistened. Fold in raisins. Do not over mix.
4. Lightly spray muffin tins with non-stick cooking spray. Fill muffin tins 2/3 full.
5. Bake at 400 F. for 15 to 20 minutes or until lightly browned.

DATE NUT BREAD

Yield 100   **Portion** 1 Slice

Calories	Carbohydrates	Protein	Fat	Cholesterol	Sodium	Calcium
189 cal	38 g	3 g	4 g	0 mg	189 mg	43 mg

Ingredient	Weight	Measure	Issue
WATER,ICE	4-1/8 lbs	2 qts	
DATES,PIECES	4-3/4 lbs	3 qts 1/4 cup	
MARGARINE	6 oz	3/4 cup	
FLOUR,WHEAT,GENERAL PURPOSE	3-1/3 lbs	3 qts	
FLOUR,WHOLE WHEAT	14-7/8 oz	3-1/2 cup	

SUGAR,GRANULATED	1-1/2 lbs	3-3/8 cup
BAKING SODA	1-1/2 oz	3 tbsp
BAKING POWDER	1-2/3 oz	3-1/3 tbsp
ORANGE PEEL,FRESH,GRATED	1/2 oz	2-1/3 tbsp
EGG WHITES,FROZEN,THAWED	14-7/8 oz	1-3/4 cup
WALNUTS,SHELLED,HALVES AND PIECES	8-1/2 oz	2 cup
COOKING SPRAY,NONSTICK	2 oz	1/4 cup 1/3 tbsp

Method
1. In a large mixer bowl combine water, dates and margarine. Let cool 5 minutes or until the dates soften.
2. Mix together flour, whole-wheat flour, sugar, baking soda, baking powder, and orange peel.
3. Add flour mixture including egg whites to the date mixture and beat at low speed until dry ingredients have moistened. Fold in chopped walnuts.
4. Lightly spray loaf pans with non-stick cooking spray.
5. Scale 2-1/2 cups of batter into each loaf pan.
6. Bake at 350 F. for 40 to 45 minutes.

APPLESAUCE CINNAMON CRUMB TOP MUFFIN

Yield 100   **Portion** 1 Muffin

Calories	Carbohydrates	Protein	Fat	Cholesterol	Sodium	Calcium
204 cal	38 g	3 g	5 g	0 mg	217 mg	76 mg

Ingredient	Weight	Measure Issue
FLOUR,WHEAT,GENERAL PURPOSE	5-3/4 lbs	1 gal 1-1/4 qts
BAKING POWDER	3-7/8 oz	1/2 cup
SALT	3/4 oz	1 tbsp
CINNAMON,GROUND	1/2 oz	2 tbsp
NUTMEG,GROUND	1/8 oz	1/3 tsp
SUGAR,GRANULATED	2-1/4 lbs	1 qts 1 cup
APPLESAUCE,CANNED,SWEETENED	5-1/4 lbs	2 qts 1-3/8 cup
EGG SUBSTITUTE,PASTEURIZED	1-1/8 lbs	2 cup
SHORTENING	10-7/8 oz	1-1/2 cup
MARGARINE	3 oz	1/4 cup 2-1/3 tbsp
FLOUR,WHEAT,GENERAL PURPOSE	1-2/3 oz	1/4 cup 2-1/3 tbsp
SUGAR,BROWN,LIGHT	6-7/8 oz	1-3/8 cup
COOKING SPRAY,NONSTICK	2 oz	1/4 cup 1/3 tbsp

Method
1. Sift together flour, baking powder, salt, cinnamon, nutmeg, and sugar into mixer bowl.
2. Add applesauce, egg substitute, and salad oil or melted shortening; mix at low speed 15 seconds until dry ingredients are moistened.
3. Lightly spray each muffin cup with non-stick cooking spray. Fill each muffin cup 2/3 full. Mix softened margarine, flour, and brown sugar until crumbly. Sprinkle on top of each muffin.
4. Bake at 400 F. for 20 to 25 minutes or until lightly brown or using a convection oven, bake at 350 F. for 23 to 26 minutes open vent, turn off fan first 10 minutes, then low fan.

APPLESAUCE BLUEBERRY MUFFINS

Yield 100   **Portion** 1 Muffin

Calories	Carbohydrates	Protein	Fat	Cholesterol	Sodium	Calcium
195 cal	36 g	3 g	4 g	0 mg	209 mg	75 mg

Ingredient	Weight	Measure	Issue
FLOUR,WHEAT,GENERAL PURPOSE	5-3/4 lbs	1 gal 1-1/4 qts	
BAKING POWDER	3-7/8 oz	1/2 cup	
SALT	3/4 oz	1 tbsp	
CINNAMON,GROUND	1/2 oz	2 tbsp	
NUTMEG,GROUND	1/8 oz	1/3 tsp	
SUGAR,GRANULATED	2-1/4 lbs	1 qts 1 cup	
APPLESAUCE,CANNED,SWEETENED	5-1/4 lbs	2 qts 1-3/8 cup	
EGG SUBSTITUTE,PASTEURIZED	1-1/8 lbs	2 cup	
SHORTENING	10-7/8 oz	1-1/2 cup	
BLUEBERRIES,FROZEN,UNSWEETENED	2-3/8 lbs	1 qts 3 cup	
COOKING SPRAY,NONSTICK	2 oz	1/4 cup 1/3 tbsp	

Method

1. Sift together flour, baking powder, salt, cinnamon, nutmeg, and sugar into mixing bowl.
2. Add applesauce, egg substitute, and salad oil or melted shortening; mix at low speed 15 seconds until dry ingredients are moistened. Fold in blueberries. Do not overmix. Batter will be lumpy.
3. Lightly spray each muffin cup with non-stick cooking spray. Fill each muffin cup 2/3 full.
4. Bake 25 to 30 minutes at 400 F. oven or at 350 F. in a convection oven for 23 to 26 minutes or until done, open vent, fan turned off first 10 minutes, then low fan.

Notes

1. In Step 2, canned drained, rinsed blueberries 6-1/4 cups per 100 portions, may be substituted for frozen thawed blueberries

CRAN-APPLE MUFFINS

Yield 100   **Portion** 1 Muffin

Calories	Carbohydrates	Protein	Fat	Cholesterol	Sodium	Calcium
201 cal	38 g	3 g	4 g	10 mg	209 mg	74 mg

Ingredient	Weight	Measure	Issue
FLOUR,WHEAT,GENERAL PURPOSE	5-3/4 lbs	1 gal 1-1/4 qts	
BAKING POWDER	3-7/8 oz	1/2 cup	
SALT	3/4 oz	1 tbsp	
CINNAMON,GROUND	1/2 oz	2 tbsp	
NUTMEG,GROUND	1/8 oz	1/3 tsp	
SUGAR,GRANULATED	2-1/4 lbs	1 qts 1 cup	
APPLESAUCE,CANNED,SWEETENED	5-1/4 lbs	2 qts 1-3/8 cup	
EGGS,WHOLE,FROZEN	8-5/8 oz	1 cup	
EGG WHITES,FROZEN,THAWED	8-1/2 oz	1 cup	
OIL, CANOLA	10-1/4 oz	1-3/8 cup	
CRANBERRY SAUCE,JELLIED	1-7/8 lbs	3 cup	
COOKING SPRAY,NONSTICK	2 oz	1/4 cup 1/3 tbsp	
ORANGE PEEL,FRESH,GRATED	1/8 oz	1/3 tsp	

Method

1. Sift together flour, baking powder, salt, cinnamon, nutmeg, and sugar into mixer bowl.
2. Add applesauce, eggs, egg whites, and salad oil; mix at low speed approximately 15 seconds until dry ingredients are moistened. Do not over mix. Batter will be lumpy.
3. Lightly spray each muffin cup with non-stick cooking spray. Fill each muffin cup 2/3 full. Make a well in the center of each muffin with the back of a spoon. Combine cranberry sauce and orange peel. Spoon 2 teaspoons of cranberry filling into each well.
4. Bake at 400 F. for 25 to 30 minutes or until done. Using a convection oven, bake at 350 F. for 23 to 26 minutes, open vent, fan off first 10 minutes, then low fan.

BREAD LOAVES (FROZEN DOUGH)

Yield 100   **Portion** 2 Rolls

Calories	Carbohydrates	Protein	Fat	Cholesterol	Sodium	Calcium
276 cal	48 g	10 g	5 g	0 mg	261 mg	32 mg

Ingredient	Weight	Measure	Issue
DOUGH,BREAD,FROZEN,WHITE	20 lbs		
COOKING SPRAY,NONSTICK	2 oz	1/4cup 1/3tbsp	

Method

1. CCP: Thaw dough under refrigeration at 41 F. or lower.
2. Preheat proof box to 90 F. Check water level. Preheat convection oven to 325 F., fan on, vent closed.
3. Spray the inside of ten 2 pound loaf pans with non-stick cooking spray. Place a loaf in each pan. Spray with non-stick cooking spray.
4. Place dough in proof box to rise until dough has doubled in size.
5. Using a convection oven, bake at 325 F. for 15 minutes.
6. Remove from oven and cool before serving.

DILL ROLLS (FROZEN DOUGH)

Yield 100   **Portion** 2 Rolls

Calories	Carbohydrates	Protein	Fat	Cholesterol	Sodium	Calcium
287 cal	50 g	10 g	5 g	0 mg	263 mg	50 mg

Ingredient	Weight	Measure	Issue
DOUGH,BREAD,FROZEN,WHITE	20 lbs		
DILL WEED,DRIED	3-1/2 oz	2 cup	
COOKING SPRAY,NONSTICK	2 oz	1/4cup 1/3tbsp	
CORNMEAL	8 oz		

Method

1. CCP: Thaw dough under refrigeration at 41 F. or lower. Allowing dough to rest for 30 minutes prior to use will make it easier to work with.
2. Preheat proof box to 90 F. Check water level. Preheat convection oven to 325 F. closed vent, fan on.
3. Cut dough into 1-1/2 ounce pieces.
4. Pour 3/4 cup dill leaves on a sheet pan. Spread herbs around the pan. Roll each piece of dough in dill leaves, shaping each one into a rope 5 inches long. Tie each rope into a loose knot. Replenish herbs as necessary.

5. Spray 4 sheet pans with non-stick cooking spray. Dust the inside of sheet pans with 1/4 cup cornmeal each.
6. Place knots on sheet pans in rows of 6x9. Place sheet pans in proof box beginning with the second shelf from the top.
7. When rolls have doubled in size, bake in a convection oven at 325 F. with fan on 12-15 minutes or until golden brown.
8. Remove from oven and cool before serving.

GARLIC HERB ROLLS (FROZEN DOUGH)

Yield 100   **Portion** 2 Rolls

Calories	Carbohydrates	Protein	Fat	Cholesterol	Sodium	Calcium
301 cal	54 g	11 g	5 g	0 mg	263 mg	95 mg

Ingredient	Weight	Measure	Issue
DOUGH,BREAD,FROZEN,WHITE	20 lbs		
COOKING SPRAY,NONSTICK	2 oz	1/4 cup 1/3 tbsp	
CORNMEAL	8 oz		
GARLIC POWDER	9-1/2 oz	2 cup	
BASIL,DRIED,CRUSHED	10-1/8 oz	1 qts	

Method
1. CCP: Thaw dough under refrigeration at 41 F. or lower. Allowing dough to rest for 30 minutes prior to use will make it easier to work with.
2. Preheat proof box to 90 F. Check water level. Preheat convection oven to 325 F. closed vent, fan on.
3. Spray 4 sheet pans with non-stick cooking spray. Dust the inside of sheet pans with 1/4 cup cornmeal each.
4. Pour 1 cup garlic powder and 2 cups crushed basil on a sheet pan. Spread herbs around the pan.
5. Cut dough into 1-1/2 inch pieces. Roll each piece of dough in garlic and basil, shaping each one into a rope 5 inches long. Tie each rope into a loose knot. Replenish herbs as necessary.
6. Place knots on sheet pans in rows of 6 x 9. Place sheet pans in proof box beginning with the second shelf from the top.
7. When rolls have doubled in size, bake in a convection oven at 325 F. with fan on 12-15 minutes or until golden brown.
8. Remove from oven and cool before serving.

HUSH PUPPIES, FROZEN

Yield 100   **Portion** 3 Ounces

Calories	Carbohydrates	Protein	Fat	Cholesterol	Sodium	Calcium
183 cal	25 g	4 g	7 g	24 mg	364 mg	151 mg

Ingredient	Weight	Measure	Issue
HUSH PUPPIES,FROZEN	12 lbs		

Method
1. Arrange frozen hush puppies on sheet pans.
2. Bake in preheated convection oven at 300 F. with fan on for 20 minutes. CCP: Hold for service at 140 F. or higher.

DINNER ROLLS (FROZEN DOUGH)

Yield 100   **Portion** 2 Rolls

Calories	Carbohydrates	Protein	Fat	Cholesterol	Sodium	Calcium
285 cal	50 g	10 g	5 g	0 mg	261 mg	32 mg

Ingredient	Weight	Measure	Issue
DOUGH,BREAD,FROZEN,WHITE	20 lbs		
COOKING SPRAY,NONSTICK	2 oz	1/4cup 1/3tbsp	
CORNMEAL	8 oz		

Method
1. CCP: Thaw dough under refrigeration at 41 F. or lower. Allowing dough to rest for 30 minutes prior to use will make it easier to work with.
2. Preheat proof box to 90 F. Check water level. Preheat convection oven to 325 F. closed vent, fan on.
3. Spray 4 sheet pans with non-stick cooking spray. Dust the inside of sheet pans with 1/4 cup cornmeal each.
4. Cut dough into 1-1/2 inch pieces. Shape dough into rolls by rolling in a circular motion.
5. Place rolls on sheet pans in rows of 6 x 9. Using a sharp knife, slash the center of each roll once. Place sheet pans in proof box beginning with the second shelf from the top.
6. When rolls have doubled in size, bake in a convection oven at 325 F. with fan on 12-15 minutes or until golden brown.
7. Remove from oven and cool before serving.

POTATO ROLLS (FROZEN DOUGH)

Yield 100   **Portion** 2 Rolls

Calories	Carbohydrates	Protein	Fat	Cholesterol	Sodium	Calcium
295 cal	52 g	10 g	5 g	0 mg	264 mg	33 mg

Ingredient	Weight	Measure	Issue
DOUGH,BREAD,FROZEN,WHITE	20 lbs		
POTATO,WHITE,INSTANT,GRANULES	10-1/8 oz	1 qts 2 cup	
COOKING SPRAY,NONSTICK	2 oz	1/4 cup 1/3 tbsp	
CORNMEAL	8 oz		

Method
1. CCP: Thaw dough under refrigeration at 41 F. or lower. Allowing dough to rest for 30 minutes prior to use will make it easier to work with.
2. Preheat proof box to 90 F. Check water level. Preheat convection oven to 325 F. closed vent, fan on.
3. Pour approximately 2 cups potato flakes into sheet pans. Spread potato flakes around evenly. Replenish as necessary.
4. Spray 4 sheet pans with non-stick cooking spray. Dust the inside of sheet pans with 1/4 cup cornmeal each.
5. Cut dough into 1-1/2 inch pieces. Shape dough into rolls by rolling in a circular motion.
6. Roll each piece of dough in potato flakes and place rolls on sheet pans in rows of 6 x 9. Using a sharp knife, slash the center of each roll once. Place sheet pans in proof box beginning with the second shelf from the top.
7. When rolls have doubled in size, bake in a convection oven at 325 F. with fan on 12-15 minutes or until golden brown.
8. Remove from oven and cool before serving.

WHOLE WHEAT ROLLS (FROZEN DOUGH)

Yield 100   **Portion** 2 Rolls

Calories	Carbohydrates	Protein	Fat	Cholesterol	Sodium	Calcium
269 cal	47 g	10 g	8 g	0 mg	480 mg	32 mg

Ingredient	Weight	Measure	Issue
DOUGH,BREAD,WHEAT,FROZEN	20 lbs		
COOKING SPRAY,NONSTICK	2 oz	1/4cup 1/3tbsp	
CORNMEAL	8 oz		

Method

1. CCP: Thaw dough under refrigeration at 41 F. or lower. Allowing dough to rest for 30 minutes prior to use will make it easier to work with.
2. Preheat proof box to 90 F. Check water level. Preheat convection oven to 325 F. closed vent, fan on.
3. Spray 4 sheet pans with non-stick cooking spray. Dust the inside of sheet pans with 1/4 cup cornmeal each.
4. Shape dough into rolls by rolling in a circular motion.
5. Place rolls on sheet pans in rows of 6 x 9. Using a sharp knife, slash the center of each roll once. Place sheet pans in proof box beginning with the second shelf from the top.
6. When rolls have doubled in size, bake in a convection oven at 325 F. with fan on 12-15 minutes or until golden brown.
7. Remove from oven and cool before serving.

OAT ROLLS (FROZEN DOUGH)

Yield 100   **Portion** 2 Rolls

Calories	Carbohydrates	Protein	Fat	Cholesterol	Sodium	Calcium
297 cal	51 g	11 g	9 g	0 mg	480 mg	37 mg

Ingredient	Weight	Measure	Issue
DOUGH,BREAD,WHEAT,FROZEN	20 lbs		
OATS,ROLLED	2 lbs	1 qts 2 cup	
COOKING SPRAY,NONSTICK	2 oz	1/4 cup 1/3 tbsp	

Method

1. CCP: Thaw dough under refrigeration at 41 F. or lower. Allowing dough to rest for 30 minutes prior to use will make it easier to work with.
2. Preheat proof box to 90 F. Check water level. Preheat convection oven to 325 F. closed vent, fan on.
3. Cut dough into 1-1/2 inch pieces.
4. Pour approximately 2 cups of oats into sheet pans. Spread the oats around the pan evenly.
5. Roll each piece in oats, shaping each one into a rope five inches long. Tie each rope into a loose knot.
6. Spray 4 sheet pans with non-stick cooking spray. Dust the inside of sheet pans with 1/4 cup corn meal each.
7. Place knots on a prepared sheet pan in rows of 6 x 9. Place in proof box beginning with the second shelf from the top.
8. When rolls have doubled in size, bake in a convection oven at 325 F. with fan on 12-15 minutes or until golden brown.
9. Remove from oven and cool before serving.

SESAME OR CARAWAY ROLLS (FROZEN DOUGH)

Yield 100   **Portion** 2 Rolls

Calories	Carbohydrates	Protein	Fat	Cholesterol	Sodium	Calcium
319 cal	50 g	11 g	8 g	0 mg	264 mg	40 mg

Ingredient	Weight	Measure	Issue
DOUGH,BREAD,FROZEN,WHITE	20 lbs		
SESAME SEEDS	1-1/4 lbs	1 qts	
COOKING SPRAY,NONSTICK	2 oz	1/4 cup 1/3 tbsp	
CORNMEAL	8 oz		

Method

1. CCP: Thaw dough under refrigeration at 41 F. or lower. Allowing dough to rest for 30 minutes prior to use will make it easier to work with.
2. Preheat proof box to 90 F. Check water level. Preheat convection oven to 325 F. closed vent, fan on.
3. Cut dough into 1-1/2 inch pieces.
4. Pour approximately 2 cups of caraway or sesame seeds on sheet pans. Spread the seeds around the pan evenly.
5. Spray sheet pans with non-stick cooking spray. Dust the inside of sheet pans with 1/4 cup corn meal each.
6. Roll each piece in seeds and place on prepared sheet pan in rows of 6 x 9. Using a sharp knife, slash the center of each roll. Place in proof box beginning with the second shelf from the top.
7. When rolls have doubled in size, bake in a convection oven at 325 F. with fan on 12-15 minutes or until golden brown.
8. Remove from oven and cool before serving.

BRAN MUFFINS (WHITE CAKE MIX)

Yield 100   **Portion** 1 Muffin

Calories	Carbohydrates	Protein	Fat	Cholesterol	Sodium	Calcium
221 cal	41 g	2 g	6 g	0 mg	306 mg	22 mg

Ingredient	Weight	Measure	Issue
COOKING SPRAY,NONSTICK	2 oz	1/4 cup 1/3 tbsp	
CAKE MIX,WHITE	10 lbs	1 gal 3-3/8 qts	
MOLASSES	11-5/8 oz	1 cup	
CEREAL,RAISIN BRAN,BULK	1-1/8 lbs	2 qts 2 cup	

Method

1. Preheat convection oven to 300 F. low fan, open vent.
2. Spray muffin pans with non-stick cooking spray.
3. Prepare white cake mix according to manufacturer's instructions.
4. Add molasses to mix.
5. Fold in raisin bran cereal.
6. Scoop 2 ounces of mix into each muffin cup.
7. Using a convection oven, bake at 300 F. for approximately 15 minutes. Muffins are cooked when tester is inserted into the center of the centermost muffin and comes out clean.
8. Remove muffins from oven. Remove muffins from pan and let cool on a rack.

Notes

1. Muffin mix can be substituted for white cake mix.

BANANA NUT MUFFINS (WHITE CAKE MIX)

Yield 100   Portion 1 Muffin

Calories	Carbohydrates	Protein	Fat	Cholesterol	Sodium	Calcium
296 cal	40 g	3 g	14 g	0 mg	279 mg	20 mg

Ingredient	Weight	Measure	Issue
COOKING SPRAY,NONSTICK	2 oz	1/4 cup 1/3 tbsp	
CAKE MIX,WHITE	10 lbs	1 gal 3-3/8 qts	
PECANS,CHOPPED	3 lbs		
EXTRACT,BANANA	1-3/8 oz	3 tbsp	
SUGAR,GRANULATED	7 oz	1 cup	

Method
1. Preheat convection oven to 300 F. low fan, open vent.
2. Spray muffin pans with non-stick cooking spray.
3. Prepare white cake mix according to manufacturer's instructions.
4. Add 3 cups of chopped pecans and banana extract to mix.
5. Scoop 2 ounces of mix into each muffin cup.
6. Sprinkle the top of each muffin with remaining chopped pecans and granulated sugar.
7. Using a convection oven, bake at 325 F. for approximately 15 minutes. Muffins are cooked when tester is inserted into the center of the centermost muffin and comes out clean.
8. Remove muffins from oven. Remove muffins from pan and let cool on a rack.

HONEY CINNAMON MUFFINS (WHITE CAKE MIX)

Yield 100   Portion 1 Muffin

Calories	Carbohydrates	Protein	Fat	Cholesterol	Sodium	Calcium
219 cal	41 g	2 g	6 g	0 mg	279 mg	23 mg

Ingredient	Weight	Measure	Issue
COOKING SPRAY,NONSTICK	2 oz	1/4 cup 1/3 tbsp	
CAKE MIX,WHITE	10 lbs	1 gal 3-3/8 qts	
CINNAMON,GROUND	1-7/8 oz	1/2 cup	
HONEY	1-1/2 lbs	2 cup	
WATER,BOILING	8-1/3 oz	1 cup	

Method
1. Preheat convection oven to 300 F. low fan, open vent.
2. Spray muffin pans with non-stick cooking spray.
3. Prepare white cake mix according to manufacturer's instructions.
4. Add cinnamon to mix.
5. Scoop 2 ounces of mix into each muffin cup.
6. Using a convection oven, bake at 325 F. for approximately 15 minutes. Muffins are cooked when tester is inserted into the center of the centermost muffin and comes out clean.
7. Combine honey and boiling water.
8. Remove muffins from oven and brush with honey. Let stand 5 minutes.
9. Remove muffins from pan and let cool.

BLUEBERRY MUFFINS (WHITE CAKE MIX)

Yield 100   **Portion** 1 Muffin

Calories	Carbohydrates	Protein	Fat	Cholesterol	Sodium	Calcium
213 cal	38 g	2 g	6 g	0 mg	279 mg	17 mg

Ingredient	Weight	Measure	Issue
COOKING SPRAY,NONSTICK	2 oz	1/4 cup 1/3 tbsp	
CAKE MIX,WHITE	10 lbs	1 gal 3-3/8 qts	
CORNSTARCH	8 oz	1-3/4 cup	
BLUEBERRIES,FROZEN,UNSWEETENED	3 lbs	2 qts 3/4 cup	

Method
1. Preheat convection oven to 300 F. low fan, open vent.
2. Spray muffin pans with non-stick cooking spray.
3. Add cornstarch to white cake mix and prepare according to manufacturer's instructions.
4. Fold frozen blueberries into mix.
5. Scoop 2 ounces of mix into each muffin cup.
6. Using a convection oven, bake at 325 F. for approximately 15 minutes. Muffins are cooked when tester is inserted into the center of the centermost muffin and comes out clean.
7. Remove muffins from oven. Remove muffins from pan and let cool on a rack.

FRENCH TOAST, FROZEN

Yield 100   **Portion** 2 Slices

Calories	Carbohydrates	Protein	Fat	Cholesterol	Sodium	Calcium
261 cal	39 g	9 g	8 g	100 mg	606 mg	131 mg

Ingredient	Weight	Measure	Issue
FRENCH TOAST,FROZEN	27 lbs		

Method
1. Prepare french toast according to instructions on package. Usual baking instructions are as follows: Bake french toast on sheet pans in a 400 F. convection oven for 3-4 minutes.

PANCAKES, BUTTERMILK, FROZEN

Yield 100   **Portion** 2 Cakes

Calories	Carbohydrates	Protein	Fat	Cholesterol	Sodium	Calcium
280 cal	53 g	6 g	4 g	11 mg	623 mg	76 mg

Ingredient	Weight	Measure	Issue
PANCAKES,FROZEN	27 lbs		

Method
1. Prepare pancakes according to instructions on the package. Usual baking instructions are as follows: Bake pancakes on sheet pans in a 400 F. convection oven for 3-4 minutes.

MUFFINS, FROZEN, BATTER

Yield 100   **Portion** 4 Ounces

Calories	Carbohydrates	Protein	Fat	Cholesterol	Sodium	Calcium
442 cal	50 g	6 g	25 g	37 mg	368 mg	39 mg

Ingredient	Weight	Measure	Issue
COOKING SPRAY,NONSTICK	2 oz	1/4 cup 1/3 tbsp	
MUFFINS,FROZEN, BATTER	27 lbs		

Method
1. Spray sheet pans with non-stick cooking spray.
2. Thaw batter in refrigerator approximately 24-36 hours for easier use. Scoop 4 ounces muffin batter into each muffin cup.
3. Using a convection oven, bake muffins 26-30 minutes at 320 F. or until lightly brown. Baking time will vary by oven type. Let muffins cool before removing from pan.

MUFFINS, FROZEN

Yield 100   **Portion** 4 Ounces

Calories	Carbohydrates	Protein	Fat	Cholesterol	Sodium	Calcium
453 cal	77 g	7 g	14 g	7 mg	693 mg	19 mg

Ingredient	Weight	Measure	Issue
MUFFINS, FROZEN	30 lbs		

Method
1. Prepare muffins according to instructions on package.

HOT OATMEAL

Yield 100   **Portion** 3/4 Cup

Calories	Carbohydrates	Protein	Fat	Cholesterol	Sodium	Calcium
106 cal	18 g	5 g	2 g	0 mg	216 mg	19 mg

Ingredient	Weight	Measure	Issue
CEREAL,OATMEAL,ROLLED	6 lbs	1 gal 3/8 qts	
SALT	1-7/8 oz	3 tbsp	
WATER,BOILING	41-3/4 lbs	5 gal	

Method
1. Add cereal and salt to boiling water; stir to prevent lumping.
2. Return to a boil; reduce heat; simmer 1 to 3 minutes, stirring occasionally.
3. Turn off heat; let stand 10 minutes before serving.

HOT FARINA

Yield 100   **Portion** 3/4 Cup

Calories	Carbohydrates	Protein	Fat	Cholesterol	Sodium	Calcium
104 cal	22 g	3 g	0 g	0 mg	216 mg	8 mg

Ingredient	Weight	Measure	Issue
SALT	1-7/8 oz	3 tbsp	
WATER	33-1/2 lbs	4 gal	
CEREAL,FARINA,DRY	6-1/4 lbs	1 gal	
WATER,COLD	8-1/3 lbs	1 gal	

Method
1. Add salt to hot water; bring to boil.
2. Mix cereal with cold water; pour into boiling salted water stirring constantly, until water returns to a boil. Reduce heat. Let simmer 2 to 5 minutes, stirring frequently. Turn off heat; let stand 5 minutes before serving.

HOMINY GRITS

Yield 100   **Portion** 2/3 Cup

Calories	Carbohydrates	Protein	Fat	Cholesterol	Sodium	Calcium
84 cal	16 g	2 g	1 g	2 mg	107 mg	4 mg

Ingredient	Weight	Measure	Issue
WATER,BOILING	33-1/2 lbs	4 gal	
SALT	7/8 oz	1 tbsp	
BUTTER	4 oz	1/2 cup	
HOMINY GRITS,QUICK COOKING	4-1/2 lbs	3 qts 1-1/8 cup	

Method
1. Add salt and butter or margarine to boiling water.
2. Add grits gradually while stirring to prevent lumping. Bring to a boil; reduce heat; cover and cook for 5 minutes. Stir occasionally.

FRIED HOMINY GRITS

Yield 100   **Portion** 3 Slices

Calories	Carbohydrates	Protein	Fat	Cholesterol	Sodium	Calcium
164 cal	16 g	2 g	10 g	2 mg	107 mg	4 mg

Ingredient	Weight	Measure	Issue
WATER,BOILING	33-1/2 lbs	4 gal	
SALT	7/8 oz	1 tbsp	
BUTTER	4 oz	1/2 cup	
HOMINY GRITS,QUICK COOKING	4-1/2 lbs	3 qts 1-1/8 cup	

Method
1. Add salt and butter or margarine to boiling water.
2. Add grits gradually while stirring to prevent lumping. Bring to a boil; reduce heat; cover and cook 5 minutes. Stir occasionally.
3. Pour hot cooked grits into bread pans or in 3 steam table pans; cover and refrigerate several hours or overnight. Cut cold grits lengthwise into 3 equal strips; cut each into 1/2-inch thick slices. If slices are moist, dip in flour; fry on 400 F. preheated well-greased griddle until lightly browned, about 8 minutes per side.

BUTTERED HOMINY

Yield 100   **Portion** 1/3 Cup

Calories	Carbohydrates	Protein	Fat	Cholesterol	Sodium	Calcium
86 cal	12 g	1 g	4 g	7 mg	208 mg	10 mg

Ingredient	Weight	Measure	Issue
HOMINY,WHOLE,CANNED	18-7/8 lbs	3 gal 1 qts	
PEPPER,BLACK,GROUND	1/8 oz	1/3 tsp	
BUTTER	12 oz	1-1/2 cup	
PARSLEY,FRESH,BUNCH,CHOPPED	1 oz	1/2 cup	1-1/8 oz

Method
1. Drain hominy. Reserve 1 quart liquid.
2. Add pepper and reserved liquid to drained hominy in pan; heat slowly for 20 minutes.
3. Add butter or margarine.
4. Garnish with parsley or 2 tbsp paprika.

FRIED HOMINY

Yield 100   **Portion** 1/3 Cup

Calories	Carbohydrates	Protein	Fat	Cholesterol	Sodium	Calcium
134 cal	12 g	1 g	9 g	0 mg	180 mg	9 mg

Ingredient	Weight	Measure	Issue
HOMINY,WHOLE,CANNED	18-7/8 lbs	3 gal 1 qts	
SHORTENING,VEGETABLE,MELTED	1-3/4 lbs	1 qts	
PEPPER,BLACK,GROUND	1/8 oz	1/8 tsp	

Method
1. Drain hominy, discard liquid.
2. Fry hominy in melted shortening or salad oil until lightly browned. Season with black pepper.

BOILED PASTA

Yield 100   Portion 1 Cup

Calories	Carbohydrates	Protein	Fat	Cholesterol	Sodium	Calcium
207 cal	41 g	7 g	1 g	0 mg	292 mg	16 mg

Ingredient	Weight	Measure	Issue
WATER	66-7/8 lbs	8 gal	
SALT	2-1/2 oz	1/4 cup 1/3 tbsp	
OIL,SALAD	1-7/8 oz	1/4 cup 1/3 tbsp	
SPAGHETTI NOODLES,DRY	12 lbs	3 gal 1 qts	

Method
1. Add salt and salad oil to water; heat to a rolling boil.
2. Slowly add pasta while stirring constantly until water boils again. Cook according to times in Note 1; stir occasionally. DO NOT OVERCOOK.
3. Drain. Rinse with cold water; drain thoroughly.

Notes
1. Macaroni or egg noodles should cook for 8 to 10 minutes; spaghetti for 10 to 12 minutes; vermicelli for 7 to 10 minutes.
2. When held on steam table, mix 1 tablespoon salad oil with pasta in each steam table pan to prevent product from sticking together.
3. To reheat pasta before serving, place desired quantity in a wire basket; lower into boiling water 2 to 3 minutes. Drain well. Place in greased steam table pans.

BUTTERED PASTA

Yield 100   Portion 1 Cup

Calories	Carbohydrates	Protein	Fat	Cholesterol	Sodium	Calcium
239 cal	41 g	7 g	5 g	10 mg	329 mg	17 mg

Ingredient	Weight	Measure	Issue
WATER	66-7/8 lbs	8 gal	
SALT	2-1/2 oz	1/4 cup 1/3 tbsp	
OIL,SALAD	1-7/8 oz	1/4 cup 1/3 tbsp	
SPAGHETTI NOODLES,DRY	12 lbs	3 gal 1 qts	
BUTTER,MELTED	1 lbs	2 cup	

Method
1. Add salt and salad oil to water; heat to a rolling boil.

2. Slowly add pasta while stirring constantly until water boils again. Cook according to times in Note 1; stir occasionally. DO NOT OVERCOOK.
3. Drain noodles and add melted butter to pasta immediately.

Notes
1. Macaroni or egg noodles should cook for 8 to 10 minutes; spaghetti for 10 to 12 minutes; vermicelli for 7 to 10 minutes.
2. To reheat pasta before serving, place desired quantity in a wire basket; lower into boiling water 2 to 3 minutes. Drain well. Place in greased steam table pans.

STEAMED RICE

Yield 100   **Portion** 3/4 Cup

Calories	Carbohydrates	Protein	Fat	Cholesterol	Sodium	Calcium
148 cal	32 g	3 g	1 g	0 mg	214 mg	26 mg

Ingredient	Weight	Measure	Issue
RICE,LONG GRAIN	8-1/2 lbs	1 gal 1-1/4 qts	
WATER,COLD	23 lbs	2 gal 3 qts	
SALT	1-7/8 oz	3 tbsp	
OIL,SALAD	1-1/2 oz	3 tbsp	

Method
1. Combine rice, water, salt, and salad oil; bring to a boil. Stir occasionally.
2. Cover tightly; simmer 20 to 25 minutes. DO NOT STIR.
3. Remove from heat; transfer to shallow serving pans.

Notes
1. In Step 2, rice may be baked in a 350 F. convection oven, 35 to 40 minutes on high fan, closed vent.

LYONNAISE RICE

Yield 100   **Portion** 3/4 Cup

Calories	Carbohydrates	Protein	Fat	Cholesterol	Sodium	Calcium
164 cal	33 g	3 g	2 g	0 mg	215 mg	29 mg

Ingredient	Weight	Measure	Issue
RICE,LONG GRAIN	8-1/2 lbs	1 gal 1-1/4qts	
WATER,COLD	23 lbs	2 gal 3 qts	
SALT	1-7/8 oz	3 tbsp	
OIL,SALAD	1-1/2 oz	3 tbsp	
ONIONS,FRESH,CHOPPED	3-1/8 lbs	2 qts 1cup	3-1/2lbs
OIL,SALAD	3-7/8 oz	1/2 cup	
PIMIENTO,CANNED,DRAINED,CHOPPED	13-1/2 oz	2 cup	

Method
1. Combine rice, water, salt, and salad oil; bring to a boil. Stir occasionally.
2. Cover tightly; simmer 20 to 25 minutes. DO NOT STIR. Remove from heat.
3. Saute onions in oil until tender.
4. Add sauteed onions and pimientos to cooked rice. Toss well. CCP: Hold for service at 140 F. or higher.

TOSSED GREEN RICE

Yield 100   **Portion** 3/4 Cup

Calories	Carbohydrates	Protein	Fat	Cholesterol	Sodium	Calcium
163 cal	33 g	3 g	2 g	0 mg	217 mg	34 mg

Ingredient	Weight	Measure	Issue
RICE,LONG GRAIN	8-1/2 lbs	1 gal 1-1/4 qts	
WATER,COLD	23 lbs	2 gal 3 qts	
SALT	1-7/8 oz	3 tbsp	
OIL,SALAD	1-1/2 oz	3 tbsp	
ONIONS,GREEN,FRESH,SLICED	1-1/3 lbs	1 qts 2 cup	1-1/2 lbs
PEPPERS,GREEN,FRESH,CHOPPED	2 lbs	1 qts 2 cup	2-3/8 lbs
OIL,SALAD	3-7/8 oz	1/2 cup	
PARSLEY,FRESH,BUNCH,CHOPPED	8 oz	3-3/4 cup	8-3/8 oz
PEPPER,BLACK,GROUND	1/8 oz	1/3 tsp	

Method
1. Combine rice, water, salt, and salad oil; bring to a boil. Stir occasionally.
2. Cover tightly; simmer 20 to 25 minutes. DO NOT STIR. Remove from heat.
3. Saute green onions with tops and sweet peppers in oil until tender.
4. Add to cooked rice. Add parsley and black pepper. Toss well. CCP: Hold for service at 140 F. or higher.

LONG GRAIN AND WILD RICE

Yield 100   **Portion** 3/4 Cup

Calories	Carbohydrates	Protein	Fat	Cholesterol	Sodium	Calcium
168 cal	34 g	7 g	1 g	0 mg	7 mg	12 mg

Ingredient	Weight	Measure	Issue
RICE,LONG GRAIN & WILD	10-1/8 lbs	1 gal 3-1/8 qts	
WATER,COLD	25-1/8 lbs	3 gal	
OIL,SALAD	1-1/2 oz	3 tbsp	

Method
1. Combine rice mix, water and salad oil; bring to a boil. Stir occasionally.
2. Cover tightly; simmer 20 to 25 minutes. DO NOT STIR.
3. Remove from heat; transfer to shallow serving pans. CCP: Hold for service at 140 F. or higher.

RICE WITH PARMESAN CHEESE

Yield 100   **Portion** 3/4 Cup

Calories	Carbohydrates	Protein	Fat	Cholesterol	Sodium	Calcium
187 cal	32 g	5 g	4 g	4 mg	329 mg	95 mg

Ingredient	Weight	Measure	Issue
RICE,LONG GRAIN	8-1/2 lbs	1 gal 1-1/4 qts	
WATER,COLD	23 lbs	2 gal 3 qts	

SALT	1-7/8 oz	3 tbsp
OIL,SALAD	1-1/2 oz	3 tbsp
MARGARINE,MELTED	8 oz	1 cup
CHEESE,PARMESAN,GRATED	1-1/8 lbs	1 qts 1 cup

Method
1. Combine rice, water, salt, and salad oil; bring to a boil. Stir occasionally.
2. Cover tightly; simmer 20 to 25 minutes. DO NOT STIR.
3. Remove from heat; transfer to shallow serving pans. Add melted butter to rice. Mix well to coat rice. Add grated Parmesan cheese. Toss well. CCP: Hold for service at 140 F. or higher.

STEAMED BROWN RICE

Yield 100   **Portion** 3/4 Cup

Calories	Carbohydrates	Protein	Fat	Cholesterol	Sodium	Calcium
168 cal	34 g	4 g	2 g	0 mg	216 mg	13 mg

Ingredient	Weight	Measure	Issue
RICE,BROWN,LONG GRAIN,RAW PARBOILED	9-3/4 lbs	1 gal 2 qts	
WATER,COLD	25-1/8 lbs	3 gal	
SALT	1-7/8 oz	3 tbsp	
OIL,SALAD	1-1/2 oz	3 tbsp	

Method
1. Combine rice, water, salt, and salad oil; bring to a boil. Stir occasionally.
2. Cover tightly; simmer for 25 minutes or until most of the water is absorbed.
3. Remove from heat; transfer to shallow serving pans. CCP: Hold for service at 140 F. or higher.

STEAMED RICE (STEAM COOKER METHOD)

Yield 100   **Portion** 3/4 Cup

Calories	Carbohydrates	Protein	Fat	Cholesterol	Sodium	Calcium
168 cal	34 g	4 g	2 g	0 mg	216 mg	13 mg

Ingredient	Weight	Measure	Issue
RICE,BROWN,LONG GRAIN,RAW PARBOILED	9-3/4 lbs	1 gal 2 qts	
WATER	25-1/8 lbs	3 gal	
SALT	1-7/8 oz	3 tbsp	
OIL,SALAD	1-1/2 oz	3 tbsp	

Method
1. Place 4-3/4 lbs rice in each pan.
2. Add 4-1/2 qts water to each pan.
3. Add 1-1/2 tbsp salt and 1-1/2 tbsp salad oil to each pan. Stir well to ensure rice is moistened.
4. Place pans in preheated steam cooker. Steam 22-27 minutes at 5 lbs PSI or 18 to 24 minutes at 15 lb PSI.

PORK FRIED RICE

Yield 100   Portion 3/4 Cup

Calories	Carbohydrates	Protein	Fat	Cholesterol	Sodium	Calcium
211 cal	29 g	8 g	6 g	55 mg	462 mg	38 mg

Ingredient	Weight	Measure	Issue
RICE,LONG GRAIN	7-1/3 lbs	1 gal 1/2 qts	
WATER,BOILING	18-3/4 lbs	2 gal 1 qts	
SALT	1-2/3 oz	2-2/3 tbsp	
OIL,SALAD	1 oz	2 tbsp	
ONIONS,FRESH,CHOPPED	2-1/2 lbs	1 qts 3 cup	2-3/4lbs
PEPPERS,GREEN,FRESH,CHOPPED	1-1/2 lbs	1 qts 1/2 cup	1-3/4lbs
CELERY,FRESH,CHOPPED	1-1/4 lbs	1 qts 1/2 cup	1-5/8lbs
OIL,SALAD	5-1/8 oz	1/2cup 2-2/3tbsp	
EGGS,WHOLE,FROZEN	2 lbs	3-3/4 cup	
PORK,COOKED,DICED	4 lbs		
PIMIENTO,CANNED,DRAINED,CHOPPED	13-1/2 oz	2 cup	
SOY SAUCE	1 lbs	1-1/2 cup	

Method
1. Place equal amounts of rice, water, salt, and salad oil in well greased pans. Stir to combine.
2. Using a convection oven, bake at 325 F. for 30 minutes on high fan, closed vent; remove from oven. Uncover. Set aside for use in Step 4.
3. Combine onions, peppers and celery; saute in shortening or salad oil about 10 minutes or until tender.
4. Add an equal quantity of sauteed vegetables to cooked rice in each pan. Mix lightly but thoroughly.
5. Pour beaten eggs on lightly greased griddle. Cook until well done. DO NOT turn. Cut into strips; add an equal amount to rice mixture in each pan.
6. Add equal amounts of pork and pimientos to rice in each pan. Mix lightly but thoroughly.
7. Using a convection oven, bake at 350 F. for 30 minutes on high fan, closed vent. CCP: Internal temperature must reach 145 F. or higher for 15 seconds.
8. Remove from oven; blend in 1/2 cup soy sauce per pan. CCP: Hold for service at 140 F. or higher.

Notes
1. In Step 6, 4 pounds diced ham may be used per 100 servings.
2. In Step 2, rice may be prepared in small batches on 350 F. griddle or tilt frying pan. Turn occasionally until brown, 10 to 15 minutes.

FILIPINO RICE

Yield 100   Portion 3/4 Cup

Calories	Carbohydrates	Protein	Fat	Cholesterol	Sodium	Calcium
250 cal	31 g	9 g	10 g	59 mg	458 mg	25 mg

Ingredient	Weight	Measure	Issue
ONIONS,FRESH,CHOPPED	2-1/2 lbs	1 qts 3 cup	2-3/4 lbs
OIL,SALAD		2 cup	
RICE,BROWN,LONG GRAIN,DRY	8-1/2 lbs	1 gal 1-1/4 qts	
WATER	23 lbs	2 gal 3 qts	
GARLIC POWDER	<1/16th oz	<1/16th tsp	
SALT	1-2/3 oz	2-2/3 tbsp	

EGGS,WHOLE,FROZEN	2 lbs	3-3/4 cup
PORK,COOKED,DICED	4 lbs	
SOY SAUCE	1 lbs	1-1/2 cup

Method

1. Saute onions in a steam jacketed kettle in salad oil until light yellow.
2. Add rice; stir until well coated.
3. Add water, garlic powder, and salt to rice mixture.
4. Bring to a boil; cover; simmer 20 to 25 minutes.
5. Pour beaten eggs on lightly greased griddle. Cook until done. DO NOT turn. Cut into strips; add an equal amount to rice mixture in each pan.
6. Add an equal amount of pork to rice in each pan. Mix lightly but thoroughly.
7. Bake 45 minutes in 350 F. CCP: Internal temperature must reach 145 F. or higher for 15 seconds.
8. Remove from oven; blend in 1/2 cup soy sauce per pan. CCP: Hold for service at 140 F. or higher.

SHRIMP FRIED RICE

Yield 100   Portion 3/4 Cup

Calories	Carbohydrates	Protein	Fat	Cholesterol	Sodium	Calcium
234 cal	19 g	12 g	7 g	90 mg	502 mg	46 mg

Ingredient	Weight	Measure	Issue
RICE,LONG GRAIN	7-1/3 lbs	1 gal 1/2 qts	
WATER,BOILING	18-3/4 lbs	2 gal 1 qts	
SALT	1-2/3 oz	2-2/3 tbsp	
OIL,SALAD	1 oz	2 tbsp	
ONIONS,FRESH,CHOPPED	2-1/2 lbs	1 qts 3 cup	2-3/4lbs
PEPPERS,GREEN,FRESH,CHOPPED	1-1/2 lbs	1 qts 1/2 cup	1-7/8lbs
CELERY,FRESH,CHOPPED	1-1/4 lbs	1 qts 3/4 cup	1-3/4lbs
OIL,SALAD	5-1/8 oz	1/2cup 2-2/3tbsp	
EGGS,WHOLE,FROZEN	2 lbs	3-3/4 cup	
COOKING SPRAY,NONSTICK	2 oz	1/4 cup 1/3 tbsp	
SHRIMP,COOKED,CHOPPED	4 lbs		
PORK,COOKED,DICED	4 lbs		
PIMIENTO,CANNED,DRAINED,CHOPPED	13-1/2 oz	2 cup	
SOY SAUCE	1 lbs	1-1/2 cup	

Method

1. Place equal amounts of rice, water, salt, and salad oil in well greased pans. Stir to combine.
2. Using a convection oven, bake at 325 F. for 30 minutes on high fan, closed vent. Remove from oven. Uncover. Set aside for use in Step 4.
3. Combine onions, peppers and celery; saute in shortening or salad oil about 10 minutes or until tender.
4. Add an equal quantity of sauteed vegetables to cooked rice in each pan. Mix lightly but thoroughly.
5. Pour beaten eggs on lightly greased griddle. Cook until well done. DO NOT TURN. Cut into strips; add an equal amount to rice mixture in each pan.
6. Add equal amounts of pork, cooked chopped shrimp and pimientos to rice in each pan. Mix lightly but thoroughly.
7. Using a convection oven, bake 45 minutes at 350 F. for 30 minutes on high fan, closed vent. CCP: Internal temperature must reach 145 F. or higher for 15 seconds.

8. Remove from oven; blend in 1/2 cup soy sauce per pan. CCP: Hold for service at 140 F. or higher.

Notes
1. In Step 6, 4 pounds diced ham may be used per 100 servings.

RICE PILAF

Yield 100   **Portion** 3/4 Cup

Calories	Carbohydrates	Protein	Fat	Cholesterol	Sodium	Calcium
201 cal	37 g	4 g	4 g	4 mg	927 mg	41 mg

Ingredient	Weight	Measure	Issue
BUTTER	6 oz	3/4 cup	
OIL,SALAD	5-3/4 oz	3/4 cup	
ONIONS,FRESH,CHOPPED	6-2/3 lbs	1 gal 3/4 qts	
RICE,LONG GRAIN	9 lbs	1 gal 1-1/2 qts	
SALT	1 oz	1 tbsp	
GARLIC POWDER	3/8 oz	1 tbsp	
PEPPER,BLACK,GROUND	1/8 oz	1/8 tsp	
CHICKEN BROTH	7-1/2 lbs	3 gal	

Method
1. Melt butter or margarine. Add salad oil or melted shortening and onions. Stir well. Saute until onions are tender, about 5 minutes.
2. Add rice to onion mixture. Cook until rice is lightly browned, about 10 minutes, stirring constantly.
3. Place about 2 quarts onion and rice mixture into each pan.
4. Prepare broth according to recipe directions. Add salt, garlic powder and pepper; stir well. Pour 3 quarts over rice mixture in each pan; cover.
5. Using a convection oven, bake at 350 F. for 40 to 45 minutes or until tender on high fan, closed vent or until rice is tender. Stir lightly. CCP: Internal temperature must reach 145 F. or higher for 15 seconds. CCP: Hold for service at 140 F. or higher.

ORANGE RICE

Yield 100   **Portion** 3/4 Cup

Calories	Carbohydrates	Protein	Fat	Cholesterol	Sodium	Calcium
221 cal	42 g	4 g	4 g	4 mg	812 mg	45 mg

Ingredient	Weight	Measure	Issue
BUTTER	6 oz	3/4 cup	
OIL,SALAD	5-3/4 oz	3/4 cup	
ONIONS,FRESH,CHOPPED	6-2/3 lbs	1 gal 3/4 qts	
RICE,LONG GRAIN	9 lbs	1 gal 1-1/2 qts	
JUICE,ORANGE	11 lbs	1 gal 1 qts	
CHICKEN BROTH	7-1/2 lbs	3 gal	

Method
1. Melt butter or margarine. Add salad oil or melted shortening and onions. Stir well. Saute until onions are tender, about 5 minutes.
2. Add rice to onion mixture. Cook until rice is lightly browned, about 10 minutes, stirring constantly.

3. Place 2 quarts of onion and rice mixture into each pan.
4. Prepare broth according to recipe directions. Add orange juice to boiling broth; stir well. Pour 3-1/4 quarts over rice mixture in each pan; cover.
5. Using a convection oven, bake at 350 F. for 40 to 45 minutes or until tender on high fan, closed vent or until rice is tender. Stir lightly. CCP: Internal temperature must reach 145 F. or higher for 15 seconds. CCP: Hold for service at 140 F. or higher.
6. May be garnished with thinly sliced oranges just before serving.

SPANISH RICE

Yield 100   Portion 3/4 Cup

Calories	Carbohydrates	Protein	Fat	Cholesterol	Sodium	Calcium
153 cal	31 g	4 g	2 g	2 mg	409 mg	55 mg

Ingredient	Weight	Measure	Issue
RICE,LONG GRAIN	5-3/4 lbs	3 qts 2 cup	
WATER,COLD	15-1/8 lbs	1 gal 3-1/4qts	
OIL,SALAD	1 oz	2 tbsp	
SALT	1-1/4 oz	2 tbsp	
BACON,RAW	1-1/2 lbs		
TOMATOES,CANNED,DICED,DRAINED	19-7/8 lbs	2 gal 1 qts	
ONIONS,FRESH,CHOPPED	4-1/4 lbs	3 qts	4-2/3lbs
PEPPERS,GREEN,FRESH,CHOPPED	2 lbs	1 qts 2 cup	2-3/8lbs
SUGAR,GRANULATED	3-1/2 oz	1/2 cup	
SALT	1 oz	1 tbsp	
THYME,GROUND	1/3 oz	2 tbsp	
PEPPER,BLACK,GROUND	1/4 oz	1 tbsp	
GARLIC POWDER	1/4 oz	3/8 tsp	
BAY LEAF,FRESH	1/8 oz	4 each	

Method
1. Cook rice according to directions on Recipe No. E 005 00. Set aside for use in Step 4.
2. Saute bacon until crisp in steam-jacketed kettle or stock pot. Drain; discard drippings.
3. Add tomatoes, onions, peppers, sugar, salt, thyme, black pepper, garlic, and bay leaves. Stir to combine; bring to boil. Cover; reduce heat; simmer 15 minutes.
4. Add rice; stir to combine; using a convection oven, bake at 325 F. 30 minutes on high fan, closed vent. CCP: Internal temperature must reach 145 F. or higher for 15 seconds. Remove bay leaves before serving. CCP: Hold for service at 140 F. or higher.

RED BEANS WITH RICE

Yield 100   Portion 1 Cup

Calories	Carbohydrates	Protein	Fat	Cholesterol	Sodium	Calcium
225 cal	41 g	10 g	3 g	3 mg	630 mg	53 mg

Ingredient	Weight	Measure	Issue
RICE,LONG GRAIN	5-3/4 lbs	3 qts 2 cup	
WATER,COLD	15-1/8 lbs	1 gal 3-1/4 qts	
OIL,SALAD	1 oz	2 tbsp	

SALT	1-1/4 oz	2 tbsp	
BACON,SLICED,RAW	3 lbs		
ONIONS,FRESH,CHOPPED	2-1/8 lbs	1 qts 2 cup	2-1/3lbs
BEANS,KIDNEY,DARK RED,CANNED,INCL LIQUIDS	27-1/8 lbs	3 gal	
PEPPER,BLACK,GROUND	1/4 oz	1 tbsp	
PEPPER,RED,GROUND	<1/16th oz	1/8 tsp	
GARLIC POWDER	1-1/8 oz	1/4 cup	

Method

1. Cook rice according to directions on Recipe No. E 005 00. Set aside for use in Step 6.
2. Cook bacon until crisp; drain. Set aside 2 ounces bacon fat per 100 servings for use in Step 3. Set aside bacon for use in Step 4.
3. Saute onions in bacon fat about 1 to 2 minutes or until lightly browned. Drain thoroughly.
4. Combine sauteed bacon and onions with undrained kidney beans, peppers and garlic powder.
5. Using a convection oven, bake at 325 F. for 30 minutes on high fan, closed vent. CCP: Internal temperature must reach 145 F. or higher for 15 seconds.
6. Serve 1/2 cup of beans over 1/2 cup of rice. CCP: Hold for service at 140 F. or higher.

HOPPING JOHN (BLACK-EYE PEAS WITH RICE)

Yield 100   Portion 2/3 Cup

Calories	Carbohydrates	Protein	Fat	Cholesterol	Sodium	Calcium
177 cal	30 g	8 g	3 g	3 mg	430 mg	32 mg

Ingredient	Weight	Measure	Issue
BACON,SLICED,RAW	3 lbs	1 qts 2 cup	
ONIONS,FRESH,CHOPPED	2-1/8 lbs	3 gal 3/4 qts	
PEAS,BLACKEYE,CANNED,INCL LIQUIDS	27 lbs	2 qts	
RICE,BROWN,LONG GRAIN,DRY	3-1/4 lbs	1 gal 1/4 qts	
WATER	8-7/8 lbs	2 tbsp	
PEPPER,BLACK,GROUND	1/2 oz	1/8 tsp	
PEPPER,RED,GROUND	<1/16th oz	1/4 cup 3 tbsp	
GARLIC POWDER	2 oz	2-1/3 lbs	

Method

1. Cook bacon until crisp; drain. Set aside 2 ounces bacon fat per 100 servings, for use in Step 2; bacon for use in Step 3.
2. Saute onions in bacon fat about 1 to 2 minutes or until lightly browned. Drain thoroughly.
3. Combine undrained black-eyed peas, rice, water, sauteed onions, cooked bacon, black pepper, red pepper, and garlic. Mix well. Bring to a boil; cover tightly; reduce heat; simmer 25 minutes or until rice is tender. CCP: Internal temperature must reach 145 F. or higher for 15 seconds. CCP: Hold for service at 140 F. or higher.

MEXICAN RICE

Yield 100   Portion 3/4 Cup

Calories	Carbohydrates	Protein	Fat	Cholesterol	Sodium	Calcium
193 cal	34 g	3 g	5 g	0 mg	244 mg	37 mg

Ingredient	Weight	Measure	Issue
RICE,LONG GRAIN	8-1/2 lbs	1 gal 1-1/4qts	
OIL,SALAD	1 lbs	2 cup	
ONIONS,FRESH,CHOPPED	1 lbs	3 cup	1-1/8 lbs
TOMATOES,CANNED,DICED,DRAINED	5 lbs	2 qts 1cup	
SALT	1-7/8 oz	3 tbsp	
PEPPER,BLACK,GROUND	3/8 oz	1 tbsp	
CUMIN,GROUND	7/8 oz	1/4 cup 1/3tbsp	
WATER	20-7/8 lbs	2 gal 2qts	

Method

1. Place 10-1/2 cups rice, 1 cup salad oil and 1-1/2 cups onions in each pan. Stir well to coat rice.
2. Place in 400 F. oven; cook until lightly brown, about 25 minutes.
3. Combine tomatoes, salt, pepper, cumin and water.
4. Pour about 1-1/2 gallons tomato mixture over rice in each pan; stir well. Cover; return to oven; bake about 1 hour in 400 F. oven or until rice is tender.
5. Stir lightly. CCP: Internal temperature must reach 145 F. or higher for 15 seconds. CCP: Hold for service at 140 F. or higher.

Notes

1. Rice may be prepared on top of range. Follow Step 1. In Step 2, heat at medium heat until rice is lightly browned; stir occasionally. Follow Step 3. In Step 4, bring rice mixture to a boil; cover; reduce heat; cook until rice is light and fluffy. Follow Step 5.
2. Rice may be prepared in steam-jacketed kettle. In Step 1, place rice, salad oil and onions in kettle. Heat until rice is lightly browned, stirring occasionally. Omit Step 2. Follow Step 3. Add tomato mixture; bring to a boil; cover; reduce heat and cook 20 minutes at medium heat. Uncover; cook an additional 5 minutes. Omit Step 4. Follow Step 5.

NOODLES JEFFERSON

Yield 100   **Portion** 3/4 Cup

Calories	Carbohydrates	Protein	Fat	Cholesterol	Sodium	Calcium
241 cal	29 g	10 g	9 g	58 mg	509 mg	143 mg

Ingredient	Weight	Measure	Issue
WATER,WARM	50-1/8 lbs	6 gal	
SALT	1-7/8 oz	3 tbsp	
OIL,SALAD	1-1/2 oz	3 tbsp	
NOODLES,EGG	9 lbs	6 gal 2-7/8 qts	
BUTTER,MELTED	1-1/4 lbs	2-1/2 cup	
SALT	5/8 oz	1 tbsp	
PEPPER,BLACK,GROUND	1/4 oz	1 tbsp	
CHEESE,PARMESAN,GRATED	2 lbs	2 qts 1 cup	

Method

1. Add salt and oil to water; heat to a rolling boil.
2. Slowly add noodles, stirring constantly, until water boils again. Cook about 8 to 10 minutes or until tender. Drain thoroughly.
3. Add butter, salt and pepper to noodles. Stir well.
4. Add cheese; toss well. CCP: Hold for service at 140 F. or higher.

STEAMED PASTA

Yield 100   **Portion** 1 Cup

Calories	Carbohydrates	Protein	Fat	Cholesterol	Sodium	Calcium
207 cal	41 g	7 g	1 g	0 mg	293 mg	17 mg

Ingredient	Weight	Measure	Issue
WATER	75-1/4 lbs	9 gal	
SALT	2-1/2 oz	1/4 cup 1/3tbsp	
OIL,SALAD	1-7/8 oz	1/4 cup 1/3tbsp	
SPAGHETTI NOODLES,DRY	12 lbs	3 gal 1 qts	

Method

1. Fill each steam table pan with 2-1/4 gallons water. Use perforated pan inside solid pan to facilitate draining.
2. Add 1 tablespoon salt and 1 tablespoon salad oil to each pan.
3. Place 3 pounds pasta in each pan. To prevent pastiness, pasta should be placed in pans just before steaming. Ensure pasta is covered with water.
4. Place pans in preheated steam cooker. Time according to type of pasta and steam cooker pressure. GUIDELINES FOR TIMING: Macaroni - 5 lb PSI, 16 minutes; 15 lb PSI, 11 minutes Noodles, Egg - 5 lb PSI, 22 minutes; 15 lb PSI, 17 minutes Spaghetti - 5 lb PSI, 20 minutes; 15 lb PSI, 15 minutes Vermicelli - 5 lb PSI, 11 minutes; 15 lb PSI, 4 minutes
5. Cooked macaroni should be rinsed in cold water and drained thoroughly to prevent sticking together. If cooked pasta is to be combined with butter or a sauce immediately, rinsing is not necessary. CCP: Hold for service at 140 F. or higher.

SPRING GARDEN RICE

Yield 100   **Portion** 3/4 Cup

Calories	Carbohydrates	Protein	Fat	Cholesterol	Sodium	Calcium
170 cal	31 g	7 g	2 g	5 mg	302 mg	160 mg

Ingredient	Weight	Measure	Issue
RICE,LONG GRAIN	6-3/4 lbs	1 gal 1/8 qts	
WATER,COLD	17-3/4 lbs	2 gal 1/2 qts	
SALT	1-1/2 oz	2-1/3 tbsp	
SQUASH,FRESH,SUMMER,SLICED	5-1/4 lbs	1gal 1-1/4qts	5-1/2lbs
CARROTS,FRESH,SHREDDED	3-1/2 lbs	3qts 2-1/2cup	4-1/4lbs
WATER	4-1/3 lbs	2 qts 1/4 cup	
MILK,NONFAT,DRY	4 oz	1-5/8 cup	
YOGURT,PLAIN,NONFAT	2-7/8 lbs	1 qts 1-1/4 cup	
CHEESE,PARMESAN,GRATED	1-1/4 lbs	1 qts 1-3/4 cup	
PEPPER,WHITE,GROUND	1/4 oz	1 tbsp	
GARLIC POWDER	1/8 oz	1/4 tsp	
BROCCOLI,FROZEN,SPEARS,THAWED,1-1/2""	3-1/4 lbs	2 qts	
MUSHROOMS,FRESH,WHOLE,SLICED	1-2/3 lbs	2 qts 3 cup	1-7/8lbs
PARSLEY,FRESH,BUNCH,CHOPPED	10 oz	1 qts 3/4cup	10-1/2oz

Method

1. Combine rice, water and salt; bring to a boil. Stir occasionally. Cover tightly; simmer 20 minutes or until most of the water is absorbed. Remove from heat; transfer to shallow serving pans. Cover.

2. Combine squash and carrots in steam-jacketed kettle. Stir; cook 5 to 7 minutes or until tender crisp.
3. Reconstitute milk.
4. Add milk, yogurt, parmesan cheese, pepper and garlic powder to vegetables in steam-jacketed kettle. Stir well.
5. Add rice, broccoli, mushrooms, and parsley; mix lightly until all ingredients are coated with sauce. Bring to a simmer while stirring, about 5 to 7 minutes. CCP: Internal temperature must reach 145 F. or higher for 15 seconds.
6. Remove to serving pans. CCP: Hold at 140 F. or higher for service.

Notes

1. In Step 1, 7 pounds 7 ounces brown rice, 9 quarts of water and 1-1/2 ounces salt may be used per 100 servings. Follow directions on Recipe No. E 005 05, Steamed Brown Rice.
2. In Steps 1 and 2, oven method may be used; use boiling water for cold water; place 3-1/2 pounds or 2 quarts rice, 4-1/4 quarts water and 2/3 ounce or 1 tablespoon salt in each steam table pan; stir. Cover tightly; bake at 350 F. in a convection oven for 35 to 40 minutes or until most of water is absorbed on high fan, closed vent.

SICILIAN BROWN RICE AND VEGETABLES

Yield 100   **Portion** 3/4 Cup

Calories	Carbohydrates	Protein	Fat	Cholesterol	Sodium	Calcium
155 cal	29 g	6 g	2 g	4 mg	542 mg	110 mg

Ingredient	Weight	Measure	Issue
RICE,BROWN,LONG GRAIN,DRY	5-1/2 lbs	3 qts 1-3/8 cup	
WATER,COLD	13-7/8 lbs	1 gal 2-5/8 qts	
SALT	1-1/4 oz	2 tbsp	
JUICE,TOMATO,CANNED	9-1/4 lbs	1 gal 1/3 qts	
TOMATOES,CANNED,DICED,DRAINED	6-5/8 lbs	3 qts	
ONIONS,FRESH,CHOPPED	2-1/3 lbs	1 qts 2-5/8cup	2-5/8lbs
TOMATO PASTE,CANNED	1-1/8 lbs	2 cup	
SUGAR,BROWN,PACKED	2-1/2 oz	1/2 cup	
SALT	1 oz	1 tbsp	
BASIL,SWEET,WHOLE,CRUSHED	1-1/8 oz	1/4 cup 3-1/3 tbsp	
GARLIC POWDER	3/8 oz	1 tbsp	
OREGANO,CRUSHED	3/4 oz	1/4 cup 1-1/3 tbsp	
PEPPER,BLACK,GROUND	1/4 oz	1 tbsp	
BAY LEAF,WHOLE,DRIED	1/3 oz	10 each	
SQUASH,FRESH,SUMMER,SLICED	2-1/2 lbs	2 qts 2 cup	2-5/8lbs
SQUASH,ZUCCHINI,FRESH,SLICED	2-1/2 lbs	2 qts 2 cup	2-5/8lbs
CARROTS,FRESH,SHREDDED	1 lbs	1 qts 1/8 cup	1-1/4lbs
BROCCOLI,FROZEN,SPEARS	2-3/4 lbs	2 qts	
MUSHROOMS,FRESH,WHOLE,SLICED	1-1/4 lbs	2 qts 1/8 cup	1-3/8lbs
PARSLEY,FRESH,BUNCH,CHOPPED	8 oz	3-3/4 cup	8-3/8lbs
CHEESE,MOZZARELLA,PART SKIM,SHREDDED	1-3/4 lbs	1 qts 3 cup	

Method

1. Combine rice, water and salt; bring to a boil. Stir occasionally. Cover tightly; simmer 30 minutes or until most of the water is absorbed. Remove from heat; transfer to shallow serving pans. CCP: Cover. Hold at 140 F. or higher for use in Step 8.

2. Place tomato juice, tomatoes, onions, tomato paste, brown sugar, salt, basil, garlic powder, oregano, pepper and bay leaves in steam-jacketed kettle. Stir; bring to a boil. Reduce heat; cover; simmer 20 minutes. Remove bay leaves.
3. Stir in rice, yellow squash, zucchini and carrots. Bring to a boil; reduce heat; simmer 3 to 5 minutes or until vegetables are tender crisp. Stir occasionally.
4. Stir in broccoli, mushrooms and parsley; bring to a simmer.
5. Place 1-1/4 gallon in each steam table pan. Sprinkle 7 ounces cheese over mixture in each pan. Using a convection oven, bake at 325 F. for 12 to 15 minutes or until mixture is bubbly and cheese is melted and lightly browned on high fan, closed vent. CCP: Internal temperature must reach 145 F. or higher for 15 seconds. CCP: Hold for service at 140 F. or higher.

Notes
1. In Steps 1 and 2, oven method may be used: Use boiling water for cold water; place 2-3/4 pounds or 6-2/3 cups rice, 3-1/8 quarts boiling water, and 2-1/2 teaspoons salt in each steam table pan. Stir, cover tightly.
2. In Step 4, 2-1/2 pounds frozen summer squash and 2-1/2 pounds frozen zucchini may be used.
3. In Step 5, 1 pound canned, drained mushrooms may be used.

ISLANDER'S RICE

Yield 100 **Portion** 3/4 Cup

Calories	Carbohydrates	Protein	Fat	Cholesterol	Sodium	Calcium
149 cal	31 g	5 g	1 g	0 mg	644 mg	43 mg

Ingredient	Weight	Measure	Issue
CHICKEN BROTH		1 gal 3-1/2qts	
BEANS,KIDNEY,DARK RED,CANNED,DRAINED	9-1/8 lbs	1 gal 1-7/8qts	
RICE,LONG GRAIN	5-3/4 lbs	3 qts 2 cup	
ONIONS,FRESH,CHOPPED	2 lbs	1 qts 1-5/8cup	2-1/4lbs
GARLIC POWDER	1-1/4 oz	1/4cup 1/3tbsp	
THYME,GROUND	5/8 oz	1/4cup 1/3tbsp	
ALLSPICE,GROUND	1/3 oz	1 tbsp	
PEPPER,RED,GROUND	1/4 oz	1 tbsp	
OREGANO,CRUSHED	1/2 oz	3 tbsp	
PEPPERS,GREEN,FRESH,CHOPPED	3-5/8 lbs	2 qts 3cup	4-3/8lbs
PIMIENTO,CANNED,DRAINED,SLICED	1-1/2 lbs	3-1/2cup	

Method
1. Prepare stock according to package directions.
2. Combine stock, beans, rice, onions, garlic powder, thyme, allspice, red pepper and oregano in steam-jacketed kettle or stock pot; bring to a boil. Stir occasionally.
3. Cover tightly; reduce heat; simmer 20 to 25 minutes or until most of the water is absorbed and rice is tender. Do not stir.
4. Add peppers and pimientos; stir well.
5. Transfer to serving pans. CCP: Hold for service at 140 F. or higher.

Notes
1. For vegetarian: double all ingredients; use 7-1/2 quarts vegetable stock. EACH PORTION: 1-1/2 cups.
2. OVEN METHOD: For 100 portions: Use steam table pans. Follow Step 1. In Step 2, place 4 pounds 13 ounces or 3 quarts beans, 3 pounds or 1-3/4 quarts of rice, and 1 pound or 3/4 quart onions in each pan; stir well. Combine stock with garlic powder, thyme, allspice, red pepper, and oregano; stir well.

Bring to a boil. Pour 3-3/4 quarts stock mixture over rice mixture in each pan. Stir well. Omit Step 3. Cover; bake in a 350 F. convection oven for 30 minutes or until most of the water is absorbed and the rice is tender on high fan, closed vent. In Step 4, add 1-1/2 quarts peppers and 2 cups pimientos to rice mixture in each pan. Stir well to mix. Follow Step 5.

MEDITERRANEAN BROWN RICE

Yield 100   **Portion** 3/4 Cup

Calories	Carbohydrates	Protein	Fat	Cholesterol	Sodium	Calcium
199 cal	38 g	4 g	4 g	0 mg	699 mg	28 mg

Ingredient	Weight	Measure	Issue
OIL,SALAD	7-2/3 oz	1 cup	
ONIONS,FRESH,CHOPPED	3-1/8 lbs	2 qts 1cup	3-1/2lbs
RICE,BROWN,LONG GRAIN,RAW PARBOILED	8-1/8 lbs	1 gal 1 qts	
CHICKEN BROTH		2gal 2-1/2qts	
RAISINS,GOLDEN	1-7/8 lbs	1 qts 2 cup	
CINNAMON,GROUND	1/2 oz	2 tbsp	
ALLSPICE,GROUND	1/4 oz	1 tbsp	
CARDAMOM SEED,GROUND	1/4 oz	1 tbsp	
CILANTRO,DRY	1/4 oz	1/4 cup 1/3 tbsp	

Method
1. Heat oil in steam jacketed kettle. Add onions; cook 5 minutes or until tender, stirring occasionally.
2. Add rice; stir well until rice is coated. Stir; cook 5 minutes or until rice is lightly browned.
3. Prepare broth according to package directions. Add stock, raisins, cinnamon, allspice, and cardamom to rice. Bring to a boil; stir.
4. Reduce heat; cover tightly; simmer 25 minutes or until most of the water is absorbed. Add cilantro; mix well. CCP: Internal temperature of cooked rice mixture must reach 145 F. or higher for 15 seconds.
5. Remove from heat; transfer to shallow serving pans. Cover. CCP: Hold for service at 140 F. or higher.

Notes
1. OVEN METHOD: For 100 portions: Omit oil. Place 6-2/3 cups rice, 3-1/2 quarts boiling stock, 3 cups onions, 2 cups raisins, 2 teaspoons cinnamon, 1-1/3 teaspoons allspice, and 1-1/3 teaspoon cardamom in each steam table pan. Stir, cover tightly, bake in 350 F. convection oven 25 minutes or until most of the water is absorbed on high fan, closed vent. Fold 1/2 cup cilantro into each pan. CCP: Internal temperature of cooked rice mixture must reach 145 F. or higher for 15 seconds. CCP: Hold for service at 140 F. or higher

SPICY BROWN RICE PILAF

Yield 100   **Portion** 3/4 Cup

Calories	Carbohydrates	Protein	Fat	Cholesterol	Sodium	Calcium
151 cal	30 g	4 g	2 g	0 mg	766 mg	36 mg

Ingredient	Weight	Measure	Issue
CHICKEN BROTH		2 gal 2-1/2 qts	
PAPRIKA,GROUND	1-1/2 oz	1/4 cup 2-2/3 tbsp	

Ingredient	Weight	Measure		
MUSTARD,DRY	1-3/4 oz	1/4 cup 2/3 tbsp		
PEPPER,BLACK,GROUND	2/3 oz	3 tbsp		
THYME,GROUND	1/2 oz	3 tbsp		
SALT	1/2 oz	3/8 tsp		
GARLIC POWDER	1/2 oz	1 tbsp		
CUMIN,GROUND	1/3 oz	1 tbsp		
OREGANO,CRUSHED	1/2 oz	3 tbsp		
BAY LEAF,WHOLE,DRIED	1/2 oz	14 each		
PEPPER,RED,CRUSHED	<1/16th oz	1/8 tsp		
RICE,BROWN,LONG GRAIN,RAW PARBOILED	7-1/3 lbs	1 gal 1/2 qts		
COOKING SPRAY,NONSTICK	3/8 oz	3/8 tsp		
ONIONS,FRESH,CHOPPED	3-1/2 lbs	2qts 1-7/8cup	3-7/8lbs	
CELERY,FRESH,CHOPPED	2-1/2 lbs	2qts 1-1/2cup	3-3/8lbs	
PEPPERS,GREEN,FRESH,CHOPPED	2-1/2 lbs	1qts 3-5/8cup	3lbs	

Method

1. Prepare broth according to package directions.
2. Add paprika, mustard flour, pepper, thyme, salt, garlic powder, cumin, oregano, bay leaves, and red pepper to stock. Stir well to blend.
3. Add rice to stock in steam jacketed kettle or stock pot. Bring to a boil. Stir. Reduce heat. Cover tightly. Simmer 25 minutes or until most of the water is absorbed and rice is tender.
4. Spray steam-jacketed kettle with non-stick cooking spray. Add onions, celery, and peppers. Stir; cook 10 to 12 minutes or until vegetables are tender crisp.
5. Place approximately 8-1/2 pounds rice in each steam table pan. Add 5-1/3 cups vegetables to each pan. Mix well. CCP: Internal temperature must reach 145 F. or higher for 15 seconds. CCP: Hold for service at 140 F. or higher.

Notes

1. OVEN METHOD: For 100 portions: Follow Steps 1 and 2. Bring stock to a boil. Place 2-1/2 pounds of rice and 3-1/2 quarts stock, in each steam table pan; stir. Cover tightly; bake in 350 F. convection oven for 30 minutes or until most of the water is absorbed on high fan, closed vent. Follow Steps 4 and 5.

BROWN RICE WITH TOMATOES

Yield 100   Portion 3/4 Cup

Calories	Carbohydrates	Protein	Fat	Cholesterol	Sodium	Calcium
167 cal	35 g	4 g	1 g	0 mg	163 mg	37 mg

Ingredient	Weight	Measure	Issue
VEGETABLE BROTH	13-1/4 lbs	1 gal 3-1/2 qts	
TOMATOES,CANNED,DICED,DRAINED	7-3/4 lbs	1 gal 2 qts	
RICE,BROWN,LONG GRAIN,RAW PARBOILED	6-1/3 lbs	1 gal 3/4 qts	
ONIONS,FRESH,CHOPPED	2-3/8 oz	1 gal 1/2 qts	
GARLIC POWDER	1/2 oz	1/2 cup	
PEPPER,BLACK,GROUND	7 lbs	2 tbsp	

Method

1. Prepare broth according to package directions in steam-jacketed kettle or stock pot.
2. Add tomatoes, brown rice, onions, garlic powder, and pepper to broth in steam-jacketed kettle or stock pot. Stir well; bring to a rolling boil, stirring occasionally. Reduce heat. Cover. Simmer 35

minutes or until most of the broth is absorbed and rice is tender. Do not stir. CCP: Internal temperature must reach 145 F. or higher for 15 seconds.

3. Stir to redistribute onions and tomatoes. Transfer to serving pans. CCP: Hold for service at 140 F. or higher.

Notes

1. Using a convection oven, bake in 2 steam table pans at 350 F. for 45 to 50 minutes on high fan, closed vent or until most of the broth is absorbed.

GINGER RICE

Yield 100   **Portion** 3/4 Cup

Calories	Carbohydrates	Protein	Fat	Cholesterol	Sodium	Calcium
183 cal	34 g	6 g	2 g	73 mg	567 mg	43 mg

Ingredient	Weight	Measure	Issue
RICE,LONG GRAIN	8-1/2 lbs	1 gal 1-1/4 qts	
WATER,BOILING	18-3/4 lbs	2 gal 1 qts	
COOKING SPRAY,NONSTICK	1/4 oz	1/4 tsp	
EGGS,WHOLE,FROZEN	3-3/4 lbs	1 qts 3 cup	
SOY SAUCE	2-1/8 lbs	3-3/8 cup	
SUGAR,GRANULATED	1-3/4 oz	1/4 cup 1/3 tbsp	
GARLIC POWDER	1/2 oz	1 tbsp	
GINGER,GROUND	1/4 oz	1 tbsp	
PEPPER,WHITE,GROUND	1/4 oz	1 tbsp	
PEPPERS,RED FRESH,DICED	1 lbs	3 cup	1-1/4lbs
CARROTS,FROZEN,SLICED	1 lbs	3-3/4 cup	
ONIONS,GREEN,FRESH,SLICED	1-1/8 lbs	1 qts 1-3/8 cup	1-1/3lbs

Method

1. Place 3 pounds rice and 3 quarts water in each lightly sprayed steam table pan; stir.
2. Cover tightly. Using a convection oven, bake at 325 F. for 30 minutes on high fan, closed vent.
3. Pour eggs on lightly sprayed griddle. Cook 1-1/2 minutes or until set. Do not turn. Cut into 4-inch strips to facilitate removal. Remove immediately. Cut into 1/2-inch squares.
4. Combine soy sauce, sugar, garlic powder, white pepper, and ginger. Stir well to dissolve sugar.
5. Add 2-1/3 cups egg strips, 1-1/2 cups soy mixture, 1 cup red peppers and 1-1/4 cups of carrots to rice in each pan. Mix lightly but thoroughly.
6. Cover. CCP: Using a convection oven, bake 15 minutes on high fan, closed vent. CCP: Internal temperature must reach 145 F. or higher for 15 seconds.
7. Add 1-3/4 cups green onions to rice in each pan. Mix lightly but thoroughly. CCP: Hold for service at 140 F. or higher.

NUTTY RICE AND CHEESE

Yield 100   **Portion** 9 Ounces

Calories	Carbohydrates	Protein	Fat	Cholesterol	Sodium	Calcium
323 cal	40 g	22 g	8 g	12 mg	835 mg	289 mg

Ingredient	Weight	Measure	Issue
WATER	20-7/8 lbs	2 gal 2 qts	
SALT	1-2/3 oz	2-2/3 tbsp	
RICE,BROWN,LONG GRAIN,DRY	8-1/8 lbs	1 gal 1 qts	
CHEESE,COTTAGE,LOWFAT	14 lbs	1 gal 3 qts	
YOGURT,PLAIN,NONFAT	10-3/4 lbs	1 gal 1 qts	
EGG WHITES,FROZEN,THAWED	5 lbs	2qts 1-3/8cup	
ONIONS,FRESH,CHOPPED	3-7/8 lbs	2 qts 3 cup	4-1/3lbs
ALMONDS,SLIVERED	1-3/8 lbs	1 qts 2 cup	
CHEESE,PARMESAN,GRATED	1-1/3 lbs	1 qts 2 cup	
FLOUR,WHEAT,GENERAL PURPOSE	6-5/8 oz	1-1/2 cup	
SALT	1-1/2 oz	2-1/3 tbsp	
PARSLEY,DEHYDRATED,FLAKED	1-1/4 oz	1-5/8 cup	
GARLIC POWDER	1-1/4 oz	1/4cup 1/3tbsp	
PEPPER,WHITE,GROUND	2/3 oz	2-2/3 tbsp	
COOKING SPRAY,NONSTICK	1/2 oz	1 tbsp	
CHEESE,PARMESAN,GRATED	7 oz	2 cup	

Method

1. Combine water, rice, and salt; bring to a boil; stir, cover tightly; simmer 25 minutes or until most of the water is absorbed.
2. Remove from heat. Transfer to sheet pans. Allow to cool 5 minutes.
3. Combine cottage cheese, yogurt, egg whites, onions, almonds, parmesan cheese, flour, salt, parsley flakes, garlic powder, and pepper in mixer bowl. Mix at low speed 1 minute. Scrape down bowl.
4. Add chilled rice to ingredients in mixer bowl. Mix at low speed 1 minute or until thoroughly blended.
5. Lightly spray steam table pans with non-stick spray. Place 12-1/4 pounds of mixture in each steam table pan. Spread evenly. Sprinkle 6 tablespoons of parmesan cheese over the top of each pan.
6. Using a convection oven, bake 55 minutes at 325 F. on high fan, open vent or until set. CCP: Internal temperature must reach 145 F. or higher for 15 seconds.
7. Cut each pan 4 by 5. CCP: Hold for service at 140 F. or higher.

ORZO WITH LEMON AND HERBS

Yield 100   Portion 3/4 Cup

Calories	Carbohydrates	Protein	Fat	Cholesterol	Sodium	Calcium
92 cal	12 g	2 g	4 g	0 mg	362 mg	19 mg

Ingredient	Weight	Measure	Issue
SALT	1-1/4 oz	2 tbsp	
MUSTARD,DIJON	1/2 oz	1 tbsp	
GARLIC POWDER	3/8 oz	1 tbsp	
BASIL,SWEET,WHOLE,CRUSHED	5/8 oz	1/4 cup 1/3tbsp	
OREGANO,CRUSHED	5/8 oz	1/4 cup 1/3tbsp	
PEPPER,BLACK,GROUND	1/4 oz	1 tbsp	
ONION POWDER	1/4 oz	1 tbsp	
JUICE,LEMON	1-1/3 lbs	2-1/2 cup	
OIL,OLIVE	11-3/8 oz	1-1/2 cup	
WATER	66-7/8 lbs	8 gal	
SALT	1-7/8 oz	3 tbsp	

OIL,SALAD	1/3 oz	1/3 tsp	
PASTA,ORZO	8-1/3 lbs	6 gal 7/8 qts	
COOKING SPRAY,NONSTICK	1-1/2 oz	3 tbsp	
ONIONS,FRESH,CHOPPED	5-1/3 lbs	3qts 3-3/8cup	5-7/8lbs

Method

1. Combine salt, mustard, garlic powder, basil, oregano, pepper, and onion powder. Add lemon juice and olive oil. Stir to blend. Cover, set aside for use in Step 6.
2. Add salt and salad oil to water; heat to a rolling boil.
3. Add pasta slowly while stirring constantly until water boils again. Cook about 9 minutes or until al dente; stirring occasionally. DO NOT OVERCOOK.
4. Drain. Rinse with cold water; drain thoroughly.
5. Stir-cook onions in a lightly sprayed steam jacketed kettle or stockpot 8 to 10 minutes or until tender, stirring constantly.
6. Add the reserved lemon and herb dressing to cooked onions. Stir to blend well. Bring to a boil; reduce heat to a simmer.
7. Add the orzo to the onion and lemon mixture. Heat to a simmer while gently stirring for 1 minute to coat the orzo with the sauce. CCP: Temperature must register 145 F. or higher for 15 seconds.
8. Place 2-1/3 gallon pasta mixture in each pan. CCP: Hold for service at 140 F. or higher.

ORZO, WITH SPINACH, TOMATO, AND ONION

Yield 100   **Portion 9-1/2 Ounces**

Calories	Carbohydrates	Protein	Fat	Cholesterol	Sodium	Calcium
62 cal	10 g	3 g	2 g	2 mg	456 mg	104 mg

Ingredient	Weight	Measure	Issue
WATER	66-7/8 lbs	8 gal	
SALT	1-7/8 oz	3 tbsp	
OIL,SALAD	1 oz	2 tbsp	
PASTA,ORZO	1-2/3 lbs	1 gal 1 qts	
ONIONS,FRESH,CHOPPED	5 lbs	3qts 2-1/8cup	5-1/2lbs
COOKING SPRAY,NONSTICK	2 oz	1/4cup 1/3tbsp	
TOMATOES,CANNED,DICED,DRAINED	13-1/4 lbs	1 gal 2 qts	
BASIL,DRIED,CRUSHED	2-1/2 oz	1 cup	
SPINACH,CHOPPED,FROZEN	4 lbs	2 qts 3-5/8 cup	
CUMIN,GROUND	7/8 oz	1/4 cup 1/3tbsp	
PEPPER,BLACK,GROUND	2/3 oz	3 tbsp	
GARLIC POWDER	5/8 oz	2 tbsp	
SALT	1 oz	1 tbsp	
CHEESE,PARMESAN,GRATED	7 oz	2 cup	

Method

1. Add salt and salad oil to water; heat to a rolling boil.
2. Add pasta slowly while stirring constantly until water boils again. Cook about 9 minutes or until tender; stirring occasionally. DO NOT OVERCOOK.
3. Drain. Rinse with cold water; drain thoroughly. Use immediately in recipe preparation or place in shallow containers and cover.
4. Stir-cook onions in a lightly sprayed steam jacketed kettle or stockpot 8 to 10 minutes or until tender, stirring constantly.

5. Add the tomatoes, spinach, basil, salt, cumin, pepper and garlic powder, stir to combine. Bring to a boil. Cover; reduce heat; simmer for 5 minutes.
6. Add the orzo; stir to blend. Bring to a boil. Cover; reduce heat; simmer for 5 minutes. CCP: Temperature must reach 140 F. or higher for 15 seconds.
7. Place 3 gallons vegetable pasta mixture in each pan.
8. Distribute 1 cup parmesan cheese evenly over vegetable pasta mixture in each pan. CCP: Hold for service at 140 F. or higher.

SOUTHWESTERN RICE

Yield 100   **Portion** 3/4 Cup

Calories	Carbohydrates	Protein	Fat	Cholesterol	Sodium	Calcium
131 cal	25 g	5 g	1 g	2 mg	192 mg	64 mg

Ingredient	Weight	Measure	Issue
RICE,LONG GRAIN	5-3/4 lbs	3 qts 2 cup	
WATER	12-1/2 lbs	1 gal 2 qts	
SALT	1 oz	1 tbsp	
COOKING SPRAY,NONSTICK	2 oz	1/4cup 1/3tbsp	
ONIONS,FRESH,CHOPPED	11-1/4 oz	2 cup	12-1/2oz
GARLIC POWDER	2-3/8 oz	1/2 cup	
PEPPERS,GREEN,FRESH,CHOPPED	6-5/8 oz	1-1/4 cup	8oz
TOMATOES,CANNED,DICED,DRAINED	3 lbs	1 qts 1-1/2 cup	
PARSLEY,DEHYDRATED,FLAKED	3/8 oz	1/2 cup	
CORN,FROZEN,WHOLE KERNEL	1-1/8 lbs	3 cup	
PEPPER,BLACK,GROUND	2/3 oz	3 tbsp	
CHILI POWDER,LIGHT,GROUND	1 oz	1/4 cup 1/3 tbsp	
WORCESTERSHIRE SAUCE	4-1/4 oz	1/2 cup	
CHEESE,MONTEREY JACK,REDUCED FAT	2 lbs	2 qts	

Method
1. Combine rice, water, and salt. Bring to a boil. Cover tightly, and simmer 20 to 30 minutes.
2. Saute onions, garlic, and peppers in vegetable spray in a steam jacketed kettle. Add tomatoes, parsley, and corn. Season with pepper, chili powder, and Worcestershire sauce. Fold in cooked drained rice and thoroughly blend.
3. Divide rice in serving pans, sprinkle with cheese. Bake in 350 F. oven for 20 minutes. CCP: Internal temperature must reach 145 F. or higher for 15 seconds. CCP: Hold at 140 F. or higher for serving.

PASTA PROVENCAL

Yield 100   **Portion** 1 Cup

Calories	Carbohydrates	Protein	Fat	Cholesterol	Sodium	Calcium
295 cal	46 g	16 g	6 g	31 mg	1288 mg	212 mg

Ingredient	Weight	Measure	Issue
WATER	54-1/3 lbs	6 gal 2 qts	
SALT	1-1/2 oz	2-1/3 tbsp	
OIL,SALAD	1/3 oz	1/3 tsp	
PASTA,PENNE	10 lbs	7 gal 1-7/8qts	

OIL,SALAD	5-3/4 oz	3/4 cup	
FLOUR,WHEAT,GENERAL PURPOSE	14-2/3 oz	3-3/8 cup	
WATER,WARM	10-1/2 lbs	1 gal 1 qts	
MILK,NONFAT,DRY	1-1/8 lbs	1 qts 3-1/2cup	
CHICKEN BROTH		1 gal 1 qts	
CHEESE,PARMESAN,GRATED	7 oz	2 cup	
SALT	1-1/4 oz	2 tbsp	
GARLIC POWDER	1-1/4 oz	1/4 cup 1/3tbsp	
THYME LEAVES,DRIED,GROUND	5/8 oz	1/4 cup 1/3tbsp	
PEPPER,BLACK,GROUND	1/2 oz	2 tbsp	
BASIL,SWEET,WHOLE,CRUSHED	5/8 oz	1/4 cup 1/3tbsp	
OREGANO,CRUSHED	7/8 oz	1/4 cup 1-2/3tbsp	
PEPPER,RED,CRUSHED	1/8 oz	1 tbsp	
TOMATOES,CANNED,DICED,DRAINED	12-1/8 lbs	1 gal 1-1/2qts	
BEANS,CANNELLINI,CANNED	8-1/2 lbs	3 qts 3 cup	
SPINACH,FROZEN	4 lbs	2 qts 1-1/2 cup	
ONIONS,FRESH,CHOPPED	4-3/8 lbs	3 qts 3/8 cup	4-7/8 lbs
HAM,CANNED,COOKED,DICED	4 lbs		
CARROTS,FRESH,CHOPPED	3-3/4 lbs	3 qts 1-1/4 cup	4-5/8 lbs
CELERY,FRESH,CHOPPED	2-3/4 lbs	2 qts 2-3/8 cup	3-3/4 lbs
PARSLEY,DEHYDRATED,FLAKED	3/4 oz	1 cup	

1. water; heat to a rolling boil.
2. Add pasta slowly while stirring constantly until water boils again. Cook 7 to 9 minutes or until tender, stirring occasionally. DO NOT OVERCOOK.
3. Drain. Rinse with cold water; drain thoroughly.
4. Blend salad oil and flour together to form a roux. Using a wire whip, stir until smooth. Cook roux for 3 minutes in a steam-jacketed kettle or stockpot stirring constantly.
5. Reconstitute milk in warm water.
6. Gradually add milk and broth to roux while stirring constantly. Bring to a boil. Cover; reduce heat; simmer 5 minutes or until thickened, stirring frequently to prevent sticking.
7. Add parmesan cheese, salt, garlic powder, thyme, black pepper, basil, oregano and red pepper to thickened sauce. Stir to blend well.
8. Add tomatoes, beans, spinach, onions, ham, carrots, celery and parsley to thickened sauce. Bring to a boil. Cover; reduce heat; simmer 7 to 10 minutes until tender, stirring occasionally.
9. Add pasta to thickened sauce and vegetable mixture. Heat to a simmer while stirring for 1 minute to coat the pasta with the vegetable sauce. CCP: Temperature must register 165 F. or higher for 15 seconds.
10. Pour 3-1/8 gal pasta-vegetable mixture into 3 ungreased steam table pans; cover. CCP: Hold for service at 140 F. or higher.

ORIENTAL RICE

Yield 100   **Portion** 4 Ounces

Calories	Carbohydrates	Protein	Fat	Cholesterol	Sodium	Calcium
67 cal	13 g	3 g	1 g	0 mg	694 mg	15 mg

Ingredient	Weight	Measure	Issue
WATER	10-1/2 lbs	1 gal 1 qts	
SOY SAUCE	1-7/8 lbs	3 cup	

GINGER,GROUND	1/4 oz	1 tbsp
HOT SAUCE	1 oz	2 tbsp
GARLIC POWDER	1-1/4 oz	1/4 cup 1/3 tbsp
RICE PILAF MIX	6 lbs	3 qts 1-1/4 cup
HONEY	9 oz	3/4 cup
WATER	8-1/3 lbs	1 gal
SALT	5/8 oz	1 tbsp
VEGETABLES,MIXED,FROZEN	6 lbs	3 qts 3 cup

Method
1. Combine water, 2 cups soy sauce, ground ginger, hot sauce and garlic powder. Bring to a boil.
2. Remove spice packet from pilaf mix and discard. Place 3 pounds of rice in each steam table pan. Add approximately 3/4 gallon of boiling liquid to each pan and cover tightly with foil. Using a convection oven, bake 25 minutes at 350 F.
3. Combine honey and remaining cup of soy sauce. Heat until honey is warm enough to blend with soy sauce. Reserve for use in Step 7.
4. Bring water to a boil in a steam jacketed kettle or stockpot. Add 1 tbsp salt.
5. Add vegetables, stir well. Return to a boil; cover.
6. Reduce heat; cook gently for 5-8 minutes or until vegetables are tender. Drain.
7. Remove rice from oven. Stir in 3 pounds of vegetables into each pan and pour the honey/soy mixture equally into each pan of rice. Cover and let stand 10 minutes before serving. CCP: Hold for service at 140 F. or higher.

WILD RICE

Yield 100   **Portion** 1/2 Cup

Calories	Carbohydrates	Protein	Fat	Cholesterol	Sodium	Calcium
37 cal	8 g	1 g	0 g	0 mg	1 mg	1 mg

Ingredient	Weight	Measure	Issue
WILD RICE BLEND MIX	8 lbs	1 gal 3/8 qts	

Method
1. Follow manufacturer's instructions which are usually to place rice and contents of spice bag from package in steam table pan and add boiling water.
2. Cover and bake in convection oven at 350 F. with fan on for twenty five minutes.
3. Fluff with spoon to mix spices that have floated to the top.
4. Hold for service at 140 F. or higher.

Notes
1. CAUTION: Amounts, portion sizes, and cooking times vary from brand to brand. Read manufacturer's label, cooking instructions, or product description before ordering or beginning food preparation.

AZTEC RICE

Yield 100   **Portion** 3/4 Cup

Calories	Carbohydrates	Protein	Fat	Cholesterol	Sodium	Calcium
135 cal	24 g	5 g	3 g	0 mg	123 mg	32 mg

Ingredient	Weight	Measure	Issue

Ingredient	Weight	Measure	Issue
RICE,MEXICAN BLEND	6 lbs	3 qts 3 cup	
GARLIC CLOVES,FRESH,MINCED	4-3/4 oz	1 cup	5-1/2oz
OIL,SALAD	7-2/3 oz	1 cup	
TOMATOES,CANNED,DICED,DRAINED	7 lbs	3 qts 3/4 cup	
BEANS,BLACK,CANNED,DRAINED	7 lbs	3 qts 3/8 cup	
CORN,FROZEN,WHOLE KERNEL	7 lbs	1 gal 7/8 qts	
PEPPER,BLACK,GROUND	2/3 oz	3 tbsp	
CHILI POWDER,LIGHT,GROUND	1 oz	1/4 cup	
CUMIN,GROUND	1-2/3 oz	1/2 cup	
ONIONS,GREEN,FRESH,CHOPPED	7 oz	2 cup	7-7/8oz

Method

1. Prepare rice according to package directions.
2. Add remaining ingredients. Mix well. Simmer 5 minutes.
3. Divide rice equally between steam table pans. CCP: Hold for service at 140 F. or higher.

MEXICAN RICE (FIESTA MIX)

Yield 100   **Portion** 1/2 Cup

Calories	Carbohydrates	Protein	Fat	Cholesterol	Sodium	Calcium
132 cal	30 g	4 g	0 g	0 mg	385 mg	21 mg

Ingredient	Weight	Measure	Issue
RICE,MEXICAN,MIX	8 lbs		
CUMIN,GROUND	7/8 oz	1/4 cup 1/3 tbsp	
CHILI POWDER,LIGHT,GROUND	1/4 oz	1 tbsp	
TOMATOES,CANNED,DICED,INCL LIQUIDS	6-7/8 lbs	3 qts	

Method

1. Prepare rice according to package directions.
2. Add cumin, chili powder to rice.
3. Cover and bake in convection oven at 350 F. with fan on for 25 minutes.
4. Carefully remove cover. Add diced tomatoes with juice. Return to oven and continue baking. CCP: Internal temperature must reach 140 F. or higher for 15 seconds. Mix well. CCP: Hold for service at 140 F. or higher.

RICE PILAF, USING MIX

Yield 100   **Portion** 1/2 Cup

Calories	Carbohydrates	Protein	Fat	Cholesterol	Sodium	Calcium
47 cal	8 g	1 g	1 g	0 mg	158 mg	6 mg

Ingredient	Weight	Measure	Issue
RICE PILAF MIX	8 lbs	1 gal 3/8 qts	

Method

1. Prepare pilaf according to manufacturer's instructions.
2. CCP: Hold for service at 140 F. or higher.

GEORGIA RICE

Yield 100   **Portion** 4 Ounces

Calories	Carbohydrates	Protein	Fat	Cholesterol	Sodium	Calcium
77 cal	16 g	2 g	1 g	0 mg	161 mg	19 mg

Ingredient	Weight	Measure	Issue
CHIVES,DRIED	4 oz		
RICE PILAF MIX	8 lbs	1 gal 3/8 qts	
PEACHES,CANNED,SLICED,JUICE PACK,INCL LIQUIDS	13 lbs	1 gal 2 qts	

Method
1. Prepare rice pilaf according to package directions. Add chives.
2. Drain peaches, reserve juice. Chop into large pieces.
3. Add peaches to rice. Cover and let stand 10 minutes before serving. CCP: Hold for service at 140 F. or higher.

DIRTY RICE

Yield 100   **Portion** 3/4 Cup

Calories	Carbohydrates	Protein	Fat	Cholesterol	Sodium	Calcium
51 cal	10 g	2 g	1 g	0 mg	159 mg	12 mg

Ingredient	Weight	Measure	Issue
RICE PILAF MIX	6 lbs	3qts 1-1/4cup	
WORCESTERSHIRE SAUCE	1 lbs	2 cup	
GARLIC POWDER	1-1/4 oz	1/4 cup 1/3tbsp	
WATER,BOILING	4-1/8 lbs	2 qts	
PEAS & CARROTS,FROZEN	5 lbs	1gal<1/16thqts	
SCALLIONS,FRESH	10-5/8 oz	3 cup	11-3/4oz
HOT SAUCE	2 oz	1/4cup 1/3tbsp	

Method
1. Combine rice pilaf blend, Worcestershire sauce and garlic in boiling water. Cover. Reduce heat and simmer for 20 minutes.
2. Chop scallions. Add peas and carrots, scallions and hot sauce. Mix well. CCP: Internal temperature must reach 140 F. or higher for 15 seconds.
3. Divide rice equally between steam table pans. CCP: Hold for service at 140 F. or higher.

BAKED MACARONI AND CHEESE

Yield 100   **Portion** 1 Cup

Calories	Carbohydrates	Protein	Fat	Cholesterol	Sodium	Calcium
359 cal	37 g	17 g	16 g	39 mg	721 mg	357 mg

Ingredient	Weight	Measure	Issue
MACARONI NOODLES,ELBOW,DRY	7-3/8 lbs	2 gal	
WATER,BOILING	50-1/8 lbs	6 gal	
SALT	1-2/3 oz	2-2/3 tbsp	
MILK,NONFAT,DRY	1-1/3 lbs	2 qts 1 cup	
WATER,WARM	20-7/8 lbs	2 gal 2 qts	
FLOUR,WHEAT,GENERAL PURPOSE	1-2/3 lbs	1 qts 2 cup	
WATER,COLD	2-1/8 lbs	1 qts	
SALT	1-7/8 oz	3 tbsp	
PEPPER,BLACK,GROUND	1/4 oz	1 tbsp	
CHEESE,CHEDDAR,SHREDDED	8 lbs	2 gal	
COOKING SPRAY,NONSTICK	2 oz	1/4 cup 1/3 tbsp	
BREADCRUMBS,DRY,GROUND,FINE	1-1/4 lbs	1 qts 1 cup	
MARGARINE,MELTED	10 oz	1-1/4 cup	

Method
1. Add macaroni slowly to boiling salted water; cook 8 to 10 minutes or until tender; stir occasionally to prevent sticking.
2. Drain. Set aside for use in Step 7.
3. Reconstitute milk; heat to just below boiling. DO NOT BOIL.
4. Combine flour and water to make a smooth mixture. Add mixture to hot milk, stirring constantly.
5. Add salt and pepper. Bring mixture to a boil; reduce heat; simmer 5 minutes or until thickened. Stir frequently to prevent scorching.
6. Add cheese to sauce; stir only until smooth; remove from heat.
7. Combine sauce and macaroni; mix well.
8. Lightly spray steam table pans with non-stick cooking spray. Place about 6-1/3 quart mixture in each sprayed pan.
9. Combine bread crumbs and melted butter or margarine; sprinkle 1-3/4 cup over mixture in each pan.
10. Using a convection oven, bake at 325 F. 15-20 minutes on high fan, open vent or until browned. CCP: Hold for service at 140 F. or higher.

NACHOS

Yield 100   **Portion** 1-1/2 Ounces

Calories	Carbohydrates	Protein	Fat	Cholesterol	Sodium	Calcium
403 cal	28 g	14 g	27 g	47 mg	1259 mg	359 mg

Ingredient	Weight	Measure	Issue
PEPPERS,JALAPENOS,CANNED,CHOPPED	9-1/2 lbs	1 gal 3-7/8 qts	
WATER	1-5/8 lbs	3 cup	
RESERVED LIQUID	3-2/3 lbs	1 qts 3 cup	
CHEESE,AMERICAN,SHREDDED	11 lbs	2 gal 3 qts	
CHIPS,TORTILLA	9 lbs		

Method

1. Drain peppers. Reserve liquid from peppers. Coarsely chop peppers. Set aside for use in Step 6.
2. Combine water and reserved jalapeno liquid in steam-jacketed kettle or stock pot. Bring to a simmer. DO NOT BOIL.
3. Add cheese to hot mixture; stir constantly until melted, about 3 to 4 minutes, or until smooth and creamy. DO NOT BOIL.
4. Remove from heat; keep warm. CCP: Hold for service at 140 F. or higher.
5. Pour 2 ounces sauce over about 20 tortilla chips.
6. Sprinkle 2 teaspoons jalapeno peppers over each portion.

Notes

1. In Step 3, DO NOT use cheddar cheese. It will not produce an acceptable product.
2. In Step 3, cheese, when combined with jalapeno liquid, begins to curdle at temperatures above 170 F. to 180 F.

NACHOS (RTU CHEESE SAUCE)

Yield 100   **Portion** 1-1/2 Ounces

Calories	Carbohydrates	Protein	Fat	Cholesterol	Sodium	Calcium
289 cal	34 g	5 g	15 g	6 mg	1028 mg	112 mg

Ingredient	Weight	Measure	Issue
PEPPERS,JALAPENOS,CANNED,CHOPPED	4-3/4 lbs	3 qts 3-7/8 cup	
RESERVED LIQUID	1-5/8 lbs	3 cup	
SAUCE, CHEESE, PREPARED	13-1/8 lbs	1 gal 2 qts	
CHIPS,TORTILLA	9 lbs		

Method

1. Drain peppers. Reserve liquid.
2. Combine jalapeno liquid with ready-to-use cheese sauce. Mix until smooth. Place in steam-jacketed kettle or stock pot. Heat, stirring constantly until hot, about 10 to 15 minutes. DO NOT BOIL.
3. Remove from heat; keep warm. CCP: Hold for service at 140 F. or higher.
4. Pour 2 ounces sauce over 20 tortilla chips.
5. Sprinkle 2 teaspoons jalapeno peppers over each portion.

Notes

1. Ready to use cheese sauce with jalapeno peppers may also be used.

EGGS AU GRATIN (SCOTCH WOODCOCK)

Yield 100   **Portion** 2/3 Cup

Calories	Carbohydrates	Protein	Fat	Cholesterol	Sodium	Calcium
223 cal	7 g	12 g	16 g	243 mg	241 mg	179 mg

Ingredient	Weight	Measure	Issue
EGG,HARD COOKED	11 lbs	100 Eggs	
MILK,NONFAT,DRY	14-3/8 oz	1 qts 2 cup	
WATER,WARM	15-2/3 lbs	1 gal 3-1/2 qts	
BUTTER,MELTED	1-1/2 lbs	3 cup	
FLOUR,WHEAT,GENERAL PURPOSE	1-1/8 lbs	1 qts	
CHEESE,CHEDDAR,SHREDDED	3 lbs	3 qts	

| BREADCRUMBS,DRY,GROUND,FINE | 5-1/8 oz | 1-3/8 cup |
| BUTTER,MELTED | 2-1/2 oz | 1/4 cup 1-1/3 tbsp |

Method

1. Place eggs in baskets as needed; cover with hot water. Bring to a boil; reduce heat; simmer 10 to 15 minutes. DO NOT BOIL. Remove from water; serve immediately. CCP: All fresh shell eggs must be heated to 155 F. or higher for 15 seconds.
2. Cool; remove shells from eggs; slice eggs in half lengthwise. Arrange 100 egg halves in each steam table pan.
3. Reconstitute milk; heat to just below boiling. DO NOT BOIL.
4. Blend butter or margarine and flour together; stir until smooth. Add milk to roux, stirring constantly. Cook until thickened.
5. Add cheese to sauce; stir until cheese is melted. Stir as necessary.
6. Pour 4-3/4 quarts sauce over egg halves in each steam table pan.
7. Combine bread crumbs and butter. Sprinkle 2/3 cup buttered crumbs over mixture in each pan.
8. Using a convection oven, bake at 325 F. 10 minutes or until browned on low fan, open vent. CCP: Hold for service at 140 F. or higher.

COOKED EGGS

Yield 100   **Portion** 2 Each

Calories	Carbohydrates	Protein	Fat	Cholesterol	Sodium	Calcium
149 cal	1 g	12 g	10 g	425 mg	126 mg	49 mg

Ingredient	Weight	Measure	Issue
EGGS,WHOLE,FRESH	22 lbs	200 each	

Method

1. HARD COOKED EGGS: Place eggs in baskets as needed; cover with hot water. Bring to a boil; reduce heat; simmer 10 to 15 minutes. DO NOT BOIL. Remove from water; serve immediately. CCP: All fresh shell eggs must be heated to 155 F. or higher for 15 seconds.
2. SOFT COOKED EGGS: Cook individual portions. Place eggs in baskets; cover with hot water. Bring to a boil; reduce heat; simmer 4 minutes. DO NOT BOIL. Remove from water; serve immediately.

Notes

1. Remove eggs from refrigeration 30 minutes before using.
2. Eggs may be placed in perforated steamer pans and steamed to desired doneness.
3. If hard cooked eggs are to be used in salads or other dishes, plunge into cold running water immediately after cooking; add ice, if necessary, to cool eggs. CCP: Refrigerate at 41 F. or lower.
4. COLD WATER METHOD FOR COOKED EGGS: Place eggs in basket asneeded; cover with cold water. Bring to a boil; reduce heat. For soft cooked eggs, simmer 1 minute. For hard cooked eggs, simmer 8 to 10 minutes. DO NOT BOIL.
5. STEAMER METHOD FOR COOKING EGGS: Grease steamer pan. Break eggs individually into a small container before dropping into greased pan. Egg depth should not exceed 2 inches. Place pan, uncovered, in steamer at 5 pound pressure for 6 to 8 minutes or 15 pound pressure for 5 to 7 minutes. Remove pan from steamer; cut eggs for easy removal. CCP: Fresh eggs must be heated to 155 F. or higher for 15 seconds. Consistency of cooked eggs can be controlled by adjusting cooking time.

DEVILED EGGS

Yield 100   **Portion** 2 Halves

Calories	Carbohydrates	Protein	Fat	Cholesterol	Sodium	Calcium
115 cal	2 g	6 g	9 g	214 mg	137 mg	26 mg

Ingredient	Weight	Measure	Issue
EGG,HARD COOKED	11 lbs	100 Eggs	
MUSTARD,PREPARED	4-3/8 oz	1/2 cup	
PICKLE RELISH,SWEET,DRAINED	8-5/8 oz	1 cup	
SALAD DRESSING,MAYONNAISE TYPE	1-1/2 lbs	3 cup	
PAPRIKA,GROUND	1/4 oz	1 tbsp	

Method

1. Cool; remove shells from eggs; slice eggs in half lengthwise. Arrange 100 egg halves in each steam table pan. CCP: All fresh shell eggs must be heated to 155 F. or higher for 15 seconds.
2. Cool; remove shells from eggs; cut eggs in half lengthwise. Remove yolks and mash thoroughly. Set whites aside for use in Step 4.
3. Blend mustard, pickle relish and salad dressing with yolks. Mix until well blended.
4. Fill the cooked whites with yolk mixture, using 1 tablespoon filling for each egg half.
5. Sprinkle paprika on top.
6. Serve immediately or cover and refrigerate until ready to serve. CCP: Hold for service at 41 F. or lower.

EGG FOO YOUNG

Yield 100   **Portion** 1 Omelet

Calories	Carbohydrates	Protein	Fat	Cholesterol	Sodium	Calcium
157 cal	4 g	10 g	12 g	134 mg	490 mg	27 mg

Ingredient	Weight	Measure	Issue
OIL,SALAD	7-2/3 oz	1 cup	
FLOUR,WHEAT,GENERAL PURPOSE	8-7/8 oz	2 cup	
CHICKEN BROTH		1 gal	
SOY SAUCE	10-1/8 oz	1 cup	
MOLASSES	1-1/2 oz	2 tbsp	
ONIONS,FRESH,CHOPPED	1-1/3 lbs	3-3/4 cup	1-1/2lbs
PEPPERS,GREEN,FRESH,CHOPPED	7-7/8 oz	1-1/2 cup	9-5/8lbs
OIL,SALAD	1-7/8 oz	1/4cup 1/3tbsp	
CHICKEN,COOKED,DICED	4 lbs		
BEAN SPROUTS,CANNED,DRAINED	1-7/8 lbs	3 qts 2 cup	
PEPPER,BLACK,GROUND	1/8 oz	1/3 tsp	
EGGS,WHOLE,FROZEN,BEATEN	6 lbs	2 qts 3-1/4 cup	
OIL,SALAD	1 lbs	2 cup	

Method

1. Blend salad oil or shortening and flour; stir until smooth.
2. Prepare broth according to package directions. Add flour mixture to broth; mix well. Bring to a boil; reduce heat; simmer 10 minutes or until thickened.
3. Add soy sauce and molasses to sauce; simmer 5 minutes.

4. Saute onions and peppers in salad oil or olive oil until tender.
5. Combine sauteed vegetables, meat, bean sprouts, and pepper; mix well.
6. Add eggs to meat mixture; blend well.
7. Place 1/3 cup mixture on 375 F. well greased griddle; cook about 3 minutes on each side or until well done. CCP: Internal temperature must reach 165 F. or higher for 15 seconds.
8. Pour 2 tablespoons sauce over each omelet just before serving. CCP: Hold for service at 140 F. or higher.

GRIDDLE FRIED EGGS

Yield 100   **Portion** 2 Each

Calories	Carbohydrates	Protein	Fat	Cholesterol	Sodium	Calcium
168 cal	1 g	12 g	12 g	425 mg	126 mg	49 mg

Ingredient	Weight	Measure	Issue
EGGS,WHOLE,FRESH	22 lbs	200 each	
OIL,SALAD	7-2/3 oz	1 cup	

Method
1. Break 2 eggs individually into a small bowl.
2. Fry eggs to order on a 325 F. lightly greased griddle. CCP: Internal temperature must reach 145 F. or higher for 15 seconds, 155 F. for fresh shell eggs.
3. CCP: Hold for service at 140 F. or higher.

PLAIN OMELET

Yield 100   **Portion** 1 Omelet

Calories	Carbohydrates	Protein	Fat	Cholesterol	Sodium	Calcium
139 cal	1 g	11 g	10 g	392 mg	121 mg	54 mg

Ingredient	Weight	Measure	Issue
EGGS,WHOLE,FROZEN	20 lbs	2 gal 1-1/3 qts	
COOKING SPRAY,NONSTICK	2 oz	1/4 cup 1/3 tbsp	

Method
1. Place thawed eggs in mixer bowl. Using wire whip, beat just enough to thoroughly blend yolks and whites.
2. Lightly spray griddle with non-stick cooking spray. Pour 1/3 cup egg mixture for individual omelets on 325 F. griddle.
3. Cook until bottom is golden brown. DO NOT STIR. If necessary, gently lift cooked portion with a spatula to permit uncooked mixture to flow underneath. Continue cooking until eggs are set and well done. CCP: Internal temperature must reach 145 F. or higher for 15 seconds, 155 F. for fresh shell eggs.
4. Fold omelet in half or into thirds making a long oval shaped omelet. CCP: Hold for service at 140 F. or higher.

PLAIN OMELET (FROZEN EGGS AND EGG WHITES)

Yield 100   **Portion** 1 Omelet

Calories	Carbohydrates	Protein	Fat	Cholesterol	Sodium	Calcium
93 cal	1 g	10 g	5 g	196 mg	132 mg	30 mg

Ingredient	Weight	Measure	Issue
EGGS,WHOLE,FROZEN	10 lbs	1 gal 2/3 qts	
EGG WHITES,FROZEN,THAWED	10 lbs	1 gal 2/3 qts	
COOKING SPRAY,NONSTICK	2 oz	1/4 cup 1/3 tbsp	

Method

1. Thaw eggs and egg whites; place eggs in mixer bowl. Using wire whip beat just enough to thoroughly blend yolks and whites.
2. Lightly spray griddle with non-stick cooking spray. Pour 1/3 cup egg mixture for individual omelets on 325 F. griddle.
3. Cook until bottom is golden brown. DO NOT STIR. If necessary, gently lift cooked portion with a spatula to permit uncooked mixture to flow underneath. Continue cooking until eggs are set and well done. CCP: Internal temperature must reach 145 F. or higher for 15 seconds, 155 F. for fresh shell eggs.
4. Fold omelet in half or into thirds making a long oval shaped omelet. CCP: Hold for service at 140 F. or higher.

CHEESE OMELET

Yield 100   **Portion** 1 Omelet

Calories	Carbohydrates	Protein	Fat	Cholesterol	Sodium	Calcium
198 cal	1 g	14 g	15 g	407 mg	212 mg	160 mg

Ingredient	Weight	Measure	Issue
EGGS,WHOLE,FROZEN	20 lbs	2 gal 1-1/3 qts	
COOKING SPRAY,NONSTICK	2 oz	1/4 cup 1/3 tbsp	
CHEESE,CHEDDAR,SHREDDED	3-1/4 lbs	3 qts 1 cup	

Method

1. Place thawed eggs in mixer bowl. Using wire whip, beat just enough to thoroughly blend.
2. Lightly spray griddle with non-stick cooking spray. Pour 1/3 cup egg mixture for individual omelets on 325 F. griddle.
3. Cook until bottom is golden brown. DO NOT STIR. If necessary, gently lift cooked portion with a spatula to permit uncooked mixture to flow underneath. Sprinkle about 2 tablespoons cheese over each omelet when partially set. Continue cooking until eggs are set and well done. CCP: Internal temperature must reach 145 F. or higher for 15 seconds, 155 F. for fresh shell eggs.
4. Fold omelet in half or into thirds making a long oval shaped omelet. CCP: Hold for service at 140 F. or higher.

GREEN PEPPER OMELET

Yield 100   **Portion** 1 Omelet

Calories	Carbohydrates	Protein	Fat	Cholesterol	Sodium	Calcium
152 cal	3 g	11 g	10 g	392 mg	121 mg	56 mg

Ingredient	Weight	Measure	Issue
COOKING SPRAY,NONSTICK	2 oz	1/4cup 1/3tbsp	
PEPPERS,GREEN,FRESH,CHOPPED	7-1/8 lbs	1gal 1-1/2qts	8-2/3lbs
EGGS,WHOLE,FROZEN	20 lbs	2 gal 1-1/3 qts	
COOKING SPRAY,NONSTICK	2 oz	1/4cup 1/3tbsp	

Method
1. Lightly spray griddle with non-stick cooking spray. Cook chopped fresh sweet peppers until tender.
2. Place thawed eggs in mixer bowl. Using wire whip, beat just enough to thoroughly blend. Lightly spray griddle with non-stick cooking spray. Pour 1/3 cup egg mixture for individual omelets on 325 F. griddle.
3. Cook until bottom is golden brown. DO NOT STIR. If necessary, gently lift cooked portion with a spatula to permit uncooked mixture to flow underneath. Sprinkle 2 tablespoons peppers over eggs when partially set. Continue cooking until eggs are set and well done. CCP: Internal temperature must reach 145 F. or higher for 15 seconds, 155 F. for fresh shell eggs.
4. Fold omelet in half or into thirds making a long oval shaped omelet. CCP: Hold for service at 140 F. or higher.

HAM OMELET

Yield 100   **Portion** 1 Omelet

Calories	Carbohydrates	Protein	Fat	Cholesterol	Sodium	Calcium
166 cal	1 g	14 g	11 g	401 mg	352 mg	55 mg

Ingredient	Weight	Measure	Issue
EGGS,WHOLE,FROZEN	20 lbs	2 gal 1-1/3 qts	
COOKING SPRAY,NONSTICK	2 oz	1/4 cup 1/3 tbsp	
HAM,COOKED,BONELESS	4 lbs		

Method
1. Place thawed eggs in mixer bowl. Using wire whip, beat just enough to thoroughly blend.
2. Lightly spray griddle with non-stick cooking spray. Pour 1/3 cup egg mixture for individual omelets on 325 F. griddle.
3. Cook until bottom is golden brown. DO NOT STIR. If necessary, gently lift cooked portion with a spatula to permit uncooked mixture to flow underneath.
4. Dice ham. Sprinkle 2 tablespoons ham over eggs when partially set. Continue cooking until eggs are set and well done. CCP: Internal temperature must reach 145 F. or higher for 15 seconds, 155 F. for fresh shell eggs.
5. Fold omelet in half or into thirds making a long oval shaped omelet. CCP: Hold for service at 140 F. or higher.

HAM AND CHEESE OMELET

Yield 100   **Portion** 1 Omelet

Calories	Carbohydrates	Protein	Fat	Cholesterol	Sodium	Calcium
180 cal	1 g	14 g	13 g	404 mg	278 mg	103 mg

Ingredient	Weight	Measure	Issue
EGGS,WHOLE,FROZEN	20 lbs	2 gal 1-1/3 qts	
COOKING SPRAY,NONSTICK	2 oz	1/4 cup 1/3 tbsp	
CHEESE,CHEDDAR,SHREDDED	1-1/2 lbs	1 qts 2 cup	
HAM,COOKED,BONELESS	2 lbs		

Method
1. Place thawed eggs in mixer bowl. Using wire whip, beat just enough to thoroughly blend.
2. Lightly spray griddle with non-stick cooking spray. Pour 1/3 cup egg mixture for individual omelets on 325 F. griddle.
3. Cook until bottom is golden brown. DO NOT STIR. If necessary, gently lift cooked portion with a spatula to permit uncooked mixture to flow underneath.
4. Dice ham. Sprinkle about 1 tablespoon cheese and 1 tablespoon ham over eggs when partially set. Continue cooking until eggs are set and well done. CCP: Internal temperature must reach 145 F. or higher for 15 seconds, 155 F. for fresh shell eggs.
5. Fold omelet in half or into thirds making a long oval shaped omelet. CCP: Hold for service at 140 F. or higher.

MUSHROOM OMELET

Yield 100   **Portion** 1 Omelet

Calories	Carbohydrates	Protein	Fat	Cholesterol	Sodium	Calcium
151 cal	3 g	11 g	10 g	392 mg	258 mg	57 mg

Ingredient	Weight	Measure	Issue
MUSHROOMS,CANNED,SLICED,DRAINED	7-1/8 lbs	1 gal 1-1/8 qts	
COOKING SPRAY,NONSTICK	2 oz	1/4 cup 1/3 tbsp	
EGGS,WHOLE,FROZEN	20 lbs	2 gal 1-1/3 qts	
COOKING SPRAY,NONSTICK	2 oz	1/4 cup 1/3 tbsp	

Method
1. Lightly spray griddle with non-stick cooking spray. Cook mushrooms until tender.
2. Place thawed eggs in mixer bowl. Using wire whip, beat just enough to thoroughly blend.
3. Lightly spray griddle with non-stick cooking spray. Pour 1/3 cup egg mixture for each individual omelet on 325 F. griddle.
4. Cook until bottom is golden brown. DO NOT STIR. When omelet is partially set, sprinkle about 1-1/2 tablespoon mushrooms over eggs and continue cooking until eggs are set and well done. If necessary when cooking, lift cooked portion with spatula to let uncooked mixture flow underneath. CCP: Internal temperature must reach 145 F. or higher for 15 seconds, 155 F. for fresh shell eggs.
5. Fold omelet in half or into thirds making a long oval shaped omelet. CCP: Hold for service at 140 F. or higher.

ONION OMELET

Yield 100   **Portion** 1 Omelet

Calories	Carbohydrates	Protein	Fat	Cholesterol	Sodium	Calcium
150 cal	3 g	11 g	10 g	392 mg	121 mg	57 mg

Ingredient	Weight	Measure	Issue
ONIONS,FRESH,CHOPPED	4-1/4 lbs	3 qts	4-2/3 lbs
COOKING SPRAY,NONSTICK	2 oz	1/4cup 1/3tbsp	
EGGS,WHOLE,FROZEN	20 lbs	2gal 1-1/3qts	
COOKING SPRAY,NONSTICK	2 oz	1/4cup 1/3tbsp	

Method

1. Lightly spray griddle with non-stick cooking spray. Cook onions until tender.
2. Place thawed eggs in a mixer bowl. Using wire whip, beat just enough to thoroughly blend.
3. Lightly spray griddle with non-stick cooking spray. Pour 1/3 cup egg mixture for each individual omelet on 325 F. griddle.
4. Cook until bottom is golden brown. DO NOT STIR. If necessary, gently lift cooked portion with a spatula to permit uncooked portion to flow underneath. Sprinkle 1 tablespoon onions over eggs when partially set. Continue cooking until eggs are set and well done. CCP: Internal temperature must reach 145 F. or higher for 15 seconds, 155 F. for fresh shell eggs.
5. Fold omelet in half or into thirds making a long oval shaped omelet. CCP: Hold for service at 140 F. or higher.

WESTERN OMELET

Yield 100   **Portion** 1 Omelet

Calories	Carbohydrates	Protein	Fat	Cholesterol	Sodium	Calcium
170 cal	4 g	13 g	11 g	396 mg	237 mg	60 mg

Ingredient	Weight	Measure	Issue
ONIONS,FRESH,CHOPPED	4-1/4 lbs	3 qts	4-2/3lbs
COOKING SPRAY,NONSTICK	2 oz	1/4cup 1/3tbsp	
PEPPERS,GREEN,FRESH,CHOPPED	5-1/4 lbs	1 gal	6-3/8lbs
HAM,COOKED,BONELESS	2 lbs		
EGGS,WHOLE,FROZEN	20 lbs	2gal 1-1/3qts	
COOKING SPRAY,NONSTICK	2 oz	1/4cup 1/3tbsp	

Method

1. Lightly spray griddle with non-stick cooking spray. Cook onions and peppers until tender.
2. Chop or grind ham. Combine cooked onions and peppers with chopped ham; mix thoroughly.
3. Place thawed eggs in mixer bowl. Using wire whip, beat just enough to thoroughly blend.
4. Lightly spray griddle with non-stick cooking spray. Pour 1/3 cup egg mixture for each individual omelet on griddle.
5. Cook until bottom is golden brown. DO NOT STIR. If necessary, gently lift cooked portion with a spatula to permit uncooked mixture to flow underneath. Sprinkle about 3 tablespoons onion/pepper/ham mixture over eggs when partially set. Continue cooking until eggs are set. CCP: Internal temperature must reach 145 F. or higher for 15 seconds, 155 F. for fresh shell eggs.
6. Fold omelet in half or into thirds making a long, oval shaped omelet. CCP: Hold for service at 140 F. or higher.

TOMATO OMELET

Yield 100   **Portion** 1 Omelet

Calories	Carbohydrates	Protein	Fat	Cholesterol	Sodium	Calcium
145 cal	2 g	11 g	10 g	392 mg	123 mg	55 mg

Ingredient	Weight	Measure	Issue
EGGS,WHOLE,FROZEN	20 lbs	2gal 1-1/3qts	
COOKING SPRAY,NONSTICK	2 oz	1/4cup 1/3tbsp	
TOMATOES,FRESH,CHOPPED	6-3/4 lbs	1gal 1/4qts	6-7/8lbs

Method

1. Place thawed eggs in mixer bowl. Using wire whip, beat just enough to thoroughly blend.
2. Lightly spray griddle with non-stick cooking spray. Pour 1/3 cup egg mixture for each individual omelet on 325 F. griddle.
3. Cook until bottom is golden brown. DO NOT STIR. If necessary, gently lift with a spatula to permit uncooked mixture to flow underneath. Sprinkle 2 tablespoons tomatoes over eggs when partially set. Continue cooking until eggs are set. CCP: Internal temperature must reach 145 F. or higher for 15 seconds, 155 F. for fresh shell eggs.
4. Fold omelet in half or into thirds making a long, oval shaped omelet. CCP: Hold for service at 140 F. or higher.

SPANISH OMELET

Yield 100   **Portion** 1 Omelet

Calories	Carbohydrates	Protein	Fat	Cholesterol	Sodium	Calcium
183 cal	9 g	12 g	11 g	392 mg	364 mg	82 mg

Ingredient	Weight	Measure	Issue
SPANISH SAUCE		2 gal 1/4 qts	
EGGS,WHOLE,FROZEN	20 lbs	2 gal 1-1/3 qts	
COOKING SPRAY,NONSTICK	2 oz	1/4 cup 1/3 tbsp	

Method

1. Prepare 1 recipe Spanish Sauce, Recipe No. O 005 01 for use in Step 6. CCP: Hold for service at 140 F. or higher.
2. Place thawed eggs in mixer bowl. Using wire whip, beat just enough to thoroughly blend.
3. Lightly spray griddle with non-stick cooking spray. Pour 1/3 cup egg mixture for individual omelets on 325 F. griddle.
4. Cook until bottom is golden brown. DO NOT STIR. If necessary, gently lift cooked portion with a spatula to permit uncooked mixture to flow underneath. Continue cooking until eggs are set. CCP: Internal temperature must reach 145 F. or higher for 15 seconds, 155 F. for fresh shell eggs.
5. Fold omelet in half or into thirds, making a long oval shaped omelet.
6. Serve each omelet with 2 ounces of heated Spanish Sauce, Recipe No. O 005 01. CCP: Hold for service at 140 F. or higher.

226

POACHED EGGS

Yield 100   **Portion** 2 Each

Calories	Carbohydrates	Protein	Fat	Cholesterol	Sodium	Calcium
149 cal	1 g	12 g	10 g	425 mg	127 mg	49 mg

Ingredient	Weight	Measure	Issue
WATER	4-1/8 lbs	2 qts	
VINEGAR,DISTILLED	1 oz	2 tbsp	
EGGS,WHOLE,FRESH	22 lbs	200 each	

Method
1. Fill a steam table pan with water to a depth of 1 inch.
2. Add vinegar; bring to a boil; reduce to a simmer.
3. Break 2 eggs individually into a small bowl; slide gently into simmering water.
4. Cook 3 to 5 minutes or until whites are set and yolks are covered with a white film. CCP: Internal temperature must reach 155 F. or higher for 15 seconds.
5. Using a perforated skimmer, lift eggs out of pan; serve immediately. CCP: Hold for service at 140 F. or higher.

SCRAMBLED EGGS

Yield 100   **Portion** 1/3 Cup

Calories	Carbohydrates	Protein	Fat	Cholesterol	Sodium	Calcium
144 cal	1 g	11 g	10 g	392 mg	121 mg	54 mg

Ingredient	Weight	Measure	Issue
EGGS,WHOLE,FROZEN	20 lbs	2 gal 1-1/3 qts	
OIL,SALAD	3-7/8 oz	1/2 cup	

Method
1. Beat eggs thoroughly.
2. Pour about 1 quart eggs on 325 F. lightly greased griddle. Cook slowly until firm, until there is no visible liquid egg, stirring occasionally. CCP: Internal temperature must reach 145 F. or higher for 15 seconds, 155 F. for fresh shell eggs. Hold for service at 140 F. or higher.

Notes
1. OVEN METHOD: Using a convection oven, bake at 350 F. 18 to 25 minutes on high fan, closed vent. After 12 minutes, stir every 5 minutes.

SCRAMBLED EGGS AND CHEESE

Yield 100   **Portion** 1/3 Cup

Calories	Carbohydrates	Protein	Fat	Cholesterol	Sodium	Calcium
217 cal	1 g	15 g	16 g	411 mg	233 mg	184 mg

Ingredient	Weight	Measure	Issue
EGGS,WHOLE,FROZEN	20 lbs	2 gal 1-1/3 qts	
OIL,SALAD	3-7/8 oz	1/2 cup	
CHEESE,CHEDDAR,SHREDDED	4 lbs	1 gal	

Method

1. Beat eggs thoroughly.
2. Pour about 1 quart eggs on 325 F. lightly greased griddle. Sprinkle cheese, using about 1 cup per 1 quart of egg mixture, over partially cooked eggs. Stir gently until cheese is melted and well blended. Cook slowly until firm or until there is no visible liquid egg, stirring occasionally. CCP: Internal temperature must reach 145 F. or higher for 15 seconds, 155 F. for fresh shell eggs. Hold at 140 F. or higher.

Notes

1. OVEN METHOD: Using a 350 F. convection oven, bake 18 to 25 minutes on high fan, closed vent. After 12 minutes, stir every 5 minutes.

SCRAMBLED EGGS AND HAM

Yield 100   Portion 1/3 Cup

Calories	Carbohydrates	Protein	Fat	Cholesterol	Sodium	Calcium
171 cal	1 g	14 g	12 g	401 mg	352 mg	55 mg

Ingredient	Weight	Measure	Issue
EGGS,WHOLE,FROZEN	20 lbs	2 gal 1-1/3 qts	
OIL,SALAD	3-7/8 oz	1/2 cup	
HAM,COOKED,BONELESS	4 lbs		

Method

1. Beat eggs thoroughly.
2. Pour about 1 quart eggs on 325 F. lightly greased griddle. Dice ham. Add diced ham, about 1 cup per 1 quart of egg mix, over partially cooked eggs. Stir well. Cook slowly until firm or until there is no visible liquid egg, stirring occasionally. CCP: Internal temperature must reach 145 F. or higher for 15 seconds, 155 F. for fresh shell eggs. Hold at 140 F. or higher.

Notes

1. Using a 350 F. convection oven, bake 18 to 25 minutes on high fan, closed vent. After 12 minutes, stir every 5 minutes.

SCRAMBLED EGGS (DEHYDRATED EGG MIX)

Yield 100   Portion 1/3 Cup

Calories	Carbohydrates	Protein	Fat	Cholesterol	Sodium	Calcium
166 cal	1 g	12 g	12 g	451 mg	140 mg	62 mg

Ingredient	Weight	Measure	Issue
EGG MIX,DEHYDRATED	5-3/4 lbs	5 #3cyl	
WATER,WARM	15-2/3 lbs	1 gal 3-1/2 qts	
OIL,SALAD	3-7/8 oz	1/2 cup	

Method

1. Combine egg mix and warm water.
2. Pour about 1 quart eggs on 325 F. lightly greased griddle. Cook slowly until firm or until there is no visible liquid egg, stir occasionally. CCP: Internal temperature must reach 145 F. or higher for 15 seconds. Hold at 140 F. or higher.

Notes

1. Using a 350 F. convection oven, bake 18 to 25 minutes on high fan, closed vent. After 12 minutes, stir every 5 minutes.

SCRAMBLED EGGS (FROZEN EGGS AND EGG WHITES)

Yield 100   **Portion** 1/3 Cup

Calories	Carbohydrates	Protein	Fat	Cholesterol	Sodium	Calcium
98 cal	1 g	10 g	6 g	196 mg	132 mg	30 mg

Ingredient	Weight	Measure	Issue
EGGS,WHOLE,FROZEN	10 lbs	1 gal 2/3 qts	
EGG WHITES,FROZEN,THAWED	10 lbs	1 gal 2/3 qts	
OIL,SALAD	3-7/8 oz	1/2 cup	

Method
1. Combine whole table eggs and frozen egg whites. Beat eggs thoroughly.
2. Pour about 1 quart eggs on 325 F. lightly greased griddle. Cook slowly until firm or until there is no visible liquid egg, stir occasionally. CCP: Internal temperature must reach 145 F. or higher for 15 seconds. Hold for service at 140 F. or higher.

Notes
1. Using a 350 F. convection oven, bake 18 to 25 minutes on high fan, closed vent. After 12 minutes, stir every 5 minutes.

MUSHROOM QUICHE

Yield 100   **Portion** 4-1/2 Ounces

Calories	Carbohydrates	Protein	Fat	Cholesterol	Sodium	Calcium
199 cal	16 g	11 g	10 g	114 mg	267 mg	231 mg

Ingredient	Weight	Measure	Issue
MUSHROOMS,CANNED,SLICED,DRAINED	4-1/8 lbs	3 qts	
ONIONS,FRESH,CHOPPED	2-1/3 lbs	1qts 2-5/8cup	2-5/8 lbs
CHEESE,SWISS,SHREDDED	3-3/4 lbs	1 gal	
COOKING SPRAY,NONSTICK	2 oz	1/4cup 1/3tbsp	
FLOUR,WHEAT,BREAD	3-1/3 lbs	2 qts 3 cup	
MILK,NONFAT,DRY	1-1/4 oz	1/2 cup	
SALT	3/8 oz	1/3 tsp	
SUGAR,GRANULATED	1-3/4 oz	1/4cup 1/3tbsp	
BAKING SODA	5/8 oz	1 tbsp	
SHORTENING	7-1/4 oz	1 cup	
MILK,NONFAT,DRY	11-3/8 oz	1 qts 3/4 cup	
WATER,WARM	11-1/2 lbs	1 gal 1-1/2qts	
EGGS,WHOLE,FROZEN	5 lbs	2 qts 1-3/8cup	
GARLIC POWDER	3/4 oz	2-2/3 tbsp	

Method
1. Lightly spray each steam table pan with non-stick cooking spray. Combine mushrooms, onions and cheese. Spread 1-3/4 quarts evenly over bottom of each sprayed and floured pan.
2. Combine flour, milk, salt, sugar and soda in mixer bowl.
3. Cut in shortening or oil until evenly distributed and granular in appearance, about 1 minute.
4. Reconstitute milk.
5. Add eggs to milk; blend in garlic powder.

6. Add egg-milk mixture gradually to flour mixture. Scrape down bowl; beat 2 minutes at medium speed.
7. Pour about 9-1/2 cups batter over cheese and vegetable mixture in each pan. Stir gently.
8. Using a convection oven, bake at 350 F. 15 minutes on low fan, closed vent; reduce heat to 325 F.; bake an additional 30 minutes or until set and lightly browned. Let stand 10 minutes. Cut 5 by 5. CCP: Internal temperature must reach 145 F. or higher for 15 seconds. Hold for service at 140 F. or higher.

BROCCOLI QUICHE

Yield 100   Portion 4-1/2 Ounces

Calories	Carbohydrates	Protein	Fat	Cholesterol	Sodium	Calcium
201 cal	16 g	12 g	10 g	114 mg	194 mg	242 mg

Ingredient	Weight	Measure	Issue
COOKING SPRAY,NONSTICK	2 oz	1/4cup 1/3tbsp	
ONIONS,FRESH,CHOPPED	1-1/8 lbs	3-3/8 cup	1-1/3lbs
BROCCOLI,FROZEN,CHOPPED	6 lbs	1 gal	
CHEESE,SWISS,SHREDDED	3-3/4 lbs	1 gal	
FLOUR,WHEAT,BREAD	3-1/3 lbs	2 qts 3 cup	
MILK,NONFAT,DRY	1-1/4 oz	1/2 cup	
SALT	3/8 oz	1/3 tsp	
SUGAR,GRANULATED	1-3/4 oz	1/4cup 1/3tbsp	
BAKING SODA	5/8 oz	1 tbsp	
SHORTENING	7-1/4 oz	1 cup	
MILK,NONFAT,DRY	11-3/8 oz	1 qts 3/4 cup	
WATER,WARM	11-1/2 lbs	1 gal 1-1/2 qts	
EGGS,WHOLE,FROZEN	5 lbs	2 qts 1-3/8 cup	
GARLIC POWDER	3/4 oz	2-2/3 tbsp	
NUTMEG,GROUND	1/8 oz	1/3 tsp	
PEPPER,BLACK,GROUND	1/3 oz	1 tbsp	

Method
1. Lightly spray each steam table pan with non-stick cooking spray. Thaw broccoli. Combine broccoli, onions and cheese. Spread about 2 quarts mixture in each sprayed and floured pan.
2. Combine flour, milk, salt, sugar and soda in mixer bowl.
3. Cut in shortening or oil until evenly distributed and granular in appearance, about 1 minute.
4. Reconstitute milk.
5. Add eggs, nutmeg and black pepper to milk; blend in garlic powder.
6. Add egg-milk mixture gradually to flour mixture. Scrape down bowl; beat 2 minutes at medium speed.
7. Pour about 9-1/2 cups batter over cheese and vegetable mixture in each pan. Stir gently.
8. Using a convection oven, bake at 350 F. 15 minutes on low fan, closed vent; reduce temperature to 325 F.; bake an additional 30 minutes or until set and lightly browned. Let stand 10 minutes. Cut 5 by 5. CCP: Internal temperature must reach 145 F. or higher for 15 seconds. Hold for service at 140 F. or higher.

BROCCOLI QUICHE (FROZEN EGGS AND EGG WHITES)

Yield 100   **Portion** 4-1/2 Ounces

Calories	Carbohydrates	Protein	Fat	Cholesterol	Sodium	Calcium
189 cal	16 g	11 g	9 g	64 mg	195 mg	236 mg

Ingredient	Weight	Measure	Issue
ONIONS,FRESH,CHOPPED	1-1/8 lbs	3-3/8 cup	1-1/3lbs
BROCCOLI,FROZEN,CHOPPED	6 lbs	1 gal	
CHEESE,SWISS,SHREDDED	3-3/4 lbs	1 gal	
COOKING SPRAY,NONSTICK	2 oz	1/4 cup 1/3 tbsp	
FLOUR,WHEAT,BREAD	3-1/3 lbs	2 qts 3 cup	
MILK,NONFAT,DRY	1-1/4 oz	1/2 cup	
SALT	3/8 oz	1/3 tsp	
SUGAR,GRANULATED	1-3/4 oz	1/4 cup 1/3 tbsp	
BAKING SODA	5/8 oz	1 tbsp	
SHORTENING	7-1/4 oz	1 cup	
MILK,NONFAT,DRY	11-3/8 oz	1 qts 3/4 cup	
WATER,WARM	11-1/2 lbs	1 gal 1-1/2 qts	
EGGS,WHOLE,FROZEN	2-3/8 lbs	1 qts 1/2 cup	
EGG WHITES,FROZEN,THAWED	2-3/8 lbs	1 qts 1/2 cup	
GARLIC POWDER	3/4 oz	2-2/3 tbsp	
NUTMEG,GROUND	1/8 oz	1/3 tsp	
PEPPER,BLACK,GROUND	1/3 oz	1 tbsp	

Method
1. Lightly spray each steam table pan with non-stick cooking spray. Thaw and cut broccoli in 1/2-inch pieces. Combine broccoli, onions and cheese. Spread about 2 quarts mixture in each sprayed and floured pan.
2. Combine flour, milk, salt, sugar and soda in mixer bowl.
3. Cut in shortening or oil until evenly distributed and granular in appearance, about 1 minute.
4. Reconstitute milk.
5. Add eggs, nutmeg, and black pepper to milk; blend in garlic powder.
6. Add egg-milk mixture gradually to flour mixture. Scrape down bowl; beat 2 minutes at medium speed.
7. Pour about 9-1/2 cups batter over cheese and vegetable mixture in each pan. Stir gently.
8. Using a convection oven, bake at 325 F. for 40 minutes on low fan, closed vent or until set and lightly browned. Let stand 10 minutes. Cut 5 by 5. CCP: Internal temperature must reach 145 F. or higher for 15 seconds. Hold for service at 140 F. or higher.

MUSHROOM QUICHE (FROZEN EGGS AND EGG WHITES)

Yield 100   **Portion** 4-1/2 Ounces

Calories	Carbohydrates	Protein	Fat	Cholesterol	Sodium	Calcium
187 cal	16 g	11 g	9 g	64 mg	269 mg	255 mg

Ingredient	Weight	Measure	Issue
MUSHROOMS,CANNED,SLICED,DRAINED	4-1/8 lbs	3 qts	
ONIONS,FRESH,CHOPPED	2-1/3 lbs	1qts 2-5/8cup	2-5/8lbs
CHEESE,SWISS,SHREDDED	3-3/4 lbs	1 gal	

COOKING SPRAY,NONSTICK	2 oz	1/4 cup 1/3tbsp
FLOUR,WHEAT,BREAD	3-1/3 lbs	2 qts 3 cup
MILK,NONFAT,DRY	1-1/4 oz	1/2 cup
SALT	3/8 oz	1/3 tsp
SUGAR,GRANULATED	1-3/4 oz	1/4 cup 1/3tbsp
BAKING SODA	5/8 oz	1 tbsp
SHORTENING	7-1/4 oz	1 cup
MILK,NONFAT,DRY	11-3/8 oz	1 qts 3/4 cup
WATER,WARM	11-1/2 lbs	1 gal 1-1/2 qts
EGGS,WHOLE,FROZEN	2-3/8 lbs	1 qts 1/2 cup
EGG WHITES,FROZEN,THAWED	2-3/8 lbs	1 qts 1/2 cup
GARLIC POWDER	3/4 oz	2-2/3 tbsp

Method

1. Lightly spray each steam table pan with non-stick cooking spray. Combine mushrooms, onions and cheese. Spread about 2 pounds 10 ounces evenly over bottom of each sprayed and floured pan.
2. Combine flour, milk, salt, sugar and soda in mixer bowl.
3. Cut in shortening until evenly distributed and granular in appearance, about 1 minute.
4. Reconstitute milk.
5. Thaw eggs under refrigeration. Add eggs to milk; blend in garlic powder.
6. Add egg-milk mixture gradually to flour mixture. Scrape down bowl; beat 2 minutes at medium speed.
7. Pour about 9-1/2 cups of batter over cheese and vegetable mixture in each pan. Stir gently.
8. Using a convection oven, bake at 325 F. for 40 minutes on low fan, closed vent or until set and lightly browned. Let stand 10 minutes. CCP: Internal temperature must reach 145 F. or higher for 15 seconds. Cut 5 by 5.

BREAKFAST BURRITO

Yield 100   **Portion** 1 Each

Calories	Carbohydrates	Protein	Fat	Cholesterol	Sodium	Calcium
302 cal	26 g	16 g	14 g	167 mg	499 mg	170 mg

Ingredient	Weight	Measure	Issue
EGG WHITES,FROZEN,THAWED	7-1/2 lbs	3 qts 2 cup	
EGGS,WHOLE,FROZEN	7-1/2 lbs	3 qts 2 cup	
CHEESE,CHEDDAR,SHREDDED	2-2/3 lbs	2 qts 2-5/8 cup	
SAUSAGE,PORK,COOKED,DICED	2 lbs		
TOMATOES,FRESH,CHOPPED	2 lbs	1qts 1cup	2lbs
ONIONS,FRESH,CHOPPED	1 lbs	2-5/8cup	1lbs
PEPPER,BLACK,GROUND	1/3 oz	1 tbsp	
OREGANO,CRUSHED	1/2 oz	3 tbsp	
COOKING SPRAY,NONSTICK	2 oz	1/4cup 1/3tbsp	
COOKING SPRAY,NONSTICK	2 oz	1/4cup 1/3tbsp	
TORTILLAS,FLOUR,8 INCH	9-1/2 lbs	100 each	

Method

1. Combine egg whites and eggs. Blend thoroughly.
2. Combine cheese, sausage, tomatoes, onions, pepper and oregano; mix thoroughly.

3. Lightly spray griddle with non-stick cooking spray. Pour about 1 quart egg mixture on 325 F. lightly sprayed griddle. Cook until partially set. Add 6 ounces cheese-sausage mixture. Cook until cheese is melted and eggs are firm. CCP: Internal temperature must reach 145 F. or higher for 15 seconds.
4. Place tortillas on lightly sprayed griddle; heat 30 seconds on each side.
5. Place about 1/2 cup cooked egg mixture in center of each tortilla; fold tortilla to cover eggs and form burrito.
6. CCP: Hold for service at 140 F. or higher.

Notes
1. In Step 2, 3-1/4 pounds (1/2 No. 10 can) of canned diced tomatoes may be used per 100 portions. Drain before using.

BREAKFAST PITA

Yield 100   **Portion** 1 Pita

Calories	Carbohydrates	Protein	Fat	Cholesterol	Sodium	Calcium
418 cal	55 g	21 g	12 g	167 mg	801 mg	198 mg

Ingredient	Weight	Measure	Issue
EGG WHITES,FROZEN,THAWED	7-1/2 lbs	3 qts 2 cup	
EGGS,WHOLE,FROZEN	7-1/2 lbs	3 qts 2 cup	
CHEESE,CHEDDAR,SHREDDED	2-2/3 lbs	2 qts 2-5/8cup	
SAUSAGE,PORK,COOKED,DICED	2 lbs		
TOMATOES,FRESH,CHOPPED	2 lbs	1 qts 1 cup	2lbs
ONIONS,FRESH,CHOPPED	1 lbs	2-5/8 cup	1lbs
PEPPER,BLACK,GROUND	1/3 oz	1 tbsp	
OREGANO,CRUSHED	1/2 oz	3 tbsp	
COOKING SPRAY,NONSTICK	2 oz	1/4 cup 1/3tbsp	
BREAD,PITA,WHITE,8-INCH	21 lbs	100 each	

Method
1. Combine egg whites and eggs. Blend thoroughly.
2. Combine cheese, sausage, tomatoes, onions, pepper and oregano; mix thoroughly.
3. Pour about 1 quart egg mixture on lightly greased griddle. Cook until partially set. Add cheese-sausage mixture. Cook until cheese is melted and eggs are firm. CCP: Internal temperature must reach 145 F. or higher for 15 seconds.
4. Cut off top third of pita pocket and place eggs in the pocket. Place pockets on sheet pans. Using a convection oven, bake at 350 F. for 5 minutes or until warm and pliable on high fan, closed vent.
5. Place about 1/2 cup egg mixture in each pocket. CCP: Internal temperature must reach 145 F. or higher for 15 seconds. Hold for service at 140 F. or higher.

Notes
1. In Step 2, 3-1/4 pounds (1/2 No. 10 can) of canned diced tomatoes may be used per 100 portions. Drain before using.

VEGGIE EGG POCKET

Yield 100   **Portion** 1 Serving

Calories	Carbohydrates	Protein	Fat	Cholesterol	Sodium	Calcium
319 cal	45 g	20 g	6 g	5 mg	952 mg	172 mg

Ingredient	Weight	Measure	Issue
MUSHROOMS,CANNED,SLICED,DRAINED	3-1/8 lbs	2 qts 1 cup	
SQUASH,ZUCCHINI,FRESH,SHREDDED	3-1/4 lbs	2 qts 3-7/8cup	3-3/8lbs
CARROTS,FRESH,SHREDDED	4-7/8 lbs	1 gal 1 qts	6lbs
FLOUR,WHEAT,GENERAL PURPOSE	11 oz	2-1/2 cup	
EGG SUBSTITUTE,PASTEURIZED	22-1/8 lbs	2 gal 2 qts	
SALT	5/8 oz	1 tbsp	
SALAD DRESSING,RANCH,FAT FREE	6-1/3 lbs	3 qts	
CHEESE,PARMESAN,GRATED	1 lbs	1 qts 1/2cup	
ONIONS,FRESH,CHOPPED	2-1/4 lbs	1 qts 2-3/8cup	2-1/2lbs
DILL WEED,DRIED	2/3 oz	1/4cup 2-1/3tbsp	
PEPPER,WHITE,GROUND	1/4 oz	1 tbsp	
COOKING SPRAY,NONSTICK	2 oz	1/4cup 1/3tbsp	
BREAD,PITA,WHITE,8-INCH	10-1/2 lbs	50 each	

Method

1. Combine mushrooms, carrots, and zucchini. Add flour; toss lightly to coat vegetables.
2. Place egg substitute, ranch dressing, cheese, onions, dillweed, salt and pepper in mixer bowl. Using a wire whip, blend at low speed 1 minute.
3. Add vegetable mixture; mix at low speed 1 minute or until blended.
4. Lightly spray each steam table pan with non-stick cooking spray. Pour 1 gallon of egg mixture in each lightly sprayed pan.
5. Using a convection oven, bake 45-55 minutes or until eggs are set. CCP: Internal temperature must reach 145 F. or higher for 15 seconds.
6. Cut pita pockets in half. Fill each half with 3/4 cup egg mixture. Serve 1 half pocket. CCP: Hold at 140 F. higher for service.

MONTEREY EGG BAKE

Yield 100   **Portion** 6 Ounces

Calories	Carbohydrates	Protein	Fat	Cholesterol	Sodium	Calcium
181 cal	14 g	19 g	6 g	5 mg	473 mg	166 mg

Ingredient	Weight	Measure	Issue
COOKING SPRAY,NONSTICK	2 oz	1/4 cup 1/3tbsp	
POTATOES,WHITE,FROZEN,SHREDDED,HASHBROWN	9-1/2 lbs	1 gal 1-1/8qts	
TOMATOES,CANNED,DICED,DRAINED	4-1/8 lbs	1 qts 3-1/2cup	
CHEESE,CHEDDAR,LOWFAT,SHREDDED	2-1/4 lbs	2 qts 1 cup	
CHEESE,MONTEREY JACK,REDUCED FAT,SHREDDED	2-1/4 lbs	2 qts 1 cup	
PEPPERS,GREEN,FRESH,CHOPPED	2 lbs	1 qts 2 cup	2-3/8lbs
CORN,FROZEN,WHOLE KERNEL	2 lbs	1 qts 1-1/2cup	
PEPPERS,CHILI,GREEN,CANNED,CHOPPED,DRAINED	12-1/4 oz	2-1/2 cup	
ONIONS,GREEN,FRESH,SLICED	1-1/8 lbs	1 qts 1-3/8cup	1-1/3lbs
SALT	1 oz	1 tbsp	
PEPPER,WHITE,GROUND	3/8 oz	1 tbsp	
EGG SUBSTITUTE,PASTEURIZED	22-1/8 lbs	2 gal 2 qts	
WATER	3 lbs	1 qts 1-3/4cup	
MILK,NONFAT,DRY	3 oz	1-1/4 cup	

Method

1. Lightly spray each steam table pan with non-stick cooking spray.
2. Combine potatoes, tomatoes, cheddar cheese, monterey jack cheese, green pepper, corn, green chilies, green onions, salt, and pepper; mix well.
3. Place 2-1/4 quarts of potato mixture into each steam table pan.
4. Combine egg substitute, water and nonfat dry milk; blend until mixed.
5. Pour 1-3/4 quarts of egg mixture into each steam table pan; stir to combine.
6. Using a convection oven, bake at 325 F. for 55 to 65 minutes. CCP: Internal temperature must reach 145 F. or higher for 15 seconds. Hold for service at 140 F. or higher.

BREAKFAST PIZZA

Yield 100   Portion 1 Piece

Calories	Carbohydrates	Protein	Fat	Cholesterol	Sodium	Calcium
346 cal	44 g	24 g	7 g	12 mg	930 mg	184 mg

Ingredient	Weight	Measure	Issue
COOKING SPRAY,NONSTICK	2 oz	1/4 cup 1/3 tbsp	
DOUGH,PIZZA	16 lbs		
SAUCE,TOMATO,CANNED	4-1/3 lbs	2 qts	
BACON,TURKEY,RAW	3 lbs		
EGG SUBSTITUTE,PASTEURIZED	15-1/2 lbs	1 gal 3 qts	
SALT	1/4 oz	1/8 tsp	
PEPPER,BLACK,GROUND	1/8 oz	1/8 tsp	
CHEESE,CHEDDAR,LOWFAT,SHREDDED	6 lbs	1 gal 2 qts	
POTATOES,WHITE,FROZEN,SHREDDED,HASHBROWN	5-1/2 lbs	2 qts 3-7/8 cup	

Method

1. Lightly spray sheet pans with nonstick cooking spray.
2. Shape dough into 4-4 lb pieces. Let dough rest 15 minutes. Place dough pieces on lightly floured working surface. Roll out each piece to 1/4-inch thickness. Transfer dough to pans, pushing dough slightly up edges of pans. Gently prick dough to prevent bubbling.
3. Using a convection oven, bake 8 minutes at 450 F. on high fan, open vent until crusts are lightly browned.
4. Spread 2 cups tomato sauce evenly over crust in each pan. Set aside for use in Step 7.
5. Cook bacon until lightly browned. Drain on absorbent paper. Finely chop.
6. Add salt and pepper to eggs. Blend well. Scramble eggs until just set. Do not over cook. Pasteurized eggs will be safe at an internal temperature of 145 F. but will not set until they reach 160 F.
7. Distribute 1-1/2 quarts cheese over sauce on each crust.
8. Distribute 1-1/2 quarts scrambled eggs over cheese on each pan.
9. Distribute 1-1/4 cups bacon over eggs on each pan.
10. Distribute 1 quart shredded potatoes over bacon in each pan.
11. Using a convection oven, bake another 8 minutes or until crust is browned and hash browns begin to turn golden brown on high fan, open vent. CCP: Internal temperature must reach 145 F. or higher for 15 seconds.
12. Cut 5 by 5. CCP: Hold for service at 140 F. or higher.

MEXICAN BREAKFAST PIZZA

Yield 100   **Portion** 1 Piece

Calories	Carbohydrates	Protein	Fat	Cholesterol	Sodium	Calcium
364 cal	50 g	26 g	6 g	6 mg	880 mg	189 mg

Ingredient	Weight	Measure	Issue
COOKING SPRAY,NONSTICK	2 oz	1/4 cup 1/3 tbsp	
DOUGH,PIZZA	16 lbs		
SAUCE,SALSA	5-3/8 lbs	2 qts 2 cup	
PEPPER,BLACK,GROUND	1/8 oz	1/8 tsp	
SALT	1/4 oz	1/8 tsp	
EGG SUBSTITUTE,PASTEURIZED	15-1/2 lbs	1 gal 3 qts	
CHEESE,MONTEREY JACK,REDUCED FAT,SHREDDED	6 lbs	1 gal 2 qts	
BEANS,BLACK,CANNED,DRAINED	5-1/3 lbs	2 qts 1-1/2 cup	
POTATOES,WHITE,FROZEN,SHREDDED,HASHBROWN	5-1/2 lbs	2 qts 3-7/8 cup	

Method

1. Lightly spray sheet pans with non-stick cooking spray.
2. Shape dough into four 4 lb pieces. Let dough rest 15 minutes. Place dough pieces on lightly floured working surface. Roll out each piece to 1/4-inch thickness. Transfer dough to pans, pushing dough slightly up edges of pans. Gently prick dough to prevent bubbling.
3. Using a convection oven, bake 8 minutes at 450 F. on high fan, open vent until crusts are lightly browned.
4. Spread 2-1/2 cups salsa evenly over crust in each pan. Set aside for use in Step 6.
5. Add salt and pepper to eggs. Blend well. Scramble eggs until just set. Do not over cook. Pasteurized eggs will be safe at an internal temperature of 145 F. but will not set until they reach 160 F.
6. Distribute 1-1/2 qt cheese over sauce on each crust.
7. Distribute 1-1/2 qt scrambled eggs over cheese on each pan.
8. Distribute 2-1/3 cup beans over eggs on each pan.
9. Distribute 1 quart shredded potatoes over beans in each pan.
10. Bake 8 minutes or until crust is browned and hash browns begin to turn golden brown on high fan, open vent. CCP: Internal temperature must reach 145 F. or higher for 15 seconds.
11. Cut 5 by 5. CCP: Hold for service at 140 F. or higher.

ITALIAN BREAKFAST PIZZA

Yield 100   **Portion** 1 Piece

Calories	Carbohydrates	Protein	Fat	Cholesterol	Sodium	Calcium
388 cal	45 g	27 g	10 g	24 mg	798 mg	281 mg

Ingredient	Weight	Measure	Issue
COOKING SPRAY,NONSTICK	2 oz	1/4 cup 1/3 tbsp	
DOUGH,PIZZA	16 lbs		
SAUCE,PIZZA,CANNED	4-7/8 lbs	2 qts	
SAUSAGE LINK,TURKEY,RAW	3-1/4 lbs		
EGG SUBSTITUTE,PASTEURIZED	15-1/2 lbs	1 gal 3 qts	
BASIL,SWEET,WHOLE,CRUSHED	1/8 oz	1/3 tsp	
PEPPER,BLACK,GROUND	1/8 oz	1/8 tsp	
SALT	1/4 oz	1/8 tsp	

OREGANO,CRUSHED	1/8 oz	1/3 tsp
CHEESE,MOZZARELLA,PART SKIM,SHREDDED	6 lbs	1 gal 2 qts
POTATOES,WHITE,FROZEN,SHREDDED,HASHBROWN	5-1/2 lbs	2 qts 3-7/8 cup

Method
1. Lightly spray sheet pans with nonstick cooking spray.
2. Shape dough into four 4 lb pieces. Let dough rest 15 minutes. Place dough pieces on lightly floured working surface. Roll out each piece to 1/4-inch thickness. Transfer dough to pans, pushing dough slightly up edges of pans. Gently prick dough to prevent bubbling.
3. Using a convection oven, bake 8 minutes at 450 F. on high fan, open vent until crusts are lightly browned.
4. Spread 2 cups pizza sauce evenly over crust in each pan. Set aside for use in Step 7.
5. Cook sausage until lightly browned. Drain on absorbent paper. Finely chop.
6. Add salt, pepper, oregano and basil to eggs. Blend well. Scramble eggs until just set. Do not overcook. Pasteurized eggs will be safe at an internal temperature of 145 F. but will not set until they reach 160 F.
7. Distribute 1-1/2 quart cheese over pizza sauce on each crust.
8. Distribute 1-1/2 quart scrambled eggs over cheese on each pan.
9. Distribute 1-3/4 cups sausage over scrambled eggs on each pan.
10. Distribute 1 quart shredded potatoes over sausage in each pan.
11. Using a convection oven, bake 8 minutes or until crust is browned and hash browns begin to turn golden brown on high fan, open vent. CCP: Internal temperature must reach 145 F. or higher for 15 seconds.
12. Cut 5 by 5. CCP: Hold for service at 140 F. or higher.

MACARONI AND CHEESE, FROZEN

Yield 100   **Portion** 5 Ounces

Calories	Carbohydrates	Protein	Fat	Cholesterol	Sodium	Calcium
249 cal	22 g	13 g	12 g	14 mg	1103 mg	123 mg

Ingredient	Weight	Measure	Issue
COOKING SPRAY,NONSTICK	2 oz	1/4 cup 1/3 tbsp	
MACARONI AND CHEESE,FROZEN	48 lbs	5 gal 2-5/8 qts	
CHEESE,CHEDDAR,SHREDDED	1 lbs	1 qts	

Method
1. Preheat convection oven to 300 F. with fan on.
2. Spray steam table pans with non-stick cooking spray.
3. Remove top from frozen macaroni and cheese. Remove contents from original container and place right side up into steam table pans. Cover.
4. Cook according to times and temperatures contained in manufacturer's instructions on package. Usual cooking time is as follows: Cook 40 minutes covered. Remove cover and top with grated cheese. Cook additional 10 minutes in preheated convection oven at 300 F.
5. Remove from oven. CCP: Hold for service at 140 F. or higher.

BREAKFAST BURRITO, FROZEN

Yield 100   **Portion** 4 Ounces

Calories	Carbohydrates	Protein	Fat	Cholesterol	Sodium	Calcium
247 cal	32 g	11 g	8 g	220 mg	464 mg	0 mg

Ingredient	Weight	Measure	Issue
COOKING SPRAY,NONSTICK	2 oz	1/4 cup 1/3 tbsp	
BREAKFAST BURRITO,FROZEN	25 lbs		

Method

1. Spray steam table pans with non-stick cooking spray.
2. Place 25 burritos in each steam table pan. Heat according to instructions on package. CCP: Hold for service at 140 F. or higher.

GUIDELINES FOR SUCCESSFUL CAKE BAKING

A. Read through entire recipe.

B. Assemble all utensils and baking pans.
    1. Preparation of Cake Pans:
        (a) Do not use warped or bent baking pans. Use only lightweight sheet pans (weighing about 4 lb) designed for baking. Shiny metal pans are best for baking cakes.
        (b) Prepare pans for baking. If cakes are to be served directly from pans, grease pans with shortening and dust with flour or spread with Pan Coating (See Note). If cakes are to be removed from pans and served as layer cakes, grease and line pans with paper to ensure easy removal.

C. Check to make sure oven racks are level and in proper position for baking. Set oven thermostat to temperature specified in recipe.

D. Assemble all ingredients. Use exact ingredients specified in recipe.
    1. Preparation and Mixing of Ingredients:
        (a) The temperature of ingredients is very important in cake preparation. Shortening should be workable, neither too cold nor warm enough to liquefy. In general, all ingredients should be at room temperature unless recipe specifies otherwise. Water should be cool, and eggs should be removed from refrigeration 30 minutes before using. Eggs are easier to separate when cold but beat to greater volume when at room temperature.
        (b) Weigh or measure all ingredients accurately. Follow the mixing procedure stated on the recipe card. DO NOT overbeat or underbeat. The correct length of time for beating at each stage indicated on the recipe card should be followed very closely.
        (c) Whenever instructions are to add dry and liquid ingredients alternately, begin and end with dry ingredients.
    2. Panning Batter:
        (a) Pour the amount of batter specified in the recipe into prepared baking pans. (See Recipe No. G-G-4.)
        (b) Spread batter evenly using a spatula.
        (c) Batter-filled baking pans should be placed immediately into a preheated oven.
    3. Baking:
        (a) Space baking pans evenly in oven to allow heat to circulate around each pan. Pans SHOULD NOT touch each other or sides of oven.
        (b) To test for doneness, touch top of cake near the center. If indentation remains, the cake is not done and should be baked 3 to 5 minutes longer and tested again, or insert a toothpick near center. If clean when removed, cake is done.
        (c) When cakes are done, they should be lightly browned and beginning to shrink from sides of pans.
    4. Cooling and Removing from Pans:
        (a) Remove baking pans from oven; place on racks away from drafts to cool.
        (b) Cool cake in pans 5 to 10 minutes before removing from pans. Remove any paper liners immediately. Turn cakes right side up to cool.
        (c) Sheet cakes may be cooled in pans and frosted, or turned out onto inverted baking pans to cool before frosting.
        (d) Allow cakes to cool thoroughly before frosting. (See Recipe No. G-G-6.)

NOTE: Use 2 lb (41/2 cups) shortening and 1 lb (1 qt) general purpose flour, sifted. Cream shortening and flour at medium speed in mixer bowl until smooth. (In cold weather, add 2 tbsp salad oil to the flour-shortening mixture to aid in spreading.)

BATTER CAKES

CHARACTERISTICS OF GOOD QUALITY

COLOR . . . . Uniform color, light golden brown crust for white or yellow cake. Crusts of dark cakes may be slightly darker than inside.

SHAPE AND SIZE . . . Cakes should be slightly rounded on top with even height at sides. Cakes should come to slightly above top of layer or sheet pans.

CRUST . . . . Thin tender crust with slight sheen. Flat bubbles may appear on surface and be slightly darker.

TEXTURE . . . . Breaks easily but does not crumble. Moist but not gummy. Light, velvety, fine to medium walled cells.

FLAVOR . . . . Determined by type of cake. Sweet, no off-flavor.

CAUSES FOR POOR QUALITY

OUTSIDE APPEARANCE

Peaks . . . . Oven too hot. Not enough liquid. Batter overmixed. Pans too close together or too close to sides of oven. Too much flour.

Sag in center . . Underbaked. Oven too cool. Too much batter in pan. Too much sugar, shortening, or leavening. Not enough eggs or flour.

COLOR

Too Dark . . . . . Oven too hot. Too much sugar or milk solids.

Too Light . . . . .Not enough batter in pan. Overmixed or undermixed. Underbaked.

CRUST

Too Thick. . . . .Oven too hot. Overbaked. Pan too deep. Batter overmixed.

Cracked. . . . . . Too much flour. Oven too hot. Overmixed.

Sticky. . . . . Underbaked. High humidity. Cake placed in pastry cabinet, refrigerator, or freezer while still warm.

Tough. . . . . Overmixed. Oven too cool. Too much flour. Not enough shortening or sugar.

Hard. . . . . Overbaked. Pan too deep.

INSIDE APPEARANCE

Coarse Grain . .Overmixed or undermixed. Oven too cool. Too much leavening.

Tunnels . . . . . . Undermixed or overmixed. Oven too hot.

TEXTURE

Too Dry . . . . . . Overbaked. Not enough liquid or shortening. Too much flour or leavening. Omission of eggs.

Crumbly . . . . . . Not enough shortening. Too much shortening. Too much leavening. Oven too cool. Undermixed or overmixed. Not enough eggs.

Tough . . . . .Overmixed. Too much or wrong type of flour. Not enough shortening or sugar. Oven too hot or too cool.

Too Tender . . . Batter undermixed.

Too Heavy . . . .Too much shortening. Underbaked.

EXCESSIVE SHRINKAGE

Overmixed. Too much grease in pan. Overbaked. Not enough batter in pan.

OFF FLAVOR . . . . . . .Ingredients not measured accurately. Rancid pan grease. Dirty pan.

HOLLOW SPOT ON BOTTOM

Not enough liquid. Too much flour. Excess bottom heat in oven. Pan not properly prepared.

UNEVENLY BAKED . Undermixed or overmixed. Uneven or dented pan. Not panned properly. Hot or cold spots in oven. Low fan not used in convection ovens.

FALLS DURING BAKING
        Overmixed. Jarred during baking. Oven too cool.
LACKS VOLUME. . . . .Not enough leavening. Undermixed or overmixed. Not enough batter in pan. Oven
        too hot or too cool.
CAKE STICKS TO PAN
        Pan not properly prepared. Oven too cool. Cake left in pan too long. Too much
        liquid. Too much sugar.

GUIDELINES FOR USING CAKE MIXES

1. Read and follow instructions on container.
2. Before starting to mix cake:
    (a) Assemble utensils and prepare baking pans.
    (b) Check to make sure oven racks are level and in proper position for baking. Set oven thermostat to
        temperature specified on container.
    (c) If making a variation of the basic mix, weigh or measure the ingredients to be added to the basic
        mix.
3. Follow the instructions on the container for mixing the cake. DO NOT UNDERMIX. If using a beater,
    time the beating precisely and use the speeds indicated. If beating by hand, use a vigorous beating
    stroke.
4. Follow instructions on the container for baking time. Test for doneness according to Guidelines for
    Successful Cake Baking, Recipe No. G-G-1.
5. Cool and then frost according to Guidelines for Frosting Cakes, Recipe No. G-G-6.
6. If making a variation of a cake mix:
    (a) Drain fruit very well before adding to the cake mix.
    (b) Chop fruits and nuts finely.
    (c) If fruit juice is to be substituted for part of the liquid, add the fruit juice as part of the last addition of
        the liquid.

GUIDELINES FOR SCALING CAKE BATTER

The size baking pan used in developing and standardizing cake recipes is included in the upper left corner
of each recipe card. Other pan sizes may be used.
When using:

9-inch Layer Pan	Pour 18 to 20 oz batter into each greased and floured layer pan. Bake 20 to 25 minutes. For 100 portions: Use 12 layer pans (6–2-layer cakes); cut 16 portions per cake.
16-inch Square Sheet Pan	Pour 4 to 6 lb batter into each greased and floured pan. Bake as directed on recipe card. For 100 portions: Use 3 pans; cut each cake 6 by 6.
16 by 19-inch Baking Pan range)	Pour 4 to 6 lb batter into each greased and floured pan. Bake as (field directed on recipe card. For 100 portions: Use 3 pans; cut each cake 6 by 6.
Loaf Pans (16 by 41/2 by 41/8)	Pour about 2 qt batter into each greased and floured pan. Bake 20 to 25 minutes. For 100 portions: Use 4 pans; cut 25 slices per pan.
Cupcakes	Fill each greased and floured or paper lined cup half full with batter. Bake 20 to 25 minutes. A 100-portion cake recipe will yield 13 dozen cupcakes.

GUIDELINES FOR CUTTING CAKES

There is a satisfactory method of cutting each kind of cake. The factors to keep in mind are the size and number of servings and the cutting utensil to be used. The size and number of servings depend upon the size and number of layers in the cake. A knife with a sharp straight-edged, thin blade is most suitable for cutting batter cakes. To make a clean cut, and to keep the knife blade free from frosting and cake crumbs, dip the blade into warm water before cutting each portion.

The following diagrams illustrate methods of cutting cakes of various sizes and shapes. The average number of servings per cake are given.

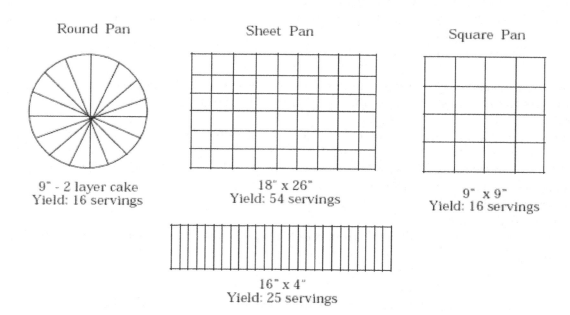

Round Pan
9" - 2 layer cake
Yield: 16 servings

Sheet Pan
18" x 26"
Yield: 54 servings

Square Pan
9" x 9"
Yield: 16 servings

16" x 4"
Yield: 25 servings

GUIDELINES FOR PREPARING FROSTINGS AND FROSTING CAKES

FROSTINGS

1. Frostings should not be so strongly flavored that they detract from the flavor of the cake. Frostings should complement the flavor of the cake.
2. If a colored frosting is desired, mix the food coloring with a small amount of the frosting and then add the colored frosting to the larger amount until the desired color is obtained. Harsh strong colors should never be used except in small amounts for some specific decoration.
3. A butter cream frosting which is too thick can be thinned with a little water or milk before it is used. Care must be taken to add the liquid in very small amounts. Butter cream frosting which is too thin can be thickened by the addition of more powdered sugar. The additional powdered sugar should be mixed into the frosting until the desired consistency is reached.

FROSTING CAKES

1. Remove loose crumbs and, if necessary, trim the cake. Use a sharp knife to remove any hard or jagged edges.
2. Form layer cakes using two 9-inch layers, or a sheet cake cut in half to form 2 layers, or two sheet cakes put together.
3. When frosting a layer cake, invert the bottom layer with the top side down. Place the thicker layer on the bottom. Use a spatula to spread a thin layer of frosting or filling evenly over bottom layer. (Top layer will slip if too much frosting or filling is used). Cover the top layer, top side up. Starting from the center and working outward, spread frosting on the top of the cake; then frost the sides.

4. When frosting cupcakes, spread the specified amount of frosting on the top of the cupcake. DO NOT frost the side.

HIGH ALTITUDE BAKING

Since atmospheric pressure decreases as altitude increases, the requirement for baking soda also decreases. Bakery mixes are formulated for use at sea level air pressure. A reduction in the soda content of mixes at higher altitudes is easily accomplished with mixes containing a separate soda packet. If the soda packet is not labeled with instructions for the amount of soda to be used at different altitudes, use the following as a guide:

2000 feet–use 80% (4/5 of package)
4000 feet–use 66% (2/3 of package)
6000 feet–use 50% (1/2 of package)
8000 feet–use 33% (1/3 of package)

When preparing cakes, hot breads, and drop cookies from basic ingredients at high altitudes, quantities of leavening agents may be adjusted as specified in the table on the back of this card.

Cakes have a tendency to stick to pans at higher altitudes; therefore the pans should be greased and dusted more heavily than those used at sea level.

Oven temperatures should be increased 25°F. at elevations of 3500 feet or more. The baking time is generally the same as at sea level; however, care should be taken to avoid overbaking since evaporation rate increases at higher altitudes.

Baking powder or baking soda in recipes for cakes, hot breads, and drop cookies prepared at higher altitudes should decreased as shown on back of this card.

Amount Basic Recipe	Amounts to be Used at Higher Altitudes			
	2000 feet	4000 feet	6000 feet	8000 feet
1 tbsp	2-1/2 tsp	2 tsp	1-2/3 tsp	1 tsp
1-2/3 tbsp	1-2/3 tbsp	1-1/3 tbsp	1 tbsp	2 tsp
2 tbsp	1-2/3 tbsp	1-1/3 tbsp	3-1/3 tsp	2-1/2 tsp
2-1/3 tbsp	2 tbsp	1-2/3 tbsp	1-1/3 tbsp	2-2/3 tsp
3-2/3 tbsp	3 tbsp	2-2/3 tbsp	2 tbsp	1-1/3 tbsp
1/4 cup	3-1/3 tbsp	2-2/3 tbsp	2-1/3 tbsp	1-2/3 tbsp
4-2/3 tbsp	3-2/3 tbsp	3 tbsp	2-2/3 tbsp	1-2/3 tbsp
5-2/3 tbsp	4-2/3 tbsp	3-2/3 tbsp	3 tbsp	2-1/3 tbsp
6-2/3 tbsp	5-2/3 tbsp	4-2/3 tbsp	3-2/3 tbsp	2-2/3 tbsp
1/2 cup	6-2/3 tbsp	5-2/3 tbsp	4-1/3 tbsp	3-1/3 tbsp
8-2/3 tbsp	7-1/3 tbsp	6 tbsp	4-2/3 tbsp	3-1/3 tbsp
9 tbsp	7-2/3 tbsp	6-1/3 tbsp	5 tbsp	3-2/3 tbsp
11 tbsp	9-1/3 tbsp	7-2/3 tbsp	6 tbsp	4-1/3 tbsp
3/4 cup	5/8 cup	1/3 cup	6-2/3 tbsp	5 tbsp
1 cup	7/8 cup	11-1/3 tbsp	8-2/3 tbsp	6-1/3 tbsp
1-1/2 cups	1-1/4 cups	1 cup	13-1/3 tbsp	5/8 cup

APPLESAUCE CAKE

Yield 100   Portion 1 Piece

Calories	Carbohydrates	Protein	Fat	Cholesterol	Sodium	Calcium
304 cal	47 g	3 g	12 g	34 mg	172 mg	43 mg

Ingredient	Weight	Measure	Issue
FLOUR,WHEAT,GENERAL PURPOSE	3-5/8 lbs	3 qts 1 cup	
BAKING POWDER	1-3/4 oz	1/4 cup	
BAKING SODA	3/4 oz	1 tbsp	
CINNAMON,GROUND	1/2 oz	2 tbsp	
CLOVES,GROUND	1/4 oz	1 tbsp	
SALT	1/4 oz	1/8 tsp	
SUGAR,GRANULATED	2-2/3 lbs	1 qts 2 cup	
RAISINS	1-1/2 lbs	1 qts 1/2 cup	
APPLESAUCE,CANNED,UNSWEETENED	3-1/4 lbs	1 qts 2 cup	
SHORTENING	1-1/2 lbs	3-3/8 cup	
EGGS,WHOLE,FROZEN	1-3/4 lbs	3-1/4 cup	
COOKING SPRAY,NONSTICK	2 oz	1/4 cup 1/3 tbsp	

Method

1. Sift together flour, baking powder, baking soda, cinnamon, cloves, salt and sugar into mixer bowl.
2. Add raisins, applesauce and shortening to dry ingredients. Beat at low speed 1 minute, then at medium speed 2 minutes. Scrape down bowl.
3. Add eggs slowly to mixture while beating at low speed about 1 minute. Scrape down bowl. Beat at medium speed 3 minutes.

4. Lightly spray each pan with non-stick cooking spray. Pour 3-3/4 quarts batter into each sprayed and floured pan.
5. Using a convection oven, bake in 325 F. oven for 20 to 25 minutes or until done on high fan, open vent.
6. Cool; frost if desired. Cut 6 by 9.

CHOCOLATE MACAROON CAKE (CAKE MIX)

Yield 100   **Portion** 1 Piece

Calories	Carbohydrates	Protein	Fat	Cholesterol	Sodium	Calcium
332 cal	51 g	4 g	13 g	30 mg	496 mg	109 mg

Ingredient	Weight	Measure	Issue
CAKE MIX,DEVILS FOOD	8-3/4 lbs		
OIL,SALAD	1 lbs	2-1/8 cup	
WATER	5-1/4 lbs	2 qts 2 cup	
EGGS,WHOLE,FROZEN	1-1/4 lbs	2-1/4 cup	
DESSERT POWDER,PUDDING,INSTANT,CHOCOLATE	1-1/2 lbs	4 cup	
COOKING SPRAY,NONSTICK	2 oz	1/4 cup 1/3 tbsp	
CAKE MIX,WHITE	2-1/2 lbs	1 qts 3-3/8 cup	
COCONUT,PREPARED,SWEETENED FLAKES	9 oz	2-3/4 cup	
WATER	1 lbs	2 cup	
VANILLA GLAZE		2-3/4 cup	

Method
1. Place Devil's Food Cake Mix, salad oil, water, eggs and dessert powder in mixer bowl. Blend at low speed until moistened, about 2 minutes. Scrape down bowl.
2. Beat at medium speed 5 to 8 minutes.
3. Pour 2 cups batter into each greased and floured pan. Set aside for use in Step 6.
4. Place White Cake Mix, coconut, and water in mixer bowl. Blend at low speed until moistened. Scrape down bowl.
5. Beat at low speed 1 minute. DO NOT OVERMIX.
6. Pour about 1 quart batter over macaroon mixture covering it completely.
7. Using a convection oven, bake 1 hour 15 minutes at 325 F. or until done on low fan, closed vent.
8. Remove from oven; cool 15 to 20 minutes; remove from pans.
9. Prepare 1 recipe of Vanilla Glaze (Recipe No. D 046 00). Drizzle 1 cup glaze over each cake.
10. Cut 20 slices per loaf.

CHOCOLATE CHIP FUDGE FROSTING

Yield 100   **Portion** 2-1/2 Quarts

Calories	Carbohydrates	Protein	Fat	Cholesterol	Sodium	Calcium
13516 cal	2295 g	89 g	496 g	728 mg	5336 mg	2634 mg

Ingredient	Weight	Measure	Issue
CHOCOLATE,COOKING CHIPS,SEMISWEET	2-1/4 lbs	1 qts 2 cup	
BUTTER	8 oz	1 cup	
SUGAR,POWDERED,SIFTED	3-2/3 lbs	3 qts 2 cup	
MILK,NONFAT,DRY	1-3/4 oz	3/4 cup	

| SALT | 1/4 oz | 1/8 tsp |
| WATER,WARM | 14-5/8 oz | 1-3/4 cup |

Method
1. Melt chocolate chips and butter or margarine over very low heat. Place in mixer bowl.
2. Sift together powdered sugar, milk, and salt; add to chocolate mixture.
3. Blend in just enough water to obtain spreading consistency. Mix at medium speed 3 minutes or until smooth.
4. Spread immediately on cool cakes.

Notes
1. In Step 1, chocolate-flavored baking chips may be substituted for semi-sweet chocolate chips.
2. For 9-inch, 2-layer cakes: Spread about 1-3/4 cups frosting per cake.
3. For cupcakes: Spread about 1 tablespoon of frosting on each cupcake.

VANILLA FROSTING (ICING MIX, VANILLA, POWDERED)

Yield 1 Portion   **Portion** 2-1/2 Quarts

Calories	Carbohydrates	Protein	Fat	Cholesterol	Sodium	Calcium
7904 cal	1808 g	6 g	94 g	0 mg	261 mg	65 mg

Ingredient	Weight	Measure	Issue
ICING MIX,POWDER,VANILLA	4-1/4 lbs		
WATER,WARM	12-1/2 oz	1-1/2 cup	

Method
1. Place icing mix in mixer bowl. Add hot water (120 F.) gradually while mixing at low speed. Scrape down bowl; beat at high speed 3 minutes or until thick and smooth.
2. Spread on cooled cakes.

ORANGE FROSTING (ICING MIX, VANILLA, POWDERED)

Yield 1 Portion   **Portion** 2-1/2 Quarts

Calories	Carbohydrates	Protein	Fat	Cholesterol	Sodium	Calcium
9135 cal	2122 g	25 g	97 g	0 mg	293 mg	1910 mg

Ingredient	Weight	Measure	Issue
ICING MIX,POWDER,VANILLA	4-1/4 lbs		
JUICE,ORANGE	11 oz	1-1/4 cup	
ORANGE,RIND,GRATED	2-1/2 lbs	2 qts 3-3/4 cup	
WATER,WARM	2-1/8 oz	1/4 cup 1/3 tbsp	

Method
1. Place icing mix in mixer bowl. Add orange juice, rind and hot water (120 F.) gradually while mixing at low speed. Scrape down bowl; beat at high speed 3 minutes or until thick and smooth.
2. Spread on cooled cakes.

BANANA CAKE (CAKE MIX)

Yield 100   **Portion** 1 Piece

Calories	Carbohydrates	Protein	Fat	Cholesterol	Sodium	Calcium
216 cal	40 g	3 g	5 g	11 mg	291 mg	26 mg

Ingredient	Weight	Measure	Issue
BANANA,FRESH	3-3/4 lbs		5-3/4 lbs
CAKE MIX,YELLOW	10 lbs		
OIL,SALAD	7-2/3 oz	1 cup	
WATER	1 lbs	2 cup	
WATER	1 lbs	2 cup	
COOKING SPRAY,NONSTICK	2 oz	1/4cup 1/3tbsp	

Method
1. Beat bananas in mixer bowl at high speed about 1 minute until smooth.
2. Add mix, contents of both soda pouches, salad oil and water to bananas. Beat at low speed 3 minutes. Scrape down bowl.
3. Add water gradually while mixing at low speed about 2 minute. Scrape down bowl. Beat at medium speed 3 minutes.
4. Lightly spray each pan with non-stick cooking spray. Pour 4-1/4 quarts of batter into each sprayed and floured pan.
5. Using a convection oven, bake at 300 F. 30 to 35 minutes or until done on low fan, open vent.
6. Cool; frost if desired.

BANANA CAKE (BANANA CAKE MIX)

Yield 100   **Portion** 1 Piece

Calories	Carbohydrates	Protein	Fat	Cholesterol	Sodium	Calcium
289 cal	50 g	3 g	9 g	0 mg	304 mg	31 mg

Ingredient	Weight	Measure	Issue
CAKE MIX,BANANA	10 lbs	1 gal 3-3/8 qts	

Method
1. Prepare mix according to instructions on container. Frost if desired.

DECORATOR'S FROSTING

Yield 100   **Portion** 1 Quart

Calories	Carbohydrates	Protein	Fat	Cholesterol	Sodium	Calcium
4494 cal	837 g	0 g	138 g	0 mg	12 mg	11 mg

Ingredient	Weight	Measure	Issue
SUGAR,POWDERED,SIFTED	1-7/8 lbs	1 qts 3 cup	
SHORTENING	4-7/8 oz	1/2cup 2-2/3tbsp	
WATER	3-1/8 oz	1/4cup 2-1/3tbsp	
EXTRACT,VANILLA	1/4 oz	1/4 tsp	

Method
1. Cream sugar and shortening in mixer bowl 1 minute at low speed. Scrape down bowl; continue beating at medium speed 2
2. Add water and vanilla slowly to creamed mixture while beating at low speed. Scrape down bowl; continue beating at medium speed until smooth.

Notes
1. Additional water may be added to reach desired consistency.
2. This icing may be used in a pastry bag for writing and all other decorative work for cakes.
3. In Step 2, for a tinted frosting, a small amount of food coloring paste may be used.

FLORIDA LEMON CAKE

Yield 100   **Portion** 1 Piece

Calories	Carbohydrates	Protein	Fat	Cholesterol	Sodium	Calcium
417 cal	52 g	4 g	22 g	53 mg	313 mg	32 mg

Ingredient	Weight	Measure	Issue
CAKE MIX,YELLOW	10 lbs		
PIE FILLING,LEMON,PREPARED	1-1/3 lbs	2-5/8 cup	
EGGS,WHOLE,FROZEN	2 lbs	3-3/4 cup	
OIL,SALAD	3-7/8 lbs	2 qts	
WATER	4-1/8 lbs	2 qts	
FLAVORING,LEMON	1-5/8 oz	3 tbsp	
COOKING SPRAY,NONSTICK	2 oz	1/4cup 1/3tbsp	
SUGAR,POWDERED,SIFTED	3-1/8 lbs	3 qts	
BUTTER,SOFTENED	3 oz	1/4cup 2-1/3tbsp	
WATER,BOILING	12-1/2 oz	1-1/2 cup	
FLAVORING,LEMON	1/2 oz	1 tbsp	

Method
1. Place cake mix and pie filling mix in mixer bowl. Blend at low speed 1 minute.
2. Add eggs; blend at low speed 1 minute. Add salad oil gradually while mixing at low speed 2 minutes. Add water and lemon flavoring while mixing; blend 3 minutes at low speed. Scrape down bowl.
3. Lightly spray each pan with non-stick cooking spray. Pour about 1-1/4 gallons batter into each sprayed and floured pan.
4. Using a convection oven, bake at 300 F. 35 to 40 minutes on low fan, open vent or until done.
5. While cake is still warm, prick entire surface with a fork.
6. Combine sugar, butter or margarine, boiling water and lemon flavoring. Mix until smooth.
7. Drizzle 2-3/4 cup glaze over each cake.
8. Cut 6 by 9.

Notes
1. In Step 3, loaf type pans may be used for sheet pans. Pour 2 quarts batter into each pan. Using a convection oven bake at 300 F. for 1 hour 15 minutes on low fan, open vent. Remove cakes from pans while still warm; prick surface with fork. Pour 1 cup glaze over each pan. Cut 20 slices per pan.

CHOCOLATE FROSTING (ICING MIX, CHOCOLATE POWDERED)

Yield 100   **Portion** 2-1/2 Quarts

Calories	Carbohydrates	Protein	Fat	Cholesterol	Sodium	Calcium
7058 cal	1669 g	24 g	94 g	0 mg	1393 mg	209 mg

Ingredient	Weight	Measure	Issue
WATER,WARM	1 lbs	2 cup	
ICING MIX,POWDER,CHOCOLATE	4 lbs		

Method
1. Place icing mix in mixer bowl. Add hot water (120 F.) gradually while mixing at low speed. Scrape down bowl; beat at high speed 3 minutes or until thick and smooth.
2. Spread on cooled cakes.

CHOC CHIP FROSTING (ICING MIX, CHOCOLATE POWDERED)

Yield 100   **Portion** 2-1/2 Quarts

Calories	Carbohydrates	Protein	Fat	Cholesterol	Sodium	Calcium
8803 cal	1871 g	47 g	199 g	75 mg	1672 mg	859 mg

Ingredient	Weight	Measure	Issue
WATER,WARM	1 lbs	2 cup	
CHOCOLATE,COOKING CHIPS,SEMISWEET	12 oz	2 cup	
ICING MIX,POWDER,CHOCOLATE	4 lbs		

Method
1. Place icing mix in mixer bowl with chocolate chips. Add hot water (120 F.) gradually while mixing at low speed. Scrape down bowl; beat at high speed 3 minutes or until thick and smooth.
2. Spread on cooled cakes.

CHOC COCONUT FROST (ICING MIX, CHOCOLATE POWDERED)

Yield 100   **Portion** 2-1/2 Quarts

Calories	Carbohydrates	Protein	Fat	Cholesterol	Sodium	Calcium
8339 cal	1791 g	31 g	185 g	0 mg	2063 mg	247 mg

Ingredient	Weight	Measure	Issue
WATER,WARM	1 lbs	2 cup	
COCONUT,PREPARED,SWEETENED FLAKES	9 oz	2-3/4 cup	
ICING MIX,POWDER,CHOCOLATE	4 lbs		

Method
1. Place icing mix in mixer bowl with coconut. Add hot water (120 F.) gradually while mixing at low speed. Scrape downbowl; beat at high speed 3 minutes or until thick and smooth.
2. Spread on cooled cakes.

MOCHA CREAM FROST (ICING MIX, CHOCOLATE POWDERED)

Yield 100   **Portion** 2-1/2 Quarts

Calories	Carbohydrates	Protein	Fat	Cholesterol	Sodium	Calcium
7084 cal	1674 g	25 g	94 g	0 mg	1397 mg	224 mg

Ingredient	Weight	Measure	Issue
WATER,WARM	1 lbs	2 cup	
COFFEE,INSTANT,FREEZE DRIED	3/8 oz	2 tbsp	
ICING MIX,POWDER,CHOCOLATE	4 lbs		

Method
1. Place icing mix in mixer bowl. Add hot water (120 F.) gradually while mixing at low speed and add coffee. Scrape down bowl; beat at high speed 3 minutes or until thick and smooth.
2. Spread on cooled cakes.

YELLOW CAKE (MIX)

Yield 100   **Portion** 1 Piece

Calories	Carbohydrates	Protein	Fat	Cholesterol	Sodium	Calcium
331 cal	51 g	2 g	14 g	1 mg	318 mg	62 mg

Ingredient	Weight	Measure	Issue
CAKE MIX,YELLOW	10 lbs		

Method
1. Prepare mix according to instructions on container.
2. Cool; frost if desired

ALMOND CAKE (YELLOW MIX)

Yield 100   **Portion** 1 Piece

Calories	Carbohydrates	Protein	Fat	Cholesterol	Sodium	Calcium
333 cal	51 g	2 g	14 g	1 mg	318 mg	62 mg

Ingredient	Weight	Measure	Issue
CAKE MIX,YELLOW	10 lbs		
FLAVORING,ALMOND	1-7/8 oz	1/4 cup 1/3 tbsp	

Method
1. Prepare mix according to instructions on container.
2. Cool; frost if desired.

BLACK WALNUT CAKE (YELLOW MIX)

Yield 100   **Portion** 1 Piece

Calories	Carbohydrates	Protein	Fat	Cholesterol	Sodium	Calcium
333 cal	51 g	2 g	14 g	1 mg	318 mg	62 mg

Ingredient	Weight	Measure	Issue
CAKE MIX,YELLOW	10 lbs		
FLAVORING,BLACK WALNUT	1-7/8 oz	1/4 cup 1/3 tbsp	

Method
1. Prepare mix according to instructions on container.
2. Cool; frost if desired.

LEMON CAKE (YELLOW MIX)

Yield 100   Portion 1 Piece

Calories	Carbohydrates	Protein	Fat	Cholesterol	Sodium	Calcium
309 cal	59 g	3 g	7 g	24 mg	363 mg	31 mg

Ingredient	Weight	Measure	Issue
CAKE MIX,YELLOW	10 lbs		
FLAVORING,LEMON	2-1/8 oz	1/4 cup 1/3 tbsp	
LEMON BUTTER CREAM FROSTING		2 qts 3 cup	

Method
1. Prepare mix according to instructions on container.
2. Cool, frost if desired.

MAPLE NUT CAKE (YELLOW MIX)

Yield 100   Portion 1 Piece

Calories	Carbohydrates	Protein	Fat	Cholesterol	Sodium	Calcium
344 cal	60 g	4 g	10 g	24 mg	363 mg	35 mg

Ingredient	Weight	Measure	Issue
CAKE MIX,YELLOW	10 lbs		
NUTS,UNSALTED,CHOPPED,COARSELY	1-1/4 lbs	1 qts	
FLAVORING,MAPLE	1-7/8 oz	1/4 cup 1/3 tbsp	
BUTTER CREAM FROSTING		2 qts 3 cup	

Method
1. Prepare mix according to instructions on container.
2. Cool; frost if desired.

MARBLE CAKE (MIX)

Yield 100   Portion 1 Piece

Calories	Carbohydrates	Protein	Fat	Cholesterol	Sodium	Calcium
327 cal	49 g	3 g	14 g	4 mg	347 mg	88 mg

Ingredient	Weight	Measure	Issue
CAKE MIX,YELLOW	5 lbs		
CAKE MIX,DEVILS FOOD	5 lbs		

Method
1. Prepare mix according to instructions on container.
2. Cool; frost if desired.

ORANGE CAKE (YELLOW MIX)

Yield 100   Portion 1 Piece

Calories	Carbohydrates	Protein	Fat	Cholesterol	Sodium	Calcium
333 cal	51 g	2 g	14 g	1 mg	318 mg	62 mg

Ingredient	Weight	Measure	Issue
CAKE MIX,YELLOW	10 lbs		
FLAVORING,ORANGE	1-7/8 oz	1/4 cup 1/3 tbsp	

Method
1. Prepare mix according to instructions on container.
2. Cool; frost if desired.

EASY CHOCOLATE CAKE

Yield 100   Portion 1 Piece

Calories	Carbohydrates	Protein	Fat	Cholesterol	Sodium	Calcium
345 cal	56 g	3 g	13 g	0 mg	315 mg	9 mg

Ingredient	Weight	Measure	Issue
FLOUR,WHEAT,GENERAL PURPOSE	5 lbs	1gal 1/2qts	
SUGAR,GRANULATED	4-3/4 lbs	2qts 2-3/4cup	
COCOA	9-7/8 oz	3-1/4 cup	
BAKING SODA	2-1/4 oz	1/4cup 1tbsp	
SALT	1 oz	1 tbsp	
OIL,SALAD	1-3/4 lbs	3-3/4 cup	
VINEGAR,DISTILLED	5-5/8 oz	1/2cup 2-2/3tbsp	
EXTRACT,VANILLA	1-3/8 oz	3 tbsp	
WATER	5-1/4 lbs	2 qts 2 cup	
COOKING SPRAY,NONSTICK	2 oz	1/4cup 1/3tbsp	

Method
1. Sift together flour, sugar, cocoa, baking soda, and salt into mixer bowl.
2. Combine salad oil, vinegar and vanilla; add to dry ingredients while mixing at low speed 2 minutes.
3. Gradually add water while mixing at low speed 1 minute; scrape down bowl.
4. Mix at medium speed 2 minutes or until ingredients are well blended.
5. Lightly spray each pan with non-stick cooking spray. Pour about 3-1/2 quarts into each sprayed sheet pan.
6. Using a convection oven, bake at 325 F. for 25 minutes or until done on low fan, open vent.
7. Cool; frost if desired. Cut 6 by 9.

DEVIL'S FOOD CAKE

Yield 100   **Portion** 1 Piece

Calories	Carbohydrates	Protein	Fat	Cholesterol	Sodium	Calcium
329 cal	49 g	4 g	14 g	49 mg	333 mg	32 mg

Ingredient	Weight	Measure	Issue
FLOUR,WHEAT,GENERAL PURPOSE	2-3/4 lbs	2 qts 2 cup	
SUGAR,GRANULATED	4-3/8 lbs	2 qts 2 cup	
SALT	1-1/2 oz	2-1/3 tbsp	
BAKING SODA	1-5/8 oz	3-1/3 tbsp	
COCOA	1-1/4 lbs	1 qts 2-1/2 cup	
MILK,NONFAT,DRY	4-1/4 oz	1-3/4 cup	
SHORTENING	1-3/4 lbs	1 qts	
WATER	2-5/8 lbs	1 qts 1 cup	
EGGS,WHOLE,FROZEN	2-1/2 lbs	1 qts 5/8 cup	
WATER	1-1/3 lbs	2-1/2 cup	
EXTRACT,VANILLA	7/8 oz	2 tbsp	
COOKING SPRAY,NONSTICK	2 oz	1/4 cup 1/3 tbsp	

Method
1. Sift together flour, sugar, salt, baking soda, cocoa and milk into mixer bowl.
2. Blend shortening with dry ingredients. Add water gradually; beat at low speed 2 minutes or until blended. Beat at medium speed 2 minutes. Scrape down bowl.
3. Combine eggs, water, and vanilla; add slowly to mixture while beating at low speed 1 minute. Scrape down bowl. Beat at medium speed 3 minutes.
4. Lightly spray each pan with non-stick cooking spray. Pour 4-1/2 quarts batter into each greased and floured pan. Spread evenly.
5. Using a convection oven, bake at 300 F. for 25 to 35 minutes or until done on low fan, open vent.
6. Cool; frost if desired. Cut 6 by 9.

DEVIL'S FOOD CAKE (CAKE MIX)

Yield 100   **Portion** 1 Piece

Calories	Carbohydrates	Protein	Fat	Cholesterol	Sodium	Calcium
322 cal	48 g	3 g	14 g	7 mg	376 mg	115 mg

Ingredient	Weight	Measure	Issue
CAKE MIX,DEVILS FOOD	10 lbs		

Method
1. Prepare mix according to instructions on container. Frost if desired.

GERMAN CHOCOLATE CAKE (MIX)

Yield 100   **Portion** 1 Piece

Calories	Carbohydrates	Protein	Fat	Cholesterol	Sodium	Calcium
335 cal	45 g	5 g	16 g	102 mg	363 mg	64 mg

Ingredient	Weight	Measure	Issue
CAKE MIX,GERMAN CHOCOLATE	10 lbs		
COCONUT PECAN FROSTING		3 qts	

Method
1. Prepare mix according to instructions on container.
2. Frost if desired.

CARROT CAKE (CAKE MIX)

Yield 100   **Portion** 1 Piece

Calories	Carbohydrates	Protein	Fat	Cholesterol	Sodium	Calcium
308 cal	51 g	4 g	11 g	20 mg	311 mg	93 mg

Ingredient	Weight	Measure	Issue
CAKE MIX,CARROT	10 lbs		
CREAM CHEESE FROSTING		2 qts 2 cup	

Method
1. Prepare mix according to instructions on container.
2. Cool; frost if desired.

PEANUT BUTTER CREAM FROSTING

Yield 100   **Portion** 3 Quarts

Calories	Carbohydrates	Protein	Fat	Cholesterol	Sodium	Calcium
11838 cal	1652 g	182 g	561 g	629 mg	5645 mg	916 mg

Ingredient	Weight	Measure	Issue
PEANUT BUTTER	1-3/8 lbs	2-1/2 cup	
BUTTER,SOFTENED	10 oz	1-1/4 cup	
HONEY	15 oz	1-1/4 cup	
SUGAR,POWDERED	2-1/2 lbs	2 qts 1-5/8 cup	
MILK,NONFAT,DRY	1-5/8 oz	1/2 cup 2-2/3 tbsp	
WATER	12-1/2 oz	1-1/2 cup	
EXTRACT,VANILLA	1/4 oz	1/4 tsp	

Method
1. Cream peanut butter, butter or margarine, and honey in mixer bowl at medium speed 3 minutes.
2. Sift together powdered sugar and milk; add alternately with water and vanilla to creamed mixture while beating at low speed. Scrape down bowl; beat at medium speed 3 minutes or until smooth.
3. Spread on cool cakes.

CHOCOLATE FUDGE FROSTING

Yield 100   **Portion** 2-1/2 Quarts

Calories	Carbohydrates	Protein	Fat	Cholesterol	Sodium	Calcium
13454 cal	2052 g	58 g	632 g	998 mg	6299 mg	749 mg

Ingredient	Weight	Measure	Issue
BUTTER	1 lbs	2 cup	
SHORTENING	8-1/8 oz	1-1/8 cup	
SUGAR,POWDERED,SIFTED	4-1/4 lbs	1 gal	
COCOA	8-1/8 oz	2-5/8 cup	
MILK,NONFAT,DRY	7/8 oz	1/4 cup 2-1/3 tbsp	
SALT	1/4 oz	1/8 tsp	
WATER,WARM	1 lbs	1-7/8 cup	
EXTRACT,VANILLA	7/8 oz	2 tbsp	

Method

1. Melt butter or margarine and shortening; pour into mixer bowl.
2. Sift together powdered sugar, cocoa, milk and salt; add to melted fats; mix at low speed until smooth.
3. Combine water and vanilla; add to mixture in bowl. Beat at medium speed until mixture obtains desired spreading consistency.
4. Spread immediately on cooled cakes.

STRAWBERRY SHORTCAKE (BISCUIT MIX)

Yield 100   **Portion** 1 Piece

Calories	Carbohydrates	Protein	Fat	Cholesterol	Sodium	Calcium
293 cal	47 g	4 g	10 g	5 mg	550 mg	106 mg

Ingredient	Weight	Measure	Issue
BISCUIT MIX	9 lbs	2 gal 1/2 qts	
SUGAR,GRANULATED	1 lbs	2-1/4 cup	
WATER	4-2/3 lbs	2 qts 1 cup	
BUTTER,SOFTENED	6 oz	1/2 cup	
WHIPPED TOPPING (DEHYDRATED)		1 gal 2-1/4 qts	
STRAWBERRIES,FROZEN,THAWED	31-1/2 lbs	3 gal 2 qts	

Method

1. Place mix, sugar and contents of pouches in mixer bowl.
2. Blend with paddle at low speed 30 seconds.
3. Divide dough into four pieces, about 3-1/2 pounds each. Place dough on lightly floured surface; fold over 2 or 3 times; press down. Roll each piece into squares, about 16 by 16 inches and 3/8 inches thick.
4. Brush 2 pieces of dough with butter or margarine. Cut with 2-1/2 inch floured biscuit cutter.
5. Place biscuits on pans in rows 6 by 9. Brush top with remaining butter or margarine.
6. Using a convection oven, bake at 350 F. 15 minutes or until golden brown, on low fan, open vent.
7. Prepare 1-1/4 recipes Whipped Topping, Recipe No. K 002 00.
8. Place 1/4 cup strawberries on bottom half of each biscuit; top with other half. Top with 1/4 cup whipped topping.

STRAWBERRY SHORTCAKE (CAKE MIX)

Yield 100   **Portion** 1 Piece

Calories	Carbohydrates	Protein	Fat	Cholesterol	Sodium	Calcium
265 cal	52 g	4 g	5 g	11 mg	304 mg	57 mg

Ingredient	Weight	Measure	Issue
CAKE MIX,YELLOW	10 lbs		
WHIPPED TOPPING (DEHYDRATED)		1 gal 2-1/4 qts	
STRAWBERRIES,FROZEN,THAWED	31-1/2 lbs	3 gal 2 qts	

Method

1. Prepare mix according to instructions on container. When cakes are cool, cut 6x9.
2. Prepare 1-1/4 recipes Whipped Topping, K 002 00.
3. Place 1/4 cup strawberries on each piece of cake. Top with 1/4 cup whipped topping.

GINGERBREAD

Yield 100   **Portion** 1 Piece

Calories	Carbohydrates	Protein	Fat	Cholesterol	Sodium	Calcium
265 cal	42 g	3 g	10 g	24 mg	266 mg	55 mg

Ingredient	Weight	Measure	Issue
FLOUR,WHEAT,GENERAL PURPOSE	4-3/8 lbs	1 gal	
SUGAR,GRANULATED	3 lbs	1 qts 2-3/4 cup	
SALT	1 oz	1 tbsp	
BAKING POWDER	1-1/8 oz	2-1/3 tbsp	
BAKING SODA	1-1/3 oz	2-2/3 tbsp	
CINNAMON,GROUND	1/2 oz	2 tbsp	
GINGER,GROUND	3/4 oz	1/4 cup 1/3 tbsp	
SHORTENING	1-1/3 lbs	3 cup	
MOLASSES	2-7/8 lbs	1 qts	
EGGS,WHOLE,FROZEN	1-1/4 lbs	2-1/4 cup	
WATER,WARM	2-5/8 lbs	1 qts 1 cup	
WATER,ICE	2-5/8 lbs	1 qts 1 cup	
COOKING SPRAY,NONSTICK	2 oz	1/4 cup 1/3 tbsp	

Method

1. Sift together flour, sugar, salt, baking powder, baking soda, cinnamon, and ginger into mixer bowl.
2. Add shortening, molasses, and eggs to dry ingredients. Beat at low speed 1 minute until blended; continue beating at medium speed 2 minutes. Scrape down bowl.
3. Add water to mixture; mix at low speed only until batter is smooth.
4. Lightly spray each pan with non-stick cooking spray. Pour about 3-1/2 quarts batter into each sprayed and floured pan.
5. Using a convection oven, bake at 300 F. for 25 to 35 minutes or until done on low fan, open vent.
6. Cut 6 by 9. Serve warm if possible.

Notes

1. If desired, top each portion with 1/4 cup Whipped Topping, Recipe No. K 002 00 or 3 tablespoons Lemon Sauce, Recipe No. K 009 00 or dust with powdered sugar.

GINGERBREAD (GINGERBREAD CAKE MIX)

Yield 100   **Portion** 1 Piece

Calories	Carbohydrates	Protein	Fat	Cholesterol	Sodium	Calcium
334 cal	54 g	3 g	12 g	0 mg	449 mg	64 mg

Ingredient	Weight	Measure	Issue
GINGERBREAD MIX	15 lbs		

Method

1. Prepare mix according to instructions on container. Top with whipped topping.

CARAMEL FROSTING

Yield 100   Portion 2-1/2 Quarts

Calories	Carbohydrates	Protein	Fat	Cholesterol	Sodium	Calcium
12575 cal	2280 g	10 g	416 g	1121 mg	4576 mg	877 mg

Ingredient	Weight	Measure	Issue
BUTTER	1-1/8 lbs	2-1/4 cup	
SUGAR,BROWN,PACKED	1-1/3 lbs	1 qts 1/4 cup	
MILK,NONFAT,DRY	5/8 oz	1/4 cup 1/3 tbsp	
WATER	8-1/3 oz	1 cup	
SUGAR,POWDERED,SIFTED	3-2/3 lbs	3 qts 2 cup	

Method

1. Melt butter or margarine. Add brown sugar; mix thoroughly while mixing at low speed. Cook over low heat 2 minutes; stir constantly.
2. Combine milk and water. Add to butter mixture. Bring mixture to a boil; stir constantly. Remove from heat.
3. Pour into mixer bowl; cool 10 minutes.
4. Add powdered sugar gradually while mixing at low speed. Mix 2 minutes at medium speed until smooth.
5. Spread immediately on cooled cakes.

BROWN SUGAR FROSTING

Yield 100   Portion 2-1/4 Quarts

Calories	Carbohydrates	Protein	Fat	Cholesterol	Sodium	Calcium
9496 cal	1997 g	12 g	185 g	502 mg	2474 mg	1336 mg

Ingredient	Weight	Measure	Issue
SUGAR,BROWN,PACKED	2-1/3 lbs	1 qts 3-1/4 cup	
BUTTER	8 oz	1 cup	
WATER	1 lbs	2 cup	
MILK,NONFAT,DRY	1 oz	1/4 cup 3-1/3 tbsp	
SUGAR,POWDERED,SIFTED	2-1/8 lbs	2 qts	
EXTRACT,VANILLA	7/8 oz	2 tbsp	

Method

1. Combine brown sugar, butter, or margarine, and water. Heat to boiling; cook 1 minute.
2. Remove from heat; pour into mixer bowl.
3. Sift together milk and powdered sugar; add slowly to cooked mixture while beating at low speed.
4. Add vanilla; mix at medium speed 5 minutes or until smooth and of spreading consistency.
5. Pour and spread immediately on cool cakes.

PEANUT BUTTER CRUMB CAKE

Yield 100   **Portion** 1 Piece

Calories	Carbohydrates	Protein	Fat	Cholesterol	Sodium	Calcium
340 cal	52 g	6 g	13 g	11 mg	340 mg	30 mg

Ingredient	Weight	Measure	Issue
CAKE MIX,YELLOW	10 lbs		
COOKING SPRAY,NONSTICK	2 oz	1/4 cup 1/3 tbsp	
FLOUR,WHEAT,GENERAL PURPOSE	1-2/3 lbs	1 qts 2 cup	
SUGAR,GRANULATED	2 lbs	1 qts 1/2 cup	
PEANUT BUTTER	1-3/4 lbs	3 cup	
MARGARINE,SOFTENED	5 oz	1/2 cup 2 tbsp	

Method
1. Prepare cake mix according to instructions on container.
2. Lightly spray each pan with non-stick cooking spray. Pour 1 gallon batter into each sprayed and floured pan.
3. Combine flour, sugar, peanut butter and butter or margarine; mix at low speed 1-1/2 minutes or until crumbs are formed.
4. Sprinkle 1-1/2 quarts crumbs over batter in each pan.
5. Using a convection oven, bake at 325 F. for 30 minutes or until done on low fan, open vent.
6. Cool. Cut 6 by 9.

PEANUT BUTTER CAKE

Yield 100   **Portion** 1 Piece

Calories	Carbohydrates	Protein	Fat	Cholesterol	Sodium	Calcium
290 cal	38 g	6 g	14 g	11 mg	345 mg	29 mg

Ingredient	Weight	Measure	Issue
CAKE MIX,YELLOW	10 lbs		
PEANUT BUTTER	2-1/2 lbs	1 qts 1/2 cup	
COOKING SPRAY,NONSTICK	2 oz	1/4 cup 1/3 tbsp	

Method
1. Prepare cake mix according to instructions on container. Add peanut butter.
2. Lightly spray each pan with non-stick cooking spray. Pour 4-1/2 quarts batter into each sprayed and floured pan.
3. Using a convection oven, bake at 325 F. for 30 minutes or until done on low fan, open vent.
4. Cool. Cut 6 by 9. Frost if desired.

POUND CAKE

Yield 100   **Portion** 1 Slice

Calories	Carbohydrates	Protein	Fat	Cholesterol	Sodium	Calcium
284 cal	35 g	4 g	14 g	60 mg	186 mg	31 mg

Ingredient	Weight	Measure	Issue
FLOUR,WHEAT,GENERAL PURPOSE	4-3/8 lbs	1 gal	
SUGAR,GRANULATED	4-1/4 lbs	2 qts 1-5/8 cup	
SALT	1-1/4 oz	2 tbsp	
BAKING POWDER	3/4 oz	1 tbsp	
MILK,NONFAT,DRY	1-5/8 oz	1/2 cup 2-2/3 tbsp	
SHORTENING	2-3/4 lbs	1 qts 2 cup	
WATER	1-7/8 lbs	3-1/2 cup	
EGGS,WHOLE,FROZEN	3 lbs	1 qts 1-5/8 cup	
EXTRACT,VANILLA	1-7/8 oz	1/4 cup 1/3 tbsp	
COOKING SPRAY,NONSTICK	2 oz	1/4 cup 1/3 tbsp	

Method
1. Sift together flour, sugar, salt, baking powder, and milk into mixer bowl.
2. Add shortening and water to dry ingredients. Beat at medium speed 7 minutes. Scrape down bowl.
3. Add eggs and vanilla slowly to mixture while beating at low speed. Beat at low speed 7 minutes. Scrape down bowl.
4. Lightly spray each pan with non-stick cooking spray. Pour 2-1/2 quarts batter into each sprayed and floured pan.
5. Using a convection oven, bake at 325 F. for 1 hour 5 minutes or until done on low fan, open vent.
6. Cool; cut 6x9.

ALMOND POUND CAKE (POUND CAKE MIX)

Yield 100   **Portion** 1 Piece

Calories	Carbohydrates	Protein	Fat	Cholesterol	Sodium	Calcium
201 cal	15 g	3 g	14 g	56 mg	177 mg	29 mg

Ingredient	Weight	Measure	Issue
CAKE MIX,POUND	10 lbs		
FLAVORING,ALMOND	1-7/8 oz	1/4 cup 1/3 tbsp	

Method
1. Prepare mix according to instructions on container. Add almond flavoring.

VELVET POUND CAKE (YELLOW CAKE MIX)

Yield 100   **Portion** 1 Piece

Calories	Carbohydrates	Protein	Fat	Cholesterol	Sodium	Calcium
289 cal	42 g	3 g	12 g	26 mg	398 mg	28 mg

Ingredient	Weight	Measure	Issue
CAKE MIX,YELLOW	10 lbs		
DESSERT POWDER,PUDDING,INSTANT,VANILLA	1-1/2 lbs	3-3/4 cup	
OIL,SALAD	1 lbs	2-1/8 cup	
EGGS,WHOLE,FROZEN	12 oz	1-3/8 cup	
WATER	4-2/3 lbs	2 qts 1 cup	
FLAVORING,ALMOND	2 oz	1/4 cup 2/3 tbsp	

Method

1. Prepare mix according to instructions on container. Add dessert powder, oil, eggs, water and flavoring to cake mix.
2. Cool; cut 25 slices per loaf.

LEMON POUND CAKE (POUND CAKE MIX)

Yield 100   **Portion** 1 Piece

Calories	Carbohydrates	Protein	Fat	Cholesterol	Sodium	Calcium
206 cal	15 g	3 g	15 g	54 mg	176 mg	29 mg

Ingredient	Weight	Measure	Issue
CAKE MIX,POUND	10 lbs		
JUICE,LEMON	2-1/8 oz	1/4 cup 1/3 tbsp	
LEMON RIND,GRATED	1/2 oz	2-2/3 tbsp	
FLAVORING,LEMON	2-1/8 oz	1/4 cup 1/3 tbsp	

Method

1. Prepare mix according to instructions on container. Add lemon juice, rind and flavoring to cake mix.

BUTTER CREAM FROSTING

Yield 100   **Portion** 2-3/4 Quarts

Calories	Carbohydrates	Protein	Fat	Cholesterol	Sodium	Calcium
13120 cal	2288 g	15 g	463 g	1248 mg	7207 mg	533 mg

Ingredient	Weight	Measure	Issue
BUTTER,SOFTENED	1-1/4 lbs	2-1/2 cup	
SUGAR,POWDERED,SIFTED	5 lbs	1 gal 3/4 qts	
SALT	1/4 oz	1/8 tsp	
MILK,NONFAT,DRY	1 oz	1/4 cup 3-1/3 tbsp	
EXTRACT,VANILLA	7/8 oz	2 tbsp	
WATER	6-1/4 oz	3/4 cup	

Method

1. Cream butter or margarine in mixer bowl at medium speed 1 to 3 minutes or until light and fluffy.
2. Sift together powdered sugar, salt and milk; add to creamed butter or margarine.
3. Add vanilla while mixing at low speed; add just enough water to obtain a spreading consistency. Scrape down bowl. Beat at medium speed 3 to 5 minutes or until mixture is light and well blended.
4. Spread immediately on cooled cakes.

ORANGE BUTTER CREAM FROSTING

Yield 100   **Portion** 2-3/4 Quarts

Calories	Carbohydrates	Protein	Fat	Cholesterol	Sodium	Calcium
13074 cal	2302 g	7 g	463 g	1242 mg	7042 mg	232 mg

Ingredient	Weight	Measure	Issue
BUTTER,SOFTENED	1-1/4 lbs	2-1/2 cup	
SUGAR,POWDERED,SIFTED	5 lbs	1 gal 3/4 qts	
SALT	1/4 oz	1/8 tsp	
ORANGE PEEL,FRESH,GRATED	1-1/8 oz	1/4 cup 1-2/3 tbsp	
JUICE,ORANGE	8-3/4 oz	1 cup	

Method

1. Cream butter or margarine in mixer bowl at medium speed 1 to 3 minutes or until light and fluffy.
2. Sift together powdered sugar and salt; add to creamed butter or margarine.
3. Add grated orange rind and orange juice while mixing at low speed to obtain a spreading consistency. Scrape down bowl. Beat at medium speed 3 to 5 minutes or until mixture is light and well blended.
4. Spread immediately on cooled cakes.

CHOCOLATE BUTTER CREAM FROSTING

Yield 100   Portion 2-3/4 Quarts

Calories	Carbohydrates	Protein	Fat	Cholesterol	Sodium	Calcium
13907 cal	2474 g	83 g	510 g	1248 mg	7283 mg	976 mg

Ingredient	Weight	Measure	Issue
BUTTER,SOFTENED	1-1/4 lbs	2-1/2 cup	
SUGAR,POWDERED,SIFTED	5 lbs	1 gal 3/4 qts	
SALT	1/4 oz	1/8 tsp	
MILK,NONFAT,DRY	1 oz	1/4 cup 3-1/3 tbsp	
COCOA	12-1/8 oz	1 qts	
EXTRACT,VANILLA	7/8 oz	2 tbsp	
WATER,BOILING	10-1/2 oz	1-1/4 cup	

Method

1. Cream butter or margarine in mixer bowl at medium speed 1 to 3 minutes or until light and fluffy.
2. Sift together powdered sugar, salt, milk and cocoa; add to creamed butter or margarine.
3. Add vanilla while mixing at low speed; add just enough boiling water to obtain a spreading consistency. Scrape down bowl. Beat at medium speed 3 to 5 minutes or until mixture is light and well blended.
4. Spread immediately on cooled cakes.

Notes

1. Unsweetened cooking chocolate may be used. For 100 portions, melt 1 pound chocolate at low heat. Cool. Reduce butter or margarine to 1-1/2 cups. Add chocolate at end of Step 1.

COCONUT BUTTER CREAM FROSTING

Yield 100   Portion 2-3/4 Quarts

Calories	Carbohydrates	Protein	Fat	Cholesterol	Sodium	Calcium
15100 cal	2476 g	27 g	603 g	1248 mg	8242 mg	592 mg

Ingredient	Weight	Measure	Issue
BUTTER,SOFTENED	1-1/4 lbs	2-1/2 cup	

SUGAR,POWDERED,SIFTED	5 lbs	1 gal 3/4 qts
SALT	1/4 oz	1/8 tsp
MILK,NONFAT,DRY	1 oz	1/4 cup 3-1/3 tbsp
EXTRACT,VANILLA	7/8 oz	2 tbsp
WATER	6-1/4 oz	3/4 cup
COCONUT,PREPARED,SWEETENED FLAKES	9 oz	2-3/4 cup
COCONUT,PREPARED,SWEETENED FLAKES	4-7/8 oz	1-1/2 cup

Method

1. Cream butter or margarine in mixer bowl at medium speed 1 to 3 minutes or until light and fluffy.
2. Sift together powdered sugar, salt and milk; add to creamed butter or margarine.
3. Add vanilla while mixing at low speed; add just enough water to obtain a spreading consistency. Scrape down bowl. Beat at medium speed 3 to 5 minutes or until mixture is light and well blended. Fold in coconut.
4. Spread immediately on cooled cakes. Sprinkle additional coconut evenly over each frosted cake.

LEMON BUTTER CREAM FROSTING

Yield 100   Portion 2-3/4 Quarts

Calories	Carbohydrates	Protein	Fat	Cholesterol	Sodium	Calcium
13075 cal	2294 g	16 g	463 g	1248 mg	7225 mg	572 mg

Ingredient	Weight	Measure	Issue
BUTTER,SOFTENED	1-1/4 lbs	2-1/2 cup	
SUGAR,POWDERED,SIFTED	5 lbs	1 gal 3/4 qts	
SALT	1/4 oz	1/8 tsp	
MILK,NONFAT,DRY	1 oz	1/4 cup 3-1/3 tbsp	
LEMON RIND,GRATED	7/8 oz	1/4 cup 1/3 tbsp	
JUICE,LEMON	3-1/4 oz	1/4 cup 2-1/3 tbsp	
WATER	6-1/4 oz	3/4 cup	

Method

1. Cream butter or margarine in mixer bowl at medium speed 1 to 3 minutes or until light and fluffy.
2. Sift together powdered sugar, salt and milk; add to creamed butter or margarine.
3. Add grated lemon rind and lemon juice while mixing at low speed; add just enough water to obtain a spreading consistency. Scrape down bowl. Beat at medium speed 3 to 5 minutes or until mixture is light and well blended.
4. Spread immediately on cooled cakes.

MAPLE BUTTER CREAM FROSTING

Yield 100   Portion 2-3/4 Quarts

Calories	Carbohydrates	Protein	Fat	Cholesterol	Sodium	Calcium
13194 cal	2291 g	15 g	463 g	1248 mg	7209 mg	536 mg

Ingredient	Weight	Measure	Issue
BUTTER,SOFTENED	1-1/4 lbs	2-1/2 cup	
SUGAR,POWDERED,SIFTED	5 lbs	1 gal 3/4 qts	
SALT	1/4 oz	1/8 tsp	
MILK,NONFAT,DRY	1 oz	1/4 cup 3-1/3 tbsp	

EXTRACT,VANILLA	1/2 oz	1 tbsp
FLAVORING,MAPLE	1-3/8 oz	3 tbsp
WATER	6-1/4 oz	3/4 cup

Method
1. Cream butter or margarine in mixer bowl at medium speed 1 to 3 minutes or until light and fluffy.
2. Sift together powdered sugar, salt and milk; add to creamed butter or margarine.
3. Add vanilla and maple flavoring while mixing at low speed; add just enough water to obtain a spreading consistency. Scrape down bowl. Beat at medium speed 3 to 5 minutes or until mixture is light and well blended.
4. Spread immediately on cooled cakes.

MOCHA BUTTER CREAM FROSTING

Yield 100   Portion 2-3/4 Quarts

Calories	Carbohydrates	Protein	Fat	Cholesterol	Sodium	Calcium
13206 cal	2332 g	28 g	478 g	1242 mg	7068 mg	315 mg

Ingredient	Weight	Measure	Issue
BUTTER,SOFTENED		2-1/2 cup	
SUGAR,POWDERED,SIFTED	1-1/4 lbs	1 gal 3/4 qts	
SALT	5 lbs	1/8 tsp	
COCOA	1/4 oz	1-3/8 cup	
COFFEE (INSTANT)	4 oz	1 cup	

Method
1. Cream butter or margarine in mixer bowl at medium speed 1 to 3 minutes or until light and fluffy.
2. Sift together powdered sugar, salt and cocoa; add to creamed butter or margarine.
3. Add double strength brewed coffee to obtain a spreading consistency. Scrape down bowl. Beat at medium speed 3 to 5 minutes or until mixture is light and well blended.
4. Spread immediately on cooled cakes.

EASY VANILLA CAKE

Yield 100   Portion 1 Piece

Calories	Carbohydrates	Protein	Fat	Cholesterol	Sodium	Calcium
356 cal	58 g	3 g	13 g	0 mg	271 mg	79 mg

Ingredient	Weight	Measure	Issue
FLOUR,WHEAT,GENERAL PURPOSE	5 lbs	1 gal 1/2 qts	
OIL,SALAD	1-3/4 lbs	3-3/4 cup	
SUGAR,GRANULATED	5-1/4 lbs	3 qts	
MILK,NONFAT,DRY	2-3/8 oz	1 cup	
BAKING POWDER	3-7/8 oz	1/2 cup	
SALT	1 oz	1 tbsp	
WATER,WARM	3-1/8 lbs	1 qts 2 cup	
EGG WHITES,FROZEN,THAWED	1-3/4 lbs	3-1/4 cup	
EXTRACT,VANILLA	3-2/3 oz	1/2 cup	
COOKING SPRAY,NONSTICK	2 oz	1/4 cup 1/3 tbsp	

Method

1. Place flour in mixer bowl.
2. Gradually add oil while mixing at low speed 2 minutes. Mixture will resemble a crumbly paste.
3. Sift together sugar, milk, baking powder and salt; add to flour-oil mixture; mix at low speed 2 minutes.
4. Combine water, egg whites and vanilla; gradually add to mixture while mixing at low speed 2 minutes; scrape down bowl.
5. Mix at medium speed 2 minutes or until well blended.
6. Lightly spray each pan with non-stick cooking spray. Pour about 3-1/2 quarts batter into each sprayed pan.
7. Using a convection oven, bake at 325 F. for 35 minutes or until done on low fan, open vent.
8. Cool; frost if desired. Cut 6 by 9.

CHOCOLATE GLAZE FROSTING

Yield 100   **Portion** 2-1/4 Cups

Calories	Carbohydrates	Protein	Fat	Cholesterol	Sodium	Calcium
2320 cal	450 g	12 g	70 g	166 mg	645 mg	99 mg

Ingredient	Weight	Measure	Issue
SUGAR,POWDERED	14-7/8 oz	3-1/2 cup	
COCOA	2 oz	1/2 cup 2-2/3 tbsp	
BUTTER	2-2/3 oz	1/4 cup 1-2/3 tbsp	
EXTRACT,VANILLA	1/8 oz	1/8 tsp	
WATER,BOILING	4-1/8 oz	1/2 cup	

Method

1. Sift together powdered sugar and cocoa into mixer bowl.
2. Combine butter or margarine and vanilla with sugar mixture at low speed. Add enough water to obtain spreading consistency. Beat at medium speed about 3 minutes or until smooth.
3. Spread immediately on cooled cakes.

Notes

1. In Step 1, 2-2/3 ounces unsweetened cooking chocolate may be used per 100 portions. Melt chocolate at low heat. Cool. In Step 2, reduce butter or margarine to 1-1/3 ounces or 2-2/3 tablespoons. Add cooled, melted chocolate to butter or margarine.

SPICE CAKE

Yield 100   **Portion** 1 Piece

Calories	Carbohydrates	Protein	Fat	Cholesterol	Sodium	Calcium
337 cal	50 g	4 g	14 g	40 mg	320 mg	76 mg

Ingredient	Weight	Measure	Issue
FLOUR,WHEAT,GENERAL PURPOSE	4-3/8 lbs	1 gal	
SUGAR,GRANULATED	3-1/2 lbs	2 qts	
SALT	1-3/8 oz	2-1/3 tbsp	
BAKING POWDER	2-3/4 oz	1/4 cup 2 tbsp	
BAKING SODA	1/2 oz	1 tbsp	
CINNAMON,GROUND	1 oz	1/4 cup 1/3 tbsp	

CLOVES,GROUND	1/2 oz	2 tbsp
ALLSPICE,GROUND	1/4 oz	1 tbsp
MILK,NONFAT,DRY	3 oz	1-1/4 cup
SHORTENING	1-7/8 lbs	1 qts 1/4 cup
WATER	2-1/2 lbs	1 qts 5/8 cup
EGGS,WHOLE,FROZEN	2 lbs	3-3/4 cup
MOLASSES	8-2/3 oz	3/4 cup
WATER	8-1/3 oz	1 cup
EXTRACT,VANILLA	1-7/8 oz	1/4 cup 1/3 tbsp
COOKING SPRAY,NONSTICK	2 oz	1/4 cup 1/3 tbsp

Method
1. Sift together flour, sugar, salt, baking powder, baking soda, cinnamon, cloves, allspice and milk into mixer bowl.
2. Add shortening and water to dry ingredients. Beat at low speed 1 minute until blended. Scrape down bowl. Continue beating at medium speed 2 minutes.
3. Combine eggs, molasses, water and vanilla. Add slowly to mixture while beating at low speed. Scrape down bowl. Beat at medium speed for 3 minutes.
4. Lightly spray each pan with non-stick cooking spray. Pour 4-1/4 quarts batter into each greased and floured pan.
5. Using a convection oven, bake at 325 F. for 35 minutes or until done on low fan, open vent.
6. Cool; frost if desired. Cut 6 by 9.

SPICE CAKE (YELLOW CAKE MIX)

Yield 100   **Portion** 1 Piece

Calories	Carbohydrates	Protein	Fat	Cholesterol	Sodium	Calcium
273 cal	52 g	3 g	7 g	11 mg	311 mg	30 mg

Ingredient	Weight	Measure	Issue
CAKE MIX,YELLOW	10 lbs		
CINNAMON,GROUND	1 oz	1/4 cup 1/3 tbsp	
CLOVES,GROUND	1/2 oz	2 tbsp	
ALLSPICE,GROUND	1/4 oz	1 tbsp	

Method
1. Prepare mix according to instructions on container. Add cinnamon, cloves and allspice. Frost if desired.

CHEESE CAKE

Yield 100   **Portion** 1 Piece

Calories	Carbohydrates	Protein	Fat	Cholesterol	Sodium	Calcium
357 cal	30 g	6 g	24 g	98 mg	323 mg	53 mg

Ingredient	Weight	Measure	Issue
MARGARINE,MELTED	1-1/2 lbs	3 cup	
CRACKERS,GRAHAM,CRUMBS	3 lbs		
SUGAR,GRANULATED	12-1/3 oz	1-3/4 cup	

CHEESE,CREAM,SOFTENED,ROOM TEMPERATURE	10-1/4 lbs	1 gal 1 qts
SUGAR,GRANULATED	3 lbs	1 qts 2-3/4 cup
FLOUR,WHEAT,GENERAL PURPOSE	4-3/8 oz	1 cup
MILK,NONFAT,DRY	1 oz	1/4 cup 3 tbsp
SALT	1/4 oz	1/8 tsp
EGGS,WHOLE,FROZEN	2-3/8 lbs	1 qts 1/2 cup
WATER	12-1/2 oz	1-1/2 cup
JUICE,LEMON	2-1/8 oz	1/4 cup 1/3 tbsp
JUICE,ORANGE	2-1/4 oz	1/4 cup 1/3 tbsp
EXTRACT,VANILLA	7/8 oz	2 tbsp
ORANGE,RIND,GRATED	3/8 oz	2 tbsp
LEMON RIND,GRATED	1/4 oz	1 tbsp

Method

1. Grind graham crackers or crush on board with rolling pin. Combine butter or margarine, crumbs, and sugar in mixer bowl. Blend thoroughly at low speed, about 1 minute.
2. Press 2 quarts crumb mixture firmly in bottom of each pan. Using a convection oven, bake 3 minutes on low fan, open vent at 325 F. Cool; set aside for use in Step 8.
3. Place cream cheese in mixer bowl. Whip at medium speed until fluffy, about 3 minutes.
4. Combine sugar, flour, milk, and salt. Mix well.
5. Add to cream cheese; whip at low speed until blended, about 2 minutes. Whip at medium speed until smooth, about 1 minute.
6. Add eggs; whip at low speed 30 seconds. Whip at medium speed until smooth, about 1 minute.
7. Combine water, lemon and orange juices, vanilla, orange and lemon rinds; add to cheese mixture. Whip at low speed until well blended, about 2 minutes.
8. Spread 5-1/4 quarts cheese filling evenly over crust in each pan.
9. Using a convection oven, bake at 325 F. for 25 to 30 minutes on low fan, open vent or until filling is firm and lightly browned.
10. Refrigerate until ready to serve. Cut 6 by 9.

CHEESE CAKE (MIX)

Yield 100   **Portion** 1 Piece

Calories	Carbohydrates	Protein	Fat	Cholesterol	Sodium	Calcium
331 cal	41 g	5 g	17 g	22 mg	440 mg	138 mg

Ingredient	Weight	Measure	Issue
MARGARINE,SOFTENED	1-1/2 lbs	3 cup	
CRACKERS,GRAHAM,CRUMBS	3 lbs		
SUGAR,GRANULATED	12 oz	1-3/4 cup	
CHEESECAKE MIX	8 lbs		

Method

1. Combine margarine or butter, crumbs and sugar in mixer bowl. Blend thoroughly at low speed about 1 minute.
2. Prepare mix according to instructions on container.

CHEESE CAKE WITH FRUIT TOPPING

Yield 100   **Portion** 1 Piece

Calories	Carbohydrates	Protein	Fat	Cholesterol	Sodium	Calcium
432 cal	50 g	6 g	24 g	98 mg	346 mg	66 mg

Ingredient	Weight	Measure	Issue
MARGARINE,MELTED	1-1/2 lbs	3 cup	
CRACKERS,GRAHAM,CRUMBS	3 lbs		
SUGAR,GRANULATED	12-1/3 oz	1-3/4 cup	
CHEESE,CREAM,SOFTENED,ROOM TEMPERATURE	10-1/4 lbs	1 gal 1 qts	
SUGAR,GRANULATED	3 lbs	1 qts 2-3/4 cup	
FLOUR,WHEAT,GENERAL PURPOSE	4-3/8 oz	1 cup	
SALT	1/4 oz	1/8 tsp	
MILK,NONFAT,DRY	1 oz	1/4 cup 3 tbsp	
EGGS,WHOLE,FROZEN	2-3/8 lbs	1 qts 1/2 cup	
WATER	12-1/2 oz	1-1/2 cup	
JUICE,LEMON	2-1/8 oz	1/4 cup 1/3 tbsp	
JUICE,ORANGE	2-1/4 oz	1/4 cup 1/3 tbsp	
EXTRACT,VANILLA	7/8 oz	2 tbsp	
ORANGE,RIND,GRATED	3/8 oz	2 tbsp	
LEMON RIND,GRATED	1/4 oz	1 tbsp	
PIE FILLING,CHERRY,PREPARED	7-1/2 lbs	3 qts 3 cup	
PIE FILLING,BLUEBERRY,PREPARED	8-7/8 lbs	3 qts 3 cup	

Method
1. Combine butter or margarine, crumbs, and sugar in mixer bowl. Blend thoroughly at low speed, about 1 minute.
2. Press 2 quarts crumb mixture firmly in bottom of each pan. Using a convection oven, bake 3 minutes at 325 F. on low fan, open vent. Cool; set aside for use in Step 8.
3. Place cream cheese in mixer bowl. Whip at medium speed until fluffy, about 3 minutes.
4. Combine sugar, flour, milk, and salt. Mix well.
5. Add to cream cheese; whip at low speed until blended, about 2 minutes. Whip at medium speed until smooth, about 1 minute.
6. Add eggs; whip at low speed 30 seconds. Whip at medium speed until smooth, about 1 minute.
7. Combine water, lemon and orange juices, vanilla, orange and lemon rinds; add to cheese mixture. Whip at low speed until well blended, about 2 minutes.
8. Spread 5-1/4 quarts cheese filling evenly over crust in each pan.
9. Using a convection oven, bake at 325 F. 25 to 30 minutes on low fan, open vent or until firm and lightly browned.
10. Chill. Spread 7-1/2 cups canned fruit pie filling over each cake. When chilled, cut 6 by 9.

Notes
1. In Step 10, suggested fruit pie fillings include peach, apple, strawberry, or cherry.

CHEESE CAKE MIX WITH FRUIT TOPPING

Yield 100   **Portion** 1 Piece

Calories	Carbohydrates	Protein	Fat	Cholesterol	Sodium	Calcium
366 cal	51 g	5 g	17 g	22 mg	460 mg	147 mg

Ingredient	Weight	Measure	Issue
MARGARINE,SOFTENED	1-1/2 lbs	3 cup	
CRACKERS,GRAHAM,CRUMBS	3 lbs		
SUGAR,GRANULATED	12 oz	1-3/4 cup	
CHEESECAKE MIX	8 lbs		
PIE FILLING,BLUEBERRY,PREPARED	8-3/4 lbs	3 qts 2-7/8 cup	

Method

1. Combine margarine or butter, crumbs and sugar in mixer bowl. Blend thoroughly at low speed, about 1 minute.
2. Prepare mix according to instructions on container.
3. Choice of toppings are blueberry, apple or cherry.

CHEESE CAKE WITH SOUR CREAM TOPPING

Yield 100   **Portion** 1 Piece

Calories	Carbohydrates	Protein	Fat	Cholesterol	Sodium	Calcium
387 cal	35 g	6 g	25 g	103 mg	333 mg	72 mg

Ingredient	Weight	Measure	Issue
MARGARINE,MELTED	1-1/2 lbs	3 cup	
CRACKERS,GRAHAM,CRUMBS	3 lbs		
SUGAR,GRANULATED	12-1/3 oz	1-3/4 cup	
CHEESE,CREAM,SOFTENED,ROOM TEMPERATURE	10-1/4 lbs	1 gal 1 qts	
SUGAR,GRANULATED	3 lbs	1 qts 2-3/4 cup	
FLOUR,WHEAT,GENERAL PURPOSE	4-3/8 oz	1 cup	
MILK,NONFAT,DRY	1 oz	1/4 cup 3 tbsp	
SALT	1/4 oz	1/8 tsp	
EGGS,WHOLE,FROZEN	2-3/8 lbs	1 qts 1/2 cup	
WATER	12-1/2 oz	1-1/2 cup	
JUICE,ORANGE	2-1/4 oz	1/4 cup 1/3 tbsp	
JUICE,LEMON	2-1/8 oz	1/4 cup 1/3 tbsp	
EXTRACT,VANILLA	7/8 oz	2 tbsp	
ORANGE,RIND,GRATED	3/8 oz	2 tbsp	
LEMON RIND,GRATED	1/4 oz	1 tbsp	
SOUR CREAM,LOW FAT	3 lbs	1 qts 2 cup	
SUGAR,GRANULATED	12-1/3 oz	1-3/4 cup	

Method

1. Combine butter or margarine, crumbs, and sugar in mixer bowl. Blend thoroughly at low speed, about 1 minute.
2. Press 2 quarts crumb mixture firmly in bottom of each pan. Using a convection oven bake at 325 F. 3 minutes on low fan, open vent. Cool; set aside for use in Step 8.
3. Place cream cheese in mixer bowl. Whip at medium speed until fluffy, about 3 minutes.
4. Combine sugar, flour, milk, and salt. Mix well.
5. Add to cream cheese; whip at low speed until blended, about 2 minutes. Whip at medium speed until smooth, about 1 minute.
6. Add eggs; whip at low speed 30 seconds. Whip at medium speed until smooth, about 1 minute.
7. Combine water, lemon and orange juices, vanilla, orange and lemon rinds; add to cheese mixture. Whip at low speed until well blended, about 2 minutes.

8. Spread 8 pounds 5 ounces, about 5-1/4 quarts cheese filling evenly over crust in each pan.
9. Using a convection oven, bake at 325 F. 25 to 30 minutes on low fan, open vent or until firm and lightly browned.
10. Combine sour cream and last sugar. Spread about 3 cups over each baked cheese cake. Using a convection oven, bake at 325 F. 3 minutes on low fan, open vent.
11. Refrigerate until ready to serve. Cut 6 by 9.

CHEESE CAKE WITH STRAWBERRIES

Yield 100   **Portion** 1 Piece

Calories	Carbohydrates	Protein	Fat	Cholesterol	Sodium	Calcium
370 cal	34 g	6 g	24 g	98 mg	324 mg	59 mg

Ingredient	Weight	Measure	Issue
MARGARINE,MELTED	1-1/2 lbs	3 cup	
CRACKERS,GRAHAM,CRUMBS	3 lbs		
SUGAR,GRANULATED	12-1/3 oz	1-3/4 cup	
CHEESE,CREAM,SOFTENED,ROOM TEMPERATURE	10-1/4 lbs	1 gal 1 qts	
SUGAR,GRANULATED	3 lbs	1 qts 2-3/4 cup	
FLOUR,WHEAT,GENERAL PURPOSE	4-3/8 oz	1 cup	
MILK,NONFAT,DRY	1 oz	1/4 cup 3 tbsp	
SALT	1/4 oz	1/8 tsp	
EGGS,WHOLE,FROZEN	2-3/8 lbs	1 qts 1/2 cup	
WATER	12-1/2 oz	1-1/2 cup	
JUICE,LEMON	2-1/8 oz	1/4 cup 1/3 tbsp	
JUICE,ORANGE	2-1/4 oz	1/4 cup 1/3 tbsp	
EXTRACT,VANILLA	7/8 oz	2 tbsp	
ORANGE,RIND,GRATED	3/8 oz	2 tbsp	
LEMON RIND,GRATED	1/4 oz	1 tbsp	
STRAWBERRIES,FROZEN,THAWED	8-3/8 lbs	3 qts 3 cup	

Method
1. Grind graham crackers or crush on board with rolling pin. Combine butter or margarine, crumbs, and sugar in mixer bowl. Blend thoroughly at low speed, about 1 minute.
2. Press 2 quarts crumb mixture firmly in bottom of each pan. Using a convection oven, bake 3 minutes on low fan, open vent at 325 F. Cool; set aside for use in Step 8.
3. Place cream cheese in mixer bowl. Whip at medium speed until fluffy, about 3 minutes.
4. Combine sugar, flour, milk, and salt. Mix well.
5. Add to cream cheese; whip at low speed until blended, about 2 minutes. Whip at medium speed until smooth, about 1 minute.
6. Add eggs; whip at low speed 30 seconds. Whip at medium speed until smooth, about 1 minute.
7. Combine water, lemon and orange juices, vanilla, orange and lemon rinds; add to cheese mixture. Whip at low speed until well blended, about 2 minutes.
8. Spread 5-1/4 quarts cheese filling evenly over crust in each pan.
9. Using a convection oven, bake at 325 F. for 25 to 30 minutes on low fan, open vent or until filling is firm and lightly browned.
10. Refrigerate until ready to serve. Place strawberries over each chilled pie. Cut 6 by 9.

CREAM CHEESE FROSTING

Yield 100   **Portion** 2-1/2 Quarts

Calories	Carbohydrates	Protein	Fat	Cholesterol	Sodium	Calcium
12009 cal	1484 g	137 g	634 g	1990 mg	5378 mg	1467 mg

Ingredient	Weight	Measure	Issue
CHEESE,CREAM,SOFTENED,ROOM TEMPERATURE	4 lbs	1 qts 3-7/8 cup	
SUGAR,POWDERED,SIFTED	3-1/8 lbs	3 qts	
EXTRACT,VANILLA	7/8 oz	2 tbsp	

Method
1. Cream softened cream cheese, powdered sugar and vanilla in mixer bowl at low speed 4 minutes or until smooth and creamy.
2. Spread immediately on cooled cakes.

STRAWBERRY CAKE (CAKE MIX)

Yield 100   **Portion** 1 Piece

Calories	Carbohydrates	Protein	Fat	Cholesterol	Sodium	Calcium
209 cal	38 g	2 g	5 g	0 mg	288 mg	17 mg

Ingredient	Weight	Measure	Issue
STRAWBERRIES,FROZEN,THAWED	2 lbs	3-1/2 cup	
DESSERT POWDER,GELATIN,STRAWBERRY	12 oz	1-1/2 cup	
CAKE MIX,WHITE	10 lbs	1 gal 3-3/8 qts	
WATER	4-1/8 lbs	2 qts	

Method
1. Thaw strawberries.
2. Prepare mix according to instructions on container. Add dessert powder and water.

PINEAPPLE UPSIDE DOWN CAKE

Yield 100   **Portion** 1 Piece

Calories	Carbohydrates	Protein	Fat	Cholesterol	Sodium	Calcium
341 cal	52 g	4 g	14 g	60 mg	340 mg	93 mg

Ingredient	Weight	Measure	Issue
PINEAPPLE,CANNED,SLICES,JUICE PACK,INCL LIQUIDS	13-1/2 lbs	1 gal 2 qts	
CHERRIES,MARASCHINO,WHOLE	1 lbs	1-3/4 cup	
BUTTER,MELTED	1-1/2 lbs	3 cup	
SUGAR,BROWN,PACKED	2-1/8 lbs	1 qts 2-1/2 cup	
FLOUR,WHEAT,GENERAL PURPOSE	4 lbs	3 qts 2-1/2 cup	
SUGAR,GRANULATED	4 lbs	2 qts 1 cup	
SALT	1-1/2 oz	2-1/3 tbsp	
BAKING POWDER	3-1/4 oz	1/4 cup 3 tbsp	

MILK,NONFAT,DRY	3 oz	1-1/4 cup
SHORTENING	1-1/2 lbs	3-3/8 cup
WATER	2-1/3 lbs	1 qts 1/2 cup
EGGS,WHOLE,FROZEN	2-1/4 lbs	1 qts 1/4 cup
WATER	12-1/2 oz	1-1/2 cup
EXTRACT,VANILLA	1-7/8 oz	1/4 cup 1/3 tbsp

Method
1. Drain pineapple well. Drain cherries; slice in half. Set fruit aside for use in Step 3.
2. Pour 1-1/2 cups butter or margarine in each pan. Sprinkle 3-1/4 cups brown sugar evenly over butter or margarine.
3. Arrange 54 pineapple slices in rows of 6 by 9, over mixture in each pan. Place 1 cherry half, cut side up, into each pineapple slice. Set aside for use in Step 5.
4. Sift together flour, sugar, salt, baking powder, and milk into mixer bowl.
5. Add shortening and water to dry ingredients; beat at low speed 1 minute until blended. Scrape down bowl; continue beating 2 minutes.
6. Combine eggs, water, and vanilla. Add slowly to mixture while beating at low speed about 2 minutes. Scrape down bowl. Beat at medium speed 3 minutes.
7. Pour 3-1/2 quarts batter evenly over fruit in each pan.
8. Using a convection oven, bake at 325 F. 25-30 minutes on low fan, open vent or until done.
9. Remove cakes from pans while still hot. Cut 6 by 9. Serve fruit side up.

PINEAPPLE UPSIDE DOWN CAKE (MIX)

Yield 100   **Portion** 1 Piece

Calories	Carbohydrates	Protein	Fat	Cholesterol	Sodium	Calcium
357 cal	60 g	3 g	13 g	26 mg	353 mg	47 mg

Ingredient	Weight	Measure	Issue
PINEAPPLE,CANNED,SLICES,JUICE PACK,INCL LIQUIDS	13-1/2 lbs	1 gal 2 qts	
CHERRIES,MARASCHINO,WHOLE	1 lbs	1-3/4 cup	
SUGAR,BROWN,PACKED	3 lbs	2 qts 1-3/8 cup	
BUTTER,SOFTENED	1-1/2 lbs	3 cup	
CAKE MIX,YELLOW	10 lbs		

Method
1. Drain pineapple well. Drain cherries; slice in half. Set fruit aside for use in Step 3.
2. Pour 1-1/2 cups butter or margarine in each pan. Sprinkle 3-1/4 cups brown sugar evenly over butter or margarine.
3. Arrange 54 pineapple slices, in rows 6 by 9, over mixture in each pan. Place 1 cherry half into each pineapple slice. Set aside.
4. Prepare mix according to instructions on container.
5. Pour 3-1/2 quarts batter evenly over fruit in each pan.
6. Using a convection oven, bake at 325 F. 25-30 minutes on low fan, open vent or until done.
7. Remove cakes from pans while still hot. Cut 6 by 9. Serve fruit side up.

FRUIT COCKTAIL UPSIDE DOWN CAKE (MIX)

Yield 100   **Portion** 1 Piece

Calories	Carbohydrates	Protein	Fat	Cholesterol	Sodium	Calcium
278 cal	41 g	3 g	12 g	11 mg	292 mg	29 mg

Ingredient	Weight	Measure	Issue
FRUIT COCKTAIL,CANNED,JUICE PACK,INCL LIQUIDS	10-1/8 lbs	1 gal 7/8 qts	
CAKE MIX,YELLOW	10 lbs		

Method
1. Drain fruit cocktail well.
2. Prepare mix according to instructions on container.

FRUIT COCKTAIL UPSIDE DOWN CAKE

Yield 100   **Portion** 1 Piece

Calories	Carbohydrates	Protein	Fat	Cholesterol	Sodium	Calcium
322 cal	47 g	4 g	14 g	60 mg	341 mg	87 mg

Ingredient	Weight	Measure	Issue
FRUIT COCKTAIL,CANNED,JUICE PACK,INCL LIQUIDS	10-1/8 lbs	1 gal 7/8 qts	
BUTTER,MELTED	1-1/2 lbs	3 cup	
SUGAR,BROWN,PACKED	2-1/8 lbs	1 qts 2-1/2 cup	
FLOUR,WHEAT,GENERAL PURPOSE	4 lbs	3 qts 2-1/2 cup	
SUGAR,GRANULATED	4 lbs	2 qts 1 cup	
SALT	1-1/2 oz	2-1/3 tbsp	
BAKING POWDER	3-1/4 oz	1/4 cup 3 tbsp	
MILK,NONFAT,DRY	3 oz	1-1/4 cup	
SHORTENING	1-1/2 lbs	3-3/8 cup	
WATER	2-1/3 lbs	1 qts 1/2 cup	
EGGS,WHOLE,FROZEN	2-1/4 lbs	1 qts 1/4 cup	
WATER	12-1/2 oz	1-1/2 cup	
EXTRACT,VANILLA	1-7/8 oz	1/4 cup 1/3 tbsp	

Method
1. Drain fruit cocktail well. Set fruit aside for use in Step 3.
2. Pour 1-1/2 cups butter or margarine in each pan. Sprinkle 3-1/4 cups brown sugar evenly over butter or margarine.
3. Spread 1-1/2 quart fruit cocktail evenly over mixture in each pan. Set aside for use in Step 5.
4. Sift together flour, sugar, salt, baking powder, and milk into mixer bowl.
5. Add shortening and water to dry ingredients; beat at low speed 1 minute until blended. Scrape down bowl; continue beating 2 minutes.
6. Combine eggs, water, and vanilla. Add slowly to mixture while beating at low speed about 2 minutes. Scrape down bowl. Beat at medium speed 3 minutes.
7. Pour 3-1/2 quarts batter evenly over fruit in each pan.
8. Using a convection oven, bake at 325 F. 25-30 minutes on low fan, open vent or until done.
9. Remove cakes from pans while still hot. Cut 6 by 9. Serve fruit side up.

WHITE CAKE

Yield 100   **Portion** 1 Piece

Calories	Carbohydrates	Protein	Fat	Cholesterol	Sodium	Calcium
306 cal	49 g	3 g	11 g	0 mg	388 mg	89 mg

Ingredient	Weight	Measure	Issue
FLOUR,WHEAT,GENERAL PURPOSE	4 lbs	3 qts 2-1/2 cup	
SUGAR,GRANULATED	4 lbs	2 qts 1 cup	
SALT	1-1/2 oz	2-1/3 tbsp	
BAKING POWDER	4-3/8 oz	1/2 cup 1 tbsp	
MILK,NONFAT,DRY	3-1/4 oz	1-3/8 cup	
SHORTENING	1-1/2 lbs	3-3/8 cup	
WATER	2-1/4 lbs	1 qts 1/4 cup	
EGG WHITES,FROZEN,THAWED	2-3/8 lbs	1 qts 1/2 cup	
WATER	8-1/3 oz	1 cup	
EXTRACT,VANILLA	1-7/8 oz	1/4 cup 1/3 tbsp	
COOKING SPRAY,NONSTICK	2 oz	1/4 cup 1/3 tbsp	

Method
1. Sift together flour, sugar, salt, baking powder, and milk into mixer bowl.
2. Add shortening and water to dry ingredients. Beat at low speed 1 minute or until blended; continue beating at medium speed 2 minutes. Scrape down bowl.
3. Combine egg whites, water, and vanilla. Add slowly to mixture while beating at low speed. Scrape down bowl. Beat at medium speed 3 minutes.
4. Lightly spray each pan with non-stick cooking spray. Pour 1 gallon batter into each greased and floured pan.
5. Using a convection oven, bake at 300 F. for 25 to 35 minutes on low fan, open vent or until done.
6. Cool; frost if desired. Cut 6 by 9.

WHITE CAKE (WHITE CAKE MIX)

Yield 100   **Portion** 1 Piece

Calories	Carbohydrates	Protein	Fat	Cholesterol	Sodium	Calcium
288 cal	50 g	2 g	9 g	0 mg	299 mg	16 mg

Ingredient	Weight	Measure	Issue
CAKE MIX,WHITE	10 lbs	1 gal 3-3/8 qts	

Method
1. Prepare mix according to instructions on container. Frost if desired.

LEMON FILLED CAKE (WHITE CAKE MIX)

Yield 100   **Portion** 1 Piece

Calories	Carbohydrates	Protein	Fat	Cholesterol	Sodium	Calcium
361 cal	64 g	2 g	11 g	12 mg	370 mg	23 mg

Ingredient	Weight	Measure	Issue
CAKE MIX,WHITE	10 lbs	1 gal 3-3/8 qts	
PIE FILLING,LEMON,PREPARED	5 lbs	2 qts 2 cup	
COCONUT BUTTER CREAM FROSTING	3-1/2 kg	2-3/4 unit	

Method

1. Prepare mix according to instructions on container. Add lemon filling to cake. Frost if desired.

RASPBERRY FILLED CAKE (WHITE CAKE MIX)

Yield 100   **Portion** 1 Piece

Calories	Carbohydrates	Protein	Fat	Cholesterol	Sodium	Calcium
286 cal	42 g	3 g	12 g	0 mg	299 mg	28 mg

Ingredient	Weight	Measure	Issue
CAKE MIX,WHITE	10 lbs	1 gal 3-3/8 qts	
RASPBERRY BAKERY FILLING	4-1/8 lbs	1 qts 3 cup	
WHIPPED TOPPING (DEHYDRATED)		1 gal 2 qts	

Method

1. Prepare mix according to instructions on container. Add raspberry filling. Frost or top with whipped topping if desired.

STRAWBERRY FILLED CAKE (WHITE CAKE MIX)

Yield 100   **Portion** 1 Piece

Calories	Carbohydrates	Protein	Fat	Cholesterol	Sodium	Calcium
313 cal	50 g	3 g	12 g	0 mg	296 mg	27 mg

Ingredient	Weight	Measure	Issue
CAKE MIX,WHITE	10 lbs	1 gal 3-3/8 qts	
JAM, STRAWBERRY	4 lbs	1 qts 1-5/8 cup	
WHIPPED TOPPING (DEHYDRATED)		1 gal 2 qts	

Method

1. Prepare mix according to instructions on container. Add strawberry jam. Frost or top with whipped topping if desired.

COCONUT PECAN FROSTING

Yield 100   **Portion** 3 Quarts

Calories	Carbohydrates	Protein	Fat	Cholesterol	Sodium	Calcium
14029 cal	1269 g	152 g	978 g	2326 mg	7540 mg	2852 mg

Ingredient	Weight	Measure	Issue
MILK,NONFAT,DRY	6-5/8 oz	2-3/4 cup	
WATER,WARM	2 lbs	3-3/4 cup	

BUTTER	1-1/4 lbs	2-1/2 cup
EGGS,WHOLE,FROZEN	8-5/8 oz	1 cup
SUGAR,GRANULATED	1-3/4 lbs	1 qts
EXTRACT,VANILLA	5/8 oz	1 tbsp
PECANS,CHOPPED	1 lbs	
COCONUT,PREPARED,SWEETENED FLAKES	1-1/4 lbs	1 qts 2 cup

Method
1. Reconstitute milk.
2. Add butter, eggs and sugar to milk; blend well.
3. Cook mixture over low heat stirring constantly about 15 minutes until thickened and just begins to bubble around edge. Remove from heat.
4. Add vanilla, nuts and coconut. Stir to mix thoroughly.
5. Chill thoroughly, about 1 hour, before spreading on cooled cakes. Refrigerate cakes after frosting.

YELLOW CAKE

Yield 100   Portion 1 Piece

Calories	Carbohydrates	Protein	Fat	Cholesterol	Sodium	Calcium
323 cal	50 g	4 g	12 g	45 mg	300 mg	75 mg

Ingredient	Weight	Measure	Issue
FLOUR,WHEAT,GENERAL PURPOSE	4-3/8 lbs	1 gal	
SUGAR,GRANULATED	4 lbs	2 qts 1 cup	
SALT	1-1/2 oz	2-1/3 tbsp	
BAKING POWDER	3-1/4 oz	1/4 cup 3 tbsp	
MILK,NONFAT,DRY	3 oz	1-1/4 cup	
SHORTENING	1-1/2 lbs	3-3/8 cup	
WATER	2-1/3 lbs	1 qts 1/2 cup	
EGGS,WHOLE,FROZEN	2-1/4 lbs	1 qts 1/4 cup	
WATER	12-1/2 oz	1-1/2 cup	
EXTRACT,VANILLA	1-7/8 oz	1/4 cup 1/3 tbsp	
COOKING SPRAY,NONSTICK	2 oz	1/4 cup 1/3 tbsp	

Method
1. Sift together flour, sugar, salt, baking powder, and milk into mixer bowl.
2. Add shortening and water to dry ingredients; beat at low speed 1 minute until blended. Scrape down bowl; continue beating 2 minutes.
3. Combine eggs, water, and vanilla. Add slowly to mixture while beating at low speed about 2 minutes. Scrape down bowl. Beat at medium speed 3 minutes.
4. Lightly spray each pan with non-stick cooking spray. Pour 3-1/2 quarts batter into each sprayed and floured pan.
5. Using a convection oven, bake at 325 F. for 30 minutes or until done on low fan, open vent.
6. Cool; frost if desired. Cut 6 by 9.

BANANA-FILLED LAYER CAKE

Yield 100   Portion 1 Piece

Calories	Carbohydrates	Protein	Fat	Cholesterol	Sodium	Calcium
369 cal	60 g	4 g	13 g	57 mg	352 mg	80 mg

Ingredient	Weight	Measure	Issue
FLOUR,WHEAT,GENERAL PURPOSE	4-3/8 lbs	1 gal	
SUGAR,GRANULATED	4 lbs	2qts 1cup	
SALT	1-1/2 oz	2-1/3tbsp	
BAKING POWDER	3-1/4 oz	1/4cup 3tbsp	
MILK,NONFAT,DRY	3 oz	1-1/4 cup	
SHORTENING	1-1/2 lbs	3-3/8 cup	
WATER	2-1/3 lbs	1 qts 1/2 cup	
EGGS,WHOLE,FROZEN	2-1/4 lbs	1 qts 1/4 cup	
WATER	12-1/2 oz	1-1/2 cup	
EXTRACT,VANILLA	1-7/8 oz	1/4cup 1/3tbsp	
COOKING SPRAY,NONSTICK	2 oz	1/4cup 1/3tbsp	
BUTTER CREAM FROSTING		2 qts 3 cup	
BANANA,FRESH,SLICED	2-1/2 lbs	1qts 3-1/2cup	3-7/8 lbs

Method

1. Sift together flour, sugar, salt, baking powder, and milk into mixer bowl.
2. Add shortening and water to dry ingredients; beat at low speed 1 minute until blended. Scrape down bowl; continue beating 2 minutes.
3. Combine eggs, water, and vanilla. Add slowly to mixture while beating at low speed. Scrape down bowl. Beat at medium speed 3 minutes.
4. Lightly spray each pan with non-stick cooking spray. Pour 3-1/2 quarts batter into each sprayed and floured pan.
5. Using a convection oven, bake at 325 F. for 30 minutes or until done on low fan, open vent.
6. Cool. Prepare Butter Cream Frosting, Recipe No. G 022 00. Spread frosting over 1 sheet cake. Thinly slice bananas; spread over frosting. Top with second sheet cake; spread remaining frosting evenly over sides and top of cake. Cut 4 by 25.

BOSTON CREAM PIE

Yield 100   Portion 1 Slice

Calories	Carbohydrates	Protein	Fat	Cholesterol	Sodium	Calcium
330 cal	57 g	4 g	10 g	48 mg	457 mg	101 mg

Ingredient	Weight	Measure	Issue
FLOUR,WHEAT,GENERAL PURPOSE	4-3/8 lbs	1 gal	
SUGAR,GRANULATED	4 lbs	2 qts 1 cup	
SALT	1-1/2 oz	2-1/3 tbsp	
BAKING POWDER	3-1/4 oz	1/4 cup 3 tbsp	
MILK,NONFAT,DRY	3 oz	1-1/4 cup	
SHORTENING	1-1/2 lbs	3-3/8 cup	
WATER	2-1/3 lbs	1 qts 1/2 cup	
EGGS,WHOLE,FROZEN	2-1/4 lbs	1 qts 1/4 cup	
WATER	12-1/2 oz	1-1/2 cup	
EXTRACT,VANILLA	1-7/8 oz	1/4 cup 1/3 tbsp	
COOKING SPRAY,NONSTICK	2 oz	1/4 cup 1/3 tbsp	
VANILLA CREAM PUDDING (INSTANT)		1 gal 1/8 qts	
CHOCOLATE GLAZE FROSTING		1 qts 1/2 cup	
SUGAR,POWDERED	10-5/8 oz	2-1/2 cup	

Method

1. Sift together flour, sugar, salt, baking powder, and milk into mixer bowl.
2. Add shortening and water to dry ingredients; beat at low speed 1 minute until blended. Scrape down bowl; continue beating 2 minutes.
3. Combine eggs, water, and vanilla. Add slowly to mixture while beating at low speed about 2 minutes. Scrape down bowl. Beat at medium speed 3 minutes.
4. Lightly spray each pan with non-stick cooking spray. Pour 2-1/3 cups batter into each sprayed and floured 9-inch pie pan.
5. Using a convection oven, bake at 325 F. for 20 to 25 minutes or until done on low fan, open vent.
6. Cool. Split cooled cakes. Prepare Vanilla Pudding, Recipe No. J 014 00 for filling; spread 1 cup filling over bottom half of each cake. Top with other half of cake. Prepare Chocolate Glaze Frosting, Recipe No. G 024 00; spread 1/3 cup over each cake, or use powdered sugar; sprinkle 3-1/3 tablespoons over each cake. Cut 8 wedges per pie.

MARBLE CAKE

Yield 100   **Portion** 1 Piece

Calories	Carbohydrates	Protein	Fat	Cholesterol	Sodium	Calcium
321 cal	50 g	4 g	13 g	47 mg	329 mg	54 mg

Ingredient	Weight	Measure	Issue
FLOUR,WHEAT,GENERAL PURPOSE	2-1/4 lbs	2 qts	
SUGAR,GRANULATED	2 lbs	1 qts 1/2 cup	
SALT	7/8 oz	1 tbsp	
BAKING POWDER	1-5/8 oz	3-1/3 tbsp	
MILK,NONFAT,DRY	1-3/4 oz	3/4 cup	
SHORTENING	10-7/8 oz	1-1/2 cup	
WATER	1-1/8 lbs	2-1/4 cup	
EGGS,WHOLE,FROZEN	1-1/8 lbs	2-1/8 cup	
WATER	6-1/4 oz	3/4 cup	
EXTRACT,VANILLA	7/8 oz	2 tbsp	
DEVIL'S FOOD CAKE (1 PIECE)	3-7/8 kg	50 unit	

Method

1. Sift together flour, sugar, salt, baking powder, and milk into mixer bowl.
2. Add shortening and water to dry ingredients; beat at low speed 1 minute until blended. Scrape down bowl; continue beating 2 minutes.
3. Combine eggs, water, and vanilla. Add slowly to mixture while beating at low speed. Scrape down bowl. Beat at medium speed 3 minutes.
4. Prepare Devil's Food Cake, Recipe Nos. G 012 00 or G 012 01.
5. Pan, alternating light and dark batters. With knife, cut carefully through batter zig-zagging to give marble effect. Using a convection oven, bake at 325 F. for 30 minutes on low fan, open vent.
6. Cool; frost if desired. Cut 6 by 9.

COCONUT CAKE

Yield 100   **Portion** 1 Piece

Calories	Carbohydrates	Protein	Fat	Cholesterol	Sodium	Calcium
305 cal	42 g	4 g	14 g	52 mg	330 mg	83 mg

Ingredient	Weight	Measure	Issue
FLOUR,WHEAT,GENERAL PURPOSE	4-3/8 lbs	1 gal	
SUGAR,GRANULATED	4 lbs	2 qts 1 cup	
SALT	1-1/2 oz	2-1/3 tbsp	
BAKING POWDER	3-1/4 oz	1/4 cup 3 tbsp	
MILK,NONFAT,DRY	3 oz	1-1/4 cup	
SHORTENING	1-1/2 lbs	3-3/8 cup	
WATER	2-1/3 lbs	1 qts 1/2 cup	
EGGS,WHOLE,FROZEN	2-1/4 lbs	1 qts 1/4 cup	
WATER	12-1/2 oz	1-1/2 cup	
EXTRACT,VANILLA	1-7/8 oz	1/4 cup 1/3 tbsp	
COOKING SPRAY,NONSTICK	2 oz	1/4 cup 1/3 tbsp	
BUTTER,MELTED	12 oz	1-1/2 cup	
SUGAR,BROWN,PACKED	13-5/8 oz	2-5/8 cup	
MILK,NONFAT,DRY	7/8 oz	1/4 cup 2-1/3 tbsp	
COCONUT,PREPARED,SWEETENED FLAKES	1-5/8 lbs	2 qts	
WATER	7-1/3 oz	3/4 cup 2 tbsp	

Method

1. Sift together flour, sugar, salt, baking powder, and milk into mixer bowl.
2. Add shortening and water to dry ingredients; beat at low speed 1 minute until blended. Scrape down bowl; continue beating 2 minutes.
3. Combine eggs, water, and vanilla. Add slowly to mixture while beating at low speed. Scrape down bowl. Beat at medium speed 3 minutes.
4. Lightly spray each pan with non-stick cooking spray. Pour 3-1/2 quarts of batter into each sprayed and floured 9-inch pie pan.
5. Using a convection oven, bake at 325 F. for 25 to 30 minutes or until done on low fan, open vent.
6. Combine melted butter or margarine, brown sugar, non-fat dry milk, prepared sweetened coconut flakes, and water. As soon as cakes are removed from oven, spread about 1 quart coconut mixture over each cake. Increase oven temperature to 400 F. ; return to oven about 7 minutes or until coconut peaks are lightly browned.
7. Cool. Cut 6 by 9.

DUTCH APPLE CAKE

Yield 100   **Portion** 1 Piece

Calories	Carbohydrates	Protein	Fat	Cholesterol	Sodium	Calcium
590 cal	120 g	4 g	12 g	54 mg	342 mg	79 mg

Ingredient	Weight	Measure	Issue
FLOUR,WHEAT,GENERAL PURPOSE	4-3/8 lbs	1 gal	
SUGAR,GRANULATED	4 lbs	2 qts 1 cup	
SALT	1-1/2 oz	2-1/3 tbsp	
BAKING POWDER	3-1/4 oz	1/4 cup 3 tbsp	
MILK,NONFAT,DRY	3 oz	1-1/4 cup	
SHORTENING	1-1/2 lbs	3-3/8 cup	
WATER	2-1/3 lbs	1 qts 1/2 cup	
EGGS,WHOLE,FROZEN	2-1/4 lbs	1 qts 1/4 cup	
WATER	12-1/2 oz	1-1/2 cup	
EXTRACT,VANILLA	1-7/8 oz	1/4 cup 1/3 tbsp	

| PIE FILLING,APPLE,PREPARED | 13 lbs | 1 gal 2-1/2 qts |
| VANILLA GLAZE | | 1 gal 2-3/4 qts |

Method
1. Sift together flour, sugar, salt, baking powder, and milk into mixer bowl.
2. Add shortening and water to dry ingredients; beat at low speed 1 minute until blended. Scrape down bowl; continue beating 2 minutes.
3. Combine eggs, water, and vanilla. Add slowly to mixture while beating at low speed. Scrape down bowl. Beat at medium speed 3 minutes.
4. Pour apple pie filling evenly over batter in each pan.
5. Using a convection oven, bake at 325 F. for 25 to 30 minutes or until done on low fan, open vent.
6. Cool. Top each portion with 1/4 cup Vanilla Glaze, Recipe No. D 046 00. Cut 6 by 9.

FILLED CAKE (WASHINGTON PIE)

Yield 100   **Portion** 1 Slice

Calories	Carbohydrates	Protein	Fat	Cholesterol	Sodium	Calcium
308 cal	56 g	4 g	8 g	45 mg	290 mg	76 mg

Ingredient	Weight	Measure	Issue
FLOUR,WHEAT,GENERAL PURPOSE	4-3/8 lbs	1 gal	
SUGAR,GRANULATED	4 lbs	2 qts 1 cup	
SALT	1-1/2 oz	2-1/3 tbsp	
BAKING POWDER	3-1/4 oz	1/4 cup 3 tbsp	
MILK,NONFAT,DRY	3 oz	1-1/4 cup	
SHORTENING	1-1/2 lbs	3-3/8 cup	
WATER	2-1/3 lbs	1 qts 1/2 cup	
EGGS,WHOLE,FROZEN	2-1/4 lbs	1 qts 1/4 cup	
WATER	12-1/2 oz	1-1/2 cup	
EXTRACT,VANILLA	1-7/8 oz	1/4 cup 1/3 tbsp	
COOKING SPRAY,NONSTICK	2 oz		
JELLY	6 lbs	2 qts 1 cup	
SUGAR,POWDERED	10-5/8 oz	2-1/2 cup	

Method
1. Sift together flour, sugar, salt, baking powder, and milk into mixer bowl.
2. Add shortening and water to dry ingredients; beat at low speed 1 minute until blended. Scrape down bowl; continue beating 2 minutes.
3. Combine eggs, water, and vanilla. Add slowly to mixture while beating at low speed. Scrape down bowl. Beat at medium speed 3 minutes.
4. Lightly spray pie pans with non-stick cooking spray. Flour 9-inch pie pans. Pour 2-3/4 cups batter into each pan.
5. Using a convection oven, bake at 325 F. for 20 to 25 minutes or until done on low fan, open vent.
6. Cool. Split cooled cakes. Spread 3/4 cup jam or jelly over bottom half of each cake. Top with other half of cake. Sprinkle about 3-1/3 tablespoon powdered sugar over each cake. Slice each layered cake into 8 slices.

YELLOW CAKE (CRUMBS)

Yield 100   **Portion** 1 Cup

Calories	Carbohydrates	Protein	Fat	Cholesterol	Sodium	Calcium
223 cal	34 g	4 g	8 g	45 mg	280 mg	74 mg

Ingredient	Weight	Measure	Issue
FLOUR,WHEAT,GENERAL PURPOSE	4-3/8 lbs	1 gal	
SUGAR,GRANULATED	4 lbs	2 qts 1 cup	
SALT	1-1/2 oz	2-1/3 tbsp	
BAKING POWDER	3-1/4 oz	1/4 cup 3 tbsp	
MILK,NONFAT,DRY	3 oz	1-1/4 cup	
SHORTENING	1-1/2 lbs	3-3/8 cup	
WATER	2-1/3 lbs	1 qts 1/2 cup	
EGGS,WHOLE,FROZEN	2-1/4 lbs	1 qts 1/4 cup	
WATER	12-1/2 oz	1-1/2 cup	
EXTRACT,VANILLA	1-7/8 oz	1/4 cup 1/3 tbsp	

Method

1. Sift together flour, sugar, salt, baking powder, and milk into mixer bowl.
2. Add shortening and water to dry ingredients; beat at low speed 1 minute until blended. Scrape down bowl; continue beating 2 minutes.
3. Combine eggs, water, and vanilla. Add slowly to mixture while beating at low speed about 2 minutes. Scrape down bowl. Beat at medium speed 3 minutes.
4. Pour about 7 pound 10 ounces of batter into each greased and floured pan.
5. Bake at 25 to 30 minutes or until done.
6. Cool; crumble into crumbs.

JELLY ROLL

Yield 100   **Portion** 1 Slice

Calories	Carbohydrates	Protein	Fat	Cholesterol	Sodium	Calcium
240 cal	53 g	3 g	2 g	59 mg	120 mg	32 mg

Ingredient	Weight	Measure	Issue
FLOUR,WHEAT,GENERAL PURPOSE	3 lbs	2 qts 3 cup	
BAKING POWDER	1-1/8 oz	2-1/3 tbsp	
SALT	1/2 oz	3/8 tsp	
EGGS,WHOLE,FROZEN,BEATEN,ROOM TEMPERATURE	3 lbs	1 qts 1-5/8 cup	
SUGAR,GRANULATED	3 lbs	1 qts 2-3/4 cup	
WATER,WARM	1 lbs	2 cup	
EXTRACT,VANILLA	1-7/8 oz	1/4 cup 1/3 tbsp	
COOKING SPRAY,NONSTICK	2 oz	1/4 cup 1/3 tbsp	
SUGAR,POWDERED,SIFTED	12-2/3 oz	3 cup	
JELLY	8 lbs	3 qts	

Method

1. Sift together flour, baking powder and salt. Set aside for use in Step 4.

2. Combine eggs and sugar in mixer bowl. Using whip, beat at high speed 10 minutes or until mixture is light and fluffy, lemon colored, and thick enough to hold a crease.
3. Combine water and vanilla; add slowly to egg mixture while beating at low speed. Beat at low speed. DO NOT OVER MIX.
4. Add dry ingredients gradually to egg mixture while beating at low speed; beat only until ingredients are blended.
5. Lightly spray each pan with non-stick cooking spray. Pour about 2-1/4 quarts batter into each lightly sprayed, paper-lined pan.
6. Cakes should be put in oven at 5 minute intervals to allow time to roll each cake while hot. Bake 9 to 10 minutes or until done in 375 F. oven.
7. Prepare work table for rolling jelly roll while cake is baking. Place 4 sheets of paper, slightly larger than sheet pan, horizontally on work table; sprinkle generously with powdered sugar.
8. Turn baked cake upside down immediately onto paper covered with powdered sugar. Remove paper liner and pan as quickly as possible. Be careful not to tear cake. Spread 3 cups jelly evenly on each cake.
9. While cake is still hot, roll tightly, using paper to assist in shaping and molding an even roll. Cool.
10. When ready to serve, remove paper; sprinkle cake with powdered sugar. Cut 25 slices, about 1-inch thick, per roll.

YELLOW CUPCAKES MIX

Yield 100   **Portion** 1 Cupcake

Calories	Carbohydrates	Protein	Fat	Cholesterol	Sodium	Calcium
276 cal	52 g	3 g	7 g	11 mg	311 mg	26 mg

Ingredient	Weight	Measure	Issue
CAKE MIX,YELLOW	10 lbs		
WATER	5 lbs	2 qts 1-1/2 cup	
COOKING SPRAY,NONSTICK	2 oz	1/4 cup 1/3 tbsp	

Method
1. Prepare mix according to instructions on container.
2. Lightly spray each muffin cup with non-stick cooking spray. Fill each sprayed muffin cup 2/3 full.
3. Using a convection oven, bake at 325 F. for 20 to 25 minutes or until done on low fan open vent.
4. Cool; frost or dust with powdered sugar, if desired.

CHOCOLATE CUPCAKES MIX

Yield 100   **Portion** 1 Cupcake

Calories	Carbohydrates	Protein	Fat	Cholesterol	Sodium	Calcium
286 cal	48 g	3 g	10 g	7 mg	376 mg	115 mg

Ingredient	Weight	Measure	Issue
CAKE MIX,DEVILS FOOD	10 lbs		
COOKING SPRAY,NONSTICK	2 oz	1/4 cup 1/3 tbsp	

Method
1. Prepare mix according to instructions on container.
2. Lightly spray each muffin cup with non-stick cooking spray. Fill each sprayed muffin cup 2/3 full.
3. Using a convection oven, bake at 325 F. for 20 to 25 minutes or until done on low fan open vent.
4. Cool; frost or dust with powdered sugar, if desired.

SPICE CAKE CUPCAKES MIX

Yield 100   **Portion** 1 Cupcake

Calories	Carbohydrates	Protein	Fat	Cholesterol	Sodium	Calcium
278 cal	52 g	3 g	7 g	11 mg	311 mg	30 mg

Ingredient	Weight	Measure	Issue
CAKE MIX,YELLOW	10 lbs	10 lbs	
CINNAMON,GROUND	1 oz	1 oz	
CLOVES,GROUND	1/2 oz	1/2 oz	
ALLSPICE,GROUND	1/4 oz	1/4 oz	
COOKING SPRAY,NONSTICK	2 oz	2 oz	

Method
1. Prepare mix according to instructions on container. Add cinnamon, cloves, and allspice. Mix well.
2. Lightly spray each muffin cup with non-stick cooking spray. Fill each sprayed muffin cup 2/3 full.
3. Using a convection oven, bake at 325 F. for 20 to 25 minutes or until done on low fan open vent.
4. Cool; frost or dust with powdered sugar, if desired.

GINGERBREAD CUPCAKES MIX

Yield 100   **Portion** 1 Cupcake

Calories	Carbohydrates	Protein	Fat	Cholesterol	Sodium	Calcium
298 cal	50 g	2 g	10 g	0 mg	318 mg	43 mg

Ingredient	Weight	Measure	Issue
GINGERBREAD MIX	10 lbs		
COOKING SPRAY,NONSTICK	2 oz	1/4 cup 1/3 tbsp	

Method
1. Prepare mix according to instructions on container.
2. Lightly spray each muffin cup with non-stick cooking spray. Fill each sprayed muffin cup 2/3 full.
3. Using a convection oven, bake at 325 F. for 20 to 25 minutes or until done on low fan open vent.
4. Cool; frost or dust with powdered sugar, if desired.

VANILLA CUPCAKES

Yield 100   **Portion** 1 Cupcake

Calories	Carbohydrates	Protein	Fat	Cholesterol	Sodium	Calcium
292 cal	50 g	2 g	9 g	0 mg	299 mg	16 mg

Ingredient	Weight	Measure	Issue
CAKE MIX,WHITE	10 lbs	1 gal 3-3/8 qts	
COOKING SPRAY,NONSTICK	2 oz	1/4 cup 1/3 tbsp	

Method
1. Prepare mix according to instructions on container.

2. Lightly spray each muffin cup with non-stick cooking spray. Fill each well-greased muffin cup 2/3 full.
3. Using a convection oven, bake at 325 F. for 20 to 25 minutes or until done on low fan open vent.
4. Cool; frost or dust with powdered sugar, if desired.

CHOCO-LITE CAKE

Yield 100   Portion 1 Piece

Calories	Carbohydrates	Protein	Fat	Cholesterol	Sodium	Calcium
225 cal	50 g	5 g	2 g	0 mg	234 mg	78 mg

Ingredient	Weight	Measure Issue
APPLESAUCE,CANNED,UNSWEETENED	3 lbs	1 qts 1-1/2 cup
EGG WHITES,FROZEN,THAWED	2-7/8 lbs	1 qts 1-1/2 cup
YOGURT,VANILLA,NONFAT	1-1/8 lbs	3 cup
WATER	12-1/2 oz	1-1/2 cup
CHOCOLATE,COOKING,UNSWEETENED,MELTED	5-7/8 oz	1-1/4 cup
EXTRACT,VANILLA	7/8 oz	2 tbsp
SUGAR,GRANULATED	4-5/8 lbs	2 qts 2-1/2 cup
FLOUR,WHEAT,GENERAL PURPOSE	3-5/8 lbs	3 qts 1 cup
COCOA	12-1/8 oz	1 qts
CORNSTARCH	9 oz	2 cup
MILK,NONFAT,DRY	4 oz	1-5/8 cup
BAKING POWDER	2-5/8 oz	1/4 cup 1-2/3 tbsp
CINNAMON,GROUND	1 oz	1/4 cup 1/3 tbsp
SALT	5/8 oz	1 tbsp
BAKING SODA	2/3 oz	1 tbsp
COOKING SPRAY,NONSTICK	2 oz	1/4 cup 1/3 tbsp
CORN SYRUP,LIGHT	8-2/3 oz	3/4 cup
WATER	6-1/4 oz	3/4 cup
SUGAR,POWDERED,SIFTED	1-1/4 lbs	1 qts 1/2 cup
COCOA	3 oz	1 cup

Method
1. Place applesauce, egg whites, yogurt, water, melted chocolate and vanilla in mixer bowl. Mix at low speed 1 minute to blend. Mix at high speed 1 minute.
2. Sift together sugar, flour, cocoa, cornstarch, milk, baking powder, cinnamon, salt, and baking soda.
3. Add dry ingredients to mixer bowl. Mix at low speed 2 minutes. Scrape down bowl. Mix at medium speed 2 minutes or until batter is smooth.
4. Lightly spray pans with non-stick cooking spray. Pour 1 gallon batter into each pan.
5. Using a convection oven bake at 325 F. for 20-25 minutes or until done on low fan, open vent.
6. To make glaze, place syrup and water in mixer bowl. Using a wire whip, mix at low speed 1 minute.
7. Sift sugar and cocoa together.
8. Add to syrup and water mixture. Mix at low speed 1 minute; scrape bowl. Mix at high speed 2 minutes.
9. Spread 1-1/2 cups chocolate glaze over each warm cake. Cool. Cut 6 by 9.

LITE CHEESE CAKE

Yield 100   **Portion** 1 Piece

Calories	Carbohydrates	Protein	Fat	Cholesterol	Sodium	Calcium
262 cal	44 g	9 g	6 g	4 mg	424 mg	101 mg

Ingredient	Weight	Measure	Issue
MARGARINE,MELTED	1-1/4 lbs	2-1/2 cup	
CRACKERS,GRAHAM,LOW FAT,GROUND	3 lbs		
SUGAR,GRANULATED	12-1/3 oz	1-3/4 cup	
CHEESE,CREAM,FAT FREE	10-1/4 lbs	1 gal 1 qts	
SUGAR,GRANULATED	3 lbs	1 qts 2-3/4 cup	
FLOUR,WHEAT,GENERAL PURPOSE	3-7/8 oz	3/4 cup 2 tbsp	
MILK,NONFAT,DRY	7/8 oz	1/4 cup 2 tbsp	
SALT	1/8 oz	1/8 tsp	
EGG WHITES,FROZEN,THAWED	2-2/3 lbs	1 qts 1 cup	
WATER	12-1/2 oz	1-1/2 cup	
JUICE,ORANGE,FRESH	2-1/4 oz	1/4 cup 1/3 tbsp	
JUICE,LEMON,FRESH	2-1/8 oz	1/4 cup 1/3 tbsp	
EXTRACT,VANILLA	3/4 oz	1 tbsp	
ORANGE,RIND,GRATED	1/3 oz	1 tbsp	
LEMON RIND,GRATED	1/4 oz	1 tbsp	

Method

1. Combine margarine or butter, crumbs, and sugar in mixer bowl. Blend thoroughly at low speed, about 1 minute.
2. Press about 2-1/4 quarts crumb mixture firmly into bottom of each pan. Using a convection oven, bake at 325 F. 3 minutes on low fan, open vent. Cool; set aside for use in Step 8.
3. Place cream cheese in mixer bowl. Whip at high speed until fluffy, about 3 minutes.
4. Combine sugar, flour, milk, and salt. Mix well.
5. Add to cream cheese; whip at medium speed until blended, about 2 minutes; scrape down bowl; whip at high speed until smooth, about 1 minute.
6. Add egg whites gradually while mixing at low speed 1 minute. Scrape down bowl. Whip at high speed until smooth, about 1 minute.
7. Combine water, orange and lemon juices, vanilla, orange and lemon rinds; add to cheese mixture. Whip at medium speed until well blended, about 2 minutes.
8. Pour about 1-1/4 gallons cheese filling evenly over crust in each pan. Spread evenly.
9. Using a convection oven bake at 325 F. 25 to 30 minutes or until firm and lightly browned on low fan, open vent.
10. CCP: Hold for service at 41 F. or lower. Cut 6 by 9. Cheesecake may be served with cherry or blueberry pie filling as topping.

GENERAL INFORMATION REGARDING COOKIES

TYPES:

1. Sliced cookies are made from a stiff dough that is generally formed into a roll, sliced, and baked on sheet pans. Care should be taken not to overmix the dough or incorporate extra flour during mixing because this will toughen the cookies. These cookies also can be rolled out and cut into squares, circles, or fancy shapes. The method of forming the dough into a roll and then slicing the roll into uniform pieces saves time and eliminates the problem of leftover dough. It is very important that the roll be uniform and that the slices be of the same thickness to ensure even baking of the cookies.
2. Drop cookies are made from a soft dough. A spoon or pastry bag may be used to drop the cookies onto the sheet pans. Drop cookies should all be the same size to ensure even baking.
3. Bars are baked and then generally cut while warm to avoid breakage. They may be formed from rolls of dough flattened in a sheet pan (See illustration) or from dough spread into a sheet pan before baking.
4. Brownies are very rich cookies. The batter is quite heavy and must be smoothed in the sheet pan to ensure an even thickness.

GUIDELINES FOR SUCCESSFUL COOKIE BAKING

1. DO NOT use warped or bent baking pans. Use only lightweight sheet pans (weighing about 4 lb) designed for baking.
2. Follow the recipe instructions regarding greasing pans as some cookies require a greased pan for baking but other cookies have enough fat in the dough to eliminate the need for greasing the pan. Heavy greasing encourages spreading of the cookies. Use cool, clean sheet pans because cookie dough will melt and spread too much if a hot sheet pan is used.
3. If cookies are to be cut into special shapes, the dough should be rolled out to 1/4 to 1/2 inch thickness on a lightly floured board, cut into the desired shapes, and baked as directed in the basic recipe. If cookie cutters are not available, an empty can of the desired size may be used. The can should have both ends removed, be thoroughly cleaned, and have the edges smoothed before it is used.
4. To cut a roll of cookie dough into even slices, it is suggested that a clean piece of wood or metal be notched according to the width desired for each cookie, and be used as a guide in slicing. For sliced cookies, a dough scraper should be used to cut the roll of cookie dough.
5. Make each cookie the same size and thickness. Space them evenly on the pan to ensure uniform baking. Cookies may be flattened with the bottom of a small can or glass dipped in sugar. Cookies may also be flattened with a fork to make a crisscross design on the top.
6. If less than a full pan of cookies is to be baked, the cookies should be spaced evenly in the center of the pan to ensure even baking.
7. Avoid overbaking cookies. Always test for doneness. Overbaked cookies become dry and lose their flavor rapidly.
8. Most cookies should be loosened from the pans and removed to other pans or racks to cool. Cookies will continue to bake if left on the hot pans and will be difficult to remove when cool.

DIRECTIONS FOR MAKE-UP OF ROLLED BAR COOKIES

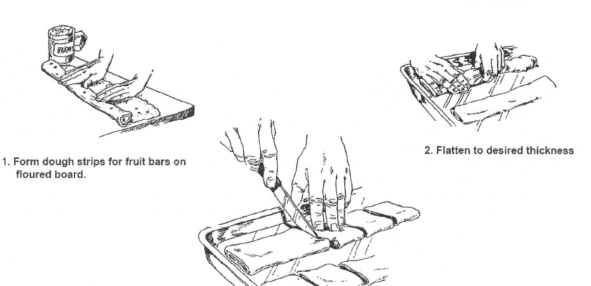

1. Form dough strips for fruit bars on floured board.

2. Flatten to desired thickness

3. Cut baked fruit bars

APPLE CAKE BROWNIES

Yield 100   **Portion** 1 Brownie

Calories	Carbohydrates	Protein	Fat	Cholesterol	Sodium	Calcium
257 cal	36 g	4 g	11 g	24 mg	246 mg	33 mg

Ingredient	Weight	Measure	Issue
FLOUR,WHEAT,GENERAL PURPOSE	2-3/4 lbs	2 qts 2 cup	
SALT	1-1/4 oz	2 tbsp	
BAKING POWDER	1-1/8 oz	2-1/3 tbsp	
BAKING SODA	3/4 oz	1 tbsp	
CINNAMON,GROUND	1/2 oz	2 tbsp	
SHORTENING	1-5/8 lbs	3-1/2 cup	
SUGAR,GRANULATED	4-1/4 lbs	2 qts 1-5/8 cup	
EGGS,WHOLE,FROZEN,BEATEN,ROOM TEMPERATURE	1-1/4 lbs	2-1/4 cup	
EXTRACT,VANILLA	1-7/8 oz	1/4cup 1/3tbsp	
APPLES,CANNED,SLICED,DRAINED	6 lbs	3 qts	
NUTS,UNSALTED,CHOPPED,COARSELY	1-1/4 lbs	1 qts	
RAISINS	7-2/3 oz	1-1/2 cup	
COOKING SPRAY,NONSTICK	2 oz	1/4cup 1/3tbsp	

Method
1. Sift together flour, salt, baking powder, baking soda, and cinnamon. Set aside for use in Step 4.
2. Cream shortening and sugar in mixer bowl for 4 minutes at medium speed.
3. Add eggs and vanilla to creamed mixture and beat for 2 minutes at medium speed. Scrape down bowl.

4. Add dry ingredients to creamed mixture while beating at low speed.
5. Add apples, nuts and raisins to mixture. DO NOT OVERMIX. Mixture will be thick.
6. Lightly spray each pan with non-stick cooking spray. Spread one half of mixture into sprayed and floured pans.
7. Bake about 40 minutes or until done at 350 F.
8. Cool and cut 6 by 9.

Notes
1. In Step 5, 3 pound 6 ounces canned applesauce or 11 ounces canned instant applesauce rehydrated with 4-1/2 cups of water may be used per 100 portions.

APPLE CAKE BROWNIES (GINGERBREAD CAKE MIX)

Yield 100   Portion 1 Brownie

Calories	Carbohydrates	Protein	Fat	Cholesterol	Sodium	Calcium
261 cal	41 g	4 g	10 g	0 mg	299 mg	50 mg

Ingredient	Weight	Measure	Issue
GINGERBREAD MIX	10 lbs		
APPLES,CANNED,SLICED,DRAINED	6 lbs	3 qts	
NUTS,UNSALTED,CHOPPED,COARSELY	1-1/4 lbs	1 qts	
RAISINS	7-2/3 oz	1-1/2 cup	
COOKING SPRAY,NONSTICK	2 oz	1/4 cup 1/3 tbsp	

Method
1. Use Gingerbread Mix. Prepare mix according to instructions on container.
2. Add apples, nuts and raisins to mixture. DO NOT OVERMIX. Mixture will be thick.
3. Lightly spray each pan with non-stick cooking spray. Spread one half of mixture into greased and floured pans.
4. Bake about 40 minutes or until done at 350 F.
5. Cool and cut 6 by 9.

Notes
1. In Step 2, 3 pounds 6 ounces canned applesauce or 11 ounces canned instant applesauce rehydrated with 4-1/4 cups of water may be used per 100 portions.

BROWNIES

Yield 100   Portion 1 Brownie

Calories	Carbohydrates	Protein	Fat	Cholesterol	Sodium	Calcium
364 cal	46 g	6 g	19 g	55 mg	132 mg	45 mg

Ingredient	Weight	Measure	Issue
FLOUR,WHEAT,GENERAL PURPOSE	3 lbs	2 qts 3 cup	
SUGAR,GRANULATED	5-1/4 lbs	3 qts	
COCOA	1-1/3 lbs	1 qts 3 cup	
BAKING POWDER	1-1/8 oz	2-1/3 tbsp	
SALT	5/8 oz	1 tbsp	
SHORTENING	2-3/4 lbs	1 qts 2 cup	
EGGS,WHOLE,FROZEN	2-3/4 lbs	1 qts 1-1/4 cup	
SYRUP	1-7/8 lbs	2-5/8 cup	
EXTRACT,VANILLA	1-3/8 oz	3 tbsp	

| NUTS,UNSALTED,CHOPPED,COARSELY | 1-7/8 lbs | 1 qts 2 cup |
| COOKING SPRAY,NONSTICK | 2 oz | 1/4 cup 1/3 tbsp |

Method

1. Place flour, sugar, cocoa, baking powder and salt in mixer bowl; blend well at low speed for 1 minute.
2. Add shortening, eggs, syrup and vanilla to dry ingredients. Mix at low speed for 1 minute then scrape down bowl. Mix at medium speed for 2 minutes or until thoroughly blended.
3. Add nuts to batter; mix at low speed for 30 seconds.
4. Lightly spray each pan with non-stick cooking spray. Spread 4-3/4 quarts batter in sprayed pans.
5. Using a convection oven, bake for 25 to 30 minutes or until done at 325 F. on high fan, open vent. DO NOT OVERBAKE. Brownies are done when a toothpick inserted in the center of baked brownies comes out clean.
6. Cool and cut 6 by 9.

BROWNIES (CHOCOLATE BROWNIE MIX)

Yield 100   Portion 1 Brownie

Calories	Carbohydrates	Protein	Fat	Cholesterol	Sodium	Calcium
375 cal	52 g	3 g	19 g	0 mg	206 mg	13 mg

Ingredient	Weight	Measure	Issue
BROWNIE MIX	15 lbs	2 gal 3-1/8 qts	

Method

1. Prepare mix according to instructions on container.

PEANUT BUTTER BROWNIES

Yield 100   Portion 1 Brownie

Calories	Carbohydrates	Protein	Fat	Cholesterol	Sodium	Calcium
377 cal	49 g	10 g	18 g	55 mg	195 mg	50 mg

Ingredient	Weight	Measure	Issue
FLOUR,WHEAT,GENERAL PURPOSE	3 lbs	2 qts 3 cup	
SUGAR,GRANULATED	5-1/4 lbs	3 qts	
COCOA	1-1/3 lbs	1 qts 3 cup	
BAKING POWDER	1-1/8 oz	2-1/3 tbsp	
SALT	5/8 oz	1 tbsp	
SHORTENING	1 lbs	2-1/4 cup	
PEANUT BUTTER	3 lbs	1 qts 1-1/4 cup	
EGGS,WHOLE,FROZEN	2-3/4 lbs	1 qts 1-1/4 cup	
SYRUP	1-7/8 lbs	2-5/8 cup	
EXTRACT,VANILLA	1-3/8 oz	3 tbsp	
NUTS,UNSALTED,CHOPPED,COARSELY	1-7/8 lbs	1 qts 2 cup	
COOKING SPRAY,NONSTICK	2 oz	1/4 cup 1/3 tbsp	

Method

1. Place flour, sugar, cocoa, baking powder and salt in mixer bowl; blend well at low speed for 1 minute.
2. Add shortening, peanut butter, eggs, syrup and vanilla to dry ingredients. Mix at low speed for 1 minute and scrape down bowl. Mix at medium speed for 2 minutes or until thoroughly blended.
3. Add nuts to batter and mix at low speed for 30 seconds.
4. Lightly spray each pan with non-stick cooking spray. Spread 4-1/4 quarts batter into each sprayed sheet pan.
5. Using a convection oven, bake at 325 F. for 25 to 30 minutes or until done on high fan, open vent. DO NOT OVERBAKE. Brownies are done when a toothpick inserted into center comes out clean.
6. Cool and cut 6 by 9.

BUTTERSCOTCH BROWNIES

Yield 100   **Portion** 1 Brownie

Calories	Carbohydrates	Protein	Fat	Cholesterol	Sodium	Calcium
328 cal	39 g	6 g	17 g	57 mg	287 mg	108 mg

Ingredient	Weight	Measure	Issue
FLOUR,WHEAT,GENERAL PURPOSE	5-1/2 lbs	1 gal 1 qts	
BAKING POWDER	4-3/8 oz	1/2 cup 1 tbsp	
SALT	5/8 oz	1 tbsp	
SUGAR,BROWN,PACKED	4-1/8 lbs	3 qts 3/4 cup	
BUTTER,MELTED	1-3/4 lbs	3-1/2 cup	
EGGS,WHOLE,FROZEN	2 lbs	3-3/4 cup	
EXTRACT,VANILLA	1-7/8 oz	1/4 cup 1/3 tbsp	
NUTS,UNSALTED,CHOPPED,COARSELY	1-7/8 lbs	1 qts 2 cup	
COOKING SPRAY,NONSTICK	2 oz	1/4 cup 1/3 tbsp	

Method

1. Sift together flour, baking powder, and salt. Set aside for use in Step 3.
2. Place brown sugar in mixer bowl; add hot butter or margarine. Beat about 2 minutes at low speed until smooth and well blended.
3. Add eggs and vanilla; beat at medium speed for 8 minutes. Scrape down bowl and add dry ingredients to mixture in mixer bowl. Beat for 2 minutes at low speed or until well blended. Scrape down bowl.
4. Fold nuts into batter.
5. Lightly spray each pan with non-stick cooking spray. Spread 3-1/4 quarts batter into sprayed and floured pans.
6. Using a convection oven, bake at 300 F. 40 to 45 minutes or until done on low fan, closed vent. DO NOT OVERBAKE. Brownies are done when a toothpick inserted into center comes out clean.
7. Cut 6 by 9 while warm.

CHEWY NUT BARS

Yield 100   **Portion** 2 Each

Calories	Carbohydrates	Protein	Fat	Cholesterol	Sodium	Calcium
225 cal	25 g	5 g	12 g	63 mg	178 mg	58 mg

Ingredient	Weight	Measure	Issue
FLOUR,WHEAT,GENERAL PURPOSE	1-7/8 lbs	1 qts 3 cup	
BAKING POWDER	1-1/8 oz	2-1/3 tbsp	
SALT	1 oz	1 tbsp	
EGGS,WHOLE,FROZEN	3-1/4 lbs	1 qts 2 cup	
SUGAR,BROWN,PACKED	3-1/2 lbs	2 qts 2-3/4 cup	
EXTRACT,VANILLA	7/8 oz	2 tbsp	
WALNUTS,SHELLED,CHOPPED	3-2/3 lbs	3 qts 2 cup	
COOKING SPRAY,NONSTICK	2 oz	1/4 cup 1/3 tbsp	

Method

1. Sift together flour, baking powder and salt. Set aside for use in Step 3.
2. Place brown sugar, eggs, and vanilla in mixer bowl. Beat at low speed for 1 minute, then at medium speed for 2 to 3 minutes or until smooth.
3. Add flour mixture; mix at low speed for 1 minute or until well blended.
4. Add nuts; mix for 1 minute at low speed.
5. Lightly spray each pan with non-stick cooking spray. Spread about 3-1/4 quarts batter into sprayed pans.
6. Using a convection oven, bake at 325 F. for 20 minutes or until done on low fan, open vent.
7. Cook; cut 6 by 18.

CONGO BARS

Yield 100   **Portion** 2 Bars

Calories	Carbohydrates	Protein	Fat	Cholesterol	Sodium	Calcium
240 cal	31 g	4 g	12 g	41 mg	175 mg	55 mg

Ingredient	Weight	Measure	Issue
FLOUR,WHEAT,GENERAL PURPOSE	3-1/3 lbs	3 qts	
BAKING POWDER	1-1/8 oz	2-1/3 tbsp	
SALT	1 oz	1 tbsp	
EGGS,WHOLE,FROZEN	2 lbs	3-3/4 cup	
OIL,SALAD	1-1/2 lbs	3 cup	
SUGAR,BROWN,PACKED	3-1/2 lbs	2 qts 2-3/4 cup	
EXTRACT,VANILLA	7/8 oz	2 tbsp	
WALNUTS,SHELLED,CHOPPED	8-1/2 oz	2 cup	
CHOCOLATE,COOKING CHIPS,SEMISWEET	1-1/2 lbs	1 qts	
COOKING SPRAY,NONSTICK	2 oz	1/4cup 1/3tbsp	

Method

1. Sift together flour, baking powder and salt. Set aside for use in Step 3.
2. Place eggs, brown sugar, vanilla and oil in mixer bowl. Beat at low speed for 1 minute, then at medium speed for 2 to 3 minutes until smooth.
3. Add flour mixture; mix at low speed 1 minute or until well blended.
4. Add nuts and chocolate chips; mix for 1 minute at low speed.
5. Lightly spray each pan with non-stick cooking spray. Spread about 6 pounds 11 ounces batter into sprayed sheet pans.
6. Using a convection oven, bake at 325 F. for 25 minutes or until done on low fan, open vent.
7. Cool; cut 6 by 18.

SHORTBREAD COOKIES

Yield 100   **Portion** 2 Cookies

Calories	Carbohydrates	Protein	Fat	Cholesterol	Sodium	Calcium
269 cal	31 g	3 g	15 g	40 mg	151 mg	9 mg

Ingredient	Weight	Measure	Issue
BUTTER,SOFTENED	4 lbs	2 qts	
SUGAR,GRANULATED	2-1/4 lbs	1 qts 1 cup	
FLOUR,WHEAT,GENERAL PURPOSE	6 lbs	1 gal 1-1/2 qts	

Method
1. Place butter in mixer bowl; beat at medium speed until creamy.
2. Gradually add sugar; continue beating until light and fluffy, about 5 minutes.
3. Add flour; mix until blended.
4. Divide dough into 10 pieces, about 1 pound 2 ounce each. Form into rolls; chill and slice each roll into 20 pieces.
5. Place in rows, 5 by 7, on ungreased pans.
6. Bake at 350 F. for 18 minutes or until cookies are firm but not browned.

CRISP TOFFEE BARS

Yield 100   **Portion** 2 Bars

Calories	Carbohydrates	Protein	Fat	Cholesterol	Sodium	Calcium
223 cal	21 g	4 g	14 g	26 mg	102 mg	27 mg

Ingredient	Weight	Measure	Issue
BUTTER	2-1/2 lbs	1 qts 1 cup	
SUGAR,BROWN,PACKED	1-1/8 lbs	3-3/8 cup	
EXTRACT,VANILLA	7/8 oz	2 tbsp	
FLOUR,WHEAT,GENERAL PURPOSE	3-1/3 lbs	3 qts	
CHOCOLATE,COOKING CHIPS,SEMISWEET	1-1/2 lbs	1 qts	
NUTS,UNSALTED,CHOPPED,COARSELY	1-1/4 lbs	1 qts	

Method
1. Place butter or margarine in mixer bowl; cream at medium speed for 5 minutes. Add brown sugar and vanilla; continue to beat for 5 minutes or until light and fluffy.
2. Add flour to mixture. Mix 1 minute at low speed or until thoroughly blended. Mixture will be stiff.
3. Fold chips and nuts into mixture.
4. Spread 2-3/4 quarts mixture into each ungreased pan. Press mixture evenly into pans.
5. Bake at 350 F. for 25 minutes or until lightly browned.
6. Cut 6 by 18 while still warm. When cool, remove from pans.

OATMEAL COOKIES

Yield 100   **Portion** 2 Cookies

Calories	Carbohydrates	Protein	Fat	Cholesterol	Sodium	Calcium
296 cal	43 g	6 g	12 g	16 mg	169 mg	48 mg

Ingredient	Weight	Measure	Issue
FLOUR,WHEAT,GENERAL PURPOSE	2-1/4 lbs	2 qts	
SALT	7/8 oz	1 tbsp	
BAKING SODA	3/8 oz	3/8 tsp	
BAKING POWDER	1-1/3 oz	2-2/3 tbsp	
EGGS,WHOLE,FROZEN	12-7/8 oz	1-1/2 cup	
WATER	4-1/8 oz	1/2 cup	
EXTRACT,VANILLA	7/8 oz	2 tbsp	
SHORTENING	2 lbs	1 qts 1/2 cup	
SUGAR,GRANULATED	1-1/2 lbs	3-1/2 cup	
SUGAR,BROWN,PACKED	1-1/3 lbs	1 qts 1/4 cup	
CEREAL,OATMEAL,ROLLED	5-1/8 lbs	3 qts 3 cup	
RAISINS	1-7/8 lbs	1 qts 2 cup	
COOKING SPRAY,NONSTICK	2 oz	1/4 cup 1/3 tbsp	

Method

1. Sift together flour, salt, baking soda, and baking powder; set aside for use in Step 2.
2. Place eggs, water, vanilla, shortening, and sugars in mixer bowl. Beat at low speed for 1 to 2 minutes or until well blended. Add dry ingredients; mix at low speed for 2 to 3 minutes or until smooth.
3. Add rolled oats and raisins; mix about 1 minute.
4. Lightly spray each pan with non-stick cooking spray. Drop about 1 tablespoon dough in rows of 5 by 7, on lightly sprayed pans.
5. Using a convection oven, bake at 325 F. for 13 to 15 minutes or until lightly browned on high fan, open vent.
6. Loosen cookies from pans while still warm.

OATMEAL CHOCOLATE CHIP COOKIES

Yield 100   **Portion** 2 Cookies

Calories	Carbohydrates	Protein	Fat	Cholesterol	Sodium	Calcium
322 cal	42 g	6 g	15 g	18 mg	177 mg	63 mg

Ingredient	Weight	Measure	Issue
FLOUR,WHEAT,GENERAL PURPOSE	2-1/4 lbs	2 qts	
SALT	7/8 oz	1 tbsp	
BAKING SODA	3/8 oz	3/8 tsp	
BAKING POWDER	1-1/3 oz	2-2/3 tbsp	
EGGS,WHOLE,FROZEN	12-7/8 oz	1-1/2 cup	
WATER	4-1/8 oz	1/2 cup	
EXTRACT,VANILLA	7/8 oz	2 tbsp	
SHORTENING	2 lbs	1 qts 1/2 cup	
SUGAR,GRANULATED	1-1/2 lbs	3-1/2 cup	
SUGAR,BROWN,PACKED	1-1/3 lbs	1 qts 1/4 cup	
CEREAL,OATMEAL,ROLLED	5-1/8 lbs	3 qts 3 cup	
CHOCOLATE,COOKING CHIPS,SEMISWEET	2-1/4 lbs	1 qts 2-1/8 cup	
COOKING SPRAY,NONSTICK	2 oz	1/4 cup 1/3 tbsp	

Method

1. Sift together flour, salt, baking soda, and baking powder; set aside for use in Step 2.

2. Place eggs, water, vanilla, shortening, and sugars in mixer bowl. Beat at low speed for 1 to 2 minutes or until well blended. Add dry ingredients; mix at low speed for 2 to 3 minutes or until smooth.
3. Add rolled oats and semisweet chocolate chips or chocolate flavored baking chips; mix about 1 minute.
4. Lightly spray each pan with non-stick cooking spray. Drop about 1 tablespoon dough in rows of 5 by 7, on lightly sprayed pans.
5. Using a convection oven, bake at 325 F. for 13 to 15 minutes or until lightly browned on high fan, open vent.
6. Loosen cookies from pans while still warm.

OATMEAL NUT COOKIES

Yield 100   **Portion** 2 Cookies

Calories	Carbohydrates	Protein	Fat	Cholesterol	Sodium	Calcium
296 cal	37 g	7 g	14 g	16 mg	169 mg	47 mg

Ingredient	Weight	Measure	Issue
FLOUR,WHEAT,GENERAL PURPOSE	2-1/4 lbs	2 qts	
SALT	7/8 oz	1 tbsp	
BAKING SODA	3/8 oz	3/8 tsp	
BAKING POWDER	1-1/3 oz	2-2/3 tbsp	
EGGS,WHOLE,FROZEN	12-7/8 oz	1-1/2 cup	
WATER	4-1/8 oz	1/2 cup	
EXTRACT,VANILLA	7/8 oz	2 tbsp	
SHORTENING	2 lbs	1 qts 1/2 cup	
SUGAR,GRANULATED	1-1/2 lbs	3-1/2 cup	
SUGAR,BROWN,PACKED	1-1/3 lbs	1 qts 1/4 cup	
CEREAL,OATMEAL,ROLLED	5-1/8 lbs	3 qts 3 cup	
NUTS,UNSALTED,CHOPPED,COARSELY	1 lbs	3-1/8 cup	
COOKING SPRAY,NONSTICK	2 oz	1/4 cup 1/3 tbsp	

Method
1. Sift together flour, salt, baking soda, and baking powder; set aside for use in Step 2.
2. Place eggs, water, vanilla, shortening, and sugars in mixer bowl. Beat at low speed for 1 to 2 minutes or until well blended. Add dry ingredients; mix at low speed for 2 to 3 minutes or until smooth.
3. Add rolled oats and unsalted nuts; mix about 1 minute.
4. Lightly spray each pan with non-stick cooking spray. Drop about 1 tablespoon dough in rows of 5 by 7, on lightly sprayed pans.
5. Using a convection oven, bake at 325 F. for 13 to 15 minutes or until lightly browned on high fan, open vent.
6. Loosen cookies from pans while still warm.

GINGERBREAD COOKIES (MIX)

Yield 100   **Portion** 2 Cookies

Calories	Carbohydrates	Protein	Fat	Cholesterol	Sodium	Calcium
222 cal	33 g	2 g	9 g	0 mg	244 mg	25 mg

Ingredient	Weight	Measure	Issue
GINGERBREAD MIX	5 lbs		
COOKIE MIX,SUGAR	5 lbs		
SHORTENING	3-5/8 oz	1/2 cup	
WATER	1-3/8 lbs	2-5/8 cup	
COOKING SPRAY,NONSTICK	2 oz	1/4 cup 1/3 tbsp	

Method

1. Place Gingerbread Cake Mix, Sugar Cookie Mix, and shortening in mixer bowl. Mix at low speed for 1 minute.
2. Add water gradually to mixture while still beating at low speed for 1 minute until sides of bowl become clean. Scrape down bowl; mix at low speed for 1 minute.
3. Divide dough into 10 pieces, about 1 pound 2 ounce each. Form into rolls about 20 inches long; slice each roll into 20 pieces.
4. Lightly spray each pan with non-stick cooking spray. Place in rows 4 by 6 on lightly sprayed sheet pans. Flatten cookies to 1/4-inch thickness.
5. Using a convection oven, bake at 350 F. for 9 minutes or until done on low fan, open vent.
6. Loosen cookies from pans while still warm.

OATMEAL COOKIES (OATMEAL COOKIE MIX)

Yield 100   Portion 2 Cookies

Calories	Carbohydrates	Protein	Fat	Cholesterol	Sodium	Calcium
253 cal	32 g	3 g	15 g	31 mg	63 mg	63 mg

Ingredient	Weight	Measure	Issue
COOKIE MIX,OATMEAL	9 lbs		
WATER	1 lbs	2 cup	
COOKING SPRAY,NONSTICK	2 oz	1/4cup 1/3tbsp	

Method

1. Place Oatmeal Cookie Mix and contents of soda pouches in mixer bowl. Mix to combine cookie mix and soda; add water; mix at low speed about 1 minute. Scrape down bowl once during mixing.
2. Lightly spray each pan with non-stick cooking spray. Drop about 1 level tablespoon of dough in rows, 5 by 7, on lightly sprayed pans.
3. Using a convection oven, bake at 325 F. for 12 to 14 minutes or until lightly browned on high fan, open vent.
4. Loosen cookies from pans while still warm.

OATMEAL RAISIN BARS (OATMEAL COOKIE MIX)

Yield 100   Portion 2 Bars

Calories	Carbohydrates	Protein	Fat	Cholesterol	Sodium	Calcium
125 cal	22 g	2 g	5 g	17 mg	34 mg	37 mg

Ingredient	Weight	Measure	Issue
COOKIE MIX,OATMEAL	9 lbs		
RAISINS	1-1/2 lbs	1 qts 5/8 cup	
WATER	1 lbs	2 cup	
COOKING SPRAY,NONSTICK	2 oz	1/4 cup 1/3 tbsp	

Method

1. Combine cookie mix and soda with raisins; mix until blended. Add water; mix.
2. Lightly spray each pan with non-stick cooking spray. Place about 5 pounds 11 ounces dough onto each lightly sprayed sheet pan. Roll evenly to 1/2-inch thickness with lightly floured rolling pin.
3. Using a convection oven, bake at 325 F. for 12 to 14 minutes or until lightly browned on high fan, open vent. DO NOT OVERBAKE.
4. Cut 6 by 18 while still warm.

OATMEAL CHOCOLATE CHIP COOKIES (OATMEAL COOKIE MIX)

Yield 100   **Portion** 2 Cookies

Calories	Carbohydrates	Protein	Fat	Cholesterol	Sodium	Calcium
199 cal	21 g	2 g	14 g	18 mg	39 mg	46 mg

Ingredient	Weight	Measure	Issue
COOKIE MIX,OATMEAL	9 lbs		
CHOCOLATE,COOKING CHIPS,SEMISWEET	1-1/2 lbs	1 qts	
WATER	1 lbs	2 cup	
COOKING SPRAY,NONSTICK	2 oz	1/4 cup 1/3 tbsp	

Method

1. Combine cookie mix and soda with chocolate chips; mix until blended. Add water; mix.
2. Lightly spray each pan with non-stick cooking spray. Drop about 1 level tablespoon dough in rows, 5 by 7, on lightly sprayed pans.
3. Using a convection oven, bake at 325 F. for 12 to 14 minutes or until lightly browned on high fan, open vent.
4. Loosen cookies from pans while still warm.

OATMEAL RAISIN COOKIES (OATMEAL COOKIE MIX)

Yield 100   **Portion** 2 Cookies

Calories	Carbohydrates	Protein	Fat	Cholesterol	Sodium	Calcium
125 cal	22 g	2 g	5 g	17 mg	34 mg	37 mg

Ingredient	Weight	Measure	Issue
COOKIE MIX,OATMEAL	9 lbs		
RAISINS	1-1/2 lbs	1 qts 5/8 cup	
WATER	1 lbs	2 cup	
COOKING SPRAY,NONSTICK	2 oz	1/4 cup 1/3 tbsp	

Method

1. Combine cookie mix and soda with raisins; mix until blended. Add water; mix.
2. Lightly spray each pan with non-stick cooking spray. Drop about 1 level tablespoon dough in rows, 5 by 7, on lightly sprayed pans.
3. Using a convection oven, bake at 325 F. for 12 to 14 minutes or until lightly browned on high fan, open vent.
4. Loosen cookies from pans while still warm.

SPICED OATMEAL NUT COOKIES (OATMEAL COOKIE MIX)

Yield 100   **Portion** 2 Cookies

Calories	Carbohydrates	Protein	Fat	Cholesterol	Sodium	Calcium
172 cal	21 g	2 g	10 g	17 mg	34 mg	41 mg

Ingredient	Weight	Measure	Issue
COOKIE MIX,OATMEAL	9 lbs		
RAISINS	1 lbs	3 cup	
CINNAMON,GROUND	5/8 oz	2-2/3 tbsp	
NUTMEG,GROUND	2/3 oz	2-2/3 tbsp	
CLOVES,GROUND	1/4 oz	1 tbsp	
NUTS,UNSALTED,CHOPPED,COARSELY	8 oz	1-1/2 cup	
WATER	1 lbs	2 cup	
COOKING SPRAY,NONSTICK	2 oz	1/4 cup 1/3 tbsp	

Method
1. Combine cookie mix and soda with raisins, ground cinnamon, nutmeg, cloves, and chopped nuts; mix until blended. Add water; mix.
2. Lightly spray each pan with non-stick cooking spray. Drop about 1 level tablespoon dough in rows, 5 by 7, on lightly sprayed pans.
3. Using a convection oven, bake at 325 F. for 12 to 14 minutes or until lightly browned on high fan, open vent.
4. Loosen cookies from pans while still warm.

CRISP CHOCOLATE COOKIES

Yield 100   **Portion** 2 Cookies

Calories	Carbohydrates	Protein	Fat	Cholesterol	Sodium	Calcium
338 cal	47 g	4 g	16 g	34 mg	167 mg	35 mg

Ingredient	Weight	Measure	Issue
SHORTENING	3-1/8 lbs	1 qts 3 cup	
EGGS,WHOLE,FROZEN,BEATEN,ROOM TEMPERATURE	1-3/4 lbs	3-1/4 cup	
WATER	4-1/8 oz	1/2 cup	
SUGAR,GRANULATED	5-3/4 lbs	3 qts 1 cup	
SALT	1 oz	1 tbsp	
BAKING POWDER	1-1/3 oz	2-2/3 tbsp	
COCOA	12-1/8 oz	1 qts	
FLOUR,WHEAT,GENERAL PURPOSE	5-1/2 lbs	1 gal 1 qts	

Method
1. Place ingredients in mixer bowl in order listed. Mix at low speed 1 to 2 minutes or until thoroughly blended. Scrape down bowl once during mixing.
2. Divide dough into 1 pound 10 ounce pieces. Form into rolls 2 inches thick. Wrap in waxed paper and chill at least 3 hours.
3. Slice each roll into 20 pieces. Place in rows, 5 by 7, on ungreased pans.
4. Bake about 10 minutes or until done in 350 F. oven.
5. Loosen cookies from pans while still warm.

CHOCOLATE COOKIES (CHOCOLATE COOKIE MIX)

Yield 100   **Portion** 2 Cookies

Calories	Carbohydrates	Protein	Fat	Cholesterol	Sodium	Calcium
277 cal	35 g	2 g	16 g	0 mg	137 mg	9 mg

Ingredient	Weight	Measure	Issue
COOKIE MIX,CHOCOLATE	10 lbs		

Method
1. Prepare Chocolate Cookie Mix in mixer bowl. Prepare according to instructions on container.

DOUBLE CHOCOLATE CHIP BARS (CHOCOLATE COOKIE MIX)

Yield 100   **Portion** 2 Bars

Calories	Carbohydrates	Protein	Fat	Cholesterol	Sodium	Calcium
254 cal	41 g	2 g	10 g	2 mg	146 mg	28 mg

Ingredient	Weight	Measure	Issue
COOKIE MIX,CHOCOLATE	10 lbs		
WATER	2-1/3 lbs	1 qts 1/2 cup	
COOKING SPRAY,NONSTICK	2 oz	1/4 cup 1/3 tbsp	
CHOCOLATE,COOKING CHIPS,SEMISWEET	2-1/4 lbs	1 qts 2-1/8 cup	

Method
1. Place Chocolate Cookie Mix and water in mixer bowl. Beat at medium speed 1 minute. Add chocolate chips or chocolate flavored baking chips; mix at low speed. Lightly spray each pan with non-stick cooking spray. Spread 7 pounds batter in each sprayed sheet pan.
2. Bake for 25 to 30 minutes in 350 F. Cut 6 by 18 per pan while warm.

DOUBLE CHOCOLATE CHIP COOKIES (CHOC COOKIE MIX)

Yield 100   **Portion** 2 Each

Calories	Carbohydrates	Protein	Fat	Cholesterol	Sodium	Calcium
254 cal	41 g	2 g	10 g	2 mg	146 mg	28 mg

Ingredient	Weight	Measure	Issue
COOKIE MIX,CHOCOLATE	10 lbs		
WATER	1-5/8 lbs	3 cup	
CHOCOLATE,COOKING CHIPS,SEMISWEET	2-1/4 lbs	1 qts 2-1/8 cup	
COOKING SPRAY,NONSTICK	2 oz	1/4 cup 1/3 tbsp	

Method
1. Place Chocolate Cookie Mix and water in mixer bowl. Mix at medium speed 1 minute. Add chocolate chips or chocolate flavored baking chips; mix on low speed. Lightly spray each pan with non-stick cooking spray. Drop by rounded tablespoon, in rows 5 by 7 on sprayed pans.
2. Bake at 375 F. for 12 to 14 minutes.
3. Loosen cookies from pans while still warm.

PEANUT BUTTER COOKIES

Yield 100   **Portion** 2 Cookies

Calories	Carbohydrates	Protein	Fat	Cholesterol	Sodium	Calcium
257 cal	27 g	5 g	15 g	24 mg	211 mg	14 mg

Ingredient	Weight	Measure	Issue
SHORTENING	1-3/4 lbs	1 qts	
SUGAR,GRANULATED	2 lbs	1 qts 1/2 cup	
SUGAR,BROWN,PACKED	1 lbs	3-1/4 cup	
EGGS,WHOLE,FROZEN	1-1/4 lbs	2-1/4 cup	
EXTRACT,VANILLA	5/8 oz	1 tbsp	
PEANUT BUTTER	2-1/2 lbs	1 qts 1/2 cup	
FLOUR,WHEAT,GENERAL PURPOSE	3-1/3 lbs	3 qts	
BAKING SODA	1-1/3 oz	2-2/3 tbsp	
SALT	3/8 oz	1/3 tsp	

Method
1. Place ingredients in mixer bowl in order listed. Mix at low speed 1 to 2 minutes or until smooth. Scrape down bowl once during mixing.
2. Divide dough into 10 pieces about 1 pound 3 ounces each. Form into rolls 1-3/4x20x1-1/4-inches; slice each roll into 20 pieces, about 1 ounce each.
3. Place in rows, 4 x 6, on ungreased sheet pans; using a fork, flatten to 1/4-inch thickness, forming a crisscross pattern.
4. Using a convection oven, bake at 325 F. for 10 minutes or until lightly browned on high fan, open vent.
5. Loosen cookies from pans while still warm.

PEANUT BUTTER COOKIES (SUGAR COOKIE MIX)

Yield 100   **Portion** 2 Cookies

Calories	Carbohydrates	Protein	Fat	Cholesterol	Sodium	Calcium
287 cal	34 g	4 g	16 g	0 mg	245 mg	12 mg

Ingredient	Weight	Measure	Issue
COOKIE MIX,SUGAR	10 lbs		
WATER	1-5/8 lbs	3 cup	
PEANUT BUTTER	2-1/2 lbs	1 qts 1/2 cup	

Method
1. Prepare sugar cookie mix according to package directions. Add water and peanut butter. Mix at low speed 1 minute. DO NOT OVERMIX.
2. Drop by slightly rounded tablespoons. Place in rows, 4 by 6, on ungreased pans; using a fork, flatten to 1/4-inch thickness, forming a crisscross pattern.
3. Using a convection oven, bake at 325 F. for 10 to 12 minutes or until lightly browned on high fan, open vent.
4. Loosen cookies from pans while still warm.

PEANUT BUTTER BARS (SUGAR COOKIE MIX)

Yield 100   **Portion** 2 Bars

Calories	Carbohydrates	Protein	Fat	Cholesterol	Sodium	Calcium
287 cal	34 g	4 g	16 g	0 mg	245 mg	12 mg

Ingredient	Weight	Measure	Issue
COOKIE MIX,SUGAR	10 lbs		
WATER	1-1/3 lbs	2-1/2 cup	
PEANUT BUTTER	2-1/2 lbs	1 qts 1/2 cup	

Method

1. Prepare sugar cookies according to package directions. Add water and peanut butter; beat on medium speed 1 minute. DO NOT OVERMIX.
2. Spread approximately 6 pounds 14 ounces dough evenly into each pan.
3. Using a convection oven, bake at 325 F. for 20 for 25 minutes until lightly browned on low fan, closed vent. DO NOT OVERBAKE. Cut 6 by 18 while still warm.

CHOCOLATE DROP COOKIES

Yield 100   **Portion** 2 Cookies

Calories	Carbohydrates	Protein	Fat	Cholesterol	Sodium	Calcium
241 cal	30 g	4 g	13 g	20 mg	158 mg	27 mg

Ingredient	Weight	Measure	Issue
SHORTENING	2-1/2 lbs	1 qts 1-1/2 cup	
EGGS,WHOLE,FROZEN,BEATEN	1 lbs	1-7/8 cup	
WATER	2-1/8 lbs	1 qts	
SUGAR,BROWN,PACKED	2-3/4 lbs	2 qts 1/2 cup	
MILK,NONFAT,DRY	1-3/4 oz	3/4 cup	
FLOUR,WHEAT,GENERAL PURPOSE	4-3/8 lbs	1 gal	
BAKING SODA	2/3 oz	1 tbsp	
SALT	7/8 oz	1 tbsp	
COCOA	12-1/8 oz	1 qts	
EXTRACT,VANILLA	1-7/8 oz	1/4 cup 1/3 tbsp	
COOKING SPRAY,NONSTICK	2 oz	1/4 cup 1/3 tbsp	

Method

1. Place ingredients in mixer bowl in order listed. Mix at low speed 1 to 2 minutes or until thoroughly blended. Scrape down bowl once during mixing.
2. Lightly spray each pan with non-stick cooking spray. Drop about 2 tablespoons dough in rows, 4 x 6, on sprayed sheet pans.
3. Using a convection oven, bake at 325 F. for 12 minutes or until done on low fan, open vent.
4. Loosen cookies from pans while still warm.

CHOCOLATE DROP COOKIES (CHOCOLATE BROWNIE MIX)

Yield 100   **Portion** 2 Cookies

Calories	Carbohydrates	Protein	Fat	Cholesterol	Sodium	Calcium
241 cal	35 g	2 g	12 g	0 mg	138 mg	9 mg

Ingredient	Weight	Measure	Issue
BROWNIE MIX	10 lbs	1 gal 3-3/8 qts	
WATER	1-5/8 lbs	3 cup	
COOKING SPRAY,NONSTICK	2 oz	1/4 cup 1/3 tbsp	

Method

1. Place Brownie Mix, contents of soda pouches and water in mixer bowl. Mix at medium speed 1 minute.
2. Lightly spray each pan with non-stick cooking spray. Drop about 1 tablespoon dough in rows, 4 by 6, on sprayed sheet pans.
3. Bake at 375 F. for 10 to 12 minutes or until done.
4. Loosen cookies from pans while still warm.

SUGAR COOKIES

Yield 100   **Portion** 2 Cookies

Calories	Carbohydrates	Protein	Fat	Cholesterol	Sodium	Calcium
243 cal	40 g	3 g	8 g	20 mg	223 mg	63 mg

Ingredient	Weight	Measure	Issue
EGGS,WHOLE,FROZEN	1 lbs	1-7/8 cup	
SHORTENING	1-1/2 lbs	3-3/8 cup	
WATER	10-1/2 oz	1-1/4 cup	
EXTRACT,VANILLA	1-3/8 oz	3 tbsp	
SUGAR,GRANULATED	4-3/8 lbs	2 qts 2 cup	
FLOUR,WHEAT,GENERAL PURPOSE	5-1/4 lbs	1 gal 3/4 qts	
SALT	1 oz	1 tbsp	
BAKING POWDER	3-1/4 oz	1/4 cup 3 tbsp	
MILK,NONFAT,DRY	5/8 oz	1/4 cup 1/3 tbsp	
SUGAR,GRANULATED	5-1/4 oz	3/4 cup	
COOKING SPRAY,NONSTICK	2 oz	1/4 cup 1/3 tbsp	

Method

1. Place ingredients in mixer bowl in order listed. Beat at low speed for 1 to 2 minutes or until smooth. Scrape down bowl once during mixing.
2. Divide dough into 1-1/4 pound pieces. Roll into rolls; slice each roll into 20 pieces.
3. Lightly spray each pan with non-stick cooking spray. Dip each piece in sugar; place sugared side up in rows, 4 by 6, on sprayed sheet pans.
4. Flatten cookies to about 1/4-inch thickness.
5. Using a convection oven, bake at 350 F. for 8 to 10 minutes or until lightly browned on low fan, open vent. DO NOT OVER BAKE.
6. Loosen cookies from pans while still warm.

SUGAR COOKIES (SUGAR COOKIE MIX)

Yield 100   **Portion** 2 Cookies

Calories	Carbohydrates	Protein	Fat	Cholesterol	Sodium	Calcium
218 cal	32 g	1 g	10 g	0 mg	191 mg	8 mg

Ingredient	Weight	Measure	Issue
COOKIE MIX,SUGAR	10 lbs		

Method
1. Prepare mix according to instructions on container. Using a convection oven, bake at 325 F. for 8 to 10 minutes on low fan, open vent.

SNICKERDOODLE COOKIES

Yield 100   **Portion** 2 Cookies

Calories	Carbohydrates	Protein	Fat	Cholesterol	Sodium	Calcium
246 cal	41 g	3 g	8 g	20 mg	223 mg	68 mg

Ingredient	Weight	Measure	Issue
EGGS,WHOLE,FROZEN	1 lbs	1-7/8 cup	
SHORTENING	1-1/2 lbs	3-3/8 cup	
WATER	10-1/2 oz	1-1/4 cup	
EXTRACT,VANILLA	1-3/8 oz	3 tbsp	
SUGAR,GRANULATED	4-3/8 lbs	2 qts 2 cup	
FLOUR,WHEAT,GENERAL PURPOSE	5-1/4 lbs	1 gal 3/4 qts	
SALT	1 oz	1 tbsp	
BAKING POWDER	3-1/4 oz	1/4 cup 3 tbsp	
MILK,NONFAT,DRY	5/8 oz	1/4cup 1/3tbsp	
SUGAR,GRANULATED	7 oz	1 cup	
CINNAMON,GROUND	1-1/4 oz	1/4cup 1-2/3tbsp	
COOKING SPRAY,NONSTICK	2 oz	1/4cup 1/3tbsp	

Method
1. Place ingredients in mixer bowl in order listed. Beat at low speed 1 to 2 minutes or until smooth. Scrape down bowl once during mixing.
2. Divide dough into 1-1/4 pound pieces. Roll into rolls; slice each roll into 20 pieces.
3. Lightly spray each pan with non-stick cooking spray. Combine granulated sugar and ground cinnamon. Dip each piece in sugar and cinnamon mixture; place sugared side up in rows, 4 by 6, on sprayed sheet pans.
4. Flatten cookies to about 1/4-inch thickness.
5. Using a convection oven, bake at 350 F. for 8 to 10 minutes or until lightly browned on low fan, open vent. DO NOT OVER BAKE.
6. Loosen cookies from pans while still warm.

SNICKERDOODLE COOKIES (SUGAR COOKIE MIX)

Yield 100   **Portion** 2 Cookies

Calories	Carbohydrates	Protein	Fat	Cholesterol	Sodium	Calcium
231 cal	34 g	1 g	10 g	0 mg	191 mg	12 mg

Ingredient	Weight	Measure	Issue
COOKIE MIX,SUGAR	10 lbs		
CINNAMON,GROUND	1-1/4 oz	1/4 cup 1-2/3 tbsp	
SUGAR,GRANULATED	7 oz	1 cup	
COOKING SPRAY,NONSTICK	2 oz	1/4 cup 1/3 tbsp	

Method
1. Prepare mix according to instructions on container.
2. Combine sugar and ground cinnamon. Dip each piece in sugar and cinnamon.
3. Lightly spray cookie pans with non-stick cooking spray. Place cookies 4 by 6.
4. Using a convection oven, bake at 325 F. for 8 to 10 minutes on low fan, open vent.

COCONUT RAISIN DROP COOKIES

Yield 100   **Portion** 2 Cookies

Calories	Carbohydrates	Protein	Fat	Cholesterol	Sodium	Calcium
192 cal	25 g	3 g	9 g	8 mg	102 mg	43 mg

Ingredient	Weight	Measure	Issue
EGGS,WHOLE,FROZEN	6-3/8 oz	3/4 cup	
SHORTENING	1 lbs	2-1/4 cup	
MOLASSES	1-5/8 lbs	2-1/4 cup	
WATER	1 lbs	2 cup	
FLOUR,WHEAT,GENERAL PURPOSE	2-3/4 lbs	2 qts 2 cup	
SUGAR,GRANULATED	1 lbs	2-1/4 cup	
MILK,NONFAT,DRY	7/8 oz	1/4 cup 2-1/3 tbsp	
BAKING POWDER	3/4 oz	1 tbsp	
BAKING SODA	3/4 oz	1 tbsp	
COCONUT,PREPARED,SWEETENED FLAKES	9-7/8 oz	3 cup	
RAISINS	1 lbs	3 cup	
NUTS,UNSALTED,CHOPPED,COARSELY	1-1/4 lbs	1 qts	
COOKING SPRAY,NONSTICK	2 oz	1/4 cup 1/3 tbsp	

Method
1. Place ingredients in mixer bowl in order listed. Mix at low speed 2 minutes or until thoroughly blended.
2. Lightly spray each pan with non-stick cooking spray. Drop about 1 ounce of dough per cookie in rows, 4 by 6, on sprayed pans.
3. Bake at 375 F. for 10 minutes or until done.

CRISP DROP COOKIES

Yield 100   **Portion** 2 Each

Calories	Carbohydrates	Protein	Fat	Cholesterol	Sodium	Calcium
249 cal	37 g	3 g	10 g	6 mg	233 mg	9 mg

Ingredient	Weight	Measure	Issue
FLOUR,WHEAT,GENERAL PURPOSE	5-1/2 lbs	1 gal 1 qts	
SUGAR,GRANULATED	12-1/3 oz	1-3/4 cup	
SUGAR,GRANULATED	3 lbs	1 qts 2-3/4 cup	

SYRUP	2-3/4 oz	1/4 cup 1/3 tbsp
SHORTENING	2 lbs	1 qts 1/2 cup
SALT	1-1/4 oz	2 tbsp
EGGS,WHOLE,FROZEN	4-7/8 oz	1/2 cup 1 tbsp
EXTRACT,VANILLA	7/8 oz	2 tbsp
MILK,NONFAT,DRY	1-1/4 oz	1/2 cup
WATER,WARM	1-1/2 lbs	2-3/4 cup
BAKING SODA	1-1/8 oz	2-1/3 tbsp
COOKING SPRAY,NONSTICK	2 oz	1/4 cup 1/3 tbsp

Method

1. Sift together flour and sugar. Set aside for use in Step 4.
2. Cream sugar, syrup, shortening, salt, eggs, and vanilla at low speed 5 minutes or until light and fluffy.
3. Reconstitute milk; add soda; add to creamed mixture. Blend thoroughly.
4. Add dry ingredients to mixture; mix only until ingredients are combined. DO NOT OVERMIX.
5. Lightly spray each pan with non-stick cooking spray. Drop by tablespoons, or through size 10 plain pastry tube, in rows 5 by 7, onto lightly sprayed pans.
6. Bake at 375 F. for 14 to 16 minutes or until lightly browned.
7. Loosen cookies from pans while still warm.

COCONUT CEREAL COOKIES

Yield 100   **Portion** 2 Cookies

Calories	Carbohydrates	Protein	Fat	Cholesterol	Sodium	Calcium
241 cal	31 g	3 g	12 g	20 mg	177 mg	12 mg

Ingredient	Weight	Measure	Issue
FLOUR,WHEAT,GENERAL PURPOSE	2-1/4 lbs	2 qts	
SALT	5/8 oz	1 tbsp	
BAKING SODA	1/2 oz	1 tbsp	
SHORTENING	2 lbs	1 qts 1/2 cup	
SUGAR,GRANULATED	2 lbs	1 qts 1/2 cup	
SUGAR,BROWN,PACKED	1-1/4 lbs	3-3/4 cup	
EGGS,WHOLE,FROZEN	1 lbs	1-7/8 cup	
EXTRACT,VANILLA	1/2 oz	1 tbsp	
COCONUT,PREPARED,SWEETENED FLAKES	1-1/8 lbs	1 qts 1-1/2 cup	
CEREAL,OATMEAL,ROLLED	1 lbs	3 cup	
CEREAL,CORN FLAKES,BULK	1 lbs	1 gal	

Method

1. Sift flour, salt and soda together. Set aside for use in Step 3.
2. Cream shortening and sugars in mixer bowl at low speed 1 minute. Mix at medium speed 3 minutes or until light and fluffy.
3. Add eggs and vanilla to creamed mixture. Beat at low speed 1 minute or until well blended. At low speed, add dry ingredients. Scrape bowl; mix at low speed 1 minute or until combined.
4. Add coconut and cereals to dough; mix at low speed only until ingredients are combined. Let dough stand about 30 minutes.
5. Divide dough into 10 pieces, about 1 pound 1 ounce each. Form into rolls; slice each roll into 20 pieces.

6. Place in rows, 4 by 6, on ungreased pans; flatten to 1/4-inch thickness.
7. Using a convection oven, bake at 325 F. for 8 to 10 minutes or until lightly browned on high fan, open vent.
8. Loosen cookies from pans while still warm.

Notes
1. In Step 4, other prepared cereals such as bran flakes, wheat flakes, puffed rice, puffed corn, or puffed wheat, or combination may be used for corn flakes.

HERMITS

Yield 100   **Portion** 2 Each

Calories	Carbohydrates	Protein	Fat	Cholesterol	Sodium	Calcium
229 cal	39 g	3 g	7 g	17 mg	50 mg	22 mg

Ingredient	Weight	Measure	Issue
SUGAR,GRANULATED	2-2/3 lbs	1 qts 2 cup	
SHORTENING	1-1/3 lbs	3 cup	
BAKING SODA	1/2 oz	1 tbsp	
EGGS,WHOLE,FROZEN	14-1/4 oz	1-5/8 cup	
NUTMEG,GROUND	1/2 oz	2 tbsp	
CINNAMON,GROUND	1/2 oz	2 tbsp	
MOLASSES	1-1/8 lbs	1-1/2 cup	
WATER	8-1/3 oz	1 cup	
RAISINS	1-7/8 lbs	1 qts 2 cup	
FLOUR,WHEAT,GENERAL PURPOSE	4-2/3 lbs	1 gal 1/4 qts	
COOKING SPRAY,NONSTICK	2 oz	1/4 cup 1/3 tbsp	

Method
1. Blend sugar, shortening, baking soda, eggs, nutmeg and cinnamon in mixer bowl at low speed 1 to 2 minutes or until well blended. Scrape down bowl.
2. Add molasses, water, and raisins; mix at medium speed about 1 minute or until blended.
3. Add flour gradually; mix at low speed only until ingredients are combined.
4. Lightly spray each pan with non-stick cooking spray. Divide dough into 12 pieces, weighing about 1 pounds each; form into strips about 22 inches long. Place 3 strips on each lightly greased sheet pan. Press strips down until each is 3 inches wide, and 3/8 inches thick.
5. Using a convection oven, bake at 325 F. for 10 to 12 minutes or until done on low fan, open vent.
6. Loosen baked strips from pans while still warm; cut each strip into 16 bars.

RAISIN NUT BARS

Yield 100   **Portion** 1 Bar

Calories	Carbohydrates	Protein	Fat	Cholesterol	Sodium	Calcium
275 cal	37 g	6 g	12 g	18 mg	191 mg	30 mg

Ingredient	Weight	Measure	Issue
EGGS,WHOLE,FROZEN	12-7/8 oz	1-1/2 cup	
WATER	12-1/2 oz	1-1/2 cup	
SHORTENING	1-1/2 lbs	3-3/8 cup	
SUGAR,BROWN,PACKED	2-1/8 lbs	1 qts 2-1/2 cup	

FLOUR,WHEAT,GENERAL PURPOSE	5-1/4 lbs	1 gal 3/4 qts
MILK,NONFAT,DRY	5/8 oz	1/4 cup 1/3 tbsp
SALT	1 oz	1 tbsp
BAKING SODA	3/4 oz	1 tbsp
CINNAMON,GROUND	1/2 oz	2 tbsp
NUTMEG,GROUND	1/8 oz	1/3 tsp
RAISINS	1-7/8 lbs	1 qts 2 cup
NUTS,UNSALTED,CHOPPED,COARSELY	1-7/8 lbs	1 qts 2 cup
COOKING SPRAY,NONSTICK	2 oz	1/4 cup 1/3 tbsp
EGGS,WHOLE,FROZEN,BEATEN	1-5/8 oz	3 tbsp
WATER	2-1/8 oz	1/4 cup 1/3 tbsp
SUGAR,GRANULATED	3-1/2 oz	1/2 cup

Method

1. Place ingredients in mixer bowl in order listed. Beat at low speed 1 to 2 minutes or until thoroughly blended. Scrape down bowl once during mixing.
2. Lightly spray each pan with non-stick cooking spray. Divide dough into 1 pound 9 ounce pieces. Form into strips about 22 inches long on lightly sprayed pans. Place 3 strips per pan. Press strips down until each strip is about 4 inches wide and 3/8 inches thick.
3. Mix egg and water together. Brush top of each strip of dough with egg and water mixture.
4. Sprinkle about 2-1/2 teaspoons sugar over each strip.
5. Using a convection oven, bake at 325 F. for 10 to 12 minutes or until done on low fan, open vent.
6. While still warm, cut each strip into 12 bars, about 1-3/4 inches wide.

GINGER RAISIN BARS (OATMEAL COOKIE & GINGRBRD MIX)

Yield 100   **Portion** 1 Bar

Calories	Carbohydrates	Protein	Fat	Cholesterol	Sodium	Calcium
100 cal	19 g	1 g	3 g	8 mg	48 mg	25 mg

Ingredient	Weight	Measure	Issue
COOKIE MIX,OATMEAL	4-1/2 lbs		
GINGERBREAD MIX	1 lbs		
WATER	1 lbs	2 cup	
RAISINS	1-7/8 lbs	1 qts 2 cup	
COOKING SPRAY,NONSTICK	2 oz	1/4 cup 1/3 tbsp	

Method

1. Prepare mix according to instructions on container.
2. Divide dough into 9 pieces, about 1-1/2 pounds each. Form strips about 22 inches long on lightly greased pans, 3 strips per pan. Press strips down until each strip is about 4 inches wide and 3/8 inch thick.
3. Using a convection oven, bake 16 to 18 minutes or until done on low fan, open vent. While still warm, cut each strip into 12 bars.

GINGER MOLASSES COOKIES (SUGAR COOKIE MIX)

Yield 100   **Portion** 2 Cookies

Calories	Carbohydrates	Protein	Fat	Cholesterol	Sodium	Calcium
231 cal	34 g	1 g	10 g	0 mg	192 mg	15 mg

Ingredient	Weight	Measure	Issue
COOKIE MIX,SUGAR	10 lbs		
GINGER,GROUND	1-1/8 oz	1/4 cup 2-1/3 tbsp	
CINNAMON,GROUND	5/8 oz	2-2/3 tbsp	
MOLASSES	8-2/3 oz	3/4 cup	
WATER	1-5/8 lbs	3 cup	
COOKING SPRAY,NONSTICK	2 oz	1/4 cup 1/3 tbsp	

Method
1. Mix cookie mix and contents of soda pouches.
2. Add ginger, cinnamon, molasses and water. Beat at medium speed 2 minutes or until blended.
3. Lightly spray cooking pans with non-stick cooking spray. Drop by tablespoons in rows of 4 by 6, on lightly sprayed pans.
4. Bake at 375 F. for 11 to 13 minutes or until done.
5. Loosen cookies from pans while still warm.

GINGER MOLASSES BARS (SUGAR COOKIE MIX)

Yield 100   **Portion** 2 Bars

Calories	Carbohydrates	Protein	Fat	Cholesterol	Sodium	Calcium
231 cal	34 g	1 g	10 g	0 mg	192 mg	15 mg

Ingredient	Weight	Measure	Issue
COOKIE MIX,SUGAR	10 lbs		
GINGER,GROUND	1-1/8 oz	1/4 cup 2-1/3 tbsp	
CINNAMON,GROUND	5/8 oz	2-2/3 tbsp	
MOLASSES	8-2/3 oz	3/4 cup	
WATER	1 lbs	2 cup	
COOKING SPRAY,NONSTICK	2 oz	1/4 cup 1/3 tbsp	

Method
1. Prepare cookie mix according to instructions on container.
2. Add ginger, cinnamon, molasses, and water. Beat at medium speed 1 minute. DO NOT OVERMIX.
3. Lightly spray pans with non-stick cooking spray. Spread dough evenly into each pan. Bake at 350 F. for 25 minutes. Cut 6 by 18 while still warm.

CHOCOLATE CHIP COOKIES

Yield 100   **Portion** 2 Cookies

Calories	Carbohydrates	Protein	Fat	Cholesterol	Sodium	Calcium
266 cal	30 g	3 g	15 g	22 mg	196 mg	29 mg

Ingredient	Weight	Measure	Issue
FLOUR,WHEAT,GENERAL PURPOSE	3-5/8 lbs	3 qts 1 cup	
BAKING SODA	3/4 oz	1 tbsp	
SALT	1 oz	1 tbsp	
SHORTENING	2 lbs	1 qts 1/2 cup	
SUGAR,BROWN,PACKED	1-1/8 lbs	3-1/2 cup	
SUGAR,GRANULATED	1-1/2 lbs	3-1/2 cup	

EGGS,WHOLE,FROZEN	1 lbs	1-7/8 cup
WATER,WARM	1 oz	2 tbsp
EXTRACT,VANILLA	1/2 oz	1 tbsp
CHOCOLATE,COOKING CHIPS,SEMISWEET	2-1/4 lbs	1 qts 2 cup

Method
1. Sift together flour, baking soda, and salt. Set aside for use in Step 4.
2. Cream shortening in mixer bowl at medium speed about 1 minute. Gradually add sugars; mix at medium speed 3 minutes or until light and fluffy. Scrape down bowl.
3. Combine slightly beaten eggs and water; add gradually to creamed mixture. Blend thoroughly about 1 minute. Add vanilla. Mix thoroughly.
4. Add dry ingredients; mix only until ingredients are combined about 1 minute.
5. Add chocolate chips; mix on low speed about 1 minute or until evenly distributed.
6. Drop by tablespoons in rows, 4 by 6, on ungreased pans.
7. Using a convection oven, bake at 325 F. for 10 to 12 minutes or until lightly browned on high fan, open vent.
8. Loosen cookies from pans while still warm.

CHOCOLATE CHIP COOKIES (SUGAR COOKIE MIX)

Yield 100   **Portion** 2 Cookies

Calories	Carbohydrates	Protein	Fat	Cholesterol	Sodium	Calcium
223 cal	32 g	1 g	10 g	0 mg	191 mg	8 mg

Ingredient	Weight	Measure	Issue
COOKIE MIX,SUGAR	10 lbs		
WATER	1-5/8 lbs	3 cup	
COOKING SPRAY,NONSTICK	2 oz	1/4 cup 1/3 tbsp	

Method
1. Prepare mix according to instructions on container. Add water.
2. Beat at medium speed 1 minute. DO NOT OVERMIX.
3. Add chocolate chips; mix on low speed about 1 minute or until evenly distributed.
4. Lightly spray sheets with non-stick cooking spray. Drop 1 tablespoon of mix onto lightly sprayed cookie sheets in rows 4 by 6.
5. Bake 12 to 14 minutes or until done. Loosen cookies from pans while still warm.

CHOCOLATE CHIP BARS (SUGAR COOKIE MIX)

Yield 100   **Portion** 2 Cookies

Calories	Carbohydrates	Protein	Fat	Cholesterol	Sodium	Calcium
223 cal	32 g	1 g	10 g	0 mg	191 mg	8 mg

Ingredient	Weight	Measure	Issue
COOKIE MIX,SUGAR	10 lbs		
WATER	1-5/8 lbs	3 cup	
COOKING SPRAY,NONSTICK	2 oz	1/4 cup 1/3 tbsp	

Method

1. Prepare mix according to instructions on container. Add water.
2. Beat at medium speed 1 minute. DO NOT OVERMIX.
3. Add chocolate chips; mix on low speed about 1 minute or until evenly distributed.
4. Lightly spray sheets with non-stick cooking spray. Place dough in lightly greased sheet pans. Roll evenly into 1/2 thickness with lightly floured rolling pin.
5. Using a convection oven, bake at 325 F. for 20 to 25 minutes ot until lightly browned on low fan, open vent. DO NOT OVERBAKE. Cut 6 by 18 while still warm.

LEMON COOKIES

Yield 100   Portion 2 Cookies

Calories	Carbohydrates	Protein	Fat	Cholesterol	Sodium	Calcium
310 cal	38 g	4 g	16 g	52 mg	231 mg	11 mg

Ingredient	Weight	Measure	Issue
EGGS,WHOLE,FROZEN	1-3/4 lbs	3-1/4 cup	
SHORTENING	1-3/4 lbs	1 qts	
BUTTER	1-3/4 lbs	3-1/2 cup	
FLAVORING,LEMON	1 oz	2 tbsp	
SUGAR,GRANULATED	3-1/8 lbs	1 qts 3 cup	
FLOUR,WHEAT,GENERAL PURPOSE	5-1/2 lbs	1 gal 1 qts	
SALT	1 oz	1 tbsp	
BAKING SODA	1/2 oz	1 tbsp	
SUGAR,POWDERED,SIFTED	1 lbs	1 qts	
COOKING SPRAY,NONSTICK	2 oz	1/4 cup 1/3 tbsp	

Method

1. Place ingredients in mixer bowl in order listed. Beat at low speed 1 to 2 minutes or until smooth. Scrape down bowl once during mixing.
2. Divide dough into ten 1-1/4 pound pieces. Roll into powdered sugar forming rolls 2 inches thick.
3. Lightly spray each pan with non-stick cooking spray. Slice each roll into 20 pieces. Dip top of each piece in powdered sugar; place in rows, 4 by 6 on sprayed pans. Do not flatten cookies.
4. Bake at 375 F. for 12 to 14 minutes or until done.
5. Loosen cookies from pans while still warm.

ALMOND COOKIES

Yield 100   Portion 2 Cookies

Calories	Carbohydrates	Protein	Fat	Cholesterol	Sodium	Calcium
310 cal	38 g	4 g	16 g	52 mg	231 mg	11 mg

Ingredient	Weight	Measure	Issue
EGGS,WHOLE,FROZEN	1-3/4 lbs	3-1/4 cup	
SHORTENING	1-3/4 lbs	1 qts	
BUTTER	1-3/4 lbs	3-1/2 cup	
FLAVORING,ALMOND	7/8 oz	2 tbsp	
SUGAR,GRANULATED	3-1/8 lbs	1 qts 3 cup	
FLOUR,WHEAT,GENERAL PURPOSE	5-1/2 lbs	1 gal 1 qts	

SALT	1 oz	1 tbsp
BAKING SODA	1/2 oz	1 tbsp
SUGAR,POWDERED,SIFTED	1 lbs	1 qts
COOKING SPRAY,NONSTICK	2 oz	1/4 cup 1/3 tbsp

Method

1. Place ingredients in mixer bowl in order listed. Beat at low speed 1 to 2 minutes or until smooth. Scrape down bowl once during mixing.
2. Divide dough into ten 1-1/4 pound pieces. Roll into powdered sugar forming rolls 2 inches thick.
3. Lightly spray each pan with non-stick cooking spray. Slice each roll into 20 pieces. Dip top of each piece in powdered sugar; place in rows, 4 by 6 on sprayed pans. Do not flatten cookies.
4. Bake at 375 F. for 12 to 14 minutes or until done.
5. Loosen cookies from pans while still warm.

ORANGE COOKIES

Yield 100   **Portion** 2 Cookies

Calories	Carbohydrates	Protein	Fat	Cholesterol	Sodium	Calcium
310 cal	38 g	4 g	16 g	52 mg	231 mg	11 mg

Ingredient	Weight	Measure	Issue
EGGS,WHOLE,FROZEN	1-3/4 lbs	3-1/4 cup	
SHORTENING	1-3/4 lbs	1 qts	
BUTTER	1-3/4 lbs	3-1/2 cup	
FLAVORING,ORANGE	7/8 oz	2 tbsp	
SUGAR,GRANULATED	3-1/8 lbs	1 qts 3 cup	
FLOUR,WHEAT,GENERAL PURPOSE	5-1/2 lbs	1 gal 1 qts	
SALT	1 oz	1 tbsp	
BAKING SODA	1/2 oz	1 tbsp	
ORANGE,RIND,GRATED	1 oz	1/4 cup 1 tbsp	
SUGAR,POWDERED,SIFTED	1 lbs	1 qts	
COOKING SPRAY,NONSTICK	2 oz	1/4 cup 1/3 tbsp	

Method

1. Place ingredients in mixer bowl in order listed. Add orange rind if desired (optional). Beat at low speed 1 to 2 minutes or until smooth. Scrape down bowl once during mixing.
2. Divide dough into ten 1-1/4 pound pieces. Roll into powdered sugar forming rolls 2 inches thick.
3. Lightly spray each pan with non-stick cooking spray. Slice each roll into 20 pieces. Dip top of each piece in powdered sugar; place in rows, 4 by 6 on sprayed pans. Do not flatten cookies.
4. Bake at 375 F. for 12 to 14 minutes or until done.
5. Loosen cookies from pans while still warm.

VANILLA COOKIES

Yield 100   **Portion** 2 Cookies

Calories	Carbohydrates	Protein	Fat	Cholesterol	Sodium	Calcium
310 cal	38 g	4 g	16 g	52 mg	231 mg	11 mg

Ingredient	Weight	Measure	Issue
EGGS,WHOLE,FROZEN	1-3/4 lbs	3-1/4 cup	
SHORTENING	1-3/4 lbs	1 qts	
BUTTER	1-3/4 lbs	3-1/2 cup	
EXTRACT,VANILLA	7/8 oz	2 tbsp	
SUGAR,GRANULATED	3-1/8 lbs	1 qts 3 cup	
FLOUR,WHEAT,GENERAL PURPOSE	5-1/2 lbs	1 gal 1 qts	
SALT	1 oz	1 tbsp	
BAKING SODA	1/2 oz	1 tbsp	
SUGAR,POWDERED,SIFTED	1 lbs	1 qts	
COOKING SPRAY,NONSTICK	2 oz	1/4 cup 1/3 tbsp	

Method

1. Place ingredients in mixer bowl in order listed. Beat at low speed 1 to 2 minutes or until smooth. Scrape down bowl once during mixing.
2. Divide dough into ten 1-1/4 pound pieces. Roll into powdered sugar forming rolls 2 inches thick.
3. Lightly spray each pan with non-stick cooking spray. Slice each roll into 20 pieces. Dip top of each piece in powdered sugar; place in rows, 4 by 6 on sprayed pans. Do not flatten cookies.
4. Bake at 375 F. for 12 to 14 minutes or until done.
5. Loosen cookies from pans while still warm.

FUDGY BROWNIES

Yield 100   **Portion** 1 Brownie

Calories	Carbohydrates	Protein	Fat	Cholesterol	Sodium	Calcium
232 cal	50 g	5 g	4 g	0 mg	234 mg	63 mg

Ingredient	Weight	Measure	Issue
FLOUR,WHEAT,GENERAL PURPOSE	3-1/3 lbs	3 qts	
SUGAR,GRANULATED	5-1/4 lbs	3 qts	
COCOA	1-1/2 lbs	2 qts	
BAKING POWDER	2-5/8 oz	1/4 cup 1-2/3 tbsp	
BAKING SODA	2/3 oz	1 tbsp	
SALT	3/4 oz	1 tbsp	
WATER	2-1/2 lbs	1 qts 3/4 cup	
PRUNE PUREE	3-1/3 lbs	1 qts 2 cup	
CHOCOLATE,COOKING,UNSWEETENED,MELTED	12-3/8 oz	2-5/8 cup	
EXTRACT,VANILLA	2-5/8 oz	1/4 cup 2 tbsp	
EGG WHITES,FROZEN,THAWED	2-1/2 lbs	1 qts 3/4 cup	
COOKING SPRAY,NONSTICK	2 oz	1/4 cup 1/3 tbsp	

Method

1. Sift together flour, sugar, cocoa, baking powder, baking soda, and salt. Set aside for use in Step 3.
2. Place prune puree, water, melted chocolate, and vanilla in mixer bowl; blend well at low speed for 1 minute. Add egg whites; mix at low speed for 30 seconds; scrape down bowl.
3. Add dry ingredients to mixer bowl; mix at low speed 1 minute. Scrape down bowl; mix at low speed 2 minutes or until thoroughly blended.
4. Lightly spray each pan with non-stick cooking spray. Spread 4-1/2 quarts into each lightly sprayed pan.

5. Using a convection oven, bake at 325 F. 18-20 minutes or until done on high fan, open vent. Do not over bake.
6. Cool; cut 6 by 9.

CRISPY MARSHMALLOW SQUARES

Yield 100   **Portion** 2 Bars

Calories	Carbohydrates	Protein	Fat	Cholesterol	Sodium	Calcium
269 cal	52 g	2 g	6 g	0 mg	364 mg	6 mg

Ingredient	Weight	Measure	Issue
COOKING SPRAY,NONSTICK	2 oz	1/4 cup 1/3 tbsp	
MARGARINE	1-1/2 lbs	3 cup	
MARSHMALLOWS,MINIATURE	8 lbs	4 gal 2-1/8 qts	
EXTRACT,VANILLA	7/8 oz	2 tbsp	
CEREAL,RICE KRISPIES,BULK	5-7/8 lbs	5 gal	

Method
1. Lightly spray sheet pans with non-stick spray.
2. Melt margarine in steam-jacketed kettle.
3. Add marshmallows and vanilla. Stir constantly until marshmallows are completely melted, about 5 to 6 minutes.
4. Turn off heat; add cereal to marshmallow mixture; stir vigorously until cereal is well coated.
5. Turn 6 pounds 14 ounces mixture into each lightly sprayed sheet pan. Using a lightly sprayed rolling pin, roll mixture firmly to spread evenly in each pan. Cut 9 by 12. Remove from pan when cool.

BANANA SPLIT BROWNIES

Yield 100   **Portion** 1 Brownie

Calories	Carbohydrates	Protein	Fat	Cholesterol	Sodium	Calcium
250 cal	53 g	3 g	4 g	0 mg	190 mg	16 mg

Ingredient	Weight	Measure	Issue
WATER,WARM	3-2/3 lbs	1qts 3cup	
BROWNIE MIX, LOWFAT CHOCOLATE	12 lbs		
BANANA,FRESH,CHOPPED	5 lbs	3qts 3-1/8cup	7-2/3 lbs
CHERRIES,MARASCHINO,CHOPPED	1-7/8 lbs	3-3/8 cup	
COOKING SPRAY,NONSTICK	2 oz	1/4cup 1/3tbsp	

Method
1. Place water in mixer bowl. Add brownie mix; mix on low speed 1 minute. Scrape down bowl. Mix on low speed 1-1/2 minutes.
2. Cut bananas 1/2 lengthwise and in 1/4 inch slices. Add bananas and cherries. Mix on low speed 15 seconds.
3. Lightly spray each sheet pan with non-stick cooking spray. Pour 4-1/2 quarts of batter into each pan. Spread evenly.
4. Using a convection oven, bake at 325 F. for 22 to 25 minutes or until done on high fan, open vent. Do not over bake.

5. Cut 6 by 9.

Notes
1. If the brownie mix package directions call for eggs, use an equal amount of egg whites. If the mix calls for oil, use an equal volume of water.

ABRACADABRA BARS

Yield 100   Portion 2 Bars

Calories	Carbohydrates	Protein	Fat	Cholesterol	Sodium	Calcium
218 cal	42 g	3 g	4 g	0 mg	205 mg	13 mg

Ingredient	Weight	Measure	Issue
FLOUR,WHEAT,GENERAL PURPOSE	4-1/2 lbs	1 gal 1/8 qts	
BAKING SODA	1-1/3 oz	2-2/3 tbsp	
SALT	7/8 oz	1 tbsp	
CINNAMON,GROUND	1/3 oz	1 tbsp	
NUTMEG,GROUND	1/4 oz	3/8 tsp	
CLOVES,GROUND	1/4 oz	3/8 tsp	
GINGER,GROUND	1/8 oz	3/8 tsp	
SWEET POTATOES,CANNED,W/SYRUP	4-7/8 lbs	2 qts 1-3/4 cup	
SUGAR,GRANULATED	3-1/3 lbs	1 qts 3-1/2 cup	
SHORTENING	12-2/3 oz	1-3/4 cup	
EXTRACT,VANILLA	2-1/2 oz	1/4 cup 1-2/3 tbsp	
RAISINS	1-7/8 lbs	1 qts 2 cup	
COOKING SPRAY,NONSTICK	2 oz	1/4 cup 1/3 tbsp	

Method
1. Combine flour, baking soda, salt, cinnamon, nutmeg, cloves, and ginger.
2. Drain sweet potatoes, mash and set aside. Cream sugar and shortening. Add sweet potatoes and vanilla to the creamed sugar and shortening, beat on medium speed 1 minute; scrape down bowl. Beat with paddle on high speed 1 minute or until light and fluffy. Scrape down bowl.
3. Gradually add dry ingredients to sweet potato mixture, while mixing on low speed 1 minutes. Scrape down bowl; mix on medium speed 30 seconds or until just blended.
4. Fold in raisins at low speed 30 seconds.
5. Spray sheet pans very lightly with non-stick cooking spray. Using a rolling pin, spread 7 pounds 5 ounces mixture evenly in each pan.
6. Using a convection oven, bake at 325 F. 16 to 18 minutes until bars are lightly browned on low fan open vent. Cool. Cut into bars 6 by 18.

COOKIES,FROZEN,OATMEAL RAISIN

Yield 100   Portion 2 Cookies

Calories	Carbohydrates	Protein	Fat	Cholesterol	Sodium	Calcium
446 cal	63 g	5 g	19 g	39 mg	311 mg	43 mg

Ingredient	Weight	Measure	Issue
COOKING SPRAY,NONSTICK	2 oz	1/4 cup 1/3 tbsp	
COOKIES,FROZEN,OATMEAL	23 lbs		

Method

1. Spray sheet pans with non-stick cooking spray.
2. Thaw cookie dough in refrigerator approximately 24-36 hours for easier use. Scoop 1-1/2 ounces of batter onto sheet pans placing each scoop 1 inch apart.
3. Using a convection oven, bake cookies at 375 F. for 7-10 minutes. Bake time will vary by oven type. Cool cookies for 20-30 minutes before removing from pan.

COOKIES,FROZEN,SNICKERDOODLE

Yield 100   Portion 2 Cookies

Calories	Carbohydrates	Protein	Fat	Cholesterol	Sodium	Calcium
459 cal	62 g	4 g	22 g	30 mg	440 mg	85 mg

Ingredient	Weight	Measure	Issue
COOKING SPRAY,NONSTICK	2 oz	1/4cup 1/3tbsp	
COOKIES,FROZEN,SNICKERDOODLE	23 lbs		

Method

1. Spray sheet pans with non-stick cooking spray.
2. Thaw cookie dough in refrigerator approximately 24-36 hours for easier use. Scoop 1-1/2 ounces of batter onto sheet pans placing each scoop 1 inch apart.
3. Using a convection oven, bake cookies at 375 F. for 7-10 minutes. Bake time will vary by oven type. Cool cookies for 20-30 minutes before removing from pan.

COOKIES, FROZEN, CHOCOLATE CHIP

Yield 100   Portion 2 Cookies

Calories	Carbohydrates	Protein	Fat	Cholesterol	Sodium	Calcium
467 cal	64 g	5 g	22 g	25 mg	218 mg	26 mg

Ingredient	Weight	Measure	Issue
COOKING SPRAY,NONSTICK	2 oz	1/4cup 1/3tbsp	
COOKIES,FROZEN,CHOCOLATE CHIP	23 lbs		

Method

1. Spray sheet pans with non-stick cooking spray.
2. Thaw cookie dough in refrigerator approximately 24-36 hours for easier use. Scoop 1-1/2 ounces of batter onto sheet pans placing each scoop 1 inch apart.
3. Using a convection oven, bake cookies at 375 F. for 7-10 minutes. Bake time will vary by oven type. Cool cookies for 20-30 minutes before removing from pan.

MAKING ONE-CRUST PIES

BAKED PIE SHELLS

1. PREPARE AND DIVIDE DOUGH: Prepare 1/2 recipe Pie Crust, (Recipe No. I-1). Divide dough into 13-71/2 oz pieces; place on lightly floured board.
2. ROLL DOUGH: Sprinkle each piece of dough lightly with flour; flatten gently. Using a floured rolling pin, roll lightly with quick strokes from center out to edge in all directions. Form a circle 1 inch larger than pie pan and about 1/8 inch thick. Shift or turn dough occasionally to prevent sticking. If edges split, pinch cracks together.
3. PLACE DOUGH IN PAN: Fold rolled dough in half; carefully place into ungreased pie pan with fold at center. Unfold and fit carefully into pie pan, being careful not to leave any air spaces between pan and dough.
4. REMOVE EXCESS DOUGH: Trim ragged edges about 1/2 inch beyond edge of pan using knife or spatula. (Incorporate excess dough into next crust, if needed.) Fold extra dough back and under; crimp with the thumb and forefinger to make a high fluted edge. Dock or prick dough on bottom and sides to prevent puffing during baking. If available, place an empty pie pan inside of shell before baking to help prevent shrinking and puffing.
5. BAKE: Bake at 450 F. about 10 minutes or until golden brown or in 400°F. convection oven 8 to 10 minutes or until golden brown on high fan, open vent.
6. FILL CRUST: Fill as specified on individual recipe card.

UNBAKED SHELL

1. Follow Steps 1 through 4; omit docking or pricking of dough in Step 4.
2. Fill and bake according to instructions on specified recipe.

MAKING TWO-CRUST PIES

1. PREPARE AND DIVIDE DOUGH: Prepare 1 recipe Pie Crust (Recipe No. I-1). Divide dough into 13-71/2 oz pieces for bottom crust and 13-7 oz pieces for top crust; place on lightly floured board.
2. ROLL DOUGH: Sprinkle each piece of dough lightly with flour; flatten gently. Using a floured rolling pin, roll lightly with quick strokes from center out to edge in all directions. Form a circle 1 inch larger than pie pan and about 1/8 inch thick. Bottom crust will be slightly thicker. Shift or turn dough occasionally to prevent sticking. If edges split, pinch cracks together.
3. BOTTOM CRUST: Fold rolled dough in half; carefully place into ungreased pie pan with fold at center. Unfold and fit carefully into pie pan, being careful not to leave any air spaces between pan and dough.
4. FILL CRUST: Fill as specified on individual recipe card.
5. TOP CRUST: Roll top crust in same manner as bottom crust. Fold in half; with knife, make several small slits near center fold to allow steam to escape during baking. Brush outer rim of bottom crust with water. Lay top crust over filling with fold at center; unfold and press edges of two crusts together lightly.
6. REMOVE EXCESS DOUGH: Trim overhanging edges of dough by using a knife or spatula. (Incorporate excess dough into next crust, if needed.) There should be little excess if skill is used in weighing and rolling dough.
7. SEAL PIE: Press edges of crust firmly together or crimp with the thumb and forefinger to make a fluted edge.
8. WASHED TOP: For a washed top, brush pies with appropriate wash as follows:

Egg and Milk Wash-This wash is used for fruit pies (apple, blueberry, cherry, peach, pineapple) that are baked 30 to 35 minutes. It SHOULD NOT be used for pies requiring longer baking time as the crust will brown excessively. See Recipe No. I-4.

Egg and Water Wash-This wash is used for berry and mincemeat pies that are baked 40 to 45 minutes. It SHOULD NOT be used for pies that are baked 30 to 35 minutes as the crusts will be too pale. Allow glaze to dry on crust before baking to eliminate dark spots. See Recipe No. I-4-1.

9. BAKE: Bake as specified on individual recipe card.

DIRECTIONS FOR MAKING TURNOVERS

1. Prepare 11/4 recipes Pie Crust (Recipe No. I-1). Divide dough into 8 pieces.
2. Place dough on lightly floured board; sprinkle each piece lightly with flour; flatten gently. Roll dough into 18 by 24-inch rectangular sheet about 1/8 inch thick. Cut into 12–6 inch squares. Brush edges of each square with water.
3. Place about 1/4 cup (2 oz or 1-No. 16 scoop) fruit filling in the center of each square. Fold opposite corner of dough together forming a triangle. Seal by crimping edges.
4. Make 2-1/2 inch slits near the center fold to allow steam to escape during baking.
5. Place 12 turnovers on each lightly greased sheet pan (18 by 26 inches).
6. Brush top of each turnover with milk and water wash. Allow to dry before baking. See Recipe No. I-4-2. DO NOT use Egg and Milk Wash (Recipe No. I-4) or Egg and Water Wash (Recipe No. I-4-1) for turnovers. The egg and milk wash will cause turnovers to brown excessively and egg and water wash will cause turnovers to be too pale in color.
7. Bake at 425 F. about 20 minutes or until lightly browned.

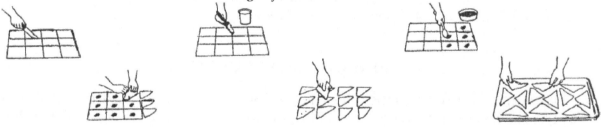

DIRECTIONS FOR MAKING DUMPLINGS

1. Prepare 11/4 recipes Pie Crust (Recipe No. I-1). Divide dough into 8 pieces.
2. Place dough on lightly floured board; sprinkle each piece lightly with flour; flatten gently. Roll dough into 18 by 24-inch rectangular sheet about 1/8 inch thick. Cut into 12-6-inch squares. Brush edges of each square with water.
3. Place 1/4 cup (2 oz or 1-No. 16 scoop) fruit filling in the center of each pastry square. Bring points of pastry up over filling as shown in diagram. Seal edges tightly.
4. Place 12 dumplings on each sheet pan (18 by 26 inches).
5. Bake at 425 F about 20 minutes or until lightly browned.
6. Serve with complementary dessert sauce. See Recipe Section K, Desserts (Sauces and Toppings).

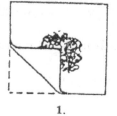

1.

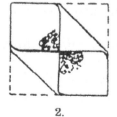

2.

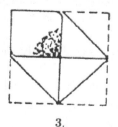

3.

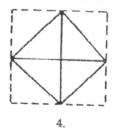

4.

PIE CRUST

Yield 100   **Portion** 1 Crust

Calories	Carbohydrates	Protein	Fat	Cholesterol	Sodium	Calcium
995 cal	92 g	12 g	64 g	0 mg	808 mg	19 mg

Ingredient	Weight	Measure	Issue
FLOUR,WHEAT,GENERAL PURPOSE	6-7/8 lbs	1 gal 2-1/4 qts	
SALT	1-7/8 oz	3 tbsp	
SHORTENING	3-5/8 lbs	2 qts	
WATER,COLD	2-1/8 lbs	1 qts	

Method

1. Sift together flour and salt in mixer bowl.
2. Add shortening to dry ingredients. Using pastry knife attachment, mix at low speed 30 seconds or until shortening is evenly distributed and mixture is granular in appearance.
3. Add water; mix at low speed 1 minute until dough is just formed.
4. Chill dough for at least 1 hour for ease in handling.
5. DIVIDE DOUGH: Divide dough into 13-7-1/2 oz pieces for bottom crust and 13-7 oz pieces for top crust; place on lightly floured board. ROLL DOUGH: Sprinkle each piece of dough lightly with flour; flatten gently. Using a floured rolling pin, roll lightly with quick strokes from center out to edge in all directions. Form a circle 1 inch larger than pie pan and about 1/8 inch thick. Bottom crust will be slightly thicker. Shift or turn dough occasionally to prevent sticking. If edges split, pinch cracks together. BOTTOM CRUST: Fold rolled dough in half; carefully place into ungreased pie pan with fold at center. Unfold and fit carefully into pie pan, being careful not to leave any air spaces between pan and dough. TOP CRUST: Roll top crust in same manner as bottom crust. Fold in half; with knife, make several small slits near center fold to allow steam to escape during baking. Brush outer rim of bottom crust with water. Lay top crust over filling with fold at center; unfold and press edges of two crusts together lightly. REMOVE EXCESS DOUGH: Trim overhanging edges of dough by using a knife or spatula. (Incorporate excess dough into next crust, if needed.) There should be little excess if skill is used in weighing and rolling dough. SEAL PIE: Press edges of crust firmly together or crimp with the thumb and forefinger to make a fluted edge. WASHED TOP: For a washed top, brush pies with appropriate wash as follows: Egg and Milk Wash -This wash is used for fruit pies (apple, blueberry, cherry, peach, pineapple) that are baked 30 to 35 minutes. It SHOULD NOT be used for pies requiring longer baking time as the crust will brown excessively. Egg and Water Wash - This wash is used for berry and mincemeat pies that are baked 40 to 45 minutes. It SHOULD NOT be used for pies that are baked 30 to 35 minutes as the crusts will be too pale. Allow glaze to dry on crust before baking to eliminate dark spots. BAKING INSTRUCTIONS FOR COOKED PIES: Bake as specified on individual recipe card. BAKING INSTRUCTIONS FOR UNCOOKED PIES: Bake crusts at 425 F. for about 15-18 minutes, or until light golden brown. Cool before filling. Proceed with the recipe directions.

Notes

1. Pie crust mix may be used. Omit steps 1 through 3. Follow manufacturer's directions for preparation. Follow steps 4 and 5. Quantity of pie crust mix required: 5 pounds pie crust mix yields 13-one crust pies; 10 pounds pie crust mix yields 13-two crust pies.

PIE CRUST (DOUGH ROLLING MACHINE)

Yield 100   **Portion** 1 Crust

Calories	Carbohydrates	Protein	Fat	Cholesterol	Sodium	Calcium
982 cal	87 g	14 g	65 g	0 mg	1260 mg	28 mg

Ingredient	Weight	Measure	Issue
FLOUR,WHEAT,BREAD	4-1/2 lbs	3 qts 3 cup	
FLOUR,WHEAT,GENERAL PURPOSE	2-1/8 lbs	1 qts 3-1/2 cup	
SALT	3 oz	1/4 cup 1 tbsp	
SUGAR,GRANULATED	1-1/3 oz	3 tbsp	
MILK,NONFAT,DRY	2/3 oz	1/4 cup 1 tbsp	
SHORTENING	3-5/8 lbs	2 qts	
WATER,COLD	1-7/8 lbs	3-1/2 cup	

Method

1. Combine sifted bread flour, sifted general purpose flour, salt, granulated sugar and nonfat dry milk in mixer bowl.
2. Add shortening to dry ingredients. Using pastry knife attachment, mix at low speed 30 seconds or until shortening is evenly distributed and mixture is granular in appearance.
3. Add water; mix at low speed 1 minute until dough is just formed.
4. Chill dough for at least 1 hour, preferably 24 hours, at 40 F. for ease in handling. Follow the equipment manufacturer's instructions for feeding/loading the dough into the machine.
5. DIVIDE DOUGH: Divide dough into 13-7-1/2 oz pieces for bottom crust and 13-7 oz pieces for top crust; place on lightly floured board. ROLL DOUGH: Sprinkle each piece of dough lightly with flour; flatten gently. Using a floured rolling pin, roll lightly with quick strokes from center out to edge in all directions. Form a circle 1 inch larger than pie pan and about 1/8 inch thick. Bottom crust will be slightly thicker. Shift or turn dough occasionally to prevent sticking. If edges split, pinch cracks together. BOTTOM CRUST: Fold rolled dough in half; carefully place into ungreased pie pan with fold at center. Unfold and fit carefully into pie pan, being careful not to leave any air spaces between pan and dough. TOP CRUST: Roll top crust in same manner as bottom crust. Fold in half; with knife, make several small slits near center fold to allow steam to escape during baking. Brush outer rim of bottom crust with water. Lay top crust over filling with fold at center; unfold and press edges of two crusts together lightly. REMOVE EXCESS DOUGH: Trim overhanging edges of dough by using a knife or spatula. (Incorporate excess dough into next crust, if needed.) There should be little excess if skill is used in weighing and rolling dough. SEAL PIE: Press edges of crust firmly together or crimp with the thumb and forefinger to make a fluted edge. WASHED TOP: For a washed top, brush pies with appropriate wash as follows: Egg and Milk Wash - This wash is used for fruit pies (apple, blueberry, cherry, peach, pineapple) that are baked 30 to 35 minutes. It SHOULD NOT be used for pies requiring longer baking time as the crust will brown excessively. Egg and Water Wash - This wash is used for berry and mincemeat pies that are baked 40 to 45 minutes. It SHOULD NOT be used for pies that are baked 30 to 35 minutes as the crusts will be too pale. Allow glaze to dry on crust before baking to eliminate dark spots. BAKING INSTRUCTIONS FOR COOKED PIES: Bake as specified on individual recipe card. BAKING INSTRUCTIONS FOR UNCOOKED PIES: Bake crusts at 425 F. for about 15-18 minutes, or until light golden brown. Cool before filling. Proceed with the recipe directions.

PIE CRUST (MANUAL MIXING METHOD)

Yield 100 **Portion** 1 Crust

Calories	Carbohydrates	Protein	Fat	Cholesterol	Sodium	Calcium
995 cal	92 g	12 g	64 g	0 mg	808 mg	19 mg

Ingredient	Weight	Measure	Issue
FLOUR,WHEAT,GENERAL PURPOSE	6-7/8 lbs	1 gal 2-1/4 qts	

SALT	1-7/8 oz	3 tbsp
SHORTENING	3-5/8 lbs	2 qts
WATER,COLD	2-1/8 lbs	1 qts

Method

1. Sift together flour and salt in mixer bowl.
2. Add shortening to dry ingredients. Cut or rub shortening until evenly distributed and granular in appearance.
3. Sprinkle half of water over flour mixture and mix. Sprinkle remaining water and mix until dough is just formed.
4. Chill dough for at least 1 hour for ease in handling.
5. DIVIDE DOUGH: Divide dough into 13-7-1/2 oz pieces for bottom crust and 13-7 oz pieces for top crust; place on lightly floured board. ROLL DOUGH: Sprinkle each piece of dough lightly with flour; flatten gently. Using a floured rolling pin, roll lightly with quick strokes from center out to edge in all directions. Form a circle 1 inch larger than pie pan and about 1/8 inch thick. Bottom crust will be slightly thicker. Shift or turn dough occasionally to prevent sticking. If edges split, pinch cracks together. BOTTOM CRUST: Fold rolled dough in half; carefully place into ungreased pie pan with fold at center. Unfold and fit carefully into pie pan, being careful not to leave any air spaces between pan and dough. TOP CRUST: Roll top crust in same manner as bottom crust. Fold in half; with knife, make several small slits near center fold to allow steam to escape during baking. Brush outer rim of bottom crust with water. Lay top crust over filling with fold at center; unfold and press edges of two crusts together lightly. REMOVE EXCESS DOUGH: Trim overhanging edges of dough by using a knife or spatula. (Incorporate excess dough into next crust, if needed.) There should be little excess if skill is used in weighing and rolling dough. SEAL PIE: Press edges of crust firmly together or crimp with the thumb and forefinger to make a fluted edge. WASHED TOP: For a washed top, brush pies with appropriate wash as follows: Egg and Milk Wash -This wash is used for fruit pies (apple, blueberry, cherry, peach, pineapple) that are baked 30 to 35 minutes. It SHOULD NOT be used for pies requiring longer baking time as the crust will brown excessively. Egg and Water Wash - This wash is used for berry and mincemeat pies that are baked 40 to 45 minutes. It SHOULD NOT be used for pies that are baked 30 to 35 minutes as the crusts will be too pale. Allow glaze to dry on crust before baking to eliminate dark spots. BAKING INSTRUCTIONS FOR COOKED PIES: Bake as specified on individual recipe card. BAKING INSTRUCTIONS FOR UNCOOKED PIES: Bake crusts at 425 F. for about 15-18 minutes, or until light golden brown. Cool before filling. Proceed with the recipe directions.

GRAHAM CRACKER CRUST

Yield 100   Portion 1 Crust

Calories	Carbohydrates	Protein	Fat	Cholesterol	Sodium	Calcium
1181 cal	144 g	9 g	65 g	0 mg	1380 mg	50 mg

Ingredient	Weight	Measure	Issue
MARGARINE	1-7/8 lbs	3-3/4 cup	
CRACKERS,GRAHAM,CRUMBS	3-5/8 lbs		
SUGAR,GRANULATED	1-1/3 lbs	3 cup	

Method

1. Grind graham crackers or crush on board with rolling pin. Combine butter or margarine, crumbs, and sugar in mixer bowl. Mix at low speed until well blended, about 2 minutes.

2. Place about 8 ounces or 1-3/4 cups crumb mixture in each pie pan. Press firmly into an even layer against bottom and sides of each pan.
3. Chill at least 1 hour before filling is added.

Notes
1. For a firmer shell, omit Step 3; using a convection oven, bake at 325 F. for 7 minutes or until lightly browned on low fan, open vent.
2. 4 lb 1 oz (13-5 oz) preformed graham cracker crusts may be used.

GRAHAM CRACKER CRUST (PERFORMED CRUST)

Yield 100   **Portion** 1 Crust

Calories	Carbohydrates	Protein	Fat	Cholesterol	Sodium	Calcium
716 cal	88 g	5 g	38 g	14 mg	313 mg	57 mg

Ingredient	Weight	Measure	Issue
PIE CRUST PREFORMED	4 lbs		

Method
1. Use 13-5 oz preformed crusts per 100 portions.

MINCEMEAT PIE

Yield 100   **Portion** 1 Slice

Calories	Carbohydrates	Protein	Fat	Cholesterol	Sodium	Calcium
330 cal	42 g	3 g	17 g	0 mg	236 mg	11 mg

Ingredient	Weight	Measure	Issue
PIE CRUST		26 each	
PIE FILLING,MINCEMEAT,CANNED	13-1/3 lbs	1 gal 2-2/3 qts	
APPLES,CANNED,DRAINED,CHOPPED	4-1/2 lbs	2 qts 1 cup	
SUGAR,GRANULATED	11-3/4 oz	1-5/8 cup	

Method
1. DIVIDE DOUGH: Divide dough into 13-7-1/2 oz pieces for bottom crust and 13-7 oz pieces for top crust; place on lightly floured board. ROLL DOUGH: Sprinkle each piece of dough lightly with flour; flatten gently. Using a floured rolling pin, roll lightly with quick strokes from center out to edge in all directions. Form a circle 1 inch larger than pie pan and about 1/8 inch thick. Bottom crust will be slightly thicker. Shift or turn dough occasionally to prevent sticking. If edges split, pinch cracks together. BOTTOM CRUST: Fold rolled dough in half; carefully place into ungreased pie pan with fold at center. Unfold and fit carefully into pie pan, being careful not to leave any air spaces between pan and dough. FILL CRUST: Fill as specified on individual recipe card. (Step 2/3). TOP CRUST: Roll top crust in same manner as bottom crust. Fold in half; with knife, make several small slits near center fold to allow steam to escape during baking. Brush outer rim of bottom crust with water. Lay top crust over filling with fold at center; unfold and press edges of two crusts together lightly. REMOVE EXCESS DOUGH: Trim overhanging edges of dough by using a knife or spatula. (Incorporate excess dough into next crust, if needed.) There should be little excess if skill is used in weighing and rolling dough. SEAL PIE: Press edges of crust firmly together or crimp with the thumb and forefinger to make a fluted edge. WASHED TOP: For a washed top, brush pies with appropriate wash as follows: Egg and Milk Wash - This wash is used for fruit pies (apple, blueberry,

320

cherry, peach, pineapple) that are baked 30 to 35 minutes. It SHOULD NOT be used for pies requiring longer baking time as the crust will brown excessively. Egg and Water Wash - This wash is used for berry and mincemeat pies that are baked 40 to 45 minutes. It SHOULD NOT be used for pies that are baked 30 to 35 minutes as the crusts will be too pale. Allow glaze to dry on crust before baking to eliminate dark spots. BAKING INSTRUCTIONS FOR COOKED PIES: Bake as specified on individual recipe card. BAKING INSTRUCTIONS FOR UNCOOKED PIES: Bake crusts at 425 F. for about 15-18 minutes, or until light golden brown. Cool before filling. Proceed with the recipe directions.

2. Combine mincemeat, apples, and sugar; mix until well blended.
3. Pour 3-1/2 cups filling into each unbaked pie shell. Cover with top crust. Seal edges.
4. Bake at 425 F. for 45 minutes or until lightly browned.
5. Cut 8 wedges per pie.

EGG AND MILK WASH

Yield 100   **Portion** 1-1/2 Cup

Calories	Carbohydrates	Protein	Fat	Cholesterol	Sodium	Calcium
91 cal	3 g	8 g	5 g	215 mg	96 mg	91 mg

Ingredient	Weight	Measure	Issue
MILK,NONFAT,DRY	1/2 oz	3 tbsp	
WATER	12-1/2 oz	1-1/2 cup	
EGGS,WHOLE,FROZEN	4-2/3 oz	1/2 cup 2/3 tbsp	

Method
1. Combine milk and water; mix until thoroughly blended.
2. Add eggs; whip until well blended.
3. Brush on pies. Allow to dry before baking. CCP: Refrigerate at 41 F. or lower until ready for use.

Notes
1. This wash will cover 13 to 15 2-crust pies that are baked 30 to 35 minutes, primarily fruit pies (apple, blueberry, cherry, peach, pineapple). It SHOULD NOT be used for pies requiring longer baking time as the crust will brown excessively.

EGG AND WATER WASH

Yield 100   **Portion** 1-1/2 Cup

Calories	Carbohydrates	Protein	Fat	Cholesterol	Sodium	Calcium
120 cal	1 g	10 g	8 g	350 mg	113 mg	51 mg

Ingredient	Weight	Measure	Issue
EGGS,WHOLE,FROZEN	7-5/8 oz	3/4 cup 2-1/3 tbsp	
WATER	1 lbs	2 cup	

Method
1. Combine eggs with water. Whip until well blended.
2. Brush on pies. Allow to dry before baking. CCP: Refrigerate at 41 F. or lower until ready for use.

Notes
1. Use on 2-crust pies (berry and mincemeat), bake 40 to 50 minutes. To prevent dark spots, allow wash to dry on crust before baking. This wash is used for berry and mincemeat pies. It SHOULD NOT be used for pies that are baked 30 to 35 minutes as the crusts will be too pale.

MILK AND WATER WASH

Yield 100   **Portion** 1-1/2 Cup

Calories	Carbohydrates	Protein	Fat	Cholesterol	Sodium	Calcium
36 cal	5 g	4 g	0 g	2 mg	59 mg	125 mg

Ingredient	Weight	Measure	Issue
MILK,NONFAT,DRY	7/8 oz	1/4 cup 2-2/3 tbsp	
WATER,WARM	14-7/8 oz	1-3/4 cup	

Method
1. Combine nonfat dry milk and warm water. Mix well.
2. Use only this wash on turnovers; allow to dry before baking. Do not use this wash on 2-crust pies.

MERINGUE

Yield 100   **Portion** 2-1/2 Cup

Calories	Carbohydrates	Protein	Fat	Cholesterol	Sodium	Calcium
401 cal	93 g	9 g	0 g	0 mg	406 mg	6 mg

Ingredient	Weight	Measure	Issue
EGG WHITES	2-3/8 lbs	1 qts 1/2 cup	
SUGAR,GRANULATED	2-2/3 lbs	1 qts 2 cup	
SALT	1/3 oz	1/4 tsp	
EXTRACT,VANILLA	1/3 oz	3/8 tsp	

Method
1. Using a whip, beat egg whites at high speed in mixer bowl until foamy, about 3 minutes.
2. Add sugar a little at a time; beat well at medium speed after each addition. Beat at high speed until stiff peaks are formed, about 6 minutes.
3. Add salt and vanilla; blend.
4. Spread about 2-1/2 cups meringue over warm pie filling, about 122 F. in each pan. Meringue should touch inner edge of crust all around and completely cover top of pie. Leave meringue somewhat rough on top.
5. Bake at 350 F. for 16 to 20 minutes or until lightly browned. CCP: Hold for service at 41 F. or lower.

MERINGUE (DEHYDRATED)

Yield 100   **Portion** 2-1/2 Cup

Calories	Carbohydrates	Protein	Fat	Cholesterol	Sodium	Calcium
225 cal	56 g	2 g	0 g	0 mg	31 mg	74 mg

Ingredient	Weight	Measure	Issue
MERINGUE POWDER	3-3/8 oz	3/4 cup	
WATER,COLD	1-5/8 lbs	3 cup	
SUGAR,GRANULATED	1-1/2 lbs	3-3/8 cup	

Method

1. Add water to mixer bowl; add meringue powder.
2. Using whip, mix at low speed 1 minute or until powder is dissolved. Beat at high speed until stiff peaks form, about 5 minutes.
3. Gradually add granulated sugar beating at high speed 1 minute or until meringue is glossy.
4. Spread about 2-1/2 cups meringue over warm pie filling, about 122 F. in each pan. Meringue should touch inner edge of crust all around and completely cover top of pie. Leave meringue somewhat rough on top.
5. Bake 16 to 20 minutes at 350 F. or until lightly browned.

VANILLA CREAM PIE

Yield 100   Portion 1 Slice

Calories	Carbohydrates	Protein	Fat	Cholesterol	Sodium	Calcium
326 cal	38 g	4 g	17 g	46 mg	268 mg	49 mg

Ingredient	Weight	Measure	Issue
PIE CRUST		13 each	
MILK,NONFAT,DRY	10-3/8 oz	1 qts 3/8 cup	
WATER,WARM	11-7/8 lbs	1 gal 1-2/3 qts	
SUGAR,GRANULATED	1-1/2 lbs	3-3/8 cup	
SALT	3/4 oz	1 tbsp	
CORNSTARCH	13-1/2 oz	3 cup	
SUGAR,GRANULATED	1-7/8 lbs	1 qts 1/8 cup	
WATER,COLD	3-1/8 lbs	1 qts 2 cup	
EGGS,WHOLE,FROZEN	2-1/3 lbs	1 qts 3/8 cup	
MARGARINE	14-7/8 oz	1-7/8 cup	
EXTRACT,VANILLA	2-1/8 oz	1/4 cup 1 tbsp	

Method

1. PREPARE AND DIVIDE DOUGH: Prepare 1/2 recipe Pie Crust (Recipe No. I 001 00). Divide dough into 13-7-1/2 oz pieces for bottom crust; place on lightly floured board. ROLL DOUGH: Sprinkle each piece of dough lightly with flour; flatten gently. Using a floured rolling pin, roll lightly with quick strokes from center out to edge in all directions. Form a circle 1 inch larger than pie pan and about 1/8 inch thick. Shift or turn dough occasionally to prevent sticking. If edges split, pinch cracks together. BOTTOM CRUST: Fold rolled dough in half; carefully place into ungreased pie pan with fold at center. Unfold and fit carefully into pie pan, being careful not to leave any air spaces between pan and dough. REMOVE EXCESS DOUGH: Trim overhanging edges of dough by using a knife or spatula. (Incorporate excess dough into next crust, if needed.) There should be little excess if skill is used in weighing and rolling dough. BAKING INSTRUCTIONS FOR UNCOOKED PIES: Bake crusts at 425 F. for about 15-18 minutes, or until light golden brown. Cool before filling. Proceed with the recipe directions.
2. Reconstitute milk. Add sugar and salt; heat to just below boiling. DO NOT BOIL.
3. Combine cornstarch, sugar and water; stir until smooth. Add gradually to hot mixture. Cook at medium heat, stirring constantly, about 10 minutes until thickened.
4. Stir about 1 quart of hot mixture into eggs. Slowly pour egg mixture into remaining hot mixture; heat to boiling, stirring constantly. Cook 2 minutes longer. Remove from heat.
5. Add butter or margarine and vanilla; stir until well blended. Cool slightly.
6. Pour 3 cups filling into each baked pie shell. Ensure cream pie filling preparation time does not exceed 4 hours total in temperatures between 40 F. to 140 F.

7. CCP: Hold for service at 41 F. or lower.
8. Cut 8 wedges per pie. Chilled pies may be topped with Whipped Cream, Recipe No. K 001 00 or Whipped Topping Recipe No. K 002 00.

Notes
1. Filling will curdle if boiled or subjected to prolonged intense heat.

BANANA CREAM PIE

Yield 100   **Portion** 1 Slice

Calories	Carbohydrates	Protein	Fat	Cholesterol	Sodium	Calcium
292 cal	40 g	4 g	13 g	46 mg	265 mg	50 mg

Ingredient	Weight	Measure	Issue
PIE CRUST	10-3/8 oz	13 each	
MILK,NONFAT,DRY	11-7/8 lbs	1 qts 3/8 cup	
WATER,WARM	1-1/2 lbs	1 gal 1-2/3 qts	
SUGAR,GRANULATED	3/4 oz	3-3/8 cup	
SALT	13-1/2 oz	1 tbsp	
CORNSTARCH	1-7/8 lbs	3 cup	
SUGAR,GRANULATED	3-1/8 lbs	1 qts 1/8 cup	
WATER,COLD	2-1/3 lbs	1 qts 2 cup	
EGGS,WHOLE,FROZEN	7-1/2 lbs	1 qts 3/8 cup	
BANANA,FRESH,SLICED	14-7/8 oz	1 gal 1-2/3 qts	
MARGARINE	2-1/8 oz	1-7/8 cup	
EXTRACT,VANILLA	11-1/2 lbs	1/4 cup 1 tbsp	

Method
1. PREPARE AND DIVIDE DOUGH: Prepare 1/2 recipe Pie Crust (Recipe No. I 001 00). Divide dough into 13-7-1/2 oz pieces for bottom crust; place on lightly floured board. ROLL DOUGH: Sprinkle each piece of dough lightly with flour; flatten gently. Using a floured rolling pin, roll lightly with quick strokes from center out to edge in all directions. Form a circle 1 inch larger than pie pan and about 1/8 inch thick. Shift or turn dough occasionally to prevent sticking. If edges split, pinch cracks together. BOTTOM CRUST: Fold rolled dough in half; carefully place into ungreased pie pan with fold at center. Unfold and fit carefully into pie pan, being careful not to leave any air spaces between pan and dough. REMOVE EXCESS DOUGH: Trim overhanging edges of dough by using a knife or spatula. (Incorporate excess dough into next crust, if needed.) There should be little excess if skill is used in weighing and rolling dough. BAKING INSTRUCTIONS FOR UNCOOKED PIES: Bake crusts at 425 F. for about 15-18 minutes, or until light golden brown. Cool before filling. Proceed with the recipe directions.
2. Reconstitute milk. Add sugar and salt; heat to just below boiling. DO NOT BOIL.
3. Combine cornstarch, sugar and water; stir until smooth. Add gradually to hot mixture. Cook at medium heat, stirring constantly, about 10 minutes until thickened.
4. Stir about 1 quart of hot mixture into eggs. Slowly pour egg mixture into remaining hot mixture; heat to boiling, stirring constantly. Cook 2 minutes longer. Remove from heat.
5. Add butter or margarine and vanilla; stir until well blended. Cool slightly. Slice bananas. Add to cooled filling. To prevent discoloration, slice bananas just before adding to filling.
6. Pour about 3-1/2 cups filling into each baked pie shell. Meringue Recipe No. I 005 00 may be spread over warm filling. Ensure cream pie filling preparation time does not exceed 4 hours total in temperatures between 40 F. to 140 F.
7. CCP: Hold for service at 41 F. or lower.

8. Cut 8 wedges per pie. Chilled pies may be topped with 1 recipe Whipped Topping, Recipe No. K 002 00.

Notes
1. Filling will curdle if boiled or subjected to prolonged intense heat.

VANILLA CREAM PIE (DESSERT POWDER, INSTANT)

Yield 100   **Portion** 1 Slice

Calories	Carbohydrates	Protein	Fat	Cholesterol	Sodium	Calcium
301 cal	43 g	3 g	13 g	1 mg	506 mg	54 mg

Ingredient	Weight	Measure	Issue
PIE CRUST		13 each	
MILK,NONFAT,DRY	13-3/4 oz	1 qts 1-3/4 cup	
WATER,COLD	15-1/8 lbs	1 gal 3-1/4 qts	
DESSERT POWDER,PUDDING,INSTANT,VANILLA	5-1/2 lbs	3 qts 1-1/2 cup	

Method
1. PREPARE AND DIVIDE DOUGH: Prepare 1/2 recipe Pie Crust (Recipe No. I 001 00). Divide dough into 13-7-1/2 oz pieces for bottom crust; place on lightly floured board. ROLL DOUGH: Sprinkle each piece of dough lightly with flour; flatten gently. Using a floured rolling pin, roll lightly with quick strokes from center out to edge in all directions. Form a circle 1 inch larger than pie pan and about 1/8 inch thick. Shift or turn dough occasionally to prevent sticking. If edges split, pinch cracks together. BOTTOM CRUST: Fold rolled dough in half; carefully place into ungreased pie pan with fold at center. Unfold and fit carefully into pie pan, being careful not to leave any air spaces between pan and dough. REMOVE EXCESS DOUGH: Trim overhanging edges of dough by using a knife or spatula. (Incorporate excess dough into next crust, if needed.) There should be little excess if skill is used in weighing and rolling dough. BAKING INSTRUCTIONS FOR UNCOOKED PIES: Bake crusts at 425 F. for about 15-18 minutes, or until light golden brown. Cool before filling. Proceed with the recipe directions.
2. Reconstitute milk in a large mixing bowl, with a wire whip.
3. Add dessert powder to milk and water. Using whip, blend at low speed 15 seconds or until well blended. Scrape down sides of bowl; whip at medium speed 2 minutes.
4. Pour about 3 cups filling into each baked pie shell.
5. CCP: Hold for service at 41 F. or lower.
6. Cut 8 wedges per pie. Chilled pies may be topped with Whipped Cream, Recipe No. K 001 00 or Whipped Topping Recipe No. K 002 00.

STRAWBERRY GLAZED CREAM PIE (INSTANT)

Yield 100   **Portion** 1 Slice

Calories	Carbohydrates	Protein	Fat	Cholesterol	Sodium	Calcium
335 cal	52 g	3 g	13 g	1 mg	508 mg	61 mg

Ingredient	Weight	Measure	Issue
PIE CRUST		13 each	
MILK,NONFAT,DRY	13-3/4 oz	1 qts 1-3/4 cup	
WATER,COLD	15-1/8 lbs	1 gal 3-1/4 qts	
DESSERT POWDER,PUDDING,INSTANT,VANILLA	5-1/2 lbs	3 qts 1-1/2 cup	
STRAWBERRY GLAZE TOPPING		3 qts 3 cup	

Method

1. PREPARE AND DIVIDE DOUGH: Prepare 1/2 recipe Pie Crust (Recipe No. I 001 00). Divide dough into 13-7-1/2 oz pieces for bottom crust; place on lightly floured board. ROLL DOUGH: Sprinkle each piece of dough lightly with flour; flatten gently. Using a floured rolling pin, roll lightly with quick strokes from center out to edge in all directions. Form a circle 1 inch larger than pie pan and about 1/8 inch thick. Shift or turn dough occasionally to prevent sticking. If edges split, pinch cracks together. BOTTOM CRUST: Fold rolled dough in half; carefully place into ungreased pie pan with fold at center. Unfold and fit carefully into pie pan, being careful not to leave any air spaces between pan and dough. REMOVE EXCESS DOUGH: Trim overhanging edges of dough by using a knife or spatula. (Incorporate excess dough into next crust, if needed.) There should be little excess if skill is used in weighing and rolling dough. BAKING INSTRUCTIONS FOR UNCOOKED PIES: Bake crusts at 425 F. for about 15-18 minutes, or until light golden brown. Cool before filling. Proceed with the recipe directions.
2. Reconstitute milk in a large mixing bowl with a wire whip.
3. Add dessert powder to milk and water. Using whip, blend at low speed 15 seconds or until well blended. Scrape down sides of bowl; whip at medium speed 2 minutes.
4. Pour about 3 cups filling into each baked pie shell.
5. CCP: Hold for service at 41 F. or lower.
6. Prepare 1 recipe Strawberry Glaze Topping, Recipe No. K 007 00 per 100 portions. Spread 11-1/2 ounces or 1-1/8 cups mixture over filling in each pie.
7. Cut pie into 8 wedges.

COCONUT CREAM PIE (INSTANT)

Yield 100   **Portion** 1 Slice

Calories	Carbohydrates	Protein	Fat	Cholesterol	Sodium	Calcium
355 cal	48 g	4 g	17 g	1 mg	535 mg	56 mg

Ingredient	Weight	Measure	Issue
PIE CRUST		13 each	
MILK,NONFAT,DRY	13-3/4 oz	1 qts 1-3/4 cup	
WATER,COLD	15-1/8 lbs	1 gal 3-1/4 qts	
DESSERT POWDER,PUDDING,INSTANT,VANILLA	5-1/2 lbs	3 qts 1-1/2 cup	
COCONUT,PREPARED,SWEETENED FLAKES	1-1/2 lbs	1 qts 3-1/4 cup	
COCONUT,PREPARED,SWEETENED FLAKES	14-3/4 oz	1 qts 1/2 cup	

Method

1. PREPARE AND DIVIDE DOUGH: Prepare 1/2 recipe Pie Crust (Recipe No. I 001 00). Divide dough into 13-7-1/2 oz pieces for bottom crust; place on lightly floured board. ROLL DOUGH: Sprinkle each piece of dough lightly with flour; flatten gently. Using a floured rolling pin, roll lightly with quick strokes from center out to edge in all directions. Form a circle 1 inch larger than pie pan and about 1/8 inch thick. Shift or turn dough occasionally to prevent sticking. If edges split, pinch cracks together. BOTTOM CRUST: Fold rolled dough in half; carefully place into ungreased pie pan with fold at center. Unfold and fit carefully into pie pan, being careful not to leave any air spaces between pan and dough. REMOVE EXCESS DOUGH: Trim overhanging edges of dough by using a knife or spatula. (Incorporate excess dough into next crust, if needed.) There should be little excess if skill is used in weighing and rolling dough. BAKING INSTRUCTIONS FOR UNCOOKED PIES: Bake crusts at 425 F. for about 15-18 minutes, or until light golden brown. Cool before filling. Proceed with the recipe directions.
2. Reconstitute milk in a large mixing bowl with a wire whip.

3. Add dessert powder to milk and water. Using whip, blend at low speed 15 seconds or until well blended. Scrape down sides of bowl; whip at medium speed 2 minutes.
4. Add prepared sweetened coconut flakes to filling; mix well. Pour 3-1/4 cups filling into each baked pie shell.
5. Sprinkle 1/3 cup coconut over each filled pie.
6. Cut 8 wedges per pie. CCP: Hold for service at 41 F. or lower. Chilled pies may be topped with Whipped Cream, Recipe No. K 001 00 or Whipped Topping, Recipe No. K 002 00.

PINEAPPLE CREAM PIE (INSTANT)

Yield 100   **Portion** 1 Slice

Calories	Carbohydrates	Protein	Fat	Cholesterol	Sodium	Calcium
310 cal	45 g	3 g	13 g	1 mg	506 mg	56 mg

Ingredient	Weight	Measure	Issue
PIE CRUST		13 each	
MILK,NONFAT,DRY	13-3/4 oz	1 qts 1-3/4 cup	
WATER,COLD	15-1/8 lbs	1 gal 3-1/4 qts	
DESSERT POWDER,PUDDING,INSTANT,VANILLA	5-1/2 lbs	3 qts 1-1/2 cup	
PINEAPPLE,CANNED,CRUSHED,JUICE PACK, DRAINED	3-1/4 lbs	1 qts 2 cup	

Method
1. PREPARE AND DIVIDE DOUGH: Prepare 1/2 recipe Pie Crust (Recipe No. I 001 00). Divide dough into 13-7-1/2 oz pieces for bottom crust; place on lightly floured board. ROLL DOUGH: Sprinkle each piece of dough lightly with flour; flatten gently. Using a floured rolling pin, roll lightly with quick strokes from center out to edge in all directions. Form a circle 1 inch larger than pie pan and about 1/8 inch thick. Shift or turn dough occasionally to prevent sticking. If edges split, pinch cracks together. BOTTOM CRUST: Fold rolled dough in half; carefully place into ungreased pie pan with fold at center. Unfold and fit carefully into pie pan, being careful not to leave any air spaces between pan and dough. REMOVE EXCESS DOUGH: Trim overhanging edges of dough by using a knife or spatula. (Incorporate excess dough into next crust, if needed.) There should be little excess if skill is used in weighing and rolling dough. BAKING INSTRUCTIONS FOR UNCOOKED PIES: Bake crusts at 425 F. for about 15-18 minutes, or until light golden brown. Cool before filling. Proceed with the recipe directions.
2. Reconstitute milk in a large mixing bowl with a wire whip.
3. Add dessert powder to milk and water. Using whip, blend at low speed 15 seconds or until well blended. Scrape down sides of bowl; whip at medium speed 2 minutes.
4. Add canned, drained, crushed pineapple. Mix well. Pour about 3-1/4 cups filling into each baked pie shell.
5. Cut 8 wedges per pie. CCP: Hold for service at 41 F. or lower. Chilled pies may be topped with Whipped Cream, Recipe No. K 001 00 or Whipped Topping, Recipe No. K 002 00.

DUTCH APPLE PIE (CANNED APPLES-CORNSTARCH)

Yield 100   **Portion** 1 Slice

Calories	Carbohydrates	Protein	Fat	Cholesterol	Sodium	Calcium
358 cal	54 g	3 g	16 g	18 mg	225 mg	17 mg

Ingredient	Weight	Measure	Issue
PIE CRUST		13 each	
APPLES,CANNED,SLICED	13-7/8 lbs	1 gal 3 qts	
SUGAR,GRANULATED	3 lbs	1 qts 2-3/4 cup	
SALT	3/8 oz	1/3 tsp	
CINNAMON,GROUND	1/3 oz	1 tbsp	
NUTMEG,GROUND	3/8 oz	1 tbsp	
CORNSTARCH	7-1/2 oz	1-5/8 cup	
WATER,COLD	1-5/8 lbs	3 cup	
JUICE,LEMON	2-1/2 oz	1/4 cup 1 tbsp	
BUTTER	4 oz	1/2 cup	
STREUSEL TOPPING		3 qts 3 cup	

Method

1. PREPARE AND DIVIDE DOUGH: Prepare 1/2 recipe Pie Crust (Recipe No. I 001 00). Divide dough into 13-7 oz pieces for pie crust and place on lightly floured board. ROLL DOUGH: Sprinkle each piece of dough lightly with flour; flatten gently. Using a floured rolling pin, roll lightly with quick strokes from center out to edge in all directions. Form a circle 1 inch larger than pie pan and about 1/8 inch thick. Shift or turn dough occasionally to prevent sticking. If edges split, pinch cracks together. CRUST: Fold rolled dough in half; carefully place into ungreased pie pan with fold at center. Unfold and fit carefully into pie pan, being careful not to leave any air spaces between pan and dough. REMOVE EXCESS DOUGH: Trim overhanging edges of dough by using a knife or spatula. (Incorporate excess dough into next crust, if needed.) There should be little excess if skill is used in weighing and rolling dough. BAKING INSTRUCTIONS FOR COOKED PIES: Bake as specified on individual recipe card.
2. Drain apples; reserve juice for use in Step 3; apples for use in Step 5.
3. Take reserved juice and add water equal 1-7/8 quart per 100 portions and combine with sugar, salt, cinnamon and nutmeg; bring to a boil.
4. Combine cornstarch and water; stir until smooth. Add gradually to boiling mixture. Cook at medium heat, stirring constantly, until thick and clear. Remove from heat.
5. Fold apples, lemon juice and butter or margarine carefully into thickened mixture. Cool thoroughly.
6. Pour 2-3/4 to 3 cups filling into each unbaked pie shell.
7. Using a convection oven, bake at 375 F. for 25 minutes or until lightly browned on high fan, open vent.
8. Prepare 1-1/2 recipes No. D 049 00 Streusel Topping per 100 portions. Spread 1/3 glaze over each pie after it has cooled.
9. Cut 8 wedges per pie.

FRENCH APPLE PIE (CANNED APPLES-CORNSTARCH)

Yield 100   **Portion** 1 Slice

Calories	Carbohydrates	Protein	Fat	Cholesterol	Sodium	Calcium
417 cal	61 g	3 g	18 g	4 mg	274 mg	10 mg

Ingredient	Weight	Measure	Issue
PIE CRUST		26 each	
APPLES,CANNED,SLICED	13-7/8 lbs	1 gal 3 qts	
SUGAR,GRANULATED	3 lbs	1 qts 2-3/4 cup	
SALT	3/8 oz	1/3 tsp	
CINNAMON,GROUND	1/3 oz	1 tbsp	

NUTMEG,GROUND	3/8 oz	1 tbsp
CORNSTARCH	7-1/2 oz	1-5/8 cup
WATER,COLD	1-5/8 lbs	3 cup
JUICE,LEMON	2-1/2 oz	1/4 cup 1 tbsp
BUTTER	4 oz	1/2 cup
VANILLA GLAZE		1 qts 1/8 cup

Method

1. PREPARE AND DIVIDE DOUGH: Prepare 1 recipe Pie Crust (Recipe No. I 001 00). Divide dough into 13-7-1/2 oz pieces for bottom crust and 13-7 oz pieces for top crust; place on lightly floured board. ROLL DOUGH: Sprinkle each piece of dough lightly with flour; flatten gently. Using a floured rolling pin, roll lightly with quick strokes from center out to edge in all directions. Form a circle 1 inch larger than pie pan and about 1/8 inch thick. Bottom crust will be slightly thicker. Shift or turn dough occasionally to prevent sticking. If edges split, pinch cracks together. BOTTOM CRUST: Fold rolled dough in half; carefully place into ungreased pie pan with fold at center. Unfold and fit carefully into pie pan, being careful not to leave any air spaces between pan and dough. FILL CRUST: Fill as specified on individual recipe card. TOP CRUST: Roll top crust in same manner as bottom crust. Fold in half; with knife, make several small slits near center fold to allow steam to escape during baking. Brush outer rim of bottom crust with water. Lay top crust over filling with fold at center; unfold and press edges of two crusts together lightly. REMOVE EXCESS DOUGH: Trim overhanging edges of dough by using a knife or spatula. (Incorporate excess dough into next crust, if needed.) There should be little excess if skill is used in weighing and rolling dough. SEAL PIE: Press edges of crust firmly together or crimp with the thumb and forefinger to make a fluted edge. BAKING INSTRUCTIONS FOR COOKED PIES: Bake as specified on individual recipe card.
2. Drain apples; reserve juice for use in Step 3; apples for use in Step 5.
3. Take reserved juice and add water equal 1-7/8 quart per 100 portions and combine with sugar, salt, cinnamon and nutmeg; bring to a boil.
4. Combine cornstarch and water; stir until smooth. Add gradually to boiling mixture. Cook at medium heat, stirring constantly, until thick and clear. Remove from heat.
5. Fold apples, lemon juice and butter or margarine carefully into thickened mixture. Cool thoroughly.
6. Pour 2-3/4 to 3 cups filling into each unbaked pie shell. Cover with top crust. Seal edges.
7. Using a convection oven, bake at 375 F. for 25 minutes or until lightly browned on high fan, open vent.
8. Prepare 1-1/2 recipes Vanilla Glaze per 100 portions, Recipe No. D 046 00; when pies are removed and still hot, spread 1/3 glaze over each top crust.
9. Cut 8 wedges per pie.

APPLE PIE (CANNED APPLES-CORNSTARCH)

Yield 100   **Portion** 1 Slice

Calories	Carbohydrates	Protein	Fat	Cholesterol	Sodium	Calcium
370 cal	50 g	3 g	18 g	2 mg	269 mg	10 mg

Ingredient	Weight	Measure	Issue
PIE CRUST		26 each	
APPLES,CANNED,SLICED	13-7/8 lbs	1 gal 3 qts	
SUGAR,GRANULATED	3 lbs	1 qts 2-3/4 cup	
SALT	3/8 oz	1/3 tsp	
CINNAMON,GROUND	1/3 oz	1 tbsp	
NUTMEG,GROUND	3/8 oz	1 tbsp	

CORNSTARCH	7-1/2 oz	1-5/8 cup
WATER,COLD	1-5/8 lbs	3 cup
JUICE,LEMON	2-1/2 oz	1/4 cup 1 tbsp
BUTTER	4 oz	1/2 cup

Method

1. PREPARE AND DIVIDE DOUGH: Prepare 1 recipe Pie Crust (Recipe No. I 001 00). Divide dough into 13-7-1/2 oz pieces for bottom crust and 13-7 oz pieces for top crust; place on lightly floured board. ROLL DOUGH: Sprinkle each piece of dough lightly with flour; flatten gently. Using a floured rolling pin, roll lightly with quick strokes from center out to edge in all directions. Form a circle 1 inch larger than pie pan and about 1/8 inch thick. Bottom crust will be slightly thicker. Shift or turn dough occasionally to prevent sticking. If edges split, pinch cracks together. BOTTOM CRUST: Fold rolled dough in half; carefully place into ungreased pie pan with fold at center. Unfold and fit carefully into pie pan, being careful not to leave any air spaces between pan and dough. FILL CRUST: Fill as specified on individual recipe card. TOP CRUST: Roll top crust in same manner as bottom crust. Fold in half; with knife, make several small slits near center fold to allow steam to escape during baking. Brush outer rim of bottom crust with water. Lay top crust over filling with fold at center; unfold and press edges of two crusts together lightly. REMOVE EXCESS DOUGH: Trim overhanging edges of dough by using a knife or spatula. (Incorporate excess dough into next crust, if needed.) There should be little excess if skill is used in weighing and rolling dough. SEAL PIE: Press edges of crust firmly together or crimp with the thumb and forefinger to make a fluted edge. BAKING INSTRUCTIONS FOR COOKED PIES: Bake as specified on individual recipe card.
2. Drain apples; reserve juice for use in Step 3; apples for use in Step 5.
3. Take reserved juice and add water equal 1-7/8 quart per 100 portions and combine with sugar, salt, cinnamon and nutmeg; bring to a boil.
4. Combine cornstarch and water; stir until smooth. Add gradually to boiling mixture. Cook at medium heat, stirring constantly, until thick and clear. Remove from heat.
5. Fold apples, lemon juice and butter or margarine carefully into thickened mixture. Cool thoroughly.
6. Pour 2-3/4 to 3 cups filling into each unbaked pie shell. Cover with top crust. Seal edges.
7. Using a convection oven, bake at 375 F. for 25 minutes or until lightly browned on high fan, open vent.
8. Cut 8 wedges per pie.

APPLE PIE (PREPARED PIE FILLING)

Yield 100   **Portion** 1 Slice

Calories	Carbohydrates	Protein	Fat	Cholesterol	Sodium	Calcium
363 cal	51 g	3 g	17 g	0 mg	256 mg	9 mg

Ingredient	Weight	Measure	Issue
PIE CRUST		26 each	
PIE FILLING,APPLE,PREPARED	22-3/4 lbs	2 gal 3-3/8 qts	

Method

1. PREPARE AND DIVIDE DOUGH: Prepare 1 recipe Pie Crust (Recipe No. I 001 00). Divide dough into 13-7-1/2 oz pieces for bottom crust and 13-7 oz pieces for top crust; place on lightly floured board. ROLL DOUGH: Sprinkle each piece of dough lightly with flour; flatten gently. Using a floured rolling pin, roll lightly with quick strokes from center out to edge in all directions. Form a circle 1 inch larger than pie pan and about 1/8 inch thick. Bottom crust will be slightly thicker. Shift or turn dough occasionally to prevent sticking. If edges split, pinch cracks together. BOTTOM

CRUST: Fold rolled dough in half; carefully place into ungreased pie pan with fold at center. Unfold and fit carefully into pie pan, being careful not to leave any air spaces between pan and dough. FILL CRUST: Fill as specified on individual recipe card. TOP CRUST: Roll top crust in same manner as bottom crust. Fold in half; with knife, make several small slits near center fold to allow steam to escape during baking. Brush outer rim of bottom crust with water. Lay top crust over filling with fold at center; unfold and press edges of two crusts together lightly. REMOVE EXCESS DOUGH: Trim overhanging edges of dough by using a knife or spatula. (Incorporate excess dough into next crust, if needed.) There should be little excess if skill is used in weighing and rolling dough. SEAL PIE: Press edges of crust firmly together or crimp with the thumb and forefinger to make a fluted edge. BAKING INSTRUCTIONS FOR COOKED PIES: Bake as specified on individual recipe card.

2. Use canned prepared apple pie filling.
3. Pour 3 cups filling into each unbaked pie shell. Cover with top crust. Seal edges.
4. Using a convection oven, bake at 375 F. for 25 minutes or until lightly browned on high fan, open vent.
5. Cut 8 wedges per pie.

DUTCH APPLE PIE (PREPARED PIE FILLING)

Yield 100   **Portion** 1 Slice

Calories	Carbohydrates	Protein	Fat	Cholesterol	Sodium	Calcium
335 cal	52 g	3 g	14 g	13 mg	204 mg	15 mg

Ingredient	Weight	Measure	Issue
PIE CRUST		13 each	
STREUSEL TOPPING		3 qts 1 cup	
PIE FILLING,APPLE,PREPARED	22-3/4 lbs	2 gal 3-3/8 qts	

Method
1. PREPARE AND DIVIDE DOUGH: Prepare 1/2 recipe Pie Crust (Recipe No. I 001 00). Divide dough into 13-7-1/2 oz pieces for bottom crust; place on lightly floured board. ROLL DOUGH: Sprinkle each piece of dough lightly with flour; flatten gently. Using a floured rolling pin, roll lightly with quick strokes from center out to edge in all directions. Form a circle 1 inch larger than pie pan and about 1/8 inch thick. Shift or turn dough occasionally to prevent sticking. If edges split, pinch cracks together. BOTTOM CRUST: Fold rolled dough in half; carefully place into ungreased pie pan with fold at center. Unfold and fit carefully into pie pan, being careful not to leave any air spaces between pan and dough. FILL CRUST: Fill as specified on individual recipe card. REMOVE EXCESS DOUGH: Trim overhanging edges of dough by using a knife or spatula. (Incorporate excess dough into next crust, if needed.) There should be little excess if skill is used in weighing and rolling dough. SEAL PIE: Press edges of crust firmly together or crimp with the thumb and forefinger to make a fluted edge. BAKING INSTRUCTIONS FOR COOKED PIES: Bake as specified on individual recipe card.
2. Prepare 1-1/4 recipes Streusel Topping per 100 portions, Recipe No. D 049 00.
3. Pour 3 cups filling into each unbaked pie shell. Omit top crust; sprinkle 1-1/8 cup topping over filling in each pan.
4. Using a convection oven, bake at 375 F. for 25 minutes or until lightly browned on high fan, open vent.
5. Cut 8 wedges per pie.

APPLE COBBLER

Yield 100   **Portion** 1 Slice

Calories	Carbohydrates	Protein	Fat	Cholesterol	Sodium	Calcium
433 cal	58 g	4 g	21 g	0 mg	311 mg	11 mg

Ingredient	Weight	Measure	Issue
PIE CRUST		32-1/2 each	
PIE FILLING,APPLE,PREPARED	24 lbs	3 gal	

Method

1. Prepare 1-1/4 recipe Pie Crust (Recipe No. I 001 00) to yield enough dough to prepare cobbler for 100 portions.
2. Divide dough into four 3-3/4 lb pieces; use 2 pieces for each sheet pan.
3. Place dough on lightly floured board; sprinkle lightly with flour; flatten gently.
4. Roll 2 pieces dough into rectangular sheets about 1/8-inch thick and large enough to fit each pan. Press dough into bottom and sides of each pan. Reserve remaining pieces for use in Step 6.
5. Pour 1-1/2 gallons filling into each pan.
6. Roll remaining pieces dough for top crusts.
7. Place top crusts carefully over filling in each pan.
8. Crimp to seal edges.
9. Cut 6 to 8 small slits, about 1/2-inch each in tops of each cobbler.
10. Using a convection oven, bake at 375 F. for 35 to 40 minutes or until lightly browned on high fan, open vent.
11. Cool; cut 6 by 9.

PEACH COBBLER

Yield 100   **Portion** 1 Serving

Calories	Carbohydrates	Protein	Fat	Cholesterol	Sodium	Calcium
484 cal	72 g	4 g	21 g	0 mg	299 mg	21 mg

Ingredient	Weight	Measure	Issue
PIE CRUST		32-1/2 each	
PIE FILLING,PEACH,PREPARED	24 lbs	3 gal	

Method

1. Prepare 1-1/4 Pie Crust, Recipe No. I 001 00 to yield enough dough to prepare cobbler for 100 portions.
2. Divide dough into four 3-3/4 pound pieces; use 2 pieces for each sheet pan.
3. Place dough on lightly floured board; sprinkle lightly with flour; flatten gently.
4. Roll 2 pieces dough into rectangular sheets about 1/8-inch thick and large enough to fit each pan. Press dough into bottom and sides of each pan. Reserve remaining pieces for use in Step 6.
5. Pour 1-1/2 gallons of filling into each pan.
6. Roll remaining pieces dough for top crusts.
7. Place top crusts carefully over filling in each pan.
8. Crimp to seal edges.
9. Cut 6 to 8 small slits, about 1/2-inch each, in tops of each cobbler.
10. Using a convection oven, bake at 375 F. for 35 to 40 minutes or until lightly browned on high fan, open vent.
11. Cool; cut 6 by 9.

BLUEBERRY COBBLER

Yield 100   **Portion** 1 Piece

Calories	Carbohydrates	Protein	Fat	Cholesterol	Sodium	Calcium
438 cal	60 g	4 g	21 g	0 mg	327 mg	35 mg

Ingredient	Weight	Measure	Issue
PIE CRUST		32-1/2 each	
PIE FILLING,BLUEBERRY,PREPARED	28-1/4 lbs	3 gal	

Method

1. Prepare 1-1/4 Pie Crust, Recipe No. I 001 00 to yield enough dough to prepare cobbler for 100 portions.
2. Divide dough into four 3-3/4 lb pieces; use 2 pieces for each sheet pan.
3. Place dough on lightly floured board; sprinkle lightly with flour; flatten gently.
4. Roll 2 pieces dough into rectangular sheets about 1/8-inch thick and large enough to fit each pan. Press dough into bottom and sides of each pan. Reserve remaining pieces for use in Step 6.
5. Pour 1-1/2 gallons of filling into each pan.
6. Roll remaining pieces dough for top crusts.
7. Place top crusts carefully over filling in each pan.
8. Crimp to seal edges.
9. Cut 6 to 8 small slits, about 1/2-inch each, in tops of each cobbler.
10. Using a convection oven, bake at 375 F. for 35 to 40 minutes or until lightly browned, on high fan, open vent.
11. Cool; cut 6 by 9.

CHERRY COBBLER

Yield 100   **Portion** 1 Piece

Calories	Carbohydrates	Protein	Fat	Cholesterol	Sodium	Calcium
449 cal	62 g	5 g	21 g	0 mg	273 mg	18 mg

Ingredient	Weight	Measure	Issue
PIE CRUST		32-1/2 each	
PIE FILLING,CHERRY,PREPARED	24 lbs	3 gal	

Method

1. Prepare 1-1/4 Pie Crust, Recipe No. I 001 00 to yield enough dough to prepare cobbler for 100 portions.
2. Divide dough into four 3-3/4 lb pieces; use 2 pieces for each sheet pan.
3. Place dough on lightly floured board; sprinkle lightly with flour; flatten gently.
4. Roll 2 pieces dough into rectangular sheets about 1/8 inch thick and large enough to fit each pan. Press dough into bottom and sides of each pan. Reserve remaining pieces for use in Step 6.
5. Pour 1-1/2 gallons of filling into each pan.
6. Roll remaining pieces dough for top crusts.
7. Place top crusts carefully over filling in each pan.
8. Crimp to seal edges.
9. Cut 6 to 8 small slits, about 1/2-inch each, in tops of each cobbler.
10. Using a convection oven, bake at 375 F. for 35 to 40 minutes or until lightly browned on high fan, open vent.
11. Cool; cut 6 by 9.

STREUSEL-TOPPED APPLE COBBLER

Yield 100   **Portion** 1 Piece

Calories	Carbohydrates	Protein	Fat	Cholesterol	Sodium	Calcium
492 cal	71 g	4 g	22 g	25 mg	303 mg	24 mg

Ingredient	Weight	Measure	Issue
PIE CRUST		19-1/2 each	
PIE FILLING,APPLE,PREPARED	24 lbs	3 gal	
STREUSEL TOPPING		1 gal 2 qts	

Method

1. Prepare 3/4 Pie Crust, Recipe No. I 001 00 to yield enough dough to prepare cobbler for 100 portions.
2. Divide dough into 2 pieces; use 1 piece for each sheet pan.
3. Place dough on lightly floured board; sprinkle lightly with flour; flatten gently.
4. Roll dough into rectangular sheets about 1/8-inch thick and large enough to fit each pan. Press dough into bottom and sides of each pan.
5. Pour 1-1/2 gallons of filling into each pan
6. Prepare 2 recipes Streusel Topping per 100 portions, Recipe No. D 049 00.
7. Spread 3 quarts topping over filling in each pan.
8. Using a convection oven, bake at 375 F. for 35 to 40 minutes or until lightly browned on high fan, open vent.
9. Cool; cut 6 by 9.

CHOCOLATE MOUSSE PIE

Yield 100   **Portion** 1 Slice

Calories	Carbohydrates	Protein	Fat	Cholesterol	Sodium	Calcium
247 cal	33 g	4 g	11 g	1 mg	377 mg	50 mg

Ingredient	Weight	Measure	Issue
PIE CRUST		13 each	
MILK,NONFAT,DRY	9-5/8 oz	1 qts	
WATER,COLD	10-1/2 lbs	1 gal 1 qts	
DESSERT POWDER,PUDDING,INSTANT,CHOCOLATE	3-3/4 lbs	2 qts 2 cup	
MILK,NONFAT,DRY	2-3/8 oz	1 cup	
WATER,COLD	2-1/8 lbs	1 qts	
WHIPPED TOPPING MIX,NONDAIRY,DRY	1-1/2 lbs	2 gal 1/2 qts	
SUGAR,GRANULATED	4 oz	1/2 cup 1 tbsp	
EXTRACT,VANILLA	1-3/8 oz	3 tbsp	

Method

1. PREPARE AND DIVIDE DOUGH: Prepare 1/2 recipe Pie Crust (Recipe No. I 001 00). Divide dough into 13-7-1/2 oz pieces for bottom crust; place on lightly floured board. ROLL DOUGH: Sprinkle each piece of dough lightly with flour; flatten gently. Using a floured rolling pin, roll lightly with quick strokes from center out to edge in all directions. Form a circle 1 inch larger than pie pan and about 1/8 inch thick. Shift or turn dough occasionally to prevent sticking. If edges split, pinch cracks together. BOTTOM CRUST: Fold rolled dough in half; carefully place into ungreased pie pan with

fold at center. Unfold and fit carefully into pie pan, being careful not to leave any air spaces between pan and dough. REMOVE EXCESS DOUGH: Trim overhanging edges of dough by using a knife or spatula. (Incorporate excess dough into next crust, if needed.) There should be little excess if skill is used in weighing and rolling dough. BAKING INSTRUCTIONS FOR UNCOOKED PIES: Bake crusts at 425 F. for about 15-18 minutes, or until light golden brown. Cool before filling. Proceed with the recipe directions.

2. Combine milk and water in mixer bowl.
3. Add dessert powder to milk and water. Using whip, blend at low speed 15 seconds or until well blended. Scrape down bowl; whip at medium speed 2 minutes. Set aside for use in Step 7.
4. Mix milk and water in mixer bowl.
5. Add topping to milk mixture in bowl. Using whip, mix at low speed until blended.
6. Gradually add sugar and vanilla to whipped topping while mixing at low speed. Scrape down bowl. Mix at high-speed 5 minutes or until peaks are formed.
7. Add topping to pudding mixture; blend until completely mixed.
8. Pour 3-1/2 cups filling into each baked pie shell.
9. Refrigerate about 4 hours until ready to serve.
10. Cut 8 wedges per pie. CCP: Hold for service at 41 F. or lower.

SWEET POTATO PIE

Yield 100   **Portion** 1 Slice

Calories	Carbohydrates	Protein	Fat	Cholesterol	Sodium	Calcium
252 cal	36 g	4 g	10 g	37 mg	221 mg	47 mg

Ingredient	Weight	Measure	Issue
PIE CRUST		13 each	
SWEET POTATOES,CANNED,VACUUM PACK	13-1/2 lbs	1 gal 2 qts	
EGGS,WHOLE,FROZEN	1-3/4 lbs	3-1/4 cup	
SUGAR,GRANULATED	1-1/8 lbs	2-5/8 cup	
SUGAR,BROWN,PACKED	1-1/8 lbs	3-1/2 cup	
MILK,NONFAT,DRY	5-1/8 oz	2-1/8 cup	
SALT	1/2 oz	3/8 tsp	
CINNAMON,GROUND	7/8 oz	1/4 cup	
NUTMEG,GROUND	3/8 oz	1 tbsp	
GINGER,GROUND	1/3 oz	1 tbsp	
CLOVES,GROUND	1/8 oz	3/8 tsp	
WATER,WARM	5-7/8 lbs	2 qts 3-1/4 cup	
BUTTER,MELTED	4 oz	1/2 cup	

Method
1. PREPARE AND DIVIDE DOUGH: Prepare 1/2 recipe Pie Crust (Recipe No. I 001 00). Divide dough into 13-7-1/2 oz pieces for bottom crust; place on lightly floured board. ROLL DOUGH: Sprinkle each piece of dough lightly with flour; flatten gently. Using a floured rolling pin, roll lightly with quick strokes from center out to edge in all directions. Form a circle 1 inch larger than pie pan and about 1/8 inch thick. Shift or turn dough occasionally to prevent sticking. If edges split, pinch cracks together. BOTTOM CRUST: Fold rolled dough in half; carefully place into ungreased pie pan with fold at center. Unfold and fit carefully into pie pan, being careful not to leave any air spaces between pan and dough. REMOVE EXCESS DOUGH: Trim overhanging edges of dough by using a knife or spatula. (Incorporate excess dough into next crust, if needed.) There should be little excess if skill is used in weighing and rolling dough. BAKING INSTRUCTIONS FOR UNCOOKED PIES: Bake

crusts at 425 F. for about 15-18 minutes, or until light golden brown. Cool before filling. Proceed with the recipe directions.

2. Mix sweet potatoes in mixer bowl at medium speed for 5 minutes or until smooth.
3. Combine eggs, sugars, milk, salt, cinnamon, nutmeg, ginger, and cloves. Stir until well blended. Add to sweet potatoes.
4. Add water and butter or margarine to sweet potato mixture; beat at low speed until well blended.
5. Pour 2-3/4 to 3 cups filling into each unbaked pie shell.
6. Bake at 425 F. for 45 to 55 minutes or until knife inserted into filling comes out clean. Center may be soft but will set when cool.
7. Cut 8 wedges per pie. CCP: Hold for service at 41 F. or lower.

PUMPKIN PIE

Yield 100   **Portion** 1 Slice

Calories	Carbohydrates	Protein	Fat	Cholesterol	Sodium	Calcium
242 cal	35 g	4 g	10 g	46 mg	370 mg	56 mg

Ingredient	Weight	Measure	Issue
PIE CRUST		13 each	
SUGAR,GRANULATED	3-5/8 lbs	2 qts 1/4 cup	
SALT	1-1/8 oz	1 tbsp	
FLOUR,WHEAT,GENERAL PURPOSE	6-5/8 oz	1-1/2 cup	
MILK,NONFAT,DRY	8 oz	3-3/8 cup	
CINNAMON,GROUND	1-1/2 oz	1/4 cup 2-1/3 tbsp	
NUTMEG,GROUND	3/8 oz	1 tbsp	
GINGER,GROUND	1/3 oz	1 tbsp	
PUMPKIN,CANNED,SOLID PACK	10-1/2 lbs	1 gal 7/8 qts	
WATER	9-3/8 lbs	1 gal 1/2 qts	
EGGS,WHOLE,FROZEN	2-1/3 lbs	1 qts 3/8 cup	

Method
1. PREPARE AND DIVIDE DOUGH: Prepare 1/2 recipe Pie Crust (Recipe No. I 001 00). Divide dough into 13-7-1/2 oz pieces for bottom crust; place on lightly floured board. ROLL DOUGH: Sprinkle each piece of dough lightly with flour; flatten gently. Using a floured rolling pin, roll lightly with quick strokes from center out to edge in all directions. Form a circle 1 inch larger than pie pan and about 1/8 inch thick. Shift or turn dough occasionally to prevent sticking. If edges split, pinch cracks together. BOTTOM CRUST: Fold rolled dough in half; carefully place into ungreased pie pan with fold at center. Unfold and fit carefully into pie pan, being careful not to leave any air spaces between pan and dough. REMOVE EXCESS DOUGH: Trim overhanging edges of dough by using a knife or spatula. (Incorporate excess dough into next crust, if needed.) There should be little excess if skill is used in weighing and rolling dough. BAKING INSTRUCTIONS FOR UNCOOKED PIES: Bake crusts at 425 F. for about 15-18 minutes, or until light golden brown. Cool before filling. Proceed with the recipe directions.
2. Combine sugar, salt, flour, milk, cinnamon, nutmeg and ginger in mixing bowl.
3. Add pumpkin to dry ingredients; mix at low speed until well blended. Mixture must set for one hour under refrigeration 41 F. or lower.
4. Add water and eggs; mix at low speed until well blended.
5. Pour 3-3/4 cups filling into each unbaked pie shell.
6. Bake at 375 F. for 50 to 55 minutes or until center is firm. Cool thoroughly.
7. Cut 8 wedges per pie. CCP: Hold for service at 41 F. or lower.

PINEAPPLE PIE (CANNED PINEAPPLE-CORNSTARCH)

Yield 100   **Portion** 1 Slice

Calories	Carbohydrates	Protein	Fat	Cholesterol	Sodium	Calcium
334 cal	43 g	3 g	17 g	0 mg	229 mg	8 mg

Ingredient	Weight	Measure	Issue
PIE CRUST		26 each	
PINEAPPLE,CANNED,CRUSHED,JUICE PACK,INCL LIQUIDS	3-3/4 lbs	1 qts 2-3/4 cup	
RESERVED LIQUID	4-2/3 lbs	2 qts 1 cup	
SUGAR,GRANULATED	3-1/4 lbs	1 qts 3-1/4 cup	
SALT	1/8 oz	1/8 tsp	
CORNSTARCH	8-1/2 oz	1-7/8 cup	
WATER,COLD	1-5/8 lbs	3 cup	
JUICE,LEMON	1-5/8 oz	3 tbsp	

Method

1. PREPARE AND DIVIDE DOUGH: Prepare 1 recipe Pie Crust (Recipe No. I 001 00). Divide dough into 13-7-1/2 oz pieces for bottom crust and 13-7 oz pieces for top crust; place on lightly floured board. ROLL DOUGH: Sprinkle each piece of dough lightly with flour; flatten gently. Using a floured rolling pin, roll lightly with quick strokes from center out to edge in all directions. Form a circle 1 inch larger than pie pan and about 1/8 inch thick. Bottom crust will be slightly thicker. Shift or turn dough occasionally to prevent sticking. If edges split, pinch cracks together. BOTTOM CRUST: Fold rolled dough in half; carefully place into ungreased pie pan with fold at center. Unfold and fit carefully into pie pan, being careful not to leave any air spaces between pan and dough. FILL CRUST: Fill as specified on individual recipe card. TOP CRUST: Roll top crust in same manner as bottom crust. Fold in half; with knife, make several small slits near center fold to allow steam to escape during baking. Brush outer rim of bottom crust with water. Lay top crust over filling with fold at center; unfold and press edges of two crusts together lightly. REMOVE EXCESS DOUGH: Trim overhanging edges of dough by using a knife or spatula. (Incorporate excess dough into next crust, if needed.) There should be little excess if skill is used in weighing and rolling dough. SEAL PIE: Press edges of crust firmly together or crimp with the thumb and forefinger to make a fluted edge. BAKING INSTRUCTIONS FOR COOKED PIES: Bake as specified on individual recipe card.
2. Drain pineapple; reserve juice for use in Step 3 and pineapple for use in Step 5.
3. Combine reserved juice, sugar, and salt; bring to a boil.
4. Combine cornstarch and water; stir until smooth. Add gradually to boiling mixture. Cook at medium heat, stirring constantly until thick and clear. Remove from heat.
5. Fold pineapple and lemon juice carefully into thickened mixture.
6. Pour 2-3/4 to 3 cups filling into each unbaked 9-inch pie shell. Cover with top crust. Seal edges.
7. Bake at 425 F. for 30 to 35 minutes or until lightly browned.
8. Cut 8 wedges per pie.

BERRY PIE (FROZEN BERRIES-CORNSTARCH)

Yield 100   **Portion** 1 Slice

Calories	Carbohydrates	Protein	Fat	Cholesterol	Sodium	Calcium
368 cal	48 g	4 g	18 g	4 mg	260 mg	10 mg

Ingredient	Weight	Measure	Issue
PIE CRUST		26 each	
BLUEBERRIES,FROZEN,UNSWEETENED	12-1/3 lbs	2 gal 1 qts	
SUGAR,GRANULATED	3-1/4 lbs	1 qts 3-1/4 cup	
SALT	1/3 oz	1/4 tsp	
CORNSTARCH	11-1/4 oz	2-1/2 cup	
WATER,COLD	2-1/3 lbs	1 qts 1/2 cup	
BUTTER	6 oz	3/4 cup	

Method

1. PREPARE AND DIVIDE DOUGH: Prepare 1 recipe Pie Crust (Recipe No. I 001 00). Divide dough into 13-7-1/2 oz pieces for bottom crust and 13-7 oz pieces for top crust; place on lightly floured board. ROLL DOUGH: Sprinkle each piece of dough lightly with flour; flatten gently. Using a floured rolling pin, roll lightly with quick strokes from center out to edge in all directions. Form a circle 1 inch larger than pie pan and about 1/8 inch thick. Bottom crust will be slightly thicker. Shift or turn dough occasionally to prevent sticking. If edges split, pinch cracks together. BOTTOM CRUST: Fold rolled dough in half; carefully place into ungreased pie pan with fold at center. Unfold and fit carefully into pie pan, being careful not to leave any air spaces between pan and dough. FILL CRUST: Fill as specified on individual recipe card. TOP CRUST: Roll top crust in same manner as bottom crust. Fold in half; with knife, make several small slits near center fold to allow steam to escape during baking. Brush outer rim of bottom crust with water. Lay top crust over filling with fold at center; unfold and press edges of two crusts together lightly. REMOVE EXCESS DOUGH: Trim overhanging edges of dough by using a knife or spatula. (Incorporate excess dough into next crust, if needed.) There should be little excess if skill is used in weighing and rolling dough. SEAL PIE: Press edges of crust firmly together or crimp with the thumb and forefinger to make a fluted edge. BAKING INSTRUCTIONS FOR COOKED PIES: Bake as specified on individual recipe card.
2. Thaw berries; drain; reserve juice.
3. Take reserved juice and add water to equal 6-3/4 cups per 100 portions and combine with sugar and salt; bring to a boil.
4. Combine cornstarch and water; stir until smooth. Add gradually to boiling mixture while stirring. Cook at medium heat, stirring constantly, until thick and clear. Remove from heat.
5. Fold berries and butter or margarine carefully into thickened mixture.
6. Pour 2-3/4 to 3 cups filling into each unbaked 9-inch pie shell. Cover with top crust. Seal edges.
7. Bake at 425 F. for 45 minutes or until lightly browned.
8. Cut 8 wedges per pie.

Notes

1. In Step 2, strawberries or raspberries may be used.

BLUEBERRY PIE (FROZEN BLUEBERRIES)

Yield 100   **Portion** 1 Slice

Calories	Carbohydrates	Protein	Fat	Cholesterol	Sodium	Calcium
407 cal	58 g	4 g	18 g	4 mg	261 mg	11 mg

Ingredient	Weight	Measure	Issue
PIE CRUST		26 each	
BLUEBERRIES,FROZEN,UNSWEETENED	13-1/2 lbs	2 gal 1-7/8 qts	
WATER	2-1/3 lbs	1 qts 1/2 cup	
SUGAR,GRANULATED	5-1/4 lbs	3 qts	
SALT	1/3 oz	1/4 tsp	

CORNSTARCH	11-1/4 oz	2-1/2 cup
WATER,COLD	2-1/3 lbs	1 qts 1/2 cup
BUTTER	6 oz	3/4 cup

Method

1. PREPARE AND DIVIDE DOUGH: Prepare 1 recipe Pie Crust (Recipe No. I 001 00). Divide dough into 13-7-1/2 oz pieces for bottom crust and 13-7 oz pieces for top crust; place on lightly floured board. ROLL DOUGH: Sprinkle each piece of dough lightly with flour; flatten gently. Using a floured rolling pin, roll lightly with quick strokes from center out to edge in all directions. Form a circle 1 inch larger than pie pan and about 1/8 inch thick. Bottom crust will be slightly thicker. Shift or turn dough occasionally to prevent sticking. If edges split, pinch cracks together. BOTTOM CRUST: Fold rolled dough in half; carefully place into ungreased pie pan with fold at center. Unfold and fit carefully into pie pan, being careful not to leave any air spaces between pan and dough. FILL CRUST: Fill as specified on individual recipe card. TOP CRUST: Roll top crust in same manner as bottom crust. Fold in half; with knife, make several small slits near center fold to allow steam to escape during baking. Brush outer rim of bottom crust with water. Lay top crust over filling with fold at center; unfold and press edges of two crusts together lightly. REMOVE EXCESS DOUGH: Trim overhanging edges of dough by using a knife or spatula. (Incorporate excess dough into next crust, if needed.) There should be little excess if skill is used in weighing and rolling dough. SEAL PIE: Press edges of crust firmly together or crimp with the thumb and forefinger to make a fluted edge. BAKING INSTRUCTIONS FOR COOKED PIES: Bake as specified on individual recipe card.
2. Use frozen blueberries. Thawing is not necessary.
3. Combine water, sugar and salt. Bring to a boil.
4. Combine cornstarch and water; stir until smooth. Add gradually to boiling mixture. Cook at medium heat, stirring constantly, until thick and clear. Remove from heat.
5. Fold berries and butter or margarine carefully into thickened mixture.
6. Pour 3 cups filling into each unbaked 9-inch pie shell. Cover with top crust. Seal edges.
7. Bake at 425 F. for 45 minutes or until lightly browned.
8. Cut 8 wedges per pie.

BLUEBERRY PIE (CANNED BLUEBERRIES-CORNSTARCH)

Yield 100   **Portion** 1 Serving

Calories	Carbohydrates	Protein	Fat	Cholesterol	Sodium	Calcium
446 cal	71 g	4 g	17 g	0 mg	267 mg	11 mg

Ingredient	Weight	Measure	Issue
PIE CRUST		26 each	
BLUEBERRIES,CANNED,HEAVY SYRUP,INCL LIQUIDS	20-1/3 lbs	2 gal 1 qts	
RESERVED LIQUID	4-2/3 lbs	2 qts 1 cup	
SUGAR,GRANULATED	5-1/4 lbs	3 qts	
SALT	1/2 oz	3/8 tsp	
CORNSTARCH	12 oz	2-5/8 cup	
RESERVED LIQUID	2 lbs	3-3/4 cup	
JUICE,LEMON	1-5/8 oz	3 tbsp	

Method

1. PREPARE AND DIVIDE DOUGH: Prepare 1 recipe Pie Crust (Recipe No. I 001 00). Divide dough into 13-7-1/2 oz pieces for bottom crust and 13-7 oz pieces for top crust; place on lightly floured board. ROLL DOUGH: Sprinkle each piece of dough lightly with flour; flatten gently. Using a

floured rolling pin, roll lightly with quick strokes from center out to edge in all directions. Form a circle 1 inch larger than pie pan and about 1/8 inch thick. Bottom crust will be slightly thicker. Shift or turn dough occasionally to prevent sticking. If edges split, pinch cracks together. BOTTOM CRUST: Fold rolled dough in half; carefully place into ungreased pie pan with fold at center. Unfold and fit carefully into pie pan, being careful not to leave any air spaces between pan and dough. FILL CRUST: Fill as specified on individual recipe card. TOP CRUST: Roll top crust in same manner as bottom crust. Fold in half; with knife, make several small slits near center fold to allow steam to escape during baking. Brush outer rim of bottom crust with water. Lay top crust over filling with fold at center; unfold and press edges of two crusts together lightly. REMOVE EXCESS DOUGH: Trim overhanging edges of dough by using a knife or spatula. (Incorporate excess dough into next crust, if needed.) There should be little excess if skill is used in weighing and rolling dough. SEAL PIE: Press edges of crust firmly together or crimp with the thumb and forefinger to make a fluted edge. BAKING INSTRUCTIONS FOR COOKED PIES: Bake as specified on individual recipe card.

2. Drain blueberries; reserve juice.
3. Combine 2-1/4 quart reserved juice, sugar, and salt; bring to a boil.
4. Combine cornstarch and 3-3/4 cups reserved juice; stir until smooth. Add gradually to boiling mixture. Cook at medium heat, stirring constantly, until thick and clear. Remove from heat.
5. Fold blueberries and lemon juice carefully into thickened mixture.
6. Pour 2-3/4 to 3 cups filling into each unbaked 9-inch pie shell. Cover with top crust. Seal edges.
7. Using a convection oven, bake at 375 F. for 20 to 25 minutes or until lightly browned on high fan, open vent.
8. Cut 8 wedges per pie.

BLUEBERRY PIE (PREPARED FILLING)

Yield 100   **Portion** 1 Slice

Calories	Carbohydrates	Protein	Fat	Cholesterol	Sodium	Calcium
351 cal	48 g	3 g	17 g	0 mg	262 mg	28 mg

Ingredient	Weight	Measure	Issue
PIE CRUST		26 each	
PIE FILLING,BLUEBERRY,PREPARED	22-3/4 lbs	2 gal 1-2/3 qts	

Method

1. PREPARE AND DIVIDE DOUGH: Prepare 1 recipe Pie Crust (Recipe No. I 001 00). Divide dough into 13-7-1/2 oz pieces for bottom crust and 13-7 oz pieces for top crust; place on lightly floured board. ROLL DOUGH: Sprinkle each piece of dough lightly with flour; flatten gently. Using a floured rolling pin, roll lightly with quick strokes from center out to edge in all directions. Form a circle 1 inch larger than pie pan and about 1/8 inch thick. Bottom crust will be slightly thicker. Shift or turn dough occasionally to prevent sticking. If edges split, pinch cracks together. BOTTOM CRUST: Fold rolled dough in half; carefully place into ungreased pie pan with fold at center. Unfold and fit carefully into pie pan, being careful not to leave any air spaces between pan and dough. FILL CRUST: Fill as specified on individual recipe card. TOP CRUST: Roll top crust in same manner as bottom crust. Fold in half; with knife, make several small slits near center fold to allow steam to escape during baking. Brush outer rim of bottom crust with water. Lay top crust over filling with fold at center; unfold and press edges of two crusts together lightly. REMOVE EXCESS DOUGH: Trim overhanging edges of dough by using a knife or spatula. (Incorporate excess dough into next crust, if needed.) There should be little excess if skill is used in weighing and rolling dough. SEAL PIE: Press edges of crust firmly together or crimp with the thumb and forefinger to make a fluted edge. BAKING INSTRUCTIONS FOR COOKED PIES: Bake as specified on individual recipe card.

2. Pour 3 cups filling into each unbaked 9-inch pie shell. Cover with top crust. Seal edges.
3. Using a convection oven, bake at 375 F. for 20 to 25 minutes or until lightly browned on high fan, open vent.
4. Cut 8 wedges per pie.

BUTTERSCOTCH CREAM PIE (DESSERT POWDER, INSTANT)

Yield 100   **Portion** 1 Slice

Calories	Carbohydrates	Protein	Fat	Cholesterol	Sodium	Calcium
301 cal	43 g	3 g	13 g	1 mg	492 mg	56 mg

Ingredient	Weight	Measure	Issue
PIE CRUST		13 each	
MILK,NONFAT,DRY	13-3/4 oz	1 qts 1-3/4 cup	
WATER,COLD	15-1/8 lbs	1 gal 3-1/4 qts	
DESSERT POWDER,PUDDING,INSTANT,BUTTERSCOTCH	5-1/2 lbs		

Method

1. PREPARE AND DIVIDE DOUGH: Prepare 1/2 recipe Pie Crust (Recipe No. I 001 00). Divide dough into 13-7-1/2 oz pieces for bottom crust; place on lightly floured board. ROLL DOUGH: Sprinkle each piece of dough lightly with flour; flatten gently. Using a floured rolling pin, roll lightly with quick strokes from center out to edge in all directions. Form a circle 1 inch larger than pie pan and about 1/8 inch thick. Shift or turn dough occasionally to prevent sticking. If edges split, pinch cracks together. BOTTOM CRUST: Fold rolled dough in half; carefully place into ungreased pie pan with fold at center. Unfold and fit carefully into pie pan, being careful not to leave any air spaces between pan and dough. REMOVE EXCESS DOUGH: Trim overhanging edges of dough by using a knife or spatula. (Incorporate excess dough into next crust, if needed.) There should be little excess if skill is used in weighing and rolling dough. BAKING INSTRUCTIONS FOR UNCOOKED PIES: Bake crusts at 425 F. for about 15-18 minutes, or until light golden brown. Cool before filling. Proceed with the recipe directions.
2. Reconstitute milk.
3. Add dessert powder. Using whip, blend at low speed 15 seconds or until well-blended. Scrape down sides of bowl; whip at medium speed for 2 minutes.
4. Pour 3 cups filling into each baked 9-inch pie shell.
5. Refrigerate until ready to serve. Chilled pies may be topped with Whipped Cream, Recipe No. K 001 00, or Whipped Topping, Recipe No. K 002 00.
6. Cut 8 wedges per pie. CCP: Hold for service at 41 F. or lower.

PEACH PIE (FROZEN PEACHES-CORNSTARCH)

Yield 100   **Portion** 1 Slice

Calories	Carbohydrates	Protein	Fat	Cholesterol	Sodium	Calcium
418 cal	64 g	4 g	17 g	0 mg	269 mg	9 mg

Ingredient	Weight	Measure	Issue
PIE CRUST		26 each	
PEACHES,FROZEN	19-7/8 lbs	2 gal 1 qts	
RESERVED LIQUID	5-1/2 lbs	2 qts 2-1/2 cup	

SUGAR,GRANULATED		3-5/8 lbs	2 qts 1/4 cup
SALT		1/2 oz	3/8 tsp
CORNSTARCH		10-1/8 oz	2-1/4 cup
WATER,COLD		1-1/8 lbs	2-1/4 cup

Method

1. PREPARE AND DIVIDE DOUGH: Prepare 1 recipe Pie Crust (Recipe No. I 001 00). Divide dough into 13-7-1/2 oz pieces for bottom crust and 13-7 oz pieces for top crust; place on lightly floured board. ROLL DOUGH: Sprinkle each piece of dough lightly with flour; flatten gently. Using a floured rolling pin, roll lightly with quick strokes from center out to edge in all directions. Form a circle 1 inch larger than pie pan and about 1/8 inch thick. Bottom crust will be slightly thicker. Shift or turn dough occasionally to prevent sticking. If edges split, pinch cracks together. BOTTOM CRUST: Fold rolled dough in half; carefully place into ungreased pie pan with fold at center. Unfold and fit carefully into pie pan, being careful not to leave any air spaces between pan and dough. FILL CRUST: Fill as specified on individual recipe card. TOP CRUST: Roll top crust in same manner as bottom crust. Fold in half; with knife, make several small slits near center fold to allow steam to escape during baking. Brush outer rim of bottom crust with water. Lay top crust over filling with fold at center; unfold and press edges of two crusts together lightly. REMOVE EXCESS DOUGH: Trim overhanging edges of dough by using a knife or spatula. (Incorporate excess dough into next crust, if needed.) There should be little excess if skill is used in weighing and rolling dough. SEAL PIE: Press edges of crust firmly together or crimp with the thumb and forefinger to make a fluted edge. BAKING INSTRUCTIONS FOR COOKED PIES: Bake as specified on individual recipe card.
2. Thaw peaches. Drain; reserve juice.
3. Combine reserved juice, sugar, and salt; bring to a boil.
4. Combine cornstarch and water; stir until smooth. Add gradually to boiling mixture. Cook at medium heat, stirring constantly, until thick and clear. Remove from heat.
5. Fold peaches carefully into thickened mixture. Cool.
6. Pour 2-3/4 to 3 cups filling into each unbaked 9-inch pie shell. Cover with top crust. Seal edges.
7. Bake at 425 F. for 30 to 35 minutes or until lightly browned.
8. Cut 8 wedges per pie.

CHERRY PIE (CANNED CHERRIES-CORNSTARCH)

Yield 100   **Portion** 1 Slice

Calories	Carbohydrates	Protein	Fat	Cholesterol	Sodium	Calcium
406 cal	61 g	4 g	17 g	0 mg	265 mg	16 mg

Ingredient	Weight	Measure	Issue
PIE CRUST		26 each	
CHERRIES,CANNED,RED,TART,WATER PACK,INCL	19-2/3 lbs	2 gal 1 qts	
LIQUIDS	2-3/4 lbs	1 qts 1-3/8 cup	
RESERVED LIQUID	5-1/4 lbs	3 qts	
SUGAR,GRANULATED	1/2 oz	3/8 tsp	
SALT	12 oz	2-5/8 cup	
CORNSTARCH	1-1/8 lbs	2-1/4 cup	
WATER,COLD	1/4 oz	1/4 tsp	
FOOD COLOR,RED			

342

Method

1. PREPARE AND DIVIDE DOUGH: Prepare 1 recipe Pie Crust (Recipe No. I 001 00). Divide dough into 13-7-1/2 oz pieces for bottom crust and 13-7 oz pieces for top crust; place on lightly floured board. ROLL DOUGH: Sprinkle each piece of dough lightly with flour; flatten gently. Using a floured rolling pin, roll lightly with quick strokes from center out to edge in all directions. Form a circle 1 inch larger than pie pan and about 1/8 inch thick. Bottom crust will be slightly thicker. Shift or turn dough occasionally to prevent sticking. If edges split, pinch cracks together. BOTTOM CRUST: Fold rolled dough in half; carefully place into ungreased pie pan with fold at center. Unfold and fit carefully into pie pan, being careful not to leave any air spaces between pan and dough. FILL CRUST: Fill as specified on individual recipe card. TOP CRUST: Roll top crust in same manner as bottom crust. Fold in half; with knife, make several small slits near center fold to allow steam to escape during baking. Brush outer rim of bottom crust with water. Lay top crust over filling with fold at center; unfold and press edges of two crusts together lightly. REMOVE EXCESS DOUGH: Trim overhanging edges of dough by using a knife or spatula. (Incorporate excess dough into next crust, if needed.) There should be little excess if skill is used in weighing and rolling dough. SEAL PIE: Press edges of crust firmly together or crimp with the thumb and forefinger to make a fluted edge. BAKING INSTRUCTIONS FOR COOKED PIES: Bake as specified on individual recipe card.
2. Drain cherries; reserve juice for use in Step 3 and cherries for use in Step 5.
3. Combine reserved juice, sugar, and salt; bring to a boil.
4. Combine cornstarch and water; stir until smooth. Add gradually to boiling mixture. Cook at medium heat, stirring constantly until thick and clear. Remove from heat.
5. Add red food coloring. Fold cherries carefully into thickened mixture. Cool.
6. Pour 3 cups filling into each unbaked 9-inch pie shell. Cover with top crust. Seal edges.
7. Using a convection oven, bake at 375 F. for 20 to 25 minutes or until lightly browned on high fan, open vent.
8. Cut 8 wedges per pie.

CHERRY PIE (PIE FILLING, PREPARED)

Yield 100   **Portion** 1 Slice

Calories	Carbohydrates	Protein	Fat	Cholesterol	Sodium	Calcium
377 cal	54 g	4 g	17 g	0 mg	219 mg	16 mg

Ingredient	Weight	Measure	Issue
PIE CRUST		26 each	
PIE FILLING,CHERRY,PREPARED	22-3/4 lbs	2 gal 3-3/8 qts	

Method

1. PREPARE AND DIVIDE DOUGH: Prepare 1 recipe Pie Crust (Recipe No. I 001 00). Divide dough into 13-7-1/2 oz pieces for bottom crust and 13-7 oz pieces for top crust; place on lightly floured board. ROLL DOUGH: Sprinkle each piece of dough lightly with flour; flatten gently. Using a floured rolling pin, roll lightly with quick strokes from center out to edge in all directions. Form a circle 1 inch larger than pie pan and about 1/8 inch thick. Bottom crust will be slightly thicker. Shift or turn dough occasionally to prevent sticking. If edges split, pinch cracks together. BOTTOM CRUST: Fold rolled dough in half; carefully place into ungreased pie pan with fold at center. Unfold and fit carefully into pie pan, being careful not to leave any air spaces between pan and dough. FILL CRUST: Fill as specified on individual recipe card. TOP CRUST: Roll top crust in same manner as bottom crust. Fold in half; with knife, make several small slits near center fold to allow steam to escape during baking. Brush outer rim of bottom crust with water. Lay top crust over filling with fold at center; unfold and press edges of two crusts together lightly. REMOVE EXCESS DOUGH:

Trim overhanging edges of dough by using a knife or spatula. (Incorporate excess dough into next crust, if needed.) There should be little excess if skill is used in weighing and rolling dough. SEAL PIE: Press edges of crust firmly together or crimp with the thumb and forefinger to make a fluted edge. BAKING INSTRUCTIONS FOR COOKED PIES: Bake as specified on individual recipe card.

2. Pour 3 cups filling into each unbaked 9-inch pie shell. Cover with top crust. Seal edges.
3. Using a convection oven, bake at 375 F. for 20 to 25 minutes or until lightly browned on high fan, open vent.
4. Cut 8 wedges per pie.

PEACH PIE (CANNED PEACHES-CORNSTARCH)

Yield 100   **Portion** 1 Slice

Calories	Carbohydrates	Protein	Fat	Cholesterol	Sodium	Calcium
374 cal	54 g	4 g	17 g	0 mg	262 mg	11 mg

Ingredient	Weight	Measure	Issue
PIE CRUST		26 each	
PEACHES,CANNED,SLICED,JUICE PACK,INCL	19-2/3 lbs	2 gal 1 qts	
LIQUIDS	6-1/4 lbs	3 qts	
RESERVED LIQUID	3-3/4 lbs	2 qts 1/2 cup	
SUGAR,GRANULATED	3/8 oz	1/3 tsp	
SALT	9 oz	2 cup	
CORNSTARCH	1-1/8 lbs	2-1/4 cup	
WATER,COLD			

Method

1. PREPARE AND DIVIDE DOUGH: Prepare 1 recipe Pie Crust (Recipe No. I 001 00). Divide dough into 13-7-1/2 oz pieces for bottom crust and 13-7 oz pieces for top crust; place on lightly floured board. ROLL DOUGH: Sprinkle each piece of dough lightly with flour; flatten gently. Using a floured rolling pin, roll lightly with quick strokes from center out to edge in all directions. Form a circle 1 inch larger than pie pan and about 1/8 inch thick. Bottom crust will be slightly thicker. Shift or turn dough occasionally to prevent sticking. If edges split, pinch cracks together. BOTTOM CRUST: Fold rolled dough in half; carefully place into ungreased pie pan with fold at center. Unfold and fit carefully into pie pan, being careful not to leave any air spaces between pan and dough. FILL CRUST: Fill as specified on individual recipe card. TOP CRUST: Roll top crust in same manner as bottom crust. Fold in half; with knife, make several small slits near center fold to allow steam to escape during baking. Brush outer rim of bottom crust with water. Lay top crust over filling with fold at center; unfold and press edges of two crusts together lightly. REMOVE EXCESS DOUGH: Trim overhanging edges of dough by using a knife or spatula. (Incorporate excess dough into next crust, if needed.) There should be little excess if skill is used in weighing and rolling dough. SEAL PIE: Press edges of crust firmly together or crimp with the thumb and forefinger to make a fluted edge. BAKING INSTRUCTIONS FOR COOKED PIES: Bake as specified on individual recipe card.
2. Drain peaches; reserve juice for use in Step 3; peaches for use in Step 5.
3. Combine reserved juice, sugar, and salt; bring to a boil.
4. Combine cornstarch and water; stir until smooth. Add gradually to boiling mixture. Cook at medium heat, stirring constantly until thick and clear. Remove from heat.
5. Fold peaches carefully into thickened mixture. Cool.
6. Pour about 3 cups filling into each unbaked 9-inch pie shell. Cover with top crust. Seal edges.
7. Using a convection oven, bake at 375 F. for 20 to 25 minutes or until lightly browned on high fan, open vent.
8. Cut 8 wedges per pie.

PEACH PIE (PREPARED PIE FILLING)

Yield 100   **Portion** 1 Slice

Calories	Carbohydrates	Protein	Fat	Cholesterol	Sodium	Calcium
410 cal	64 g	4 g	17 g	0 mg	245 mg	19 mg

Ingredient	Weight	Measure	Issue
PIE CRUST		26 each	
PIE FILLING,PEACH,PREPARED	22-3/4 lbs	2 gal 3-3/8 qts	

Method

1. PREPARE AND DIVIDE DOUGH: Prepare 1 recipe Pie Crust (Recipe No. I 001 00). Divide dough into 13-7-1/2 oz pieces for bottom crust and 13-7 oz pieces for top crust; place on lightly floured board. ROLL DOUGH: Sprinkle each piece of dough lightly with flour; flatten gently. Using a floured rolling pin, roll lightly with quick strokes from center out to edge in all directions. Form a circle 1 inch larger than pie pan and about 1/8 inch thick. Bottom crust will be slightly thicker. Shift or turn dough occasionally to prevent sticking. If edges split, pinch cracks together. BOTTOM CRUST: Fold rolled dough in half; carefully place into ungreased pie pan with fold at center. Unfold and fit carefully into pie pan, being careful not to leave any air spaces between pan and dough. FILL CRUST: Fill as specified on individual recipe card. TOP CRUST: Roll top crust in same manner as bottom crust. Fold in half; with knife, make several small slits near center fold to allow steam to escape during baking. Brush outer rim of bottom crust with water. Lay top crust over filling with fold at center; unfold and press edges of two crusts together lightly. REMOVE EXCESS DOUGH: Trim overhanging edges of dough by using a knife or spatula. (Incorporate excess dough into next crust, if needed.) There should be little excess if skill is used in weighing and rolling dough. SEAL PIE: Press edges of crust firmly together or crimp with the thumb and forefinger to make a fluted edge. BAKING INSTRUCTIONS FOR COOKED PIES: Bake as specified on individual recipe card.
2. Pour 3 cups filling into each unbaked 9-inch pie shell. Cover with top crust. Seal edges.
3. Using a convection oven, bake at 375 F. for 20 to 25 minutes or until lightly browned on high fan, open vent.
4. Cut 8 wedges per pie.

CREAMY COCONUT PIE

Yield 100   **Portion** 1 Slice

Calories	Carbohydrates	Protein	Fat	Cholesterol	Sodium	Calcium
296 cal	23 g	4 g	21 g	23 mg	214 mg	43 mg

Ingredient	Weight	Measure	Issue
PIE CRUST		13 each	
MILK,NONFAT,DRY	3-5/8 oz	1-1/2 cup	
WATER,COLD	3-7/8 lbs	1 qts 3-1/2 cup	
MILK,NONFAT,DRY	2-3/8 oz	1 cup	
WATER,WARM	3 lbs	1 qts 1-5/8 cup	
CHEESE,CREAM,SOFTENED,ROOM TEMPERATURE	4-1/2 lbs	2 qts 3/4 cup	
SUGAR,GRANULATED	8 oz	1-1/8 cup	
COCONUT,PREPARED,SWEETENED FLAKES	3-1/8 lbs	3 qts 3 cup	
FLAVORING,ALMOND	1-3/8 oz	3 tbsp	
WHIPPED TOPPING MIX,NONDAIRY,DRY	5-2/3 oz	2 qts	

Method

1. PREPARE AND DIVIDE DOUGH: Prepare 1/2 recipe Pie Crust (Recipe No. I 001 00). Divide dough into 13-7-1/2 oz pieces for bottom crust; place on lightly floured board. ROLL DOUGH: Sprinkle each piece of dough lightly with flour; flatten gently. Using a floured rolling pin, roll lightly with quick strokes from center out to edge in all directions. Form a circle 1 inch larger than pie pan and about 1/8 inch thick. Shift or turn dough occasionally to prevent sticking. If edges split, pinch cracks together. BOTTOM CRUST: Fold rolled dough in half; carefully place into ungreased pie pan with fold at center. Unfold and fit carefully into pie pan, being careful not to leave any air spaces between pan and dough. REMOVE EXCESS DOUGH: Trim overhanging edges of dough by using a knife or spatula. (Incorporate excess dough into next crust, if needed.) There should be little excess if skill is used in weighing and rolling dough. BAKING INSTRUCTIONS FOR UNCOOKED PIES: Bake crusts at 425 F. for about 15-18 minutes, or until light golden brown. Cool before filling. Proceed with the recipe directions.
2. Combine milk and water in mixer bowl. CCP: Refrigerate at 41 F. or lower for use in Step 5.
3. Combine 2nd milk and 2nd water in mixer bowl.
4. Combine cream cheese, sugar, coconut and almond flavoring with milk in mixer bowl. Whip at low speed 1 minute; scrape down sides of bowl. Whip 3 minutes at low speed, or until well blended. Set aside for use in Step 6.
5. Place cold milk and water (from Step 2) in mixer bowl. Add topping. Blend 3 minutes at low speed. Scrape down sides of bowl. Whip at high speed about 5 to 10 minutes or until stiff peaks are formed.
6. Add whipped topping to cream cheese mixture. Blend at low speed 1 minute; scrape down sides of bowl. Blend at low speed 1 minute or until smooth.
7. Pour 4-2/3 cups filling into each crust.
8. Toasted coconut, chopped unsalted nuts, or chopped maraschino cherries may be sprinkled over pies before placing in freezer. Place pies in freezer 4 hours or until firm.
9. Let pies stand at room temperature 5 minutes before cutting. Cut 8 wedges per pie. CCP: Hold for service at 41 F. or lower.

Notes

1. 4 pound and 1 ounce preformed, graham cracker pie crusts may be used per 100 servings

CREAMY BANANA COCONUT PIE

Yield 100   **Portion** 1 Slice

Calories	Carbohydrates	Protein	Fat	Cholesterol	Sodium	Calcium
307 cal	26 g	4 g	21 g	23 mg	214 mg	44 mg

Ingredient	Weight	Measure	Issue
PIE CRUST		13 each	
MILK,NONFAT,DRY	3-5/8 oz	1-1/2 cup	
WATER,COLD	3-7/8 lbs	1 qts 3-1/2 cup	
MILK,NONFAT,DRY	2-3/8 oz	1 cup	
WATER,WARM	3 lbs	1 qts 1-5/8 cup	
CHEESE,CREAM,SOFTENED,ROOM TEMPERATURE	4-1/2 lbs	2 qts 3/4 cup	
SUGAR,GRANULATED	8 oz	1-1/8 cup	
COCONUT,PREPARED,SWEETENED FLAKES	3-1/8 lbs	3 qts 3 cup	
BANANA,FRESH	3 lbs		4-5/8
WHIPPED TOPPING MIX,NONDAIRY,DRY	5-2/3 oz	lbs 2 qts	

Method

1. PREPARE AND DIVIDE DOUGH: Prepare 1/2 recipe Pie Crust (Recipe No. I 001 00). Divide dough into 13-7-1/2 oz pieces for bottom crust; place on lightly floured board. ROLL DOUGH: Sprinkle each piece of dough lightly with flour; flatten gently. Using a floured rolling pin, roll lightly with quick strokes from center out to edge in all directions. Form a circle 1 inch larger than pie pan and about 1/8 inch thick. Shift or turn dough occasionally to prevent sticking. If edges split, pinch cracks together. BOTTOM CRUST: Fold rolled dough in half; carefully place into ungreased pie pan with fold at center. Unfold and fit carefully into pie pan, being careful not to leave any air spaces between pan and dough. REMOVE EXCESS DOUGH: Trim overhanging edges of dough by using a knife or spatula. (Incorporate excess dough into next crust, if needed.) There should be little excess if skill is used in weighing and rolling dough. BAKING INSTRUCTIONS FOR UNCOOKED PIES: Bake crusts at 425 F. for about 15-18 minutes, or until light golden brown. Cool before filling. Proceed with the recipe directions.
2. Combine milk and water in mixer bowl. CCP: Refrigerate at 41 F. or lower for use in Step 5.
3. Combine 2nd milk and 2nd water in mixer bowl.
4. Combine cream cheese, sugar, coconut and peeled ripe bananas with milk in mixer bowl. Whip at low speed 1 minute; scrape down sides of bowl. Whip 3 minutes at low speed, or until well blended. Set aside for use in Step 6.
5. Place cold milk and water (from Step 2) in mixer bowl. Add topping. Blend 3 minutes at low speed. Scrape down sides of bowl. Whip at high speed about 5 to 10 minutes or until stiff peaks are formed.
6. Add whipped topping to cream cheese mixture. Blend at low speed 1 minute; scrape down sides of bowl. Blend at low speed 1 minute or until smooth.
7. Pour 1-1/4 quart filling into each 9-inch pie crust.
8. Toasted coconut, chopped unsalted nuts, or chopped maraschino cherries may be sprinkled over pies before placing in freezer. Place pies in freezer 4 hours or until firm.
9. Let pies stand at room temperature 5 minutes before cutting. Cut 8 wedges per pie. CCP: Hold for service at 41 F. or lower.

Notes

1. 13 5-ounce pie crusts, preformed, graham cracker pie crusts, may be used per 100 portions

AMBROSIA PIE

Yield 100   **Portion** 1 Slice

Calories	Carbohydrates	Protein	Fat	Cholesterol	Sodium	Calcium
314 cal	28 g	4 g	21 g	23 mg	214 mg	44 mg

Ingredient	Weight	Measure	Issue
PIE CRUST		13 each	
MILK,NONFAT,DRY	3-5/8 oz	1-1/2 cup	
WATER,COLD	3-7/8 lbs	1 qts 3-1/2 cup	
JUICE,ORANGE	5-1/2 lbs	2 qts 2 cup	
MILK,NONFAT,DRY	2-3/8 oz	1 cup	
CHEESE,CREAM	4-1/2 lbs	2 qts 3/4 cup	
SUGAR,GRANULATED	1 lbs	2-1/4 cup	
COCONUT,PREPARED,SWEETENED FLAKES	3-1/8 lbs	3 qts 3 cup	
FOOD COLOR,YELLOW	1/4 oz	1/4 tsp	
FOOD COLOR,RED	1/8 oz	1/8 tsp	
WHIPPED TOPPING MIX,NONDAIRY,DRY	5-2/3 oz	2 qts	

Method

1. PREPARE AND DIVIDE DOUGH: Prepare 1/2 recipe Pie Crust (Recipe No. I 001 00). Divide dough into 13-7-1/2 oz pieces for bottom crust; place on lightly floured board. ROLL DOUGH: Sprinkle each piece of dough lightly with flour; flatten gently. Using a floured rolling pin, roll lightly with quick strokes from center out to edge in all directions. Form a circle 1 inch larger than pie pan and about 1/8 inch thick. Shift or turn dough occasionally to prevent sticking. If edges split, pinch cracks together. BOTTOM CRUST: Fold rolled dough in half; carefully place into ungreased pie pan with fold at center. Unfold and fit carefully into pie pan, being careful not to leave any air spaces between pan and dough. REMOVE EXCESS DOUGH: Trim overhanging edges of dough by using a knife or spatula. (Incorporate excess dough into next crust, if needed.) There should be little excess if skill is used in weighing and rolling dough. BAKING INSTRUCTIONS FOR UNCOOKED PIES: Bake crusts at 425 F. for about 15-18 minutes, or until light golden brown. Cool before filling. Proceed with the recipe directions.
2. Combine milk and water in mixer bowl. CCP: Refrigerate at 41 F. or lower for use in Step 5.
3. Combine nonfat dry milk with orange juice.
4. Combine cream cheese, sugar, and coconut with milk in mixer bowl. Add yellow and red food coloring. Whip at low speed 1 minute; scrape down sides of bowl. Whip 3 minutes at low speed, or until well blended. Set aside for use in Step 6.
5. Place cold milk and water (from Step 2) in mixer bowl. Add topping; blend 3 minutes at low speed. Scrape down sides of bowl. Whip at high speed about 5 to 10 minutes or until stiff peaks are formed.
6. Add whipped topping to cream cheese mixture. Blend at low speed 1 minute; scrape down sides of bowl. Blend at low speed 1 minute or until smooth.
7. Pour 4-2/3 cups filling into each 9-inch pie crust.
8. Toasted coconut, chopped unsalted nuts, or chopped maraschino cherries may be sprinkled over pies before placing in freezer. Place pies in freezer 4 hours or until firm.
9. Let pies stand at room temperature 5 minutes before cutting. Cut 8 wedges per pie. CCP: Hold for service at 41 F. or lower.

Notes

1. 13-5 ounce pie crusts, preformed, graham cracker pie crusts, may be used.

CHERRY CRUMBLE PIE

Yield 100   Portion 1 Slice

Calories	Carbohydrates	Protein	Fat	Cholesterol	Sodium	Calcium
456 cal	77 g	4 g	16 g	0 mg	185 mg	16 mg

Ingredient	Weight	Measure	Issue
FLOUR,WHEAT,GENERAL PURPOSE	8 lbs	1 gal 3-1/4 qts	
SALT	1-1/2 oz	2-1/3 tbsp	
SUGAR,GRANULATED	4-3/8 lbs	2 qts 2 cup	
SHORTENING	3-1/8 lbs	1 qts 3 cup	
CHERRIES,CANNED,RED,TART,WATER PACK,INCL	19-2/3 lbs	2 gal 1 qts	
LIQUIDS	1-1/2 lbs	3-3/8 cup	
SUGAR,GRANULATED	2-1/4 lbs	1 qts 1 cup	
SUGAR,GRANULATED	7-7/8 oz	1-3/4 cup	
CORNSTARCH	1/8 oz	1/8 tsp	
SALT	1 lbs	2 cup	
WATER,COLD	3 oz	1/4 cup 2-1/3 tbsp	
MARGARINE	1/4 oz	1/4 tsp	
FOOD COLOR,RED			

Method

1. Mix flour, salt, sugar, and shortening in a mixer bowl 1 minute at low speed to form a crumbly mixture.
2. Place 1-1/2 cups of mixture in each pan; press firmly into an even layer against bottom and sides of pan. Set remaining crumb mixture aside for use in Step 5.
3. Drain cherries. Set aside juice for use in Step 7.
4. Combine cherries and sugar. Spread 2 cups mixture over crumbs in each pan.
5. Spread 1 cup reserved crumb mixture over cherries in each 9-inch pan.
6. Using a convection oven, bake 35 to 40 minutes at 350 F. or until done on low fan, open vent.
7. Take reserved juice add water to equal 1 gallon per 100 portions and combine with sugar; bring to a boil.
8. Combine cornstarch, salt, and water; stir until smooth. Add gradually to boiling mixture. Stir until well blended; cook at medium heat about 5 minutes. Add margarine or butter and food coloring.
9. Pour 1-1/2 cups of sauce over each baked pie.
10. Cool; cut 8 wedges per pie.

CHOCOLATE CREAM PIE

Yield 100   **Portion** 1 Slice

Calories	Carbohydrates	Protein	Fat	Cholesterol	Sodium	Calcium
333 cal	43 g	5 g	16 g	31 mg	257 mg	60 mg

Ingredient	Weight	Measure	Issue
PIE CRUST		13 each	
MILK,NONFAT,DRY	13-1/4 oz	1 qts 1-1/2 cup	
WATER,WARM	14-1/8 lbs	1 gal 2-3/4 qts	
SUGAR,GRANULATED	1-7/8 lbs	1 qts 1/4 cup	
SALT	3/4 oz	1 tbsp	
CORNSTARCH	1-1/8 lbs	1 qts	
SUGAR,GRANULATED	1-7/8 lbs	1 qts 1/4 cup	
COCOA	9-7/8 oz	3-1/4 cup	
WATER,COLD	1-1/3 lbs	2-1/2 cup	
EGGS,WHOLE,FROZEN	1-1/2 lbs	2-7/8 cup	
MARGARINE	10-5/8 oz	1-3/8 cup	
EXTRACT,VANILLA	1 oz	2-1/3 tbsp	

Method

1. PREPARE AND DIVIDE DOUGH: Prepare 1/2 recipe Pie Crust (Recipe No. I 001 00). Divide dough into 13-7-1/2 oz pieces for bottom crust; place on lightly floured board. ROLL DOUGH: Sprinkle each piece of dough lightly with flour; flatten gently. Using a floured rolling pin, roll lightly with quick strokes from center out to edge in all directions. Form a circle 1 inch larger than pie pan and about 1/8 inch thick. Shift or turn dough occasionally to prevent sticking. If edges split, pinch cracks together. BOTTOM CRUST: Fold rolled dough in half; carefully place into ungreased pie pan with fold at center. Unfold and fit carefully into pie pan, being careful not to leave any air spaces between pan and dough. REMOVE EXCESS DOUGH: Trim overhanging edges of dough by using a knife or spatula. (Incorporate excess dough into next crust, if needed.) There should be little excess if skill is used in weighing and rolling dough. BAKING INSTRUCTIONS FOR UNCOOKED PIES: Bake crusts at 425 F. for about 15-18 minutes, or until light golden brown. Cool before filling. Proceed with the recipe directions.
2. Reconstitute milk. Add sugar and salt; heat to just below boiling. DO NOT BOIL.

3. Combine cornstarch, sugar, cocoa, and water; stir until smooth. Add gradually to hot mixture. Cook at medium heat, stirring constantly, about 10 minutes until thickened.

4. Stir 1 quart of hot mixture into eggs. Slowly pour egg mixture into remaining hot mixture; heat to boiling stirring constantly. Cook 2 minutes longer. Remove from heat.

5. Add margarine or butter and vanilla; stir until well blended. Cool slightly.

6. Pour 3 cups of filling into each 9-inch baked pie shell. Meringue, Recipe No. I 005 00 or I 005 01 may be spread over chilled filling, about 50 F. Ensure cream pie filling preparation time does not exceed 4 hours total in temperatures between 40 F. to 140 F.

7. Refrigerate until ready to serve. CCP: Hold for service at 41 F. or lower.

8. Cut 8 wedges per pie. Chilled pies may be topped with Whipped Cream, Recipe No. K 001 00 or Whipped Topping, Recipe No. K 002 00.

Notes
1. Filling will curdle or scorch if boiled or subjected to prolonged intense heat.

CHOCOLATE CREAM PIE (DESSERT POWDER, INSTANT)

Yield 100   **Portion** 1 Slice

Calories	Carbohydrates	Protein	Fat	Cholesterol	Sodium	Calcium
331 cal	50 g	4 g	14 g	1 mg	620 mg	64 mg

Ingredient	Weight	Measure	Issue
PIE CRUST		13 each	
MILK,NONFAT,DRY	15 oz	1 qts 2-1/4 cup	
WATER,COLD	16-3/4 lbs	2 gal	
DESSERT POWDER,PUDDING,INSTANT,CHOCOLATE	7-1/2 lbs	1 gal 1 qts	

Method
1. PREPARE AND DIVIDE DOUGH: Prepare 1/2 recipe Pie Crust (Recipe No. I 001 00). Divide dough into 13-7-1/2 oz pieces for bottom crust; place on lightly floured board. ROLL DOUGH: Sprinkle each piece of dough lightly with flour; flatten gently. Using a floured rolling pin, roll lightly with quick strokes from center out to edge in all directions. Form a circle 1 inch larger than pie pan and about 1/8 inch thick. Shift or turn dough occasionally to prevent sticking. If edges split, pinch cracks together. BOTTOM CRUST: Fold rolled dough in half; carefully place into ungreased pie pan with fold at center. Unfold and fit carefully into pie pan, being careful not to leave any air spaces between pan and dough. REMOVE EXCESS DOUGH: Trim overhanging edges of dough by using a knife or spatula. (Incorporate excess dough into next crust, if needed.) There should be little excess if skill is used in weighing and rolling dough. BAKING INSTRUCTIONS FOR UNCOOKED PIES: Bake crusts at 425 F. for about 15-18 minutes, or until light golden brown. Cool before filling. Proceed with the recipe directions.

2. Combine nonfat dry milk and cold water, 50 F. in mixer bowl. Add dessert powder pudding, instant, chocolate to milk and water.

3. Using whip, blend at low speed for 15 seconds or until well blended.

4. Scrape down sides of bowl; whip at medium speed 2 minutes.

5. Pour 3 cups filling into each baked 9-inch pie shell. Meringue, Recipe No. I 005 00 or I 005 01 may be spread over chilled filling, about 50 F. Ensure cream pie filling preparation time does not exceed 4 hours total in temperatures between 40 F. to 140 F.

6. Refrigerate until ready to serve.

7. Chilled pies may be topped with Whipped Cream, Recipe No. K 001 00 or Whipped Topping, Recipe No. K 002 00. Cut 8 wedges per pie. CCP: Hold for service at 41 F. or lower.

Notes
1. Filling will curdle or scorch if boiled or subjected to prolonged intense heat.

CHOCOLATE AND VANILLA CREAM PIE (INSTANT)

Yield 100   **Portion** 1 Slice

Calories	Carbohydrates	Protein	Fat	Cholesterol	Sodium	Calcium
290 cal	40 g	4 g	13 g	1 mg	446 mg	58 mg

Ingredient	Weight	Measure	Issue
PIE CRUST		13 each	
MILK,NONFAT,DRY	14-3/8 oz	1 qts 2 cup	
WATER,COLD	15-2/3 lbs	1 gal 3-1/2 qts	
DESSERT POWDER,PUDDING,INSTANT,CHOCOLATE	2-1/4 lbs	1 qts 2 cup	
DESSERT POWDER,PUDDING,INSTANT,VANILLA	2-1/2 lbs	1 qts 2 cup	
WHIPPED TOPPING MIX,NONDAIRY,DRY	1 oz	1-1/2 cup	
SUGAR,GRANULATED	5/8 oz	1 tbsp	
EXTRACT,VANILLA	5/8 oz	1 tbsp	

Method

1. PREPARE AND DIVIDE DOUGH: Prepare 1/2 recipe Pie Crust (Recipe No. I 001 00). Divide dough into 13-7-1/2 oz pieces for bottom crust; place on lightly floured board. ROLL DOUGH: Sprinkle each piece of dough lightly with flour; flatten gently. Using a floured rolling pin, roll lightly with quick strokes from center out to edge in all directions. Form a circle 1 inch larger than pie pan and about 1/8 inch thick. Shift or turn dough occasionally to prevent sticking. If edges split, pinch cracks together. BOTTOM CRUST: Fold rolled dough in half; carefully place into ungreased pie pan with fold at center. Unfold and fit carefully into pie pan, being careful not to leave any air spaces between pan and dough. REMOVE EXCESS DOUGH: Trim overhanging edges of dough by using a knife or spatula. (Incorporate excess dough into next crust, if needed.) There should be little excess if skill is used in weighing and rolling dough. BAKING INSTRUCTIONS FOR UNCOOKED PIES: Bake crusts at 425 F. for about 15-18 minutes, or until light golden brown. Cool before filling. Proceed with the recipe directions.
2. Combine milk and water in mixer bowl.
3. Pour 3-1/2 quarts chilled milk into mixer bowl; add dessert powder. Using whip, blend at low speed 15 seconds or until well blended. Scrape down sides of bowl. Whip at medium speed 2 minutes or until smooth.
4. Pour 1-1/3 cups filling into each baked pie shell.
5. Pour 1 gallon chilled milk into mixer bowl; add dessert powder. Using whip, blend 15 seconds at low speed or until well blended. Scrape down sides of bowl. Whip at medium speed 2 minutes or until smooth. Set aside for use in Step 7.
6. Pour 1-1/2 cups chilled milk into mixer bowl; add topping, sugar and vanilla. Whip at low speed 3 minutes or until blended. Scrape down sides of bowl. Whip at high speed until stiff.
7. Fold whipped topping into vanilla pie filling. Spread 1-3/4 cups over chocolate filling in each baked pie shell.
8. Refrigerate at least 1 hour or until ready to serve.
9. Cut 8 wedges per pie. CCP: Hold for service at 41 F. or lower. Chilled pies may be topped with Whipped Cream, Recipe No. K 001 00 or Whipped Topping, Recipe No. K 002 00.

Notes

1. 1 pound 5 ounces canned dessert topping and frozen bakery products, may be used. Omit Step 6.

FRIED APPLE PIE

Yield 100   **Portion** 1 Pie

Calories	Carbohydrates	Protein	Fat	Cholesterol	Sodium	Calcium
366 cal	52 g	5 g	16 g	0 mg	340 mg	73 mg

Ingredient	Weight	Measure	Issue
FLOUR,WHEAT,GENERAL PURPOSE	9-7/8 lbs	2 gal 1 qts	
MILK,NONFAT,DRY	2-2/3 oz	1-1/8 cup	
BAKING POWDER	3-1/4 oz	1/4 cup 3 tbsp	
SALT	1-7/8 oz	3 tbsp	
SHORTENING	1-1/3 lbs	3 cup	
WATER	2-7/8 lbs	1 qts 1-1/2 cup	
PIE FILLING,APPLE,PREPARED	14 lbs	1 gal 3 qts	

Method
1. Sift together flour, milk, baking powder, and salt into mixer bowl.
2. Blend shortening into dry ingredients at low speed until mixture resembles coarse crumbs.
3. Add water; mix at low speed only enough to form soft dough.
4. On lightly floured board, roll dough into a rectangular sheet, about 1/8-inch thick. Cut into 6 circles.
5. Place 1/4 cup filling in the center of each circle. Wash edges of circle with water. Fold over to form a half circle; seal edges with a fork.
6. Fry pies, a few at a time, 2 minutes on one side, turn and fry 2 minutes on other side until golden brown. Drain on absorbent paper.

Notes
1. Pie crust mix may be used. Omit steps 1 through 3. Use 6 pounds 14 ounces of pie crust mix. Follow manufacturer's directions for mixing. Follow Steps 4 through 6.

FRIED LEMON PIE

Yield 100   **Portion** 1 Pie

Calories	Carbohydrates	Protein	Fat	Cholesterol	Sodium	Calcium
349 cal	47 g	5 g	16 g	0 mg	338 mg	76 mg

Ingredient	Weight	Measure	Issue
FLOUR,WHEAT,GENERAL PURPOSE	9-7/8 lbs	2 gal 1 qts	
MILK,NONFAT,DRY	2-2/3 oz	1-1/8 cup	
BAKING POWDER	3-1/4 oz	1/4 cup 3 tbsp	
SALT	1-7/8 oz	3 tbsp	
SHORTENING	1-1/3 lbs	3 cup	
WATER	2-7/8 lbs	1 qts 1-1/2 cup	
PIE FILLING,LEMON,PREPARED	14 lbs	1 gal 3 qts	

Method
1. Sift together flour, milk, baking powder, and salt into mixer bowl.
2. Blend shortening into dry ingredients at low speed until mixture resembles coarse crumbs.
3. Add water; mix at low speed only enough to form soft dough.
4. On lightly floured board, roll dough into a rectangular sheet, about 1/8-inch thick. Cut into 6 circles.
5. Place 1/4 cup filling in the center of each circle. Wash edges of circle with water. Fold over to form a half circle; seal edges with a fork.

6. Fry pies, a few at a time, 2 minutes on one side, turn and fry 2 minutes on other side until golden brown. Drain on absorbent paper.

Notes
1. Pie crust mix may be used. Omit steps 1 through 3. Use 6 pounds 14 ounces of pie crust mix. Follow manufacturer's directions for mixing. Follow Steps 4 through 6.

FRIED CHERRY PIE

Yield 100   **Portion** 1 Pie

Calories	Carbohydrates	Protein	Fat	Cholesterol	Sodium	Calcium
375 cal	54 g	5 g	16 g	0 mg	318 mg	78 mg

Ingredient	Weight	Measure	Issue
FLOUR,WHEAT,GENERAL PURPOSE	9-7/8 lbs	2 gal 1 qts	
MILK,NONFAT,DRY	2-2/3 oz	1-1/8 cup	
BAKING POWDER	3-1/4 oz	1/4 cup 3 tbsp	
SALT	1-7/8 oz	3 tbsp	
SHORTENING	1-1/3 lbs	3 cup	
WATER	2-7/8 lbs	1 qts 1-1/2 cup	
PIE FILLING,CHERRY,PREPARED	14 lbs	1 gal 3 qts	

Method
1. Sift together flour, milk, baking powder, and salt into mixer bowl.
2. Blend shortening into dry ingredients at low speed until mixture resembles coarse crumbs.
3. Add water; mix at low speed only enough to form soft dough.
4. On lightly floured board, roll dough into a rectangular sheet, about 1/8-inch thick. Cut into 6 circles.
5. Place 1/4 cup filling in the center of each circle. Wash edges of circle with water. Fold over to form a half circle; seal edges with a fork.
6. Fry pies, a few at a time, 2 minutes on one side, turn and fry 2 minutes on other side until golden brown. Drain on absorbent paper.

Notes
1. Pie crust mix may be used. Omit steps 1 through 3. Use 6 pounds 14 ounces of pie crust mix. Follow manufacturer's directions for mixing. Follow Steps 4 through 6.

FRIED PEACH PIE

Yield 100   **Portion** 1 Pie

Calories	Carbohydrates	Protein	Fat	Cholesterol	Sodium	Calcium
395 cal	59 g	5 g	16 g	0 mg	333 mg	79 mg

Ingredient	Weight	Measure	Issue
FLOUR,WHEAT,GENERAL PURPOSE	9-7/8 lbs	2 gal 1 qts	
MILK,NONFAT,DRY	2-2/3 oz	1-1/8 cup	
BAKING POWDER	3-1/4 oz	1/4 cup 3 tbsp	
SALT	1-7/8 oz	3 tbsp	
SHORTENING	1-1/3 lbs	3 cup	
WATER	2-7/8 lbs	1 qts 1-1/2 cup	
PIE FILLING,PEACH,PREPARED	14 lbs	1 gal 3 qts	

Method

1. Sift together flour, milk, baking powder, and salt into mixer bowl.
2. Blend shortening into dry ingredients at low speed until mixture resembles coarse crumbs.
3. Add water; mix at low speed only enough to form soft dough.
4. On lightly floured board, roll dough into a rectangular sheet, about 1/8-inch thick. Cut into 6 circles.
5. Place 1/4 cup filling in the center of each circle. Wash edges of circle with water. Fold over to form a half circle; seal edges with a fork.
6. Fry pies, a few at a time, 2 minutes on one side, turn and fry 2 minutes on other side until golden brown. Drain on absorbent paper.

Notes

1. Pie crust mix may be used. Omit steps 1 through 3. Use 6 pounds 14 ounces of pie crust mix. Follow manufacturer's directions for mixing. Follow Steps 4 through 6.

FRIED BLUEBERRY PIE

Yield 100   **Portion** 1 Pie

Calories	Carbohydrates	Protein	Fat	Cholesterol	Sodium	Calcium
358 cal	50 g	5 g	16 g	0 mg	344 mg	85 mg

Ingredient	Weight	Measure	Issue
FLOUR,WHEAT,GENERAL PURPOSE	9-7/8 lbs	2 gal 1 qts	
MILK,NONFAT,DRY	2-2/3 oz	1-1/8 cup	
BAKING POWDER	3-1/4 oz	1/4 cup 3 tbsp	
SALT	1-7/8 oz	3 tbsp	
SHORTENING	1-1/3 lbs	3 cup	
WATER	2-7/8 lbs	1 qts 1-1/2 cup	
PIE FILLING,BLUEBERRY,PREPARED	14 lbs	1 gal 2 qts	

Method

1. Sift together flour, milk, baking powder, and salt into mixer bowl.
2. Blend shortening into dry ingredients at low speed until mixture resembles coarse crumbs.
3. Add water; mix at low speed only enough to form soft dough.
4. On lightly floured board, roll dough into a rectangular sheet, about 1/8-inch thick. Cut into 6 circles.
5. Place 1/4 cup filling in the center of each circle. Wash edges of circle with water. Fold over to form a half circle; seal edges with a fork.
6. Fry pies, a few at a time, 2 minutes on one side, turn and fry 2 minutes on other side until golden brown. Drain on absorbent paper.

Notes

1. Pie crust mix may be used. Omit steps 1 through 3. Use 6 pounds 14 ounces of pie crust mix. Follow manufacturer's directions for mixing. Follow Steps 4 through 6.

PECAN PIE

Yield 100   **Portion** 1 Slice

Calories	Carbohydrates	Protein	Fat	Cholesterol	Sodium	Calcium
504 cal	77 g	6 g	21 g	126 mg	396 mg	25 mg

Ingredient	Weight	Measure	Issue
PIE CRUST		13 each	

EGGS,WHOLE,FROZEN	6 lbs	2 qts 3-1/4 cup
SUGAR,GRANULATED	4-7/8 lbs	2 qts 3 cup
BUTTER,MELTED	12 oz	1-1/2 cup
CORN SYRUP,LIGHT	11-5/8 lbs	1 gal
EXTRACT,VANILLA	1-7/8 oz	1/4 cup 1/3 tbsp
SALT	1-1/2 oz	2-1/3 tbsp
PECANS,CHOPPED	2-1/2 lbs	

Method

1. PREPARE AND DIVIDE DOUGH: Prepare 1/2 recipe Pie Crust (Recipe No. I 001 00). Divide dough into 13-7-1/2 oz pieces for bottom crust; place on lightly floured board. ROLL DOUGH: Sprinkle each piece of dough lightly with flour; flatten gently. Using a floured rolling pin, roll lightly with quick strokes from center out to edge in all directions. Form a circle 1 inch larger than pie pan and about 1/8 inch thick. Shift or turn dough occasionally to prevent sticking. If edges split, pinch cracks together. BOTTOM CRUST: Fold rolled dough in half; carefully place into ungreased pie pan with fold at center. Unfold and fit carefully into pie pan, being careful not to leave any air spaces between pan and dough. REMOVE EXCESS DOUGH: Trim overhanging edges of dough by using a knife or spatula. (Incorporate excess dough into next crust, if needed.) There should be little excess if skill is used in weighing and rolling dough.
2. Place eggs in mixer bowl; add sugar gradually while beating at low speed. Add butter or margarine; mix thoroughly.
3. Add corn syrup, vanilla, and salt; beat at low speed until smooth.
4. Place 3/4 cup pecans into each unbaked pie shell.
5. Pour 2-3/4 cups filling over pecans in each 9-inch pie pan.
6. Bake at 350 F. for 35 minutes or until filling is set. DO NOT OVERBAKE.
7. Refrigerate until ready to serve.
8. Cut 8 wedges per pie. CCP: Hold for service at 41 F. or lower.

WALNUT PIE

Yield 100   **Portion** 1 Slice

Calories	Carbohydrates	Protein	Fat	Cholesterol	Sodium	Calcium
502 cal	76 g	6 g	21 g	126 mg	397 mg	32 mg

Ingredient	**Weight**	**Measure**	**Issue**
PIE CRUST		13 each	
EGGS,WHOLE,FROZEN	6 lbs	2 qts 3-1/4 cup	
SUGAR,GRANULATED	4-7/8 lbs	2 qts 3 cup	
BUTTER,MELTED	12 oz	1-1/2 cup	
CORN SYRUP,LIGHT	11-5/8 lbs	1 gal	
EXTRACT,VANILLA	1-7/8 oz	1/4 cup 1/3 tbsp	
SALT	1-1/2 oz	2-1/3 tbsp	
WALNUTS,SHELLED,CHOPPED	2-1/2 lbs	2 qts 1-1/2 cup	

Method

1. PREPARE AND DIVIDE DOUGH: Prepare 1/2 recipe Pie Crust (Recipe No. I 001 00). Divide dough into 13-7-1/2 oz pieces for bottom crust; place on lightly floured board. ROLL DOUGH: Sprinkle each piece of dough lightly with flour; flatten gently. Using a floured rolling pin, roll lightly with quick strokes from center out to edge in all directions. Form a circle 1 inch larger than pie pan and about 1/8 inch thick. Shift or turn dough occasionally to prevent sticking. If edges split, pinch cracks

together. BOTTOM CRUST: Fold rolled dough in half; carefully place into ungreased pie pan with fold at center. Unfold and fit carefully into pie pan, being careful not to leave any air spaces between pan and dough. REMOVE EXCESS DOUGH: Trim overhanging edges of dough by using a knife or spatula. (Incorporate excess dough into next crust, if needed.) There should be little excess if skill is used in weighing and rolling dough.

2. Place eggs in mixer bowl; add sugar gradually while beating at low speed. Add butter or margarine; mix thoroughly.
3. Add corn syrup, vanilla, and salt; beat at low speed until smooth.
4. Place 3/4 cup chopped walnuts into each unbaked pie shell.
5. Pour 2-3/4 cups filling over walnuts in each 9-inch pie pan.
6. Bake at 350 F. for 35 minutes or until filling is set. DO NOT OVERBAKE.
7. Refrigerate until ready to serve.
8. Cut 8 wedges per pie. CCP: Hold for service at 41 F. or lower.

LEMON CHIFFON PIE

Yield 100   **Portion** 1 Slice

Calories	Carbohydrates	Protein	Fat	Cholesterol	Sodium	Calcium
216 cal	30 g	3 g	10 g	0 mg	151 mg	10 mg

Ingredient	Weight	Measure	Issue
PIE CRUST		13 each	
DESSERT POWDER,GELATIN,LEMON	3-1/4 lbs	1 qts 2-1/2 cup	
SUGAR,GRANULATED	5-1/4 oz	3/4 cup	
WATER,BOILING	5-1/2 lbs	2 qts 2-1/2 cup	
WATER,COLD	3-1/8 lbs	1 qts 2 cup	
JUICE,LEMON	12-7/8 oz	1-1/2 cup	
WATER,COLD	1-1/2 lbs	2-7/8 cup	
WHIPPED TOPPING MIX,NONDAIRY,DRY	12 oz	1 gal 1/4 qts	
MILK,NONFAT,DRY	1-1/3 oz	1/2 cup 1 tbsp	
SUGAR,GRANULATED	2-2/3 oz	1/4 cup 2-1/3 tbsp	
EXTRACT,VANILLA	3/4 oz	1 tbsp	
LEMON RIND,GRATED	7/8 oz	1/4 cup 1/3 tbsp	

Method

1. PREPARE AND DIVIDE DOUGH: Prepare 1/2 recipe Pie Crust (Recipe No. I 001 00). Divide dough into 13-7-1/2 oz pieces for bottom crust; place on lightly floured board. ROLL DOUGH: Sprinkle each piece of dough lightly with flour; flatten gently. Using a floured rolling pin, roll lightly with quick strokes from center out to edge in all directions. Form a circle 1 inch larger than pie pan and about 1/8 inch thick. Shift or turn dough occasionally to prevent sticking. If edges split, pinch cracks together. BOTTOM CRUST: Fold rolled dough in half; carefully place into ungreased pie pan with fold at center. Unfold and fit carefully into pie pan, being careful not to leave any air spaces between pan and dough. REMOVE EXCESS DOUGH: Trim overhanging edges of dough by using a knife or spatula. (Incorporate excess dough into next crust, if needed.) There should be little excess if skill is used in weighing and rolling dough. BAKING INSTRUCTIONS FOR UNCOOKED PIES: Bake crusts at 425 F. for about 15-18 minutes, or until light golden brown. Cool before filling. Proceed with the recipe directions.
2. Dissolve gelatin and sugar in boiling water; add cold water. Mix until well blended.
3. Add juice to gelatin mixture; mix until blended.
4. Refrigerate until gelatin is thickened but not firm.

5. Pour cold water into chilled mixer bowl; add topping, milk, sugar, and vanilla. Using whip, beat at low speed 3 minutes or until well blended. Scrape down whip and bowl. Whip at high speed 5 to 10 minutes or until mixture forms stiff peaks. Set aside for use in Step 7.
6. Using whip, beat thickened gelatin at high speed 10 minutes or until foamy and soft peaks form.
7. Fold whipped topping and lemon rind into gelatin. Mix carefully at low speed until well blended.
8. Pour 1-1/4 quart filling into each baked pie shell.
9. Refrigerate about 2 hours or until set. CCP: Hold for service at 41 F. or lower.
10. Cut 8 wedges per pie.

Notes
1. In Step 5, 2 pound 10 ounces of canned dessert topping and frozen bakery products may be used for all ingredients, per 100 servings

PINEAPPLE CHIFFON PIE

Yield 100   **Portion** 1 Slice

Calories	Carbohydrates	Protein	Fat	Cholesterol	Sodium	Calcium
216 cal	30 g	3 g	10 g	0 mg	149 mg	10 mg

Ingredient	Weight	Measure	Issue
PIE CRUST		13 each	
DESSERT POWDER,GELATIN,LEMON	3-1/4 lbs	1 qts 2-1/2 cup	
WATER	4-2/3 lbs	2 qts 1 cup	
WATER,COLD	1-1/2 lbs	2-7/8 cup	
MILK,NONFAT,DRY	1-1/3 oz	1/2 cup 1 tbsp	
SUGAR,GRANULATED	2-2/3 oz	1/4 cup 2-1/3 tbsp	
EXTRACT,VANILLA	3/4 oz	1 tbsp	
PINEAPPLE,CANNED,CRUSHED,JUICE PACK,DRAINED	2-1/2 lbs	1 qts 1/2 cup	
WHIPPED TOPPING MIX,NONDAIRY,DRY	12 oz	1 gal 1/4 qts	

Method
1. PREPARE AND DIVIDE DOUGH: Prepare 1/2 recipe Pie Crust (Recipe No. I 001 00). Divide dough into 13-7-1/2 oz pieces for bottom crust; place on lightly floured board. ROLL DOUGH: Sprinkle each piece of dough lightly with flour; flatten gently. Using a floured rolling pin, roll lightly with quick strokes from center out to edge in all directions. Form a circle 1 inch larger than pie pan and about 1/8 inch thick. Shift or turn dough occasionally to prevent sticking. If edges split, pinch cracks together. BOTTOM CRUST: Fold rolled dough in half; carefully place into ungreased pie pan with fold at center. Unfold and fit carefully into pie pan, being careful not to leave any air spaces between pan and dough. REMOVE EXCESS DOUGH: Trim overhanging edges of dough by using a knife or spatula. (Incorporate excess dough into next crust, if needed.) There should be little excess if skill is used in weighing and rolling dough. BAKING INSTRUCTIONS FOR UNCOOKED PIES: Bake crusts at 425 F. for about 15-18 minutes, or until light golden brown. Cool before filling. Proceed with the recipe directions.
2. Dissolve gelatin in boiling water; add cold water. Mix until well blended.
3. Refrigerate until gelatin is thickened but not firm.
4. Pour cold water into chilled mixer bowl; add topping, milk, sugar, and vanilla. Using whip, beat at low speed 3 minutes or until well blended. Scrape down whip and bowl. Whip at high speed 5 to 10 minutes or until mixture forms stiff peaks. Set aside for use in Step 7.
5. Using whip, beat thickened gelatin at high speed 10 minutes or until foamy and soft peaks form.
6. Fold whipped topping and drained pineapple into gelatin. Mix carefully at low speed until well blended.

7. Pour 5-3/4 cups filling into each baked pie shell.
8. Refrigerate about 2 hours or until set. CCP: Hold for service at 41 F. or lower.
9. Cut 8 wedges per pie.

Notes
1. In Step 5, 2 pound 10 ounces of canned dessert topping and frozen bakery products may be used for all ingredients, per 100 servings

STRAWBERRY CHIFFON PIE

Yield 100   **Portion** 1 Slice

Calories	Carbohydrates	Protein	Fat	Cholesterol	Sodium	Calcium
209 cal	28 g	3 g	10 g	0 mg	145 mg	13 mg

Ingredient	Weight	Measure	Issue
PIE CRUST		13 each	
DESSERT POWDER,GELATIN,STRAWBERRY	2 lbs	1 qts 1-1/2 cup	
WATER,BOILING	5-1/2 lbs	2 qts 2-1/2 cup	
WATER,COLD	4-2/3 lbs	2 qts 1 cup	
WATER,COLD	1-1/2 lbs	2-7/8 cup	
MILK,NONFAT,DRY	1-1/3 oz	1/2 cup 1 tbsp	
SUGAR,GRANULATED	2-2/3 oz	1/4 cup 2-1/3 tbsp	
EXTRACT,VANILLA	3/4 oz	1 tbsp	
WHIPPED TOPPING MIX,NONDAIRY,DRY	12 oz	1 gal 1/4 qts	
STRAWBERRIES,FROZEN,THAWED	5 lbs	2 qts 1 cup	

Method
1. PREPARE AND DIVIDE DOUGH: Prepare 1/2 recipe Pie Crust (Recipe No. I 001 00). Divide dough into 13-7-1/2 oz pieces for bottom crust; place on lightly floured board. ROLL DOUGH: Sprinkle each piece of dough lightly with flour; flatten gently. Using a floured rolling pin, roll lightly with quick strokes from center out to edge in all directions. Form a circle 1 inch larger than pie pan and about 1/8 inch thick. Shift or turn dough occasionally to prevent sticking. If edges split, pinch cracks together. BOTTOM CRUST: Fold rolled dough in half; carefully place into ungreased pie pan with fold at center. Unfold and fit carefully into pie pan, being careful not to leave any air spaces between pan and dough. REMOVE EXCESS DOUGH: Trim overhanging edges of dough by using a knife or spatula. (Incorporate excess dough into next crust, if needed.) There should be little excess if skill is used in weighing and rolling dough. BAKING INSTRUCTIONS FOR UNCOOKED PIES: Bake crusts at 425 F. for about 15-18 minutes, or until light golden brown. Cool before filling. Proceed with the recipe directions.
2. Dissolve gelatin in boiling water; add cold water. Mix until well blended.
3. Refrigerate until gelatin is thickened but not firm.
4. Pour cold water into chilled mixer bowl; add topping, milk, sugar, and vanilla. Using whip, beat at low speed 3 minutes or until well blended. Scrape down whip and bowl. Whip at high speed for 5 to 10 minutes or until mixture forms stiff peaks. Set aside for use in Step 7.
5. Using whip, beat thickened gelatin at high speed for 10 minutes or until foamy and soft peaks form.
6. Fold whipped topping and thawed, drained strawberries into gelatin. Mix carefully at low speed until well blended.
7. Pour 5-3/4 cups filling into each baked pie shell.
8. Refrigerate 2 hours or until set. Keep refrigerated until ready to serve.
9. Cut 8 wedges per pie. CCP: Hold for service at 41 F. or lower.

Notes
1. In Step 5, 2 pound 10 ounces of canned dessert topping and frozen bakery products may be used for all ingredients, per 100 servings

LEMON MERINGUE PIE

Yield 100   **Portion** 1 Slice

Calories	Carbohydrates	Protein	Fat	Cholesterol	Sodium	Calcium
327 cal	53 g	3 g	12 g	39 mg	317 mg	11 mg

Ingredient	Weight	Measure	Issue
PIE CRUST		13 each	
SUGAR,GRANULATED	7 lbs	1 gal	
SALT	1-3/8 oz	2-1/3 tbsp	
LEMON RIND,GRATED	2-1/2 oz	3/4 cup	
WATER	9-3/8 lbs	1 gal 1/2 qts	
CORNSTARCH	1-3/8 lbs	1 qts 1 cup	
WATER,COLD	2-1/3 lbs	1 qts 1/2 cup	
EGGS,WHOLE,FROZEN,BEATEN	1-5/8 lbs	3 cup	
BUTTER	12 oz	1-1/2 cup	
JUICE,LEMON	2-1/8 lbs	1 qts	
FOOD COLOR,YELLOW	<1/16th oz	2 drop	
MERINGUE	532 gm	7-1/2 unit	

Method

1. PREPARE AND DIVIDE DOUGH: Prepare 1/2 recipe Pie Crust (Recipe No. I 001 00). Divide dough into 13-7-1/2 oz pieces for bottom crust; place on lightly floured board. ROLL DOUGH: Sprinkle each piece of dough lightly with flour; flatten gently. Using a floured rolling pin, roll lightly with quick strokes from center out to edge in all directions. Form a circle 1 inch larger than pie pan and about 1/8 inch thick. Shift or turn dough occasionally to prevent sticking. If edges split, pinch cracks together. BOTTOM CRUST: Fold rolled dough in half; carefully place into ungreased pie pan with fold at center. Unfold and fit carefully into pie pan, being careful not to leave any air spaces between pan and dough. REMOVE EXCESS DOUGH: Trim overhanging edges of dough by using a knife or spatula. (Incorporate excess dough into next crust, if needed.) There should be little excess if skill is used in weighing and rolling dough. BAKING INSTRUCTIONS FOR UNCOOKED PIES: Bake crusts at 425 F. for about 15-18 minutes, or until light golden brown. Cool before filling. Proceed with the recipe directions.
2. Combine sugar, salt, lemon rind, and water. Bring to a boil.
3. Combine cornstarch and water; stir until smooth. Add gradually to boiling mixture; cook at medium heat, stirring constantly until thick and clear.
4. Stir about 1 quart hot mixture into eggs. Slowly pour egg mixture into remaining hot mixture, stirring constantly. Cook at medium heat; stirring frequently, until mixture returns to a boil. Remove from heat.
5. Add butter or margarine, lemon juice, and food coloring; stir until well blended. Cool slightly.
6. Pour 2-3/4 to 3 cups filling into each baked 9-inch pie shell.
7. Prepare 1 recipe Meringue, Recipe No. I 005 00 or I 005 01 per 100 portions. Spread 2-1/2 cups completely over warm filling, about 122 F., in each pan. Meringue should touch inner edge of crust all around and completely cover top of pie. Leave meringue somewhat rough on top.
8. Bake at 350 F. for 15 to 20 minutes or until lightly browned.
9. Refrigerate until ready to serve.
10. Cut 8 wedges per pie. CCP: Hold for service at 41 F. or lower.

LEMON MERINGUE PIE (PIE FILLING PREPARED)

Yield 100   **Portion** 1 Slice

Calories	Carbohydrates	Protein	Fat	Cholesterol	Sodium	Calcium
213 cal	33 g	2 g	9 g	0 mg	156 mg	11 mg

Ingredient	Weight	Measure	Issue
PIE CRUST		13 each	
PIE FILLING,LEMON,PREPARED	21 lbs	2 gal 2-1/2 qts	
MERINGUE	532 gm	7-1/2 unit	

Method

1. PREPARE AND DIVIDE DOUGH: Prepare 1/2 recipe Pie Crust (Recipe No. I 001 00). Divide dough into 13-7-1/2 oz pieces for bottom crust; place on lightly floured board. ROLL DOUGH: Sprinkle each piece of dough lightly with flour; flatten gently. Using a floured rolling pin, roll lightly with quick strokes from center out to edge in all directions. Form a circle 1 inch larger than pie pan and about 1/8 inch thick. Shift or turn dough occasionally to prevent sticking. If edges split, pinch cracks together. BOTTOM CRUST: Fold rolled dough in half; carefully place into ungreased pie pan with fold at center. Unfold and fit carefully into pie pan, being careful not to leave any air spaces between pan and dough. REMOVE EXCESS DOUGH: Trim overhanging edges of dough by using a knife or spatula. (Incorporate excess dough into next crust, if needed.) There should be little excess if skill is used in weighing and rolling dough. BAKING INSTRUCTIONS FOR UNCOOKED PIES: Bake crusts at 425 F. for about 15-18 minutes, or until light golden brown. Cool before filling. Proceed with the recipe directions.
2. Heat filling to 122 F. ; pour about 3-1/4 cups of filling into each baked 9-inch pie shell.
3. Prepare Meringue, Recipe No. I 005 00. Spread 2-1/2 cups completely over warm filling, about 122 F., in each 9-inch pie pan. Meringue should touch inner edge of crust all around and completely cover top of pie. Leave meringue somewhat rough on top.
4. Bake at 350 F. for 15 to 20 minutes or until lightly browned.
5. Refrigerate until ready to serve.
6. Cut 8 wedges per pie. CCP: Hold for service at 41 F. or lower.

FRUIT TURNOVERS

Yield 100   **Portion** 1 Turnover

Calories	Carbohydrates	Protein	Fat	Cholesterol	Sodium	Calcium
315 cal	38 g	3 g	17 g	0 mg	236 mg	11 mg

Ingredient	Weight	Measure	Issue
PIE CRUST		26 each	
PIE FILLING,APPLE,PREPARED	12 lbs	1 gal 2 qts	
MILK AND WATER WASH		3 cup	

Method

1. Prepare Pie Crust, Recipe No. I 001 00 to yield enough dough to prepare cobbler for 100 portions. Divide dough into 8 pieces.
2. Place dough on lightly floured board; sprinkle each piece lightly with flour; flatten gently. Roll dough into 18 by 24-inch rectangular sheet about 1/8-inch thick. Cut into twelve 6-inch squares. Brush edges of each square with water.
3. Place 1/4 cup of fruit filling in the center of each square. Fold opposite corner of dough together forming a triangle. Seal by crimping edges.

4. Make 2-1/2 inch slits near the center fold to allow steam to escape during baking.
5. Place 12 turnovers on each lightly greased sheet pan.
6. Brush top of each turnover with Milk and Water wash. Allow to dry before baking. See Recipe No. I 004 02. Do not use Egg and Milk wash or Egg and Water wash for turnovers. The egg and milk will cause the turnovers to brown excessively and egg and water wash will cause turnovers to be too pale in color.
7. Bake at 425 F. for 20 minutes or until lightly browned.

FRUIT DUMPLINGS

Yield 100   **Portion** 1 Each

Calories	Carbohydrates	Protein	Fat	Cholesterol	Sodium	Calcium
378 cal	44 g	4 g	21 g	0 mg	287 mg	8 mg

Ingredient	Weight	Measure	Issue
PIE CRUST	7-1/4 kg	32-1/2 unit	
PIE FILLING,APPLE,PREPARED	12 lbs	1 gal 2 qts	

Method
1. Prepare Pie Crust, Recipe No. I 001 00 to yield enough dough to prepare cobbler for 100 portions. Divide dough into 8 pieces.
2. Place dough on lightly floured board; sprinkle each piece lightly with flour; flatten gently. Roll dough into 18x24-inch rectangular sheet, about 1/8-inch thick. Cut into 12, 6-inch squares. Brush edges of each square with water.
3. Place 1/4 cup of fruit filling in the center or each pastry square. Bring points of pastry up over filling. Seal edges tightly.
4. Place 12 dumplings on each sheet pan.
5. Bake at 425 F. 20 minutes or until lightly browned.
6. Serve with dessert sauce. See Recipe Section K.

KEY LIME PIE

Yield 100   **Portion** 1 Slice

Calories	Carbohydrates	Protein	Fat	Cholesterol	Sodium	Calcium
337 cal	60 g	4 g	10 g	73 mg	177 mg	20 mg

Ingredient	Weight	Measure	Issue
COOKIES,CHOCOLATE,CRUSHED	5 lbs	1 gal 1-1/8 qts	
SHORTENING	10-7/8 oz	1-1/2 cup	
EGGS,WHOLE,FRESH	3-3/4 lbs	34 each	
JUICE,LIME	1 lbs	2 cup	
LIMES,FRESH	14-1/4 oz	6 each	
FLOUR,WHEAT,GENERAL PURPOSE	1-1/4 lbs	1 qts 1/2 cup	
SUGAR,GRANULATED	7 lbs	1 gal	
MARGARINE	8 oz	1 cup	
WATER	10-1/2 lbs	1 gal 1 qts	
SUGAR,GRANULATED	1-1/3 lbs	3 cup	

Method
1. Crush chocolate wafer cookies to equal 5 quarts. In a mixer, combine the crushed cookies and shortening. Mix on low speed for 3 minutes. Divide among large sheet pans. Press crust evenly into bottom of pans.

2. Separate egg yolks from whites. In a heavy saucepan or steam kettle, beat egg yolks with lime juice and 2 tablespoon lime zest. Place over low heat.
3. Beat in flour, sugar, margarine, and water, alternating each ingredient so as to maintain a smooth consistency. Cook stirring constantly for 3 minutes on medium low heat. CCP: Internal temperature must reach 155 F. or higher for 15 seconds. Pour into the cookie crust.
4. In a mixer, beat egg whites until stiff, but not dry. Gradually add sugar and whip for 3 minutes. Spread over filling. Bake at 450 F. for 10 minutes or until meringue is brown.
5. Chill for 1 hour before serving. Cut 6 by 9. CCP: Hold for service at 41 F. or lower.

PIES, FROZEN

Yield 100   **Portion** 1 Slice

Calories	Carbohydrates	Protein	Fat	Cholesterol	Sodium	Calcium
84 cal	8 g	1 g	5 g	0 mg	106 mg	3 mg

Ingredient   **Weight**   **Measure**   **Issue**
PIES,FROZEN,8""   4-1/8 lbs   13 each

Method
1. Follow manufacturer's cooking instructions.
2. Cooking times and temperatures vary with type of pie.

Notes
1. Because products and appliances vary, heating times, portion size and weights are appropriate.

ELEPHANT EARS (FROZEN PUFF PASTRY)

Yield 100   **Portion** 2 Cookies

Calories	Carbohydrates	Protein	Fat	Cholesterol	Sodium	Calcium
75 cal	9 g	1 g	4 g	0 mg	44 mg	7 mg

Ingredient	Weight	Measure	Issue
PUFF PASTRY SHEETS,FROZEN	6-1/4 lbs		
CINNAMON,GROUND	1-7/8 oz	1/2 cup	
SUGAR,GRANULATED	1-3/4 lbs	1 qts	
WATER	2-1/8 oz	1/4 cup 1/3 tbsp	
COOKING SPRAY,NONSTICK	2 oz	1/4 cup 1/3 tbsp	

Method
1. Preheat convection oven to 325 F. with fan on.
2. Thaw puff pastry sheet for 10 minutes or until soft and pliable.
3. Combine cinnamon and sugar in a sheet pan.
4. Brush pastry sheets lightly with water. Press wet side down into cinnamon and sugar mixture first and then press dry side into mixture.
5. Roll each side of sheet to form a scroll. Fold one side on top of the other and press down lightly. Cut into 1/2 inch pieces.
6. Spray sheet pans with non-stick cooking spray. Lay cookies on sheet pans one inch apart in rows of 5x10 cookies.
7. Using a convection oven, bake at 325 F. with fan on for 12-15 minutes or until golden brown.
8. Remove from oven. Remove cookies from pans and let cool.

APPLE CRISP (PIE FILLING & COOKIE MIX)

Yield 100   **Portion** 1 Piece

Calories	Carbohydrates	Protein	Fat	Cholesterol	Sodium	Calcium
190 cal	34 g	1 g	7 g	12 mg	103 mg	30 mg

Ingredient	Weight	Measure	Issue
PIE FILLING,APPLE,PREPARED	18 lbs	2 gal 1 qts	
COOKIE MIX,OATMEAL	6-3/4 lbs		
MARGARINE,SOFTENED	1 lbs	2 cup	

Method
1. Place 10-1/2 pounds of the pie filling in each pan.
2. Combine oatmeal cookie mix with margarine.
3. Sprinkle 3 pounds 13 ounces of oatmeal-margarine mixture evenly over apples, in each pan.
4. Using a convection oven, bake at 350 F. for 30 minutes or until top is bubbling and lightly browned on low fan, open vent.
5. Cut 6 by 9. Serve with serving spoon or spatula.

VANILLA SOFT SERVE ICE CREAM (DEHY)

Yield 100   **Portion** 3/4 Cup

Calories	Carbohydrates	Protein	Fat	Cholesterol	Sodium	Calcium
166 cal	40 g	1 g	0 g	1 mg	71 mg	29 mg

Ingredient	Weight	Measure	Issue
ICE MILK-MILKSHAKE,DEHYDRATED,VAN	10 lbs		
WATER	20-7/8 lbs	2 gal 2 qts	

Method
1. Stir dehydrated mix into water. Mix thoroughly with wire whip or mixer. Cover container.
2. Chill 4 to 24 hours in refrigerator to 35 F. to 40 F.
3. Stir until smooth. Pour mixture into top hopper of soft serve ice cream freezer; start dasher motor; turn on refrigeration according to manufacturer's directions. Freeze to a temperature of 18 F. to 22 F., about 10 minutes or until product can be drawn with a stiff consistency that will hold a peak.

CHOCOLATE SOFT SERVE ICE CREAM (DEHY)

Yield 100   **Portion** 3/4 Cup

Calories	Carbohydrates	Protein	Fat	Cholesterol	Sodium	Calcium
166 cal	40 g	1 g	1 g	1 mg	168 mg	29 mg

Ingredient	Weight	Measure	Issue
ICE MILK-MILKSHAKE,DEHYDRATED,CHOC	10 lbs		
WATER	20-7/8 lbs	2 gal 2 qts	

Method

1. Stir dehydrated mix into water. Mix thoroughly with wire whip or mixer. Cover container.
2. Chill 4 to 24 hours in refrigerator until 35 F. to 40 F.
3. Stir until smooth. Pour mixture into top hopper of soft serve ice cream freezer; start dasher motor; turn on refrigeration according to manufacturer's directions. Freeze to a temperature of 18 F. to 22 F., about 10 minutes or until product can be drawn with a stiff consistency that will hold a peak.

CHOCOLATE MILK SHAKE (DEHY MIX)

Yield 100   Portion 8 Ounces

Calories	Carbohydrates	Protein	Fat	Cholesterol	Sodium	Calcium
166 cal	40 g	1 g	1 g	1 mg	169 mg	29 mg

Ingredient	Weight	Measure	Issue
ICE MILK-MILKSHAKE,DEHYDRATED,CHOC	10 lbs		
WATER	25-1/8 lbs	3 gal	

Method

1. Stir dehydrated mix into water. Mix thoroughly with wire whip or mixer. Cover container.
2. Chill 4 to 24 hours in refrigerator until 35 F. to 40 F.
3. Stir until smooth. Pour mixture into top hopper of milk shake mix machine, according to manufacturer's directions. Freeze to a temperature of 27 F. to 30 F., about 10 minutes.

STRAWBERRY SOFT SERVE ICE CREAM (DEHY)

Yield 100   Portion 3/4 Cup

Calories	Carbohydrates	Protein	Fat	Cholesterol	Sodium	Calcium
176 cal	43 g	1 g	0 g	1 mg	71 mg	33 mg

Ingredient	Weight	Measure	Issue
ICE MILK-MILKSHAKE,DEHYDRATED,VAN	10 lbs		
WATER	17-1/4 lbs	2 gal 1/4 qts	
STRAWBERRIES,FROZEN,THAWED	6-1/2 lbs	2 qts 3-1/2 cup	
FOOD COLOR,RED	1/8 oz	1/8 tsp	

Method

1. Stir dehydrated mix into water. Mix thoroughly with wire whip or mixer. Cover container.
2. Chill 4 to 24 hours in refrigerator to 35 F. to 40 F. Crush strawberries; red food coloring may be added.
3. Stir until smooth. Pour mixture into top hopper of soft serve ice cream freezer; remove mix feed and air control units. Start dasher motor; turn on refrigeration according to manufacturer's directions. Stir occasionally. Freeze to a temperature of 18 F. to 22 F., about 10 minutes or until product can be drawn with a stiff consistency that will hold a peak.

VANILLA MILK SHAKE (DEHY MIX)

Yield 100   **Portion** 1 Cup

Calories	Carbohydrates	Protein	Fat	Cholesterol	Sodium	Calcium
166 cal	40 g	1 g	0 g	1 mg	72 mg	29 mg

Ingredient	Weight	Measure	Issue
ICE MILK-MILKSHAKE,DEHYDRATED,VAN	10 lbs		
WATER	25-1/8 lbs	3 gal	

Method
1. Stir dehydrated mix into water. Mix thoroughly with wire whip or mixer. Cover container.
2. Chill 4 to 24 hours in refrigerator to 35 F. to 40 F.
3. Stir until smooth. Pour mixture into top hopper of milk shake machine, according to manufacturer's directions; freeze to a temperature of 27 F. to 30 F.

BAKED APPLES

Yield 100   **Portion** 1 Serving

Calories	Carbohydrates	Protein	Fat	Cholesterol	Sodium	Calcium
207 cal	51 g	0 g	1 g	2 mg	34 mg	11 mg

Ingredient	Weight	Measure	Issue
APPLES,COOKING,FRESH,UNPEELED	28-1/8 lbs	100 each	33-1/8 lbs
SUGAR,GRANULATED	7 lbs	1 gal	
CINNAMON,GROUND	1/8 oz	1/3 tsp	
SALT	1/4 oz	1/8 tsp	
WATER,ICE	5-1/4 lbs	2 qts 2 cup	
BUTTER	4 oz	1/2 cup	

Method
1. Score apples once around middle to prevent bursting. Place apples on pans.
2. Mix sugar, cinnamon and salt thoroughly.
3. Combine with water and butter or margarine. Pour 1-1/2 quarts of syrup over apples in each pan.
4. Using a convection oven, bake at 325 F. for 30 minutes or until tender on low fan, closed vent. Baste occasionally.
5. Serve each apple with 2 tablespoons syrup.

BAKED APPLES WITH RAISIN NUT FILLING

Yield 100   **Portion** 1 Serving

Calories	Carbohydrates	Protein	Fat	Cholesterol	Sodium	Calcium
264 cal	58 g	4 g	5 g	2 mg	35 mg	16 mg

Ingredient	Weight	Measure	Issue
APPLES,COOKING,FRESH,UNPEELED	28-1/8 lbs	100 each	33-1/8lbs
RAISINS	1-1/2 lbs	1 qts 1/2cup	
PECANS,CHOPPED	1-1/4 lbs		

SUGAR,GRANULATED		7 lbs	1 gal
CINNAMON,GROUND		1/8 oz	1/3 tsp
SALT		1/4 oz	1/8 tsp
WATER,ICE		5-1/4 lbs	2 qts 2cup
BUTTER		4 oz	1/2 cup

Method

1. Score apples once around middle to prevent bursting. Place apples on pans.
2. Mix raisins with finely chopped, unsalted nuts. Fill cavity in center of each apple with 1-2/3 tablespoons of mixture.
3. Mix sugar, cinnamon and salt thoroughly.
4. Combine with water and butter or margarine. Pour 1-1/2 quart syrup over apples in each pan.
5. Using a convection oven, bake at 325 F. for 30 minutes or until tender on low fan, closed vent, basting occasionally.
6. Serve each apple with 2 tablespoon of syrup.

Notes

1. In Step 4, baking time will vary depending on variety and size of apples.

BAKED APPLES WITH RAISIN COCONUT FILLING

Yield 100   **Portion** 1 Serving

Calories	Carbohydrates	Protein	Fat	Cholesterol	Sodium	Calcium
241 cal	58 g	0 g	2 g	2 mg	42 mg	14 mg

Ingredient	Weight	Measure	Issue
APPLES,COOKING,FRESH,UNPEELED	28-1/8 lbs	100 each	33-1/8 lbs
RAISINS	1-1/2 lbs	1 qts 1/2cup	
COCONUT,PREPARED,SWEETENED FLAKES	9-7/8 oz	3 cup	
SUGAR,GRANULATED	7 lbs	1 gal	
CINNAMON,GROUND	1/8 oz	1/3 tsp	
SALT	1/4 oz	1/8 tsp	
WATER,ICE	5-1/4 lbs	2 qts 2cup	
BUTTER	4 oz	1/2 cup	

Method

1. Score apples once around middle to prevent bursting. Place apples on pans.
2. Mix raisins with prepared, sweetened, flaked coconut. Fill cavity in center of each apple with 1 tablespoon of mixture.
3. Mix sugar, cinnamon and salt thoroughly.
4. Combine with water and butter or margarine. Pour 1-1/2 quart syrup over apples in each pan.
5. Using a convection oven, bake at 325 F. for 30 minutes or until tender on low fan, closed vent, basting occasionally.
6. Serve each apple with 2 tablespoons of syrup.

VANILLA SOFT SERVE ICE CREAM (LIQUID MIX)

Yield 100   **Portion** 3/4 Cup

Calories	Carbohydrates	Protein	Fat	Cholesterol	Sodium	Calcium
101 cal	16 g	3 g	3 g	0 mg	0 mg	84 mg

Ingredient	Weight	Measure	Issue
ICE MILK MIX,LIQ,VAN,CHILLED	29-1/4 lbs	3 gal 2 qts	

Method
1. Pour mix into top hopper of soft serve ice cream freezer; start dasher motor; turn on refrigeration according to manufacturer's directions.
2. Freeze to a temperature of 18 F. to 22 F., about 10 minutes or until product can be drawn with a stiff consistency that will hold a peak.

STRAWBERRY SOFT SERVE ICE CREAM (LIQUID MIX)

Yield 100   **Portion** 3/4 Cup

Calories	Carbohydrates	Protein	Fat	Cholesterol	Sodium	Calcium
111 cal	18 g	3 g	3 g	0 mg	1 mg	89 mg

Ingredient	Weight	Measure	Issue
FOOD COLOR,RED	1/8 oz	1/8 tsp	
ICE MILK MIX,LIQ,VAN,CHILLED	29-1/4 lbs	3 gal 2 qts	
STRAWBERRIES,FROZEN,THAWED	6-1/2 lbs	2 qts 3-1/2 cup	

Method
1. Pour mix into top hopper of soft serve ice cream freezer; start dasher motor; turn on refrigeration according to manufacturer's directions. Crush strawberries; drain. Red food coloring may be added.
2. Add strawberry mixture to soft serve mixture. Freeze to a temperature of 18 F. to 22 F., about 10 minutes or until product can be drawn with a stiff consistency that will hold a peak.

Notes
1. While drawing ice cream, strawberries must be stirred up occasionally from the bottom of freezer hopper.

VANILLA MILK SHAKE (LIQUID MIX)

Yield 100   **Portion** 1 Cup

Calories	Carbohydrates	Protein	Fat	Cholesterol	Sodium	Calcium
115 cal	18 g	3 g	4 g	0 mg	1 mg	97 mg

Ingredient	Weight	Measure	Issue
ICE MILK MIX,LIQ,VAN,CHILLED	33-3/8 lbs	3 gal	
WATER,COLD	8-1/3 lbs	1 gal	

Method
1. Combine liquid milk shake mix and cold water.
2. Pour sufficient amount into top hopper of soft serve ice cream freezer; start dasher motor; turn on refrigeration. Prepare according to manufacturer's directions; freeze to a temperature of 27 F. to 30 F.

CHOCOLATE MILK SHAKE (LIQUID MIX)

Yield 100   **Portion** 1 Cup

Calories	Carbohydrates	Protein	Fat	Cholesterol	Sodium	Calcium
130 cal	20 g	4 g	4 g	0 mg	0 mg	108 mg

Ingredient	Weight	Measure	Issue
ICE MILK,MIX,LIQ,CHOC,CHILLED	37-5/8 lbs	4 gal 2 qts	

Method
1. Pour mix into top hopper of soft serve ice cream freezer; start dasher motor; turn on refrigeration according to manufacturer's directions.
2. Freeze to a temperature of 27 F. to 30 F.

CHOCOLATE SOFT SERVE ICE CREAM (LIQUID MIX)

Yield 100   **Portion** 3/4 Cup

Calories	Carbohydrates	Protein	Fat	Cholesterol	Sodium	Calcium
101 cal	16 g	3 g	3 g	0 mg	0 mg	84 mg

Ingredient	Weight	Measure	Issue
ICE MILK,MIX,LIQ,CHOC,CHILLED	29-1/4 lbs	3 gal 2 qts	

Method
1. Pour mix into top hopper of soft serve ice cream freezer; start dasher motor; turn on refrigeration according to manufacturer's directions.
2. Freeze to a temperature of 18 F. to 22 F., about 10 minutes, or until product can be drawn with a stiff consistency that will hold a peak.

FLUFFY FRUIT CUP

Yield 100   **Portion** 1/2 Cup

Calories	Carbohydrates	Protein	Fat	Cholesterol	Sodium	Calcium
82 cal	20 g	1 g	0 g	0 mg	5 mg	20 mg

Ingredient	Weight	Measure	Issue
PINEAPPLE,CANNED,CHUNKS,JUICE PACK,DRAINED	7-7/8 lbs	1 gal 1/2 qts	
CHERRIES,MARASCHINO,WHOLE	1-2/3 lbs	3 cup	
ORANGE,FRESH,SECTIONS	4 lbs	2qts 2-1/8cup	5-1/2lbs
GRAPES,FRESH,CUT IN HALVES	2-7/8 lbs	2qts 1/8cup	3lbs
BANANA,FRESH,SLICED	4-1/3 lbs	3qts 1-1/8cup	6-2/3lbs
MARSHMALLOWS,MINIATURE	1 lbs	2 qts 1 cup	
WATER,COLD	1 lbs	2 cup	
WHIPPED TOPPING MIX,NONDAIRY,DRY	1-3/8 oz	2 cup	
MILK,NONFAT,DRY	7/8 oz	1/4cup 2-1/3tbsp	
SUGAR,GRANULATED	1/2 oz	1 tbsp	
EXTRACT,VANILLA	1/2 oz	1 tbsp	

Method

1. Drain pineapple. Drain cherries; cut into halves.
2. Combine pineapple, cherries, oranges, grapes, bananas and marshmallows; mix well. Set aside for use in Step 4.
3. Pour cold water into mixer bowl; add topping, milk, sugar and vanilla. Whip at low speed for 3 minutes or until thoroughly blended.
4. Fold mixed fruit into whipped topping. Mix carefully until thoroughly blended.
5. Refrigerate until ready to serve. CCP: Hold for service at 41 F. or lower.

YOGURT FRUIT CUP

Yield 100   **Portion** 1/2 Cup

Calories	Carbohydrates	Protein	Fat	Cholesterol	Sodium	Calcium
90 cal	21 g	2 g	0 g	1 mg	16 mg	50 mg

Ingredient	Weight	Measure	Issue
PINEAPPLE,CANNED,CHUNKS,JUICE PACK,DRAINED	7-7/8 lbs	1 gal 1/2 qts	
CHERRIES,MARASCHINO,WHOLE	1-2/3 lbs	3 cup	
ORANGE,FRESH,SECTIONS	4 lbs	2qts 2-1/8cup	5-1/2lbs
GRAPES,FRESH,CUT IN HALVES	2-7/8 lbs	2qts 1/8cup	3lbs
BANANA,FRESH,SLICED	4-1/3 lbs	3qts 1-1/8cup	6-2/3lbs
MARSHMALLOWS,MINIATURE	1 lbs	2 qts 1 cup	
YOGURT,PLAIN,LOWFAT	4 lbs	1 qts 3-1/2 cup	

Method

1. Drain pineapple. Drain cherries; cut into halves.
2. Combine pineapple, cherries, oranges, grapes, bananas and marshmallows; mix well. Set aside for use in Step 3.
3. Fold yogurt into mixed fruit. Mix lightly until just combined.
4. Refrigerate until ready to serve. CCP: Hold for service at 41 F. or lower.

FRUIT CUP

Yield 100   **Portion** 1/2 Cup

Calories	Carbohydrates	Protein	Fat	Cholesterol	Sodium	Calcium
153 cal	16 g	1 g	0 g	0 mg	3 mg	15 mg

Ingredient	Weight	Measure	Issue
PEACHES,CANNED,SLICED	6-1/2 lbs	3 qts	
PEARS,CANNED,SLICES	6-1/2 lbs	3 qts	
PINEAPPLE,CANNED,CHUNKS,JUICE PACK,INCL LIQUIDS	6-5/8 lbs	3 qts	
ORANGE,FRESH,CHOPPED	3 lbs	1qts 3-7/8cup	4-1/8 lbs
APPLES,FRESH,MEDIUM,UNPEELED,DICED	3-1/2 lbs	3qts 1/8cup	4-1/8 lbs

Method

1. Drain peaches and pears. Reserve juices. Cut fruit into 3/4-inch pieces.
2. Combine pineapple, peaches, pears, oranges, apples and juices from all fruit. Mix thoroughly.
3. Cover; CCP: Hold for service at 41 F. or lower.

AMBROSIA

Yield 100   Portion 1/2 Cup

Calories	Carbohydrates	Protein	Fat	Cholesterol	Sodium	Calcium
85 cal	18 g	1 g	2 g	0 mg	15 mg	16 mg

Ingredient	Weight	Measure	Issue
PEACHES,CANNED,SLICED,JUICE PACK,INCL LIQUIDS	6-1/2 lbs	3 qts	
PEARS,CANNED,JUICE PACK,SLICES,INCL LIQUID	6-1/2 lbs	3 qts	
PINEAPPLE,CANNED,CRUSHED,JUICE PACK,INCL LIQUIDS	6-5/8 lbs	3 qts	
ORANGE,FRESH,CHOPPED	3-1/8 lbs	1qts 3-7/8cup	4-1/4lbs
APPLES,FRESH,MEDIUM,UNPEELED,DICED	3-1/3 lbs	3qts 1/8cup	3-7/8lbs
COCONUT,PREPARED,SWEETENED FLAKES	1 lbs	1 qts 1 cup	

Method
1. Drain peaches and pears. Reserve juices. Cut fruit into 3/4-inch pieces.
2. Combine pineapple, peaches, pears, oranges, apples and sweetened coconut flakes and juices from all fruit. Mix thoroughly.
3. Cover. CCP: Hold for service at 41 F. or lower.

BANANA FRUIT CUP

Yield 100   Portion 1/2 Cup

Calories	Carbohydrates	Protein	Fat	Cholesterol	Sodium	Calcium
82 cal	21 g	1 g	0 g	0 mg	1 mg	14 mg

Ingredient	Weight	Measure	Issue
BANANA,FRESH,SLICED	11-1/2 lbs	2 gal 2/3 qts	17-2/3lbs
PINEAPPLE,CANNED,CHUNKS,JUICE PACK,INCL LIQUIDS	6-5/8 lbs	3 qts	4-1/4lbs
ORANGE,FRESH,CHOPPED	3-1/8 lbs	1 qts 3-7/8 cup	3-7/8lbs
APPLES,FRESH,MEDIUM,UNPEELED,DICED	3-1/3 lbs	3 qts 1/8 cup	

Method
1. Combine bananas, pineapple, oranges and apples. Mix thoroughly.
2. Cover. CCP: Hold for service at 41 F. or lower.

MELON FRUIT CUP

Yield 100   Portion 1/2 Cup

Calories	Carbohydrates	Protein	Fat	Cholesterol	Sodium	Calcium
54 cal	14 g	1 g	0 g	0 mg	3 mg	14 mg

Ingredient	Weight	Measure	Issue
PEACHES,CANNED,SLICED,JUICE PACK,INCL LIQUIDS	6-1/2 lbs	3 qts	
PEARS,CANNED,JUICE PACK,SLICES,INCL LIQUID	6-1/2 lbs	3 qts	
WATERMELON,FRESH,DICED	7 lbs	1gal 1-1/4qts	13-1/2lbs

| ORANGE,FRESH,SECTIONS,PEELED,DICED | 3-1/8 lbs | 1qts 3-7/8cup | 10-7/8each |
| APPLES,FRESH,MEDIUM,UNPEELED,DICED | 3-1/3 lbs | 3qts 1/8cup | 3-7/8lbs |

Method
1. Drain peaches and pears. Reserve juices. Cut fruit into 3/4 inch pieces.
2. Seed melon. Combine melon with oranges, peaches, pears, apples and juices from fruit. Mix thoroughly.
3. Cover; CCP: Hold for service at 41 F. or lower.

STRAWBERRY FRUIT CUP

Yield 100   **Portion** 1/2 Cup

Calories	Carbohydrates	Protein	Fat	Cholesterol	Sodium	Calcium
58 cal	14 g	1 g	0 g	0 mg	3 mg	21 mg

Ingredient	Weight	Measure	Issue
PEACHES,CANNED,SLICED,JUICE PACK,INCL LIQUIDS	6-1/2 lbs	3 qts	
PINEAPPLE,CANNED,CHUNKS,JUICE PACK,INCL LIQUIDS	6-5/8 lbs	3 qts	
ORANGE,FRESH,SECTIONS,PEELED,DICED	3-1/8 lbs	2 qts	11 each
STRAWBERRIES,FRESH,SLICED	8-3/4 lbs	1gal 2qts	1gal 2-3/8qts
KIWIFRUIT,FRESH,CHOPPED	2-7/8 lbs	1qts 3-1/4cup	3-1/4lbs

Method
1. Drain peaches. Reserve juices. Cut fruit into 3/4-inch pieces.
2. Combine pineapple, peaches, oranges and juices from all fruit.
3. Slice strawberries into quarters. Combine strawberries with fruit mixture; mix thoroughly. Cut kiwi into 3/8-inch slices. Garnish with kiwifruit. Place 1 slice kiwifruit on each portion.
4. Cover; CCP: Hold for service at 41 F. or lower.

FRUIT COCKTAIL FRUIT CUP

Yield 100   **Portion** 1/2 Cup

Calories	Carbohydrates	Protein	Fat	Cholesterol	Sodium	Calcium
58 cal	15 g	1 g	0 g	0 mg	4 mg	14 mg

Ingredient	Weight	Measure	Issue
ORANGE,FRESH,CHOPPED	3-1/8 lbs	1qts 3-7/8cup	4-1/4lbs
FRUIT COCKTAIL,CANNED,JUICE PACK,INCL LIQUIDS	20-1/4 lbs	2gal 1-2/3qts	
APPLES,FRESH,MEDIUM,UNPEELED,DICED	3-1/3 lbs	3qts 1/8cup	3-7/8lbs

Method
1. Quickly combine apples and oranges with canned fruit cocktail to prevent discoloration; mix thoroughly.
2. Cover; CCP: Hold for service at 41 F. or lower.

SPICED FRUIT CUP

Yield 100   **Portion** 1/2 Cup

Calories	Carbohydrates	Protein	Fat	Cholesterol	Sodium	Calcium
58 cal	15 g	0 g	0 g	0 mg	3 mg	18 mg

Ingredient	Weight	Measure	Issue
FRUIT COCKTAIL,CANNED,JUICE PACK,INCL LIQUIDS	12-1/2lbs	1 gal 2 qts	
CINNAMON,GROUND	1/8 oz	1/8 tsp	
NUTMEG,GROUND	1/8 oz	1/3 tsp	
SUGAR,BROWN,PACKED	8-1/2 oz	1-5/8 cup	
APPLES,FRESH,MEDIUM,UNPEELED,DICED	4 lbs	3qts 2-1/2cup	4-3/4lbs
ORANGE,FRESH,SECTIONS,PEELED,DICED	5-1/4 lbs	3qts 1-3/8cup	18-1/3each

Method
1. Drain fruit cocktail and reserve juice for Step 2. Combine drained juice with ground cinnamon, ground nutmeg, and packed brown sugar. Bring to a boil; reduce heat; simmer 5 minutes. Chill.
2. Combine fruit cocktail, apples and oranges. Pour chilled syrup over fruits; mix lightly.
3. Cover; CCP: Hold for service at 41 F. or lower.

MANDARIN ORANGE AND PINEAPPLE FRUIT CUP

Yield 100   **Portion** 1/2 Cup

Calories	Carbohydrates	Protein	Fat	Cholesterol	Sodium	Calcium
74 cal	19 g	1 g	0 g	0 mg	4 mg	20 mg

Ingredient	Weight	Measure	Issue
PINEAPPLE,CANNED,CHUNKS,JUICE PACK,DRAINED	20-1/4 lbs	1 gal 3-3/8 qts	
ORANGES,MANDARIN,CANNED,DRAINED	15-1/4 lbs	1 gal 3 qts	
CHERRIES,MARASCHINO,HALVES	1-1/8 lbs	2 cup	

Method
1. Combine pineapple and mandarin oranges.
2. Top each portion with 1/2 a maraschino cherry, if desired.
3. Cover; CCP: Hold for service at 41 F. or lower.

FRUIT GELATIN

Yield 100   **Portion** 2/3 Cup

Calories	Carbohydrates	Protein	Fat	Cholesterol	Sodium	Calcium
116 cal	28 g	2 g	0 g	0 mg	65 mg	8 mg

Ingredient	Weight	Measure	Issue
FRUIT COCKTAIL,CANNED,JUICE PACK,INCL LIQUIDS	12-1/2 lbs	1 gal 2 qts	
DESSERT POWDER,GELATIN,STRAWBERRY	5-1/8 lbs	2 qts 2-1/2 cup	
WATER,BOILING	12-1/2 lbs	1 gal 2 qts	
RESERVED LIQUID	6-1/4 lbs	3 qts	
WATER,COLD	6-1/4 lbs	3 qts	

Method

1. Drain fruit; reserve juice for use in Step 3 and fruit for use in Step 5.
2. Dissolve gelatin in boiling water.
3. Add juice and water; stir to mix well.
4. Pour about 1 gallon into each pan. Chill until slightly thickened.
5. Fold an equal quantity of fruit into gelatin in each pan. Chill until firm. CCP: Hold for service at 41 F. or lower.

Notes

1. In Step 1, 2 No. 10 cans of the following canned fruit may be used per 100 servings: Canned Fruit Cocktail, Canned Mixed Fruit Chunks, Canned Peaches, quarters or slices, Canned Pears, quarters or slices, Canned Pineapple, chunks or tidbits.

BANANA GELATIN

Yield 100   Portion 2/3 Cup

Calories	Carbohydrates	Protein	Fat	Cholesterol	Sodium	Calcium
130 cal	32 g	2 g	0 g	0 mg	64 mg	6 mg

Ingredient	Weight	Measure	Issue
DESSERT POWDER,GELATIN,STRAWBERRY	5-1/8 lbs	2 qts 2-1/2 cup	
WATER,BOILING	12-1/2 lbs	1 gal 2 qts	
WATER,COLD	12-1/2 lbs	1 gal 2 qts	
BANANA,FRESH,SLICED	9-3/4 lbs	1 gal 3-3/8 qts	15lbs

Method

1. Dissolve gelatin in boiling water.
2. Add cold water; stir to mix well.
3. Pour 1 gallon into each pan. Chill until slightly thickened.
4. Fold 2-1/4 quarts of banana into gelatin in each pan. Chill until firm.

FRUIT FLAVORED GELATIN

Yield 100   Portion 1/2 Cup

Calories	Carbohydrates	Protein	Fat	Cholesterol	Sodium	Calcium
90 cal	21 g	2 g	0 g	0 mg	63 mg	3 mg

Ingredient	Weight	Measure	Issue
DESSERT POWDER,GELATIN,STRAWBERRY	5-1/8 lbs	2 qts 2-1/2 cup	
WATER,BOILING	12-1/2 lbs	1 gal 2 qts	
WATER,COLD	12-1/2 lbs	1 gal 2 qts	

Method

1. Dissolve gelatin in boiling water.
2. Add water; stir to mix well.
3. Pour 1 gallon into each steam table pan. Chill until firm.

FRUIT GELATIN (CRUSHED ICE METHOD)

Yield 100   Portion 2/3 Cup

Calories	Carbohydrates	Protein	Fat	Cholesterol	Sodium	Calcium
116 cal	28 g	2 g	0 g	0 mg	65 mg	7 mg

Ingredient	Weight	Measure	Issue
FRUIT COCKTAIL,CANNED,JUICE PACK,INCL LIQUIDS	12-1/2 lbs	1 gal 2 qts	
DESSERT POWDER,GELATIN,STRAWBERRY	5-1/8 lbs	2 qts 2-1/2 cup	
RESERVED LIQUID	9-3/8 lbs	1 gal 1/2 qts	
ICE CUBES	12-1/2 lbs	3 gal 3-5/8 qts	

Method
1. Drain fruit; reserve juice for use in Step 2 and fruit for use in Step 3.
2. Dissolve gelatin in boiling water and juice.
3. Crush the ice. Add crushed ice, stirring constantly until ice is melted and gelatin begins to thicken. Add fruit; stir until blended; pour into pans. Chill until firm.

Notes
1. In Step 1, 2 No. 10 cans of the following canned fruit may be used per 100 servings: Canned Fruit Cocktail, Canned Mixed Fruit Chunks, Canned Peaches, quarters or slices, Canned Pears, quarters or slices, Canned Pineapple, chunks or tidbits.

STRAWBERRY GELATIN

Yield 100   Portion 2/3 Cup

Calories	Carbohydrates	Protein	Fat	Cholesterol	Sodium	Calcium
117 cal	28 g	2 g	0 g	0 mg	64 mg	14 mg

Ingredient	Weight	Measure	Issue
DESSERT POWDER,GELATIN,STRAWBERRY	5-1/8 lbs	2 qts 2-1/2 cup	
WATER,BOILING	14-5/8 lbs	1 gal 3 qts	
STRAWBERRIES,FROZEN,THAWED	16-7/8 lbs	1 gal 3-1/2 qts	
JUICE,LEMON	4-1/3 oz	1/2 cup	

Method
1. Dissolve strawberry flavored gelatin in boiling water.
2. Add strawberries and lemon juice to gelatin. Stir until strawberries are completely thawed and separated.
3. Pour 5-1/2 quarts of gelatin mixture into each pan. Chill until firm.

PEACH GELATIN

Yield 100   Portion 2/3 Cup

Calories	Carbohydrates	Protein	Fat	Cholesterol	Sodium	Calcium
160 cal	39 g	2 g	0 g	0 mg	66 mg	4 mg

Ingredient	Weight	Measure	Issue
DESSERT POWDER,GELATIN,ORANGE	5-1/8 lbs	2 qts 2-1/2 cup	

| WATER,BOILING | 14-5/8 lbs | 1 gal 3 qts |
| PEACHES,FROZEN | 16-1/2 lbs | 1 gal 3-1/2 qts |

Method
1. Dissolve orange flavored gelatin in boiling water.
2. Add partially thawed sliced or quartered peaches to orange flavored gelatin. Stir peaches until thawed and separated.
3. Pour 5-1/2 quarts into each pan. Chill until firm.

PEACH CRISP

Yield 100   **Portion** 1 Piece

Calories	Carbohydrates	Protein	Fat	Cholesterol	Sodium	Calcium
203 cal	32 g	2 g	8 g	0 mg	211 mg	23 mg

Ingredient	Weight	Measure	Issue
PEACHES,CANNED,SLICED	19-2/3 lbs	2 gal 1 qts	
COOKING SPRAY,NONSTICK	2 oz	1/4 cup 1/3 tbsp	
SUGAR,GRANULATED	1 lbs	2-1/4 cup	
FLOUR,WHEAT,GENERAL PURPOSE	6-5/8 oz	1-1/2 cup	
SALT	1/4 oz	1/8 tsp	
CINNAMON,GROUND	1/4 oz	1 tbsp	
NUTMEG,GROUND	1/8 oz	1/3 tsp	
FLOUR,WHEAT,GENERAL PURPOSE	1-3/8 lbs	1 qts 1 cup	
BAKING POWDER	1/4 oz	1/4 tsp	
BAKING SODA	1/4 oz	1/4 tsp	
SALT	5/8 oz	1 tbsp	
CEREAL,OATMEAL,ROLLED	1 lbs	2-7/8 cup	
SUGAR,BROWN,PACKED	1-2/3 lbs	1 qts 1-3/8 cup	
MARGARINE,SOFTENED	2 lbs	1 qts	

Method
1. Drain fruit; reserve juice.
2. Spray each pan with non-stick cooking spray. Arrange about 3 quarts of peaches in each pan. Pour 3 cups reserve juice over peaches in each pan.
3. Combine sugar, flour, salt, cinnamon, and nutmeg; sprinkle about 2 cups evenly over peaches in each pan. Stir lightly to moisten flour mixture.
4. Combine flour, baking powder, baking soda, salt, rolled oats, brown sugar and margarine; mix only until blended.
5. Sprinkle 2-1/2 quarts of mixture over the fruit in each pan.
6. Using a convection oven, bake at 350 F. for 30 minutes or until top is lightly browned on low fan, open vent.
7. Cut 6 by 9 and serve with serving spoon or spatula.

CHERRY CRISP (PIE FILLING COOKIE MIX)

Yield 100   **Portion** 1Piece

Calories	Carbohydrates	Protein	Fat	Cholesterol	Sodium	Calcium
215 cal	41 g	1 g	6 g	8 mg	69 mg	30 mg

Ingredient	Weight	Measure	Issue
PIE FILLING,CHERRY,PREPARED	24-1/2 lbs	3 gal 1/4 qts	
COOKING SPRAY,NONSTICK	2 oz	1/4 cup 1/3 tbsp	
COOKIE MIX,OATMEAL	4-1/2 lbs		
MARGARINE,SOFTENED	1 lbs	2 cup	

Method

1. Pour 5-1/2 quarts of prepared pie filling into each pan.
2. Combine cookie mix and margarine. Sprinkle half of mixture evenly over cherries in each pan.
3. Using a convection oven, bake at 350 F. for 30 minutes or until top is lightly browned on low fan, open vent.
4. Cut 6 by 9. Serve with serving spoon or spatula.

CHERRY CRISP

Yield 100   **Portion** 1 Piece

Calories	Carbohydrates	Protein	Fat	Cholesterol	Sodium	Calcium
232 cal	39 g	2 g	8 g	0 mg	209 mg	30 mg

Ingredient	Weight	Measure	Issue
CHERRIES,CANNED,RED,TART,WATER PACK,INCL LIQUIDS	19-2/3 lbs	2 gal 1 qts	
COOKING SPRAY,NONSTICK	2 oz	1/4 cup 1/3 tbsp	
SUGAR,GRANULATED	1 lbs	2-1/4 cup	
FLOUR,WHEAT,GENERAL PURPOSE	6-5/8 oz	1-1/2 cup	
SALT	1/4 oz	1/8 tsp	
CINNAMON,GROUND	1/4 oz	1 tbsp	
NUTMEG,GROUND	1/8 oz	1/3 tsp	
FLOUR,WHEAT,GENERAL PURPOSE	1-3/8 lbs	1 qts 1 cup	
BAKING POWDER	1/4 oz	1/4 tsp	
BAKING SODA	1/4 oz	1/4 tsp	
SALT	5/8 oz	1 tbsp	
CEREAL,OATMEAL,ROLLED	1 lbs	2-7/8 cup	
SUGAR,BROWN,PACKED	1-2/3 lbs	1 qts 1-3/8 cup	
MARGARINE,SOFTENED	2 lbs	1 qts	

Method

1. Drain fruit; reserve juice.
2. Spray each pan with non-stick cooking spray. Arrange about 3 quarts of peaches in each pan. Pour 3 cups reserve juice over peaches in each pan.
3. Combine sugar, flour, salt, cinnamon, and nutmeg; sprinkle about 2 cups evenly over cherries in each pan. Stir lightly to moisten flour mixture.
4. Combine flour, baking powder, baking soda, salt, rolled oats, brown sugar and margarine; mix only until blended.
5. Sprinkle 2-1/2 quarts of mixture over the fruit in each pan.
6. Using a convection oven, bake at 350 F. for 30 minutes or until top is lightly browned on low fan, open vent.
7. Cut 6 by 9 and serve with serving spoon or spatula.

PEACH CRISP (PIE FILLING COOKIE MIX)

Yield 100   **Portion** 1 Piece

Calories	Carbohydrates	Protein	Fat	Cholesterol	Sodium	Calcium
250 cal	51 g	1 g	6 g	8 mg	96 mg	33 mg

Ingredient	Weight	Measure	Issue
PIE FILLING,PEACH,PREPARED	24-1/2 lbs	3 gal 1/4 qts	
COOKING SPRAY,NONSTICK	2 oz	1/4 cup 1/3 tbsp	
COOKIE MIX,OATMEAL	4-1/2 lbs		
MARGARINE,SOFTENED	1 lbs	2 cup	

Method

1. Lightly spray each pan with non-stick cooking spray. Pour about 5-1/2 quarts of pie filling into each sprayed pan.
2. Combine canned oatmeal cookie mix with softened margarine; mix until crumbly.
3. Sprinkle 2-1/2 quarts of mixture over fruit in each pan.
4. Using a convection oven, bake at 350 F. for 30 minutes or until top is lightly browned on low fan, open vent.
5. Cut 6 by 9 and serve with serving spoon or spatula.

BLUEBERRY CRISP (PIE FILLING COOKIE MIX)

Yield 100   **Portion** 1 Serving

Calories	Carbohydrates	Protein	Fat	Cholesterol	Sodium	Calcium
219 cal	35 g	1 g	10 g	8 mg	158 mg	44 mg

Ingredient	Weight	Measure	Issue
PIE FILLING,BLUEBERRY,PREPARED	24-1/2 lbs	2 gal 2-3/8 qts	
COOKING SPRAY,NONSTICK	2 oz	1/4 cup 1/3 tbsp	
COOKIE MIX,OATMEAL	4-1/2 lbs		
MARGARINE,SOFTENED	2 lbs	1 qts	

Method

1. Lightly spray each pan with non-stick cooking spray. Pour about 5-1/2 quarts of pie filling into each sprayed pan.
2. Combine canned oatmeal cookie mix with margarine; mix until crumbly.
3. Sprinkle 2-1/2 quarts of mixture over fruit in each pan.
4. Using a convection oven, bake at 350 F. for 30 minutes or until top is lightly browned on low fan, open vent.
5. Cut 6 by 9 and serve with serving spoon or spatula.

APPLE CRUNCH (APPLE PIE FILLING)

Yield 100   **Portion** 1 Piece

Calories	Carbohydrates	Protein	Fat	Cholesterol	Sodium	Calcium
231 cal	42 g	2 g	7 g	6 mg	236 mg	18 mg

Ingredient	Weight	Measure	Issue
PIE FILLING,APPLE,PREPARED	18 lbs	2 gal 1 qts	
COOKING SPRAY,NONSTICK	2 oz	1/4 cup 1/3 tbsp	
JUICE,LEMON	3-1/4 oz	1/4 cup 2-1/3 tbsp	
CAKE MIX,YELLOW	5 lbs		
COCONUT,PREPARED,SWEETENED FLAKES	1 lbs	1 qts 1 cup	
MARGARINE,SOFTENED	1 lbs	2 cup	

Method
1. Spray each pan with non-stick cooking spray. Spread 4-1/2 quarts filling in each sprayed sheet pan. Sprinkle 3 tablespoons of lemon juice on top of mixture in each pan.
2. Combine cake mix and coconut; add margarine; mix until crumbly.
3. Sprinkle 2-3/4 quarts of mixture over each pan.
4. Using a convection oven, bake at 325 F. for 30 minutes or until lightly brown on low fan, open vent.
5. Cut 6 by 9.

Notes
1. In Step 2, 1 pound chopped unsalted nuts may be substituted for coconut per 100 servings.

BLUEBERRY CRUNCH (BLUEBERRY PIE FILLING)

Yield 100   **Portion** 1 Serving

Calories	Carbohydrates	Protein	Fat	Cholesterol	Sodium	Calcium
235 cal	43 g	2 g	7 g	6 mg	249 mg	36 mg

Ingredient	Weight	Measure	Issue
PIE FILLING,BLUEBERRY,PREPARED	21-1/4 lbs	2 gal 1 qts	
COOKING SPRAY,NONSTICK	2 oz	1/4 cup 1/3 tbsp	
JUICE,LEMON	3-1/4 oz	1/4 cup 2-1/3 tbsp	
CAKE MIX,YELLOW	5 lbs		
COCONUT,PREPARED,SWEETENED FLAKES	1 lbs	1 qts 1 cup	
MARGARINE,SOFTENED	1 lbs	2 cup	

Method
1. Spray each pan with non-stick cooking spray. Spread 4-1/2 quarts of pie filling into each sprayed sheet pan. Sprinkle 3 tablespoons of lemon juice on top of mixture in each pan.
2. Combine cake mix and coconut; add margarine; mix until crumbly.
3. Sprinkle 2-3/4 quarts of mixture over each pan.
4. Using a convection oven, bake at 325 F. for 30 minutes or until lightly browned on low fan, open vent.
5. Cut 6 by 9.

Notes
1. In Step 2, 1 pound chopped unsalted nuts may be substituted for coconut, per 100 servings.

CHERRY CRUNCH (CHERRY PIE FILLING)

Yield 100   **Portion** 1 Piece

Calories	Carbohydrates	Protein	Fat	Cholesterol	Sodium	Calcium
243 cal	44 g	2 g	7 g	6 mg	207 mg	24 mg

Ingredient	Weight	Measure	Issue
PIE FILLING,CHERRY,PREPARED	18 lbs	2 gal 1 qts	
COOKING SPRAY,NONSTICK	2 oz	1/4 cup 1/3 tbsp	
JUICE,LEMON	3-1/4 oz	1/4 cup 2-1/3 tbsp	
CAKE MIX,YELLOW	5 lbs		
COCONUT,PREPARED,SWEETENED FLAKES	1 lbs	1 qts 1 cup	
MARGARINE,SOFTENED	1 lbs	2 cup	

Method
1. Spray each pan with non-stick cooking spray. Spread 4-1/2 quarts of pie filling into each sprayed sheet pan. Sprinkle 3 tablespoons of lemon juice on top of mixture in each pan.
2. Combine cake mix and coconut; add margarine; mix until crumbly.
3. Sprinkle 2-3/4 quarts of mixture over each pan.
4. Using a convection oven, bake at 325 F. for 30 minutes on low fan, open vent or until lightly browned.
5. Cut 6 by 9.

Notes
1. In Step 2, 1 pound chopped unsalted nuts may be substituted for coconut, per 100 servings.

PEACH CRUNCH (PEACH PIE FILLING)

Yield 100   Portion 1Piece

Calories	Carbohydrates	Protein	Fat	Cholesterol	Sodium	Calcium
269 cal	52 g	2 g	7 g	6 mg	227 mg	26 mg

Ingredient	Weight	Measure	Issue
PIE FILLING,PEACH,PREPARED	18 lbs	2 gal 1 qts	
COOKING SPRAY,NONSTICK	2 oz	1/4 cup 1/3 tbsp	
JUICE,LEMON	3-1/4 oz	1/4 cup 2-1/3 tbsp	
CAKE MIX,YELLOW	5 lbs		
COCONUT,PREPARED,SWEETENED FLAKES	1 lbs	1 qts 1 cup	
MARGARINE,SOFTENED	1 lbs	2 cup	

Method
1. Spray each pan with non-stick cooking spray. Spread 4-1/2 quart filling in each sprayed sheet pan. Sprinkle 3 tablespoons of lemon juice on top of mixture in each pan.
2. Combine cake mix and coconut; add margarine and butter; mix until crumbly.
3. Sprinkle 2-3/4 quarts of mixture over each pan.
4. Using a convection oven bake at 325 F. for 30 minutes or until lightly browned on low fan, open vent.
5. Cut 6 by 9.

Notes
1. In Step 2, 1 pound chopped unsalted nuts may be used for coconut per 100 servings.

BANANA SPLIT

Yield 100   Portion 1 Each

Calories	Carbohydrates	Protein	Fat	Cholesterol	Sodium	Calcium
361 cal	53 g	5 g	16 g	30 mg	110 mg	132 mg

Ingredient	Weight	Measure	Issue
BANANA,FRESH	13 lbs		20 lbs
JUICE,ORANGE	1-1/8 lbs	2 cup	
ICE CREAM,VANILLA	15-1/8 lbs	3 gal 1 qts	
ICE CREAM TOPPING,FUDGE	8-5/8 lbs	3 qts 1 cup	
WHIPPED TOPPING,12 OZ CAN	1-1/4 lbs	2 qts	
PECANS,CHOPPED	8 oz		
CHERRIES,MARASCHINO,SLICED	1-1/8 lbs	2 cup	

Method
1. Peel and slice bananas lengthwise into quarters; place on pan.
2. Pour juice over bananas; cover with waxed paper; refrigerate until ready to serve.
3. Make banana splits to order. Place 1/2 cup ice cream in soup bowl. Drain 2 banana quarters; place 1 on each side of ice cream. Ladle 2 tablespoons of topping over ice cream. Top with 1 tablespoon whipped topping, 1 teaspoon chopped pecans and 1/2 maraschino cherry.

Notes
1. In Step 3, Chocolate Sauce, Recipe No. K 005 00, or Butterscotch, Fudge, Marshmallow, Pineapple, or Strawberry Topping, or Whipped Topping, Recipe No. K 002 00 may be used.

VANILLA SOFT SERVE YOGURT (DEHYDRATED)

Yield 100   **Portion** 3/4 Cup

Calories	Carbohydrates	Protein	Fat	Cholesterol	Sodium	Calcium
166 cal	40 g	1 g	0 g	1 mg	71 mg	29 mg

Ingredient	Weight	Measure	Issue
YOGURT MIX,DEHYDRATED,VANILLA	10 lbs		
WATER	10 lbs		

Method
1. Stir dehydrated mix into water. Mix thoroughly with wire whip or mixer. Cover container.
2. Chill 4 to 24 hours in refrigerator to 35 F. to 40 F.
3. Stir until smooth. Pour mixture into top hopper to soft serve ice cream freezer; start dasher motor; turn on refrigeration according to manufacturer's directions. Freeze to temperature of 18 F. to 22 F., about 10 minutes, or until product can be drawn with a stiff consistency that will hold a peak.

CHOCOLATE SOFT SERVE YOGURT (DEHYDRATED)

Yield 100   **Portion** 3/4 Cup

Calories	Carbohydrates	Protein	Fat	Cholesterol	Sodium	Calcium
166 cal	40 g	1 g	1 g	1 mg	169 mg	30 mg

Ingredient	Weight	Measure	Issue
YOGURT MIX,DEHYDRATED,CHOCOLATE	10 lbs		
WATER	10 lbs		

Method
1. Stir dehydrated mix into water. Mix thoroughly with wire whip or mixer. Cover container.

2. Chill 4 to 24 hours in refrigerator to 35 F. to 40 F.
3. Stir until smooth. Pour mixture into top hopper to soft serve ice cream freezer; start dasher motor; turn on refrigeration according to manufacturer's directions. Freeze to temperature of 18 F. to 22 F., about 10 minutes, or until product can be drawn with a stiff consistency that will hold a peak.

TAPIOCA PUDDING

Yield 100   Portion 1/2 Cup

Calories	Carbohydrates	Protein	Fat	Cholesterol	Sodium	Calcium
119 cal	21 g	3 g	3 g	36 mg	139 mg	92 mg

Ingredient	Weight	Measure	Issue
MILK,NONFAT,DRY	1-1/2 lbs	2 qts 2 cup	
WATER,WARM	23-1/2 lbs	2 gal 3-1/4 qts	
BUTTER	8 oz	1 cup	
TAPIOCA,QUICK-COOKING	14-1/3 oz	2-5/8 cup	
SUGAR,GRANULATED	3 lbs	1 qts 2-3/4 cup	
SALT	5/8 oz	1 tbsp	
EGGS,WHOLE,FROZEN	1-1/2 lbs	2-7/8 cup	
EXTRACT,VANILLA	1-3/8 oz	3 tbsp	

Method
1. Reconstitute milk. Reserve 2 cups for use in Step 3.
2. Heat remaining milk in steam jacketed kettle or stock pot to a boil. Add butter or margarine.
3. Combine reserved milk with tapioca, sugar, salt, and eggs.
4. Add tapioca mixture to hot milk in steam-jacketed kettle or stock pot. Bring to just a boil; reduce heat; cook without boiling, stirring occasionally until slightly thickened, about 5 minutes. The mixture will be thin. Turn off heat; cool in kettle 15 to 20 minutes.
5. Add vanilla; blend well. Pour 1 gallon into each pan. Cover surface of pudding with waxed paper. Refrigerate until ready to serve. Mixture will thicken as it cools. CCP: Hold for service at 41 F. or lower.

Notes
1. Garnish with Whipped Topping, Recipe No. K 002 00 and maraschino cherry half (optional).

VANILLA CREAM PUDDING (INSTANT)

Yield 100   Portion 3/4 Cup

Calories	Carbohydrates	Protein	Fat	Cholesterol	Sodium	Calcium
136 cal	32 g	2 g	0 g	1 mg	503 mg	77 mg

Ingredient	Weight	Measure	Issue
MILK,NONFAT,DRY	1-1/3 lbs	2 qts 3/4 cup	
WATER,COLD	23 lbs	2 gal 3 qts	
DESSERT POWDER,PUDDING,INSTANT,VANILLA	6-7/8 lbs	1 gal 1/4 qts	

Method
1. Reconstitute milk. Chill to 50 F. Place in mixer bowl.
2. Add dessert powder. Using whip, blend at low speed 15 seconds or until well blended. Scrape sides and bottom of bowl; whip at medium speed 2 minutes or until smooth.

3. Pour 4-1/2 quarts pudding into each pan. Cover surface of pudding with waxed paper.
4. Refrigerate at least 1 hour or until ready to serve. Pudding may be garnished with well-drained fruit or whipped topping. CCP: Hold for service at 41 F. or lower.

BANANA CREAM PUDDING (INSTANT)

Yield 100   **Portion** 1/2 Cup

Calories	Carbohydrates	Protein	Fat	Cholesterol	Sodium	Calcium
134 cal	32 g	2 g	0 g	1 mg	403 mg	63 mg

Ingredient	Weight	Measure	Issue
MILK,NONFAT,DRY	1 lbs	1 qts 3 cup	
WATER,COLD	18-1/4 lbs	2 gal 3/4 qts	
DESSERT POWDER,PUDDING,INSTANT,VANILLA	5-1/2 lbs	3qts 1-1/2cup	
BANANA,FRESH,SLICED	6 lbs	1gal 1/2qts	9-1/4lbs

Method
1. Reconstitute milk. Chill to 50 F. Place in mixer bowl.
2. Add dessert powder. Using whip, blend at low speed 15 seconds or until well blended. Scrape sides and bottom of bowl; whip at medium speed 2 minutes or until smooth.
3. Pour 3-2/3 quarts pudding into each pan. Fold 1-1/2 quarts of banana into each pan. Cover surface of pudding with waxed paper.
4. Refrigerate at least 1 hour or until ready to serve. Pudding may be garnished with well-drained fruit or whipped topping. CCP: Hold for service at 41 F. or lower.

Notes
1. To prevent discoloration, slice bananas just before adding to pudding

COCONUT CREAM PUDDING (INSTANT)

Yield 100   **Portion** 1/2 Cup

Calories	Carbohydrates	Protein	Fat	Cholesterol	Sodium	Calcium
178 cal	36 g	2 g	3 g	1 mg	525 mg	78 mg

Ingredient	Weight	Measure	Issue
MILK,NONFAT,DRY	1-1/3 lbs	2 qts 3/4 cup	
WATER,COLD	23 lbs	2 gal 3 qts	
DESSERT POWDER,PUDDING,INSTANT,VANILLA	6-7/8 lbs	1 gal 1/4 qts	
COCONUT,PREPARED,SWEETENED FLAKES	1-7/8 lbs	2 qts 1 cup	

Method
1. Reconstitute milk. Chill to 50 F. Place in mixer bowl.
2. Add dessert powder. Using whip, blend at low speed 15 seconds or until well blended. Scrape sides and bottom of bowl; whip at medium speed 2 minutes or until smooth.
3. Pour 4-1/2 quarts pudding into each pan. Fold coconut into pudding. Cover surface of pudding with waxed paper.
4. Refrigerate at least 1 hour or until ready to serve. Pudding may be garnished with well drained fruit or whipped topping. CCP: Hold for service at 41 F. or lower.

PINEAPPLE CREAM PUDDING (INSTANT)

Yield 100   Portion 1/2 Cup

Calories	Carbohydrates	Protein	Fat	Cholesterol	Sodium	Calcium
128 cal	31 g	2 g	0 g	1 mg	403 mg	66 mg

Ingredient	Weight	Measure	Issue
MILK,NONFAT,DRY	1 lbs	1 qts 3 cup	
WATER,COLD	18-1/4 lbs	2 gal 3/4 qts	
DESSERT POWDER,PUDDING,INSTANT,VANILLA	5-1/2 lbs	3 qts 1-1/2 cup	
PINEAPPLE,CANNED,CRUSHED,JUICE PACK,DRAINED	7-1/4 lbs	1 #10cn	

Method
1. Reconstitute milk. Chill to 50 F. Place in mixer bowl.
2. Add vanilla dessert powder. Using whip, blend at low speed 15 seconds or until well blended. Scrape sides and bottom of bowl; whip at medium speed 2 minutes or until smooth.
3. Pour 3-2/3 quarts of pudding into each pan. Fold drained pineapple into pudding. Cover surface of pudding with waxed paper.
4. Refrigerate at least 1 hour or until ready to serve. Pudding may be garnished with well-drained fruit or whipped topping. CCP: Hold for service at 41 F. or lower.

BUTTERSCOTCH CREAM PUDDING (INSTANT)

Yield 100   Portion 1/2 Cup

Calories	Carbohydrates	Protein	Fat	Cholesterol	Sodium	Calcium
136 cal	32 g	2 g	0 g	1 mg	485 mg	79 mg

Ingredient	Weight	Measure	Issue
MILK,NONFAT,DRY	1-1/3 lbs	2 qts 3/4 cup	
WATER,COLD	23 lbs	2 gal 3 qts	
DESSERT POWDER,PUDDING,INSTANT,BUTTERSCOTCH	6-7/8 lbs		

Method
1. Reconstitute milk. Chill to 50 F. Place in mixer bowl.
2. Add butterscotch dessert powder. Using whip, blend at low speed 15 seconds or until well blended. Scrape sides and bottom of bowl; whip at medium speed 2 minutes or until smooth.
3. Pour 4-1/2 quarts pudding into each pan. Cover surface of pudding with waxed paper.
4. Refrigerate at least 1 hour or until ready to serve. Pudding may be garnished with well-drained fruit or whipped topping. CCP: Hold for service at 41 F. or lower.

CHOCOLATE CREAM PUDDING (INSTANT)

Yield 100   Portion 1/2 Cup

Calories	Carbohydrates	Protein	Fat	Cholesterol	Sodium	Calcium
128 cal	30 g	3 g	1 g	1 mg	465 mg	81 mg

Ingredient	Weight	Measure	Issue
MILK,NONFAT,DRY	1-1/3 lbs	2 qts 3/4 cup	
WATER,COLD	22-1/4 lbs	2 gal 2-2/3 qts	
DESSERT POWDER,PUDDING,INSTANT,CHOCOLATE	6-5/8 lbs	1 gal 3/8 qts	

Method

1. Reconstitute milk. Chill to 50 F. Place in mixer bowl.
2. Add chocolate dessert powder. Using whip, blend at low speed 15 seconds or until well blended. Scrape sides and bottom of bowl; whip at medium speed 2 minutes or until smooth.
3. Pour 4-1/2 quarts pudding into each pan. Cover surface of pudding with waxed paper.
4. Refrigerate at least 1 hour or until ready to serve. Pudding may be garnished with well-drained fruit or whipped topping. CCP: Hold for service at 41 F. or lower.

BAKED RICE PUDDING

Yield 100   **Portion** 1/2 Cup

Calories	Carbohydrates	Protein	Fat	Cholesterol	Sodium	Calcium
173 cal	30 g	4 g	4 g	48 mg	156 mg	62 mg

Ingredient	Weight	Measure	Issue
RICE,LONG GRAIN	3-1/4 lbs	2 qts	
WATER,COLD	12-1/2 lbs	1 gal 2 qts	
SALT	3/4 oz	1 tbsp	
MILK,NONFAT,DRY	10-3/4 oz	1 qts 1/2 cup	
WATER,WARM	11-1/2 lbs	1 gal 1-1/2 qts	
EGGS,WHOLE,FROZEN	2-3/8 lbs	1 qts 1/2 cup	
MARGARINE,MELTED	12 oz	1-1/2 cup	
SUGAR,GRANULATED	2 lbs	1 qts 1/2 cup	
EXTRACT,VANILLA	1-3/8 oz	3 tbsp	
CINNAMON,GROUND	1/4 oz	1 tbsp	
NUTMEG,GROUND	1/8 oz	1/8 tsp	
COOKING SPRAY,NONSTICK	2 oz	1/4 cup 1/3 tbsp	
RAISINS	1-7/8 lbs	1 qts 2 cup	

Method

1. Combine rice, water, and salt. Bring to a boil, stirring occasionally. Reduce heat; cover tightly; simmer 20 to 25 minutes or until water is absorbed.
2. Reconstitute milk; add eggs, margarine or butter, sugar, vanilla, cinnamon and nutmeg; blend thoroughly.
3. Spray each pan with non-stick cooking spray. Place 1-3/4 quarts of cooked, cooled rice and 1-1/2 cup of raisins in each sprayed pan. Blend thoroughly.
4. Pour 2 quarts egg mixture over rice-raisin mixture in each pan.
5. Using a convection oven, bake at 325 F. 30 to 35 minutes or until lightly browned on low fan, open vent and a knife inserted in center comes out clean.
6. Cover, refrigerate until ready to serve. CCP: Hold for service at 41 F. or lower.
7. Cut 4 by 6.

BAKED RICE PUDDING (FROZEN EGGS AND EGG WHITES)

Yield 100   **Portion** 1/2 Cup

Calories	Carbohydrates	Protein	Fat	Cholesterol	Sodium	Calcium
168 cal	30 g	4 g	4 g	24 mg	157 mg	59 mg

Ingredient	Weight	Measure	Issue
RICE,LONG GRAIN	3-1/4 lbs	2 qts	
WATER,COLD	12-1/2 lbs	1 gal 2 qts	
SALT	3/4 oz	1 tbsp	
MILK,NONFAT,DRY	10-3/4 oz	1 qts 1/2 cup	
WATER,WARM	11-1/2 lbs	1 gal 1-1/2 qts	
EGGS,WHOLE,FROZEN	1-1/4 lbs	2-1/4 cup	
EGG WHITES	1-1/4 lbs	2-1/4 cup	
MARGARINE,MELTED	12 oz	1-1/2 cup	
SUGAR,GRANULATED	2 lbs	1 qts 1/2 cup	
EXTRACT,VANILLA	1-3/8 oz	3 tbsp	
CINNAMON,GROUND	1/4 oz	1 tbsp	
NUTMEG,GROUND	1/8 oz	1/8 tsp	
COOKING SPRAY,NONSTICK	2 oz	1/4 cup 1/3 tbsp	
RAISINS	1-7/8 lbs	1 qts 2 cup	

Method

1. Combine rice, water, and salt. Bring to a boil, stirring occasionally. Reduce heat; cover tightly; simmer 20 to 25 minutes or until water is absorbed.
2. Reconstitute milk; add eggs, egg whites, margarine or butter, sugar, vanilla, cinnamon and nutmeg; blend thoroughly.
3. Spray each pan with non-stick cooking spray. Place 1-3/4 quarts cooked cooled rice and 1-1/2 cups raisins in each sprayed pan. Blend thoroughly.
4. Pour 2 quarts egg mixture over rice-raisin mixture in each pan.
5. Using a convection oven, bake 30 to 35 minutes in 325 F. oven or until lightly browned on low fan, open vent and a knife inserted in center comes out clean.
6. Cover, refrigerate until ready to serve. CCP: Hold for service at 41 F. or lower.
7. Cut 4 by 6.

BREAD PUDDING

Yield 100   **Portion** 2/3 Cup

Calories	Carbohydrates	Protein	Fat	Cholesterol	Sodium	Calcium
205 cal	34 g	5 g	6 g	30 mg	310 mg	93 mg

Ingredient	Weight	Measure	Issue
BREAD,WHITE,CUBED	4-1/8 lbs	3 gal 1-1/2 qts	
COOKING SPRAY,NONSTICK	2 oz	1/4 cup 1/3 tbsp	
MARGARINE,MELTED	1 lbs	2 cup	
EGGS,WHOLE,FROZEN	1-1/2 lbs	2-3/4 cup	
EGG WHITES,FROZEN,THAWED	1-1/2 lbs	2-3/4 cup	
SUGAR,GRANULATED	2-2/3 lbs	1 qts 2 cup	
SALT	1 oz	1 tbsp	
NUTMEG,GROUND	1/4 oz	1 tbsp	
EXTRACT,VANILLA	1-7/8 oz	1/4 cup 1/3 tbsp	

MILK,NONFAT,DRY	1 lbs	1 qts 3 cup
WATER,WARM	18-3/4 lbs	2 gal 1 qts
RAISINS	2-7/8 lbs	2 qts 1 cup

Method

1. Spray each pan with non-stick cooking spray. Place 4-1/2 quarts bread in each sprayed steam table pan. Pour margarine or butter over bread cubes and toss lightly. Toast in oven until light brown.
2. Add sugar, salt, nutmeg, and vanilla to eggs; blend thoroughly.
3. Reconstitute milk; combine with egg mixture. Pour 1 gallon over bread cubes in each pan.
4. Add 3 cups raisins to each pan.
5. Bake at 350 F. for 15 minutes: stir to distribute the raisins. Bake 45 minutes or until firm.
6. Cover; refrigerate until ready to serve. CCP: Hold for service at 41 F. or lower.
7. Cut 4 by 8.

CHOCOLATE CHIP BREAD PUDDING

Yield 100   **Portion** 2/3 Cup

Calories	Carbohydrates	Protein	Fat	Cholesterol	Sodium	Calcium
218 cal	30 g	6 g	9 g	32 mg	318 mg	106 mg

Ingredient	Weight	Measure Issue
BREAD,WHITE,CUBED	4-1/8 lbs	3 gal 1-1/2 qts
COOKING SPRAY,NONSTICK	2 oz	1/4 cup 1/3 tbsp
MARGARINE,MELTED	1 lbs	2 cup
EGGS,WHOLE,FROZEN	1-1/2 lbs	2-3/4 cup
EGG WHITES	1-1/2 lbs	2-3/4 cup
SUGAR,GRANULATED	2-2/3 lbs	1 qts 2 cup
SALT	1 oz	1 tbsp
NUTMEG,GROUND	1/4 oz	1 tbsp
EXTRACT,VANILLA	1-7/8 oz	1/4 cup 1/3 tbsp
MILK,NONFAT,DRY	1 lbs	1 qts 3 cup
WATER,WARM	18-3/4 lbs	2 gal 1 qts
CHOCOLATE,COOKING CHIPS,SEMISWEET	2-1/4 lbs	1 qts 2-1/8 cup

Method

1. Spray each pan with non-stick cooking spray. Place 4-1/2 quarts bread in each sprayed steam table pan. Pour margarine or butter over bread cubes, toss lightly. Toast in oven until light brown.
2. Add sugar, salt, nutmeg, and vanilla to eggs; blend thoroughly.
3. Reconstitute milk; combine with egg mixture. Pour 1 gallon over bread cubes in each pan.
4. Add 12 ounces of chocolate chips to each pan.
5. Bake 1 hour or until firm in 350 F. oven.
6. Cover; CCP: Hold for service at 41 F. or lower.
7. Cut 4 by 8.

COCONUT BREAD PUDDING

Yield 100   **Portion** 2/3 Cup

Calories	Carbohydrates	Protein	Fat	Cholesterol	Sodium	Calcium
208 cal	28 g	5 g	8 g	30 mg	331 mg	88 mg

Ingredient	Weight	Measure	Issue
COOKING SPRAY,NONSTICK	2 oz	1/4 cup 1/3 tbsp	
BREAD,WHITE,CUBED	4-1/8 lbs	3 gal 1-1/2 qts	
COCONUT,PREPARED,SWEETENED FLAKES	1-7/8 lbs	2 qts 1 cup	
MARGARINE,MELTED	1 lbs	2 cup	
EGGS,WHOLE,FROZEN	1-1/2 lbs	2-3/4 cup	
EGG WHITES	1-1/2 lbs	2-3/4 cup	
SUGAR,GRANULATED	2-2/3 lbs	1 qts 2 cup	
SALT	1 oz	1 tbsp	
NUTMEG,GROUND	1/4 oz	1 tbsp	
EXTRACT,VANILLA	1-7/8 oz	1/4 cup 1/3 tbsp	
MILK,NONFAT,DRY	1 lbs	1 qts 3 cup	
WATER,WARM	18-3/4 lbs	2 gal 1 qts	

Method

1. Lightly spray each pan with non-stick cooking spray. Place 4-1/2 quarts bread in each pan. Pour margarine over bread cubes; toss flaked coconut with bread cubes. Toast in oven until lightly brown.
2. Add sugar, salt, nutmeg, and vanilla to eggs; blend thoroughly.
3. Reconstitute milk; combine with egg mixture. Pour 1 gallon over bread cubes in each pan.
4. Bake 1 hour or until firm in 350 F. oven.
5. Cover; CCP: Hold for service at 41 F. or lower.
6. Cut 4 by 8.

CREAM PUFFS

Yield 100   **Portion** 1 Each

Calories	Carbohydrates	Protein	Fat	Cholesterol	Sodium	Calcium
139 cal	10 g	3 g	10 g	90 mg	121 mg	14 mg

Ingredient	Weight	Measure	Issue
BUTTER	2 lbs	1 qts	
WATER,BOILING	4-1/8 lbs	2 qts	
FLOUR,WHEAT,GENERAL PURPOSE	2-3/4 lbs	2 qts 2 cup	
SALT	1/4 oz	1/8 tsp	
EGGS,WHOLE,FROZEN	3-5/8 lbs	1 qts 2-5/8 cup	
COOKING SPRAY,NONSTICK	2 oz	1/4 cup 1/3 tbsp	

Method

1. Combine butter or margarine and water; bring to a boil.
2. Add flour and salt all at once, stirring rapidly. Cook 2 minutes or until mixture leaves sides of pan and forms a ball.
3. Remove from heat; place in mixer bowl. Cool slightly.
4. Add eggs, while beating at high speed, using a flat paddle. Beat until mixture is thick and shiny.
5. Spray each pan with non-stick cooking spray. Drop 2-1/2 tablespoons of batter in rows, 2 inches apart on sprayed pans.
6. Bake 10 minutes at 400 F.; reduce oven temperature to 350 F.; bake 30 minutes longer or until firm. Turn off oven.
7. Open oven door slightly; leave puffs in oven 8 to 10 minutes to dry out after baking. Shells should be slightly moist inside.
8. Using a pastry tube, fill shells. See Note 1.

9. CCP: Hold for service at 41 F. or lower.

Notes
1. Fill shells with 2/3 recipe Vanilla Cream Pudding Recipe No. J 014 00, 1 recipe Whipped Topping Recipe No. K 002 00, or commercial prepared hard ice cream may be used. Fill shells with 1/3 cup filling. Sprinkle with sifted powdered sugar or cover with Chocolate Glaze Frosting, Recipe No. G 024 00.

ECLAIRS

Yield 100   **Portion** 1 Each

Calories	Carbohydrates	Protein	Fat	Cholesterol	Sodium	Calcium
139 cal	10 g	3 g	10 g	90 mg	121 mg	14 mg

Ingredient	Weight	Measure	Issue
BUTTER	2 lbs	1 qts	
WATER,BOILING	4-1/8 lbs	2 qts	
FLOUR,WHEAT,GENERAL PURPOSE	2-3/4 lbs	2 qts 2 cup	
SALT	1/4 oz	1/8 tsp	
EGGS,WHOLE,FROZEN	3-5/8 lbs	1 qts 2-5/8 cup	
COOKING SPRAY,NONSTICK	2 oz	1/4 cup 1/3 tbsp	

Method
1. Combine butter and water; bring to a boil.
2. Add flour and salt all at once stirring rapidly. Cook 2 minutes or until mixture leaves the sides of the pan and forms a ball.
3. Remove from heat; place in mixer bowl. Cool slightly.
4. Add eggs, while beating at high speed, using a flat paddle. Beat until mixture is thick and shiny.
5. Spray each pan with non-stick cooking spray. Use a pastry bag or drop 2-1/2 tablespoons of batter 2 to 6 inches apart on sprayed pans; spread each mound into a 1x4-1/2 inch rectangle, rounding sides or piling batter on top.
6. Bake at 400 F. for 10 minutes; reduce oven temperature to 350 F. ; bake 30 minutes longer or until firm. Turn off oven.
7. Open oven door slightly; leave puffs in oven 8 to 10 minutes to dry out after baking. Shells should be slightly moist inside.
8. Using a pastry tube, fill shells. See Note 1.
9. Refrigerate filled shells until served.

Notes
1. Fill shells with 2/3 recipe Vanilla Cream Pudding Recipe No. J 014 00, 1 recipe Whipped Topping Recipe No. K 002 00, or commercial prepared hard ice cream may be used. Fill shells with 1/3 cup filling. Sprinkle with sifted powdered sugar or cover with Chocolate Glaze Frosting, Recipe No. G 024 00.

VANILLA CREAM PUDDING

Yield 100   **Portion** 1/2 Cup

Calories	Carbohydrates	Protein	Fat	Cholesterol	Sodium	Calcium
154 cal	25 g	3 g	5 g	58 mg	193 mg	58 mg

Ingredient	Weight	Measure	Issue
MILK,NONFAT,DRY	13-3/4 oz	1 qts 1-3/4 cup	
WATER,WARM	15-2/3 lbs	1 gal 3-1/2 qts	
SUGAR,GRANULATED	2 lbs	1 qts 1/2 cup	
SALT	1 oz	1 tbsp	
CORNSTARCH	1-1/8 lbs	1 qts	
SUGAR,GRANULATED	2 lbs	1 qts 1/2 cup	
WATER	5-1/4 lbs	2 qts 2 cup	
EGGS,WHOLE,FROZEN	2-3/8 lbs	1 qts 1/2 cup	
BUTTER	1 lbs	2 cup	
EXTRACT,VANILLA	2-3/4 oz	1/4 cup 2-1/3 tbsp	

Method

1. Reconstitute milk. Add sugar and salt. Heat to just below boiling. DO NOT BOIL.
2. Combine cornstarch, sugar, and water; stir until smooth. Add gradually to hot mixture. Cook at medium heat, stirring constantly, about 10 minutes or until thickened.
3. Stir 1 quart of hot mixture into eggs. Slowly pour egg mixture into remaining hot milk mixture; heat to boiling, stirring constantly. Cook about 2 minutes longer. Remove from heat.
4. Add butter or margarine and vanilla; stir until well blended.
5. Pour 1 gallon of pudding into each pan. Cover surface of pudding with waxed paper.
6. Refrigerate until ready to serve. CCP: Hold for service at 41 F. or lower.

Notes

1. Pudding will curdle if boiled or subjected to prolonged intense heat.

CHOCOLATE CREAM PUDDING

Yield 100   **Portion** 1/2 Cup

Calories	Carbohydrates	Protein	Fat	Cholesterol	Sodium	Calcium
181 cal	36 g	2 g	4 g	11 mg	180 mg	56 mg

Ingredient	Weight	Measure	Issue
MILK,NONFAT,DRY	13-3/4 oz	1 qts 1-3/4 cup	
WATER,WARM	15-2/3 lbs	1 gal 3-1/2 qts	
SUGAR,GRANULATED	4 lbs	2 qts 1 cup	
SALT	1 oz	1 tbsp	
COCOA	12-1/8 oz	1 qts	
CORNSTARCH	1-1/8 lbs	1 qts	
SUGAR,GRANULATED	2 lbs	1 qts 1/2 cup	
WATER	5-1/4 lbs	2 qts 2 cup	
BUTTER	1 lbs	2 cup	
EXTRACT,VANILLA	2-3/4 oz	1/4 cup 2-1/3 tbsp	

Method

1. Reconstitute milk. Add sugar and salt. Heat to just below boiling. DO NOT BOIL.
2. Combine cocoa with cornstarch, sugar, and water; stir until smooth. Add gradually to hot mixture. Cook at medium heat stirring constantly, about 10 minutes or until thickened.
3. Add butter or margarine and vanilla; stir until well blended.
4. Pour 1 gallon of pudding into each pan. Cover surface of pudding with waxed paper.
5. Refrigerate until ready to serve. CCP: Hold for service at 41 F. or lower.

Notes

1. Pudding will curdle if boiled or subjected to prolonged intense heat.

CREAMY RICE PUDDING

Yield 100   **Portion** 1/2 Cup

Calories	Carbohydrates	Protein	Fat	Cholesterol	Sodium	Calcium
170 cal	30 g	3 g	4 g	49 mg	254 mg	63 mg

Ingredient	Weight	Measure	Issue
RICE,LONG GRAIN	2-2/3 lbs	1 qts 2-1/2 cup	
WATER,BOILING	6-3/4 lbs	3 qts 1 cup	
SALT	5/8 oz	1 tbsp	
SUGAR,GRANULATED	2 lbs	1 qts 1/2 cup	
CORNSTARCH	7-7/8 oz	1-3/4 cup	
MILK,NONFAT,DRY	12 oz	1 qts 1 cup	
SALT	1 oz	1 tbsp	
CINNAMON,GROUND	1/8 oz	1/8 tsp	
NUTMEG,GROUND	1/8 oz	1/8 tsp	
WATER,WARM	7-1/3 lbs	3 qts 2 cup	
EGGS,WHOLE,FROZEN	2 lbs	3-3/4 cup	
WATER,BOILING	6-1/4 lbs	3 qts	
BUTTER	14 oz	1-3/4 cup	
EXTRACT,VANILLA	1-3/8 oz	3 tbsp	
RAISINS	1-7/8 lbs	1 qts 2 cup	
CINNAMON,GROUND	1/8 oz	1/3 tsp	

Method
1. Cook rice in boiling, salted water 20 to 25 minutes or until tender. Cover; set aside for use in Step 6.
2. In a steam jacketed kettle, combine sugar, cornstarch, milk, salt, cinnamon, and nutmeg; mix until well blended.
3. Add water to dry mixture; stir until smooth.
4. Add eggs; blend well.
5. Slowly add water to egg mixture, stirring with a wire whip. Cook until thickened, stirring constantly.
6. Turn off heat; add cooked rice, butter or margarine, vanilla, and raisins.
7. Pour 1 gallon of pudding into each pan.
8. Sprinkle cinnamon or nutmeg over pudding in each pan.
9. Cover surface of pudding with waxed paper. CCP: Hold for service at 41 F. or lower.

Notes
1. Pudding may be served hot. Omit Step 9.

FLUFFY PINEAPPLE RICE CUP

Yield 100   **Portion** 1/2 Cup

Calories	Carbohydrates	Protein	Fat	Cholesterol	Sodium	Calcium
140 cal	22 g	2 g	6 g	0 mg	56 mg	22 mg

Ingredient	Weight	Measure	Issue
WATER,COLD	3-1/8 lbs	1 qts 2 cup	
RICE,LONG GRAIN	1-1/4 lbs	3 cup	
SALT	1/4 oz	1/8 tsp	
OIL,SALAD	1/2 oz	1 tbsp	

Ingredient	Weight	Measure
PINEAPPLE,CANNED,CRUSHED	6-5/8 lbs	3 qts
CHERRIES,MARASCHINO,CHOPPED,DRAINED	8-7/8 oz	1 cup
RESERVED LIQUID	3-7/8 lbs	1 qts 3-1/2 cup
WHIPPED TOPPING MIX,NONDAIRY,DRY	2 lbs	2 gal 3-1/4 qts
MILK,NONFAT,DRY	3-1/4 oz	1-3/8 cup
EXTRACT,VANILLA	1-7/8 oz	1/4 cup 1/3 tbsp
MARSHMALLOWS,MINIATURE	1-1/4 lbs	2 qts 3 cup
COCONUT,PREPARED,SWEETENED FLAKES	1 lbs	1 qts 1 cup

Method

1. Combine water, rice, salt and salad oil; bring to a boil. Stir occasionally.
2. Cover tightly; simmer 20 to 25 minutes. DO NOT STIR.
3. Remove from heat and refrigerate for use in Step 5.
4. Drain pineapple; reserve juice for use in Step 6.
5. Combine rice, pineapple and cherries. Refrigerate for use in Step 7.
6. Pour reserved juice and water into mixer bowl; add topping, milk and vanilla. Using whip at low speed, whip 3 minutes or until thoroughly blended. Scrape down bowl. Whip at high speed 5 to 10 minutes or until stiff peaks form.
7. Combine rice mixture and marshmallows and coconut. Mix thoroughly. Fold in whipped topping. Mix lightly.
8. Refrigerate until ready to serve. CCP: Hold for service at 41 F. or lower.

BREAKFAST BREAD PUDDING

Yield 100   **Portion 2/3 Cup**

Calories	Carbohydrates	Protein	Fat	Cholesterol	Sodium	Calcium
206 cal	39 g	7 g	3 g	1 mg	300 mg	99 mg

Ingredient	Weight	Measure	Issue
COOKING SPRAY,NONSTICK	2 oz	1/4 cup 1/3 tbsp	
PEACHES,CANNED,QUARTERS,DICED,DRAINED	8-3/4 lbs	1 gal	
BREAD,WHITE,CUBED	4-1/8 lbs	3 gal 1-1/2 qts	
MILK,NONFAT,DRY	15 oz	1 qts 2-1/4 cup	
EGG SUBSTITUTE,PASTEURIZED	3 lbs	1 qts 1-1/2 cup	
WATER,WARM	15-2/3 lbs	1 gal 3-1/2 qts	
SUGAR,BROWN,PACKED	1-3/8 lbs	1 qts 3/8 cup	
EXTRACT,VANILLA	1-7/8 oz	1/4 cup 1/3 tbsp	
SALT	7/8 oz	1 tbsp	
CINNAMON,GROUND	1/4 oz	1 tbsp	
GINGER,GROUND	1/8 oz	1/3 tsp	
CEREAL,GRANOLA,TOASTED OAT MIX,LOW FAT	4-5/8 lbs	1 gal 3/4 qts	

Method

1. Lightly spray steam table pans with non-stick cooking spray. Place 1 quart peaches and 3-1/2 quarts bread in each pan. Mix lightly.
2. Reconstitute milk; add egg substitute, brown sugar, vanilla, salt, cinnamon, and ginger to milk, blend thoroughly.
3. Pour 2-1/2 quarts egg mixture over bread mixture in each pan.
4. Evenly distribute 4-3/4 cups granola on top of each pan.

5. Using a convection oven, bake 30 minutes at 325 F. or until lightly browned and a knife inserted in center comes out clean on low fan, open vent. CCP: Internal temperature must reach 145 F. or higher for 15 seconds.
6. CCP: Hold for service at 140 F. or higher.
7. Cut 4 by 6.

BAKED CINNAMON APPLE SLICES

Yield 100   **Portion** 1/2 Cup

Calories	Carbohydrates	Protein	Fat	Cholesterol	Sodium	Calcium
106 cal	26 g	0 g	1 g	0 mg	4 mg	8 mg

Ingredient	Weight	Measure	Issue
APPLES,CANNED,SLICED	27-3/4 lbs	3 gal 2 qts	
EXTRACT,VANILLA	2-1/2 oz	1/4 cup 1-2/3 tbsp	
SUGAR,GRANULATED	3-1/2 oz	1/2 cup	
CINNAMON,GROUND	1/2 oz	2 tbsp	
NUTMEG,GROUND	1/8 oz	1/4 tsp	
SUGAR,GRANULATED	14-1/8 oz	2 cup	
CINNAMON,GROUND	1/4 oz	1 tbsp	

Method
1. Blend sugar, cinnamon, and nutmeg. Combine with apples and vanilla. Place 3-1/3 quarts mixture in each pan.
2. Blend 2nd sugar and cinnamon. Sprinkle 1/2 cup evenly over apples in each pan.
3. Using a convection oven, bake at 375 F. for 20 minutes or until mixture begins to simmer and sugar begins to brown on high fan, open vent. CCP: Hold at 140 F. or higher for service.

BREAD PUDDING WITH HARD SAUCE

Yield 100   **Portion** 1 Piece

Calories	Carbohydrates	Protein	Fat	Cholesterol	Sodium	Calcium
243 cal	43 g	5 g	6 g	1 mg	206 mg	54 mg

Ingredient	Weight	Measure	Issue
BREAD,WHITE,CUBED	1-2/3 lbs	3 gal 3 qts	
APPLES,COOKING,FRESH,PARED,CHOPPED	1-7/8 lbs	1 qts 3 cup	
RAISINS	3-1/3 lbs	1 qts 2 cup	
EGG SUBSTITUTE,PASTEURIZED	3-5/8 oz	1 qts 2 cup	
MILK,NONFAT,DRY	3-7/8 lbs	1-1/2 cup	
WATER	1 lbs	1 qts 3-1/2 cup	
MARGARINE	3-1/2 lbs	2 cup	
SUGAR,GRANULATED	1/2 oz	2 qts	
NUTMEG,GROUND	7/8 oz	2 tbsp	
EXTRACT,VANILLA	1/2 oz	2 tbsp	
CINNAMON,GROUND	8-1/3 oz	2 tbsp	
WATER	1-3/4 lbs	1 cup	
SUGAR,GRANULATED	2-3/4 oz	1 qts	
FLAVORING,RUM	4 oz	1/4 cup 2-1/3 tbsp	
MARGARINE	11-3/4 oz	1/2 cup	
EGG SUBSTITUTE,PASTEURIZED	2-1/8 lbs	1-3/8 cup	

Method

1. Preheat oven to 350 F. Place bread in steam table pans.
2. Combine apples and raisins. Divide apples and raisins evenly among pans.
3. Reconstitute milk. Combine margarine, egg substitute, sugar, nutmeg, vanilla, cinnamon, and milk. Pour over bread and fruit. Fold lightly. Bake 20 to 30 minutes until set.
4. In medium saucepan, heat water, sugar, and extract until sugar is dissolved. Add margarine a little at a time until melted and combined. Temper the eggs with hot mixture, then add eggs. Stir and heat until sauce thickens slightly. Pour sauce over pudding. CCP: Internal temperature must reach 145 F. or higher for 15 seconds. Hold for service at 140 F. or higher.

BAKED BANANAS

Yield 100   **Portion** 1/2 Cup

Calories	Carbohydrates	Protein	Fat	Cholesterol	Sodium	Calcium
169 cal	44 g	1 g	0 g	0 mg	4 mg	13 mg

Ingredient	Weight	Measure	Issue
SUGAR,BROWN,LIGHT	1-3/8 lbs	1 qts 3/8 cup	
WATER	2-1/8 lbs	1 qts	
HONEY	3 lbs	1 qts	
BANANA,FRESH	25 lbs		38-1/2 lbs

Method

1. Heat brown sugar, water, and honey in a saucepan over low heat until sugar is dissolved, about 5 minutes.
2. Cut bananas in half crosswise. Place 25 halves into each steam table pan. Pour 3/4 cup of syrup over each pan of bananas.
3. Using a convection oven, bake at 350 F. for 10 minutes until lightly browned.
4. Serve with sauce. CCP: Hold for service at 140 F. or higher.

WHIPPED CREAM

Yield 100   **Portion** 2 Tablespoons

Calories	Carbohydrates	Protein	Fat	Cholesterol	Sodium	Calcium
72 cal	2 g	0 g	7 g	26 mg	7 mg	12 mg

Ingredient	Weight	Measure	Issue
CREAM,WHIPPING,COLD	4-1/4 lbs	2 qts	
SUGAR,POWDERED,SIFTED	5-1/4 oz	1-1/4 cup	
EXTRACT,VANILLA	7/8 oz	2 tbsp	

Method
1. Pour cream into chilled mixer bowl. Using whip at medium speed, whip 1 gallon of cream 3 to 7 minutes or until slightly thickened.
2. Gradually add sugar and vanilla. Whip 7 to 8 minutes or until stiff. DO NOT OVER WHIP.
3. Cover; refrigerate until ready to serve. CCP: Hold for service at 41 F. or lower.

WHIPPED TOPPING (DEHYDRATED)

Yield 100   **Portion** 3 Tablespoons

Calories	Carbohydrates	Protein	Fat	Cholesterol	Sodium	Calcium
29 cal	3 g	0 g	2 g	0 mg	8 mg	7 mg

Ingredient	Weight	Measure	Issue
WATER,COLD	2 lbs	3-3/4 cup	
WHIPPED TOPPING MIX,NONDAIRY,DRY	1 lbs	1 gal 1-5/8 qts	
MILK,NONFAT,DRY	1-5/8 oz	1/2 cup 2-2/3 tbsp	
EXTRACT,VANILLA	7/8 oz	2 tbsp	

Method
1. Place cold water in mixer bowl; add topping, milk, and vanilla. Using whip at low speed, whip 3 minutes or until well blended. Scrape down bowl.
2. Whip at high speed 5 to 10 minutes or until stiff peaks form. Cover; refrigerate until ready to serve. CCP: Hold for service at 41 F.or lower.

Notes
1. When topping is used for icing cakes, fold 2 cups sifted powdered sugar into whipped topping.

WHIPPED TOPPING (FROZEN)

Yield 100   **Portion** 3 Tablespoons

Calories	Carbohydrates	Protein	Fat	Cholesterol	Sodium	Calcium
14 cal	1 g	0 g	1 g	0 mg	1 mg	0 mg

Ingredient	Weight	Measure	Issue
WHIPPED TOPPING,FROZEN,NONDAIRY	1 lbs	1 qts 2 cup	

Method

1. Thaw topping in chilled mixer bowl. Using whip at medium speed, whip topping 10 to 20 minutes or until stiff peaks form. Cover; refrigerate until ready to serve. CCP: Hold for service at 41 F. or lower.

Notes

1. When topping is used for icing cakes, fold 2 cups sifted powdered sugar into whipped topping.

RUM SAUCE

Yield 100   **Portion** 2 Tablespoons

Calories	Carbohydrates	Protein	Fat	Cholesterol	Sodium	Calcium
130 cal	12 g	0 g	9 g	25 mg	101 mg	18 mg

Ingredient	Weight	Measure	Issue
BUTTER	2-1/2 lbs	1 qts 1 cup	
SUGAR,BROWN,PACKED	2-3/4 lbs	2 qts 1/2 cup	
MILK,NONFAT,DRY	1-1/4 oz	1/2 cup	
WATER	1 lbs	2 cup	
FLAVORING,RUM	1-7/8 oz	1/4 cup 1/3 tbsp	

Method

1. Melt butter or margarine; add brown sugar. Cook on low heat for 2 minutes, stirring constantly.
2. Reconstitute milk; add to sugar mixture. Cook, stirring constantly, until mixture comes to a boil.
3. Remove immediately from heat; cool 10 minutes.
4. Add rum flavoring; stir until well blended.

CHERRY SAUCE

Yield 100   **Portion** 2-1/2 Tablespoons

Calories	Carbohydrates	Protein	Fat	Cholesterol	Sodium	Calcium
46 cal	12 g	0 g	0 g	0 mg	4 mg	4 mg

Ingredient	Weight	Measure	Issue
PIE FILLING,CHERRY,PREPARED	8-3/4 lbs	1 gal 3/8 qts	
WATER	8-1/3 oz	1 cup	

Method

1. Combine pie filling with water in mixer bowl and mix well.

CHOCOLATE SAUCE

Yield 100   **Portion** 2 Tablespoons

Calories	Carbohydrates	Protein	Fat	Cholesterol	Sodium	Calcium
83 cal	16 g	1 g	3 g	6 mg	31 mg	19 mg

Ingredient	Weight	Measure	Issue
MILK,NONFAT,DRY	4-1/4 oz	1-3/4 cup	

WATER,WARM	3-1/8 lbs	1 qts 2 cup
SUGAR,GRANULATED	3 lbs	1 qts 2-3/4 cup
COCOA	9-1/8 oz	3 cup
WATER,COLD	1 lbs	2 cup
BUTTER	10 oz	1-1/4 cup
EXTRACT,VANILLA	1/2 oz	1 tbsp

Method
1. Reconstitute milk. Set aside for use in Step 3.
2. Mix sugar and cocoa with water to form a paste. Bring to a boil, stirring constantly; cool slightly.
3. Add milk stirring constantly. Bring to a boil; cook 3 minutes. Remove from heat immediately.
4. Add butter or margarine and vanilla; stir. Serve warm or at room temperature.

Notes
1. In Step 2, for 100 portions, 1 pound unsweetened, cooking chocolate may be used for cocoa. In Step 4, reduce butter or margarine to 1/4 cup. Add chocolate with butter or margarine.

CHOCOLATE COCONUT SAUCE

Yield 100   **Portion** 2 Tablespoons

Calories	Carbohydrates	Protein	Fat	Cholesterol	Sodium	Calcium
109 cal	18 g	1 g	4 g	6 mg	45 mg	20 mg

Ingredient	Weight	Measure	Issue
MILK,NONFAT,DRY	4-1/4 oz	1-3/4 cup	
WATER,WARM	3-1/8 lbs	1 qts 2 cup	
SUGAR,GRANULATED	3 lbs	1 qts 2-3/4 cup	
COCOA	9-1/8 oz	3 cup	
WATER,COLD	1 lbs	2 cup	
BUTTER	10 oz	1-1/4 cup	
EXTRACT,VANILLA	1/2 oz	1 tbsp	
COCONUT,PREPARED,SWEETENED FLAKES	1-1/8 lbs	1 qts 1-1/2 cup	

Method
1. Reconstitute milk. Set aside for use in Step 3.
2. Mix sugar and cocoa with water to form a paste. Bring to a boil, stirring constantly; cool slightly.
3. Add milk stirring constantly. Bring to a boil; cook 3 minutes. Remove from heat immediately.
4. Add butter or margarine and vanilla; stir.
5. Just before serving, add sweetened, flaked coconut to sauce and mix well.

Notes
1. In Step 2, for 100 portions, 1 pound unsweetened, cooking chocolate may be used for cocoa. In Step 4, reduce butter or margarine to 1/4 cup. Add chocolate with butter or margarine.

CHOCOLATE MARSHMALLOW SAUCE

Yield 100   **Portion** 2 Tablespoons

Calories	Carbohydrates	Protein	Fat	Cholesterol	Sodium	Calcium
97 cal	19 g	1 g	3 g	6 mg	33 mg	19 mg

Ingredient	Weight	Measure	Issue
MILK,NONFAT,DRY	4-1/4 oz	1-3/4 cup	
WATER,WARM	3-1/8 lbs	1 qts 2 cup	
SUGAR,GRANULATED	3 lbs	1 qts 2-3/4 cup	
COCOA	9-1/8 oz	3 cup	
WATER,COLD	1 lbs	2 cup	
BUTTER	10 oz	1-1/4 cup	
EXTRACT,VANILLA	1/2 oz	1 tbsp	
MARSHMALLOWS,MINIATURE	1 lbs	2 qts 1 cup	

Method
1. Reconstitute milk. Set aside for use in Step 3.
2. Mix sugar and cocoa with water to form a paste. Bring to a boil, stirring constantly; cool slightly.
3. Add milk stirring constantly. Bring to a boil; cook 3 minutes. Remove from heat immediately.
4. Add butter or margarine and vanilla; stir.
5. Just before serving, add miniature marshmallows to sauce and mix well.

Notes
1. In Step 2, for 100 portions, 1 pound unsweetened, cooking chocolate may be used for cocoa. In Step 4, reduce butter or margarine to 1/4 cup. Add chocolate with butter or margarine.

CHOCOLATE NUT SAUCE

Yield 100   Portion 2 Tablespoons

Calories	Carbohydrates	Protein	Fat	Cholesterol	Sodium	Calcium
109 cal	16 g	2 g	5 g	6 mg	32 mg	23 mg

Ingredient	Weight	Measure	Issue
MILK,NONFAT,DRY	4-1/4 oz	1-3/4 cup	
WATER,WARM	3-1/8 lbs	1 qts 2 cup	
SUGAR,GRANULATED	3 lbs	1 qts 2-3/4 cup	
COCOA	9-1/8 oz	3 cup	
WATER,COLD	1 lbs	2 cup	
BUTTER	10 oz	1-1/4 cup	
EXTRACT,VANILLA	1/2 oz	1 tbsp	
NUTS,UNSALTED,CHOPPED,COARSELY	1 lbs	3-1/8 cup	

Method
1. Reconstitute milk. Set aside for use in Step 3.
2. Mix sugar and cocoa with water to form a paste. Bring to a boil, stirring constantly; cool slightly.
3. Add milk stirring constantly. Bring to a boil; cook 3 minutes. Remove from heat immediately.
4. Add butter or margarine and vanilla; stir.
5. Just before serving, add chopped unsalted nuts to sauce and mix well.

Notes
1. In Step 2, for 100 portions, 1 pound unsweetened, cooking chocolate may be used for cocoa. In Step 4, reduce butter or margarine to 1/4 cup. Add chocolate with butter or margarine.

CHOCOLATE MINT SAUCE

Yield 100   Portion 2 Tablespoons

Calories	Carbohydrates	Protein	Fat	Cholesterol	Sodium	Calcium
83 cal	16 g	1 g	3 g	6 mg	31 mg	19 mg

Ingredient	Weight	Measure	Issue
MILK,NONFAT,DRY	4-1/4 oz	1-3/4 cup	
WATER,WARM	3-1/8 lbs	1 qts 2 cup	
SUGAR,GRANULATED	3 lbs	1 qts 2-3/4 cup	
COCOA	9-1/8 oz	3 cup	
WATER,COLD	1 lbs	2 cup	
BUTTER	10 oz	1-1/4 cup	
FLAVORING,PEPPERMINT	1/2 oz	1 tbsp	

Method
1. Reconstitute milk. Set aside for use in Step 3.
2. Mix sugar and cocoa with water to form a paste. Bring to a boil, stirring constantly; cool slightly.
3. Add milk stirring constantly. Bring to a boil; cook 3 minutes. Remove from heat immediately.
4. Add butter or margarine and peppermint flavoring; stir. Serve warm or at room temperature.

Notes
1. In Step 2, for 100 portions, 1 pound unsweetened, cooking chocolate may be used for cocoa. In Step 4, reduce butter or margarine to 1/4 cup. Add chocolate with butter or margarine.

CHERRY JUBILEE SAUCE

Yield 100   Portion 1/4 Cup

Calories	Carbohydrates	Protein	Fat	Cholesterol	Sodium	Calcium
86 cal	22 g	0 g	0 g	0 mg	25 mg	6 mg

Ingredient	Weight	Measure	Issue
CHERRIES,CANNED,DARK,SWEET,PITTED,INCL LIQUIDS	13-3/8 lbs	1 gal 2 qts	
CORNSTARCH	3-3/8 oz	3/4 cup	
SALT	1/4 oz	1/8 tsp	
SUGAR,GRANULATED	1-3/4 lbs	1 qts	
FLAVORING,BRANDY	1-3/8 oz	3 tbsp	

Method
1. Drain cherries; set aside for use in Step 5. Take cherry juice and add water to equal 1 gallon per 100 portions.
2. Combine cornstarch, salt, and sugar. Add liquid; mix well.
3. Cook over medium heat until mixture comes to a boil.
4. Reduce heat; continue cooking slowly, stirring occasionally until sauce is thick and clear.
5. Remove from heat; add brandy flavoring and cherries.
6. Serve warm or cold.

STRAWBERRY GLAZE TOPPING

Yield 100   **Portion** 2-1/2 Tablespoons

Calories	Carbohydrates	Protein	Fat	Cholesterol	Sodium	Calcium
36 cal	9 g	0 g	0 g	0 mg	2 mg	7 mg

Ingredient	Weight	Measure	Issue
STRAWBERRIES,FROZEN,THAWED	9 lbs	1 gal	
CORNSTARCH	7-1/2 oz	1-5/8 cup	
SUGAR,GRANULATED	12-1/3 oz	1-3/4 cup	
RESERVED LIQUID	4-2/3 lbs	2 qts 1 cup	

Method

1. Drain strawberries. Set juice aside for use in Step 2; berries for use in Step 3.
2. Combine cornstarch, sugar and strawberry juice. Bring to a boil. Cook at medium heat, stirring constantly until thick and clear. Remove from heat.
3. Fold strawberries per 100 portions into thickened mixture.
4. Chill topping.